The Challenge to the Auspices

The Challenge to the Auspices

*Studies on Magisterial Power in
the Middle Roman Republic*

C. F. KONRAD

OXFORD
UNIVERSITY PRESS

Great Clarendon Street, Oxford, OX2 6DP,
United Kingdom

Oxford University Press is a department of the University of Oxford.
It furthers the University's objective of excellence in research, scholarship,
and education by publishing worldwide. Oxford is a registered trade mark of
Oxford University Press in the UK and in certain other countries

© C. F. Konrad 2022

The moral rights of the author have been asserted

First Edition published in 2022

Impression: 1

All rights reserved. No part of this publication may be reproduced, stored in
a retrieval system, or transmitted, in any form or by any means, without the
prior permission in writing of Oxford University Press, or as expressly permitted
by law, by licence or under terms agreed with the appropriate reprographics
rights organization. Enquiries concerning reproduction outside the scope of the
above should be sent to the Rights Department, Oxford University Press, at the
address above

You must not circulate this work in any other form
and you must impose this same condition on any acquirer

Published in the United States of America by Oxford University Press
198 Madison Avenue, New York, NY 10016, United States of America

British Library Cataloguing in Publication Data

Data available

Library of Congress Control Number: 2022933852

ISBN 978–0–19–285552–7

DOI: 10.1093/oso/9780192855527.001.0001

Printed and bound in the UK by
TJ Books Limited

Links to third party websites are provided by Oxford in good faith and
for information only. Oxford disclaims any responsibility for the materials
contained in any third party website referenced in this work.

VXORI OPTIMAE

Preface

No public action of the Roman State, the *populus Romanus*, at home or at war, was to be carried out without prior permission from Iuppiter Optimus Maximus: permission obtained, through auspices, by the magistrate (usually a Consul, Praetor, Censor, or Dictator) in charge of the intended action. It was for the individual magistrate to take the auspices, and either proceed with the action or—should Iuppiter withhold permission—refrain from it; but if a question arose as to the correct meaning of the god's answer or message, a greater degree of expertise was called for. It was furnished by the Augurs, nine experts—and usually senators—who could advise a magistrate individually, or as a body submit a formal interpretation to the Senate, who would issue the necessary directives to comply with whatever augural law required.

Auspices thus occupy a fundamental place in the—unwritten—constitution of the Roman State. They are an instrument of Roman government; they are also part of Roman religion. The study of the latter has undergone wide-ranging changes over the past generation or two. In the context of this book, the most significant—and salutary—development has been the abandonment, by and large, of a view that saw little more than empty ritual in Roman religious practices as a whole, and mostly cynical manipulation for political purposes in the practice of augury in particular.[1] Recent work more specifically on aspects of Roman government, especially in the area of warfare and military command, carefully and judiciously considers the role of auspices.[2]

This book examines, in a collection of related studies, a range of situations in which auspices led to questions about the legitimacy of a magistrate's action or status, and became a matter of political contention. It is primarily concerned with the institutions affected by those events: an attempt to understand, as precisely as possible (and readers will be keenly aware of just how difficult it is to extract reliable information from the evidence that has survived), their functioning, their rules, their practices. It has little to offer in the way of theoretical discussion; although, to some extent, my views on the larger questions that surround the role of augury in Roman religion and government may become clear from my treatment of individual issues. In general terms, I proceed from an assumption that the Romans, high and low alike, took their gods to be real, and took them seriously.

---

[1] Champion (2017) offers a perceptive up-to-date approach.
[2] Note especially Rüpke (1990), Vervaet (2014), and Berthelet (2015).

The gods to be taken seriously included, first and foremost, Iuppiter Best and Greatest, the god of auspices. As a whole, the Roman ruling class—the Nobles—at least during the period of the Middle Republic, the third and second centuries BC, appears to have embraced and observed the rules imposed by augural law scrupulously and without contention; it would be difficult to argue with Craige Champion's recent conclusion that "Roman elites believed in their gods, in the sense that they held a collective conviction that proper observance of orthopraxy's demands had a direct bearing on the well-being of the empire."[3] To ask Iuppiter's permission and act in accordance with his response, to observe his messages and heed their meaning (especially if a warning), was treated as a form of genuine communication, evolved over the primordial centuries of the community, and indispensable for its continued existence. Moreover, as Lindsay Driediger-Murphy observes, "Roman institutions worked ultimately only through the compliance of the elite"; in consequence, "the pre-eminence of consensus and peer pressure in Republican life would have compelled compliance with the rules of the augural system as the majority defined them at any given point in time."[4] Without doubt, this puts the matter accurately—as a whole. But any society has its doubters and unbelievers, professed or covert; and individuals do not always act in accordance with collective conviction.

The book takes its origin from a curious entry in the *Fasti Capitolini*, which under the year 217 BC list the second dictatorship of Q. Fabius Maximus Verrucosus as having been *interregni caussa*, "for reason of an *interregnum*." No connection seems conceivable between the Dictator and an *interregnum*, the situation that obtained when, for one reason or another, no regular magistrates were in office, and the auspices reverted collectively to the *patres*, the patrician members of the Senate (or perhaps all Patricians). A caretaker—the Interrex—chosen *auspicato* by the *patres* for five days at a time managed the *res publica* until he could successfully conduct the election of new Consuls; in this way, since no auspices carried over from the magistrates of the previous year to those newly elected, the auspices were renewed *de integro*. The strange appellation *interregni causa*, occasionally noted by scholars but rarely discussed, called for explanation; and the explanation prompted two distinct—albeit related—further avenues of investigation.

In 223 BC the College of Augurs concluded that the Consuls of that year were *vitio creati*, elected under flawed auspices, and the Senate duly instructed them to abdicate their office, in order for the auspices to be renewed in untainted form through the process of an *interregnum*. But one of the Consuls, Gaius Flaminius, balked at the order, and openly disputed the Augurs' ruling. He refused to abdicate, at least at first; eventually, though, he yielded, and the desired *interregnum*

---

[3] Champion 200.   [4] Driediger-Murphy 2019: 45–46.

ensued. What made him step down? The circumstances may have required a magistrate with greater power—a Dictator, "for reason of an *interregnum*."

The attempt to solve the puzzle made it necessary to re-examine the nature of the dictatorship and the role of *imperium* and auspices as markers of legitimate power for Roman magistrates. But this remarkable instance of a Consul publicly challenging a ruling by the College of Augurs also led to a second line of inquiry, one that gave this book its title: an investigation into a series of attempts—mostly in the third century BC—by leading actors in the *res publica* to question the traditional role of auspices in the proper conduct of warfare.

For Flaminius in 223 was not the first Roman magistrate who refused to submit to the rules that represented the augural side of the republican constitution, nor the last. During the lifetime of one generation in the third century, a number of instances are known in which senior Roman magistrates chose to contest the rule of auspices and the authority of the Augurs. One case is reported even earlier, in the fourth century; two more in 249 BC; another in 242 or 241; and in 217, Flaminius in his second consulship again made a point of ignoring the auspices. All those instances are well known, but merely seen as isolated incidents. The present study aims to understand them as expressions of a larger sense of disaffection among elements of the Roman political class. Observing auspices according to all the augural rules could restrict, sometimes severely, a military commander's freedom of action in the field. To encounter five attempts, in a span of just over thirty years (between 249 and 217), at challenging the practice suggests the presence of a set of mind that did not subscribe to the inescapable necessity of obtaining Iuppiter's permission, through auspices, for all public acts; and some of those in a position to launch a challenge chose to seize the opportunity. Had any of them prevailed, more might have been encouraged to follow; and each time a military operation was conducted successfully without the proper observance of augural rules, upholding and enforcing such rules in future would have become ever more difficult. If auspices could be shown to be unnecessary in the sphere of war, moreover, their efficacy in the realm of domestic government could be called into question as well.

This book is a composite work rather than a straightforward monograph. Its overarching themes (if such a term may be applied here) are the nature of Roman magistrates' auspices and *imperium*—the essential elements in their legitimate exercise of power—and attempts to challenge the necessity of auspices. It makes no pretense at a comprehensive treatment: what follows is a series of studies (pursued over the course of some twenty years) that investigate individual cases and problems, and that, in exploring points of detail, hope to shed light on wider matters. To set the stage, it begins (Chapter 1) with the first reported instance of a Roman magistrate openly acting contrary to orders from his superior, and justifying his action by disputing the subordinate status of his own auspices: the famous dust-up pitting the Dictator L. Papirius Cursor against his Magister Equitum, Q. Fabius Maximus Rullianus, in the late fourth century. Chapter 2 reconsiders our knowledge of *imperium* and auspices, particularly insofar as both concepts relate to the constitutional qualification to command an army. Chapter 3 examines in depth the peculiar position of the dictatorship within the framework of Roman magistracies, under the aspects of both public and augural law: the nature of the Dictator's *imperium* and auspices, and the state of his powers relative to the Consuls (and, by extension, lower magistrates).[5] Yet the Dictator, when appointed, did not manage the *res publica* all by himself. As his first official act he named a deputy, the Master of the Horse. It was this deputy that first contested the auspices, and this office, as we shall see, would be instrumental in defusing the constitutional crisis of 223 BC; it was the subject of a constitutional dispute as late as 47 BC. Of all Roman magistracies, the Magister Equitum may be the most shadowy and least understood. What was his precise relation to the Dictator? Could he exist independently of the latter? Could he triumph? The answers are attempted in several case studies (Chapter 4).

From there, the book returns to its other theme. The final years of the First Punic War saw three attempts by Roman Consuls to go against or at least without the auspices: P. Claudius Pulcher drowning the augural Chickens when they refused to eat, in 249; his colleague, L. Iunius Pullus, sailing his fleet into a devastating storm despite a prohibitive response from Iuppiter; and C. Lutatius Catulus (or perhaps his brother, Q. Lutatius Cerco) proposing to take up his command without obtaining the traditional auspices in 242 (or 241). All three cases are discussed in Chapter 5. Next, the aforementioned refusal in 223 of C. Flaminius to abdicate his consulship (Chapter 6). Finally, Chapter 7 examines the—from an augural point of view—most elaborate and serious challenge, when Flaminius, Consul again in 217, departed the City before taking office, hence without obtaining valid auspices to begin with, and suffered disaster at Lake Trasumene.

Flaminius' catastrophe put an end to such attempts to free commanders from the constraints imposed by augural rules. It did not persuade individual skeptics that the *res publica* could not survive without scrupulous observance of the auspices; but it rendered politically indefensible further attempts to publicly question them, let alone any display of outright opposition and contempt in the manner of Flaminius. In the years that followed, influential leaders such as Fabius Maximus and M. Claudius Marcellus, Augurs both, demonstratively paid heed to Iuppiter's messages, even when (as in the case of Marcellus' second consulship, in 215) doing so was costly from a personal point of view. When, half a century later, the Augurs found the Consuls of 162 to be *vitio creati*, both instantly and without complaint obeyed the Senate's directive to abdicate their magistracy. Scattered

---

[5] Wilson's thorough and stimulating *Dictator* (2021) appeared too late to be fully taken into account; a few points of disagreement are briefly indicated in the notes.

instances of auspices ignored, in a military context, are known from the second and first centuries, but none were accompanied by the public spectacles of opposition to the ancient practice that had marked those of the Punic Wars. Chapter 8 addresses this aftermath.

We learn best about the ancient world by examining it step by step, detail by detail. And much of what we think we know may prove, on closer inspection, to not be so. Close inspection demands close attention to the ancient sources. For the reader's convenience, and to make clear how I understand a given passage, I have tried to translate or paraphrase most longer quotations from Greek and Latin; unless noted otherwise, translations are my own—as literal as I could manage, since smooth renderings lend themselves more to obscuring the information offered in the source than to preserving it.

I am deeply grateful to those who have read drafts of the book in whole or in part. Jerzy Linderski and Jeffrey Tatum gave invaluable advice, which I am afraid I have not always followed. The generous and constructive comments by the anonymous readers of the Press prompted me to rethink the structure of the work from the ground up; I hope the result offers a more coherent argument. Among others who made this book possible, I must single out the staff of the Interlibrary Loan office at Texas A&M University's Sterling C. Evans Library; without their tireless efforts at obtaining publications for me, I could not have completed the work. Faculty Development Leaves granted by the University in 2003 and 2014 provided helpful relief from teaching duties. Marc Addington, as a student ages ago, got it all started with a question about *dictator interregni caussa* in the *Fasti*. My colleague, Craig Kallendorf, encouraged me to send the manuscript to Oxford. What I know about auspices and augury—little enough, in comparison to him—I learned from Jerzy Linderski; what I owe him as a scholar is beyond evaluation.

My thanks go out to the editorial staff at Oxford University Press. First and foremost, I am indebted to Charlotte Loveridge, who took an immediate interest in the proposed book, and graciously put up with innumerable questions and special requests. Cathryn Steele, Nico Parfitt, and Nivedha Vinayagamurthy made the process of turning manuscript into book a smoother experience than I could have imagined. Mike Adams produced a proper map from my hand-drawn draft. And my copy editor, Neil Morris, in his painstaking examination of the manuscript offered invaluable advice on improving the text.

Nothing, however, could have come of this without the inspiration and boundless patience of the one who, for two decades now and counting, has given me the support of a comforting home, and constant love. To Robyn I dedicate this book.

C. F. K.

Contents

List of Map	xvii
List of Abbreviations	xix

1. Dictator and Magister Equitum ... 1
    1.1 The Quarrel ... 1
        1.1.1 A Victory or Two—or a Defeat? ... 2
        1.1.2 The Missing Magister Equitum ... 4
        1.1.3 Facts, Traditions, and Pictor's Version ... 6
    1.2 Rullianus as Magister Equitum ... 8
        1.2.1 Competing Chronologies ... 9
        1.2.2 The Story Not Told ... 13
    1.3 The Challenge ... 15
        1.3.1 Dictator vs. Master of the Horse: *Imperium* and Auspices ... 16
        1.3.2 Mercy, Disobedience, and the Shadow of Defeat ... 18
    1.4 The Play ... 21
    1.5 The Aftermath ... 23
        1.5.1 Cotta at Lipara ... 24
        1.5.2 Minucius Rufus ... 26

2. *Imperium* and Auspices ... 30
    2.1 *Imperium* ... 30
        2.1.1 Mommsen and Alternatives ... 30
        2.1.2 All *Imperia* Are Equal (but Some Are More Equal than Others) ... 32
        2.1.3 *Potestas* and *Imperium* ... 37
    2.2 *Auspicia*: Basic Concepts ... 39
        2.2.1 Augurs, Augury, and Magistrates ... 39
        2.2.2 The *Vinculum Temporis* ... 43
    2.3 The "Auspices of Investiture" ... 45
    2.4 The "Auspices of Departure": the Evidence ... 48
        2.4.1 The *Praetor* Approved by the Birds ... 48
        2.4.2 *Votis in Capitolio nuncupatis paludatus cum lictoribus profectus* ... 50
    2.5 The "Auspices of Departure"—a Modern Fiction ... 52
        2.5.1 The Departure of Gaius Flaminius ... 53
        2.5.2 Taking the Auspices along from Home ... 55
    2.6 Repeating the Auspices ... 56
        2.6.1 The Significance of Place ... 57
        2.6.2 *Vitium in Auspicio* ... 59
        2.6.3 *Auspicia Militiae*? ... 61

3. Dictator — 66
3.1 The Lictors — 66
- 3.1.1 Ahenobarbus' *Fasces* — 67
- 3.1.2 Cicero and His Laureled Lictors — 68
- 3.1.3 The Magistrate Without His Lictors — 71
- 3.1.4 The Turnus — 74
- 3.1.5 No Lictors, No Action — 76

3.2 Cessation or Termination? — 78
- 3.2.1 Polybios and Plutarch — 78
- 3.2.2 Dionysios — 82

3.3 The Nature of the Office — 84
- 3.3.1 Peculiar Aspects — 85
- 3.3.2 What's in a Name? — 87
- 3.3.3 *Dic(t)ator Latinus* — 89
- 3.3.4 *Dictator* and *Magister Populi* — 92
- 3.3.5 *Imperium Valentius* — 94

3.4 Term Limits — 100
- 3.4.1 The *Dictio* — 100
- 3.4.2 *Dictator sine Magistro Equitum* — 103
- 3.4.3 The Magister Equitum as Dictator — 105
- 3.4.4 The Six-month Limit — 109

4. Magister Equitum — 112
4.1 The Auspices of the Magister Equitum — 112
4.2 Auspices and Triumph — 116
- 4.2.1 Catulus and Falto — 116
- 4.2.2 Salinator and Nero — 119
- 4.2.3 Furius Purpurio — 120
- 4.2.4 Helvius — 121
- 4.2.5 *Suis Auspiciis* — 125

4.3 The Consul as Magister Equitum — 127
- 4.3.1 Cases of Cumulation — 128
- 4.3.2 Lepidus as Magister Equitum — 130

4.4 The Magister Equitum and the Augurs — 131
- 4.4.1 Caesar and Antonius: the Time Frame — 132
- 4.4.2 The Magister Equitum Named by the Consul: Constitutional Considerations — 133
- 4.4.3 No Decree for Caesar — 137
- 4.4.4 Lepidus' Enabling Act and the Auspices — 141
- 4.4.5 The Objection to Antonius — 142

5. Drowning the Chickens — 148
5.1 The *Pulli* — 148
- 5.1.1 The Evidence — 149
- 5.1.2 Servius, the Tribune, and the Chickens — 152

	5.2	The Auspices at Sea	156
		5.2.1 Augural Waters	157
		5.2.2 Making a Move, on Land and at Sea	158
	5.3	The Location of the *Vitium*: Claudius and Iunius	159
	5.4	*Vitium* and *Perduellio*	163
	5.5	The *Sortes Praenestinae*	165
		5.5.1 Consultation at Praeneste	165
		5.5.2 An Alternative to Auspices	167
6.	*Dictator Interregni Caussa*	169
	6.1	An Inconvenient Document	169
		6.1.1 Sumner's Interrex	170
		6.1.2 The Dictator as Interrex Substitute	172
		6.1.3 A Very Special Interrex	173
		6.1.4 The Missing Gerundive	174
	6.2	The *Fasti*	176
		6.2.1 Death and the *Fasti*	176
		6.2.2 More Oddities	178
	6.3	Flaminius in Gaul	179
	6.4	*Consules vitio facti*	182
		6.4.1 Augurs and Omens	183
		6.4.2 Augural Sabotage (a Fantasy)	185
		6.4.3 The Triumph	187
		6.4.4 Abdication and the Consular Year	189
	6.5	Contesting the Auspices	193
	6.6	Abdication, *Interregnum*, and the Need for a Dictator	197
		6.6.1 The Abdication of Sergius and Verginius	197
		6.6.2 Abdication Forced by a Dictator?	200
	6.7	The First Dictatorship of Fabius Maximus	203
		6.7.1 Removing Flaminius: a Moderate Solution	203
		6.7.2 The Name of the Dictator	206
		6.7.3 The *Sorex*	209
7.	The Road to Perdition	212
	7.1	Hannibal's Pass	212
		7.1.1 Hannibal's Options	213
		7.1.2 The Floods of the Arno	217
		7.1.3 Where was Flaminius?	219
		7.1.4 Where was Faesulae?	222
	7.2	Hannibal's Surprise	224
		7.2.1 The Race to Arezzo	225
		7.2.2 The Campaign in Gaul	228
		7.2.3 Flaminius at Arretium	233
	7.3	Going after Hannibal	235

    7.4 *Ostenta Flaminiana*   238
        7.4.1 The Signs   238
        7.4.2 The Fall off the Horse   240
        7.4.3 The Chickens and the Standard   241
        7.4.4 Auspices Valid and Invalid   243
        7.4.5 Coelius, Cicero, and Livy—an Augural Perspective   245
        7.4.6 Flaminius at the Lake   247
    7.5 *Inauspicato Consul*   249
        7.5.1 Redeployments for 217   249
        7.5.2 Strategy   252
        7.5.3 The Fog of Contempt   253

8. The Auspices Prevail   255
    8.1 Disaster and Dictator   255
        8.1.1 Emergency   256
        8.1.2 *Vitium*   258
        8.1.3 After Cannae   262
    8.2 *Contra Auspicia*   266
        8.2.1 The Challengers   266
        8.2.2 The Cunctator and his Deputy   268
    8.3 Upholding the Auspices   270
        8.3.1 The Second Consulship of Marcellus   270
        8.3.2 The Nature of the *Vitium*   274
        8.3.3 *Augur Optumus*   276
    8.4 The Triumph of the Augurs   278
        8.4.1 The *Vitium* of the First Marcellus   278
        8.4.2 *Vitium* and Its Consequences   280
        8.4.3 The Final Test   283
    8.5 Last Notes   287

Appendix: Consular Abdication and Interregnum   291

Bibliography   295
General Index   309
Index Locorum   329

List of Map

1. North-Central Italy and Appennine Passes   214

List of Abbreviations

Unless indicated otherwise below, authors whose work appears with only a single entry in the Bibliography are normally cited by author's name and page number(s) only. Ancient authors and texts are cited as in the *Oxford Classical Dictionary*, with occasional self-evident adjustments (e.g., Varro *LL* for Varro *Ling.*) Periodicals are abbreviated according to *L'année philologique*, with the customary modifications (e.g., *CP* instead of *CPh* for *Classical Philology*).

AL	Linderski, J. 1986. "The Augural Law." *ANRW* II.16.3: 2146–2312.
ANRW	*Aufstieg und Niedergang der römischen Welt: Geschichte und Kultur Roms im Spiegel der neueren Forschung.* J. Vogt, H. Temporini, and W. Haase (eds.). (Berlin and New York, 1972–).
AS	Kromayer, J., and G. Veith. *Antike Schlachtfelder: Bausteine zu einer antiken Kriegsgeschichte.* 4 vols. (Berlin, 1903–31).
CEF	Bailey, D. R. Shackleton. *Cicero: Epistulae ad Familiares.* 2 vols. (Cambridge, 1977).
CIL	*Corpus Inscriptionum Latinarum.* Consilio et auctoritate Academiae Litterarum Regiae Borussicae editum. (Berlin, 1863–).
CL	Oakley, S. P. *A Commentary on Livy, Books VI–X.* 4 vols. (Oxford, 1997–2005).
CLA	Bailey, D. R. Shackleton. *Cicero's Letters to Atticus.* 7 vols. (Cambridge, 1965–70).
FRH	Beck, H., and U. Walter. *Die Frühen Römischen Historiker.* 2 vols. (1: 2nd ed.). (Darmstadt, 2004–5).
FRHist	Cornell, T. J., E. H. Bispham, J. W. Rich, C. J. Smith, et al. *The Fragments of the Roman Historians.* 3 vols. (Oxford, 2013).
FS	Rüpke, J. *Fasti sacerdotum: Die Mitglieder der Priesterschaften und das sakrale Funktionspersonal römischer, griechischer, orientalischer und jüdisch-christlicher Kulte in der Stadt Rom von 300 v. Chr. bis 499 n. Chr.* 3 vols. (Stuttgart, 2005).
GdK	Meltzer, O., and U. Kahrstedt. *Geschichte der Karthager.* 3 vols. (Berlin, 1879–1913).
GramLat	Keil, H. *Grammatici Latini.* 8 vols. (Leipzig, 1855–80).
HCP	Walbank, F.W. *A Historical Commentary on Polybius.* 3 vols. (Oxford, 1957–79).
HRR	Peter, H. *Historicorum Romanorum reliquiae.* 2 vols. (1: 2nd ed.). (Leipzig, 1906–14).
ILS	Dessau, H. *Inscriptiones Latinae Selectae.* 3 vols. (Berlin, 1892–1916).
InscrItal	Degrassi, A. *Inscriptiones Italiae.* Rome.
	Vol. 13.1: *Fasti Consulares et Triumphales.* (1947).
	Vol. 13.2: *Fasti anni Numani et Iuliani.* (1963).
	Vol. 13.3: *Elogia.* (1937).
K–G	Kühner, R., and B. Gerth. *Ausführliche Grammatik der griechischen Sprache.* Part 2: *Satzlehre.* 2 vols., 2nd ed. (Hanover, 1898).

K–S   Kühner, R., and C. Stegmann. *Ausführliche Grammatik der lateinischen Sprache.* Part 2: *Satzlehre.* 2 vols., 2nd ed. (Hanover, 1914; 5th ed. 1976).
MRR   Broughton, T. R. S. *The Magistrates of the Roman Republic.* Vols. 1–2. (New York, 1951–2). Vol. 3, *Supplement.* (Atlanta, 1986).
OLD   *Oxford Latin Dictionary.* P. G. W. Glare (ed.). (Oxford, 1982).
PRR   Brennan, T. C. *The Praetorship in the Roman Republic.* 2 vols. (Oxford and New York, 2000).
RA   Lange, L. *Römische Alterthümer.* 3 vols. (Berlin, 1863–71).
RE   *Paulys Realencyclopädie der classischen Altertumswissenschaft.* G. Wissowa, W. Kroll, K. Mittelhaus, and K. Ziegler (eds.). (Stuttgart, 1893–1980).
RQ   Linderski, J. *Roman Questions: Selected Papers.* (Stuttgart, 1995).
RQ2   Linderski, J. *Roman Questions II: Selected Papers.* (Stuttgart, 2007).
RStat Crawford, M. H., et al. *Roman Statutes.* 2 vols. (London, 1996).
Schw–D Schwyzer, E., and A. Debrunner. *Griechische Grammatik.* 4 vols. (Munich, 1934–71; 2nd–6th eds., 1980–94).
SdR   De Sanctis, G. *Storia dei Romani.* 4 vols. (Turin, 1907–23).
ServGr Thilo, G., and H. Hagen. *Servii Grammatici qui feruntur in Vergilii carmina commentarii.* 3 vols. (Leipzig, 1881–1902).
SRR   Willems, P. *Le sénat de la république romaine: Sa composition et ses attributions.* 3 vols. (Louvain and Paris, 1878–85).
StO   Kunkel, W., and R. Wittmann. *Staatsordnung und Staatspraxis der Römischen Republik.* Part 2, *Die Magistratur.* (Munich, 1995).
StR   Mommsen, Th. *Römisches Staatsrecht.* 3 vols. (1–2: 3rd ed.). (Leipzig, 1887–8).
VM   Bailey, D. R. Shackleton. *Valerius Maximus: Memorable Doings and Sayings.* 2 vols. (Cambridge, Mass., and London, 2000).
W–M   Weissenborn, W., and H. J. Müller. *Titi Livi Ab urbe condita libri.* 10 vols., 2nd–10th eds. (Berlin, 1880–1924).

1
Dictator and Magister Equitum

In Samnium incertis itum auspiciis est, "the Romans advanced into Samnium under uncertain auspices." Thus begins Livy's account of the epic quarrel between the Dictator L. Papirius Cursor (*cos. I* 326) and his Master of the Horse, Q. Fabius Maximus Rullianus (*cos. I* 322), in 324 V (8.30.1–36.1).[1] The tale is well known: alerted by the *pullarius* to a problem with his auspices,[2] the Dictator returns to Rome *ad auspicium repetendum,* leaving the army under the command of his Magister Equitum, with strict orders not to engage the enemy (8.30.2); Fabius, young and chafing at his subordinate position, disobeys, and wins a splendid victory over the Samnites (8.30.3–7). Rejoining his army, the Dictator, infuriated at the disobedience, resolves to have his deputy put to death; but Rullianus escapes. Back in Rome, the Magister Equitum, aided by Tribunes of the Plebs and his distinguished father, M. Fabius Ambustus (*cos. III* 354; *dict.* 351), seeks protection by mobilizing public opinion against his superior; Papirius Cursor, in turn, insists on the absolute authority invested in his office to enforce his command. The ensuing contest of wills, played out *in contione* in the Forum, revolves—in Livy's telling— around a fundamental question: was the Master-of-Horse entirely and without exception subordinate to the Dictator, or could he plausibly claim his auspices as his own, not subject to those of the Dictator, and assert a right to independent action regardless of the latter's orders? It is the first recorded instance of a Magister Equitum—indeed, of anyone—publicly disagreeing with a Dictator and challenging the legitimacy of his power, under public as well as augural law.

1.1 The Quarrel

Exactly what events led to the quarrel is far from evident. Livy's sources here displayed a stunning range of differing accounts: some knew of two battles fought by Rullianus, both victorious; but in the earliest authors, only one was to be

---

[1] Or FC 429 = AUC 430, the second of the four "dictator" years. Dates before 300 BC will be marked "V" for "Varronian," as a reminder that the traditional chronology of the fifth and fourth centuries BC is hopelessly unreliable and confused. Thus, for instance, the year in question, 324 V, is (like all the dictator years) unknown to Livy, who reports its events *L. Furio II D. Iunio coss.,* the year we call 325 V; in reality, both probably correspond, if to anything, to the actual year 322 BC.

[2] It remains uncertain whether the phrase *incerta auspicia* denotes auspices that were merely ambiguous, or auspices that were or had become invalid: Linderski 1993: 62 = *RQ* 617; Konrad 2004: 172 n. 6, 202–203.

found; and in some annals, the "entire matter" was passed over in silence. *Auctores habeo bis cum hoste signa conlata dictatore absente, bis rem egregie gestam; apud antiquissimos scriptores una haec pugna invenitur; in quibusdam annalibus tota res praetermissa est* (8.30.7). It will be desirable to establish some clarity on that count before addressing the constitutional issues raised in connection with the dispute.

1.1.1 A Victory or Two—or a Defeat?

Among the *antiquissimi scriptores* noted here we may count Q. Fabius Pictor, whom Livy cites when explaining what happened next: Rullianus had all the spoils of the battle burnt, be it on account of a vow he had made to that effect, be it—as Fabius Pictor had it—to prevent the Dictator from taking credit for the victory and displaying the spoils in his triumph (*seu votum id deorum cuipiam fuit seu credere libet Fabio auctori eo factum ne suae gloriae fructum dictator caperet nomenque ibi scriberet aut spolia in triumpho ferret*, 8.30.8–9).[3] Evidently, the first historian did not believe that any vows had been involved, and was prepared to ascribe a less-than-pious-and-heroic motive to the action of his famous *gentilis*, preferring jealous ambition instead.[4] Livy earlier had advanced two competing explanations of why Rullianus chose to disobey orders: either the young man, lacking self-control, resented that all decisions lay with the Dictator, or he simply could not pass up an opportunity for successful action (*seu ferox adulescens indignitate accensus quod omnia in dictatore viderentur reposita esse seu occasione bene gerendae rei inductus*, 8.30.4); it will be reasonable to conclude that the first of them, again stressing jealous ambition, also derived from Pictor.

Now, in both those instances of motivation that we can deduce as having been attributed by Pictor—for giving battle and for burning the spoils—the language stresses not merely Rullianus' ambition but his constitutional subordination under the Dictator, and resentment thereof. In consequence, that feature is certain to have been present already in Pictor, not merely introduced by Livy or some intermediary: the entire point of burning the spoils rested on the Dictator's ability to claim them for himself, on the grounds that any battle fought by the Magister Equitum was fought under the Dictator's auspices; mere private ambition or rivalry would render the act absurd. It stands in stark contrast to the alternative motives offered: a military opportunity too good to pass up, and fulfillment of a vow previously made—neither of which has any bearing on the Master-of-Horse's

---

[3] Oakley *CL* 2: 694–697, 704–707, 711–714; 4: 584; Forsythe 1999: 60–61. Against the notion, once popular, that Livy did not directly consult Fabius Pictor or other second-century authors: Northwood *passim*; Oakley *CL* 1: 17–18 (with earlier literature); 4: 474; Rich 2005: 147. Ridley sums it up decisively: "One of the most outrageous and totally unproven charges against Livy is that he was lying when he claimed to have consulted Fabius" (2014: 470).

[4] Timpe 953; Frier 1979: 244 n. 47; 269; Beck 2003: 82–83, 88–89; Beck–Walter *FRH* 1: 121–122; 2: 171.

being subordinate to the Dictator, or on the ensuing power struggle between two magistrates. But just as with the "jealousy" pair of motivations, so with the alternatives: they form a consistent picture in which Rullianus acts as would any good Roman commander, seizing the opportunity and honoring the gods who granted him victory. Jealousy plays no part in his decisions, and nothing hints at the fact that he was challenging a higher authority. Oakley noted that Pictor's comment about Rullianus' treatment of the spoils "shows that already in his day there was rivalry over aristocratic self-advertisement." Yet the close coupling of the jealousy motif with Rullianus' subordination under the Dictator shows something more: not only the critical—not truly hostile, to be clear about that—elements in Livy's portrayal of Rullianus in this scene can be traced to Fabius Pictor, but also the implied debate, in Livy's subsequent account, on the Dictator's powers vis-à-vis his Magister Equitum.[5]

As regards Rullianus' victory, Livy's "earliest authors" (surely Pictor, and perhaps some others[6]) knew of only a single battle (8.30.7). Later writers had two, both victorious: no doubt they were also the ones who preferred to attribute Rullianus' action to military opportunity and vows to be honored. But in yet another group of accounts, says Livy, *tota res praetermissa est*. The statement is intriguing. Were it not for Livy's assurance that his oldest sources told of one battle, one would naturally conclude that those who omitted the matter preserved what really happened—the one- and two-battle versions both being later accretions to the story. To complicate things further, a fourth version of the tale can perhaps still be extracted from the sources: it may help solve the puzzle.

Twenty-one years later (by his reckoning), Livy tells of a Dictator who returned to Rome *auspiciorum repetendorum causa*, leaving his Magister Equitum in command of the army. The latter, intent on foraging, walked into an ambush, was beaten with heavy loss of life, and forced to withdraw into camp again (10.3.5–6):

(5) profectus dictator cum exercitu proelio uno Marsos fundit...(6) tum in Etruscos versus bellum; et, cum dictator auspiciorum repetendorum causa profectus Romam esset, magister equitum **pabulatum** egressus **ex insidiis circumvenitur** signisque aliquot amissis foeda militum **caede** ac fuga in castra est compulsus.

Virtually the same thing had happened in 324 V: while Papirius was haggling with the Senate and People in Rome over whether to execute his insubordinate Master of the Horse, a group of foragers was ambushed and slaughtered (in virtually

---

[5] Oakley *CL* 2: 714; Beck 2003: 86–87. Cf. Frier 1979: 244 n. 47 ("The severe criticism of Rullianus in Livy...shows an appreciation of the constitutional issue involved"); 269, noting the "constitutional significance" of burning the spoils.
[6] Oakley *CL* 2: 711: "almost certainly a reference to Fabius Pictor and perhaps to Fabius alone."

4 THE CHALLENGE TO THE AUSPICES

identical language: *frumentatores cum circumventi ex insidiis caesi loco iniquo essent*); but the *legatus* now left in charge of the camp, mindful of what would happen to him should he disobey the Dictator's orders to stay put, dared not act to rescue them (8.35.10–11).[7]

1.1.2 The Missing Magister Equitum

The Dictator in 301 V was M. Valerius Maximus;[8] as his Magister Equitum, Livy reports M. Aemilius Paullus—but he was not so sure about the latter (10.3.3–4, 7–8). To wit:

(4) id magis credo quam Q. Fabium ea aetate atque eis honoribus Valerio subiectum; ceterum ex Maximi cognomine ortum errorem haud abnuerim…(7) qui terror non eo tantum a Fabio abhorret quod, si qua alia arte cognomen suum aequavit, tum maxime bellicis laudibus, (8) sed etiam quod memor Papirianae saevitiae nunquam ut dictatoris iniussu dimicaret adduci potuisset.

It was hard to believe that Rullianus, at his age and with his distinguished career, would have held a subordinate position under Valerius (and the common surname "Maximus" might have caused the error); more to the point, not only did Fabius' military skill and reputation render such a defeat improbable, but given his past experience of "Papirian" severity, he surely could never have been led to engage the enemy against the Dictator's command. The comment reveals something not expressly stated in the narrative: on this occasion, as in 324 V, the Magister Equitum engaged the enemy in violation of the Dictator's orders (*dictatoris iniussu*) to stay put.

"Although [Livy] does not mention any discrepancy in his sources, it is plain that he found one." Certainly, but what exactly did that discrepancy consist of? "Perhaps some sources made Paullus hold the post, others Maximus."[9] Perhaps some did; but the unusual coyness—Livy having no trouble, normally, saying just that—suggests that he faced a bigger problem. Some sources, evidently, did not

---

[7] Cf. Chaplin 110.
[8] Or FC 452 = AUC 453, the last dictator year; Livy reports the events *M. Livio M. Aemilio coss.*, or 302 V. (With the dictator years done, all those dates now resolve into 301 BC, insofar as any consistent chronology can be attempted.) It is fairly certain that Livy thought of Valerius not as Corvus but as his son: he never calls Corvus "Maximus" in those instances where identity is not in doubt, and the avoidance of "Corvus" in all reference to the man he calls "M. Valerius" (with or without "Maximus") in Book 10 suggests the son. If so, Livy apparently did not accept the well-established tradition of Corvus' six consulships, held forty-six years apart from first to last. See Oakley *CL* 2: 238–239; in favor of Corvus: *MRR* 1: 170 n. 2.
[9] Oakley *CL* 4: 70. Walt 282 entertains confusion with Rullianus' son, Fabius Maximus Gurges (*cos. I* 292).

simply have Rullianus, but also Paullus, as Magister Equitum; more precisely, they had Rullianus, followed in the office by Paullus. One such source survives (whether Livy consulted this particular one is immaterial): the *Fasti Capitolini*.

[Q. Fabius] M. f . N. n. Maxi[mus Rullianus II abd(dicavit) mag(ister)
   eq(uitum). in e(ius) l(ocum) f(actus) e(st)]
[M. Ai]milius L. f. L. [n. Paullus mag(ister) eq(uitum)]

Though *abd(dicavit)* is not preserved (*InscrItal* 13.1: 38–39), the presence of a second Master of the Horse in the same year, 301 V, leaves nothing else to restore. It makes Rullianus the only recorded Magister Equitum to abdicate while the Dictator remained in office—enough of an anomaly to call for explanation. Oakley suggests that he "may have fallen ill." In fact, the historian's concluding remark (10.3.8) leaves no doubt about the nature of his embarrassment: some sources did not merely have Rullianus as Magister Equitum but ascribed to him that ignominious defeat, incurred while acting *iniussu dictatoris*. And in at least some of those sources the defeat had humiliating consequences for Rullianus: he abdicated, and was replaced. Almost the same thing, again, had happened in 324 V: after giving in, at last, to the pleas of Senate, Tribunes, and the People, Papirius the Dictator refrained from punishing Rullianus, but suspended him from acting as Magister Equitum: *dictator praeposito in urbe L. Papirio Crasso, magistro equitum Q. Fabio vetito quicquam pro magistratu agere, in castra rediit* (Livy 8.36.1). No wonder Livy found it past belief that, in all those years, one of Rome's most distinguished field commanders should have learned nothing in the areas of discipline and elementary tactics—and twice suffered the disgrace of being removed from office.

As Livy continues his narrative in Book 10, the Magister Equitum suffers no punishment or reproach. When the Dictator, with fresh levies, returns to the camp, he finds that his deputy has things well in hand: *omnia spe tranquilliora et composita magistri equitum cura...invenit*; the camp relocated to a safer position, the defeated units punished, the troops eager to engage the enemy and redeem themselves (10.4.3–4). Soon a full-scale battle is fought, a splendid victory achieved; but it is a close affair, as the Dictator deliberately allows the enemy to surround and nearly overwhelm a Roman detachment (10.4.6–5.11). Only a headlong cavalry charge at the last moment wins the day (*emissus eques libero cursu in hostem invehitur...itaque, ut prope serum auxilium iam paene circumventis, ita universa requies data est*, 10.5.7–8).

Rullianus' victory in 324, too, was the work of his cavalry, charging in wild abandon (8.30.6). Valerius Maximus also tells the story (3.2.9), but with a twist not in Livy: Rullianus' army was on the verge of suffering defeat (*manus cum hoste, sed tam infeliciter quam temere conseruit: procul enim dubio superabatur*), when the cavalry saved the day, and the Magister Equitum from being accused of having commenced battle in poor judgment (*strenuus ille quoque flos ordinis equestris, cuius mira virtute...male commissi proelii crimine levatus est*).

A further oddity obtrudes. After the quarrel in 324 V, no Magister Equitum is mentioned as accompanying Papirius on his victorious campaign against the Samnites (8.36): naturally, since Rullianus had been prohibited from acting in his official capacity. No such prohibition is recorded, or can be inferred, for the Master-of-Horse in 301 V; yet in like manner, from Livy's long, vivid description of the battle in Etruria, he is conspicuously absent, in stark contrast to other such pieces:[10] a *legatus* has taken his place in the narrative (at 10.4.7), virtually from the point the Dictator returned to the camp and found his deputy in control of the situation. After the victory, *dictator triumphans in urbem rediit* (10.5.1–13). Then again, a discrepancy: *habeo auctores sine ullo memorabili proelio pacatam ab dictatore Etruriam esse*. Some authors told of the Dictator putting down the Etruscans without any battle worth mentioning (and, presumably, without noting any presence of the Magister Equitum in Etruria).

That alternative "exposes [Livy's] longer version as the product of annalistic elaboration and invention."[11] The Dictator of 301 V (assuming there was one) fought no battle against the Etruscans, in the earliest tradition. We should not, however, rashly apply the same reasoning to the story about the Master of the Horse. The latter's defeat is told in brief, sparse narrative, without any of the romantic and anecdotal detail that fills chapters 4 and 5 (the Dictator's return and victorious campaign); we can rightfully expect better of annalistic invention. Although coming under the label of the Etruscan War, the incident stands isolated—carefully so, one almost senses—in Livy's narrative; its actual place is with the Marsian campaign (told in equal brevity), separated by a dozen lines of text (10.3.7–4.4) from the "long" version of the maneuvering and fighting near Rusellae. Most of all disturbing, the involvement of Rullianus. Why invent a defeat and abdication in disgrace at this point in the man's career? (It clearly was not needed to make the "long" version of the Etruscan War look plausible.) Invent it so clumsily, and patently parallel to what had happened in 324 V, that any reader, not just Livy, could see that something was amiss?

1.1.3 Facts, Traditions, and Pictor's Version

If we look at what we find in Livy, his sources, Valerius Maximus, and the *Fasti*, not from the prospect of a finished history but from the perspective of what later

---

[10] E.g., 2.20.7–9 (Aebutius at Lake Regillus, 499 or 496 V); 4.33.7 (Cossus at Fidenae, 426 V); 6.12.10 (Quinctius Capitolinus against the Volscians, 385 V); 6.29.1–2 (Sempronius Atratinus against Praeneste, 380 V); 7.15.6–7 (Valerius Poplicola against the Gauls, 358 V); 8.38.14–39.5 (M. Fabius Ambustus against the Samnites, 322 V); 9.22.4–10 (Aulius Cerretanus at Saticula, 315 V); 9.23.6, 15 (C. Fabius Ambustus at Lautulae, 315 V); 9.40.8–10 (Iunius Bubulcus at Longulae, 309 V).

[11] Oakley *CL* 4: 46.

ages had to tell about Fabius Rullianus (differently put, if for a moment we suspend the chronological fixation of those events, in particular what appears, in the finished history, as a twenty-one-year interval between two identical acts of disobedience), a measure of clarity emerges.

(1) Rullianus was Magister Equitum.
(2) When the Dictator goes back to Rome to repeat the auspices, Rullianus, against his orders, engages the enemy.
(3) His action results in:
 (a) two battles, both victorious;
 (b) one battle and victory,
  (bb) though according to some only after almost certain defeat;
 (c) nothing worth reporting;
 (d) a defeat.
(4) By the time the Dictator returns to the camp, his deputy has the situation under control. (Note how, at precisely this point, the Magister Equitum disappears from Livy's "long" version of the fighting in 301 V.)
(5) The Dictator decides to execute Rullianus; both return to Rome.
(6) A group of foragers is ambushed and cut down.
(7) After much recrimination, argument, and begging for mercy, the Dictator refrains from punishment, but
(8) suspends Rullianus from office.
(9) Rullianus abdicates as Master of the Horse.
(10) The Dictator returns to his army, wins a splendid victory without any known participation of a Magister Equitum, and triumphs.

What transpires is a perfectly coherent tradition about Rullianus' experience as Magister Equitum—except for #3 and, to a lesser degree, ##8–9. Even here, though, we find an element common to defeat (3d) and victory (3a and/or 3b): all those versions know of Roman foragers caught and destroyed in an ambush, the difference being that, in (3d), the Master-of-Horse leads out the main body of the army (*pabulatum egressus...signis amissis*, Livy 10.3.6), whereas in #3a/b = 6 the *legatus* left in command of the camp during the Dictator's absence fails to come to the rescue of the *frumentatores* (Livy 8.35.10–11). Livy does not mention this event until after the conflict between Dictator and Magister Equitum has been resolved; it is part epilogue, part transition to the next chapter (8.36), which focusses on the continuing political education of Papirius Cursor. That the Romans should be bloodied in a skirmish (6) so as to illustrate the deleterious effects of the Dictator's *saevitia* comes as no surprise in writers who took up Rullianus' cause, or tried—like Livy—to see merit in both sides of the dispute; that the details of that skirmish should so closely imitate those of #3d is too much coincidence for comfort.

We can now reconstruct, with a fair degree of probability, the elements of the story as told by the first historian. Fabius Pictor presented the one-battle version (3b), along with ##1–2, 5, and 7. Since he reported a victory, he need not emphasize #4, although Rullianus' long *contio* (Livy 8.31) clearly shows the Magister Equitum in control of camp and army. This part in Livy, of course, might derive from the two-battles-and-victories (3a) tradition, and in any case contains much subsequent elaboration, but the repeated stress on the Master's independence—alleged or desired—from the Dictator suggests that it was not entirely missing from Pictor's account. Whether he included the slaughter of the foragers (6), and at what point in his narrative, is hard to tell: the incident's distinctly anti-Papirian bent in Livy does not obviously point to Pictor, nor rule him out; in any case, Livy must have found it in representatives of either the #3a or 3b tradition, if not both. Pictor further gave either #8 or 9; had he shown no consequences at all suffered by Rullianus, Livy certainly would have noted that. If Pictor had Rullianus abdicate (9), the *praepositus in urbe* L. Papirius Crassus may have been, in his account, the suffect Magister Equitum; but one would expect the latter to accompany the Dictator on his renewed campaign: hence Livy's version (8 = 8.36.1) is perhaps more likely to reflect Pictor's. As for #10, Livy makes much of the Dictator's realization that he must balance *severitas* with *comitas* (8.36.2–7): in other words, Papirius Cursor develops the very quality Rullianus' supporters had found wanting in him, and which he had attacked in them. That, too, might point to Fabius Pictor, but it could equally well be Livy's own contribution—or, as we shall see, belong to an even earlier version of the tale.[12] That Pictor omitted the Dictator's battle and triumph seems improbable. Unlike the writers in the two-battles (3a) tradition, with their strong (it appears) endorsement of Rullianus, his version was critical of the Magister Equitum, hence, presumably, not outright hostile to Papirius. #3a would be less likely to mention a triumph—not necessarily, though, out of sheer malice; but those authors certainly would lack the incentive to create one for Papirius.

1.2 Rullianus as Magister Equitum

It passes belief that Fabius Rullianus should have, as Master of the Horse, disobeyed the Dictator, suffered defeat, and been removed from office twice in his career, twenty-one years apart; we may with confidence embrace Livy's judgment in that regard. And yet, there are grounds to suspect that at least one source (not necessarily used by Livy) did imply just that.

---

[12] Lipovsky 115, 126–128; cf. Oakley *CL* 2: 705–707.

1.2.1 Competing Chronologies

Under 301 V, the *Fasti Capitolini* noted Rullianus' abdication as Magister Equitum. No iteration survives on the stone, but the Chronographer of 354 lists *Corvo II et Rulliano II*: coming from a tradition very close to the *FC*, this may be safely taken to reflect what stood in the marble. Nor would anyone expect otherwise: surely the *Fasti* could not omit the man's first turn at that office, in 324 V (by the document's reckoning). By the time they were compiled, he and Papirius had become inseparable: witness the latter's elogium (*InscrItal* 13.3: 39 no. 62), *bello Samnitium cum auspicii repetendi caussa Romam redisset atque interim Q. Fabius Amb[usti f.] Maximus mag[ister] equitum iniu[ssu eiu]s proelio c[onflixisset—]*.

But the stone for 324 V is not extant, and the late chronographers offer an intriguing variant. The one from 354 simply indicates a dictator year (*hoc anno dictatores non [sic] fuerunt*), without names. The *Fasti Hydatiani*, however, have *dictator…Papinius [sic] Cursor et magister equitum Drusus*, which finds its parallel in the *Chronicon Paschale*: Παπίνιος Κούρσωρ ἀντιγραφεὺς…, Δροῦσος στρατηγὸς ἱππέων. The mysterious Drusus has long since been identified with the ancestor of the Livii Drusi, presumably father of M. Livius Denter (*cos.* 302); Suetonius attests a *magisterium equitum* for the family (*Tib.* 3.1).[13] The *Fasti* must have shown Rullianus as Master of the Horse, given their virtually certain iteration under 301, and the near impossibility of omitting his service under Papirius Cursor. What of Drusus?

Under 301 V, the *Fasti Hydatiani* list *Corvinus dictator et Aemilius magister equitum*; no mention of Rullianus. Yet the *FC* had both, one after the other. Why not the same in 324—Rullianus followed by Drusus? Both are dictator years, the product of chronological manipulation (would that we understood the how and why!); for each, some of the literary sources had Rullianus as Magister Equitum, disobedient and disgraced. (That cannot be contested, even if one were to reject the conclusion reached above, namely, that some of Livy's sources for 324 V reported Rullianus' battle as a defeat.) In both years, the *Fasti Hydatiani* omit Rullianus: if their source showed him as having abdicated on both occasions, his presence in the office may not have seemed worth noting. No rational argument can be adduced why the *FC*, noting his abdication in 301, should not also note it on the earlier occasion, if a substantial strand of the tradition thus reported it. That such a strand existed has been argued above. Now a Livius Drusus could not have been substituted for Rullianus, of all men, in an even exchange:[14] if ever there was a tradition that had Drusus, and only Drusus, as Master of the Horse to Papirius Cursor, it would have to be earlier than the latter's association with Rullianus. Perhaps there was; but it cannot possibly have been the *FC*'s version.

---

[13] F. Münzer "Livius" *RE* 13.1 (1926) 811–812; Broughton *MRR* 1: 148–149.
[14] As Bandel 92 thought possible.

Once Rullianus entered the record for 324 V, a pre-existing Drusus as Magister Equitum must either disappear or become Rullianus' suffect; if Rullianus belonged to Papirius' dictatorship from the very beginning, Drusus could only enter the record as suffect—or be ignored by those who preferred to have Rullianus end his term suspended, rather than abdicate. That a Drusus-only version (if such did exist at all) survived in Livian family tradition, and re-emerged in Suetonius, is conceivable; that it produced, from independent compilation, the entries in the late chronographers is not. The *Fasti Capitolini*, under 324 V, had two Magistri Equitum: first Fabius Rullianus, *abdicavit*; then Livius Drusus.[15]

We should not rashly assume falsification when mere confusion will suffice. The chronology of early Rome (the fourth century in particular) is a morass with preciously few islands of firm ground, and the ancient historians experienced no fewer challenges, or better success, in navigating across it than do their modern counterparts. That the same event—Rullianus in disgrace as Magister Equitum— should eventually be reported, in different sources, some twenty years apart may be disturbing, but it has parallels.[16]

The *Fasti* show C. Maenius (*cos.* 338) as Dictator in 320 and 314 V (*InscrItal* 13.1: 36–37), both times with M. Folius Flaccinator (*cos.* 318) for Magister Equitum; yet the literary sources know of only one dictatorship, in 314 V. That appointment was prompted by anti-Roman activities in Capua; Diodoros writes of a full-fledged rebellion that folded without a fight when confronted by the Dictator's army (19.76.3–5; cf. 19.73.1), while Livy describes Maenius' designation as *quaestionibus exercendis* (9.26.7, 14). Both agree that the Campanian ringleaders took their own lives rather than face the *ingens terror* of a trial conducted by a Dictator; Livy tells how, subsequently, the Dictator's investigation was expanded to conspiratorial activities in Rome itself, where it ran into such vociferous opposition from the "Nobles" that Dictator and Magister Equitum thought it best to abdicate (9.26.8–20).

In the *Fasti*, Maenius' and Folius' appointment in 314 is listed as *rei gerund(ae) caussa* and identified as their second one, after an earlier turn at Dictator and Magister Equitum in 320 (no designation survives). The discrepant designations under the year 314 need not perturb. Diodoros' account would seem to bear out the stone's *rei gerundae*; Livy's *quaestionibus exercendis* may simply have anticipated what he himself clearly describes as a redirection, subsequent to the initial appointment, of Maenius' activity after the conspiracy at Capua had collapsed.

---

[15] Thus, essentially, already Jahn 91–92. But the *Fasti* certainly did not have a third; Tarpin's assertion (276 n. 107) that the Dictator named L. Papirius Crassus as a second Magister Equitum, side by side with the suspended Rullianus, has no basis in the evidence. Crassus (*praeposito in urbe*, Livy 8.36.1) was most likely the Praetor of 325 V (the same year as 324 V, unless the dictator years are real); of the Consuls, one was fighting with his army among the Vestini, and the other's illness had prompted the appointment of the Dictator (Livy 8.29.6–14).

[16] Càssola 1999: 10, on the phenomenon in general.

(In fact, the highly unusual dative of the gerundive—the sole occurrence in Livy—to denote the Dictators' task, as opposed to the genitive with *causa* that normally expresses the reason for the appointment, may indicate that Livy did not intend here to give the original appellation.)[17] Now, under 310 V, Livy, in the speech of the Tribune Sempronius, recalls how Maenius had been forced from office: *nuper intra decem annos C. Maenius dictator...cum quaestiones severius quam quibusdam potentibus tutum erat exerceret...dictatura se abdicavit* (9.34.14). "Within ten years (past)" surely points back farther, from 310 V, than to 314: indeed, it squares admirably with a dictatorship in 320 V, as reported by the *Fasti*.[18] It does not, of course, support that document's notion of two dictatorships for Maenius, six years apart—both Diodoros and Livy, clearly, knew of only one dictatorship in the man's career. As did, we may say with confidence, the entire tradition prior to the Capitoline *Fasti*. Degrassi, unfortunately, accepted the FC evidence and accused Livy of carelessly transferring the designation *quaestionibus exercendis* from Maenius' first appointment in 320 V to the "second" in 314, without considering that *quaestionibus exercendis* cannot be separated from the story told by Livy and Diodoros.[19] Which is to say, no trace has survived in the literary record of a dictatorship *rei gerundae causa*—except in Diodoros, whose account concerns the same event as does Livy's, in the same year.

The problem, and discrepancy, lie in the date of Maenius' dictatorship: one strand of the tradition (what we may call the "low" chronology) placed it in the year we know as 314 V; another (the "high" chronology), in 320. Both, probably, put it in the year after the Caudine Forks. It is a discrepancy that plagues the entire Second Samnite War (indeed, much of the fourth century). Our surviving accounts—Livy and the *Fasti* alike—did not consistently follow either the "high" or the "low" tradition: the historian, although attempting to produce a coherent account, frequently, if unawares, moves from one to the other, as did no doubt already some of his predecessors. The FC, with disastrous consequences, "resolved" at least some discrepancies of such nature by incorporating both traditions, creating thus (among numerous other doublets, contradictions, and temporal dislocations) two dictatorships for C. Maenius—and two humiliating stints at Magister Equitum for Fabius Rullianus.[20]

It is surely no coincidence that, of the four dictator years, two (324 V and 301 V) feature Rullianus as Magister Equitum, and two (324 V again, and 309 V) Papirius Cursor as Dictator; Rullianus, in fact, is tied to all three instances, as Consul (*II*)

---

[17] Hartfield 439–440; cf. Baroni 780–782.
[18] I am not persuaded by Oakley's argument (*CL* 3: 443) that *intra decem annos* is simply "a vague Livian generalization." Ridley 1989: 241 is surely correct.
[19] *InscrItal* 13.1: 109.
[20] For a possible example of another twenty-year dislocation see Holloway 123, arguing that the Carthaginian invasion of Sicily reported by Livy—and nowhere else—under 431 V (4.29.8) is really the well-known one of 409 BC.

in 310 V and "Proconsul" in 309. No satisfactory explanation of why those particular years, along with 333 V, should have ended up as dictator years has ever been advanced, and none will be attempted here; but given our general understanding that the dictator years originated as a device to manage fourth-century chronology,[21] Rullianus' prominence among them accords well with the view pursued above, namely, that his career was subject to substantial chronological displacement in Roman historiography.

Indeed, the bizarre attribution of a second curule aedileship to Rullianus[22] in 299 BC by Licinius Macer and Aelius Tubero (Livy 10.9.10–11, 11.9) may have its root in the same problem. What would seem, at first glance, the easiest explanation—Rullianus confused with his son, Gurges—is highly unlikely. Whatever their shortcomings and sins as historians, Macer and Tubero knew the *cursus honorum* as thoroughly as do we; if anything, they would be inclined to retroject such a pattern to a period when it had not yet solidified. If they had found a Fabius Maximus, without further identification, listed as Curule Aedile in 299, they would naturally have assumed that this must be Gurges, soon to be Consul (in 292) and at the right stage in his public life—not the great Rullianus, Censor, Dictator, and thrice Consul by that time.[23] Confusion arising out of conflicting and intractable information is one thing; downright stupidity is quite another. It should not be made the basis of our explanation without grave reason or conclusive evidence. Clearly, the record(s) that contained the troublesome aedileship in 299 BC specified Fabius Rullianus, not just Fabius Maximus: the very story of how he came to hold that office so improbably late (Livy 10.9.10–13) shows that Macer and Tubero saw the problem, and tried to address it.[24] Livy, of course, did not see the original record (whatever it was), but merely what his two authorities made of it; he noticed that it conflicted with the Aediles Piso listed under the same year (or, rather, what Livy took to be the same year[25]), but suspected any errors to have been caused by that year's superfetation with men called "Maximus" (Fabius, Domitius Calvinus, and Carvilius). That Fabius Maximus Gurges might have been the Aedile did not occur to him. No one, evidently, raised eyebrows at

---

[21] Mommsen 1859: 102, 114–117, suggesting that, in the original *fasti*, the four consular pairs in question for chronological reasons each occupied two years; but again, why this should have happened in those particular years remains unexplained. Drummond 1978 offers a full if ultimately aporistic discussion.

[22] Assuming he was the Q. Fabius Maximus holding the office in 331 V (Livy 8.18.4–5).

[23] Livy almost certainly knew Gurges as Curule Aedile in 295: *eo anno Q. Fabius Gurges consulis filius aliquot matronas ad populum stupri damnatas pecunia multavit; ex quo multaticio aere Veneris aedem quae prope Circum est faciendam curavit*, 10.31.9. It is difficult to see in what other function Gurges could have fined anyone; cf. F. Münzer "Fabius (112)" *RE* 6.2 (1909) 1798; *MRR* 1: 178; Oakley *CL* 4: 187.

[24] Walt 282–284.

[25] It probably was not, as 299 BC ought to be a "patrician" year, and Piso's Aediles are plebeians; but whether this is due to a mistake of Piso, or of Livy, or (as I suspect) an unresolved chronological dislocation, cannot be pursued here: see Münzer "Fabius (114)" *RE* 6.2 (1909) 1807; Forsythe 1994: 348; Oakley *CL* 4: 140.

Rullianus' supposed colleague, L. Papirius Cursor; that name called for no explanation—precisely because everyone assumed, naturally, that he was the son (*cos. I* 293).[26] The aedileship in 299 and the second stint as Magister Equitum in 301 V are the product not of wholesale fiction, but derive initially from an account that placed—or was taken by later writers, correctly or from misunderstanding, to place—the man (and, quite possibly, many of the related events) about two or three decades closer to the First Punic War than in what was, or became, the standard tradition.

For our current discussion, the actual year in which Rullianus was Magister Equitum is of no consequence. By Fabius Pictor's day, his association with Papirius Cursor the Dictator appears to have been well established: indeed, the complete absence of the great quarrel in Livy's narrative of 301 V (his sources for that year told of Rullianus' office, disobedience, defeat, and disgrace, and he was troubled by it; but apparently he knew of no claims that this time, too, the Dictator aimed to execute his Master of the Horse) suggests—but does not prove, of course—that this connection was equally accepted in Fabian, Papirian, and popular tradition, and probably original. Rullianus' appearance in 301 V should be considered the result of an unresolved discrepancy in the temporal fixation of his career, producing eventually a second, unhistorical tenure of the office under the Dictator Valerius Maximus.

1.2.2 The Story Not Told

As Livy noted at the outset, his sources on the incident came in three kinds: those with one battle that ended in a victory, those with two victories, and some others, *in quibus...tota res praetermissa est*. What, though, was "the matter" (*res*) they passed over?

Oakley assumed that *res* simply referred to the battle ("others did not record any fighting at all"), and though calling such omission "worrying," he suggested "haste or even anti-Fabian spite" to explain those writers' silence.[27] But if those authors omitted the battle fought in disobedience of the Dictator's orders, they could not have told of the ensuing quarrel between Papirius and his Magister Equitum; and yet, if they were anti-Fabian, that quarrel, ending even under the most favorable spin (3a) in Rullianus' disgrace, would be hard to pass up. Or does *tota res* here not mean what one would expect? The phrase might, conceivably,

---

[26] Oakley *CL* 4: 149 would also allow reference, "conceivably," to the father: quite improbable. Forsythe 1994: 347 assumes the father without question, and would see the story as a "patriotic moral" in which "the two great military men put their past differences aside and pulled in unison for the good of the state," turning "their talents from war to peace in insuring that a severe grain shortage did not endanger the state." None of this is found in Livy.

[27] *CL* 2: 697.

be intended to cover not merely the battle but the entire subsequent quarrel; but Livy had yet to tell that story—only hinted at, obliquely, in the opening paragraph (*cuius rei vitium non in belli eventum…sed in rabiem atque iras imperatorum vertit*, 8.30.1). If that is what he meant, he took care to camouflage it. The context in which he placed the comment—immediately after narrating the battle, rather than at the end of the whole episode—naturally leads the reader to think that fighting is what Livy had in mind.[28]

What kind of fighting, though? One could not tell the story of the quarrel without reporting a battle first—but not necessarily a battle that Rullianus won. The unambiguous references to the first two groups of Livy's sources speak of victory, but in at least one of the single-battle versions (3bb = Val. Max. 3.2.9), defeat had been imminent, and the decision to engage the enemy is described as taken in poor judgment (*male commissi proelii*). Livy surely knew of the near disaster alleged in #3bb, but chose to omit that detail, and went straight to the cavalry's glorious charge, without a hint that this was what turned catastrophe into triumph. By the time his narrative of the conflict is concluded, some eleven pages later, few readers would come back to wonder if the quarrel, too, fell under the *res praetermissa*, or how any writers that omitted all the fighting could still have reported the dispute.

Hence three possibilities offer for the third group: it omitted the entire episode of Papirius and Rullianus (3c); or it had the Magister Equitum suffer a defeat (3d); or it included authors answering to either description. If this group's authorities consisted of #3c throughout, it is difficult to see why Livy should not clearly say so. But if they represented, at least in part, the #3d tradition, his ambiguity shows purpose: he will allow, truthfully, that some authors made no mention of Rullianus' victorious battle(s), without divulging that they told of a defeat.

In his account of 301 V, Livy did acknowledge, with evident and considerable discomfort, that some of his sources reported a case of disobedience and defeat under the name of Fabius Rullianus, Magister Equitum. Why not acknowledge the same in the earlier context, in 324 V? No source for 301 V appears to have ascribed a victory to Rullianus, let alone two: the problem here, for Livy, was to decide whether Rullianus had held the office at all in that year. For 324 V, the historian had the word of Fabius Pictor, supported by numerous (it seems) other accounts—and Pictor's was the earliest, hence, preferable.[29]

And Livy (as he makes clear at 10.3.7) found it exceedingly hard to believe that a consummate commander such as Fabius Rullianus should have suffered a defeat caused by his own ineptitude. Note, for illustration, how Livy treats the campaign

---

[28] Cf. Livy 7.9.3–5, *dictatorem T. Quinctium Poenum eo anno fuisse satis constat*; but Licinius Macer maintained that Quinctius was merely *comitiorum habendorum causa: cum mentionem eius rei* (i.e., not the dictatorship but this specific purpose) *in vetustioribus annalibus nullam invenio*.

[29] Forsythe 1999: 18, 60–61; Ridley 2014: 470.

of 315 V: a splendid performance by Rullianus (now Dictator) at Saticula, with the fatal heroics of his Magister Equitum (9.22), followed by the initial, indecisive fight at Lautulae, told in distant, impersonal language (*ancipiti proelio dimicatum est*, 9.23.4) without mentioning Rullianus. Then, barely, a note that some authors reported that second battle as a Roman defeat, and that it was here that Aulius the Magister Equitum lost his life: *invenio apud quosdam adversam eam pugnam Romanis fuisse atque in ea cecidisse Q. Aulium magistrum equitum* (9.23.5).[30] Once the situation is restored, the eventual victory at Lautulae is again painted in full color (9.23.7–17).

Which leaves the question: When did the authors of #3d have Rullianus suffer the defeat (and effective removal from office), and under which Dictator—and how many times? Here, clearly, at least two further variants obtained: one (3d1) associating the event with the (first) dictatorship of Papirius Cursor in 324 V, the other (3d2) with that of Valerius Maximus in 301. The latter variant, however, does not appear (to judge from Livy 10.3) to have contained a dramatic struggle between Dictator and Master of the Horse, but limited itself to a matter-of-fact account of disobedience, defeat, and abdication. One might be tempted to conclude that #3d2 must be the earlier and (more) original one, lacking the magnificent embellishment we read in Book 8. But much of that embellishment could have accrued later; it does not disprove the originality of a bare-bones version that told of the quarrel. The struggle with Papirius, as we have seen, was integral to the story of Rullianus probably from the beginning; it would resist transfer to a different context and Dictator. The underlying events were not so protected.

We still cannot eliminate the possibility that some of Livy's sources did omit the entire episode, but we must note that it is far from certain. More likely, what the authors behind Livy's third variant (3c) of what happened when the Dictator left Rullianus in command in 324 V—nothing—passed over was Rullianus' victory, not the ensuing quarrel nor any fighting as such; instead, they reported a defeat. In other words, Livy's third variant (3c) may be a phantom, identical in reality with the fourth variant (3d), defeat, that we have tried to rescue from oblivion.

1.3 The Challenge

Livy did not exclusively base his narrative of the episode on Fabius Pictor and representatives of the one-battle (3b) tradition. At the end of his great speech, M. Fabius Ambustus invokes his son's two battles, both victorious through the gods' help he had sought (*deosque ab se duobus proeliis haud frustra advocatos*, 8.33.21). Oakley suggests that Livy either "was deliberately making the elder

---

[30] "The true version of the tale," notes Oakley *CL* 3: 292.

Fabius exaggerate or…had forgotten the views of the older annalists."[31] Neither seems probable.

1.3.1 Dictator vs. Master of the Horse: *Imperium* and Auspices

At the debate in Rome, the theme of dictatorial powers versus those of the Magister Equitum, as we have seen, almost certainly goes back to Pictor. The constitutional position is expressed in general assertions that the Dictator holds authority over all officials. The Dictator's *imperium* is supreme, and even the Consuls—the regal power!—do obey him, as do the Praetors, elected under the same auspices as the Consuls: you would think it only just that the Magister Equitum should obey his command (8.30.11, *cum summum imperium dictatoris sit pareantque ei consules, regia potestas, praetores, iisdem auspiciis quibus consules creati, aequum censeas necne magistrum equitum dicto audientem esse*; cf. 8.32.3, 34.2–3, 34.5–6, 35.5).

In like manner, his auspices take precedence over those of his deputy: if a religious fault posed an obstacle for the Dictator to conduct a campaign, surely the Master of the Horse could not be unaffected and free of it (8.32.4–7, *quae dictatori religio impedimento ad rem gerendam fuerit, num ea magister equitum solutus ac liber potuerit esse*; 8.34.4); which specific insistence is countered with claims that the Magister Equitum ought to be more than a mere attendant (8.31.4, *quod se Q. Fabius magistrum equitum duxerit ac non accensum dictatoris*) and that he fought under his own auspices (8.31.1, *cuius ductu auspicioque vicissent*; 8.33.22). We need not assume that Pictor presented a scene of similar length and complexity as we find in Livy; a few sentences stating the respective positions of the Dictator and his opponents would have sufficed.

Yet Livy offers another strand of argumentation in behalf of Rullianus. It revolves around the question of whether the Dictator is, or ought to be, subject to *provocatio* and the tribunician *ius auxilii* (8.33.8, *tribunos plebis appello et provoco ad populum…videro cessurusne provocationi sis*; countered at 8.34.6: *optare ne potestas tribunicia, inviolata ipsa, violet intercessione sua Romanum imperium neu populus [in] se potissimum dictatore[m et] ius dictaturae exstinguat*[32]). It emphasizes the restraint shown by earlier dictators in dealing with troublesome subordinates (8.33.12, *se quoque*—the speaker is Rullianus' father—*dictatorem Romae fuisse nec a se quemquam, ne plebis quidem hominem, non centurionem, non militem, violatum*; 8.33.14–15); but the historic examples cited involve, remarkably, only instances of military incompetence and defeat—not disobedience and victory. A general reminder follows to the effect that the People, *penes quem potestas*

---

[31] *CL* 2: 736; similarly Forsythe 2005: 296; *contra* Chaplin 111.
[32] For the text, Oakley *CL* 2: 739.

omnium rerum esset, had never punished more harshly than with a fine any commander who, *temeritate atque inscitia*, had lost his army: to this day, none had ever faced a trial for his life (*capite anquisitum ob rem bello male gestam de imperatore nullo ad eam diem esse*, 8.33.17).[33] How could a worse fate befall one who had conquered in two battles, under his own auspices? Not once in Ambustus' speech does the question of (dis)obeying orders—let alone auspices—find mention.

Clearly none of such reasoning is connected with the relative powers of Dictator and Magister Equitum, or the Dictator's authority over all other (that is to say, "patrician") magistrates, or the need to maintain military discipline; and the fundamental issue that had triggered the whole incident—should a battle be waged *incertis auspiciis*—is dismissed with a peremptory but unargued claim that the Magister Equitum fought *suis auspiciis*. All of it is designed to sidestep the constitutional dispute between the Dictator and his deputy, and change the debate into a popular referendum on the powers inherent in the dictatorship vis-à-vis the Tribunes and the People on the one hand, and, on the other, whether prowess in command combined with the favor of the gods, as demonstrated in two victories—*deosque ab se duobus proeliis haud frustra advocatos*—should absolve from all sins (8.33.21). Such would have been the line of defense taken by any competent *patronus* when the law unequivocally put his client in the wrong. The question for us is: How much of it can we expect to have stood in Pictor's account?

The latter point in particular, and in slightly modified form—that victory gave proof of the validity of a commander's auspices—would be raised again a century later in an attempt to contest a ruling by the College of Augurs that both Consuls were *vitio creati*.[34] It ties in perfectly with the alternative reasons Livy offered for Rullianus' actions at the outset: *seu occasione bene gerendae rei inductus* (8.30.4), and *seu votum id deorum cuipiam fuit* (8.30.9). Those explanations Livy did not find in Fabius Pictor; indeed, the argument in its unreserved support for Rullianus undercuts Pictor's portrait of a young man jealous of, and chafing under, the Dictator's authority. It surely is the product of those authors that increased the number of Rullianus' battles and victories from one to two. Hence Livy incorporated ample material from that tradition (3a), especially in the arguments brought in defense of Rullianus.

The conflict, in Livy, is eventually resolved when the Dictator acknowledges that, in the last resort, he lacks the means—not the legal power!—to enforce his will on the People and the Tribunes, and warns that if through their continued resistance they prevent the punishment of Rullianus, the dictatorship itself and its legal powers, not just the extent of their practical application, will be diminished, respect for the auspices will vanish, and military discipline will suffer beyond the

---

[33] Not entirely true: Oakley *CL* 2: 733–734.   [34] Chapter 6.5.

point of repair (8.34.4–11). The People, the Tribunes, Rullianus himself, and old Fabius Ambustus understand, and do their part to offer Papirius a face-saving way out of the crisis: they cease to argue their case as a matter of right, and plead for mercy instead, acknowledging thereby that the Magister Equitum had done wrong, and that the Dictator was right to punish him. His authority now unchallenged, Papirius waives the execution of his guilty subordinate, as a favor to the Roman People and the Tribunes (8.35.1–9).

1.3.2 Mercy, Disobedience, and the Shadow of Defeat

The pleas for mercy (*veniam errori humano, veniam adulescentiae Q. Fabi daret; satis eum poenarum dedisse*, 8.35.2) resume an approach encountered earlier, after Papirius' initial confrontation with Rullianus in the camp, when the Dictator's staff urged calm and forgiveness. That scene on the tribunal is instructive; it constitutes—leaving aside Rullianus' wonderfully incoherent response to the Dictator's questions (8.32.8–10)—the first of three distinct attempts to reason in favor of the Magister Equitum. It stands in stark contrast to the second, namely, his father's: no hint here that Rullianus' victory somehow justified his transgression, or that the Dictator's decision to execute him might be challenged on constitutional grounds. The Dictator, his officers advise, should postpone the matter and give his anger room to cool, his judgment time to think;[35] Fabius' youthful behavior had been sufficiently chastised, his victory sufficiently disgraced (*orabant ut rem in posterum diem differet et irae suae spatium et consilio tempus daret: satis castigatam adulescentiam Fabi esse, satis deformatam victoriam*, 8.32.14–15). That clearly acknowledges Rullianus' misconduct, and the Dictator's right to punish him; the appeal is directed entirely at the wisdom and necessity of doing so—especially in view of who he is: it would not do to go for the most extreme penalty, nor to inflict such humiliation on a very special young man, his father—that eminent personage—and the Fabian clan (*ne ad extremum finem supplicii tenderet neu unico iuveni neu patri eius, clarissimo viro, neu Fabiae genti eam iniungeret ignominiam*, 8.32.15). Nor was the punishment of a commander popular with the troops apt to restore discipline: it might trigger a mutiny instead (8.32.16). That line of reasoning is consistent with what we have been able to identify as Fabius Pictor's version of the incident; the pointed reference to the *gens Fabia*, carefully balanced with the officers' volunteering to swear to it that leniency was not motivated by hopes of currying personal favor with Fabius Rullianus but by reasons of state (*postremo, ne id se gratiae dare Q. Fabi crederet, se ius iurandum dare paratos*

---

[35] Lipovsky 118.

esse non videri e re publica in Q. Fabium eo tempore animadverti,[36] 8.32.18), leads in the same direction.

Hence the Dictator's officers in the camp approach the task of saving Rullianus in fundamentally the same manner as will eventually succeed, in the third and final attempt: not through claims that victory had justified his actions and rendered him blameless, nor by challenging the Dictator's legal powers, but through arguing public utility and political reality, and asking to forgive an act of youthful irresponsibility. Such, then, seems to have been Pictor's position on the dispute: the Magister Equitum acted illegally and out of irrational jealousy; the Dictator reacted in—irrational—anger yet within his rights, but in the end yielded to entreaties and wiser counsel. The authors in the two-victories (3a) tradition, in contrast, mounted an all-out defense of Rullianus: his success in battle, now suitably enhanced, was all that counted; the subordination of Magister Equitum to Dictator could be ignored, along with the delicate matter of the auspices; the powers of the dictatorship itself are called into question, by introducing the theme of *provocatio*, tribunician *auxilium*, and the will of the People, surely more powerful than any Dictator (*populum...tibi...iudicem fero, qui certe unus plus quam tua dictatura potest polletque*, 8.33.8). In Livy, such reasoning issues from the mouth of Fabius Ambustus: which now prompts the conclusion—at first blush, counterintuitive—that little of that speech, if any, could be found in Fabius Pictor. Perhaps a father's pleading for the life of his son, but not the arguments Livy treats us to. As for the version that Rullianus simply suffered a defeat (3d), it has left no trace in Livy's narrative of 324 V. Or has it?

Satis eum poenarum dedisse, the Tribunes say when they, eventually, beg for Rullianus' life (8.35.2). An odd statement, it might seem, considering that he had not suffered any visible punishment so far. It echoes the Dictator's staff in camp (*satis castigatam adulescentiam Fabi esse, satis deformatam victoriam*, 8.32.15)— not surprisingly, as we have seen how Livy's third take of the debate essentially resumes the first. Presumably, Rullianus' victory had been "sufficiently disgraced" by the Dictator's harangue, and his having come within a hair's breadth of flogging and death—the lictors were already ripping his clothes (8.32.2–11)—might be thought to constitute "punishment enough."

Yet other comments create unease. The charge against Rullianus is disobedience; his father counters it by holding Papirius' overbearing cruelty against the

---

[36] *Id se...dare* is ambiguous: *se* can refer to the subject of the governing clause (the *legati*), or to the subject of its own clause (Papirius). If the first, clarity might have prompted Livy to substitute *eos* (K–S 1: 609–612, and cf. Livy 23.19.5, *praedictum erat dictatoris, ne quid absente eo rei gereret*). On the other hand, the phrase seems a bit compressed for meaning "lest he believe that he was (i.e., would be suspected of) making this concession"—on *dare* in that sense, Oakley *CL* 2: 726—"as a favor to Q. Fabius," and one might expect *daturum esse*, since (unlike his officers) the Dictator has yet to come around to the view that Rullianus should be spared. All in all, though, an offer by his staff to protect the Dictator against a potential accusation of favoritism better fits the tenor of the argument than a mere assertion of their own lack of self-interest.

way the ancients had acted in comparable situations. After rescuing the force trapped at the Algidus, the Dictator Cincinnatus put the Consul Minucius, who had failed so disastrously, back in charge of the army—albeit as a mere *legatus*, having forced him to abdicate the consulship (8.33.14; cf. 3.29.2–3); the great Camillus as Consular Tribune not only forgave his rash and foolhardy colleague L. Furius but asked him to share his next command (8.33.15; cf. 6.23.3–25.6). The People themselves had never sought to take the life of a commander who had lost an army, *temeritate atque inscitia*—through recklessness and incompetence (8.33.17). In like manner Valerius Maximus characterized Rullianus' engagement with the Samnites as luckless and reckless in equal degree (*tam infeliciter quam temere*, 3.2.9: not from Livy), and in Dio, old Fabius Ambustus concedes as much: he notes the human propensity to draw courage from inexperience and act recklessly when in a position of power (ἀπειρίας τε θρασύτητι καὶ ἐξουσίας προπετείᾳ, fr. 36.2), and warns that extreme punishments in such situations do not make others act with more restraint (ἀλλ' εὖ ἴσθι ὅτι αἱ μὲν ἀνήκεστοι ἐν τοῖς τοιούτοις τιμωρίαι...τοὺς ἄλλους οὐδὲν μᾶλλον σωφρονίζουσιν).

None of those examples of ancient *moderatio*, invoked forcefully by Fabius Ambustus, has direct bearing on his son's predicament: they all belong in the realm of military defeat, not disobedience—let alone disobedience crowned by victory. (Admittedly, a suitable example of the latter kind might be hard to come by; young Titus Manlius would not do.[37]) He does go on to play up the contrast between the old forgiving ways in the face of failure and the Dictator's newfangled insistence on punishing a deed that better merits a triumph (8.33.18–19). Still, one cannot help but notice how those examples make a perfect fit for someone arguing that Rullianus should be spared, not because he won a battle but in spite of having lost, *temeritate atque inscitia*: the ancients had forgiven worse defeats— and his was punishment enough. (On the matter of outright disobedience, toward the Dictator and the auspices, no one could really make a case for leniency by drawing on *exempla* from the past; it simply had to be ignored.)

The peculiar character of these arguments for leniency gives further support to the view that Livy was aware of a tradition that had Rullianus suffer defeat—a tradition almost certainly older than the "victorious" one. We can also see more clearly now why Livy chose to suppress it.

To give full credit to those who wrote of a defeat could, in this particular instance, create a serious narrative obstacle: so much of the drama in what follows depends on Rullianus' having conquered. Had Livy simply followed Pictor and the #3b tradition, acknowledgment of the dissenters (3d) might have been possible, since Pictor's arguments for leniency worked equally well in the case of a defeat; but once he chose to incorporate substantial elements of the #3a tradition

---

[37] His ghost, of course, hovers above the entire episode: 8.30.11; 8.34.2, 9; cf. Lipovsky 115; Chaplin 108–112.

into his debate, with their insistence that Rullianus' (double) victory justified his actions, any hint that the Magister Equitum might in fact have reaped defeat from disobedience would pose a jarring and undesirable distraction.

1.4 The Play

Livy considered the authors of the one-victory version (3b), led by Fabius Pictor, his earliest sources on the incident. As literary historical narratives go, that is undoubtedly correct. But it stands to reason that the #3d tradition—having Rullianus suffer defeat—is even older: its unadorned survival under 301 V (as in 3d2) is difficult to imagine if that tradition was born of an anti-Fabian reaction to the single victory (3b) or double victory (3a) version. The process of embellishment, not only in the course of, but even before, the onset of annalistic invention, is much more likely to have transformed a Fabian defeat into a victory than vice versa, especially as it involved one of the great heroes of the Samnite Wars; and the unmistakable—and undeniable—disgrace in which Rullianus ended his term as Magister Equitum even in as sympathetic an account as Livy's does not have the look of later accretion. The examples from *mos maiorum* advanced in favor of leniency all revolve around defeat, caused by reckless incompetence: they are unlikely to have first been assembled with victory in mind.

But, thus Livy tells us, Rullianus sent a letter (or two, if he conquered twice) announcing his successful action(s)—directly to the Senate, not to the Dictator; this was taken as further evidence of his being unwilling to share the credit with the latter (*litterae quoque de re prospere gesta ad senatum non ad dictatorem missae argumentum fuere minime cum eo communicantis laudes*, 8.30.10). If authentic, the document surely would preclude the "defeat" tradition from being earlier than the "victory" one. Frier suggests that the letter was still available to Pictor in Fabian family archives. That this information and its interpretation (*fuere* marks it out as not just Livy's own) stood in Pictor is possible; but scholars are perhaps too sanguine in embracing the view that the first historian saw the actual letter in "the family archives of the Fabii."[38] Even if there was such a letter, it was addressed to the Senate, and, unless Rullianus kept a copy, it is doubtful that it would have ended up in any family collection.

It is not at all certain, however, that Pictor mentioned the letter: Livy introduces it not as an integral part of Pictor's version (8.30.9), but as additional evidence

---

[38] Frier 1979: 269, followed by Hölkeskamp 1987: 27 n. 118; Beck 2003: 83; Beck–Walter *FRH* 1: 121. Münzer *RE* 6.2 (1909): 1801 was certain that family tradition informed Fabius' presentation of the entire episode, whereas Timpe: 950 more cautiously entertains it as one source among others. Oakley *CL* 2: 714 is skeptical about the letter ("likely to be...Livian or annalistic reconstruction"); certainly nothing in Livy warrants the claim that it was personally known ("die dem Fabius Pictor bekannten *litterae*," Beck 2003: 83) to Pictor.

supporting the latter's interpretation of Rullianus' motive for burning the spoils. Which does not prove, or even imply, that the earliest source mentioning the letter intended it to have just that effect. The letter could have originated as easily with the two-battles (3a) tradition that sought to portray the Magister Equitum as, essentially, the Dictator's equal colleague, as with the "victorious" but critical one (3b) embraced by Pictor: Rullianus seized a military opportunity, won a double victory, honored the gods, and duly notified the Senate of those events.

What form could #3d, the defeat version, have taken before Fabius Pictor wrote the first history? Fabian and Papirian family traditions—one hesitates to say "records"—for one, certainly. The stage, however, would have offered the best opportunity to firmly anchor the story in the general public's remembrance of things past, while embodying it with detail, and reshaping it to meet the requirements of dramatic effect and historical, not to mention political, education. The retelling and re-enacting of famous moments in a family's history were a common element in aristocratic funerals, which in turn could be accompanied by games and theatrical performances.[39] In recent years, Wiseman has revived, with powerful arguments, a nineteenth-century view first championed by Ranke, Jahn, and Ribbeck: drama, in particular—yet by no means exclusively—the *fabula praetexta*, made significant contributions to the formation of the Roman historical tradition, both before and after the advent of literary narrative at the end of the third century.[40] The story of Papirius and Rullianus has all the makings of a play:

Prologue: Setting of story. (Dictator alerted by *pullarius*; ordered Magister Equitum not to move, then left for Rome.—Master-of-Horse chafed under restriction; led army out for forage/fight.)

Scene 1: Rome, outside the *curia*. News of battle and defeat [or victory, in the "Fabian" variant] arrives; Dictator emerges from *curia*, furious; announces his immediate departure for camp, to punish Rullianus.

Scene 2: The camp. Magister Equitum holds *contio*. Soliloquy of Rullianus: justifies his actions, appeals to troops for support against Dictator's wrath.—Dictator arrives, summons Magister Equitum before *contio*: harangue, met with inarticulate response. Lictors lay hands on Rullianus; he jumps off the tribunal and seeks

---

[39] Flower 1996: 92, 104–105, 122, 128, 145–150; Manuwald 2001: 110–119; 2011: 47, 142; Blösel 55–62; Kragelund 32–45.

[40] Wiseman 1994: 1–48; 1995: 129–144; and esp. 1998: 1–74, with a survey (1–16) of earlier scholarship advancing this view. *Contra* Flower 1995: 173–175, although allowing that "much ancient evidence points to the theatre as a political forum in Rome" (188): but if so, it is difficult to square with her contention that *praetextae* were very rarely performed; see also Wiseman 1998: 15. On the development of Roman drama in the fourth and third centuries in general, Manuwald 2011: 30–40; on *ludi scaenici* and *fabulae praetextae* in particular, 41–45, 140–145; cf. 2001: 97–110. She is skeptical (2001: 102; 2011: 141) about Wiseman's thesis. But Kragelund 3–68 makes a persuasive argument in its favor.

shelter among the *triarii* (offstage?).—The *legati* (chorus?) intercede for Rullianus; Dictator is unmoved.

Scene 3: Rome, the *curia*. Magister Equitum, having furtively left the camp, convenes Senate, agitates against Papirius. Dictator suddenly arrives; attempts arrest; Fabius Ambustus implores *provocatio*.

Scene 4: Rome, the Forum. Grand speech of Ambustus, invoking *moderatio antiquorum* in comparable or worse cases of reckless failure [or implying, in the "Fabian" version, that victory justified transgression].—Grand speech of Papirius, defending dictatorial powers, military discipline, auspices; warns of consequences if forced to give in.—People and Tribunes (chorus?) beg for mercy; Dictator relents, but orders Magister Equitum to step aside [or offers reconciliation to Rullianus]. General rejoicing.

Here the play ought to end; indeed, after Livy's vivid picture of public celebration and congratulation, it comes as a bit of a surprise when Papirius suspends Rullianus from office,[41] before returning to his army (8.35.7–9, 36.1). Livy clearly felt the incongruity, and tried to dampen it by inserting the incident of the foraging party (cut down because the *legatus* left in charge of the camp dared not move to rescue them, 8.35.10–12: originally this was probably what occasioned Rullianus' defeat, as in 10.3.6) between reconciliation and suspension. Back in command, the Dictator finds the troops sullen, hostile, and dispirited, and promptly suffers a reverse (8.36.2–4). Now, at last, he comes to understand that discipline must be tempered by *comitas*. Making extra efforts to ensure the well-being of his wounded, he restores morale and wins back his soldiers' loyalty (8.36.5–7). Great victory ensues, bereft of all narrative detail (and without participation of the Magister Equitum), though Livy emphasizes the Dictator's generosity in letting the troops retain all the booty (8.36.8–10). Papirius returns to Rome in triumph, a better man for having conquered his own temper and unbending sternness.[42]

1.5 The Aftermath

In theme, Livy's epilogue fits smoothly with the rest of that long drama; why, then, is it so imperfectly joined to it?[43] The earliest (that is, pre-Pictor) version of the

---

[41] W–M *ad loc.*: "Livius will die Großmut des Papirius darstellen, obgleich 36,1 damit nicht übereinstimmt."

[42] Lipovsky 126–128.

[43] "The final section stands somewhat apart from the rest of the episode, but presents an important coda" (Oakley *CL* 2: 705). On Livy's approach to dramatic technique, see Feldherr's stimulating study (165–217).

story probably ended at the same point as our hypothetical play: the Dictator granting mercy, but forcing Rullianus from office (entirely or effectively, by prohibiting his exercise thereof). That did not, however, exhaust the tale's dramatic (and moralistic) potential; Livy's epilogue—whether inherited or his own production—renders the character of Papirius Cursor substantially more complex, and human. And there were those, doubtless from early on, who wished to brighten up the portrait of Fabius Rullianus. A victory would leave intact the splendid military reputation he was to gain later in life, without distorting or diminishing, in itself, the nature and magnitude of his transgression, or subverting the Dictator's position in the dispute; suspension from office would soften the humiliation of forced abdication (which, given the remnant tradition of a Livius Drusus as Magister Equitum in the same year, probably belonged to the earliest story), yet just as effectively remove him from the scene. Reconciliation, though, amidst popular rejoicing would provide the best conclusion, especially if the tale were told with full support for Rullianus. As we have seen, Ambustus' arguments in Livy are heavy with the double victory (3a) tradition: the historian probably crafted the old man's discourse from a version that concluded the entire episode with the public celebration in the Forum, and made no mention of Rullianus' abdication or suspension. Livy knew, of course, and would not go so far as to suppress it; but why ruin a grand and uplifting finale? He chose to separate the matter, and report it after the foragers' incident. As to exactly which consequence Rullianus suffered, if Fabius Pictor told of suspension rather than abdication, Livy would follow him, just as he had in the question of one victory or two, or none at all.

It would be unwise to banish the whole incident into the realm of legend or historical fiction. Fabius Rullianus served as Magister Equitum under Papirius Cursor, and was forced from office for an act of disobedience resulting in defeat. That much can safely be accepted. The Dictator's dramatic determination to execute his deputy is another matter.[44]

1.5.1 Cotta at Lipara

In 252 BC, the Consul C. Aurelius Cotta laid siege to Lipara, off the coast of Sicily. At some point during the operation, he found it necessary to return to Rome (via Messana) to repeat his auspices: evidently, something had occurred to render them *incerta*. What happened next will sound familiar:

---

[44] Münzer *RE* 6.2 (1909): 1800–1801; Beck 2003: 83, 88–89; Beck-Walter *FRH* 1: 121. J. H. Richardson 2012: 84–105 makes an attractive case for a Roman historiographic tradition in which young Fabii characteristically get into trouble from rash and irresponsible behavior, with their aged—hence wiser and more composed—fathers coming to the rescue. The pattern is clearly present; but it is difficult to believe that it could already have shaped Fabius Pictor's version of events.

P. Aurelium Pecuniolam sanguine sibi iunctum, quem obsidioni Liparitanae ad auspicia repetenda Messanam transiturus praefecerat, virgis caesum militiae munere inter pedites fungi coegit, quod eius culpa agger incensus, paene castra erant capta. (Val. Max. 2.6.4)

Having left in charge one Aurelius Pecuniola, a relative by blood, the Consul on his return to the army had him flogged and demoted to the rank of common soldier, because he had allowed the enemy to set the siege works on fire and nearly take the Roman camp. Thus Valerius Maximus reports; Frontinus almost verbatim repeats the story.[45] Dio (to judge from Zonaras) made the chastised officer a Tribune by the name of Q. Cassius,[46] and specified what one would have to conclude anyway from the fact that the Consul left because of trouble with the auspices: the Tribune had been ordered to avoid battle, disobeyed, and launched an assault on Lipara town that failed—disastrously.

μετὰ δὲ τοῦτο Αὐρήλιος...ἔπλευσεν εἰς Λιπάραν, καὶ ἐν αὐτῇ Κυΐντον Κάσσιον χιλίαρχον καταλιπὼν προσεδρεύσοντα μάχης ἄνευ, ἀπῆρεν οἴκαδε. Κυΐντος δὲ μὴ φροντίσας τῆς ἐντολῆς προσέμιξε τῇ πόλει καὶ πολλοὺς ἀπέβαλεν. ὁ μέντοι Αὐρήλιος μετὰ ταῦτα ἐκείνους ἑλὼν πάντας ἀπέκτεινε καὶ τὸν Κάσσιον τῆς ἀρχῆς ἔπαυσε. (Zonar. 8.14)

If the story of Papirius and Rullianus was already current in its essential details, Cotta simply acted on example. If, on the other hand, all he and his contemporaries knew about Rullianus was that he abdicated in disgrace, the Consul took the punishment a step further, in having his disobedient deputy flogged. Once that example had been set, the story of Papirius' reaction could not fail to escalate: if a Consul had his deputy flogged, how could the Dictator facing an identical case of disobedience do less—or try, at least? Either way, there are no grounds to wait for Fabius Pictor to give the tale the basic shape we read in Livy.

What about version #3a, the one where Fabius Rullianus emerged victorious not once but twice, and whose representatives challenged not just the wisdom but the right of the Dictator to punish his Magister Equitum, and defended the latter's action with an appeal to military prowess and success? Fabius Pictor did not

---

[45] Frontin. *Strat.* 4.1.31, *idem P. Aurelium sanguine sibi iunctum, quem obsidioni Lipararum, ipse ad auspicia repetenda Messanam transiturus, praefecerat, cum agger incensus et capta castra essent, virgis caesum in numerum gregalium peditum referri et muneribus fungi iussit.* Given the verbal parallels, this comes either from Valerius Maximus directly, or from an earlier collection of *exempla* used by both.

[46] Broughton *MRR* 1: 212 thought that Aurelius Pecuniola and Q. Cassius were punished on two separate occasions, each "similarly degraded for a similar offence." But Dio/Zonaras clearly refers to the same incident as do Valerius and Frontinus. See Konrad 2008 for a discussion of the offending officer's identity, and for the possibility that Cotta held more than one of his officers accountable for the debacle.

subscribe to that view, and it may not yet have gained wide currency when he wrote his history. But there is reason to think that it arose during his time.

1.5.2 Minucius Rufus

In 217, a vociferous disagreement over what strategy to pursue against Hannibal erupted between the Dictator, Q. Fabius Maximus, and his Master of the Horse, M. Minucius Rufus (*cos.* 221); the troops largely favored Minucius' aggressive approach.[47] When the Dictator was called back to Rome *sacrorum causa*, he ordered Minucius not to attack the enemy during his absence.[48] The Master-of-Horse promptly proceeded to attack anyway, and fought a successful engagement with Hannibal near Gereonium; whereupon, in the widening popular outrage over the Cunctator's delaying strategy and his public announcement that he would hold Minucius accountable for his disobedience, the Magister Equitum by plebiscite was granted *imperium* equal to that of the Dictator. (In fact, he and his contemporaries appear to have interpreted his new status as that of a second Dictator, side by side with Fabius.) Not much afterwards, Minucius found himself and his army trapped by Hannibal and facing annihilation; only Fabius' timely arrival prevented another Roman disaster. Minucius renounced his newfound dictatorial powers, and returned under the Dictator's command as Master of the Horse.[49]

The heated debate in Rome on the proper conduct of the war during the summer of 217 was apt to invoke the—by then—celebrated previous quarrel between Dictator and Magister Equitum. The (few) supporters of Fabius Maximus could cite it as proof that the Dictator must not be challenged by his deputy, no matter what the circumstances. But if version #3b, transforming Rullianus' defeat into a victory, was already current (as seems likely), Minucius' success at Gereonium would open the door to a more radical reinterpretation of the tale. The Master's case in the City was being championed by a relative of his, the Tribune of the Plebs M. Metilius, with arguments strongly reminiscent of those Livy put in the mouth of Fabius Rullianus and his defenders.

---

[47] Polyb. 3.90.6, 92.4; Livy 22.12.11-12, 14.4-15, 15.5; Plut. *Fab.* 5.5-6; Appian *Hannib.* 12.51-52; Zonar. 8.26.

[48] Polyb. 3.94.9; Livy 22.18.9-10, 25.13; Plut. *Fab.* 8.1. In Polybios, Minucius is "ordered" to focus on avoiding defeat rather than attempt to inflict it on the enemy (ἐνετείλατο μὴ τοσαύτην ποιεῖσθαι σπουδὴν ὑπὲρ τοῦ βλάψαι τοὺς πολεμίους ἡλίκην ὑπὲρ τοῦ μηδὲν αὐτοὺς παθεῖν δεινόν). Livy's account is in complete agreement, though more elaborate; evidently, the common source (presumably Pictor) did not report, or at least emphasize, that Fabius issued a blanket prohibition against all fighting: but no offensive moves were to be undertaken. At 22.25.13 the Dictator accuses Minucius of disobeying orders (*quod contra dictum suum pugnasset*), and the latter had, in fact, done just that in taking the initiative (22.24; cf. Polyb. 3.102). For the possibility that here, too, a question of auspices was in play, see Chapter 8.2.2.

[49] Polyb. 3.103; Livy 22.25-26; Plut. *Fab.* 9.1-3. On Minucius' titulature, Chapter 3.4.3.

The Dictator is criticized for not joining in the general rejoicing over his subordinate's victory:

> 22.25.2, cum laeta civitate dictator unus nihil nec famae nec litteris crederet <et>, ut vera omnia essent, secunda se magis quam adversa timere diceret, tum M. Metilius Tribunus plebis id unum enimvero ferendum esse negat, non praesentem solum dictatorem obstitisse rei bene gerendae sed absentem etiam gestae obstare.
>
> — 8.30.10, ita certe dictator id factum accepit, ut laetis aliis victoria parta prae se ferret iram tristitiamque; 8.31.2–3, furere quod se absente res publica egregie gesta esset; malle, si mutare fortunam posset, apud Samnites quam Romanos victoriam esse; imperium dictitare spretum, tamquam non eadem mente pugnari vetuerit qua pugnatum doleat.

He is accused of actively preventing his Master of the Horse from seizing any opportunity to inflict damage on the enemy, keeping him and the troops virtual prisoners in the camp, deprived of their arms:

> 22.25.6, M. Minucium magistrum equitum, ne hostem videret, ne quid rei bellicae gereret, prope in custodia habitum; 22.25.8–9, exercitum cupientem pugnare et magistrum equitum clausos prope intra vallum retentos; tamquam hostibus captivis arma adempta. tandem, ut abscesserit inde dictator, ut obsidione liberatos, extra vallum egressos fudisse ac fugasse hostes.
>
> —8.31.3–4, et tunc invidia impedire virtutem alienam voluisse cupidissimisque arma ablaturum fuisse militibus, ne se absente moveri possent; et nunc id furere, id aegre pati, quod sine L. Papirio non inermes, non manci milites fuerint, quod se Q. Fabius magistrum equitum duxerit ac non accensum dictatoris.

The difference here in the underlying accusations—Fabius essentially being called a coward, Papirius a glory hog—does nothing to diminish the significance of finding identical arguments advanced against both. By the late third century, the character of Papirius Cursor was too firmly established to permit being recast as lacking offensive spirit.

Finally, the appeal to the ultimate source of power in the Roman State—the People and the Plebs, each superior to even the Dictator:

> 22.25.10, quas ob res, si antiquus animus plebei Romanae esset, audaciter se laturum fuisse de abrogando Q. Fabi imperio; nunc modicam rogationem promulgaturum de aequando magistri equitum et dictatoris iure.
>
> —8.33.8, tribunos plebis appello et provoco ad populum eumque tibi...iudicem fero, qui certe unus plus quam tua dictatura potest polletque; 8.33.17, nam populi quidem, penes quem potestas omnium rerum esset....

The *rogatio Metilia* passed, and in making the powers of the Magister Equitum equal to those of the Dictator, it legitimized the conduct of Minucius Rufus. And not only his: for once he had been declared right, by law, to disobey the Dictator's orders, the same justification must, surely, apply to Fabius Rullianus, who could now be made to serve as a historic precedent for Minucius' heroic initiative and manly challenge of the Dictator's power. Victory absolves from all sins. That his own (great-)grandfather should thus be employed to put the craven Delayer in his place would have made it twice as sweet.[50] Small wonder the Pictorian tradition about Papirius and Rullianus did not join that route. But with public sentiment rampant against Fabius Maximus in 217, we should not be surprised if in September, at the *ludi Romani*,[51] or at the Plebeian Games in November, a play was staged that presented, for the first time, that old story from the perspective of Livy's #3a tradition: handing two victories to the Magister Equitum, and ending with the Dictator not giving in to pleas for mercy, but submitting to the greater power of the Tribunes and the People.[52]

Minucius Rufus fell at Cannae, and never had an opportunity to redeem himself in high command. His eventual submission to Fabius Maximus put an end to their personal rivalry, and healed a dangerous rift that threatened to paralyze Rome's ability to confront the enemy; it did not settle the debate over strategy— far from it. Almost another year would pass before the beat-Hannibal-in-a-decisive-battle view was discredited, and nothing makes us believe that Minucius had changed his fundamental outlook on how to fight the war; another of his vocal backers in 217, C. Terentius Varro (*cos.* 216), certainly had not. Yet even after Cannae, there were some who favored a more aggressive approach to Hannibal, and a decade later, one of them prevailed over the cautious old man and took the war to Africa. Through all those years, the memory of Minucius Rufus will not have been cultivated solely by his detractors, and a family of plebeian nobility that had succeeded in tracing their consular origins to the fifth and fourth centuries may be expected to salvage his record as best they could. Had the Romans won at Cannae, and finished Hannibal then and there, the story of Minucius and Fabius would no doubt read differently today; as things stood, little could be done to improve Minucius' image. But the arguments advanced on his behalf—challenging the absolute power of the Dictator, forcing him under the authority of the People and the Tribunes, and, most of all, the idea that military

---

[50] On the question of how many generations came between Rullianus and the Cunctator, Münzer "Fabius (116)" *RE* 6.2 (1909): 1814–1815 argued for two (Gurges and an unknown son), cf. Sumner 1973: 30–32. Feig Vishnia 2007: 20–23 recently made a case for one (Gurges); cf. J. H. Richardson 2012: 93 n. 183.

[51] The Cunctator returned to Rome from Campania *extracta prope aestate* (Livy 22.18.9; cf. 22.15.1, *aestatis reliquum extraxit*), probably in late August: Walbank *HCP* 1: 430, 433. Minucius' successful engagement could have occurred before the middle of September (the *ludi* ran from the 4th through the 13th).

[52] See Kragelund 58–68 on the use of plays to promote political partisan points of view.

success, *res bene gestae*, should count for more than rules and discipline: those arguments could be kept alive, and passed on to future generations; and clad in the guise of version #3a of the Rullianus tale, they could be transmitted untainted by Minucius' embarrassment. Others, alas, remembered earlier versions of that tale.[53]

That is significant, for it renders unavailable a favorite tool for disposing of the evidence: we cannot dismiss the disputes over the constitutional subordination of the Magister Equitum under the Dictator (as presented by Livy, in this case and that of Fabius Rullianus) as the mere product of antiquarian speculation in an age that had not seen a "traditional" (that is, pre-Sullan) Dictator and his deputy up close. Those elements of the tale about Rullianus and Papirius Cursor were present already in Fabius Pictor, the oldest narrative Livy had access to, and hence reflect views—not necessarily unanimous ones—current in the late third century BC. The same goes for Minucius' rivalry with the Cunctator. Perhaps we can learn something from those tales, after all.

---

[53] Cf. Wiseman 1998: 90–105; on the persistence of minority traditions—both oral and written—preserving a more accurate version of an event, see Càssola 1999: 6–7.

2
Imperium and Auspices

The story of Papirius and Rullianus indicates that, at least by the time the various annalistic traditions took shape in the second and first century BC, diverging views could exist as to the precise powers and respective constitutional positions of the Dictator and his Magister Equitum; as we will see later on, similar questions could be asked regarding the Consul and the Dictator. Before delving into the particular cases examined in this volume, it may be advisable to address, in the next three chapters, a number of institutional matters of general import. The status of Dictator and Magister Equitum will be the subject of Chapters 3 and 4; but first, two disputed issues in the realm of *Staatsrecht*: the nature of *imperium* and the auspices under which the magistrate goes to war. No comprehensive survey will be attempted here. As regards *imperium*, the aim is not so much to argue a case—although some argument will ensue—nor to revisit at length the scholarship surrounding that debate, but to make clear the positions taken herein. Where the auspices are concerned, however, the evidence of the sources, carefully examined, demands a radical (though not entirely unprecedented) departure from certain tenets of the *communis opinio*.

2.1 *Imperium*

In Livy's telling, Papirius Cursor as Dictator claimed supreme and unqualified power over all other magistrates, even the Consuls, holders of the *regia potestas* (8.30.11). That the Consul's powers in turn outranked those of the Praetor is generally agreed. For the military sphere, however, that principle has recently been called into question, with consequences also for the Dictator's position vis-à-vis the Consul.[1]

2.1.1 Mommsen and Alternatives

Theodor Mommsen saw in *imperium* the supreme military and civil (in that order) power invested in Roman officials, noting that, as a technical term, it

---
[1] Below, Subsection 2.1.2.

occurs far more often in its military application—not surprisingly, since the military high command constituted the true core of the supreme official power, and cannot formally be separated from it.[2] He postulated the existence of two distinct spheres in which official power ("Amtsgewalt") was exercised: *domi*, comprising essentially all governmental functions pertaining to or carried out in or near the City, and *militiae*, comprising all functions outside the City, first and foremost those of a military nature; the *pomerium* formed the fundamental dividing line between the two spheres. He took pains to point out that the spheres could overlap: the muster of an army, or convening the Centuriate Assembly, fell into the sphere *domi*, even though by nature and location both acts belonged outside the City; and the triumph, even though it was an act falling into the sphere *militiae*, took place in the City, with the "triumphator" exercising his military command there.[3] Mommsen scrupulously avoided the nowadays common (and decidedly un-Roman) expressions *imperium domi* and *imperium militiae* (which misleadingly evoke the impression of two different types of *imperium*[4]), speaking instead of the "Amtführung" (exercise of official power) in the respective spheres *domi* and *militiae*; and while on occasion allowing himself the phrase "militärisches Imperium"—he much preferred "Commando"—he noted that Latin does not use *imperium militare* any more than *imperium domesticum*.[5] Mommsen's view, if sometimes distorted in the aforementioned notion of two types of *imperium*, to this day commands the scholarly consensus.[6]

Yet not without disagreement. Nearly eighty years ago, Alfred Heuß argued that the magistrate acquired *imperium* not automatically, *qua* magistrate, but only through passage of the *lex curiata*, which in turn was concerned exclusively with

---

[2] *StR* 1: 22 ("bezeichnet in seinem allgemeinsten technischen Wert die oberste mit Commando und Jurisdiction ausgestattete Amtsgewalt") with n. 4; 116: "*Imperium*...wird weit häufiger und in nicht minder technischer Weise im eminenten Sinn verwendet für das militärische Commando. Es beruht dies darauf, dass der militärische Oberbefehl der eigentliche Kern der obersten Beamtengewalt und formell von ihr untrennbar ist."

[3] *StR* 1: 61–63, 70–71.

[4] E.g., Drogula 2007: 421: "[Mommsen] reasoned that *imperium* must have existed in two basic types: *imperium militiae*...and *imperium domi*." He did not. The same unfortunate formulation can be found even more recently in Rafferty 19 ("...divided into two types, with *imperium domi* operative within the *pomerium* and *imperium militiae* beyond it"); although Rafferty subsequently (21) clarifies the matter, correctly: "There was not any separation between *imperium domi* and *militiae*: *imperium* was a unitary power, and *domi* and *militiae* qualify its meaning, indicating in which sphere *imperium* was being exercised." Then why obfuscate the matter and prompt conceptual misunderstandings by employing misleading terminology?

[5] *StR* 1: 22 n. 4; 61 n. 1; 62–71;116–119 and *passim*; cf. 131, "ausserstädtische[s] Imperium." On rare occasions (I count three), the master admitted the now popular expressions (*StR* 1: 61 n. 1, "weil man späterhin das *imperium militiae* als *imperium* schlechtweg zu bezeichnen pflegt"; 2.1: 94 n. 1, "blieb auch jetzt noch das *imperium militiae* in Italien rechtlich zulässig, was es in Rom nicht war"; 2.1: 101: "Die Civilgerichtsbarkeit...ging mit der Einrichtung der Prätur...dem Consulat verloren, indem das militärisch-jurisdictionelle Imperium des bisherigen Oberbeamten in das consularische *imperium militiae* und das prätorische *imperium domi* aufgelöst ward").

[6] Recently affirmed by Kunkel *StO* 24 (emphasizing, like Mommsen, the military origin and dominant usage of the term); Lintott 96; Brennan *PRR* 1: 14–15; Vervaet 2014: 17–22; Rafferty 19–21.

military matters: hence *imperium* originally meant nothing but—and not just primarily—the power of military command. Moreover, since the nature of early Roman law—operating almost entirely within the *gentes*, families, and through self-help—would have left virtually no room for judicial intervention, civilly or criminally, by a government official, Heuß reasoned that, the magistrate's civil functions being minimal, *imperium* cannot have existed, and denoted the magistrate's power, in the sphere *domi*. This would change over time, though, largely in consequence of the Conflict of the Orders: patrician attempts to cow and thwart plebeian aspirations resulted in the gradual importation of *imperium*, military power, from the sphere *militiae* into the sphere *domi*—a process eventually tamed by the *lex Valeria de provocatione* of 300 BC. Though often seen as a challenge to Mommsen, for the historical period Heuß's view is essentially the same: *imperium* now denoted the magistrate's powers in both spheres, *militiae* as well as *domi*.[7]

A similar view, but with different reasoning, was put forward by Jochen Bleicken. The magistrate's official power originally was *auspicium*, pure and simple; but for the military sphere, auspices required a separate grant by way of the *lex curiata*. This power of command in the military sphere from early on became also known as *imperium*: at first, simply the commander's ability to issue orders to his troops, rather than an abstract responsibility for the sphere *militiae* (covered by *auspicium*); but over time, *imperium* acquired that quality side by side with *auspicium*, and eventually came to overshadow the latter as the prevailing—although never exclusive—term denoting not just the chief magistrate's military power of command but official powers in general.[8]

2.1.2 All *Imperia* Are Equal (but Some Are More Equal than Others)

A more radical departure from Mommsen's view has been advanced recently. Fred Drogula makes a sustained argument that, at least throughout the Republic, *imperium* technically never belonged to the sphere *domi*, but existed exclusively in the sphere *militiae* (other than in certain extraordinary situations, such as a Dictator, whose—military—*imperium* extended over the City). All the Consul's civil and judicial functions, even convening the Centuriate Assembly, were covered by the *consularis potestas*, which did not include *imperium*; the latter was an entirely separate power granted only through the *lex curiata*, and of

---

[7] Heuß 1944, esp. 67–78, 84–104, 125–133.
[8] Bleicken 1981, esp. 255–275 [5–21], 287–295 [33–39]. Cf. Voci *passim*, who saw *imperium* as originating in the purely military power of Rome's Etruscan rulers (he refrained from calling them "Kings") of the late Regal Period, which over the course of the Early Republic was appropriated by the chief magistrates and combined with their civil functions (inherited, at least in part, from the Regal Period) such as *iuris dictio*; thus *imperium* became the all-encompassing power—civil and military—that the term denotes in historical times.

consequence exclusively for his military functions.[9] In principle, this corresponds to the view of Heuß as to the primordial definition; but Drogula would not allow for any concept of *imperium* existing *domi* in subsequent developments.

In his basic contention that *imperium* "im streng staatsrechtlichen Sinne" always was military in nature, and that magistrates did not exercise *imperium* at all in the sphere *domi*—more precisely, perhaps, *in Urbe*—Drogula is probably correct, up to a point. (It remains difficult to believe that convening the Centuriate Assembly, the technical term for which is *exercitum imperare*, should not require *imperium*.[10]) The fact that Latin sources, especially in official language, never see a need to qualify *militiae* when speaking of *imperium* in that sphere, and that in reference to the sphere *domi* the term occurs with much less frequency (no more common than *potestas*, if as much[11]), does point in support. If accepted, we may welcome this as a constitutional clarification; little, though, is gained in substance beyond the realm of terminology (which, in itself, is not insignificant). In the end, Drogula's *imperium* existing only in the sphere *militiae* is no different from Mommsen's *imperium* exercised in that sphere as opposed to *domi*. Certainly the Roman political class of the first century, and indeed well before, had no compunction about saying *"imperium"* when, technically, all that may have been involved in a Consul's exercise of power *domi* were the various non-"imperial" powers included in his *potestas* (such as *coercitio*, the *ius agendi cum patribus*, or *cum populo*, and so forth): Mommsen's definition, though terminologically less narrow, reflects the common parlance of our sources; and Mommsen, one should not forget, had always understood that the military power, rather than the civil one, lay at the core of *imperium*.[12] A pedantic avoidance, in scholarly discourse, of the word *imperium* when dealing with matters of domestic governance seems unwarranted; but one may hope (hope springs eternal) to see the abominable locutions *imperium domi* and *imperium militiae*—used as if they denoted two different categories—disappear.

Yet Drogula has gone much further in his attempt to redefine *imperium*. In his view, the generally accepted *maior potestas* of the Consul vis-à-vis the Praetor's *minor potestas* applied only to the sphere *domi*; but *militiae*, every commander's *imperium* was the same: the Consul's was not *maius* compared to that of the

---

[9] Drogula 2007; 2015: 81–130 and *passim*; no *imperium* needed for *comitia centuriata*: 2015: 83, 109 n. 207.

[10] Varro *LL* 6.88, 95; Laelius Felix *apud* Gell. 15.17.5. Note that when explaining the Censors' ability to convene the *comitia centuriata* for the purpose of the *lustrum*, Varro pointedly uses *constituere* rather than *imperare*, in contrast to the actual magistrates with *imperium*—Consul, Dictator, Interrex: *quod censor exercitum centuriato constituit quinquennalem cum lustrare et in urbem ad vexillum ducere debet; dictator et consul in singulos annos, quod hic exercitui imperare potest quo eat, id quod propter centuriata comitia imperare solent* (6.93).

[11] Mommsen *StR* 1: 116; Kunkel *StO* 22.

[12] *StR* 1: 22; Kunkel *StO* 24; cf. above, note 2. For *imperium* used in technical parlance when discussing magisterial powers and functions that clearly belonged into the sphere *domi*, see Varro *apud* Gell. 13.12.6; Tuditanus and Messalla *apud* Gell. 13.15.4.

Praetor, nor the Dictator's in any way superior to that of the Consul. The exercise of *imperium* was tied to the magistrate's assigned *provincia*, and no supersession of a lower-ranking commander—say, Praetor or Propraetor—by a higher-ranking one (Dictator, Consul, or Proconsul) could occur within the former's *provincia*, other than by a formal transfer of the *provincia* to the latter.[13] In this scheme, the Dictator becomes nothing more than an assistant to the Consuls, who remain fully independent commanders within their own *provinciae*, or an additional commander if one was needed (what Mommsen would have called "(ein) Aushülfsbeamter"), unable to give orders to anyone other than perhaps his Magister Equitum, and limited to his assigned *provincia*. Since the sources never employ that term in connection with a Dictator, Drogula takes it to be the equivalent of the *causa* specified for the Dictator's appointment, instead of exploring if this strange silence ought not to make us ask whether the concept of *provincia* applied at all to the Dictator.[14] How a phrase such as *rei gerundae causa*, "for the sake of managing the Thing"—the whole Thing, the whole war effort, not just part of it—could be compatible with the notion that this purpose was limited to a specific *provincia*, separate from and exclusive of independent *provinciae* of other commanders, is never discussed. On the face of it, *rei gerundae causa* describes a purpose seen as all-encompassing, hence not restricted (or restrictable) to a *provincia*: to maintain otherwise requires evidence, or sustained reasoning.

It is certainly true that *imperium* simply was *imperium*, and did not exist at objectively distinct levels: the Praetor's *imperium* did not lack any of the powers inherent in the Consul's. But in case of conflict, the Praetor's was considered *minus* as compared to that of the Consul, precisely because the *praetoria potestas* was inferior to the *consularis potestas*. The expressions *consulare imperium* (very common) and *praetorium imperium* (rather rare) do not represent different types or levels of *imperium*; they simply indicate precedence among magistrates of different rank in case of disagreement.[15] At the same time, they undeniably imply a distinction in those powers relative to each other. Nor is it in question that the provincial assignment played a major part in regulating conflicts of

---

[13] Drogula 2015: 131–231. The theory asserted there rests in its entirety on a highly speculative view of warfare and command in archaic Rome, prior to the third century (8–130). Such reconstructions, according to one's own imagination, of poorly documented areas can be illuminating; but they are not evidence, and cannot support the wholesale rejection of what evidence—even if most of it dates from later periods—we actually have. See Bellomo 27–29 for a recent critical assessment of Drogula's view.

[14] Drogula 2015: 161–180; Dictators even "mere understudies" of the Consuls: 164; *causa* and *provincia*: 169–170.

[15] Cf. Brennan *PRR* 1: 29. Vervaet 2014: 11 (and throughout) talks of three *genera imperii* (a terminology not attested in this form, to my knowledge), yet at the same time notes, correctly, that the *imperia* of the Dictator, Consul, and Praetor were "essentially the same kind of official authority," exercised at different strengths relative to each other (cf. Chapter 3.3.1, note 54). That definition, with emphasis on "relative to each other," is correct; yet if we are dealing with the same kind of authority, we should not use misleading formulations such as *genus imperii*. On the peculiar position of the Dictator, see Chapter 3.3.

authority (and claims to a triumph) among commanders.[16] But to make his case that the *provincia* constituted the sole means of determining precedence in command, Drogula is compelled to dismiss any and all of the sources' abundant evidence attesting to the Consul's *imperium* being *maius* compared to the Praetor's as not meaning what they patently do,[17] or to roundly declare them in error. Apparently, the Romans themselves knew less about how these things worked in their own day than we do now.[18]

To take a case in point. In a number of instances, Livy refers to a magistrate as *adiutor* of another in the same *provincia*: sometimes both are of the same rank, but on at least three occasions, we encounter a (Pro)Praetor as the (Pro)Consul's *adiutor*. Drogula's hypothesis here forces him into a bizarre conclusion: the *adiutor* (an appellation he elevates to the level of a title) was *pari imperio* with the higher-ranking magistrate, who held the *provincia*; but the *adiutor* did not have a *provincia* assigned to himself "in which to exercise his *imperium*." In consequence, a Praetor as *adiutor* was operating in the Consul's *provincia*, not his own, and thus "the consul's *imperium* always enjoyed priority over that of the *adiutor*."[19]

Now the notion that a magistrate or promagistrate would have a defined assignment but no *provincia* is so revolutionary that one should expect some concrete evidence to be presented in its support, not just an arbitrary reimagination of what we find in the sources. As it happens, the idea can be refuted readily. In 195 BC, the Consul drew Hispania for his province; *praetores deinde provincias sortiti*. Ap. Claudius Nero drew Hispania Ulterior; *P. Manlius in Hispaniam citeriorem adiutor consuli datus* (Livy 33.43.5). Next, the Proconsul T. Quinctius in Greece had his *imperium* prorogued for another year (33.43.6). Clearly, P. Manlius' assignment as *adiutor consulis* was part of the *provinciarum sortitio*, and his *provincia* was Hispania Citerior—the same as the Consul's. Better still, we next learn that Manlius was decreed the same number of reinforcements as were given to Claudius Nero in Farther Spain, as well as the legion that had been in Citerior under the previous commander (33.43.8). Hence Manlius the Praetor had his

---

[16] For examples and discussion, see Chapter 4.2.   [17] Drogula 2015: 193,197–204.

[18] Drogula 2015: 190–192, in a discussion replete with tendentious misrepresentation of the evidence. "Cicero and Messala admit that their obscure (and apparently incorrect) claims were rejected by their respective colleagues in the college of augurs" (192 with n. 28). They admit no such thing. Cicero makes clear (*Att.* 9.3.3.) that only four—out of fifteen—Augurs were prepared to support Caesar's contention that a Praetor should be able to create Consuls or name a Dictator. Even allowing for the absence of several Augurs from Rome at the time, it is quite clear that these four did not constitute a majority of those present (for discussion, see Chapter 4.4.3). To say that Cicero "points out that many augurs accepted the legitimacy of Caesar's claims" is absurd. As for Messalla's noting that "praetors did indeed supervise the election of praetors in his day" (Gell. 13.15.4), *his temporibus* clearly refers to the abusive practice started under Caesar, and perhaps continued subsequently (see Linderski *AL* 2192–2193; cf. Drummond *FRHist* 3: 386 n. 9); it cannot be invoked to maintain that there had been augural disagreement on this question prior to the Civil War. The supercilious arrogance with which two Roman authorities, Consuls and Augurs both, are dismissed as clueless on a question relating to their most pertinent expertise is remarkable.

[19] Drogula 2015: 158–160; 203–204.

own *imperium*, and his own *exercitus*—but no *provincia*? The mind boggles. Likewise in 176, the decision (in the previous year) that the Propraetor T. Aebutius (*pr.* 178) should remain in his *provincia* of Sardinia as *adiutor* to the Consul who had drawn that same *provincia* is reported as part of the *provinciarum sortitio* (41.15.4–7). The evidence is uncontestable: a Praetor assigned as *adiutor* to a Consul was given the same *provincia* as the latter.[20] If both had *par imperium*, there could have been no way of resolving a conflict between them under Drogula's rule, especially as he does not believe that the Consul's auspices were superior even to the Quaestor's, let alone the Praetor's.[21]

Nor does Drogula's treatment of the celebrated dispute between Lutatius Catulus and Valerius Falto in 241 (Val. Max. 2.8.2) help his case. Acknowledging that in the process of the *sponsio* the Praetor admitted that both the Consul's *imperium* and auspices were superior to his, Drogula flatly refuses to accept the unequivocal evidence ("...this conclusion cannot be supported"): because, if so, there could have been no dispute in the first place as to who should get the triumph.[22] Like many others, Drogula misunderstands the issue: Falto was not trying to deny Catulus his triumph, but wanted one for himself as well, on the grounds that he had been in actual command of the fleet at the Aegates Islands, and hence won the battle *suo ductu*. Drogula, oddly enough, does not entertain the obvious possibility that the Praetor had been assigned as *adiutor* to the Consul; instead, he insists that either he must have had his own *provincia*, in Sicily, apart from the Consul's, "but took command of the consul's navy when the consul was disabled," or "some unusual exception was made to allow each to celebrate separate triumphs for the same victory." If Falto had his own *provincia*, he would automatically fall under the Consul's authority, under Drogula's rule of *cuius provincia, eius imperium*, once he took command of the fleet in the Consul's *provincia*: it offers no support for the claim that the Praetor's *imperium* as such was equal to the Consul's. If the Praetor here was the Consul's *adiutor*, without a *provincia* (in Drogula's view) of his own but with equal *imperium*, the legal question should have turned on whether *suo ductu* could apply to a man who lacked a *provincia*, which it manifestly did not: it was decided solely on the basis *utrum quod consul an quod praetor imperasset maius habiturum fuerit momentum* ("whether what the Consul ordered or what the Praetor ordered would have had greater force") and *si diversa auspicia accepissetis, cuius magis auspicio staretur* ("if you had received different auspices, according to whose *auspicium* would things rather have stood")? And nothing, of course, can be concluded from all this if what happened was an "unusual exception."

---

[20] This has long been known and understood: Giovannini 1983: 68–69; Vervaet 2012: 60 n. 56; 2014: 199–202.
[21] Drogula 2015: 69–70; cf. 161: "...all commanders possessed the exact same *imperium* and *auspicium*."
[22] Drogula 2015: 204–205; similarly Bergk 72. For detailed discussion of that case, see Chapter 4.2.1.

Then there are the lictors. It remains an uncontestable fact that, by at least the first half of the second century, the Praetor commanding an army (hence holding *imperium*) was accompanied by six lictors; the Consul had twelve, and the Dictator, twenty-four. Now the *fasces* are commonly seen as representing the magistrate's *imperium*: with the axes in the sphere *militiae*, not subject to *provocatio*; without them *domi*. Of course, if *imperium* by definition can only be exercised *militiae*, the *fasces* can only represent it when they contain the axes, as Drogula points out at length.[23] (Which is no different in substance from Mommsen's view that, with the axes, the *fasces* signify *imperium* exercised in the sphere *militiae*.) Whether *fasces* without axes also represent *imperium* (in the sphere *domi*), or merely the magistrate's *coercitio* subject to *provocatio*, is of no consequence for the matter at stake here; the crucial point is that Drogula accepts the *fasces* containing axes as representing *imperium* in the sphere *militiae*.

But if the Praetor's *imperium* was the same as the Consul's, and not inferior in any way, why would he not carry the same number of *fasces*? One might reason (Drogula does not) that in the City, the Consul's unquestionable *maior potestas* would naturally be expressed by twice the number of *fasces*, and that this practice simply carried over into the sphere *militiae*, where they signify *imperium* with the axes added. But in Drogula's view *imperium* was an entity entirely separate from the *consularis* or *praetoria potestas*: it was the same for all commanders, regardless of rank, and always had been. If all commanders were equal in the sphere *militiae*, no need ought ever to have arisen for distinguishing them according to their respective rank *domi*—quite the contrary. And since the Dictator supposedly does not outrank the Consul in any sense whatsoever (all that distinguishes him is that he also has—military—*imperium in Urbe*), no such transfer from the sphere *domi* to the sphere *militiae* could be invoked to explain why he has twice a Consul's lictors.

2.1.3 *Potestas* and *Imperium*

It seems probable enough that *imperium* refers, *sensu stricto*, exclusively to the military sphere, the common parlance of the Late Republic (and beyond) notwithstanding. What must be rejected is the claim that *imperium*, as a constitutional concept, was something disconnected from the magistrate's *potestas*. It is all very well to say that the Consul (or Praetor) was able to carry out all his civil functions by virtue of his *potestas*, and required *imperium* only for his military ones; it is an altogether different thing to maintain that without a special transaction

---

[23] Drogula 2007: 431–434; 2015: 93–96.

(the much-conjured *lex curiata*) he did not even have *imperium*.[24] It must be stated firmly that no concrete ancient evidence (and barely anything that would rise to ambiguous), let alone conclusive argument, has ever been produced to the effect that *imperium* was bestowed by that mysterious procedure. The notion stands and falls on a wholly speculative reconstruction (as any such reconstruction inevitably must be) of what the *lex curiata* meant.[25] That is not a sound foundation on which to erect a major constitutional theory.

In all of Latin usage, *potestas* refers to the full and complete range of a man's legal power, not merely a fraction of it. Hence the *consularis potestas* ought to include, by definition, *imperium* (that is, in the military sphere), from the moment the Consul entered office; ditto for the *praetoria* and *dictatoria potestas*. Mommsen saw and expressed this clearly enough ("Gegenüber dem *imperium* ist *potestas* der weitere Begriff"), but then, in consequence of his definition of *imperium*, proceeded to cloud the issue. For magistrates who held *imperium*, the term *potestas* is synonymous and covers the same range of powers ("...und hier also mit dem *imperium* zusammenfällt"); but in common parlance ("im Sprachgebrauch"), *imperium* is reserved for the higher magistrates, while *potestas* is primarily used for those who lack *imperium*. Hence the terms come to be employed in opposition to each other ("...so dass *imperium* und *potestas* in Gegensatz zu einander treten"): the higher magistracies are called *cum imperio*, the lower ones *cum potestate*.[26]

No doubt it was Mommsen's unfortunate way of putting this that has prompted, in subsequent scholarship, the misleading and pernicious habit of saying that

---

[24] The idea is neither novel nor exclusive to Drogula. J. S. Richardson 1991: 2–4 claimed as much, pointing out that promagistrates had *imperium*, without being magistrates. That *imperium* was separable from the magistracy is not in doubt; it does not prove that, for a magistrate to acquire it, a formal act beyond his election was necessary. Richardson's erroneous statement (3) that by the first century BC Proconsuls were able to hear cases under the *ius civile* in Rome rests on a misunderstanding of Mommsen *StR* 2.1: 102–103.

[25] The complex of questions surrounding the Curiate Law cannot be addressed here; I hope to discuss the matter in a separate study. Briefly, though, my position is this. The *lex curiata* did not confer on the magistrate any powers he did not already possess, *qua* magistrate, on account of having been duly elected or appointed; specifically, it granted neither *imperium* nor auspices. The Curiate Law's essential purpose was confirmatory, with regard to the magistrate and his powers *in toto*. It represented a formal pronouncement by the *populus* that the magistrate was in possession of valid auspices, as demonstrated by his affirmative "auspices of investiture," and probably contained language ordaining that the auspices obtained by the magistrate should count as being obtained on behalf of the entire *populus*, and to deny valid auspication *de re publica* to anyone else. (Similarly Staveley 1956: 89–90, surely correct; cf. Catalano 1960: 450–475; Berthelet 128–137.) In this way, the *lex curiata* made his office a *iustus magistratus* (as explained by Messalla *De auspiciis* apud Gell. 13.15.4: *minoribus creatis magistratibus tributis comitiis magistratus, sed iustus curiata datur lege; maiores centuriatis comitiis fiunt*). The law further ordered the magistrate to act as the lawful holder of his office, with the consequence that he should exercise, *domi militiaeque*, over his fellow citizens all the powers inherent in his office. This view is fundamentally, if not in every detail, in agreement with, e.g., Mommsen *StR* 1: 609–614; Botsford 188–193; Nicholls *passim*; Versnel 350; Keaveney 161–163; Rüpke 1990: 47–51 = 2019: 48–52; Kunkel *StO* 96–103; Stasse *passim*; Van Haeperen 2012 and 2017 *passim*; Fiori 2014b: 106–115; Vervaet 2014: 310–340.

[26] *StR* 1: 23–24.

higher magistrates have *imperium*, whereas the lower ones "only" have *potestas* (a distinction Mommsen would hardly have countenanced in this form). Precise terminology does matter; it affects the way we think about an issue, approach a question, and endeavor to solve a problem.[27] (Which is why Drogula's definition of *imperium* as strictly military must be taken seriously, not brushed away.) It may be wiser to formulate the matter thus: all magistrates have *potestas*; for the higher ones this includes *imperium*, but for the lower ones it does not. And *imperium* was part and parcel of the *consularis potestas*, not a power separately conferred by the *lex curiata*.

For our present inquiry, we may conclude that the Consul's *imperium*, in the sphere *militiae*, was *maius* compared to that of the Praetor, just as his powers were greater in the sphere *domi* in case of collision. All the ancient evidence attests to that, and none indicates otherwise. When it comes to the Dictator and the Consul, though, the matter, as we shall see, is more complicated.

2.2 *Auspicia*: Basic Concepts

At home and at war (*domi militiae*), all acts of managing the *res publica* required the permission of Iuppiter Optimus Maximus. Public sacrifice, Assemblies of the People, meetings of the Senate, military operations—such and a host of other proceedings demanded that the magistrate in charge obtain Iuppiter's assent before commencing the intended action. It was a cardinal rule, immutable and not open to exceptions.[28]

2.2.1 Augurs, Augury, and Magistrates

All communications with Iuppiter on matters of state fell into the area termed *auspicia*, distinct from worship of the gods through acts of ceremony (*sacra*, chiefly prayer and sacrifice) and from prediction of future events through interpretation of portents (*prodigia*). The *sacra* came under the responsibility of the various public priesthoods associated with the Pontifical College (*pontifices, flamines*, and Vestal Virgins), whereas the interpretation of portents was entrusted partly to

---

[27] To think in terms of some magistrates having *imperium*, while others "only" have *potestas*, can lead to strange results. It is doubtful that, with reflection on the proper relationship between the two terms as they are used in Latin, Badian (1990: 469) and Brennan (*PRR* 1: 51–53) would have argued that the *tribuni militum consulari potestate*, because that and not *consulari imperio* is the prevailing appellation in the sources, did not have *imperium* but "only" *potestas*. Vervaet 2014: 339 n. 113 correctly rejects the idea as "an absurdity"; cf. Linderski *RQ* 675 ("not likely").

[28] Cic. *Div.* 1.3, *exactis regibus nihil publice sine auspiciis nec domi nec militiae gerebatur*; Livy 1.36.6, *auguriis certe sacerdotioque augurum tantus honos accessit ut nihil belli domique postea nisi auspicato gereretur*; 6.41.4, *auspiciis bello ac pace domi militiaeque omnia geri, quis est qui ignorat?*

the Decemviri *sacris faciundis*, keepers of the Sibylline Books, partly to the *haruspices*—Etruscan diviners summoned by the Roman government on a case-by-case basis.[29] The auspices, however, were the realm of the College of Public Augurs (*augures publici populi Romani*), nine in number since 300 BC and almost always senators, hence active politicians. They served as the guardians of augural law: experts to advise Senate and magistrates on questions relating to the auspices, and to act as the "interpreters of Iuppiter" (*interpretes Iovis*, Cic. *Leg.* 2.20) in cases where his message might not be self-evident.[30]

Permission to act was secured through *auspicium*: the process of asking Iuppiter if it was *fas*, "proper," to perform the planned activity on this day, in this location; an action carried out with such permission was considered to occur *auspicato*, "with auspices obtained." The answer held good for only that day: if permission was granted, the act could not be carried out on a later date without first auspicating again; if permission was denied, it could be sought again the next day.[31] The question must be asked (the technical term is *auspicari*, commonly rendered as "taking the auspices") by the magistrate intending to perform the action, and it is to him that Iuppiter gives his response: an Augur has no part in the auspication, unless to provide advice or assistance, if so summoned by the magistrate. Auspices could be sought *de caelo*, "from the sky" (Iuppiter's response would come by way of a celestial phenomenon, usually lightning or thunder); *ex avibus*, "from the birds" (the response would come through certain kinds of birds); or *ex tripudio*, "from the dance" (the feeding of the *pulli*, the augural Chickens). In the most general terms, signs from the sky and from the birds conveyed their meaning—Iuppiter granting permission, or withholding it—through their orientation: where precisely they appeared within a defined area of observation. The Chickens offered Iuppiter's response through the manner of their eating: affirmative when they fed greedily, with crumbs of dough "dancing" upon

---

[29] Cic. ND 3.5, *cumque omnis populi Romani religio in sacra et auspicia divisa sit, tertium adiunctum sit si quid praedictionis causa ex portentis et monstris Sibyllae interpretes haruspicesve monuerunt*. For an overview of Roman priests (*sacerdotes publici populi Romani*), see Wissowa 479–566; North 1990b: 582–590.

[30] Cic. ND 1.122, *quod ni ita sit...cur sacris pontifices, cur auspiciis augures praesunt?* cf. *Dom.* 41, *si et sacrorum iure pontifices et auspiciorum religione augures...evertunt tribunatum tuum*; 42, *intellegis omni genere iuris, quod in sacris, quod in auspiciis, quod in legibus sit, te tribunum non fuisse*; *Har. resp.* 18, (sc. *maiores nostri*) *statas solemnisque caerimonias pontificatu, rerum bene gerendarum auctoritates augurio...contineri putaverunt*. (The speeches' polemical context has no bearing on the accuracy of Cicero's description of the Augurs' and Pontiffs' respective responsibility in law and religion.) See also Linderski *AL* 2147–2151; and cf. Giovannini 1998: 106: "Il apparaît ainsi que les augures, loin d'être les charlatans dont se moquent certains des historiens modernes, étaient en réalité les gardiens de la constitution romaine."

[31] *Auspicium* must be distinguished from *augurium*, an act that permanently transformed certain persons, places, or ceremonies into a peculiar augural state, in a procedure, known as *inauguratio*, that only an Augur could perform. Here Iuppiter's answer was final: if permission was denied, it could not be sought again. (*Augurium*, "augury," can also denote the entire augural science, comprising *auspicia* and *auguria*.) Kings, Flamines, and Augurs—but not magistrates—were inaugurated, as were most (though not all) temples. See Catalano 1960: 42–45; Linderski *AL* 2295; 1986b: 338 = *RQ* 493.

dropping to the ground; prohibitive, when they refused to eat. In all instances, the answer was unambiguous—"yes" or "no"; and in all instances, it merely gave or denied permission to proceed with the intended act on this day. An affirmative response, naturally, could be taken to signal Iuppiter's approval of the objective behind the action in question, just as a negative one presumably signified his opposition (on that day—not necessarily in principle); but in no instance did his permission to go ahead imply a promise of success, a guarantee that the act's desired objective would indeed be achieved. Denial of permission, on the other hand, constituted a clear warning that if the magistrate were to proceed nonetheless, the outcome of the action would be to the detriment of the *res publica*. (Differently put, permission to engage the enemy in battle today was not an assurance of victory; but prohibition disregarded almost certainly assured defeat.)[32] From an augural perspective, for an action to occur *inauspicato*, "without auspices," it did not matter whether it was performed in spite of a negative response or without seeking permission in the first place; nor did it matter if the action was performed in a mistaken belief to possess affirmative auspices (an error during the auspication, for instance, would invalidate the permission apparently granted): any act committed without valid affirmative auspices caused *vitium*, a ritual flaw under augural law. Unless and until mended (insofar as possible—usually by repeating the act, this time with affirmative auspices), *vitium* attached to the magistrate who caused it and all his subsequent actions that depended on the vitiated one.[33]

Individually, Augurs were mostly occupied with the performance of *auguria* and the ritual maintenance of augurally significant locations in Rome and the *ager Romanus*, along with advising or assisting magistrates at their auspications, if so required. Their principal role in the working of the *res publica*, however, they carried out collectively. The College of Augurs formed the sole body able and authorized to officially interpret the *ius augurale publicum*. Their rulings, issued as decrees (*decreta*) on their own initiative or as responses (*responsa*) to questions submitted—usually by the Senate, sometimes a magistrate—to the College, constituted binding interpretations of Iuppiter's will. Yet such a ruling did not in itself

---

[32] Cf. Champion 213: "Religious orthopraxy worked to create the optimal conditions for what was desired in this world; it was not a practice with eschatological aims. And it could not guarantee successful outcomes, as the relationship between human and divine in elite religious practices was unequal, quasi-contractual, but not reciprocal."

[33] Linderski *AL* 2162–2168, 2185 (comparing *vitium* to a "contagious disease"). Linderski's work (with an indispensable annotated bibliography) remains the standard treatment of augury and auspices; earlier studies still essential are those of Valeton (1889, 1890, and 1891) and Catalano (1960 and 1978). A spirited recent discussion by Driediger-Murphy (2019) questions, not always persuasively, a number of long-held tenets, but offers a welcome affirmation of the view that in Rome augury was taken seriously: "it made an independent contribution to Roman life, providing religious motives for behaviour even to the detriment of self-interest. In this sense, the perceived will of Jupiter bound the Roman politician as tightly in practice as it did in theory" (201).

have the force of law: it required a directive of the Senate, to be executed by a magistrate, to give it effect.[34]

Now, moderns do not, for the most part, believe in Iuppiter or the reality of auspices. How, then, was it possible for the *res publica* to function, when, as a simple matter of long-term random distribution, half of all responses from Iuppiter ought to be negative? We happen to know the answer: in the taking of auspices, the god's response was being helped along by presuming it to come in the affirmative, and by employing practices apt to produce the desired result. Thus the Chickens normally were never fed, except when auspicating; a lusty attack on their food— an affirmative response—was pretty much assured.[35] Cynical manipulation, some will say. Not if one actually believes that Iuppiter communicates with us through auspices: for the god has power to render moot all such human efforts at gaining a particular response, if he wishes it so, and send a message contrary to the one desired. To believe this requires no more conviction than any other religious doctrine. We may call it manipulation, but in fairness only in the basic sense of the word: the proper handling of a tool.[36]

But any tool can fail; any method of auspication can unexpectedly produce an answer opposite to the one desired; and people make mistakes—forget to auspicate when necessary, or overlook a small detail in the ritual. (There are no minor details as regards significance: the slightest error is fatal.) If cynical manipulation were behind it all, one should expect a system in place to defang such slip-ups and mishaps, so as not to interfere with the smooth running of the *res publica* or the personal ambitions and objectives of the individual actors. Yet clearly no such system existed; when Iuppiter's message was not as hoped for, everyone accepted it all the same, sometimes at great personal disappointment.[37] Or, as we shall see later, almost everyone.

Could augury be used to influence the outcome of political decisions or disagreements? Certainly, and at times it surely was. But notwithstanding sweeping assertions in modern scholarship of ubiquitous exploitation for political gain, attested—or at least plausibly conjectured—concrete instances are hard to find

---

[34] See Linderski *AL* 2151–2190 on the workings of the College; 2190–2225 on individual Augurs.

[35] Cic. *Div.* 1.27, *necesse est enim offa obiecta cadere frustum ex pulli ore cum pascitur*; 1.77, *praeclara vero auspicia, si esurientibus pullis res geri poterit, saturis nihil geretur* (cf. 2.72); 2.73, *nunc vero inclusa in cavea et fame enecta* (sc. *avis*) *si in offam pultis invadit et si aliquid ex eius ore cecidit, hoc tu auspicium aut hoc modo Romulum auspicari solitum putas?*; Fest. 285L, *puls potissimum dabatur pullis in auspiciis, quia ex ea necesse erat aliquid decidere, quod tripudium faceret*. Driediger-Murphy 2019: 112–113 implausibly dismisses Cicero's depiction as "a selective caricature or distortion of the real ritual." See also Cicero's caustic summary (*Div.* 2.83) of augural practices: ...*necesse est fateri partim horum errore susceptum esse, partim superstitione, multa fallendo* ("a mixture of error, superstition and above all fraud," Linderski 1982: 15 = *RQ* 461).

[36] Linderski 1985: 226 = *RQ* 515; cf. Liebeschuetz 19–25.

[37] "Roman politicians must often have had to accept augural results which they might otherwise have preferred to ignore or evade": Driediger-Murphy 2019: 46.

prior to the more freewheeling employment, in the Late Republic, of prohibitive signs reported to prevent a legislative or elective assembly from meeting.[38]

2.2.2 The *Vinculum Temporis*

All magistrates have auspices—the right to request permission from Iuppiter Optimus Maximus to proceed with an intended act of state on the present day. Our inquiry in this subsection will concern only the holders of the *auspicia maxima* (Consuls, Praetors, Censors, and—surely—Dictators), as defined by the Consul (53 BC) and Augur M. Valerius Messalla Rufus (Gell. 13.15.4). It will focus mostly on auspices as they relate to a military context, there being few known instances of disputes limited to the sphere *domi*. For a proper understanding of the augural issues discussed in what follows, it will be helpful to briefly consider the nature of so-called oblative auspices: their function and—occasional—interaction with impetrative auspices.

Iuppiter was not limited to giving a response when asked (what is known as "impetrative" auspices); he could send auspices of his own accord. Such "oblative" messages served to express encouragement or—more frequently, it appears—deliver a warning; if unheeded, *vitium* would result, although more often than not a ritual augural flaw already committed would be what triggered the warning. Moreover, the god was known to change his mind: he might grant permission to the magistrate when asked at dawn, but later on revoke it; and the only way in which he could alert the magistrate that permission had been rescinded was through an oblative sign. Therein, however, lay a problem: not only must the magistrate observe the prohibitive sign in time to abandon his intended action—now deprived of approval—today, or terminate it if already commenced: he must be able to tell, with a fair degree of certainty, whether any unusual occurrence was indeed an *auspicium* and not merely a *prodigium*, and if so, to what particular action it pertained.

Prodigia—omens, portents, and so forth—indicated divine concern with the state of the *res publica*, whether actual displeasure or a warning of dangers lying ahead; either way, they signalled a need to seek the *pax deorum*. They could originate with any deity, but in and of themselves carried no augural significance. Their management (after interpretation by the Decemviri or the *haruspices*) fell under the immediate responsibility of the *pontifices*, not the Augurs, and they did

---

[38] Commonly nowadays referred to as *obnuntiatio*; in reality, a complex mix of augurally distinct procedures that, fortunately, have no bearing on the present study. On the augural details, see Linderski *AL* 2195–2199; 1986b: 333–335 = *RQ* 488–490; Driediger-Murphy 2019: 127–160; on political use, de Libero 56–64; Görne 215–229.

as such not count as auspices. But one and the same sign could, in fact, serve both purposes.[39] What added an augural dimension in such cases was time and place.

For a sign to count, in the augural discipline, as an oblative *auspicium*—a message sent by Iuppiter pertaining to a specific action—it must occur and be observed while that action was in progress, not before or after. This constituted a fundamental requirement: lacking the nexus between time and action, any portents reported were not *auspicia oblativa* but "mere" *prodigia*; and some events might not be even such, but simply natural occurrences. This augural rule, nowadays commonly known as the *vinculum temporis*, allowed the magistrate to suspect and the Augurs to determine whether, for example, a bolt of lightning seen or a growl of thunder heard was a sign from Iuppiter, or merely weather.[40]

A negative response to impetrative auspices fundamentally consists in Iuppiter's refusal to send the desired affirmative sign—for instance, by keeping the Chickens from eating; though for auspices taken *de caelo* or *ex avibus*, the negative response will usually be more pronounced, by way of a prohibitive sign within the requested category—a *fulmen adversum* or *avis remora*.[41] Anything else (such as a bird, or thunder, when a *fulmen sinistrum* was sought) observed at that moment is not a response to the impetrative *auspicium* requested, but an oblative sign—which, when negative in character, usually does not simply deny permission for the day but alerts to the presence of *vitium*.[42] The oblative sign may come instead of the response sought, or simultaneously with it—in the *vinculum temporis*. If, for example, the Consul auspicating before dawn receives the desired affirmative response (say, lightning or a bird "on the left," or the Chickens feeding lustily), while simultaneously thunder is heard "on the right," the latter will be taken as an

---

[39] On the difference (but also overlap), see Linderski 1993: 58–59 = *RQ* 613–614: "The *auspicium oblativum* pertained solely to a concrete action during the exercise of which it was sighted. The *prodigium* referred to the state of the republic, and it could be observed at any time and practically at any place…The subtle part is that the same sign could function at the same time both as an *auspicium oblativum* and a *prodigium*. That *prodigia* were fundamentally different from *auspicia* is demonstrated by the fact that the augurs are never called upon, in Livy and in other sources, to interpret the prodigies."

[40] See Valeton 1890: 447–448; 1891: 94–99; Linderski *AL* 2196–2197. Driediger-Murphy 2018: 197 n. 64 questions this theory, noting that the phrase *vinculum temporis* is "a modern coinage of Valeton's" and suggesting that it "may not have governed all oblative auspices." Valeton developed his theory from an exhaustive examination of the evidence, reaching a carefully argued rational conclusion. It may be called into question by demonstrating that the underlying principle is wrong; that the name he chose to give that principle, *vinculum temporis*, does not occur in the sources is irrelevant to the theory's validity as long as the evidence supports the theory: and Driediger-Murphy adduces neither contrary evidence nor reasoning. To seriously entertain the notion that the *vinculum temporis* may not have applied to all oblative auspices, it would be necessary to offer, at a minimum, an explanation of how augural law could otherwise determine whether a given sign referred to a particular action; actual evidence in support of the notion would be desirable.

[41] Signs *de caelo*—lightning and thunder—and *ex avibus* normally signalled Iuppiter's approval when observed "on the left" (i.e., in the east), prohibition when "on the right" (in the west): see Valeton 1889: 288–299; and especially Linderski's exhaustive study, *AL* 2170, 2280–2286; cf. 1986b: 338–339 = *RQ* 493–494. On the tendency in augural terminology to avoid *dexter* when referring to prohibitive impetrative signs, Valeton 1889: 286–289; cf. Pease 135.

[42] See Linderski *AL* 2169–2171.

oblative *auspicium* warning of *vitium* (the how and why would be for the Augurs to determine): it will be impossible to go through with the intended action for which permission had been sought, and—seemingly—granted. Likewise, if the Consul obtains an affirmative response at dawn and later in the day, as he commences the corresponding action, observes a negative sign, it will constitute an oblative *auspicium*, effectively cancelling the permission Iuppiter had given at dawn (what is known, in augural parlance, as *dirimere auspicia*[43]). But any thunder or lightning occurring between the auspication and the action itself will be just that—severe weather.

2.3 The "Auspices of Investiture"

The magistrate is in office *de iure* from midnight of the first day of his term. However, a set of ceremonies—most spectacular in the case of the Consuls—surrounds his formal assumption of the office. First and before venturing on any other public business, he must ask Iuppiter for auspices.

The magistrate—regardless of rank—spends the previous night on a bed under the open sky, in a practice known as *incubatio*.[44] At dawn he rises and puts his question to Iuppiter; upon receiving an affirmative response—the *fulmen sinistrum*, a flash of lightning from left to right[45]—the Consul now dons the *toga prae-*

---

[43] See Linderski *AL* 2197.

[44] Fest. 326.16L,...*ubi incubare posset auspicii repetendi causa* (the conjectural lemma <*Romanus ager*> appears to lack an evidentiary basis); 474.7–15L, <*silentio surgere...ai*>*t dici, ubi qui post mediam* <*noctem...auspic*>*andi causa ex lectulo suo si*<*lens surr*>*exit et liberatus a lecto, in solido...*<*se*>*detque, ne quid eo tempore deiciat,* <*cavens, donec s*>*e in lectum reposuit: hoc enim est* <*proprie sil*>*entium, omnis vitii in auspiciis vacuitas. Veranius ait, non utique ex lecto, sed ex cubili, ne*<*c*> *rursus ex in lectum reponere necesse esse* (and cf. 470.35, *mane surg*<*ens*>); Dion. Hal. 2.5.1–2, 6.1–2; Livy 8.23.15, *cum consul oriens de nocte silentio diceret dictatorem*; 9.38.14, *nocte deinde silentio...dictatorem dixit* (cf. Cic. *Leg.* 3.9, *isque ave sinistra dictus populi magister esto*); Gell. 3.2.10; Macrob. *Sat.* 1.3.7; see Mommsen *StR* 1: 79–83, 102 n. 1; 105; Valeton 1890: 249–255; Vaahtera 112–122; Linderski 2006: 90–91 = *RQ2* 5; cf. *AL* 2276 on Serv. ad *Aen.* 4.200, *amplius uno exitu in eo* [sc. *templo*, confused here with *tabernaculum*] *esse non oportet, cum ibi sit cubiturus auspicans*; cf. also Varro *LL* 6.86, *ubi noctu in templum censor auspicaverit atque de caelo nuntium erit.*

[45] Rafferty 32 would have the auspication be made *ex tripudiis*, with reference to Van Haeperen 2012: 76. The latter argued correctly that Dionysios' ὀρνιθοσκόποι (2.6.2), drawing pay from the *aerarium* (μισθὸν ἐκ τοῦ δημοσίου φερόμενοι), cannot be Augurs, and must be *pullarii* (thus already Linderski *AL* 2191 n. 164; Kunkel *StO* 90 n. 133); although one should perhaps consider the possibility that Dionysios was thrown off by the phrase *augures publici* in his Latin source: he appears to have similarly mistaken the paid (hence free) Greek translators assisting the *Xviri sacris faciundis* (Zonar. 7.11) for public slaves (δημοσίοι θεράποντες, 4.62.4; cf. Wissowa 536). But Van Haeperen did not conclude that the magistrate's initial auspices were provided by the Chickens. On the contrary: Dionysios' description of the ritual speaks, unambiguously and undeniably, of a flash of lightning from the left (ἀστραπὴ ἐκ τῶν ἀριστερῶν) to the right (2.5.2, ἀστραπὴ διῆλθεν ἐκ τῶν ἀριστερῶν ἐπὶ τὰ δεξιά). With the auspicant facing east, he would observe the flash running from northeast to southeast—the two most favorable regions of the sky (Linderski *AL* 2265–2266, 2280–2285). Van Haeperen sums up (79) the character of these auspices as ones *de caelo* ("basées sur l'observation du ciel et plus précisément de la foudre"). That the *pullarii* were not responsible solely for the Chickens but assisted regularly with *auspicia de caelo* is evident from Cicero *Div.* 2.74: *iam de caelo servare non ipsos censes solitos qui*

texta and proceeds to the Capitol, where he and his colleague take their seats on the *sella curulis*; thus they preside over the sacrifice, solving—since he had kept the City safe throughout the past year—the vow made to Iuppiter by their predecessors, and pronounce the same vow to be solved by their successors, should he keep the City safe throughout the coming year. The first Senate meeting of the year follows right away.[46]

The precise question the Consul puts to Iuppiter at the dawn of his first day in office is not reported; but the objective seems clear enough. As in the case of Romulus himself, it was an auspication περὶ τῆς ἀρχῆς, hence *de magistratu* or *de imperio* (in the colloquial, "Mommsenian" sense);[47] Romulus had asked Iuppiter and all the other gods for a favorable sign εἰ βουλομένοις αὐτοῖς ἐστι βασιλεύεσθαι τὴν πόλιν ὑφ' ἑαυτοῦ, if it was their will that the City should be ruled by him (Dion. Hal. 2.5.1). This practice continued to be observed even after the expulsion of the Kings, in the election of Consuls, Praetors, and all other magistrates established by law (διέμεινε ... τὸ περὶ τοὺς οἰωνισμοὺς νόμιμον, οὐ μόνον βασιλευομένης τῆς πόλεως, ἀλλὰ καὶ μετὰ κατάλυσιν τῶν μονάρχων ἐν ὑπάτων καὶ στρατηγῶν καὶ τῶν ἄλλων τῶν κατὰ νόμους ἀρχόντων αἱρέσει, Dion. Hal. 2.6.1). *Mutatis mutandis*, the Consul's question therefore must have been not merely for permission to enter office on that day,[48] but whether it was *fas* for him to be Consul at all. Having been chosen, *auspicato*, by the People in the *comitia*, and properly renunciated as such by his predecessor presiding over the Assembly, he was Consul *iure publico* from the moment the day began, at midnight;[49] but without Iuppiter's assent under the *ius augurale*, it was unthinkable that he should assume and exercise the powers of his office.

Now the Consul's legitimacy under the *ius augurale* depended not on his identity, but on his auspices: on his ability to lawfully ask Iuppiter to ask for them, and Iuppiter's willingness to grant them. Iuppiter's assent could only be expressed in that form: approval of the Consul's person could not be separated from the validity of his auspices. If Iuppiter disapproved of the People's choice (a choice made *after* he had granted permission, through auspices, to the presiding magistrate to go ahead with the election: permission to proceed might imply a presumption, but did not constitute a guarantee, that Iuppiter would approve of the result[50]),

---

auspicabantur? nunc imperant pullario; ille renuntiat (or *ille renuntiat fulmen sinistrum*, depending on how one chooses to punctuate).

[46] Dion. Hal. 2.6.2, cf. 2.5.2, for the details of the initial auspication; for the ceremonies on the Capitol, see Mommsen *StR* 1: 616; Van Haeperen 2007.

[47] Cf. Nicholls 265; Van Haeperen 2012: 91.

[48] As Catalano argued, 1960: 43–45. (I reasoned along the same lines at Konrad 2004: 175 n. 12, but no longer hold to that view: see what follows.) Catalano himself acknowledged (45–46) that certain auspices could pertain to a person rather than an action, as in the auspication to determine the *praetor* of the Latin League (Fest. 276–277L; below, Subsection 2.4.1 #1).

[49] Even if *vitio creatus*, as it might later be discovered: *magistratus vitio creatus nihilo setius magistratus*, Varro *LL* 6.30.

[50] Noted by Van Haeperen 2012: 88.

surely he would not validate such a man's auspices when asked to do so; and why would he withhold valid auspices from a man he approved of?[51]

Hence we may take it for virtually certain that the question put to Iuppiter pertained specifically to the validity of the Consul's auspices:[52] *si est fas me L. Titium consulem meo auspicio rem publicam populi Romani gerere*, or something to that effect. In a fundamental sense, it was through this first auspication that he acquired his auspices, by ascertaining their validity.[53] In consequence, the Consul's initial auspices form the basis for all his auspices asked and obtained throughout his year in office; if they were flawed, so would be all his subsequent ones, and every act he performed under such flawed auspices would be augurally—not legally—invalid, *vitiosus*. A negative response would be considered final, not open to another try at obtaining an affirmative one on a subsequent day.[54] (Iuppiter could be inscrutable at times, but not perverse: to randomly delay the new Consul's entry into office when he had no objection to his person would serve no purpose.)

Perhaps Nicholls summed the matter up best: election (or, in the case of a Dictator, *dictio*) *auspicato* gave the man thus chosen the right to ask Iuppiter for auspices on behalf of the Roman People; but it was the act of asking for, and receiving, an affirmative response, not countermanded by an oblative sign under the *vinculum temporis*, that gave the new magistrate his valid auspices.[55] Which raises the question whether there is room for a second fundamental act of auspication within the Consul's term of office, this time pertaining to the departure for war: a military equivalent of the magistrate's initial auspices on entering office.

---

[51] Dion. Hal. 3.35.5–6 expressly contemplates the possibility of divine disapproval; but we cannot tell whether this is his own conclusion or drawn from an authoritative source. Kunkel *StO* 90 with n. 134 would allow, grudgingly ("allenfalls"), that the question put to Iuppiter asked whether the magistrate met his approval ("ob er…als Beamter willkommen sei"); but he denied the magistrate's initial auspication any constitutional or "sakralrechtliche" significance: solely the auspices obtained at the magistrate's election were of legal consequence. This conflates the magistrate's status *iure publico* (determined by his election in the *comitia*) with that *iure augurali* (determined by the validity of his auspices). An affirmative response at his initial auspices did not bestow his office on the magistrate, any more than a negative response, in and of itself, would deprive him of it. Iuppiter's response confirmed or denied the validity of the magistrate's auspices; in case of the latter, his election and magistracy remained legally unimpaired (*magistratus vitio factus nihilo setius magistratus*, Varro *LL* 6.30), but tainted by *vitium*—hence impossible to continue.

[52] Linderski *AL* 2169 with n. 74, rejected—*perperam*—by Konrad 2004: 175 n. 12.

[53] Magdelain 1964: 429–431 = 1990: 343–345; cf. 1968: 36–40, arguing against the concept of a transmission of the auspices from his predecessor to the magistrate: it is Iuppiter himself who grants to the new magistrate, at the time of his election *auspicato*, the right to ask him for auspices, and at the moment of the initial auspication—with an affirmative response—upon entering office, renews in the person of the new magistrate his pact with the Roman People.

[54] No instance of this is actually on record: the case of M. Claudius Marcellus (*cos. II* 215) involved an oblative sign—thunder—observed in connection (the *vinculum temporis*) with his entrance into office, which was ruled by the College of Augurs to signify that he was *vitio creatus*; Marcellus promptly abdicated his office. For discussion, see Chapter 8.3.

[55] Nicholls 274 n. 36; cf. Fiori 2014b: 76–79 with n. 85.

2.4 The "Auspices of Departure": the Evidence

The Consul (or Praetor, or Dictator) leaving the City in order to go to war must do so under auspices obtained from Iuppiter. These auspices form the overriding divine authorization for his entire campaign; if for any reason they lost their validity (or were not validly acquired in the first place), or their validity came into doubt, the commander must return to Rome, and repeat them.

2.4.1 The *Praetor* Approved by the Birds

That much is generally considered certain. Yet questions remain. We are not told specifically where magistrates took their auspices for war, or how. Mommsen placed the procedure on the Capitol, immediately before the *votorum nuncupatio*.[56] In this, he relied on the antiquarian (L.) Cincius,[57] who wrote of a ceremony that served to determine, prior to the end of the Latin League in 340 V, the Roman commander of the Latin federal forces:

> (1) Fest. 276.15–277.2L: praetor ad portam nunc salutatur is qui in provinciam pro praetore aut pro consule exit: cuius rei morem ait Cincius in libro de consulum potestate talem:…itaque quo anno Romanos imperatores ad exercitum mittere oporteret iussu nominis Latini, conplures nostros in Capitolio a sole oriente auspicis operam dare solitos. ubi aves adixissent…illum quem aves addixerant, praetorem salutare solitum, qui eam provinciam optineret praetoris nomine.

> "As *praetor* is hailed at the gate nowadays he who goes out to his province *pro praetore* or *pro consule*; the reason for this custom Cincius, in his book *On the Powers of the Consuls*, says to be as follows: 'Thus in any year in which the Romans were to send commanders to the army as decided by the Latin League, several of ours would observe auspices on the Capitol at sunrise; once the birds had indicated their consent…it was the custom to hail as *praetor* the one whom the birds had indicated, as he would obtain that *provincia* under the title of *praetor*.'"

---

[56] *StR* 1: 99, 63–64: "Der in den Krieg ziehende Feldherr hat speciell zu diesem Zweck am Morgen des Tages, an dem er die Stadt verlässt, die Auspicien auf dem Capitol einzuholen." Thus also Magdelain 1968: 40–42.

[57] Not to be confused with L. Cincius Alimentus, Rome's second historian. Cincius the Antiquarian very likely wrote in the first century BC, as a contemporary of Cicero and Varro, if not earlier; his work was extensively used by Verrius Flaccus, as is evident from the numerous citations in Festus' excerpt of the latter: see Bispham–Cornell *FRHist* 1: 181–183; cf. G. Wissowa "Cincius (3)" *RE* 3.2 (1899) 2555–2556; R. Helm "Pompeius (145) Festus" *RE* 21.2 (1952) 2316–2319; A. Dihle "Verrius (2)" *RE* 8A.2 (1958) 1636–1645.

But an auspication that served to determine which Roman should become the federal commander (*praetor*) of the Latin League cannot simply be assumed to apply to the Consul's auspices on the day of departure: Festus—which is to say, presumably, Verrius Flaccus—cited this to explain why in his own time (*nunc*), promagistrates (not Consuls or Praetors) leaving Rome to command an army or province, be they *pro consule* or *pro praetore*, are saluted at the City gates as *praetor*, and commonly—generically, if you wish—addressed and referred to as such.[58] He does not imply that the ancient ritual described by Cincius was still in use in the first century BC for purposes different than the Latin League command. Moreover, the sole unambiguous—or perhaps not, as we shall see—reference to auspices in connection with the rituals of departure clearly implies that the Consul took them before he ascended onto the Capitol for his profession of vows: *ne auspicato profectus in Capitolium ad vota nuncupanda, paludatus inde cum lictoribus in provinciam iret* (Livy 21.63.9). With good reason, several scholars have rejected the Capitol as location, without being able to offer an alternative.[59]

The procedure itself is unlikely to describe the auspices taken at a Consul's *profectio*. The auspication is performed by *conplures nostri*; that much (and little else) is clear. The man approved by the birds must either belong to that group, hence be one of the auspicants, or he is not included among the *conplures nostri*, in which case he is not taking these auspices himself. If the latter, the ceremony cannot possibly describe the commander's auspices of departure, as Iuppiter would give those directly to him, not to a third party.[60] If the former, we are confronted with an otherwise unknown process (save for the twins' primordial contest) of choosing a commander—what Adam Ziółkowski calls "sheer absurdity." Even accepting this as an authentic practice in archaic times for the purpose of determining a Latin federal commander supplied by Rome, it could not simply be taken as evidence for how commanders of a Roman army were selected; and, obviously, in historical times a commander's departure from Rome did not entail an auspical contest with others.

---

[58] For an example of such usage, see Cic. *Fam.* 2.17.6, *quod ego officio quaestorio te adductum reticere de praetore tuo non moleste ferebam* (the *praetor* in question was M. Calpurnius Bibulus, cos. 59, and now *pro consule*, cf. *Fam.* 15.3.2). The federal commanders of the Latin League were known as *praetores* (apparently two in number) in the fourth century, and probably at all times: Chapter 3.3.3 with note 76.

[59] E.g., Valeton 1890: 222; Keaveney 163; Rüpke 1990: 45–46 = 2019: 46–47; Konrad 2004: 172 (where, in n. 5, Valeton should have been referenced); Ziółkowski 2011 *passim*. The Capitol is still maintained by Dalla Rosa 2003: 189; Hurlet 2010: 45; Humm 77; Berthelet 119. Against the notion (espoused by, e.g., Humm and Berthelet, followed by Rafferty 41 n. 61) that the auspication took place not on the Capitol proper but at the *auguraculum* on the Arx see, correctly, G. Wissowa "auspicium" *RE* 2.2 (1896) 2585. The *auguraculum* was used by the Augurs (*auguraculum appellabant antiqui, quam nos arcem dicimus, quod ibi augures publice auspicarentur*, Fest. 17.14–15L); not a shred of evidence connects it with any magistrate taking auspices.

[60] "This should be enough to rule out the procedure…being the auspices of departure": Ziółkowski 2011: 468.

Recently, Pierre Sánchez has made an attempt to vindicate Cincius for the auspices of departure. While persuasive in most of its interpretation regarding what the passage tells us about Rome's relations with the Latin League, it founders on the grounds already laid out by Ziółkowski. Sánchez assumes *conplures* to mean *augures*, and questions the apparent selection purpose of the ritual, arguing that Cincius was not thinking of several candidates competing for the command, but merely of a single nominee looking to be confirmed by Iuppiter.[61] That may well be so; but it does not alter the fact that, in such a reconstruction, the commander does not obtain his auspices himself.

2.4.2 *Votis in Capitolio nuncupatis paludatus cum lictoribus profectus*

Pinpointing where the Consul (or Praetor) took his auspices for war, however, is the least of our troubles. The ancient evidence—or rather, lack of it—calls into question the entire modern theory of "auspices of war" or "auspices of departure": neither those terms themselves nor their underlying concept find attestation in the sources. We read repeatedly of a set of ceremonies observed on the day of the *profectio*: the Consul performs the solemn *votorum nuncupatio* on the Capitol, then walks down to the *pomerium*, where along with his lictors he exchanges the toga for military garb (the scarlet *paludamentum*), and with trumpets blaring, leaves the City.[62] No source, however, ever spells out the precise objective, place,

---

[61] Sánchez 25–39, reviving a view long ago advanced by Schwegler 2: 344 n. 2; cf. Valeton 1890: 241, suspecting *conplures* to be corrupt and referring to *sacerdotes*. Coli 1951: 163 proposed to read *consules* for *conplures*, arguing that Cincius' ceremony constituted an *augurium*, exactly like the inauguration of the King. If so, a more plausible conjecture would indeed be *augures*, being the performers of *auguria*. On Coli's own view that the King, created *augurato* and not merely *auspicato*, had no need of *auspicia* (93–95), this would mean that the Roman chosen to command the Latin Army likewise functioned without auspices and the need of them: a most improbable scenario. (Coli did not seem to realize this consequence.) In any case, the conclusion that the King (or any leader) chosen in a procedure involving *augurium* would have no further need of auspices seems far from compelling. The notion that "*conplures nostri* should be understood here as all those *magistrati praeteriti* to whom the task had been allotted" (Koortbojian 70) is unhelpful.

[62] See Varro *LL* 7.37 on the change of vestments and the trumpets: *haec* (sc. *paludamenta*) *insignia atque ornamenta militaria: ideo ad bellum cum exit imperator ac lictores mutarunt vestem et signa incinuerunt, paludatus dicitur proficisci*. From Cic. *Pis*. 55, *togulae lictoribus ad portam praesto fuerunt; quibus illi acceptis sagula reiecerunt* (on occasion of Piso's return from Macedonia), one may conclude that the change of vestments took place at the *pomerium*, not on the Capitol (cf. Rüpke 1990: 35 = 2019: 37). It should be noted (*contra* Mignone 430–431) that the change of vestments and attachment of axes to the *fasces* occurred only when the Consul was setting out for war, not at every routine crossing of the *pomerium*, such as to hold a Centuriate Assembly (attested by Livy 24.9.1–2, and implied by the totality of the evidence). There is no evidence that crossing the line as such required auspication; the case of Ti. Gracchus in 163 BC (Chapter 8.4.3) involved special circumstances: the Consul had auspicated for the *comitia centuriata* in the Field of Mars at dawn, then had returned into the City to hold a Senate meeting, and eventually had gone back to the Campus to conduct the Assembly. Crossing the line after receiving auspices *extra pomerium* cancelled these auspices, unless permission to retain their validity (for the Assembly to take place later) was obtained by way of auspicating when crossing the *pomerium*. Either when returning to the City or—less likely—to the Field of Mars,

or manner of whatever auspication occurred in that context; in fact, among some thirty occasions that refer, either clearly or possibly, to a commander's departure from the City *paludatus*, only three (##2, 3, and 11 below) mention auspices at all (although one of them, #3, does so four times).[63]

By far the most prominent element among the ceremonies surrounding *profectio* is the *votorum nuncupatio*, the solemn profession of vows for a victorious completion of the campaign; it is also the sole element directly attested to have taken place on the Capitol (##2–10, below), and almost always coupled with a reference to the commander (or his lictors) clad in the *paludamentum*. To wit.

(2) Livy 21.63.8–9: et **Capitolium** et sollemnem **votorum nuncupationem** fugisse, ne die initi magistratus Iovis Optimi Maximi templum adiret, ne senatum...consuleretque, ne Latinas indiceret Iovique Latiari sollemne sacrum in monte faceret, (21.63.9) ne *auspicato* profectus in **Capitolium ad vota nuncupanda, paludatus** inde cum lictoribus in provinciam iret.

(3) Livy 22.1.6–7: duos se consules creasse, unum habere; quod enim illi (*sc.* Flaminio) iustum imperium, quod *auspicium* esse? magistratus *id* (*sc.* auspicium) a domo, publicis privatisque penatibus, Latinis feriis actis, sacrificio in monte perfecto, **votis** rite in **Capitolio nuncupatis** secum ferre; (22.1.7) nec privatum *auspicia* sequi nec **sine** *auspiciis* **profectum** in externo ea solo nova atque integra concipere posse.

(4) Livy 31.14.1: secundum **vota in Capitolio nuncupata paludatis** lictoribus profectus ab urbe.

(5) Livy 38.48.16: ut...et ipse triumphans **in Capitolium** escenderem, unde **votis** rite **nuncupatis** profectus sum.

(6) Livy 41.10.7: cum is more maiorum secundum **vota in Capitolio nuncupata** lictoribus **paludatis** profectus ab urbe esset.

(7) Livy 41.10.13: **paludatis** lictoribus **votisque in Capitolio nuncupatis** in provinciam...abiit.

Gracchus forgot to auspicate, and thus lost the auspices granted to him at dawn: hence the Consuls elected at that day's *comitia* were *vitio creati*.

[63] There is also a curious reference to T. Quinctius Flamininus (*cos.* 198), now *pro consule*, ostensibly during the Battle of Kynoskephalai in 197 BC: *auspicantem immolantemque et vota nuncupantem sacrificuli vatis modo in acie vidisse* (Livy 35.48.13: cf. Plut. *Flam.* synkr. 2(23).6). It is part of a tirade launched, in 192 BC, against Flamininus by the Aitolian ambassador to the Akhaian League, one Arkhidamos, who accuses the Roman of falling short in the duties of a general (*quo enim illum unquam imperatoris functum officio esse?*) by praying for victory instead of personally leading his troops into battle. Obviously, a Roman *imperator* would not engage in any of the activities ridiculed here— auspication, sacrifice, and profession of vows—in the midst of battle: the jibe does not reflect any actual observation of Flamininus' actions during the battle, let alone before his departure from Rome six years earlier; it simply serves to illustrate Greek condescension towards Roman preoccupation with religious ritual in all areas of public life. Cf. Briscoe 1981: 212–214; Scheid 2015: 251–253; but note Linderski 1993: 69 n. 29 = *RQ* 624: "here Livy implies *e contrario* that it was not solely Roman armies but above all Roman *religio* that triumphed over the Greeks."

(8) Livy 41.27.3: consules **votis in Capitolio nuncupatis** in provincias profecti sunt.

(9) Livy 42.49.1: **votis in Capitolio nuncupatis paludatus** ab urbe profectus est.

(10) Livy 45.39.11 consul proficiscens praetorve **paludatis** lictoribus in provinciam et ad bellum **vota in Capitolio nuncupat**: victor perpetrato <...> eodem **in Capitolium** triumphans ad eosdem deos quibus **vota nuncupavit** merita † bonaque pr*. trans † redit.[64]

(11) Cic. *2Verr.* 5.34: cum **paludatus** exisset **votaque** pro imperio suo communique re publica **nuncupasset**, noctu stupri causa lectica in urbem introferri solitus est ad mulierem nuptam uni, propositam omnibus, contra fas, **contra auspicia**, contra omnis divinas atque humanas religiones.

(12) Cic. *Phil.* 5.24: neque sacrificiis sollemnibus factis neque **votis nuncupatis** non profectus est, sed profugit **paludatus**.[65]

(13) Caes. *BCiv* 1.6.6: **paludatique votis nuncupatis** exeunt.

(14) Festus 176.7–9 L: **vota nuncupata** dicuntur, quae consules praetores cum in provinciam proficiscuntur faciunt.

(15) Livy 41.10.5: non **votis nuncupatis**, non **paludatis** lictoribus…nocte profectus praeceps in provinciam abiit.

(16) Livy 41.10.11: quo minus **votis nuncupatis paludatus** ab urbe exiret.[66]

It will be readily apparent that, in the rigidly formulaic language describing a magistrate's departure for war, the operative terms are *paludatus* and *votis nuncupatis*; if auspices were accorded a particular significance in this context, one should reasonably expect *auspicato* to occur with comparable frequency. Instead, mention of auspices is almost non-existent.

2.5 The "Auspices of Departure"—a Modern Fiction

Along with his improbable interpretation of Festus, Mommsen based the theory of special "auspices of war" on the two Livy passages 21.63.8–9 and 22.1.6–7

---

[64] For possible restorations, see Briscoe's Teubner edition (1986) 383; Madvig's *dona portans redit* (accepted by Mommsen *StR* 1: 64 n. 1) seems least invasive and fits the sense. Instead of postulating a lacuna, *perpetrato* <...> *eodem in Capitolium* (thus Kreyssig; *Capitolio* mss.) *triumphans*, Mommsen proposed *perpetrato <eo> eodem [in Capitolio] triumphans*, perhaps rightly. Cf. Livy 42.49.6, *triumphantemne mox cum exercitu victore scandentem in Capitolium ad eosdem deos a quibus proficiscatur visuri*.

[65] There is no allegation here, one may note, that Antonius proceeded without auspices: a strange silence if "auspices of departure" constituted a fundamental element of the *profectio*.

[66] Another fifteen references to commanders leaving *paludati* contain no mention of vows or auspices: Cic. *Fam.* 8.10.2; 13.61; 15.17.3; 15.19.2; *Sest.* 71; *Pis.* 31, 55; Varro *LL* 7.37; Livy 2.49.3; 36.3.14; 37.4.3; 40.26.6; 41.5.8; 41.17.6; 42.27.8.

(##2 and 3, above).⁶⁷ Both belong to the controversy arising from C. Flaminius' decision, in 217, to enter his second consulship not in Rome but at Ariminum, and thus to skip not only the ritual of departure for war but an even more fundamental one: the complex of ceremonies surrounding the new Consuls taking office on March 15—beginning with their first auspices.

2.5.1 The Departure of Gaius Flaminius

The two Livy passages reward closer scrutiny. In the first one (21.63.8-9, #2 above), Flaminius is chided for a long string of inappropriate acts, or rather, omissions: (a) avoiding the solemn profession of vows on the Capitol (*et Capitolium et sollemnem votorum nuncupationem fugisse*); (b) failing to visit the temple of Iuppiter Optimus Maximus on the day he entered his magistracy (*ne die initi magistratus Iovis Optimi Maximi templum adiret*); (c) failing to consult the Senate (*ne senatum...consuleretque*); (d) failing to announce the Latin Festival and perform the solemn sacrifice to Iuppiter Latiaris on the Alban Mountain (*ne Latinas indiceret Iovique Latiari sollemne sacrum in monte faceret*); (e) failure to proceed, *auspicato*, onto the Capitol for the profession of vows, and from there to go his province, *paludatus* and with his lictors (*ne auspicato profectus in Capitolium ad vota nuncupanda, paludatus inde cum lictoribus in provinciam iret*). Indeed, he left the City while still *privatus*, in secret and without lictors.⁶⁸

Of the two professions of vows noted here, the first (#a) certainly refers to the all-important one on the first day of the year, March 15;⁶⁹ the second (#e) to the one on the actual day of departure. Both frame the intervening rituals: the entire sequence, from the day the Consul enters office to the day he leaves the City, forms a coherent and connected whole, not merely an enumeration of isolated ceremonies. The crucial word, *auspicato*, occurs only at the end, with that second *nuncupatio votorum*, before the Consul ascends the Capitol to perform it. If auspices were taken before that second *nuncupatio*, on the day of departure, they cannot have been absent from the first one, on March 15. But surely we are not to assume that an auspication on the day of departure held greater significance for the Consul than his first auspices on entering the magistracy; the latter must have been *eo ipso* more fundamental than any auspication that came afterwards. Yet not a hint at them in Livy—or is there? In fact, all the acts preceding #e must have been performed *auspicato*, and the Consul could perform them thus only because

---

⁶⁷ *StR* 1: 99 nn. 3 and 5 ("die besonderen Kriegsauspicien"); cf. 1: 63 ("nachdem für diesen Act besondere Auspicien auf dem Capitol eingeholt sind"). On Festus 276–277L, see above, #1.
⁶⁸ Livy 21.63.5, *simulato itinere privatus clam in provinciam abiit*; 21.63.9, *lixae modo sine insignibus, sine lictoribus profectum clam, furtim, haud aliter quam si exsilii causa solum vertisset.*
⁶⁹ Cf. Ovid *Pont.* 4.4.30, *et fieri faciles in tua vota deos*; Dio fr. 102.12, θυόντων τῶν Ῥωμαίων ἱσταμένου τοῦ ἔτους τὰ ἐσιτήρια, καὶ τῇ ἡγεμονίᾳ τὰς εὐχὰς κατὰ τὰ πάτρια ποιουμένων.

Iuppiter had granted him auspices at dawn on the first day. Flaminius had failed to obtain those and, consequently, was incapable of doing anything *auspicato*. Rather than imparting a special, unique significance to auspices taking on the day of departure, Livy's placement of *auspicato* sums up the entire sequence of ritual acts that, performed with proper observation of all required auspices,[70] enabled the Consul to go out from the City *paludatus*, commanding an army of the Roman People. (It will be helpful to remind ourselves that Livy wrote for an audience familiar—intimately so, in many cases—with all those things, and not in need of lengthy exposition.) Which, so far, leaves us with still only one instance of fundamental auspices attested in the sources: those of "investiture."

Livy returns to the issue in his report of the initial Senate meeting in 217, held by the other Consul, Cn. Servilius Geminus, on the Ides of March (21.1.6–7, #3 above). Again, much criticism of the absent Flaminius, but this time with a pronounced focus on the auspices. Having (f) elected two Consuls, they really now had only one: for how could Flaminius be in possession of *iustum imperium*, in possession of *auspicium* (*duos se consules creasse, unum habere; quod enim illi iustum imperium, quod **auspicium** esse*)? (g) The magistrate carried his auspices with him from home, from the divine protectors of the state and of his private dwelling (*magistratus id [sc. auspicium]a domo, publicis privatisque penatibus…secum ferre*), having (h) celebrated the Latin Festival, performed the sacrifice on the Mountain, and in proper form professed his vows on the Capitol (*Latinis feriis actis, sacrificio in monte perfecto, **votis** rite in **Capitolio** nuncupatis*). And (j) the auspices did not follow a private citizen (*nec privatum **auspicia** sequi*), nor (k) could anyone who had set out without auspices ask for and obtain them, new and unblemished, on foreign soil (*nec **sine auspiciis profectum** in externo ea solo nova atque integra concipere posse*).

As Consul, one must concede, Flaminius had *imperium*—but not *iustum*, of a fully legitimate kind.[71] That was because he had no auspices at all (from what fol-

---

[70] For a careful examination of the term *(in)auspicato* in Latin sources, see Fiori 2014b: 85–89, who cautions against mechanically translating *auspicato* as "after obtaining auspices"; as a more accurate rendering he suggests (87) "*agere* 'correttamente da un punto di vista augurale,'" to act in proper manner from an augural point of view. In almost all instances in the record surveyed, naturally, this involved an auspication at some point in the ritual; but it is clear that *(in)auspicato* can refer also to the effects of oblative signs or even sortition. The augural significance of the latter, however, must not be overstated. Lots had to be drawn in a *templum*, hence sortition came under the *ius augurale* (Linderski AL 2174–2175, 2194 n. 173; Fiori 2014b: 92 n. 137); but Rosenstein has shown conclusively that the result of a sortition was not understood to express the divine will: Iuppiter guaranteed the lot's impartiality, without influencing its outcome. That sortition must be preceded by auspication is possible though uncertain: Linderski 2175 was skeptical of Mommsen's assertion to that effect (*StR* 1: 96 n. 4; 103. n. 1); Rosenstein 1995: 57 n. 50 makes a strong case in favor. Feldherr 53–63 offers a perceptive study of Livy's use of auspices as a literary device.

[71] He also lacked the *lex curiata*, which—among whatever else it may have done—served to render *iustus* the magistrate elected by the *comitia tributa* or *centuriata* (above, n. 25). Livy takes no notice of this additional flaw in Flaminius' status; neither, perhaps, did his sources. Given his repeated emphasis on Flaminius' lack of auspices, his silence here does not help the case of those who would ascribe to

lows, in Livy, it is apparent that *iustum* is not intended to modify *auspicium*). The Consul takes the auspices with him when he leaves Rome; but first he must validly acquire them: and Flaminius had not done so, at dawn on the Ides of March. He had left the city when still *privatus*, and the auspices do not come along with private citizens. Worse, they could not be obtained *in externo solo*, on foreign soil—only at home, in Rome. (Whether that meant *in Urbe*, or anywhere *in agro Romano*, remains to be seen.) Thus Flaminius was Consul, in a purely legal sense, but not in the sense that mattered really; anything he did would be done *vitio*.[72]

2.5.2 Taking the Auspices along from Home

Which auspices does the Consul take with him (#g), though? Livy does not say. Now the string of accusations is presented at the first Senate meeting, on the Ides of March, and the complaint that Flaminius lacked auspices *tout court* (#f, *quod [sc. illi] auspicium esse*) can, in this context, only be based on his failure to obtain his initial auspices where he must, on that very day, in Rome. Immediately next comes the key comment: the magistrate carries the auspices with him from home. How could those be different from the ones Livy has just mentioned, the auspices "of investiture"? Unlike in #e, Livy makes no reference here to auspices in connection with the *votorum nuncupatio* on the day of departure (#h): the auspices the magistrate carries with him (#g) come at the beginning of the sequence of rituals, extending over several days at least (and usually, weeks), that culminates in the profession of vows and his departure, *paludatus*. It is difficult to see how the two concluding instances (#j, the auspices do not follow a *privatus*, and #k, cannot be obtained *de novo* on foreign soil) could suddenly pertain to an altogether different set of auspices, never identified, than the ones (#f) that mattered on the first day of the year.

We learn still more from this. The Consul carries the auspices with him *a domo, publicis privatisque penatibus*: "from home, from the divine protectors of the state and of his private dwelling."[73] *A domo* often means the City or community as a whole,[74] but *(a) privatis penatibus* can only refer to the Consul's private home.

---

the *lex curiata* some particular significance with regard to the Consul's auspices, especially or at least in the sphere *militiae*.

[72] Livy's *nec privatum auspicia sequi* (22.1.7) is not meant to characterize Flaminius as *privatus* after entering office on March 15, or to imply that "technically, Flaminius was no magistrate;" nor is there any hint that he could not take the auspices along because "they had not been confirmed by a *lex curiata*" (thus Koortbojian 61–62). The augural flaw rests in his departing from Rome before he entered office—still *privatus*—and thus being unable to acquire his auspices at the proper time and place.

[73] For the phrase *penates publici privatique*, see also Livy 3.17.11; 25.18.10; 45.24.12.

[74] E.g., Livy 8.22.6, *classe qua advecti ab domo fuerant*; 9.22.2, *accitis ab domo novis militibus*; 26.12.9, *nec ab domo quicquam mittebatur*; 36.10.1, *cum audisset profectam ab domo popularium suorum classem*; 40.33.4, *Celtiberi qui a domo profecti erant deditionis ignari*; 45.17.7, *ut incohata omnia*

Indeed Livy had made the same point once already: in choosing to enter office at Ariminum, not Rome, Flaminius preferred to don the scarlet-bordered toga in some guest house rather than in his own home (*magis... in deversorio hospitali quam apud penates suos praetextam sumpturum*, 21.63.10). Hence *a domo* here covers both the City and the Consul's private home, the public Penates and his own; and it is in his own home that he asks Iuppiter for his first auspices.[75] And those auspices are the only ones that Livy ever unambiguously identifies. The "auspices of departure" are a phantom of modern scholarship, without basis in the evidence.

Not that they have remained unquestioned until now. A generation ago, Jörg Rüpke noted both the complete lack of direct evidence in the sources and the absence of any hint at any particular category of auspices in connection with *profectio*. He allowed that it probably was customary to obtain auspices on the day of departure, but denied them any particular significance, comparing them to "regular" auspices such as those obtained for electoral assemblies: they were valid for this day only. Of course, any *vitium* that attached to them would render invalid all subsequent actions that depended on them, and thus occasionally require the magistrate's return to Rome so as to repeat them.[76] Herein lies the problem.

2.6 Repeating the Auspices

The Livy passages discussed above make it clear enough that without taking the auspices with him from home, the magistrate could not properly go to war: hence they were not merely "customary." But it is the procedure known as *repetere auspicia* that suggests a particular significance.

We have five instances, during the Republic, of commanders returning to the City in order to repeat their auspices.[77] We know, from Livy, that the Consul going to war "carries" the auspices with him from the City: but only in his capacity as a magistrate (not as a *privatus*, hence not as an attribute attached to his person regardless of office). We further read that the Consul having left the City without auspices (or, which comes down to the same thing, without valid ones) cannot

---

legati ab domo ferre ad imperatores possent; and, perhaps most pertinent, 8.32.4, *cum me incertis auspiciis profectum ab domo scirem.*

[75] As Mommsen noted, "wie es scheint, in seiner Privatwohnung": *StR* 1: 616; cf. Keaveney 161; Kunkel *StO* 90. Note also Cic. *2Verr*.1.104, *nam ut praetor factus est, qui auspicato a Chelidone surrexisset, sortem nactus est urbanae provinciae*: Verres rising *auspicato* from his mistress's bed does not suggest an act in a public venue. Humm 75–76 and Berthelet 119, without considering the evidence, place the "auspices of investiture" on the Capitoline Arx. See also above, note 59.

[76] Rüpke 1990: 45–46 = 2019: 46–47.

[77] Livy 8.30.1–2 (Dictator, in 324 V; cf. Val. Max. 3.2.9); 10.3.6 (Dictator, in 301 V); 23.19.3 (Dictator, in 216); 23.36.9–10 (Consul, in 215); Val. Max. 2.7.4 (Consul, in 252; cf. Front. *Strat*. 4.1.31); on the latter case, Konrad 2008.

(re-)acquire them *in externo solo*—outside the *ager Romanus*. In what sense does he carry the auspices from the City?

2.6.1 The Significance of Place

The answer can perhaps be found in the long speech of Camillus that concludes Livy's Fifth Book. The Dictator's arguments against the proposal to relocate Rome to Veii are constructed, carefully and consistently, around the belief that all essential religious functions of the *populus Romanus*, both *sacra* and *auspicia*, are unalterably tied to the physical location of the City, and cannot properly be observed or carried out elsewhere:[78]

> Urbem auspicato inauguratoque conditam habemus; nullus locus in ea non religionum deorumque est plenus...hos omnes deos publicos privatosque, Quirites, deserturi estis? (5.52.2–3).

> "We have a City founded under auspices and with proper rites of inauguration; there is no location in it that is not filled with observance of religion and gods...all those gods, public and private ones, are you, Citizens, going to abandon them?"

> Forsitan aliquis dicat aut Veiis ea nos facturos aut huc inde missuros sacerdotes nostros qui faciant; quorum neutrum fieri salvis caerimoniis potest (5.52.5).

> "Perhaps someone might say that we will either perform those observances at Veii, or send our priests here from there to perform them; neither of which can be done without invalidating the rituals."

> Quid alia quae auspicato agimus omnia fere intra pomerium, cui oblivioni aut cui neglegentiae damus? comitia curiata, quae rem militarem continent, comitia centuriata, quibus consules tribunosque militares creatis, ubi auspicato, nisi ubi adsolent, fieri possunt? (5.52.15–16)

> "And those other acts, almost all of whom we carry out under auspices within the *pomerium*—to what kind of oblivion shall we consign them, to what neglect? The Curiate Assembly, which contains the military matters, the Centuriate Assembly, in which you elect Consuls and Military Tribunes—where can these take place, in an augurally correct manner, except at their customary sites?"

> Hic Capitolium est, ubi quondam capite humano invento responsum est eo loco caput rerum summamque imperii fore; hic cum augurato liberaretur Capitolium, Iuventas Terminusque maximo gaudio patrum vestrorum moveri se non passi (5.54.7).

---

[78] Ogilvie 745.

"Here is the Capitol, where once a human head was found, and the response given was that in this place, there would be the head of all things and the sum total of all power; here, when the Capitol was being freed (from ritual constraints) in an act of auguration, Iuventas and Terminus—to the enthusiastic jubilation of your fathers—would not allow themselves to be moved."

The underlying suggestion here is that the auspices are tied to Rome: a relocation of the City to Veii would not effect a transfer of the auspices to that place. "In Rome," though not exclusively *in Urbe*: the Centuriate Assembly must meet *extra pomerium*, and auspices may be obtained throughout the *ager Romanus*.[79] The latter, like the *urbs*, is *effatus*, an area augurally delimited and capable of receiving auspices: its outer boundary, marked by *termini*, constituted the limit for *auspicia de caelo*.[80]

From Servius auctus we learn that auspices—unlike *auguria*—could be obtained anywhere, by anyone: *auspicia omnium rerum sunt, auguria certarum; auspicari enim cuivis etiam peregre licet, augurium agere nisi in patriis sedibus non licet* (ad Aen. 3.20).[81] This is surely correct in principle; but if the *ager effatus* marked the limit for (impetrative) auspices from the sky, the ability to auspicate anywhere cannot have extended to every type of auspices: presumably it included such as the *peremnia*, *ex tripudiis*, and the mysterious *auspicia ex acuminibus*. Different rules, though, applied to different locations: in the *ager Gabinus*, though *peregrinus*, auspices were preserved just as in the *ager Romanus* (differently put, crossing from one into the other did not annul auspices previously obtained); in this sense, the *ager Gabinus* possessed its own distinct auspices that separated it from the rest of the *ager peregrinus*.[82] To cross from *ager Romanus* or *Gabinus* into *ager*

---

[79] As augurally defined: the primordial territory of the Roman State, extending a mere 6 miles beyond the *pomerium*, and not to be confused with the *fines populi Romani*: Varro LL 5.33; Festus 232.23–28L (cf. 326.16L); Ovid Fasti 2.682; Strabo 5.3.2 C230. See Mommsen StR 3.1: 824–825; Magdelain 1968: 58–67; Catalano 1978: 479–482, 491–502.

[80] Varro LL 6.53, *augures finem auspiciorum caelestum extra urbem agri<s> sunt effati ut esset*; Cic. Leg. 2.21, *urbemque et agros et templa liberata et effata habento* (sc. *augures*); Gell. 13.14.1, *pomerium est locus intra agrum effatum per totius urbis circuitum pone muros regionibus certeis determinatus, qui facit finem urbani auspicii*; Serv. ad Aen. 6.197, *proprie effata sunt augurum preces: unde ager post pomeria, ubi captabantur auguria, dicebatur effatus*. Strictly speaking, only the *pomerium* or any other augural line of demarcation could be *effatum*, not the *urbs* itself: Linderski, AL 2156–2157 n. 31. For the view that the *ager effatus* comprised the entire *ager Romanus*, not merely part of it, see Magdelain 1968: 58–60 (cautiously endorsed by Catalano 1978: 501 n. 250), and Rüpke 1990: 32–35 = 2019: 34–37 (implausibly denying any significance to the *pomerium* as the *finis urbani auspicii*).

[81] Catalano 1960: 93–94, showing that the terms *auspicium* and *augurium* are used here in their classical, technical sense (above, note 31).

[82] Varro LL 5.33, *ut nostri augures publici disserunt, agrorum sunt genera quinque: Romanus, Gabinus, peregrinus, hosticus, incertus. Romanus dicitur unde Roma ab Romo; Gabinus ab oppido Gabiis; peregrinus ager pacatus, qui extra Romanum et Gabinum, quod uno modo in his servantur auspicia; dictus peregrinus a pergendo, id est a progrendiendo: eo enim ex agro Romano primum progrediebantur: quocirca Gabinus quoque peregrinus, sed quod auspicia habet singularia, ab reliquo discretus; hosticus dictus ab hostibus; incertus is, qui de his quattuor qui sit ignoratur*; Marius Victorinus Ars gramm. 4.42 (GramLat 6: 14.21–22): *pertermine dicitur auspicium quod fit cum de fine Romano in*

peregrinus required special authorization, known as *auspicium pertermine*. Even though no auspication was necessary to cross from *ager Romanus* into *ager Gabinus*, it does not follow that the *ager Gabinus* was suitable for auspices that must be obtained *in agro Romano* (let alone *in Urbe*). Presumably the same rules as for *ager peregrinus* (if not more restrictive ones) applied in turn for magistrates moving in(to) *ager hosticus* and *incertus*.

The Consul at war thus may auspicate on a daily basis wherever necessary, because he "has" the auspices, having taken them along when he left the City. But he can only take them along because he is *magistratus*: if he departs from the City while still *privatus*, before entering office, he cannot carry them with him; and, once abroad, he cannot obtain them there. Livy's point at 22.1.6–7 is quite clear. The auspices the magistrate takes with him when he goes to war are the ones that enable him to auspicate at all—the ones granted him by Iuppiter on his first day in office, at dawn. And they are the only ones.

2.6.2 Vitium in Auspicio

As Rüpke notes, the Consul probably did take auspices on the day he left the City, presumably to obtain Iuppiter's permission to go ahead with the various ritual observances, especially the *votorum nuncupatio* on the Capitol. A *vitium in auspicio* would taint all subsequent actions that depended on the one whose auspices were flawed; once the fault was discovered, it would become necessary for the magistrate to return to Rome and repeat them.[83] Yet how could the Consul, weeks or months after leaving the City, know that it was precisely the auspices obtained on the day of his departure that were flawed? It is clear from the record that a mere negative response, even if received repeatedly, at an auspication was not sufficient to cause doubts about the general validity of the commander's auspices: it would take an oblative sign from Iuppiter to alert him to the problem.[84] Ordinarily, the *vinculum temporis* ought to offer some assistance in determining

---

agrum peregrinum transgrediuntur. For discussion, see Catalano 1978: 492–498; Linderski *AL* 2157 n. 31; Rüpke 1990: 33–34 = 2019: 35–36 (whose grammatically contorted attempt, 34 n. 41 = 36 n. 40, to make *quod uno modo in his servantur auspicia* refer to the *ager peregrinus* fails to persuade); Fiori 2014a: 307–309.

[83] Rüpke 1990: 45–46 = 2019: 46–47.

[84] *Contra* Keaveney 163 ("If on any of these occasions the consul received unfavourable signs it would mean that the auspices for his military power as whole were flawed"); but the evidence is unambiguous. In 209 BC, Fabius Maximus on several days in a row received a negative response; nothing indicates that this called into question the validity of his auspices (Livy 27.16.15); and it is evident from the incidents reported of Papirius Cursor in 293 (Livy 10.40) and Gaius Flaminius in 217 (Cic. *Div.* 1.77, *pullarius diem proeli committendi differebat*) that a negative response merely denied permission to act for that day. Impetrative signs alone, by their very nature, were unsuitable to determine the validity of one's auspices: see Konrad 2004: 172–178, 202–203, where, however, the implication of oblative signs—their occurrence or absence—in this context was neglected.

the nature of the flaw: if, for instance, thunder was heard while the Consul was engaged in the *auspicium pullarium*, it very likely signalled that something was wrong with his auspices, and that the Chickens' hearty appetite signified nothing more than that they were hungry—not Iuppiter's assent. But it would be of no help in identifying the precise cause of the *vitium*: it could have arisen at this very auspication, or with any of the numerous auspices the Consul would have taken while on campaign, since the day he left the City. Not only since that day, though: the span of time in question extends, in fact, over all the days that had passed since the Consul entered office. Any auspication, on any one of those days, could have incurred the *vitium*; without the expert guidance of an Augur (or all of them), the magistrate would be hard pressed to decide which auspices he must repeat, along with the acts for which they had been obtained.

And we hear nothing about any doubts of that sort. The magistrate simply returns to Rome and repeats "the auspices." Now to repeat an auspication that was not, in fact, flawed would do no good: it could not rectify the *vitium* caused at another one, whether prior or subsequent, and revalidate the magistrate's auspices. Perhaps in all the attested instances, the commander somehow knew, for certain, that he had committed an error in the auspices at his *profectio*? But at least one such commander clearly did not know the cause: his auspices were *incerta*, not even flawed for certain.[85]

It follows that the auspices to be repeated had to be of a more fundamental nature than those obtained on the day of departure, for purposes relating to the ceremonies of *profectio*. To repeat the latter would have no effect if a *vitium*, until now undiscovered, had rendered the Consul's auspices *incerta* or invalid already before his departure. Given what the sources tell us—which is to say, not a word about special auspices "of departure"—those auspices can only be those "of investiture," obtained on the magistrate's first day.[86] Anything less, such as repeating merely the auspices taken in connection with the *profectio*, risked leaving the flaw unremedied. Differently put, when the Consul's auspices become invalid or uncertain, he must return to Rome and put the question—again—to Iuppiter: *si est fas me L. Titium consulem meo auspicio rem publicam populi Romani gerere*. No doubt if the answer were to come down in the negative (or affirmative quickly countermanded by an oblative sign), he would be left with no choice but to abdicate.[87]

---

[85] L. Papirius Cursor, in 324 V: *in Samnium incertis itum auspiciis est…dictator a pullario monitus cum ad auspicium repetendum Romam proficisceretur*, Livy 8.30.1–2; cf. 8.32.4, *cum me incertis auspiciis profectum ab domo scirem*.

[86] Scheid 2012: 119 notes that Consuls might return to Rome to renew "leur auspices d'investiture," without making it clear whether this reflects a position similar to the one argued above; elsewhere, though, he twice refers to "auspices de départ" (2015: 253).

[87] For a similar argument against "auspices of departure," Fiori 2014b: 89–96; also skeptical Koortbojian 66–71.

When returning to the City to repeat his auspices, did the Consul or Dictator do so *in Urbe*, after crossing the *pomerium*? The Dictator, perhaps; for the Consul, though, it seems unlikely. Crossing the *pomerium* would almost certainly end the Consul's ability to exercise *imperium* in the sphere *militiae* in its fullest sense, as the commander of an army, with capital *coercitio sine provocatione*, and make it necessary to repeat not only the auspices but the entire ritual of *profectio*—the *votorum nuncupatio* on the Capitol, the march down to the *pomerium*, the change of dress into the *paludamentum*, the axes added to the lictors' *fasces*, and so forth.[88] As the *ager effatus* marked the limit for *auspicia de caelo*, there should have existed no obstacle to asking Iuppiter for auspices anywhere within it: outside the *pomerium*, but *in agro Romano*. In consequence, the Consul normally would repeat his auspices *ad Urbem*, without entering the City proper.[89] The Dictator, on the other hand, exercised *imperium* (in its fullest sense) everywhere: it may not have mattered whether he crossed the *pomerium* or not. No Dictator, in fact, is attested to have gone through the ceremony of *profectio*.[90]

2.6.3 *Auspicia Militiae?*

Surely, though, the fact that we only hear of *auspicia repetenda* when commanders in the field are compelled to return to Rome proves that the auspices in question must be peculiar to the sphere *militiae*? Not necessarily. We hear of those occasions— five in all—because of the disruption they caused in military operations, compounded each time by either setbacks or delays (301 V, 252 BC, 216, 215) or a political crisis (324 V).[91] There is no telling how often other commanders may have returned to Rome to repeat their auspices, without their campaigns suffering a negative impact, and without the matter leaving a mark in the tradition. The Kings,

---

[88] From Cic. *2Verr.* 1.149 one may conclude that Verres (*pr. urb.* 74) left the City *votis nuncupatis paludatus* after December 13, but before the end of the year (see Hurlet 2010: 64–65). His nightly visits to his mistress after that moment each time involved crossing the *pomerium* and entering the City (Cic. *2Verr.* 5.34, above Subsection 2.4.2 #11), and thus would cancel his ability to exercise *imperium* in the sphere *militiae*; to observe the rules, he would have to repeat all the rituals of *profectio* under valid auspices. If his visits continued beyond December 29 (as is virtually certain: Brennan *PRR* 2: 486; Rafferty 104), now *pro magistratu*, he would no longer be able to do so even if he wanted, having lost *imperium* and auspices for good: hence *contra fas, contra auspicia, contra omnes divinas atque humanas religiones*, as Cicero puts it. *Contra* Berthelet 123, there is no allusion here to special "auspices of departure," let alone proof.
[89] Rüpke 1990 = 2019: 46; cf. above, n. 80.
[90] Which is not to say that Dictators commonly left the City without the customary ritual; certainly the phrase *paludatus exire* could be applied to them, as it was to M. Aemilius Lepidus the Magister Equitum in 44 BC: *FC = InscrItal* 13.1: 58–59, *ut, qum M. [Lep]idus paludatu[s exisset, iniret]*; cf. now FPrivern b, lines 15–16 (Zevi 292–303), *M. Valerius Meṣ[sal(la) mag(ister) eq(uitum) desig(natus) ut, cum Lepidus] | paludatus [exisset, iniret]*. The question is whether the Dictator needed the ceremony in order to exercise his *imperium*.
[91] For the individual instances, above, n. 77. A sixth occasion can perhaps, with due caution, be conjectured for 217 BC; if so, political crisis would be the salient element—see Chapter 8.2.2.

Augurs, and Flamines were inaugurated, hence enjoyed Iuppiter's permanent approval: nothing could cast doubt on it, and nothing short of formal *exauguratio* could terminate it. The auspices of magistrates held no such secure status. Nothing we know excludes the possibility that a Consul's auspices could become invalid or uncertain back home in the City, and would have to be repeated: if there was no recorded case where such an event led to a significant problem, we should not expect our surviving sources to dwell on it. (Such instances might, however, lurk behind some unexplained abdications of magistrates found *vitio creati*.)

In 309 V, L. Papirius Cursor was named Dictator for a second time.[92] Having appointed his Master-of-Horse, he enacted the *lex curiata*; but trouble arose:

> Papirius C. Iunium Bubulcum magistrum equitum dixit; atque ei legem curiatam de imperio ferenti triste omen diem diffidit, quod Faucia curia fuit principium, duabus insignis cladibus, captae urbis et Caudinae pacis, quod utroque anno eiusdem curiae fuerat principium...dictator postero die auspiciis repetitis pertulit legem; et profectus cum legionibus eqs.   (Livy 9.38.15–39.1)

The *curia* Faucia was the first to vote: a dreadful omen, as the same *curia* had voted first when the Curiate Law was passed for the commanders who had suffered disaster at the Allia River (leading to the capture of the City by the Gauls) and at the Caudine Forks. Rather than proceed with the vote, the Dictator chose to postpone it (literally, "the omen postponed the day for him"). The next day, having repeated the auspices, he enacted the law, evidently without further complications (a different *curia* now voting first).

Which auspices did Livy have in mind here, though? The ones for holding the *comitia curiata*, it is generally assumed.[93] But everywhere else in Livy, *auspicia repetere* unambiguously is employed of commanders returning to Rome to repeat the auspices.[94] Indeed, it is strange that he should emphasize an auspication that, with the assembly meeting again on a different day, was required as a matter of course—a perfectly routine event, especially as the postponement had been caused by the omen of the Faucia, not by a negative response at the Dictator's impetrative auspices.

But the omen could be a *prodigium*, and a *prodigium* could function as an oblative *auspicium*; in which case it usually alerted to the presence of *vitium*.[95] Considering that and Livy's consistent usage of *auspicia repetere*, a more probable

---

[92] Or FC 444 = AUC 445, the third dictator year. Livy has the dictatorship Q. *Fabio II C. Marcio coss.*, or 310 V; the actual date probably corresponds to 308 BC.

[93] W–M *ad loc.*; Versnel 328; Linderski 1993: 69 n. 31 = *RQ* 624.

[94] Livy 8.32.4; 10.3.6; 23.19.3; 23.36.10; to which add 5.17.3, *ut...auspicia de integro repeterentur et interregnum iniretur*: the augurally correct term here would have been *renovarentur*, but it is clear that, for Livy, *auspicia repetere* implies a more fundamental act than merely taking the auspices again after having received a negative response the day before. See Linderski 1993: 69 n. 31 = *RQ* 624.

[95] Above, Subsection 2.2.2.

understanding of the passage emerges. When the lot brought up the *curia* Faucia to vote first, Papirius—mindful of the *vinculum temporis*—took it as an oblative sign that warned him of a problem with his auspices. But the auspices in question cannot have been those of departure; he could and did not leave the city until after the passage of the Curiate Law. The auspices are those of investiture: in the space of a mere few hours (he had received the *fulmen sinistrum* just before dawn, presumably), they had become *incerta* or invalid.[96] And so he repeated them: *si est fas me L. Papirium dictatorem meo auspicio rem publicam populi Romani gerere.*

In 177 BC, the Consul (and Augur, since 195: Livy 33.44.3) C. Claudius Pulcher had drawn Histria for his province. While he was still in Rome, seeing legislation through the *comitia*, word arrived that there might be threat of peace: the Histrians had sent envoys to that effect, and given hostages, to the current Roman commanders in the province—the Consuls of the previous year, A. Manlius Vulso and M. Iunius Brutus. Fearing that this development, if left unchecked, might deprive him of the chance to command a province with an army, Claudius, notifying only his colleague of his whereabouts, set out from the City at night, and in unseemly haste travelled to Histria, without the customary ceremonies of *profectio*: *non votis nuncupatis, non paludatis lictoribus* (Livy 41.10.4–5).

Yet on arriving at his destination, he encountered an unpleasant surprise: when he ordered his predecessors in command to leave the province, they refused to comply and hand over the army to him until he completed the necessary ceremonies: *tum consulis imperio dicto audientes futuros esse dicerent, cum is more maiorum secundum vota in Capitolio nuncupata lictoribus paludatis profectus ab urbe esset* ("they would be obedient to the Consul's *imperium* at that moment when, in accordance with the custom of the ancients, after professing his vows on the Capitol, he had left the City with his lictors in their war cloaks," 41.10.6–7). Enraged, the Consul commanded Vulso's Proquaestor to put Brutus and Vulso in chains (in his hurry, Claudius evidently had not brought his own Quaestor along); the Proquaestor likewise refused. By now, the troops were rallying in support of their old commanders; humiliated, Claudius returned to Rome. In a mere three days—a record time, perhaps?—he performed the requisite rituals: he offered his vows on the Capitol and set back out, with his lictors cloaked for war, toward his province as rapidly as in his first attempt (*non ultra triduum moratus Romae, paludatis lictoribus votisque in Capitolio nuncupatis in provinciam aeque ac prius praecipiti celeritate abit*, 41.10.11–13). Arriving there with his newly levied legions (ordered in the meantime to assemble at Aquileia), he dismissed the previous army and commanders, this time without incident (*vetere exercitu cum suis ducibus dimisso*, 41.11.2).

---

[96] Oakley 3: 496 with 2: 708 and 4: 583 similarly does not think of auspices for the *comitia curiata*, but of departure.

The word *auspicia* does not occur in Livy's narrative here, nor even the faintest allusion to it. Its absence in a context that has at its center the most formal ritual—we might say, "constitutional"—conditions for a Consul's legitimate exercise of military command offers perhaps the most damning evidence against the notion of "auspices of departure." Surely Claudius had brought along his lictors: without them, he could not wield any consular powers. But they were not *paludati*,[97] hence did not carry axes in their *fasces*: which means, he was unable to fully exercise *imperium* in the sphere *militiae*. To render his lictors *paludati*, and himself depart the City in like fashion, the Consul must complete the necessary rituals, beginning with the *votorum nuncupatio* on the Capitol. What disqualified Claudius from being a *iustus imperator* was not a lack of auspices, nor of a *lex curiata*: it was his omission of the ceremonies attached to *profectio*.[98]

If there are no separate "auspices of departure," the entire notion—not resting, in any case, on actual evidence in the sources—of military auspices as a category somehow distinct from other auspices must be rejected.[99] The word *auspicium/a* occurs a total of four times in connection with the term *militiae* or *belli*:

(17) Cic. *Div.* 1.3: exactis regibus nihil publice sine auspiciis nec domi nec militiae gerebatur.

"Once the Kings had been expelled, nothing was done as a matter of state without auspices, neither at home nor at war."

(18) Livy 1.36.6: auguriis certe sacerdotioque augurum tantus honos accessit ut nihil belli domique postea nisi auspicato gereretur.

"Certainly such respect was acquired by augury and the priesthood of the Augurs that in future nothing was done at home or at war except with auspices."

(19) Livy 6.41.4: auspiciis hanc urbem conditam esse, auspiciis bello ac pace domi militiaeque omnia geri, quis est qui ignorat?

"That this City was founded with auspices, that everything is done under auspices in war and peace, at home and in the military sphere—who is there that does not know it?"

---

[97] Early editors—chiefly Gronovius—wished to emend (*non*) *paludatis lictoribus* here (41.10.5, 7, 13) and in identically worded passages elsewhere (31.14.1; 45.39.11) to *non paludatus <sine> lictoribus* or *paludatus <cum> lictoribus*, as appropriate, on the basis (presumably) of 21.63.9, *ne auspicatus profectus in Capitolium ad vota nuncupanda, paludatus inde cum lictoribus in provinciam iret: lixae modo sine insignibus, sine lictoribus profectus clam, furtim, eqs*. But Flaminius had left the City before he took office, not as Consul, but while still *privatus*; of course, he could not do so with lictors, *paludati* or otherwise. Claudius in 177 was already Consul (as were the magistrates in the other two passages from Livy), hence possessed lictors; the point here is that neither he nor they were properly equipped for war: without his lictors wearing their correct ritual garb, the Consul could not exercise his *imperium* in the military sphere. Staveley, in an eminently sensible discussion (1963: 461–462), apparently followed an edition thus emended. On the need for lictors, see Chapter 3.1.

[98] Rafferty 40–44.

[99] Versnel 331 n. 5, correctly: "There are *auspicia urbana* (Varro l.l. 5.143), but there is no distinction between *auspicia domi* and *auspicia militiae*"; cf. Wissowa "auspicium" *RE* 2.2 (1896) 2584.

(20) Livy 10.8.9: penes vos auspicia esse, vos solos gentem habere, vos solos iustum imperium et auspicium domi militiaeque.

"That the auspices are in your possession, that you alone have a *gens*, you alone lawful *imperium* and *auspicium*, at home and at war."

There is no difference between *auspiciis domi militiaeque omnia geri* (#19) or *ut nihil belli domique nisi auspicato gereretur* (#18) and Livy's frequent turn of phrase, *domi militiaeque gesta*.[100] In all four instances above, the emphasis is on auspices *tout court*, applicable equally in both the spheres *domi* and *militiae*, *bello ac pace*, the two spheres of existence in which Iuppiter sends auspices, in which *imperium* and *auspices* are active—the same auspices in both. What makes the difference is the *pomerium*: auspices granted on one side of it do not carry over to the other; an act for which auspices are obtained *domi* cannot be carried out in the sphere *militiae*, and vice versa. Nothing even hints at two different kinds of auspices, distinct in their nature: the distinction is one of locality and circumstance, not category.[101] *Auspicium militiae* does not constitute a category of auspices distinct from those obtained *domi* any more than *imperium militiae* (as noted earlier, strictly the only sphere in which *imperium* normally operates) represents a category of *imperium* different from that exercised *domi*.[102]

However deeply ingrained in the prevailing understanding of the matter, the entire concept of "auspices of war" or "auspices of departure" constitutes a scholarly fiction unsupported and unsupportable by the ancient evidence. Along with the notion of military auspices as a category somehow separate from other or "domestic" auspices, it must be rejected. The Consul (and every other magistrate) has auspices: that is all. Depending on his location, different rules may pertain to their effect and persistence; but his auspices themselves are the same wherever he goes. If a doubt arises as to their continued validity, he must repeat his initial auspices, the ones "of investiture," and put the question to Iuppiter again.

---

[100] Livy 1.15.6; 2.8.9; 5.10.1; 8.17.12; 28.10.6; 39.32.15; cf. also 45.39.18, *ad rem publicam bene gerendam domi militiaeque*.

[101] Fiori 2014a: 310: "L'*auspicium* non ha una diversa natura a seconda del luogo in cui viene assunto ma...il pomerium interrompe la continuità dell'*auspicium*, così come interrompe la continuità dell'*imperium*; 311: "il pomerium...interferisce in modo rilevante con gli auspici, impedendo ogni continuità tra gli auspici assunti *domi* e quelli assunti *militiae*: le attività autorizzate in un àmbito spaziale non possono essere compiute nell'altro"; cf. 2014b: 63 n. 16. (*Contra* Rüpke 1990: 32–35 = 2019: 34–37.)

[102] The only *auspicium militare* actually attested is the one *ex acuminibus*—St. Elmo's fire dancing on the soldiers' spear-tips (Cicero *Div*. 2.77, *nam ex acuminibus quidem, quod totum auspicium militare est, M. Marcellus ille quinquies consul totum omisit*). If this was an oblative sign (thus Pease 475–476), it would have no bearing anyway on the question whether *auspicia militiae* existed as a category distinct from those obtained *domi*; but an argument can be made that it was impetrative (cf. *StR* 1: 87 n. 6).

3
Dictator

Papirius Cursor, at least in Livy's telling, held that the Dictator's powers were superior and unrestricted with regard to his Magister Equitum, as well as all other magistrates. Let us examine this claim with a closer look at the status of the Consuls (and by extension the lower officers) when a Dictator had been named.

3.1 The Lictors

A curious detail involving Fabius Maximus in the Hannibalic War informs us that the Consuls were not to approach the Dictator with their lictors and insignia of office, such as *toga praetexta* and *sella curulis*, but essentially as *privati* (or so Plutarch puts it), and that he could enforce that rule by ordering them to comply—perhaps this was one of the rituals accompanying a Dictator's "investiture," such as the request for permission to mount a horse.[1] Certainly (as Jeffrey Tatum reminds in a private communication) with sources that ultimately go back to the annalists, it is often unclear whether a given detail "was routine but not routinely included in narratives, or something singular." But Livy—in a different context, the appointment of Iunius Pera as Dictator after Cannae, in 216—makes it clear that the request for permission to mount a horse was in fact routine (*ut solet*). In connection with Fabius' appointment in 217, Livy mentions only the order that Servilius approach without his lictors: no word about other insignia or mounting the horse. Now Plutarch's discussion of the taboo against mounting a horse occurs not on the occasion of Pera's dictatorship (*Fab.* 9.4), but with Fabius Maximus here. Which makes it probable that the biographer was not simply elaborating on Livy's account of Fabius' accession but followed a common (Latin) source that spelled out the entire ceremonial, noting the Dictator's twenty-four lictors (*Fab.* 4.3) and specifying the requirement that the Consul shed his lictors and other insignia, as well as the implications of their absence: without them the Consul was effectively rendered *privatus*. (The tenor of the entire passage is how Fabius

---

[1] Livy 22.11.5, *viatore misso qui consuli nuntiaret ut sine lictoribus ad dictatorem veniret*; Plut. *Fab.* 4.3, καὶ τοῦ ἑτέρου τῶν ὑπάτων ἀπαντῶντος αὐτῷ, τὸν ὑπερέτην πέμψας ἐκέλευσε τοὺς ῥαβδούχους ἀπαλλάξαι καὶ τὰ παράσημα τῆς ἀρχῆς ἀποθέμενον ἰδιώτην ἀπαντᾶν; cf. Livy 23.14.2, *dictator…latoque, ut solet, ad populum ut equum escendere liceret*, and Plut. *Fab.* 4.1–2.

strove to meet the appearance expected of a proper Dictator.) What precisely was the significance of a magistrate without his lictors?

3.1.1 Ahenobarbus' *Fasces*

In February of 49 BC, L. Domitius Ahenobarbus (*cos*. 54), newly appointed *pro consule* for Gallia Transalpina, surrendered to Caesar at Corfinium. A few days later, Atticus, then in Rome, in a letter to Cicero at Formiae had noted that he did not know whether Domitius (still) had the *fasces* with him; when he found out he would tell Cicero (*ignoras Domitius cum fascibusne sit; quod cum scies, facies ut sciamus*, Cic. *Att*. 8.15.1). Cicero in turn was eager to learn what Domitius' next move would be, as the latter's (and others') example had a bearing on how to solve his own quandary: stay in Italy, or leave? (*omnino ad id de quo dubito pertinet me scire quid Domitius acturus sit, quid noster Lentulus*, 8.14.3.) As regards Domitius' *fasces*, he seems to have already known, or assumed to know, the answer: in debating what to do, he points out that of those senators who were planning to leave Italy (or had left already), almost all except Ap. Claudius (*cos*. 54, *cens*. 50) were legally entitled to do so,[2] because they either held *imperium* or served as Legates (*memento praeter Appium neminem esse fere qui non ius habeat transeundi; nam aut cum imperio sunt, ut Pompeius, ut Scipio, Sufenas, Fannius, Voconius, Sestius, ipsi consules...aut legati sunt eorum*, 8.15.3). Domitius is pointedly omitted from the list of those that hold *imperium*. As Caesar put it, Domitius at Corfinium, having thrown away his *fasces* and laid down his *imperium*, had come into another man's power as a captive and *privatus* (*BCiv* 2.32.9, *cum proiectis fascibus et deposito imperio privatus et captus ipse in alienam venisset potestatem*). Cicero, it appears, took the same view.

Noting, however, "whether or not a magistrate was attended by lictors, his *imperium* persisted," Tatum concludes that "*something* extraordinary happened to Domitius at Corfinium: in a letter to Atticus...Cicero refers to a general ignorance over whether or not Domitius still possesses his *fasces* (again, this had nothing to do with Domitius' actual *imperium*)."[3] On the contrary, it had everything to do with it. What possible interest could the question of Domitius' *fasces* and their physical whereabouts, or his having them in his physical possession, hold for Atticus (and, presumably, others in Rome) if the answer had no bearing on Domitius' official status? Why would Atticus consider the matter important enough to promise forwarding that information to Cicero as soon as he could

---

[2] Senators not on official business abroad were not permitted to leave Italy without special dispensation: see Mommsen *StR* 3.1: 912–913. Besides Appius, Cicero later mentions C. Cassius (*Att*. 9.1.4; cf. 7.21.2; Cassius was Tribune of the Plebs); "it is difficult to believe that there were not more" (Shackleton Bailey *CLA* 4: 355).
[3] Tatum 126.

obtain it (*quod cum scies, facies ut sciamus*)? In the letter, Cicero is wholly occupied with sorting out who was legally entitled—being *cum imperio* or someone's *legatus*—to leave Italy or not, and what all of it implied for his own situation. To him and Atticus, wondering whether Domitius had his *fasces* was not a matter of idle curiosity.

As regards the persistence of a magistrate's *imperium* with or without the presence of his lictors, Tatum may well be correct. Yet Domitius—and Cicero: the point is crucial—was not a magistrate, but *pro magistratu*, and, in that case, having lictors evidently made a difference (as will be seen further below). Nor can it be maintained that "Domitius remained a promagistrate, as even Caesar recognized when he allowed him to take away from Corfinium his public funds." *HS sexagies...Domitio reddit, etsi eam pecuniam publicam esse constabat* (Caes. *BCiv* 1.23.4): Caesar let him have the money even though (*etsi*) it was comprised of public funds. The implication is clear: in Caesar's view, Domitius had no claim to the money, being no longer a promagistrate. (In all likelihood, Caesar did not recognize Domitius' appointment as Proconsul in the first place: *audio enim eum ea senatus consulta improbare quae post discessum tribunorum facta sunt* (Cic. *Att.* 11.7.1.).

3.1.2 Cicero and His Laureled Lictors

The *consularis disertus* himself had a tale to tell when it came to lictors. Acclaimed *imperator* in Cilicia in 51 (*Att.* 5.20.3), Cicero returned to Italy late in the following year, his lictors carrying *fasces* duly wrapped in laurel. Yet as the Civil War broke out, he soon found his lictors an encumbrance, not to say embarrassment. Having reached the outskirts of the City on January 4, he saw the vote on his much-expected triumph postponed (*Fam.* 14.11.3); on the 18th, on news of Caesar's rapid advance, he left for Campania before dawn, to avoid talk or spectacle, *lictoribus praesertim laureatis* (*Att.* 7.10): he—as others—was keenly aware of the incongruity of an *imperator* moving *away* from Rome with laureled *fasces*, especially when claiming a triumph. Within a few days, as it became clear that Pompeius might not put up a fight in Italy but go overseas, Cicero was wrestling with a difficult decision: how far should he commit himself? Some eminent friends had already drawn the line at leaving Italy, and his lictors posed an obstacle (*scribe...si Pompeius Italia cedit, quid nobis agendum putes; M'. quidem Lepidus...eum finem statuit, L. Torquatus eundem; me cum multa tum etiam lictores impediunt*, 7.12.4). Among the considerations that advocated staying were the inclement time of year, his lictors, and the incompetence of the republican leaders (*ad manendum hiems, lictores, improvidi et neglegentes duces*, 7.20.2). By mid-February, he could see the day when the City would be full of men of substance, including not a few consulars, that chose to stay behind: and he would join them, were it not for those awkward lictors (*etsi prope diem video bonorum*, *id est lautorum et locupletum, urbem refertam fore…quo ego in numero essem, si hos lictores molestissimos non haberem, nec me M'. Lepidi, L. Vulcati, Ser. Sulpici comitum paeniteret*, 8.1.3). Then again, to leave Italy with his laureled *fasces*, those foot-chains, would be just as awkward (*age iam, has compedes, fascis, inquam, hos laureatos efferre ex Italia quam molestum est!* 8.3.5). Better, perhaps, to stay and join Caesar—except that here, too, the *fasces* are a problem: what if Caesar were to offer him his triumph? To reject it could be dangerous, to accept would put him in bad odor with the *boni* (8.3.6). On March 6, finally, a decision: first from Formiae to Arpinum, then on to the Adriatic to join Pompeius—still at Brundisium—and the *boni*; the lictors he would put aside, or dismiss altogether (*remotis sive omnino missis lictoribus*, 9.1.3).

Yet two days later, Cicero had second thoughts (9.2a). By March 13, he thought it best to remain for now at Formiae and meet with Caesar, in hopes of being allowed to remain in Italy and out of public view, or come to Rome but not be forced to participate in measures against Pompeius; and he would readily let go of the triumph (*de triumpho tibi adsentior, quem quidem totum facile et libenter abiecero*, 9.7.2–5; cf. 9.9.1; 9.11A.3; 9.15.1). Another five days, and he was again determined to leave and join Pompeius (*nunc si vel periculosum experiundum erit, experiar certe ut hinc avolem*, 9.10.3; cf. 9.12.4), though not right away—he still wanted to talk with Caesar first. That interview, on the 28th, did not go well (9.18), and Cicero now pursued his plan to depart from Italy as soon as the season permitted and opportunity offered (9.19.3). By April 3, however, a new twist developed: he would go overseas, but seek a neutral location rather than join the optimates' camp (10.1.2). Then again, perhaps it was more honorable to either follow the *boni* or come out openly against the scoundrels (10.1a). On April 14, C. Scribonius Curio paid a visit; Cicero explained that he wanted to leave Italy for a place of retirement and solitude—especially as he had his lictors (*ego me recessum et solitudinem quaerere, maxime quod lictores haberem*, 10.4.10), five weeks after indicating that he would get rid of them (9.1.3). On the 3rd or 4th of May, he told Caelius Rufus that he would happily stay in Italy, if it were not for that bothersome train of lictors and his title of *imperator* (*Fam.* 2.16.2, *accedit etiam molesta haec pompa lictorum meorum nomenque imperi quo appellor*); the laurel on his *fasces* gave rise to ill-willed looks and comments. About the same time, he had written in a similar vein to Antony: he wanted to leave Italy, being unwilling to hurry back and forth with his lictors (*Att.* 10.10.1, *me autem, quia cum lictoribus invitus cursarem, abesse velle*). On June 7, Cicero sailed for Greece (*Fam.* 14.7).

He returned to Italy, at Brundisium, well over a year later, in the fall of 48, still with his lictors, although on making his way through the crowd when approaching the town, he had them exchange their *fasces* for a single staff each,[4] to avoid trouble

---

[4] In the manner of municipal lictors: Cic. *Leg. agr.* 2.93, *anteibant lictores* (sc. *Capuae*) *non cum bacillis, sed, ut hic praetoribus urbanis anteeunt, cum fascibus binis*; Mommsen *StR* 1: 373 n. 3.

with the troops stationed there; since then, he remained indoors (*Att*.11.6.2, *quos* [sc. *lictores*] *ego †non paulisper† cum bacillis in turbam conieci ad oppidum accedens, ne quis impetus militum fieret; reliquo tempore me domo tenui*). And how was he to come closer to Rome, as Atticus advised, without the lictors which the People had granted him, and which could not be taken away from him as long as he retained his status (*Att*.11.6.2, *propius accedere, ut suades, quo modo sine lictoribus quos populus dedit possum? qui mihi incolumi adimi non possunt*)? By mid-December, though, things were looking up: Balbus and Oppius, Caesar's men in Rome, told Atticus that Cicero should continue to use the same lictors as he had now (*ita faciam igitur ut scribis istis placere, isdem istis lictoribus me uti*, 11.7.1).[5] And so it happened. The man who was sole *imperator* in the empire of the Roman People permitted Cicero to be the other one, and keep his laureled *fasces* for as long as he should wish (*Lig*. 7, *qui me, cum ipse imperator in toto imperio populi Romani unus esset, esse alterum passus est; a quo...concessos fascis laureatos tenui quoad tenendos putavi*). For another year, Cicero remained at Brundisium. In October of 47, he returned to Rome, and finally dismissed his lictors before crossing the *pomerium*.[6]

The lictors with their *fasces* symbolize the magistrate's powers, *coercitio* in the most immediate manner, and *imperium* more generally; that much is not in doubt.[7] Yet the instances assembled above point to something more. Cicero had left Rome for Cilicia in the summer of 51, *cum imperio pro consule*. Under Sulla's legislation, and by long-established practice, he retained his *imperium*—not his province!—until he returned to Rome and crossed the *pomerium*: that, too, is not in doubt.[8] Once the outbreak of civil war had rendered a triumph doubtful and, if ever to be realized, a thing of the distant future, the lictors—laureled, no less—became an embarrassment, all the more in the case of a man who did everything to avoid being associated with a military command in those circumstances.[9] One ought to think that, as symbols without substance, they could have been dismissed without much ado, and resumed in case a triumph did materialize. Yet Cicero clung to them for almost three years, long past the point at which he still

---

[5] A concession also made to P. Sestius (*pro pr*. Cilicia 49): *quod concessum Sestio sit*. Or so Atticus thought; but Cicero immediately set him straight: *he* had his own lictors (i.e., granted by the People), but Sestius had not been allowed to keep his—merely those given to him by Caesar, on changing sides (*cui non puto suos esse concessos sed ab ipso datos*). For Caesar, reportedly, considered void all Senate votes that had occurred after the "flight" of the Tribunes on January 7, 49, which included Sestius' appointment to Cilicia: hence he would be able to approve of Cicero's keeping his lictors, without appearing to be inconsistent (*audio enim eum ea senatus consulta improbare quae post discessum tribunorum facta sunt; qua re poterit, si volet sibi constare, nostros lictores comprobare*).

[6] Shackleton Bailey *CLA* 5: 298.

[7] Mommsen *StR* 1: 374–378; Kunkel *StO* 119–120; Lintott 96; cf. Chapter 2.1.2.

[8] Cic. *Fam*. 1.9.25, *se, quoniam ex senatus consulto provinciam haberet, lege Cornelia imperium habiturum quoad in urbem introisset* (the "speaker" is Ap. Claudius, *cos*. 54); Mommsen *StR* 1: 641; Kunkel *StO* 101 n. 180; Lintott 194; Vervaet 2014: 56–62; Rafferty 37, 43. Cf. Chapter 4.2.4 with notes 43 and 44.

[9] Shackleton Bailey *CLA* 4: 438–440.

entertained some hope of a triumph, and even when their public appearance posed a danger to his safety.[10] The reason is not far to seek. Cicero explicitly connects his lictors with his *nomen imperii* (*Fam.* 2.16.2), with his status *cum imperio pro consule*, granted by the People (*Att.* 11.6.2): the lictors could not be taken from him without depriving him of this status as well. No lictors, no *imperium*. (He made the same connection with regard to Domitius, who relinquished his *fasces* at Corfinium.)

3.1.3 The Magistrate Without His Lictors

In 185 BC, the Consul M. Sempronius Tuditanus had drawn by lot the presidency over the elections; but his colleague, Ap. Claudius Pulcher, returned to Rome from their joint province, Liguria, first: his brother Publius was seeking the consulship, with scant prospects of success, given that year's competition (Livy 39.32.5–9).[11] Back in the City, Appius canvassed for his brother without lictors, and with abandon, which triggered vocal criticism from competitors and within the Senate: Claudius ought to remember that he was Consul first and foremost, not Publius' brother (*Claudius consul sine lictoribus cum fratre toto foro volitando, clamitantibus adversariis et maiore parte senatus meminisse eum debere se prius consulem populi Romani quam fratrem P. Claudi esse*, 39.32.10–11).

When Appius campaigned for his brother in this fashion, he evidently meant to separate his canvassing activity from his official position as the Consul[12]—yet that precisely is the criticism directed at him: in his eagerness to support his brother, he had forgotten that he was Consul. And for the Consul, the only proper role during elections was to sit on his tribunal and either conduct them or be a silent spectator: *quin ille sedens pro tribunali aut arbitrum aut tacitum spectatorem comitiorum se praeberet* (Livy 39.32.11).[13] Only as a *privatus* could Appius campaign for his brother without impropriety; whatever he did while appearing to exercise the *consularis potestas* could not be separated from official action as

---

[10] He abandoned the quest for a triumph in his letter of March 13, 49 (*Att.* 9.7.5), and never mentions the matter again; it is not entirely clear, though, whether he had given up for good, or for the time being—a republican victory, even years down the road, might still revive the opportunity. On the potential for trouble at Brundisium, see *Att.* 11.6.2.

[11] Pina Polo 196 lists Appius as presiding over the elections, but if that is what eventually happened, it occurred contrary to the original assignment. Livy is quite clear: *prior tamen Claudius quam Sempronius, cui sors comitia habendi obtigerat, Romam venit*.

[12] Briscoe 2008: 332: "to make it clear that he is campaigning as Publius' brother, not as consul."

[13] Briscoe 2008: 332 holds that there is "no suggestion that he should preside at the election instead of his colleague" (*contra* W–M *ad loc.*), but Livy's wording is maddeningly opaque here: Wiseman 1979: 100 and Pina Polo 201 take the passage to mean that Appius did, in fact, seize control of the elections. His colleague's complete absence in Livy's actual narrative of the proceedings, together with the emphasis on Appius' arriving in Rome first (which, if it were merely a matter of canvassing, need not have constituted a significant advantage), may point in that direction.

Consul. Hence no lictors. Without them, it would be inappropriate for him to exercise his powers, and thus, without them, he was free to act like any *privatus*. But by ridding himself of his lictors, he effectively ceased to function—for the duration of that condition—as Consul, thus opening himself to charges that he had put family interest ahead of his public duties, in effect suspending, for the time being, his office, while yet retaining it: for obviously, he still remained Consul. If symbolism without substance were at stake here, one should expect the attempt thus to separate his private persona from his public one to have drawn accusations of abusing his consular powers, rather than opprobrium for neglecting them.

In 62 BC, the Senate decreed that one of the Praetors, C. Iulius Caesar, should be removed from managing public affairs (*donec ambo*[14] *administratione rei publicae decreto patrum submoverentur*, Suet. *DIul* 16.1). At first refusing to comply (*nihilo minus permanere in magistratu et ius dicere ausus*), Caesar quickly bowed to the threat of armed violence: he dismissed his lictors, shed the scarlet-bordered toga, and withdrew to his home (*ut comperit paratos, qui vi ac per arma prohiberent, dimissis lictoribus abiectaque praetexta domum clam refugit*). But a few days later, he defused an angry crowd demonstrating in his support outside his house, which prompted the Senate to repeal the decree and reinstate him (*senatus...in integrum restituit inducto priore decreto*, 16.2).

Caesar's actions conform to the view developed here. The Senate had voted him removed from managing the *res publica*; but the Senate lacked the constitutional means to enforce such a removal: they must of necessity rely on the magistrate's cooperation.[15] Hence, when Caesar balked, the threat of using violence. Dismissing his lictors was not merely a symbolic action, necessary only to show that Caesar did not want to extend his conflict with the Senate: there was no other way he could remove himself, effectively and visibly, from public affairs.[16] As long

---

[14] The other individual thus affected was the Tribune Q. Metellus Nepos.

[15] As had happened a few months earlier, on December 3, 63 BC, when P. Lentulus Sura, Praetor and Catilinarian, abdicated his office. In brief mention, the sources commonly speak of Lentulus' being compelled to do so (Cic. *Cat.* 4.5, *P. Lentulum se abdicare praetura coegistis*; Appian *BCiv* 2.5.16, ἡ μὲν βουλὴ Λέντλον παρέλυσε τῆς ἀρχῆς; Dio 37.34.2, κἀκ τούτου ὁ Λέντουλος ἀπειπεῖν τὴν στρατηγίαν ὑπὸ τῆς γερουσίας ἀναγκασθεὶς ἐν φρουρᾷ...ἐγένετο); but from the more detailed accounts it is clear that the compulsion consisted in Lentulus' being confronted with overwhelming evidence of his complicity, and the Senate's judging that he had forfeited both his status as a Praetor and a citizen, whereupon Lentulus abdicated (*nam P. Lentulus, quamquam patefactis indiciis, confessionibus suis, iudicio senatus non modo praetoris ius verum etiam civis amiserat, tamen magistratu se abdicavit*, Cic. *Cat.* 3.15). In so doing, he obligingly removed any *religio* that might attach to the execution of a sitting magistrate—never mind that it had not stopped Marius from killing Claudia (*ut quae religio C. Mario, clarissimo viro, non fuerat quo minus C. Glauciam de quo nihil nominatim erat decretum praetorem occideret, ea nos religione in privato P. Lentulo puniendo liberaremur*). Thus the Senate simply voted to have Lentulus taken into custody, *cum se praetura abdicasset* (Cic. *Cat.* 3.14; cf. Sall. *Cat.* 47.3, *senatus decernit uti abdicato magistratu Lentulum itemque ceteri in liberis custodiis habeantur*, and Plut. *Cic.* 19.3, ἐξελεγχθεὶς ὁ Λέντλος ἀπωμόσατο τὴν ἀρχήν). Cf. Mommsen *StR* 1: 262 n. 1.

[16] It may be noted that the Consuls are strangely absent from this story. Presumably either of them could forbid Caesar to do anything *pro magistratu*. If such a prohibition had in fact been issued, *de*

as he had lictors, he exercised the *praetoria potestas* in anything he did: by definition and default, he was involved in the *administratio rei publicae*.

In 58 BC, Cicero spent most of his exile in Macedonia, sheltered by his friend the Quaestor Cn. Plancius. While the governor, L. Appuleius (*pr.* by 59), maintained a neutral distance towards the *exsul*, Plancius met him at Dyrrachium, without lictors or insignia (*lictoribus dimissis, insignibus abiectis*), and escorted him to his official residence in Thessalonica (*Thessalonicam me in quaestoriumque perduxit*, Cic. *Planc.* 98–99). Plancius persisted in his solicitous attitude for the duration of Cicero's stay, rejecting the role of Quaestor for that of a companion (*abiecta quaestoris persona comitisque sumpta*, 100).

Like Ap. Claudius, the Consul in 185, Plancius was at pains to separate his public persona from his private one, and, like Appius, his endeavor brought only limited success. In meeting Cicero without lictors and insignia, Plancius wanted to be seen as not exercising his official powers when welcoming a fugitive, but effectively acting as a private citizen. But setting aside his powers for the time being was not the same thing as renouncing his office altogether: he remained Quaestor just as Appius had remained Consul (or Caesar, Praetor). Thus he still resided in the *quaestorium*, and indeed could find no better place for his exiled guest to stay.

How did Plancius come by his lictors, though? As a rule, Quaestors were not entitled to them (Varro *apud* Gell. 13.12.6). If Appuleius the governor was not (yet) *in provincia* when Cicero arrived, Plancius could have been Quaestor *pro praetore*, acting governor, surely with lictors; we know nothing in that regard, of course. But it seems that, in the first century, Legates in the provinces were commonly granted lictors by their commanders; even senators travelling abroad on private business under a *legatio libera* could expect to be so endowed.[17] It would not surprise if provincial Quaestors, too, by this time had acquired lictors as a matter of course; again, there seems to be no evidence apart from this passage. Now, if a Quaestor held his lictors—as did the *legati*—merely by way of a grant from the provincial governor, rather than *lege publica*, dismissing them could hardly affect Plancius' official appearance: of necessity, he must be seen as acting *pro magistratu* even without them, having no legal claim to such instruments. Dropping his quaestorian insignia would have offered greater meaning but, naturally, less spectacle.

---

senatus sententia, his recalcitrance in the face of *maior potestas* would call for a forcible response. But the silence of the sources makes it doubtful that the Consuls got involved; in any case, the *senatus consultum*, as reported by Suetonius (*DIul* 16.1), was directed at both Caesar and Metellus Nepos: and no Consul could prohibit a Tribune from doing anything.

[17] Legates: Cic. *2Verr.* 1.67, 72; *Fam.* 12.30.7, with Shackleton Bailey *CEF* 2: 561, noting, *contra* Mommsen, that the gentlemen in question—Venuleius, Latin<i?>us, and Horatius—surely were the previous governor's *legati*, still remaining in the province. For senators, see Cic. *Fam.* 12.21, with *StR* 1: 387; Kunkel *StO* 121–122. The evidence suffices to refute Vervaet's sweeping assertion (2014: 12 n. 7) that "the *fasces* were the exclusive *insignia imperii*."

Under normal circumstances, the magistrate was virtually inseparable from his lictors: they accompany him wherever he goes or stays, be it the Forum or the bath, the battlefield or a dinner party.[18] No one was allowed to step between the *lictor proximus* (the one immediately preceding the magistrate, or otherwise standing next to him) and the magistrate, except the latter's *filius praetextatus*—wearing the same outfit (Val. Max. 2.2.4). The only known exceptions are the private home (the magistrate's own, or that of anyone he visited), where the lictors remain in the vestibule,[19] and—perhaps—the brothel: *si praecedentibus fascibus praetor deducetur in lupanar, maiestatem laedet*, we are told (Sen. *Contr.* 9.2.17). Inside a private home, the magistrate is effectively *privatus*; and in the bordello, that is what he ought to be, should a visit become unavoidable.[20] Manumission before the Praetor (that is, *vindicta*) may be secured anywhere he can be found, in the theater or the bath, not only *pro tribunali*; but it requires the presence of his lictors—unless the transaction occurs in the privacy of his home.[21]

3.1.4 The Turnus

Lastly, there is the ancient and well-known principle of limiting the active management of the *res publica* to one of the two Consuls at a time, alternating monthly in the City, and daily in the field (if with the same army). Only the Consul "in charge"—*penes quem sunt fasces*—is preceded by his twelve lictors, carrying the rods. His colleague goes about with an *accensus* leading the way; that much is clear, but little else.[22] Both Livy and Cicero seem to imply the physical alternation of a single set of lictors.[23] Dionysios, though, envisaged two sets of

---

[18] For the bath, Livy 25.17.1 (the Proconsul Ti. Gracchus going for a swim in the river *cum lictoribus ac tribus servis*); Gaius *Inst.* 1.20; cf. *Dig.* 40.2.7; for the party, Petron. *Satyr.* 65.3–4. The full evidence is assembled by Mommsen (*StR* 1: 376 n. 1) and Gladigow; the latter's study, along with Marshall's, remains essential to the discussion.

[19] Livy 39.12.2; and it is clear from the subsequent narrative (39.12.3–13.14) that the Consul's interrogation of Hispala Faecenia proceeded in an interior room of his mother-in-law's house, without anyone but the latter present, in as unofficial a setting as could be mustered. See also Gell. 2.2.1–10 and Meister 49–50. (We may assume that the lictor at Petr. *Satyr.* 65.3–4 did not accompany Habinnas into the *triclinium*, but, having announced the Sevir, withdrew to the vestibule of Trimalchio's house.)

[20] Gladigow 297 takes this to mean that the magistrate was required to take his lictors along even into a brothel; but the passages discussed above show that a temporary separation from the lictors could be used to effect a suspension of official capacity. Hence the Praetor entering the *lupanar* without lictors did so not *qua* Praetor—which would have offended the majesty of the Roman People—but like a *privatus*.

[21] Even so, the exception does not seem to have taken hold until well into imperial times: *ego cum in villa cum praetore fuissem, passus sum apud eum manumitti, etsi lictoris praesentia non esset*, noted Ulpian (*Dig.* 40.2.8; cf. Gaius *Inst.* 1.20; *Dig.* 40.2.7; Mommsen *StR* 1: 376 n. 1).

[22] Livy 3.33.8, *penes praefectum iuris fasces duodecim erant: collegis novem singuli accensi apparebant*. This refers to the (first) Decemvirs, but clearly represents the normal consular practice.

[23] Cic. *Rep.* 2.55, *Publicola... secures de fascibus demi iussit, postridieque sibi collegam Sp. Lucretium subrogavit, suosque ad eum quod erat maior natu lictores transire iussit, instituitque primus ut singulis consulibus alternis mensibus lictores praeirent, ne plura insignia essent imperii in libero populo quam in*

lictors: one with axes (πελέκεις) for the Consul in charge; the other with rods only, as some of his sources told it, for his colleague, or with some kind of clubs or staffs as well (5.2.1, τοῦ δ' ἑτέρου δώδεκα ὑπηρέτας ῥάβδους ἔχοντας μόνον, ὡς δέ τινες ἱστοροῦσι, καὶ κορύνας).[24] This has been thought confused and conflated with the removal of the axes *intra pomerium*, but Dionysios subsequently reports the latter under the measures ascribed to Poplicola.[25] Now, Caesar as Consul in 59 BC is said to have revived—at least in part—the ancient custom of ordering his lictors to walk behind him in the off-months, rather than in front.[26] That clearly implies two sets of lictors, as in Dionysios. It also implies that from some point on prior to the first century—when exactly remains unknown—both Consuls appeared in public preceded by their lictors at all times; but the evidence amply demonstrates that they continued to take turns, month by month, at actually administering the *res publica*: even though both now appeared with lictors before them, only one at any given time was considered, constitutionally, to be holding the *fasces*, and capable of independent action.[27] Did the lictors accompanying the Consul not in charge carry *fasces*?

In 28 BC, Imp. Caesar, Consul for the sixth time and observing all the practices prescribed by *mos* since ancient times, handed over his bundles of rods—in accordance with what was due—to M. Agrippa his colleague, and himself used the others (τοὺς φακέλους τῶν ῥάβδων τῷ Ἀγρίππᾳ συνάρχοντί οἱ κατὰ τὸ ἐπιβάλλον παρέδωκεν, αὐτός τε ταῖς ἑτέραις ἐχρήσατο, Dio 53.1.1). The "others" (αἱ ἕτεραι) can only refer to the rods (αἱ ῥάβδοι), not to the bundles (οἱ φάκελοι): Dio draws a contrast here between *fasces* and *virgae*. As so often, Staveley saw the correct explanation more clearly than most: only the lictors of the Consul *penes quem fasces* carried a full set of rods, tied up in a bundle; those of his colleague carried something else, and visibly different.[28] Staveley called this "dummy rods"; but

---

regno fuissent; Livy 2.1.8, *id modo cautum est ne, si ambo fasces haberent, duplicatus terror videretur; Brutus prior, concedente collega, fasces habuit.* (Plutarch evidently understood it the same way: ᾧ τῆς ἡγεμονικωτέρας ἐξιστάμενος ὄντι πρεσβυτέρῳ τάξεως παρέδωκε τοὺς καλουμένους φάσκης, *Popl.* 12.5.)

[24] That καί can have adversative force, "or," is well known; usually in such a case, it offers an alternative between two characteristics applying to the same subject not simultaneously, but viewed according to circumstances; the effect is one of connection rather than separation: see Ramsay 337–341; K–G 2: 248; Schw–D 2: 567 n. 5. But it would be difficult to make Dionysios say here that he had conflicting information to the effect that these lictors either carried only ῥάβδοι or only κορύναι; the implication of his parenthetical ὡς δέ τινες ἱστοροῦσι and the force of καί clearly must be that some of his authorities only mentioned the rods, but most had the lictors carry both "rods" and "staffs."

[25] Dion. Hal. 5.19.3, ἀφεῖλεν ἀπὸ τῶν ῥάβδων τοὺς πελέκεις; cf. Mommsen *StR* 1: 37 n. 4.

[26] Suet. *DIul* 20.1, *antiquum etiam re<t>tulit morem, ut quo mense fasces non haberet, accensus ante eum iret, lictores pone sequerentur*; Mommsen *StR* 1: 40, 375–377; Gladigow 298. In ritual terms, this probably differed from appearing with no lictors at all: the *accensus* walking in front still marked him out as *magistratus*, not *privatus*; and the lictors walking behind were still present—not dismissed, as with Appius the Consul in 185 or Caesar as Praetor in 62.

[27] Cf. Wittmann *StO* 192 and Appian *BCiv* 2.11.37, οὐ γὰρ...ἐξῆν τῷ ἑτέρῳ τῶν ὑπάτων συναγαγεῖν αὐτήν (sc. τὴν βουλήν); and see Staveley 1963: 466; Vervaet 2014: 32.

[28] Staveley 1963: 466–467; but Syme, in a paper only recently published, had reached the same conclusion five years earlier ([1958] 2016: 259–264).

Dio's contrast between bundle and rod suggests that each such lictor carried only a single rod, not multiple ones. Lictors, it seems, usually carried the *fasces* over their left shoulder, while holding a shorter staff in their right hand, presumably to keep others at an appropriate distance from the magistrate.[29] The staffs are surely identical with the κορύναι known from Dionysios, hence still carried by the lictors of the Consul not in charge:[30] were they "the others"? But Dionysios—who would have seen it all in action—clearly thought of those lictors as carrying two distinct implements, ῥάβδοι and κορύναι. Now the lictors in Roman colonies and *municipia* did not carry *fasces* in the form of an actual bundle of rods, but a single staff (*bacillum*) each; and when Cicero, on his return to Italy in 48 BC, wanted to enter Brundisium with a minimum of public visibility, he had his lictors appear in the same manner.[31] Almost certainly, this explains Dio's "other" set: the lictors of the Consul not in charge did not carry a bundle (φάκελος) each, but a single rod (ῥάβδος) over their left shoulder, presumably along with a staff (Dionysios' κορύνη) in their right hand. "What matters is not the lictors but the emblems they carried."[32]

The Consul not in charge retained his capacity to obstruct—*intercessio* and *obnuntiatio*—his colleague's actions; he retained full command of his own army, including the right to auspicate.[33] But he was unable to initiate acts of state, except in agreement with his colleague and, of course, whenever the latter was unable to do so himself due to illness, death, or absence from the scene.[34]

3.1.5 No Lictors, No Action

It is evident that the physical presence of the lictors was closely associated with the magistrate's ability to exercise the powers of his office, as the Consul in charge, or being perceived as *magistratus* rather than *privatus*. Yet, as so often, the principle does not neatly translate into rigid constitutional rules. For an incumbent magistrate, dismissing his lictors and shedding the trappings of office evidently did not amount to ending the latter: Appius remained Consul, Caesar remained Praetor, and Plancius, Quaestor. Premature termination of an annual magistracy required a formal renunciation under oath.[35]

---

[29] Apparently the same as a Flamen's *commoetaculum* (Festus 56.29L); see B. Kübler *RE* 13.1 (1926) 508; Gladigow 298; 306 n. 77; 314; and cf. Mommsen *StR* 1: 374–376. The staff is visible, e.g., in the right hands of Augustus' lictors on the Boscoreale cups, or on the funeral stele of the lictor M. Coelius Dionysius (*CIL* 6.1898).
[30] Thus Staveley 1963: 467 n. 42, tentatively ("possibly identifiable"); cf. above, note 24.
[31] Cic. *LegAgr* 2.93; *Att.* 11.6.2; Mommsen *StR* 1: 373 n. 3; and above, note 4.
[32] Syme 2016 [1958]: 260–261.   [33] Livy 22.49.7–9 is instructive.
[34] The evidence is assembled in *StR* 1: 37–43; Kunkel *StO* 191–199; cf. Linderski *AL* 2178–2179 n. 115; Brennan *PRR* 1: 41.
[35] Coli 1953: 402–404; Kunkel *StO* 253–254 with n. 7; Brennan *PRR* 2: 397–398.

DICTATOR 77

The temporary relegation of lictors to a place behind the Consul during the periods in which he did not hold the *fasces* signified an incapacity for independent action; but their physical—and visible—presence, along with the antecedence of the *accensus*, made it clear that he was not acting in any capacity other than his official one. But to appear in public without lictors or other insignia signalled that the magistrate, on this occasion, was not to be considered such: whatever he did while without them was to be seen as the action of a *privatus*, not an exercise of official powers. In effect, a magistrate without his lictors was deemed suspended from office, be it as part of a regular rotation or for some other reason.[36] Even if in theory the absence itself of lictors did not render the magistrate unable to exercise his powers, it made little difference: as a practical matter, in a culture so steeped in ritual, it would be well-nigh unthinkable for him to do so except in the most routine kind of business.[37]

A man commanding *pro consule*, although holding *imperium consulare* and the outward trappings of curule office, and in that regard the equal of a Consul,[38] clearly was not in possession of the full *consularis potestas*: he lacked, for instance, the ability to convene the People or the Senate even *extra pomerium*, or to engage in any governmental activity within the City. In fact, his *imperium* existed only outside the *pomerium*; to cross into the City meant the end of it, without further ado and ceremony. Hence he could not have lictors in the City, and must dismiss them before entering it: he crossed the *pomerium* as *privatus*, not *pro magistratu*.[39] Yet something more is clear from Cicero: to a promagistrate, the lictors were

---

[36] Hölkeskamp 2011: 165–166: "In a culture of spectacular visibility, the language or 'poetics' of power is necessarily visual…it is simply not enough to exercise power by pulling strings behind the scenes—power only becomes real when and if it is seen to be exercised, it needs publicity and performance"; "leaving the fasces behind means for a magistrate that he foregoes his *dignitas* and quality of a magistrate" (169); "a consul who is summoned to appear before the dictator even has to dismiss his lictors with his fasces—just as if he resigned his office and was demoted to the status of *privatus*" (171).

[37] The matter is incapable of proof, but in light of the principle *quod si tum imprudens id verbum emisit* (sc. *praetor*) *ac quem manumisit, ille nihilo minus est liber, sed vitio, ut magistratus vitio creatus nihilo setius magistratus* (Varro *LL* 6.30), one ought to assume that simply being *magistratus* constituted all the legal basis necessary to exercise the powers of the office. Certainly Plancius could hardly have put up Cicero in the *quaestorium* at Thessalonica except by virtue of exercising his quaestorial powers, the absence of insignia (and lictors) notwithstanding. Nor did being preceded by his lictors, in the years before Caesar revived the ancient custom, enable the Consul to act independently of his colleague during the months in which he did not hold the *fasces*. On the other hand, the fact that as late as the third century AD the legal validity of manumission by the Praetor in his own home, without a lictor present, could be questioned (Ulpian *Dig.* 40.2.8) makes it clear how essential those ritual accompaniments were in the eyes of the public.

[38] Any and all attempts to postulate a subordination of the Proconsul under the Consul solely on the basis of *imperium* are futile: see Staveley 1963: 472–478, to which nothing further needs to be said.

[39] For *privati cum imperio*, this surely meant that they were not accompanied by lictors until they had crossed the *pomerium* outbound. Failure to observe this practice in January, 49, gave cause for castigation, at least in the judgment of a scrupulous observer of *mos* and constitutional correctness: *lictoresque habent in urbe et Capitolio privati contra omnia vetustatis exempla* (Caes. *BCiv* 1.6.7; for a novel interpretation, perceptive if ultimately unconvincing, see Frolov).

inseparable from his appointment. To dismiss them anywhere (even under duress, like Domitius at Corfinium) meant the end of his *imperium*, hence of his tenure.[40]

Even so, Cicero at one point appears to contemplate their removal as distinct from complete dismissal (*Att.* 9.1.3, *remotis sive omnino missis lictoribus*: in early March, 49): could he have gone without them temporarily without giving up his *imperium* and status *pro consule*? (A magistrate, as we have seen, certainly could.) Yet except for this one brief instance, Cicero never mentions that possibility, nor did he adopt what would seem to us the obvious course of action that would have solved the problem of the lictors' inconvenient and embarrassing presence. In fact, the distinction is imaginary; *sive* here, as commonly (and in Cicero especially), serves not to offer a true alternative, but to correct the first of the two elements it connects, or express it with greater precision: "with my lictors removed, or rather discharged altogether."[41]

3.2 Cessation or Termination?

It is on the very occasion of Fabius' dictatorship in 217 that we first encounter, in Polybios, the universal view of Greek writers (insofar as they comment on the matter) that all magistracies—other than the Tribunes of the Plebs—cease when a Dictator is appointed: οὗτος δ' ἔστιν αὐτοκράτωρ στρατηγός, οὗ καταστᾰθέντος παραχρῆμα διαλύεσθαι συμβαίνει πάσας τὰς ἀρχὰς ἐν τῇ Ῥώμῃ πλὴν τῶν δημάρχων (3.87.8). Mommsen dismissed it as an error, albeit a puzzling one, coming from Polybios.[42]

3.2.1 Polybios and Plutarch

It is clear enough from the Latin evidence that all magistrates stayed in office during a dictatorship. Yet it is difficult to believe that the Greeks, with such unanimity from Polybios (not noted for easily misunderstanding things Roman) on down, should have so thoroughly got this wrong, dependent as they all were, ultimately, on Roman sources of information. As so often, we may with greater benefit assume that they simplified the matter, but did not misrepresent it altogether.

Indeed, Polybios did not imagine that all other magistrates were actually terminated under a Dictator, and had to be elected *de novo* afterwards.

---

[40] Lacey 18 notes this correctly, but in his subsequent discussion (21, 34–37) does not observe the distinction, demanded by the evidence, between promagistrates and magistrates in this regard.
[41] See K-S 2: 437–438 (adducing, among others, this very passage), and cf. 2: 107–111 on *vel/-ve* in corresponding usage.
[42] *StR* 2.1: 155 n. 4: "...diese falsche Vorstellung, der bei Polybius zu begegnen...mit Recht befremdet." But Lange *RA* 1: 636–637 saw the matter correctly.

He terms Servilius "the current Consul" (τὸν ὑπάρχοντα στρατηγόν[43]) when the Dictator deprives him of his command by land (3.88.8), and, after Fabius' abdication, reintroduces Servilius and Atilius as "the previously serving Consuls" (οἱ προϋπάρχοντες ὕπατοι, 3.106.2), while noting that Atilius had been elected after the death of Flaminius—by implication, while Fabius was Dictator. He states expressly that the διάλυσις affected all magistrates except the Tribunes of the Plebs. The exception is significant. One is hard pressed to see how it could be the result of a misunderstanding: it rather shows that he was following good information that made the crucial distinction between (*patricii*) *magistratus* and *tribuni plebis*. He understood the matter as something other than removal from office.

Appian, commenting on the question in the same context as did Polybios, clearly imagined termination (ἕως ἀφικόμενος Φάβιος Μάξιμος ὁ δικτάτωρ Σερουίλιον μὲν ἐς Ῥώμην ἔπεμπεν ὡς οὔτε ὕπατον οὔτε στρατηγὸν ἔτι ὄντα δικτάτορος ᾑρημένου, *Hannib*. 12.50). Mommsen thought that this, like Plutarch *Ant*. 8.5 and *QR* 81, derived simply from Polybios, and was inclined to see in him the informant of Dionysios as well.[44] The matter is perhaps more complicated.

Plutarch comments on constitutional aspects of the dictatorship on seven occasions, as follows:

(1) *Marc*. 24.11: ὁ γὰρ δικτάτωρ οὐκ ἔστιν ὑπὸ τοῦ πλήθους οὐδὲ τῆς βουλῆς αἱρετός, ἀλλὰ τῶν ὑπάτων τις ἢ τῶν στρατηγῶν προελθὼν εἰς τὸν δῆμον ὃν αὐτῷ δοκεῖ λέγει δικτάτορα.

"For the Dictator is not chosen by popular majority or by the Senate, but one of the Consuls or the Praetors, stepping in front of the People, names as Dictator the man whom he thinks best."

The description of the mode of appointment stays close to the Latin terminology *dictatorem dicere* (thus also in the surrounding narrative: εἰπεῖν δικτάτορα, 24.10; λέγειν δικτάτορα and τοῦτον <ἂν>ειπεῖν, 25.1; ἀνεῖπε, 25.2). The biographer continues (24.12–13) with two explanations of the word *dictator*. One hails from *dicere*, in line with Varro's and Cicero's.[45] The other derives the title from the Dictator's not being subject to votes and elections, and his powers to issue ordinances (*edicta*) at his sole discretion: ἔνιοι δέ <φασι> τὸν δικτάτορα τῷ μὴ προτιθέναι ψῆφον ἢ χειροτονίαν, ἀλλ' ἀφ' αὑτοῦ τὰ δόξαντα προστάττειν καὶ λέγειν οὕτως ὠνομάσθαι· καὶ γὰρ τὰ διαγράμματα τῶν ἀρχόντων Ἕλληνες <μὲν> διατάγματα, Ῥωμαῖοι δ' ἔδικτα προσαγορεύουσιν. With the possible exception of *QR* 81 (below, #8), this ought to be Plutarch's earliest discussion of the office. It contains no hint of other magistrates' ceasing to hold office during a dictatorship.

---

[43] On Polybios' routinely calling Consuls στρατηγοί even in a non-military context, see Luce 24.
[44] *StR* 2.1: 155 n. 4.   [45] Varro *LL* 5.82; 6.61; Cic. *Rep*. 1.63.

(2) *Cam.* 18.6: καίτοι πρότερόν γε καὶ πρὸς ἐλάττονας ἀγῶνας εἵλοντο πολλάκις **μονάρχους,** οὓς δικτάτορας καλοῦσιν, οὐκ ἀγνοοῦντες ὅσον ἐστὶν εἰς ἐπισφαλῆ καιρὸν ὄφελος μιᾷ χρωμένους γνώμῃ πρὸς **ἀνυπεύθυνον** ἀρχὴν ἐν χερσὶ τὴν δίκην ἔχουσαν εὐτακτεῖν.

"And yet they had previously, and for lesser contests, frequently chosen single commanders, whom they call Dictators—understanding full well how useful it is to be under the discipline, in a dangerous situation, of an unrestricted office holding the law in its hands, relying on a single judgment."

(3) *Fab.* 3.6–7: πάντες δ' εἰς μίαν γνώμην συνηνέχθησαν, **ἀνυπευθύνου** τε δεῖσθαι τὰ πράγματα **μοναρχίας,** ἣν δικτατορίαν καλοῦσι.

"All agreed unanimously that the circumstances required the unrestricted rule of a single man, which they call dictatorship."

(4) *Cam.* 29.3: ἤδη γὰρ αὐτοῦ δικτάτορος ᾑρημένου καὶ **μηδενὸς ἄρχοντος ἑτέρου** νόμῳ, πρὸς οὐκ ἔχοντας ἐξουσίαν ὁμολογηθῆναι.

"For since he had already been chosen Dictator and there was no other magistrate under the law, the treaty had been concluded with those who had no power to do so."

(5) *Cam.* 5.1: ἡ δὲ σύγκλητος εἰς τὸ δέκατον ἔτος τοῦ πολέμου **καταλύσασα** τὰς ἄλλας ἀρχὰς δικτάτορα Κάμιλλον ἀπέδειξεν.

"In the tenth year of the war, the Senate, having dissolved all the other magistracies, named Camillus Dictator."

(6) *Fab.* 9.2: ὁ δὲ Μετίλιος ἔχων τὴν ἀπὸ τῆς δημαρχίας ἄδειαν—μόνη γὰρ αὕτη δικτάτορος αἱρεθέντος ἡ ἀρχὴ τὸ κράτος οὐκ ἀπόλλυσιν, ἀλλὰ μένει τῶν ἄλλων **καταλυθεισῶν.**

"Metilius enjoyed the safety granted by his being Tribune of the Plebs; for this office alone does not lose its power when a Dictator has been chosen, but continues even though all the other magistracies have been dissolved."

(7) *Ant.* 8.4–5: Ἀντώνιον δ' ἵππαρχον ἑλόμενος εἰς Ῥώμην ἔπεμψεν. ἔστι δ' ἡ ἀρχὴ δευτέρα τοῦ δικτάτορος παρόντος· ἂν δὲ μὴ παρῇ, πρώτη καὶ μόνη σχεδόν· ἡ γὰρ δημαρχία διαμένει, τὰς δ' ἄλλας **καταλύουσι** πάσας δικτάτορος αἱρεθέντος.

"Having picked Antonius as Master of the Horse, he sent him to Rome. This magistracy is the second highest when the Dictator is present; but when he is absent, it is the highest and almost the only one: for the tribunate of the Plebs remains, but the other magistracies are all dissolved once a Dictator has been chosen."

(8) *QR* 81 (*Mor.* 283B): οὐδὲ **παύονται** (sc. οἱ δήμαρχοι) δικτάτωρος αἱρεθέντος ἀλλὰ πᾶσαν ἀρχὴν ἐκείνου μετατιθέντος εἰς ἑαυτὸν αὐτοὶ μόνοι διαμένουσιν, ὥσπερ οὐκ ὄντες ἄρχοντες ἀλλ' ἑτέραν τινὰ τάξιν ἔχοντες.

"For the Tribunes of the Plebs do not cease to function when a Dictator has been chosen, but while he transfers any other office unto himself, they alone remain, precisely because they are not magistrates, but have some other status."

In four (##5–8) out of eight discussions of the office, Plutarch explicitly states that all other magistrates cease to function under a dictatorship, and his description of the office as an "unaccountable monarchy" in two more (##2, 3) can accommodate such a view. A fifth passage (#4) implies that, under a Dictator, there are no other magistrates; yet the narrative here very closely follows Livy, who makes it clear that other magistrates still remained in office—though bereft of power: *negat eam pactionem ratam esse quae postquam ipse dictator creatus esset iniussu suo ab inferioris iuris magistratu facta esset* (5.49.2). In three of the instances stating cessation (##5–7), the verb employed (καταλύω) corresponds to Polybios' διαλύομαι. Yet παύομαι (#8) may evoke more of an indefinite halt than complete termination, and the phrase μόνη αὕτη ἡ ἀρχὴ τὸ κράτος οὐκ ἀπόλλυσιν (#6), taken literally, implies that the other magistracies do not simply disappear, but— unlike the tribunate—lose their power. On three occasions (##6–8), Plutarch notes the same exception as did Polybios: the Tribunes of the Plebs. But his additional comment, in the QR (#8), that the exception applies because the Tribunes are not magistrates—again, coming from a source knowledgeable and accurate in such matters, if not revealing the biographer's own understanding—along with the intriguing notion of the Dictator's absorbing all other magistracies into himself (δικτάτωρος...πᾶσαν ἀρχὴν...μετατίθεντος εἰς ἑαυτόν) plainly cannot be read into what Polybios wrote.[46] It is part of a lengthy and learned—indeed, highly percipient—disquisition on the constitutional character of the tribunate (*Mor.* 283B–D); he did not come upon the material for any of this in the extant work of Polybios. Nor could all of it derive from lost parts of the work: Curio's quip about a Tribune being the public's doormat (τὸν δὲ δήμαρχον...καταπατεῖσθαι δεῖ) was uttered a century after the historian wrote. The underlying thoughts, however, are fully compatible with what we have; if Polybios eventually did produce his promised treatment of the dictatorship in detail (οὐ μὴν ἀλλὰ περὶ μὲν τούτων ἐν ἄλλοις ἀκριβεστέραν ποιησόμεθα τὴν διαστολήν, 3.87.9), it will have come within a systematic description of Roman institutions after 6.18.[47] Plutarch in that case is likely enough to have taken much of QR 81 from it. It is improbable that Polybios in that lost treatment would have expressed himself less clearly on the subject than he did in Book 3; unfortunately, we cannot assume a greater degree of clarity, either:

---

[46] *Pace* Mommsen, the latter idea could have been prompted by Caesar's dictatorship in 45 BC, with no magistrates in office until his return from Spain in the fall, and the City governed by his *praefecti*. But even in Caesar's years that was exceptional, and it is difficult to believe that Plutarch himself would have drawn a general rule from this singular occurrence.

[47] See Walbank *HCP* 2: 635–636, 697. Polybios notes elsewhere that Tribunes are not subordinate to the Consuls (6.12.2).

it may never have occurred to him that readers could mistake his words for implying the actual abdication of all magistrates. (His narrative in Book 3 had implied the opposite.) Nor can we be certain that Plutarch thought of actual abdication in the instances he implies cessation (##5, 6, 7, and 8): the language, so close to Polybios', supports a temporary loss of power as readily as termination.

Plutarch, though, comes close to suggesting abdication in the *Fabius*:

> (9) Having been made Dictator, Fabius orders the surviving Consul to dismiss his lictors and meet him as a private citizen (καὶ τὰ παράσημα τῆς ἀρχῆς ἀποθέμενον ἰδιώτην ἀπαντᾶν, 4.3); and when the Dictator's term is up, Consuls are elected again (14.1)—who turn out to be not those of 216, but an unnamed pair (in reality, Servilius and his suffect colleague), adhering closely to Fabius' precepts.

That Plutarch imagined termination when he had Fabius dismiss Servilius as a private citizen is possible; something similar to Γνάιον μὲν τὸν ὑπάρχοντα στρατηγὸν ἀπολύσας τῆς κατὰ γῆν στρατείας (Polyb. 3.88.8) could have been misunderstood, in light of the Dictator's ordering the Consul to approach without lictors. (Appian certainly thought the same.) But the "election" of new Consuls after the Dictator's term was up may be more readily attributed to a sloppy reading of his source—probably not Polybios[48] but the one that furnished him with additional details he could not have found in the latter or in Livy (Fabius requesting permission to mount a horse, his twenty-four *fasces*, and his ordering Servilius to approach him without lictors, 4.1–3). That source was well informed on minutiae of Roman ceremonial: it is unlikely to have presented Servilius' dismissal as an actual abdication.

On the other hand, the comment in *Antony* (#7) fairly closely parallels Polybios in the information furnished, in particular as regards the Magister Equitum being not merely a second-in-command, but a deputy capable of—in the Dictator's absence—independent action (οὗτος δὲ τέτακται μὲν ὑπὸ τὸν αὐτοκράτορα, γίνεται δ' οἷον εἰ διάδοχος τῆς ἀρχῆς ἐν τοῖς ἐκείνου περισπασμοῖς, 3.87.9). One need not conclude, from its appearance only in a relatively late life, that the biographer had been unaware of it when he wrote the *Fabius*, although an explanation of the Master's position might have been as useful in that life as in the *Antony*. (But Minucius was an incidental character, not the hero.)

3.2.2 Dionysios

Cessation—even termination—of other magistracies is also the case in Dionysios' view. His long disquisition on the establishment of the dictatorship in 498 V repeatedly emphasizes it as characteristic of the office:

---

[48] Polyb. 3.106.2–9, 107.6–7, describing how Servilius and Atilius, Proconsuls now, continued to command the field armies in the spring of (consular) 217, strictly adhering to "Fabian" strategy.

(10) The consular power is temporarily "removed," for a maximum period of six months; afterwards, the Consuls again assume control of the government: ἔκρινε τὴν μὲν ὑπατικὴν ἐξουσίαν ἀνελεῖν κατὰ τὸ παρόν...χρόνου δ' εἶναι μέτρον τῇ νέᾳ ἀρχῇ μῆνας ἕξ, μετὰ δὲ τὴν ἑξάμηνον αὖθις ἄρχειν τοὺς ὑπάτους (5.70.1-2).

(11) The Consuls and all others holding public office are to lay down their powers: τοὺς τότε ὑπατεύοντας ἀποθέσθαι τὴν ἐξουσίαν, καὶ εἴ τις ἄλλος ἀρχήν τινα εἶχεν ἢ πραγμάτων τινῶν κοινῶν ἐπιμέλειαν (5.70.4).

(12) The Consul Q. Cloelius, having named his colleague, T. Larcius, Dictator, promptly abdicates his office: ἀναστὰς ὁ Κλοίλιος ἀναγορεύει τε αὐτόν...καὶ τὴν ὑπατείαν αὐτὸς ἐξόμνυται (5.72.3).

(13) Having completed his task, Larcius the Dictator sees to the appointment of new Consuls, then abdicates his office; clearly, Dionysios does not envisage him and his (former) colleague resuming their consulship: ὑπάτους ἀποδείξας ἀπέθετο τὴν ἀρχήν (5.77.1).

(14) Frequently it has been necessary to eliminate the lawful offices and place the entire government under a single man: πολλάκις ἀναγκασθείσης τῆς πόλεως **καταλῦσαι** τὰς νομίμους ἀρχὰς καὶ πάντα ποιῆσαι τὰ πράγματα ὑφ' ἑνί (5.77.2).

(15) The same view recurs in a much later context, on recalling Cincinnatus' dictatorship in a speech directed against the Decemvirs: "Gathering in the Curia at midnight, you appointed a single office to exercise supreme command in war and peace, and in doing so you dissolved all the other offices" (περὶ μέσας νύκτας εἰς τὸ βουλευτήριον συνελθόντες ἀρχὴν ἀπεδείξατε μίαν αὐτοκράτορα πολέμου καὶ εἰρήνης, ἁπάσας τὰς ἄλλας **καταλύσαντες** ἀρχάς, 11.20.3). Yet in his actual Cincinnatus narrative, Dionysios had both Consuls remain in office (below, #16).

The first of these passages (#10) certainly, and two more (##14, 15) possibly, could be taken as implying a temporary cessation of Consuls and other magistrates, along the lines of Polybios. But another two (##12, 13) expressly speak of termination through abdication, and while #11 in isolation could be understood either way, depending on whether ἐξουσία is to mean "power" or "office," its contextual proximity to ##12 and 13 renders abdication more likely by far. It would require a considerable stretch—much more so than Plutarch's in ##7 and 8—to trace that notion to Polybios' curt notice, or, for that matter, his longer treatise on the magistracies. Not that Dionysios was entirely consistent:

(16) Both Consuls stay in office under Cincinnatus as Dictator; the unfortunate L. Minucius is not forced to resign until the crisis has been resolved (ταῦτα πράξας καὶ τὸν Μηνύκιον ἀποθέσθαι τὴν ἀρχὴν ἀναγκάσας ἀνέστρεψεν εἰς τὴν Ῥώμην (10.25.2), and C. Nautius triumphs well after the Dictator has abdicated (10.25.4).

The notion that all magistrates are removed from office—as opposed to losing the ability to independently exercise their powers—under a Dictator is not Polybian, as we have seen; and although a careless use of his work might have led others to such a misconception, all the completely unambiguous expressions of that view other than Appian's—which is to say, Dionysios at ##11, 12, and 13—occur in contexts that cannot be reduced to Polybios' extant work. Another source, perhaps more directly concerned with the origins of the dictatorship, appears probable. That source, unfortunately, may still have been Polybios: his lost *"archaeologia"* of how Rome's constitution developed, from the kings to the decemvirate,[49] likely enough included the establishment of the dictatorship, and a fuller discussion of the office could have been found in his treatise of Roman institutions, if not directly in the *"archaeologia."* Termination would still result from a misunderstanding of what Polybios meant; and perhaps of something else. Unless Dionysios made it up out of whole cloth, one of his sources must have reported the abdication of Q. Cloelius the Consul in 498 V after he named his colleague Dictator; but that source need not have presented it as a requirement of the dictatorship. That may have been the rhetorician's own inference, "guided" by what he thought he had read in Polybios.

Nor—it must at last be noted—is the Polybian view entirely absent from the Latin evidence. In 390 V, Camillus stops payment of ransom, agreed to by Q. Sulpicius the Military Tribune, to Brennus and the Gauls: *cum illi* (sc. *Galli*) *renitentes pactos dicerent sese, negat eam pactionem ratam esse quae postquam ipse dictator creatus esset iniussu suo ab inferioris iuris magistratu facta esset* (Livy 5.49.2). If, with a Dictator in office, anything done by another magistrate—and in this case, one *consulari potestate*—can be deemed *eo ipso* invalid unless approved or confirmed by the Dictator,[50] such other magistrate can obviously not be seen as being able to exercise his regular powers independently. If full weight is allowed to *omne imperium*, Cicero's comment that, during a dictatorship, all public power was to be concentrated in the hands of a single man (*Rep.* 1.63, *sine collega omne imperium nostri penes singulos esse voluerunt*) supports precisely such a view. A closer look at the nature of the office held by that single man will come next.

3.3 The Nature of the Office

The appointment of a Dictator threw the Consuls and all lower magistrates (save Tribunes of the Plebs) into a state of suspension. What were the terms that

---

[49] Polyb. 6.11a; see Walbank *HCP* 2: 663–673.
[50] Cf. Plut. *Cam.* 29.3 (above, #4). Note how in Plutarch this turns into an "absence of other magistrates" under a Dictator. Livy's statement is too sweeping to be taken for merely a florid assertion of the right to *intercessio vi maioris imperii* here. Ogilvie 738 ascribes it to "the spirit of legalistic quibbling...characteristic of Sullan annalists." Not likely, as the idea that the dictatorship "put all other magistracies into suspension" is as old, at least, as Polybios.

governed its appointment and duration, and what precisely were its powers compared to those of the Consuls?

3.3.1 Peculiar Aspects

Mommsen saw in the Dictator nothing but a *collega maior* of the Consuls, just as the Praetor was a *collega minor*. Corey Brennan's discussion has rendered that view untenable; the Dictator, for one, was not elected—unlike the Praetor—under the same auspices as the Consul, and his complete absence from Messalla's discussion of the *auspicia maxima* (those of Consuls, Praetors, and Censors) and their relation to, and interaction with, each other precludes any notion of collegiality.[51] Instead, Brennan defined the Dictator's *imperium* in terms diametrically opposite to Mommsen's: rather than being of the same kind as the Consul's, though *maius*, it was not technically *maius* but somehow "different"; indeed, the Dictator's powers were in no way greater than the Consuls'.[52]

That latter contention, however, runs into difficulties of its own. It rests on two lines of reasoning. First, an axiomatic assertion: "The consul had the *imperium* and *auspicia* of the kings of Rome; logically, the dictator could have no more"— but where is it written that there can be no power greater than the King's? Livy, for one, certainly thought that the Dictator's power could be understood in precisely that fashion: the Dictator's *imperium* is supreme, and the Consuls—the regal power!—do obey him (*cum summum imperium dictatoris sit pareantque ei consules, regia potestas*, 8.32.3).[53]

Next, Cicero's provision in *Leg.* 3.9, *oenus ne amplius sex menses...idem iuris quod duo consules teneto, isque ave sinistra dictus populi magister esto*. Brennan, by implication of his argument, takes *idem iuris...teneto* for synonymous with *aequum* (sive *par*) *imperium...habeto*, and concludes that the Dictator had twenty-four lictors "to mark him clearly as the full equal of a consular pair, with the ability to give either consul orders"; yet, by the same token, he supposedly could not override both Consuls together. This contradicts everything we know about the Roman concept of *imperium*, which was never cumulative, but indivisible in the person of every holder: each Consul exercised the *imperium consulare* in full, not just one half of it, and two Praetors together possessed no more of *imperium* than did a third one by himself, alone. Nor did two Consuls have

---

[51] *StR* 2.1: 155: "Demnach hat der Dictator eine gleichartige, aber stärkere Amtsgewalt als der Consul und der Prätor." *Contra* Brennan *PRR* 1: 41; cf. Messalla *apud* Gell. 13.15.4.

[52] *PRR* 1: 39–43; but note 1: 56, where it is allowed that the Dictator's powers are "effectively superior." On what follows, cf. Konrad 2003.

[53] For Livy's view that the *consularis potestas* did constitute the *regia potestas* limited in time rather than scope, see 2.1.7–8; 4.2.8, 3.9; it was shared by Cicero: *uti consules potestatem haberent tempore dumtaxat annuam, genere ipso ac iure regiam* (*Rep.* 2.56). See Oakley 2: 720–721.

more power, in a quantitative sense, than one. Hence Cicero's contrasting *oenus* (sc. *populi magister*) with *duo consules* cannot mean, as Brennan would have it, that the Dictator had "*idem iuris*, 'just as much power' as the two consuls, but no more": either he held as much power as one Consul, in which case he could not "give orders" to any magistrate of that rank (being his equal), or he possessed more power than one Consul, in which case he could "give orders" to (which is to say, override, rescind, or forbid) any number of Consuls simultaneously—but such "more" power could not derive from a cumulation of the two Consuls' individual powers, their sum being no greater than each of its components. It is not too difficult to see what Cicero had in mind: his *magister populi* had "the same legal status" as the two Consuls not in a quantitative sense, but in a qualitative one. In other words, he took their place.[54]

Almost certainly, Claudius Caesar furnished us with a clue (*ILS* 212) when he noted that in times of severe emergency, military or domestic, the ancients had found the Dictator's *imperium* to be *valentius*—"stronger, more powerful, more effective"—than the Consuls': *dictaturae hoc ipso consulari imperium valentius repertum apud maiores nostros, quo in a[s]perioribus bellis aut in civili motu difficiliore uterentur.* (Claudius' phrasing is curiously reminiscent of Cicero's, *Leg.* 3.9: *ast quando duellum gravius discordiaeve civium escunt.*) Brennan doubted that Claudius here alluded to a characteristic of the Dictator's constitutional position, and preferred to ascribe *valentius* to the emperor's "desire for literary variation."[55] There is no good reason to think so. The connotation of superior force in general inherent in *valere*, and of special ability to achieve a desired objective in particular, eminently fits the Dictator's function as an extraordinary official appointed to deal with extraordinary situations. Nor does the word lack religious overtones; witness the *faustum omen* associated with the name "Valerius," especially in a military context.[56]

Long ago, in a study that has drawn scant attention, Cohen conclusively demonstrated how the Dictator was more than simply an exalted version of the Consul: he possessed a religious, near-magical dimension altogether lacking in

---

[54] Note also the immediately following sentence: *ast quando consulis magisterve populi nec erunt.* This clearly expects a situation in which there were Consuls, but no Dictator—or a Dictator, but no Consuls. Cicero makes his view clear enough in *Rep.* 1.63: *gravioribus vero bellis etiam sine collega omne imperium nostri penes singulos esse voluerunt, quorum ipsum nomen vim summae potestatis indicat. nam dictator quidem ab eo appellatur quia dicitur, sed in nostris libris vides eum, Laeli, magistrum populi appellari.* This hardly agrees with giving the Dictator more power than one Consul, but not more than both together. Vervaet 2014: 11 would define the difference in the *imperium* of Dictator, Consul, and Praetor as "'quantitative' rather than 'qualitative' in that all *imperia* were essentially of the same kind of higher official authority but the *dictatorium imperium* was twice as strong as the *consulare imperium*," and the latter "twice as strong as the *praetorium imperium*." Other than using the terms "quantitative" and "qualitative" in the opposite sense as I do above, and aside from the unhelpful notion of "twice as strong"—"stronger" is all that is attested by the evidence, and needed—this is essentially correct.
[55] *PRR* 1: 41.   [56] Cic. *Scaur.* 29–30; Schol. Ambros. ad *Scaur.* 274St.

the latter.[57] The Dictator's *edictum* is said to be *pro numine semper observatum*, his *imperium* described as *sua vi vehemens*,[58] and the office itself was thought to instill an elementary, visceral fear never associated with the consulship. Repeatedly the enemy withdraws, or sues for peace, or commits suicide, on the mere news that Rome has named a Dictator: *tantus eius magistratus terror erat*.[59] That such *ingens terror* was also felt at home could be explained, perhaps, by the Dictator's freedom from *provocatio* and tribunician veto; but it is out of the question that this constitutional peculiarity should be of concern to non-Romans, or that the Romans should expect it to cause fright and panic among others. It was a quality associated with the Dictator, and with him alone—not with any other magistrate.[60]

3.3.2 What's in a Name?

The title of the office may provide illumination. No other magistracy's appellation (with the exception, perhaps, of *consul*) has defied understanding as tenaciously as the word *dictator*. The earliest surviving etymology has it derive from *dicere*: *hinc dictator magister populi, quod is a consule debet dici* (Varro *LL* 6.61), and

---

[57] Cohen 304–318. Note the prohibition against riding on a horse (Livy 23.14.2; Plut. *Fab.* 4.1–2; Zonar. 7.13), a taboo the Dictator shares with the Flamen Dialis (Fest. 71L; Pliny *NH* 28.146; Plut. *QR* 40 = *Mor.* 274C; Gell. 10.15.3; Serv. auct. ad *Aen.* 8.552). Attempts to find a "practical" or "rational" explanation for this—e.g., the dictator as *magister populi* has his proper place with the infantry (Mommsen *StR* 2.1: 159; more recently Valditara 1988), or is barred from horseback to set him apart from the *rex*, who always led in that fashion (Wittmann *StO* 675–676)—are fundamentally misguided. (So is Wilson's argument, 179–183, based on Zonaras' confused notice at 7.13, that the prohibition applied only to the Dictator riding on a horse within the City: why in the world would he want to?) The *populus* at all times comprised the *equites*, and we have no right to act as if *magister populi* were a synonym for *magister peditum*—unless the appellation *magister populi* goes back to a time before the introduction of cavalry, in which case the prohibition can only be understood as a religious taboo—or, better, protection—against a dangerous (though useful, even necessary) *res nova*, akin to the Dialis' taboo against iron shears (Serv. ad *Aen.* 1.448; Latte 202–203, 402–403). As for Wittmann's *rex*, we know of course nothing at all about his manner of leading the army (assuming he did lead it, which is perhaps not as certain an assumption as scholars like to think: Voci 77–78), and Romulus held his triumphs on foot (Plut. *Rom.* 16.7–8, adducing compelling evidence against Dion. Hal. 2.34.2). Philipp's observation (107–109) that there was no ritual prohibition, for the Dictator and the Dialis, against riding in a horse-drawn chariot may come as close to a convincing explanation as we can hope: chariot warfare is older than cavalry, and riding in a chariot is more distinguished than on a horse; it remained at all times a rare privilege of certain officials on certain occasions—the *imperator* triumphant, the *rex sacrorum*, the *flamines*, and the Vestal Virgins (*StR* 1: 393–396). Cf. Sini 422–423.
[58] Livy 2.30.4; 8.43.2.   [59] Livy 6.28.4; cf. 2.18.9; 7.20.1; 9.26.7; Diod. 19.76.3–5.
[60] Oakley *CL* 1: 617 notes that "the appearance of this notion in D. H. [5.75.2–3; 6.39.2] shows that it was not a fantasy of L[ivy]'s own invention, but rooted in the annalistic tradition." But his explanation of this "mystique" as something having accrued to the dictatorship during its long period of disuse, and that "the experience of Sulla and Caesar sharpened the annalistic portrait of the office," lacks conviction; and in any case it is hard to see how Sulla's and Caesar's dictatorships could have given rise to the notion that this office struck terror into the minds of Rome's foreign enemies. If anything, the annalistic portrait seems determined to bring out the contrast between the "classic" dictatorship and its "later counterfeit form" (the phrase is Ridley's, 2013: 46).

dictator quidem ab eo appellatur quia dicitur (Cic. *Rep.* 1.63). Already Varro combines this with a second, albeit subordinate, explanation: *dictator quod a consule dicebatur, cui dicto audientes omnes essent* (*LL* 5.82). In a similar vein, and clearly following a Latin source, Dionysios and Plutarch connect the title to *edicere/edictum*, on the grounds that the Dictator could issue public ordinances ("edicts") solely according to his own judgment; both offer the manner of appointment, by being "named," as an alternative.[61] Priscian simply has *dictator…a dictando* (*Inst.* 8.78 = *GramLat* 2: 432.25).

As Mommsen noted, nothing suggests that the Dictator was in any special way associated with issuing edicts—no more so than other magistrates with *imperium*.[62] Varro's derivation from *dicere* is generally rejected as absurd, seeing how the title, in that case, ought to be *dict(at)us*, not *dictator*. It has found endorsement, however, by no less an authority than Rix: being "named" rather than elected was indeed a feature unique to the Dictator, and a hypothetical appellation (*praetor*) *dictatus* could have been transformed to *dictator* by analogy with *nomina agentis* such as *praetor, quaestor*, or *imperator*.[63] But Rix was unable to offer a Latin parallel for such an "Umgestaltung," and his solution lacks conviction. Against the derivation from *dictare* (in the sense of *cui dicto audientes omnes essent*), finally, speaks the scant evidence that this verb expressed the notion of giving orders.

And yet *dictare* holds the answer. As Rix points out, the word in origin cannot have had the narrow meaning of "dictate, recite" in which it is mostly attested; it simply is an intensive variant of *dicere*, just as *captare/capere, iactare/iacere, tractare/trahere*. Now, students of Roman law and religion well know the magical properties of the spoken word, the elementary importance of the correctly recited formula or prayer. Varro (*LL* 6.30) sets out the fundamental concept:

> dies nefasti, per quos dies nefas fari praetorem "do dico addico": itaque non potest agi: necesse est aliquo uti verbo, cum lege quid peragitur. quod si tum imprudens id verbum emisit ac quem manumisit, ille nihilo minus est liber, sed vitio, ut magistratus vitio creatus nihilo setius magistratus.

If on a *dies nefastus* the Praetor, carelessly or by mistake, speaks the ritually prescribed words, the legal business thus transacted is valid nonetheless. The Consul is elected by the People, but what made a man a magistrate was not the People's vote: only the formal announcement (*renuntiatio*) by the presiding officer lends legal force and effect to the assembly's vote.[64] This held true even if the election occurred under a ritual augural flaw (*vitium*). "The formula '*do dico addico*' was

---

[61] Dion. Hal. 5.37.1; Plut. *Marc.* 24.12.   [62] *StR* 2.1: 144 n. 2.   [63] Rix 90–92.
[64] Botsford 183–184; Magdelain 1968: 34; Rüpke 1990: 50–51 = 2019: 50–52. In the strictest sense, one might say that all magistrates were appointed, not elected; the People prescribed to the Consul whom to appoint as his successor, but it was the formal announcement, hence appointment, not the prescription, that legally created the new magistrate: Mommsen *StR* 1: 212–214, 578–581; 3.1:

more powerful than the sacral division of time";[65] the announcement *L. Titius consul factus est* overrode the fact that Iuppiter had not given his permission to hold elections on that day. In augury throughout, mere observation of a sign by a third party is of no consequence to its intended recipient: to have effect, it must be properly and formally reported; and even a false report, if properly made, becomes as valid and effective as if the sign had truly been observed.[66] The spoken word creates reality.[67]

Here, surely, is where we must seek both the origin of the name *dictator* and the reason for his being "named." He is "the One Who Speaks": his word is more powerful than any obstacle or limit, more efficacious than any word spoken by anybody else; it overcomes all opposition and resistance, at home and abroad. His word is strong enough to shape reality in favor of the Roman People.

3.3.3 Dic(t)ator Latinus

Yet the office was originally called *magister populi*. We know that appellation was used in early days, and always in the *libri augurales* (Cic. *Rep.* 1.63);[68] we do not know for a fact that it was older than the term *dictator*, or that at any time it was used exclusively. We also know that, in a number of Latin communities, a *dictator* served as the annual chief magistrate, often associated with religious functions, but nowhere resembling the Roman emergency official; occasionally, the title occurs together with other (lower) officials, but never with a *magister equitum*.[69] Licinius Macer believed that at Alba after the death of Numitor, an annual magistrate

---

346–347; Meyer 1961: 66–67, noting that the common Latin term for electing magistrates, *creare*, denotes a personal act of bringing into existence; cf. Philipp 106.

[65] Linderski *AL* 2162–2164, esp. nn. 48–49.

[66] Linderski *AL* 2206–2207. In her sustained—and stimulating—attempt to call into question the augural principle stated here, Driediger-Murphy 2019, esp. 51–126 (and 2018 *passim*), although aware of the Varro passage (121 n. 184), does not consider its implications for the realm of augury.

[67] See Latte 62, 198. The idea is not limited to Rome. In making a persuasive case for deriving *censor/censere* from the Indo-European root *$\widetilde{k}$ens-* "wirkungsmächtig sprechen," "to speak so that the spoken word has consequences," Rix 94–96 adduces perhaps the most famous instance of them all— Genesis 1:3. God creates the world not by doing anything, but by speaking.

[68] Cic. *Rep.* 1.63, *nam dictator quidem ab eo appellatur quia dicitur, sed in nostris libris vides eum, Laeli, magistrum populi appellari*; Sen. *Ep.* 108.31, *notat* (sc. Cicero) *eum quem nos dictatorem dicimus et in historia ita nominari legimus, apud antiquos magistrum populi vocatum. hodieque id extat in auguralibus libris et testimonium est quod qui ab illo nominatur magister equitum est.*

[69] Dictators are found in Aricia, Fidenae, Lanuvium, Nomentum, Tusculum, as well as at the eventual *municipia* Caere and Fabrateria Vetus: see W. Liebenam "Dictator" *RE* 5.1 (1903) 370–390 at 389. Rudolph 7–35 rejected the existence of original Latin *dictatores* out of hand, arguing that officials of that title—with purely religious functions—were imposed by Rome on the *municipia* created after the dissolution of the League in 338, which local titulature in the course of the third century came to be adopted for the Roman *magister populi*, first when representing Rome at the Latin Festival, and eventually across the board; against this, see Ridley 1979: 307. At Tusculum, the Dictator may have exercised military command (Ridley 1979: 307), if *dux uterque suos adhortatur* (Livy 3.18.7) may be taken to refer to L. Mamilius, *Tusculi tum dictator* (3.18.2).

called *dictator* replaced the King while holding the same power as the latter, and that the Romans derived their dictatorship from Alba.[70]

There is also some—albeit tenuous—evidence that *dictator* at some point was the title of a Latin federal official. Priscian (*Inst.* 4.21 = *GramLat* 2: 129.11-15) preserves a fragment of Cato's *Origines* (*HRR* F 58/*FRHist* 5 F 36): *lucum Dianium in nemore Aricino Egerius Laevius Tusculanus dedicavit dictator Latinus*; Festus probably refers to the same event (*Manius Eger<ius lucum> Nemorensem Dianae consecravit*, 128.15-16L). This has been taken to mean that the Latin League was headed by an (annual) magistrate called *dictator*, with civil, religious, and— especially—military authority who eventually may have stood model for the Roman Dictator.[71] But all we know is that Egerius Laevius (or perhaps Baebius, as in some codices) dedicated the grove at Aricia, and that, although a citizen of Tusculum, he did so in his capacity as *dictator Latinus*. It follows that this was a federal office, but Cato's note tells us nothing about its nature: the occasion reported manifestly does not imply military functions.

Nor is *dictator* entirely certain as Egerius' title: one of Priscian's codices (R = Parisinus 7496) has *dicator*. The same word occurs in an inscription from the third century BC, where at Spoletium we encounter a *dicator* empowered to levy fines on persons violating a sacred grove: *honce loucom ne qui[s] violatod neque exvehito neque exferto quod louci siet…sei quis scies violasit dolo malo Iovei bovid piaclum datod et a(sses) CCC moltai suntod. eius piacli moltaique dicator[ei] moltai suntod.*[72] Mommsen wanted to see in this *dicator* not an official title but simply a reference to the dedicating magistrate and his successors in office. But in a general prohibition such as this, it would be highly unusual to focus on one specific dedicator, and if *dicator* indeed merely denotes the person dedicating the grove, then nothing in the wording implies that the power to levy fines devolves on

---

[70] Dion. Hal. 5.74.4 = Macer *HRR* F 10/*FRHist* 27 F 15; cf. Plut. *Rom.* 27.1. In historical times, a *dictator Albanus* still performed priestly duties connected with the Alban cults: *CIL* 6.2161 = *ILS* 4955; Mommsen *StR* 2.1: 171. It is doubtful that Alba Longa ever existed in the form of an actual *urbs*, or city-state: Grandazzi 1986 and 2008; Cornell 1995: 55, 70-72. But the persistence of religious institutions specifically tied to that name, rather than the Latin one—e.g., the *pontifices Albani* (*CIL* 6.2168 = *ILS* 4956; 9.1595 = *ILS* 1345; 14.2264 = *ILS* 887), *salii Albani* or *arcis Albanae* (*CIL* 6.2170, 2171 = *ILS* 5010; 14.2947 = *ILS* 2749), *virgines Vestales arcis Albanae* (*CIL* 6.2172 = *ILS* 5011) or *virgines Albanae* (Ascon. *Mil.* 36.23St; *CIL* 14.2410 = *ILS* 6190)—is difficult to explain unless the Iron Age villages in the Alban Hills did at some time constitute an organized community.

[71] E.g., Soltau 1914: 359-368, claiming for the *dictator Albanus* "unbeschränktes Befehlsrecht über das Bundesaufgebot" and arguing that, until the end of the Latin League in 338, Roman Dictators were only appointed as federal commanders, for wars jointly conducted by Rome and the League; similarly Momigliano 31-34 ("la dittatura si introduceva così in Roma non già come magistratura civica, ma come magistratura federale"). Alföldi 36-37, 42-43 accepts a Latin federal Dictator, chosen by the member states in rotation, on which office the local *dictatores* in various Latin towns as well as the Roman one were modelled; the latter, though, like his Latin counterparts, originated as an annual magistrate that replaced the King. Ridley 1979: 306-308 (cf. 2013: 34) likewise favors the Latin League Dictator as model for the Roman, adding the intriguing argument that Livy (2.18.3-4) hints, by implication, at just such a connection.

[72] *CIL* 11.4766 = *ILS* 4911; for the date, Buecheler 627.

anyone else. Surely the natural assumption should be that *dicator* is the title of a local magistrate.⁷³ The question is: What was this magistracy?

Instinsky followed Mommsen in seeing in the *dicator* the dedicating magistrate and his successors, on which basis he preferred the reading in Priscian's *R* as the correct one: the *dicator* (not *dictator*) *Latinus* Egerius Laevius was a Latin federal official, albeit not a regular one, but named specifically for the purpose of dedicating the grove at Aricia.⁷⁴ Adducing against this view, however, multiple examples from both Greek and Latin glossaries that equate δικάτωρ/*dicator* with δικτάτωρ/*dictator*, Buecheler and Mazzarino have made a strong case that *dicator* represents a linguistic variant of *dictator*, not a separate institution.⁷⁵

Whichever form one accepts for Egerius Laevius, it will be prudent to remain skeptical about the notion of a Dictator as the regular commander of Latin League forces. Without exception, the unambiguous references to the Latin federal military command describe it as a dual magistracy called *praetores* as far back as the days of King Tullus.⁷⁶ On the other hand, there is no reason to avoid the clear implication of Cato's testimony: there existed a *dic(t)ator* as a federal magistrate of the League, responsible for religious matters (and perhaps civil ones, if such there were), be it as a permanent office or one filled only for specific occasions.⁷⁷

The apparent variation of *dicator/dictator* as an appellation for the same office would reinforce the view that the official thus named received his title from performing acts of speaking. In a largely preliterate society, such acts could encompass virtually anything to do with government and religion. Any directive or ritual would, of necessity, be spoken; but it is the act of speaking—and speaking it exactly in the correct form—that gives it effect.⁷⁸ Therein lies the task, and the power, of the magistrate, and therefore he can be known simply as *dic(t)ator*, the

---

⁷³ Mommsen 1899: 811 n. 5 ("vermuthlich der dedicirende Magistrat einschliesslich seiner Amtsnachfolger"; *contra* Dessau *ILS* 4911 ("sed tamen hic videtur significari magistratus Spoletinus") and Buecheler 627–628, pointing to the similar inscription from Luceria (*CIL* 9.782 = *ILS* 4912, *in hoce loucarid stircus ne [qu]is fundatid neve cadaver proiecitad neve parentatid...seive mag[li]steratus volet moltare [li]cetod*) which clearly enables the (any?) magistrate to levy the fine; cf. also Instinsky 119–120.

⁷⁴ Instinsky 120–122; cf. Rudolph 12–13.

⁷⁵ Buecheler 627–628; Mazzarino 426–427; *contra* Jordan 26–27, arguing for *dicator* = *curator luci*, which Instinsky (121) has shown to be untenable.

⁷⁶ Dion. Hal. 3.34.3, αἱροῦνται δύο στρατηγοὺς αὐτοκράτορας, and thus again in the first years of the Republic (5.61.3; 6.4.1), which surely reflects the two *praetores* attested for 340 V by Livy 8.3.9, and more generally by Festus 276.15–277.2L (Chapter 2.4.1); cf. Mommsen *StR* 3.1: 617; Liebenam "Dictator" *RE* 5.1 (1903) 389. Alföldi 37, 43–45, 119–120, suggested that the federal Dictator was replaced at an unknown time (though probably during the fifth century) by two *praetores*. Ridley 1979: 308, although noting that Livy never calls Octav(i)us Mamilius *dictator* (he is *Latinus dux*, 2.19.10, or *imperator Latinus*, 2.20.7), concludes that Mamilius was "obviously dictator of the Latin league." Conceivably that is how Livy saw him, but not Dionysios, who knew of Mamilius and Sextus Tarquin as joint supreme commanders: τούτους γὰρ ἀπέδειξαν στρατηγοὺς αὐτοκράτορας, 5.61.3.

⁷⁷ Cf. Cornell *FRHist* 3: 83.

⁷⁸ Birt 201–202. On Rome as a preliterate society prior to the third century BC, see Wiseman 1995: 129.

Speaker. If the King—perhaps, yet by no means certainly—was endowed with the same ability, it was for life instead of just a year or a specific task.

We must allow, then, room for the possibility that *dictator* was, in fact, originally a title found both as that of a Latin federal institution and in many, though not necessarily all, Latin communities in which the King had disappeared. One cannot even rule out the possibility that in those towns which did have Kings (attested only, it seems, for Alba and Rome) a *dictator* existed, beside or under the King, to perform acts of speaking which the *rex*, for whatever reason, could not. But (with the possible exception of the federal office) all the attested Latin Dictators have in common that they are regular, annual, and—presumably, after whatever fashion—elected magistrates, which stands in sharp contrast to the Roman variant.[79] The evidence, such as it is, thus points to the conclusion that *dictator* and *magister populi* initially denoted two distinct offices.

3.3.4 *Dictator* and *Magister Populi*

The Roman *magister populi* almost certainly existed already in the Regal Period, as a military commander to serve instead of the King whenever the latter was indisposed, incapable, or for some other reason prevented from taking the field, or conceivably even as the regular actual commander in the presence of the King.[80] Such a position would have been held either permanently, or by appointment for each specific campaign, but hardly on an annual basis. If a similar institution existed in other Latin communities, it is likely that it went by the same title, and improbable that it provided the basis for the annual magistrate called *dictator* that eventually replaced the King. The title *magister populi* is descriptive of the institution's principal function; presumably, so is the Latin *dictator*—the one who speaks and, in so doing, shapes reality.

At Rome, however, institutions underwent a development different from that in many Latin towns. The King was replaced not by a single *dictator* but by two annual magistrates, of equal or unequal collegiality, most likely known until at

---

[79] Ridley 1979: 304.
[80] Meyer 1961: 41–42; Heuß 1982: 437; Giovannini 1984: 19–21; 1993: 88–89; and, for an exhaustive treatment, Valditara 1989. Brennan repeatedly notes the "primitive" character of the dictatorship (*PRR* 1: 40; 2: 599–600) without drawing the logical conclusion that if the "Consuls" (i.e., a dual magistracy under whatever title) date to the beginning of the Republic—as Brennan holds, correctly—an office that is primitive by comparison must necessarily be older, hence go back to the Regal Period. The common assumption that the King exercised direct military command at all times should perhaps not be taken for granted as much as it is: see the cautionary remarks of Voci 77–78 (who, though, thinks of the *tribuni celerum* rather than the *magister populi*). One may note that the term *magister populi*, "master of the people-in-arms," almost exactly corresponds to the Mycenaean *lawagetas*. (That the King held *imperium* need not be doubted; the question is whether he invariably discharged such power in person, or could do so through a stand-in.)

least the mid-fifth century as *iudices* or *praetores*.[81] The *magister populi* survived, though not as the regular military commander (a function assumed, it would seem, by the new chief magistrates): he was called upon to assume command—not merely of the army but the entire State—in a time of crisis. The office thus acquired a function significantly different from the one it had held originally, a function that now included—unlimited—civil authority and the expectation to shape events in favor of the Roman People. The ability—previously attached to the official known as *dictator*—to "speak with effect" would be integral to its new purpose.[82] To make it so, it would be essential that he himself be "spoken," *dictus*, and that this be done under conditions ensuring the most stringent augural correctness, *de nocte silentio*, by night in ritual silence (Livy 8.23.15; 9.38.14); this manner of appointment presumably belonged to the *magister populi* already in regal times, and must continue to be observed unalterably, lest his efficacy be put in jeopardy. As the *iudex* could be called *praetor*, especially in a military context,[83]

---

[81] In the formula used to convene the Centuriate Assembly, the summoning magistrate is called *iudex*: Varro *LL* 6.88, *in commentariis consularibus scriptum sic invenit: qui exercitum imperaturus erit, accenso dicito:* 'C. Calpurni, voca in licium omnes Quirites huc ad me.' *accensus dicit sic:* 'omnes Quirites, in licium visite huc ad iudices.' — 'C. Calpurni,' cos. dicit, 'voca ad conventionem omnes Quirites huc ad me.' *accensus dicit sic:* 'omnes Quirites, ite ad conventionem huc ad iudices.' *dein consul eloquitur ad exercitum:* 'impero qua convenit ad comitia centuriata.' The formula is ancient (Mommsen <IBT>*StR* 2.1: 74–77</IBT>: "seit ältester Zeit unverändert beibehaltene[r] Heroldsruf") and must represent the title in use for the chief magistrate before *praetor* or *consul* became (more) common; since the formula twice specifies that it is the army being summoned, one cannot maintain (with Mommsen, ibid., and others, e.g., *OLD iudex* 1.c.) that *iudex* here emphasizes the magistrate's civil or non-military functions; cf. Yaron 352. Note that even though the summons in the example is ordered by only one Consul, the formula invariably employs the plural *iudices*. Livy knew that the Consuls were also known as *iudices*, but thought it to be a post-decemviral appellation (3.55.11–12); Cicero applied all three terms to the office: *regio imperio duo sunto, iique praeeundo, iudicando, consulendo praetores, iudices, consules appellamino* (*Leg.* 3.8). That *praetor* was in use during the fifth century seems likely enough, but cannot be shown: its appearance in the Twelve Tables remains doubtful (see Crawford et al. *RStat* 2: 557, 719). I do not intend to visit here the interminable debate about the development of the Roman chief magistracy; suffice it to say that I remain unpersuaded by attempts to produce a tripartite chief magistracy centered on a *praetor maximus* (e.g., Bunse; Tietz has now demonstrated that the phrase did not constitute the official title of a specific magistrate), though Bleicken 1981: 278–287 [24–33] offers the perhaps most cogent reasoning against a dual magistracy with *par potestas* prior to the fourth century. For a brief yet incisive argument in favor of the dual magistracy from the beginning, see Giovannini 1984: 19–21, 26–29; 1993: 91–93; Cornell 1995: 226–230; and for a recent sober survey with ample bibliography, Smith 2011.

[82] Wittmann's explanation (*StO* 676–678) of *dictator* as "Einschwörer," the one who recites the "Fahneneid" (*sacramentum*) to be repeated by the soldiers, though ingenious and attractive, runs into the same objection as the derivation from *edicere*: administering the military oath was no more peculiar to the Dictator (as opposed to the Consul) as was the issuing of edicts—unless we postulate a primordial state of affairs in which the *dictator* (not the *rex* or another magistrate) functioned as the sole military commander. In emphasizing the Dictator's connection with speaking *concepta verba*, however, Wittmann has correctly identified the essential element in the magistracy's title.

[83] But see Giovannini 1984: 15–19 and 1993: 90–93, raising serious doubts that *praeire* could ever have had a specifically military connotation, and favoring a derivation of *praetor* from *praeire verbis* (cf. Varro *LL* 5.80, *praetor dictus qui praeiret iure et exercitu*, which can hardly mean "who walks in front of the law"): "il praetor è colui che fa ripetere una formula sacra e solenne 'alla giurisdizione ed all'*exercitus*." This would be no stranger than the—attested—summoning of the *exercitus* by an official known as *iudex* (note 81, above). Then again, it is worth here heeding Daube's observations (2–10) on

so the *magister populi* could now be called *dictator*, without either losing his original appellation in ritual parlance—the *iudices* remained thus in the *commentarii consulares*, and the *magister populi* in the *libri augurales*.[84] Nor does it necessarily follow that the term *dictator* overshadowed *magister populi* from its first republican manifestation; it may have entered common parlance as late as the fourth century, when Dictators came to be named with increasing frequency for special, non-military purposes: first *clavi figendi causa*, in 363 V and again in 331, on numerous occasions to hold elections (352, 351, 350, 349, 335, 327, 321, 306), and once each *feriarum constituendarum causa* (344) and *ludorum faciendorum causa* (322[85]).

One may object that our sources show no awareness of this "speaking-with-effect" aspect of the office. Not consciously, it is true; but neither do they exhibit much conscious awareness of most archaic concepts underlying Roman cult and government. When Varro wrote how the Praetor's saying the magic words *do dico addico* on a *dies nefastus* gave legal force to the matter despite the ritual flaw attached, he surely did not think of it in terms of the spoken word creating reality: he knew the way things worked, not necessarily the reason why. Livy's consistent picture of the Dictator as an office imbued with a degree of terror not quite of this world is credible precisely because it remains unexplained (and not consciously understood) by him: antiquarian speculation or invention would have told us everything.

3.3.5 Imperium Valentius

According to Brennan, the Dictator's *imperium*, rather than being of the same nature as the Consul's, albeit *maius*,[86] was not technically *maius* but of an altogether different kind that caused the Consuls (and all other magistrates) to lose their

---

agent nouns, especially, e.g., the contrast between *spondere* "to promise" and *sponsor* "guarantor, surety"—never used in the sense of "promiser."

[84] The view proposed here owes much to Heuß 1982: 434–450, who envisaged for the earliest Republic a tripartite annual magistracy consisting of *rex* (responsible for religious matters), *magister populi* (military), and *dictator* (civil authority), analogous to the pre-Solonic Athenian set of Basileus, Polemarch, and Archon. The *rex* was soon pushed aside and transformed into a pure priesthood as *rex sacrorum*, while *dictator* and *magister populi* gradually lost their functions over the course of the fifth century to the *tribuni militum*; the *dictator* as an office disappeared altogether, but the *magister populi* survived as the emergency magistrate known in the historical period, and in the process of reinvention absorbed the title of *dictator*. This reconstruction remains unpersuasive in some of its details, and especially in its view of why the *magister populi* should have become known as *dictator*. Heuß (450) thought the ancient appellation cumbersome and outmoded: "Freilich klang sein uralter Titel umständlich und altmodisch. Eine neue Nomenklatur wäre erwünscht gewesen." If *dictator* is understood as argued above, we have an explanation.

[85] According to Livy's main narrative (8.38.1–39.15; cf. Zonar. 7.26), this dictatorship was *rei gerundae causa*; but a different version (8.40; Acta Tr. = InscrItal 13.1: 70–71) ascribed victory and triumph to the Consuls, while the Dictator filled in for the ailing Praetor at the *Ludi Romani*.

[86] Thus Mommsen's view, *StR* 2.1: 155.

powers in the presence of the Dictator; in that sense, it could be termed *valentius*. Wherever the Dictator went, he was the sole magistrate *penes quem fasces*, "and so always had the capacity for independent action"; in consequence, the Consuls' *imperium*, in his presence, "lay dormant," with both of them reduced to the same state simultaneously as each experienced, under normal circumstances, every other month when his colleague held the *fasces*.[87] In principle, this is surely correct. Yet nothing in Claudius' comment compels the notion that the Dictator's *imperium* as such was defined differently from the Consul's: *imperium*, even in the Late Republic, simply was *imperium*; qualifiers such as *maius, minus, consulare*, or *praetorium* did not describe distinct types or kinds of *imperium*, but merely served to regulate precedence among magistrates of different or equal rank. Surely *valentius* falls into the same category; we ought to proceed under the assumption that it describes effect rather than nature. The Dictator's *imperium* was more powerful than the Consul's not because it belonged to a different kind; indeed, no source suggests that the Romans had any concept of such a difference, let alone a word for it.[88] (Even the term *valentius* occurs just once, in Claudius' address.) What rendered the Dictator's *imperium* more "effective" was something else, abundantly attested in the sources: the peculiar nature of the dictatorship.[89]

Alone among magistrates, the Dictator could be expected to cause a turn of events in favor of the Roman People merely by being *dictator*; alone among magistrates, he not only lacked a colleague but effected the cessation of all other offices (save the Tribunes of the Plebs, of course) as independent agents. Ordering the Consul to appear before the Dictator without lictors and insignia did not cause this cessation: it simply gave visible expression to it. As we have seen, an incumbent magistrate who appeared in public without his lictors or insignia remained a magistrate; but the gesture signalled that he was not going to exercise his powers for the time being, and that his actions while in such a state of "undress" were to be seen as those of a *privatus*, not *pro magistratu*. The Consul could forbid a Praetor to exercise the powers of his office (*vetari quicquam agere pro magistratu*) and thus effectively suspend him, or deprive him of his insignia by having his curule chair smashed, or *toga praetexta* ripped: but all attested instances of this kind represent disciplinary measures against Praetors who had treated the Consul with disrespect, or otherwise defied higher authority.[90] Yet we have no evidence that the Consul could order the Praetor to approach him without lictors, let alone did so as a matter of routine ceremonial, and when Fabius ordered Servilius to appear before him in such fashion in 217, it is out of the question that he intended it to signal punishment or humiliation for some

---

[87] Brennan *PRR* 1: 38–43, esp. 41 ("…we ought to regard the dictator's powers as the same as the consuls', but different") and 42 (as quoted in text).
[88] I owe this caveat to Jeffrey Tatum.   [89] Similarly already Lange *RA* 1: 636–637.
[90] Dio 36.41.2; 42.23.3; Auct. *De vir. ill.* 72.6; Mommsen *StR* 1: 262.

infraction.⁹¹ Hence the relation of the Consul to the Dictator was different in character from that of the Praetor to the Consul.

These observations confirm—paradoxically, at first glance—Brennan's view that the Dictator did not possess an *imperium maius* vis-à-vis the Consul in the same sense as the latter's *imperium* was *maius* compared to that of the Praetor: otherwise, there would be no need to make the Consuls dismiss their lictors. Even with their *fasces*, they would not be able to oppose the Dictator any more than the Praetors were able to oppose the Consul. Brennan likened the relationship between Consul and Dictator to that between the Consul "not in charge" and his colleague *penes quem fasces*, while emphasizing—correctly—that the Dictator was not a colleague, *maior* or otherwise, of the Consul: hence the latter was unable to obstruct him.⁹² Yet the Consul holding the *fasces* could not order his colleague to appear before him without his lictors (or other insignia): the Dictator could. Nor could the Consul "in charge" remove the other Consul from command of an army, and assign him a different military task instead: the Dictator could, and did.⁹³ Not only was the relation between Consul and Dictator different from that between Praetor and Consul; it also differed from that between the Consul holding the *fasces* and his colleague. From all we have seen concerning the presence of lictors, it follows that when facing the Dictator without lictors, the Consuls stood on the same footing, essentially, with regard to him as a private citizen stood with regard to the Consul. (Plutarch's καὶ τὰ παράσημα τῆς ἀρχῆς ἀποθέμενον ἰδιώτην ἀπαντᾶν, *Fab*. 4.3, is not far off the mark.) A Consul could not issue a direct order to the Praetor: the latter, although subordinate to the Consul, held his powers, including his auspices, directly from Iuppiter and the People, and was answerable to them independently for all his actions. In consequence, the Consul could make the Praetor do something against his will only by forbidding him, *vi maioris imperii*, to do the thing he wanted to.⁹⁴ But against a Dictator, the Consuls were not in a position to freely exercise the powers of their office, and consequently could not be held responsible for carrying out his orders: he even had no need to couch those in the language of prohibition.

---

⁹¹ *Contra* Wilson 178 with n. 76, who sees Fabius' "humiliation of Servilius" as part of a "smear campaign" aimed at discrediting "the previous consuls for having neglected their religious duties"; but the evidence adduced (Livy 22.9; Plut. *Fab*. 4.4–5.1) exclusively concerns Flaminius, with not a hint of criticism directed at Servilius.

⁹² *PRR* 1: 42–43.

⁹³ Witness Fabius' reassignment of Servilius Geminus in 217, from commanding the army to overseeing the protection of the City and making preparations against an invasion of Italy by sea (Polyb. 3.88.8; Livy 22.11.7). There is nothing to support Drogula's claim (2015: 174) that "Livy makes clear that Geminus received his naval *provincia* from the state, and not from the dictator." From the City, a letter was delivered—clearly addressed to the Dictator, not the Consul—with reports of Punic naval activity near Ostia (22.11.6); *itaque exemplo consul Ostiam proficisci iussus eqs.*: "in consequence (*itaque*), the Consul was ordered immediately to proceed to Ostia." In this context, *itaque...iussus* can only refer to Fabius as the one giving the order: it was not contained in the letter from Rome.

⁹⁴ Mommsen *StR* 1: 258 n. 2; and see Chapter 6.6.2 with note 103.

As Brennan notes, Servilius in 217 did not lose his lictors the moment Fabius assumed office as Dictator: that happened only later, when they met in person, and only at the Dictator's express orders.[95] It is the Dictator's actual presence, not merely his existence, that matters: wherever he goes, all other magistrates' *imperia* are in abeyance. In this context, it is unfortunate that Messalla's treatment of magistrates' *auspicia*, as preserved in Gellius (13.15.4), omits the Dictator. The reason is probably not, as Brennan entertained, that Dictator and Magister Equitum were not considered "proper magistrates" in augural parlance; it is difficult to see how an official called *magister* (be it *populi* or *equitum*) could not be *magistratus*—an obvious abstraction of the former.[96] Gellius quoted the passage to explain the distinction between *magistratus maiores* and *minores*, but this is incidental to Messalla's disquisition, which concerns itself with the auspices "of the Patricians": *patriciorum auspicia in duas sunt divisa potestates; maxima sunt consulum, praetorum, censorum...reliquorum magistratuum minora sunt auspicia*. Presumably, Messalla—if he thought it necessary to discuss them at all—treated the auspices of the Dictator in a passage nearby,[97] as well as those of another official who undoubtedly possessed the *patriciorum auspicia maxima*—the Interrex. Now Messalla explains at length how the auspices of Consuls and Praetors interact with each other (all of them being colleagues), prevailing or overriding as the case may be, but not with those of the Censors, the latter not being colleagues of the former (*neque consules aut praetores censoribus neque censores consulibus aut praetoribus turbant aut retinent auspicia*). Hence, within the group of *auspicia maxima*, the relative strength of auspices affects only those who are colleagues within the same office: the Consuls' take precedence over those of the Praetors, but have no effect on those of the Censors, and vice versa (*at censores inter se, rursus praetores consulesque inter se et vitiant et obtinent*). The separate nature of the Censors' auspices, though *maxima*, is further indicated by the fact that, unlike all other patrician magistrates, Censors upon election are confirmed by a *lex centuriata* instead of a *lex curiata* (Cic. *LegAgr* 2.26). Like Consul and Praetor, but unlike the Censors, the Dictator requires a *lex curiata* (as attested explicitly by Livy 9.38.15); he is no one's colleague, but named directly by the Consul with the Consul's own auspices. It stands to reason that the Dictator's auspices cannot fall into a category separate from those of the Consuls, as opposed to the Censors' auspices.[98] In other words, the auspices of the Dictator are of the same nature as

---

[95] *PRR* 1: 263 n. 80.
[96] *PRR* 1: 41, adding—in fairness—that "one should not push this negative argument too far." Against the notion, Coli 1951: 12 n. 41: "il dittatore è sempre e soltanto un magistrato (*magister!*)."
[97] Cf. Badian 1990: 465 n. 16.
[98] "The dictator (like the consul) had the regal *auspicia*, yet did not have to fear interference from a consul. The dictator's auspices were incommensurable with those of the consul. The dictator should not have been a colleague of the consuls, since he was not created under the same auspices, that is, in the Centuriate Assembly" (Brennan *PRR* 2: 599–600). This is simply muddled. If both the Dictator and the Consul had the regal *auspicia*, they must have been of the same nature, and therefore not

the *auspicia consulum*.⁹⁹ But, in his presence, there are no Consuls able to exercise their powers, hence no *auspicia consulum* other than his own—and no possibility of collision.

Yet Consuls, and Praetors, evidently did not cease to function altogether. The crucial qualifier was, as Brennan saw, the presence of the Dictator on the scene, be it in the City or *militiae*. The qualifier is not without parallel: one may compare the Tribune's sacrosanctity—and, consequently, veto power—affecting everyone and everything in his presence, but extending no further. In 43 BC, Cicero proposed, unsuccessfully, that C. Cassius Longinus, *pro consule* in Syria, be granted a *maius imperium* with regard to the commanders in the Eastern provinces, whenever Cassius entered any of these provinces (*Phil*. 11.30: *utique, quamcumque in provinciam eius belli gerendi causa advenerit, ibi maius imperium C. Cassi pro consule sit quam eius erit qui eam provinciam tum obtinebit cum C. Cassius pro consule in eam provinciam venerit*): his "personal presence" was made "a condition of the operation of his *imperium maius*."¹⁰⁰ Away from the Dictator, Consuls and other magistrates continued to tend to the duties of their office, including those that entailed military command. There are no grounds for thinking that they did so without the usual trappings, lictors and all;¹⁰¹ if Servilius the Consul was entitled to retain his lictors until coming face to face with the Dictator, he ought to be entitled to resume them after departing. We know for certain that the Consul, in the Dictator's absence, retained his auspices: in 216, Varro returned to Rome in order to name a second Dictator while the other was with the army (Livy 23.22.10–11); which nomination could only happen *auspicato*. In theory, thus, a Consul might attempt to act contrary to the Dictator's orders once the two had parted; in reality, the chance of such was nil. The Dictator could, at any moment, re-establish his presence: at which point, the Consul would be rendered effectively *privatus*, and subject to be dealt with like any other recalcitrant citizen.

As with the auspices, so with *imperium*. The Dictator's was technically no different from the Consul's; what rendered it *valentius* was the appointee's near-magical ability to shape events in favor of the Roman People—an ability that must

---

incommensurable with each other. The Censor was elected in the Centuriate Assembly, like the Consul, yet was not the latter's colleague.

⁹⁹ The same, in all likelihood, is true of the Interrex: the auspices under which he creates the Consul are no different from the *auspicia consulum*. In this case, of course, an election by the People is involved, and one might argue that the situation is analogous to the creation of the Censors, elected by the People under the Consul's auspices, yet not his colleagues. But if the *consularis potestas* was the *regia potestas*, the *potestas* of the Interrex could be nothing less, or else he would be unable to create a Consul—a power greater than his own. In consequence, his auspices, like those of the Dictator, ought to be the same. The *censoria potestas*, on the other hand, was separate from but no greater than the *consularis potestas*: hence Censors were created by the Consul, but not his colleagues, and their auspices did not interact with his.

¹⁰⁰ Last 162.   ¹⁰¹ Brennan *PRR* 1: 42; Vervaet 2004: 66 n. 113.

not be jeopardized by allowing any other powers to exist beside him (let alone any power of the same kind). Hence the incapacity of the Consuls to exercise their *imperium* in his presence. From which it does not follow, though, that the Dictator had no more power than the Consul. This unique aspect of his office made the Dictator *eo ipso* superior not merely to one but both Consuls at the same time, and allowed him to issue direct orders to either or both of them, just as to any private citizen. In practical terms, it gave the Dictator exclusive control over the *res publica*; insofar, Livy naturally and justifiably describes his *imperium* as *maius* or *summum*.[102] Or as the Greeks would put it, with a Dictator in office, all other magistrates, save Tribunes, lose their powers. The Consuls indeed are not "lower" magistrates compared to the Dictator: they simply cease to function as independent magistrates during a dictatorship. Which is not to be confused with ceasing to function as magistrates at all: they (as do the other magistrates) clearly carry on with their regular tasks and duties, including military operations—but all under the direction and at the discretion of the Dictator. The apparent contradiction between the Consul's naming the Dictator and the fundamental rule that no magistrate can create another that holds an *imperium* greater than his own[103] is thus resolved. The Consul does not appoint a magistrate with *maius imperium*; he names one in whose presence no other magistrate can freely exercise his powers, and whose *imperium*, by virtue of that exclusive character of his office, remains the only one in force whenever other magistrates are present. That the ancients should find it to be *valentius*, stronger and more effective than the Consuls', need hardly surprise.[104]

---

[102] Livy 6.38.3, *trepidi patres ad duo ultima auxilia, summum imperium summumque ad civem decurrunt*; 7.3.8, *ad dictatores, quia maius imperium erat, sollemne clavi figendi translatum est*; 8.32.3, *cum summum imperium dictatoris sit pareantque ei consules, regia potestas, praetores, iisdem auspiciis quibus consules creati*; 22.10.10, *Veneri Erycinae aedem...dictator vovit, quia ita ex fatalibus libris editum erat ut is voveret cuius maximum imperium in civitate esset*; 30.24.3, *dictator...pro iure maioris imperii consulem in Italiam revocavit*. Cf. also 2.18.6, [sc. *dictatorem*] *moderatorem et magistrum consulibus appositum*; and Pompon. *Dig.* 1.2.2.18, *placuit maioris potestatis magistratum constitui, itaque dictatores proditi sunt*.

[103] Messalla *apud* Gell. 13.15.4, *a minore imperio maius aut maiori conlega rogari iure non potest* (misquoted, embarrassingly, in Konrad 2003: 345); cf. Cic. *Att.* 9.9.3, *quod maius imperium a minore rogari non sit ius*. See Linderski *AL* 2182 with n. 130.

[104] Last 159, correctly noting the Dictator's ability to subordinate Consuls and other magistrates to his will in a manner and degree quite different from—and exceeding—anything inherent in the *consularis potestas*, postulated the existence of two different kinds of *imperium maius*: one ("type A") in the form generally recognized, regulating precedence—usually on the basis of magisterial rank—among different holders of *imperium* in case of conflict; the other ("type B") in the form of the Dictator's *imperium valentius*, requiring the other magistrates to "work under general instructions received from him," and reducing them to a status tending towards "something like the Dictator's *legati*." In consequence, they were "relieved of the ultimate responsibility for their official acts," such responsibility passing on to the Dictator. This fairly enough describes the condition of the other magistracies during a dictatorship, but fails to explain how the holder of such an *imperium maius* could be appointed by one with *imperium minus*; nor (as noted earlier) does the evidence support a conceptual distinction between different kinds or types of *imperium*.

3.4 Term Limits

What was it that, practically speaking, put an end to a Dictator's tenure? The office had no fixed term like the one-year duration of the permanent magistracies; in principle, its tenure was indefinite, until the completion of the Dictator's task, up to a maximum of six months. Yet even on reaching that six-month limit the office did not terminate automatically—unlike the annual magistracies, which expired with the last day of their term. For most Dictators, Livy notes their abdication: this cannot be an empty gesture, but must reflect a ritual necessity. Every Dictator (whether "special" or *rei gerundae causa*) was expected to abdicate as soon as the situation that had prompted his appointment was resolved; but his office ended only with that abdication.[105] Moreover, it appears that, until the late third century, the six-month limit applied only to Dictators named *rei gerundae causa*.

3.4.1 The *Dictio*

In 216 BC, after M. Iunius Pera (*cos.* 230; *cens.* 225) had assumed office as Dictator *rei gerundae causa*, M. Fabius Buteo (*cos.* 245; *cens.* 241) was named Dictator *senatus legendi causa*—for six months, but without a Magister Equitum. In a *contio* immediately upon assuming office, Fabius found much—indeed, everything—wrong with his own appointment: two Dictators at the same time (which had never happened before); no Master of the Horse; censorial authority allowed to a single man, and to the same man twice; and *imperium* given to a Dictator for six months, for reasons other than *rei gerundae*.[106] That last objection implies both that for "special" Dictators the six-month appointment was an innovation, and that for Dictators *rei gerundae causa* it was well established, or at least had precedent. But how exactly was the limit imposed?

The Dictator received his powers through the *dictio*: being named (*dictus*), with auspices *ave sinistra*, by the Consul. As Mommsen saw long ago, the auspical formula pronounced by the Consul when asking Iuppiter for permission to name a Dictator contained the limits of the appointment: *Iuppiter pater, si est fas me hic hodie magistrum populi dicere in sex menses*, or something to that effect. All that was necessary to create a Dictator not subject to that limit was to omit the phrase

---

[105] Mommsen *StR* 1: 594–596, 624–626; 2.1: 159–161; fully demonstrated by Coli (with an important clarification of Mommsen) 1953: 397–398, 404–412. See further Janssen 72–143, and Wittmann *StO* 670–672, on the Dictator's *Abdikationspflicht*; cf. Vervaet 2010: 100–102.

[106] Livy 23.22.11–23.2: (sc. C. Terentius consul) *nocte proxima, ut mos est, M. Fabium Buteonem ex senatus consulto sine magistro equitum dictatorem in sex menses dixit. is ubi cum lictoribus in rostra escendit, neque duos dictatores tempore uno, quod nunquam antea factum esset, probare se dixit, neque dictatorem sine magistro equitum, nec censoriam vim uni permissam et eidem iterum, nec dictatori, nisi rei gerundae causa creato, in sex menses datum imperium.*

in sex menses at the auspication for the *dictio*.[107] But the terms of the question put to Iuppiter were a matter of the *ius augurale*, and could not as such determine the length of office. Their force lay elsewhere: the Dictator held his auspices for as long as they had been requested, by the Consul naming him, from Iuppiter. When that time expired, so did his auspices. He remained Dictator, though—but lacking valid auspices, *vitium* now attached to anything he undertook; hence he must abdicate and thus terminate his office. If no particular duration was specified in the *dictio*, he retained his auspices until he abdicated.

Mommsen further thought that, for Dictators named to complete a special task, the mention of that reason alone—say, *clavi figendi causa*—in the auspical formula constituted the limit of their term originally. Reasonable and attractive as that conclusion appears at first glance, it runs into obstacles. For one, while the case of Fabius Buteo shows that a temporal clause such as *in sex menses* could be added in the *dictio* (and usually was added for those named *rei gerundae causa*), we do not know for certain if the reason for the Dictator's appointment was specified in the *dictio*. (That of Fabius Buteo, as reported by Livy 23.22.11, did not contain the words *senatus legendi causa*.) The fact that Sulla in 82 deemed it necessary to have his extraordinary commission—*legibus scribundis et rei publicae constituendae*—spelled out by comitial legislation[108] rather suggests that its mere inclusion in the *dictio* would not have been sufficient to expand the powers of the office beyond those normally associated with it. Insofar as the *dictio* established the Dictator's auspices—and, if *in sex menses*, also limited their duration—inclusion of a particular task would have restricted, presumably, their validity to actions related to that task, rather than create a requirement to abdicate upon completion of the task. Yet whether such a restriction of auspices to a particular task was augurally possible is doubtful; no examples appear to be on record. Magistrates had auspices, plain and simple; any constraints in their use were imposed by the powers of the office held: a magistrate could not auspicate for a task that he was legally not capable of performing.[109] The Censors, for instance, held *auspicia maxima*, just like Consuls and Praetors, and, like the latter, they held them by virtue of their office (Messalla *apud* Gell. 13.15.4). They were not auspices custom-tailored to the needs and limits of that office; it was the office that limited their applicable use to its functions.

It seems certain that any Dictator, regardless of designation, possessed the undiminished *imperium* and unrestricted auspices of the office, and could attend to any business that came his way.[110] The only limitation imposed on a special-purpose Dictator (sometimes termed by moderns, improperly, *imminuto iure*)

---

[107] *StR* 2.1: 161 n. 2; cf. Wittmann *StO* 670, 705.
[108] On this, see Mommsen *StR* 1: 170; 2.1: 703–704, 710–711; and at length Vervaet 2004: 38–51.
[109] Linderski *AL* 2217.
[110] Mommsen *StR* 2.1: 157; cf. Nicosia's compelling discussion, 1987; see also Jehne, offering the sole plausible explanation of Festus (216L) *dictator optima lege*.

was one of duration, the completion of the task for which he was named, upon which he was supposed to abdicate. The formulation of this reason—normally by way of a *senatus consultum*—did, of course, serve to prescribe the moment when his abdication would be expected, but it appears that this limit was not enshrined in comitial legislation. No doubt it was considered *fas* and *ius*, but for enforcement one must rely on each Dictator's willingness to obey the rule—and on public pressure, if necessary.[111] When L. Manlius Imperiosus, named *clavi figendi causa* in 363 V, proceeded to call up the levy for an impending war against the Hernici after completing the nailing ceremony, public opposition forced him to step down (*perinde ac rei gerendae ac non solvendae religionis gratia creatus esset, bellum Hernicum adfectans dilectu acerbo iuventum agitavit; tandemque omnibus in eum tribunis plebis coortis seu vi seu verecundia victus dictatura abiit*, Livy 7.3.9): not because as Dictator *clavi figendi causa* he could not call up the army, but because, having dealt with the situation that had occasioned the reason for his appointment, he was not supposed to remain in office. In Livy's account, there is no hint at a violation of *ius*, be it *publicum* or *augurale*. But Cicero's comment on the matter (*Off.* 3.112, *L. Manlio A. f., cum dictator fuisset, M. Pomponius tr. pl. diem dixit, quod is paucos sibi dies ad dictaturam gerendam addidisset*) shows that the Dictator's failure to abdicate when expected could result in prosecution, once he was *privatus* again. At the same time, Cicero's characterization of the offense— Manlius had added a few days to exercising his dictatorship—is instructive: the office itself is not described as having already expired (for instance, *quod is dictatura functus per paucos dies magistratum continuisset*).[112] One doubts that Manlius would have prepared for a military campaign if his auspices were understood to have lapsed the moment he drove the nail into the temple wall.

In fact, the manner of Buteo's appointment rather suggests that no reason for it was mentioned in the *dictio*. Evidently Varro the Consul had included the phrase *in sex menses* when he named him. Now, Livy rather makes it sound as if that limit, along with the peculiar lack of a Magister Equitum, was part of the decree ordering Buteo's appointment (*M. Fabium Buteonem ex senatus consulto sine magistro equitum dictatorem in sex menses dixit*). Naming a Dictator without permitting him a Master of the Horse (more on which shortly) marked this dictatorship out as irregular—most likely in an attempt to mitigate the anomaly of

---

[111] See Wittmann *StO* 667, pointing out that especially for Dictators with religious functions (e.g., *clavi figendi* or *feriarum Latinarum causa*) a restriction incorporated into the *dictio* would essentially undercut the need to have these ceremonies carried out by the magistrate with the greatest power possible. Wittmann correctly believes that the auspical formula for naming the Dictator did not contain any definition of the task; but his contention that the Dictator was nonetheless legally—not merely *de facto*—restricted to that task by virtue of the *senatus consultum* authorizing his appointment is problematic for those who, like the present writer, hold that no *s.c.* could ever *de iure* bind a magistrate.

[112] Cf. Val. Max. 5.4.3, *quod occasione bene conficiendi belli inductus legitimum optinendi imperii tempus excessisset*. The *tempus legitimum* was reached with the completed hammering of the nail, but the dictatorship did not legally end with it. Cf. Jehne 564; Vervaet 2010: 142–143.

having two Dictators in office simultaneously.[113] (The year before, when Minucius the Magister Equitum had his *imperium* made equal to the Dictator's, neither he nor Fabius Maximus appointed another Master of the Horse.) Conceivably, the measure could have been designed to prevent Buteo from attending to military matters, as Manlius Imperiosus had attempted a century and a half before. But why such an extreme measure should have been deemed necessary in this case is hard to imagine: no special-purpose Dictator after old Manlius had sought to exceed his commission. Moreover, the Senate decree, although it did not specify Fabius Buteo by name, had left no room for doubt as to who would be appointed: the Dictator was to be a former Censor, and the most senior among the ones still living (Livy 23.22.10, *dictatorem, qui censor antea fuisset vetustissimusque ex iis qui viverent censoriis esset, creari placuit qui senatum legeret*). Hence Buteo, like every senator, had known what was coming, and we may safely assume that he voiced his objections to the procedure not only in the *contio* upon taking office but also previously in the Senate meeting in which the decision was made. That anyone should suspect him of aiming to abuse his position passes belief. The same consideration applies to his six months. No one, surely, worried that Buteo might draw out the *lectio senatus* for more than a few days, and thus had better be constrained in the same manner as a Dictator *rei gerundae causa*.

Indeed, Fabius' criticism clearly implies that he saw this less as a limitation on his office than as an undue extension: the Dictator *rei gerundae causa* was given up to six months because the situation he was to deal with might require that much time; for a special commission, this had hitherto been unthinkable. It follows that, in consequence of his having been named *in sex menses*, Buteo could remain in office for up to six months, without violating *fas* or *ius*, or even *mos* (otherwise, why grouse about it?), even if he accomplished the task in a matter of days. His appointment *in sex menses* thus runs counter to any limitation that may have been intended in not allowing him to name a Magister Equitum.

3.4.2 *Dictator sine Magistro Equitum*

To turn to that other anomaly in Buteo's appointment: how could the Consul name a Dictator *sine magistro equitum*? It would have to be included in the request of auspices for the *dictio* (*Iuppiter pater, si est fas hic hodie me magistrum populi dicere in sex menses, ita uti is sine magistro equitum sit* vel *ita uti is magistrum equitum dicat neminem*), there being no other conceivable way of preventing the Dictator from carrying out what ordinarily would be his first official act. A further thought arises. Did the *dictio*, perhaps, at all times contain a reference

---

[113] Cf. Wittmann *StO* 670, 694 n. 147; Masi Doria 142–144.

to the naming of a Master of the Horse: *si est fas me magistrum populi dicere (in sex menses), ita uti is magistrum equitum dicat (in sex menses)*? Such a ritual would readily lead to the loose parlance, in Livy and—perhaps—even the Augur Cicero, that has the nominator name both the Dictator and his deputy; and if indeed the Consul was able to name a Magister Equitum directly,[114] that too would have to be contained within the auspical formula (*si est fas me magistrum populi et magistrum equitum dicere*), for otherwise, once the Dictator had been named, the Consul might lack the power to do so. If this be correct, the mere omission of *ita uti is magistrum equitum dicat* would suffice to keep the Dictator thus named from appointing a Master of the Horse. The auspical formula would also offer a ready procedure in those cases where comitial legislation prescribed the identity of both men to be named: the Consul would be instructed to ask Iuppiter, for example, *si est fas me dicere magistrum populi L. Titium, ita uti L. Titius magister populi dicat C. Seium magistrum equitum*.

Buteo's is the fourth of five occasions known in which a Dictator served without a Master of the Horse. In the first such case, in 249, the unhappy M. Claudius Glicia, *qui scriba fuerat*, was forced to abdicate before he had a chance to name his deputy.[115] In the last, in 49, Caesar did not name a Master of the Horse (evident from the *Fasti*, but not recorded in any literary source). The reason is unknown. He had gone to the trouble of procuring comitial legislation that empowered the Praetor to name a Dictator, and, on the precedents set in 217 (?), 210, and 82, we might expect the law to prescribe the names both of the Dictator and the Master of the Horse—unless in this instance it directed the Praetor to name Caesar Dictator *sine magistro equitum*. In any case, Caesar was at Massilia when he learned of his appointment as Dictator (Caes. *BCiv* 2.21.5). Being away from Italy, in Gaul, he could not name a Magister Equitum there without violating augural law. He was Dictator from the moment Lepidus named him; when Dio notes that he entered office after he arrived in Rome (41.36.2), it can only mean that he waited to obtain his initial auspices until then. He clearly intended to complete his business as quickly as possible, and abdicated after eleven days (Caes. *BCiv* 3.2.1); he may simply not have bothered with a Master of the Horse—the absence of which, in turn, might serve as a concession to those who held that this dictatorship, like Fabius Buteo's in 216, was irregular. With the Augural College presumably on record as opposing nomination by the Praetor, it may have seemed prudent—the Civil War was far from decided, and support or, at least, neutrality could depend on small gestures.[116]

---

[114] On this, see Chapter 4.4.2.

[115] *FC = InscrItal* 13.1: 42–43; Livy *Per.* 19; Suet. *Tib.* 2.2. Conceivably, no one was found willing to serve in that capacity, as Suolahti 101 suggests. The second and third instances are Fabius Maximus and Minucius Rufus in 217.

[116] Full discussion in Chapter 4.4.

As Varro had named Iunius Pera Dictator without anomalies earlier in the year, the appointment of Fabius Buteo without a Magister Equitum cannot be ascribed to inadvertence on the Consul's part; he clearly acted as directed by the Senate. The six-month limit is more difficult to understand; no plausible explanation offers why the Senate should have wanted it thus. Did Varro include *in sex menses* by mistake, because he had used that formula earlier when naming Iunius Pera? (Once the words had been spoken, their effect could not be recalled.)

3.4.3 The Magister Equitum as Dictator

The remaining two instances of a Dictator serving without a Magister Equitum require a separate discussion. The appointment in 216 of Fabius Buteo as Dictator *senatus legendi causa*, to hold office side by side with the Dictator *rei gerundae causa*, Iunius Pera, marked a constitutional anomaly; yet an even more spectacular one (*quod nunquam ante eam diem factum erat*, Livy 22.8.6) had occurred in the year before: the grant in 217, by plebiscite, of *imperium* equal to that of the Dictator, Q. Fabius Maximus, to his Master of the Horse, M. Minucius Rufus.

Polybios leaves his readers in no doubt as to the significance of that step, calling attention to it twice in as many sentences:

τὸν δὲ Μάρκον ἐπὶ τοσοῦτον ηὖξον διὰ τὸ συμβεβηκὸς ὥστε τότε γενέσθαι τὸ μηδέποτε γεγονός· αὐτοκράτορα γὰρ κἀκεῖνον κατέστησαν...καὶ δὴ δύο δικτάτορες ἐγεγόνεισαν ἐπὶ τὰς αὐτὰς πράξεις, ὃ πρότερον οὐδέποτε συνεβεβήκει παρὰ Ῥωμαίοις (3.103.4).

Minucius, too, was made Dictator, in an unprecedented move; and now indeed there were two Dictators in office for the same task, something that had never happened before. Did Polybios know of two Dictators in office together on an earlier occasion, but for different tasks (such as one *rei gerundae*, the other *clavi figendi causa*)? Perhaps, but it seems unlikely:[117] the emphasis on the same task was probably prompted by the next instance of two simultaneous Dictators, just a year later—one *rei gerundae causa*, the other *senatus legendi*. Certainly Plutarch made that connection: the Romans voted that Minucius should pursue the war as an equal in command, and with the same powers as the Dictator—something that had never occurred previously at Rome, but was to happen again soon afterwards, in the wake of Cannae, when M. Iunius was Dictator in charge of the army and in the City Fabius Buteo was chosen, as a second Dictator, to replenish the ranks of the Senate.

---

[117] Cf. Walbank *HCP* 1: 434.

τὸν δὲ Μινούκιον ἐψηφίσαντο τῆς στρατηγίας ὁμότιμον ὄντα διέπειν τὸν πόλεμον ἀπὸ τῆς αὐτῆς ἐξουσίας τῷ δικτάτορι, πρᾶγμα μὴ πρότερον ἐν Ῥώμῃ γεγονός, ὀλίγῳ δ' ὕστερον αὖθις γενόμενον μετὰ τὴν ἐν Κάνναις ἀτυχίαν. καὶ γὰρ τότ' ἐπὶ τῶν στρατοπέδων Μᾶρκος Ἰούνιος ἦν δικτάτωρ, καὶ κατὰ πόλιν τὸ βουλευτικὸν ἀναπληρῶσαι δεῆσαν...ἕτερον εἵλοντο δικτάτορα Φάβιον Βουτεῶνα (Fab. 9.3-4).

That Polybios knew of Minucius as Dictator plain and simple, not just as a Magister Equitum with *aequatum imperium*, is clear enough (cf. also 3.106.2, οἱ μὲν δικτάτορες ἀπέθεντο τὴν ἀρχήν, "the Dictators laid down their office"). But Plutarch's narrative in all other elements seems to follow Livy step by step; even the process of Minucius' "promotion" is couched in terms (ἐψηφίσαντο...δικτάτορι) that parallel Livy's *rogatio de aequando magistri equitum et dictatoris iure* (22.25.10), and the end of the affair is quite the same, with Minucius referring to Fabius as "the Dictator" (ὑμῖν δὲ τῶν μὲν ἄλλων ἐστὶν ἄρχων ὁ δικτάτωρ, Fab. 13.4)—by implication the only one—and returning under his command (*Fab.* 13).[118] Only in the digression on the two Dictators of 216 does the biographer think of Minucius as Dictator; and while he could have found the information about Fabius Buteo in Livy,[119] he would also have found there the claim that this, not 217, was the first such case of a dual dictatorship (*neque duos dictatores tempore uno, quod nunquam antea factum est, probare se dixit*, 23.23.2). Hence the comparison with the events of 217 is his own.

Or is it? Nothing in Livy could have given Plutarch the idea that Minucius was no longer Magister Equitum but Dictator. Another source,[120] surely, alerted him to that distinction, and to the repetition of the anomaly in the next year. Polybios remains a possibility, either in his lost discussion of Roman institutions in Book 6, or in his narrative of events after Cannae in Book 7. (That he commented on Iunius Pera and Fabius Buteo is likely enough.) Indeed, Plutarch returns to the main story with the words τὸν δὲ Μινούκιον ἐπὶ τὰς αὐτὰς τῷ δικτάτορι πράξεις ἀποδείξαντες, "having appointed Minucius for the same purpose as the Dictator" (*Fab.* 10.1): an obvious echo of Polybios. But one rather suspects a source common

---

[118] Plutarch's principal source for the *Fabius* has been variously identified as Livy (Hesselbarth 288-291, 312, 320), Coelius Antipater (Peter 1865: 51-56; Soltau 1870: 69-104), or Fabius Pictor (M. Buchholz, *Quibus auctoribus Plutarchus in vitis Fabii Maximi et Marcelli usus sit*, Diss. Greifswald, 1865, p. 30 [*non vidi*]; cited by Soltau 1870: 71 n. 1; cf. Klotz 1935: 126 n. 1). Klotz argued persuasively against Livy, and (with Peter and Soltau) for an author used by both Livy and the biographer; an author who, given Plutarch's consistent proximity to Polybios, also relied on the same source(s) as the Megalopolitan: not, however, Coelius, but Valerius Antias. The crucial observation remains that, regardless of the name attached to Plutarch's main source, it frequently represents material that must have come from Fabius Pictor (Peter 1865: 55-56; Klotz 1935, esp. 128, 132-133, 135-136, 139-140, 146).

[119] Or Antias, if Klotz is correct in identifying him as Livy's source for the Buteo episode (1940/41: 155; cf. above, note 118).

[120] Not Antias, assuming that he served as the source of both Livy and Plutarch in the Fabius-Minucius narrative (Klotz 1935: 136-41; 1940/41: 141-142). As Klotz notes, the essentials of that narrative could be found already in Fabius Pictor.

to the biographer and Polybios—hence belonging to the earliest stratum of the tradition—that included the comparison with 216 at this point in its narrative, prompting Plutarch to adopt it here as well, and perhaps expand it with the brief story of Buteo's one-day dictatorship (*Fab.* 9.5): a story carefully omitted, along with that of Iunius Pera, from his long account of Cannae's aftermath (*Fab.* 17–18).

Livy does not portray Minucius as Dictator, calling him *magister equitum* (and Fabius *dictator*) throughout the period of his independent command.[121] The magnitude of the innovation is noted, though only in Minucius' voice (*quod nulla memoria habeat annalium*, 22.27.3), not the historian's own. Yet, in an unguarded moment, he lets the Polybian view slip into his narrative: when the Consuls resume command toward the end of the year, Atilius takes over Fabius' army, Servilius that of Minucius (22.32.1, *consules Atilius Fabiano, Geminus Servilius Minuciano exercitu accepto*). After all the talk about Minucius with his army returning under the Dictator's orders (*sub imperium auspiciumque tuum redeo et signa haec legionesque restituo... tu, quaeso, placatus me magisterium equitum, hos ordines suos quemque tenere iubeas*, 22.30.4), it transpires that Minucius retained command of his own army until the end of his term.[122]

The other sources essentially adopt the Livian view—an upgrade of *imperium* without the title of Dictator, and resignation or return to his subordinate position after his rescue at the hands of Fabius.[123] Zonaras' account is of particular interest (8.26, οὐδ' ἀνέμεινε τὸν δῆμον ἀναψηφίσασθαι, ἀλλ' ἐθελοντὴς τὴν ἡγεμονίαν...ἀφῆκε): in Dio, it appears, the story took Minucius' humiliation a step further, by reporting a threat that the People might revoke his *imperium* after

---

[121] Minucius: Livy 22.27.3, 11; 22.30.2, 5; Fabius: 22.27.3–4; 22.30.1, 3.

[122] Cf. Meyer 1972: 978 (*contra* Vervaet 2007: 210 n. 42, arguing that Livy merely meant to indicate that Atilius received the army commanded by Minucius during his period of independence). This does not contradict Polybios' notice that, after his debacle, Minucius resumed cooperation with Fabius and shared the same camp (3.105.10).

[123] Nepos *Hann.* 5.3, *magistrum equitum pari ac dictatorem imperio...fugavit*; Val. Max. 3.8.2, *dictatori ei magistrum equitum Minucium iure imperii senatus aequaverat*; 5.2.4, *dictatori ei magister equitum Minucius scito plebis, quod numquam antea factum fuerat, aequatus;...deposito aequalis imperii iugo magisterium equitum, sicut par erat, dictaturae subiecit*; Appian *Hannib.* 12.52, ἡ βουλή, ἐπανεληλυθότος ἐς τὸ στρατόπεδον ἤδη τοῦ Φαβίου, ἴσον ἰσχύειν αὐτῷ τὸν ἵππαρχον ἀπέφηνεν (clearly confused with what Livy reports at 22.26.7, *acceptisque in ipso itinere litteris senatus de aequato imperio*; cf. the same error at Val. Max. 3.8.2); 13.55, ὁ δὲ Μινούκιος...ἀπέθετο τὴν ἀρχὴν καὶ τὸ μέρος τοῦ στρατοῦ παρέδωκε τῷ Φαβίῳ; Dio fr. 57.16, καὶ διὰ τοῦτο αὐτὸν μὲν οὐκ ἔπαυσαν, τῷ δὲ ἱππάρχῳ τὴν αὐτὴν οἱ ἐξουσίαν ἔδωκεν, ὥστ' ἀμφοτέρους ἅμα ἀπὸ τῆς ἴσης ἄρχειν; fr. 57.17, ὁ Ῥοῦφος ἀπεστρατοπεδεύσατο, ἵνα καὶ τῷ ἔργῳ διάδηλος, ὅτι αὐτὸς καθ' ἑαυτόν, ἀλλ' οὐχ ὑπὸ τῷ δικτάτορι ἄρχοι, γένοιτο; fr. 57.19, ὁ Ῥοῦφος ἰσομοιρίαν λαχὼν τῷ δικτάτορι...ἐθελοντὴς τὴν ἡγεμονίαν ἀφῆκε; Zonar. 8.26, ἀλλ' ἐκεῖνον μὲν...οὐκ ἔπαυσαν, τῷ δὲ ἱππάρχῳ τὴν αὐτὴν ἐξουσίαν προσένειμαν, ὥστ' ἄμφω ἀπὸ τῆς ἴσης ἄρχειν;...ὁ Ῥοῦφος ἀπεστρατοπεδεύσατο, ἵνα διάδηλος ᾖ ὅτι καθ' ἑαυτόν ἄρχει, ἀλλ' οὐχ ὑπὸ τῷ δικτάτορι;...τὴν ἀρχὴν παραδέδωκεν, οὐδ' ἀνέμεινε τὸν δῆμον ἀναψηφίσασθαι, ἀλλ' ἐθελοντὴς τὴν ἡγεμονίαν, ἣν παρ' αὐτοῦ μόνος ἱππάρχων ἔλαβεν, ἀφῆκε; Auct. *De vir. ill.* 43.3, *Minucium magistrum equitum imperio sibi aequari passus est*.

his luck against Hannibal ran out, or even (as Vervaet argues) an actual plebiscite repealing the Metilian Law subsequent to Minucius' self-subordination.[124]

Livy's version has found champions among moderns. It will not do. The famous inscription of Minucius' altar agrees with Polybios (and Plutarch): *Hercolei sacrum M. Minuci C. f. dictator vovit* (*ILS* 11).[125] Nor do we have reason to think that Polybios, in a matter whose constitutional significance he emphasized not once, but twice (3.103.3–4), carelessly glossed over or mistook the true nature of Minucius' enhanced position. The oldest tradition treated Minucius as Dictator. Was he *dictus*?

The *lex Metilia* gave the Magister Equitum *imperium* equal to that of the Dictator; that much is not in doubt. To permit him the title *dictator* as well, the legislation could have instructed the Consul M. Atilius Regulus, suffected just days before the passage of the plebiscite (Livy 22.25.16), to name Minucius Dictator. The insistence of Metilius the Tribune that Fabius see to the election of a Consul suffect before the vote on his bill (Livy 22.25.11) may point to that solution. But the Dictator, if uncooperative in the diminution of his power, could simply forbid the Consul to perform such a *dictio*: hence Metilius' threat that he was prepared to have Fabius' *imperium* abrogated altogether (Livy 22.25.10). Now Polybios and Livy agree on a pertinent point: Minucius' term in office ended on the same day as did that of Fabius.[126] Had he been *dictator dictus a M. Atilio consule*, his six-month term would have continued for several months beyond that of Fabius.

We have a further sign that the *lex Metilia* did not simply create a second Dictator in the normal sense of the office: nothing indicates that Minucius appointed a Magister Equitum of his own, or that Fabius replaced him with another deputy. When Fabius Buteo was named as a second Dictator the next year, it was with the express proviso *sine magistro equitum* (to which he objected, Livy 23.22.11–23.2): irregular, and presumably intended to mark this dictatorship as such.[127] Did the plebiscite contain the same proviso, and extend it to Fabius as well: two Dictators *rei gerundae causa*, commanding at the same time, but each without a Master of the Horse?

It appears certain that Minucius' dictatorship was not one established *de novo*—as would have been the inevitable effect of a *dictio*—but an extension of his *magisterium equitum*. If Minucius was *dictus* by the Dictator at his initial appointment, it may not have been augurally necessary to repeat the *dictio*—not even

---

[124] Note Zonar. 8.26, καὶ ὁ Φάβιος αὐτίκα μηδὲν ἐνδοιάσας πᾶσαν (sc. τὴν ἡγεμονίαν) ἐδέξατο, καὶ ὁ δῆμος αὐτὸ ἀπεδέξατο, and cf. Livy 22.30.4, *itaque plebei scito, quo oneratus <sum> magis quam honoratus, primus antiquo abrogoque* (thus Minucius). See Vervaet 2007: 217–218.

[125] See Chapter 6.7.2.

[126] As clearly follows from Polyb. 3.106.2, οἱ μὲν δικτάτορες ἀπέθεντο τὴν ἀρχήν, and Livy 22.31.7, 32.1. Cf. Schmitt 311.

[127] See above, Subsection 3.4.2.

proper, in all likelihood, without his abdicating first. (If Fabius himself was not, indeed, a *dictator dictus*,[128] the question would be moot in any case.) Hence the tradition of an *aequatio imperii*, without *dictio* by the Consul, is probably correct insofar as it describes the process that gave Minucius his enhanced position. Whether in consequence he could call himself "Dictator" would depend on the exact language used in the law.

At a minimum, we should expect something like *velitis iubeatis ut M. Minucius magister equitum aequo* (sive *pari*) *sit imperio* (sive *iure*) *ac Q. Fabius dictator*. If it continued, for instance, *ita uti rem uterque gerat sine magistro equitum*, Minucius (and contemporaries) could reasonably conclude that the prohibition to name a Master of the Horse made him, by implication, *dictator*, there being no other official with the power to make such an appointment. Others, of course, could conclude that the identical prohibition addressed to Fabius, along with the absence of the word *dictator* in direct reference to Minucius, implied that the latter was still Magister Equitum. In the light of Minucius' inscription, Polybios, and Plutarch, there can be little doubt that the first interpretation prevailed at the time.[129] Nor can we be certain that the law did not apply the word *dictator* to Minucius: *velitis iubeatis ut dictator sit M. Minucius magister equitum aequo* (sive *pari*) *imperio* (sive *iure*) *ac Q. Fabius dictator*, or *ita uti dictator rem uterque gerat sine magistro equitum*. With the passing of time, Minucius' lasting humiliation in virtually the entire surviving tradition, and Fabius' ever-increasing stature as an exemplary leader, would ensure ready acceptance of a version, once put forth, that denied him the title of Dictator altogether.

3.4.4 The Six-month Limit

Whether the six-month limit had existed from primordial days we cannot say for certain; in the first century BC, Livy and perhaps most Romans thought so, despite traces of an earlier tradition that some Dictators held office for considerably longer than six months.[130] The first such case is Camillus in 396 V: attested as Dictator on October 31 at the instauration of the Latin Festival, he proceeded to capture Veii, and after his triumph dedicated the temple of Mater Matuta, almost certainly on June 11. Those dates amount to a tenure of about eight months.[131] The most explicit instance involves again Camillus, in 390 V: *eaque causa fuit non abdicandae post triumphum dictaturae, senatu obsecrante ne rem publicam in*

---

[128] Thus Livy implies, 22.31.8–11; I intend to discuss the circumstances of Fabius' appointment in a separate study.
[129] Vervaet's discussion of Minucius' titulature, 2007: 218–220, is rather unsatisfactory.
[130] See Wittmann *StO* 671–672.
[131] *Fasti feriarum Latinarum* = *InscrItal* 13.1: 146–147; Livy 5.19.1, 23.7; Wissowa 111; for discussion, see Janssen 83.

incerto relinqueret statu (Livy 5.49.9); *neque eum abdicare se dictatura nisi anno circumacto passi sunt* (Livy 6.1.4). Mommsen, following Weissenborn and Müller, points out that *anno circumacto*, far from implying a year-long dictatorship, means that Camillus remained in office until the end of the consular year.[132] But the consular year had started on July 1 (Livy 5.32.1), and the Gauls sacked Rome in the last third of that month. Livy does not give a date for Camillus' appointment, but clearly envisages it at a point in time well before the Gauls' departure seven months later.[133] Whoever devised that version of the story was thinking of a dictatorship that lasted longer than six months, though not an entire year; and it may be significant that Livy makes no mention of a six-month limit here.[134]

Sulla has been thought to have stood model for Camillus' dictatorship in 390 V, on grounds that "the whole notion of a dictator re-establishing the constitution is unparalleled from the fifth and fourth centuries."[135] Certainly; but Livy says—and implies—nothing about the Dictator's re-establishing the constitution, and Camillus' reputation as a Second Founder of Rome "was already current" by the late second century.[136] It goes without saying (or so it should) that the silence of Polybios has no bearing on the issue. He evidently knew of—or believed in—no Roman victory over the Gauls (2.18.2-3, 22.4-5); but he was not concerned, in this or any part of his narrative, with constitutional details such as whether or not the Romans had named a Dictator on that occasion, or whether Camillus had any part in it. The silence of Diodoros might seem to carry more significance, since he does report the (third) dictatorship the other sources give to Camillus for the following year (14.117): but his account combines the defeats of Volsci, Aequi, and Sutrium with a victory over the retreating Gauls, complete with Camillus' recovery of the Roman ransom; nor does he indicate that those events happened in the consular year after the sack. In other words, one cannot assert that Diodoros did not know of a dictatorship at all in connection with the Gallic catastrophe.

In 316 V (L. Aemilius Mamercinus, 9.21.1, 22.1) and 315 V (Q. Fabius Rullianus, 9.22.1, 24.1), Livy's narrative clearly—though, perhaps, unawares—implies that those Dictators held office for approximately a year. To dismiss the inconvenient datum as "ein staatsrechtliches Unding"[137] assumes as proven fact—without the slightest contemporary, that is, fifth- and fourth-century evidence—the very thing being called into question by that earlier source we glimpse through Livy: the notion that the six-month limit had always applied. To explain the

---

[132] Mommsen *StR* 2.1: 160 n. 3; cf. W–M *ad loc.*; indeed, Livy 6.1.5 is clear enough.

[133] See W–M *ad* 6.1.4; note the Dictator's slow preparations and the long and increasingly desperate wait for his arrival in Rome, 5.48; for the duration of the occupation, Polyb. 2.22.5; Plut. *Cam.* 30.1.

[134] Unlike Plutarch, *Cam.* 31.3: ἡ βουλὴ τὸν μὲν Κάμιλλον οὐκ εἴασε βουλόμενον ἀποθέσθαι τὴν ἀρχὴν ἐντὸς ἐνιαυτοῦ, καίπερ ἐξ μῆνας οὐδενὸς ὑπερβαλόντος ἑτέρου δικτάτορος. This could be Plutarch's own comment, to emphasize the measure's significance in terms of trust and honor shown to the hero; but it could equally come from a source more explicit here than Livy.

[135] Oakley *CL* 1: 387; cf. Gaertner 32.   [136] See Ogilvie 739.

[137] Bandel 99. Janssen 150–151 and Wilson 258 rightly accept these year-long dictatorships.

discrepancy as "concocted by late historians ignorant about the nature of the long-disused dictatorship"[138] takes no account of the fact that all but one of the "late historians" that have survived to comment on the matter—Dionysios, Livy, Plutarch, Appian, Dio, even Lydus—know the limit as original to the office.[139] (The exception being, perhaps, Polybios, who in describing how the Dictator differed from the Consul says nothing about a six-month term: 3.87.7-9.) Are we to believe that the annalists of the second century, much closer in time to the real thing, were ignorant of how it worked, but those of the first somehow discovered the truth?

Lastly, the dictator years—however fictitious—indicate that in the eyes of some antiquarians a dictatorship exceeding six months was seen as at least a theoretical possibility for the more distant past.[140] All in all, it is very little to go on. Perhaps the fact that the six-month limit was not applied to special-purpose Dictators until 216 BC provides a clue. The first such Dictators appear in the fourth century (beginning, in fact, with L. Manlius Imperiosus, *clavi figendi causa* in 363).[141] It seems odd that the phrase *in sex menses* should be omitted in their *dictio* if it already constituted a fixed element in the naming of every Dictator; after all, the absence of such a limit would not increase the pressure to abdicate once the task was completed—if anything, it would invite temptation to prolong a man's time in the office. By the late third century, the six months seem to have become established for the Dictator *rei gerundae causa*, perhaps even prescribed by legislation—which, however, would not alter the fact that only abdication could terminate his tenure.[142]

---

[138] Oakley *CL* 3: 278.   [139] See *StR* 2.1: 160 n. 1 for references.

[140] Coli 1953: 408; Janssen 151-153; and see Wittmann *StO* 671-672, against ("kaum glaubhaft") Drummond's suggestion (1978: 569-572) that the dictator years were invented to lend legitimacy to Caesar's year-long dictatorship in 48 BC.

[141] The Dictators of 494 and 439 are often identified as *seditionis sedandae causa* in modern works (e.g., Bandel 11, 51; Degrassi *InscrItal* 13.1: 88, 95), but the reason for their appointment is not attested, and M'. Valerius in 494 triumphed (*Acta Tr.* = *InscrItal* 13.1: 66-67; Livy 2.31.3), hence *rei gerundae*. The only Dictator formally recorded with that function, P. Manlius Capitolinus in 368, is shown as *seditionis sedandae et r(ei) g(erundae) c(aussa)* in the *Fasti* (*InscrItal* 13.1: 32-33). No doubt Mommsen concluded correctly that *seditionis sedandae* was not so much a special purpose than a "domestic" use of the Dictator *rei gerundae causa*, and that the former reason officially occurred only together with the latter (*StR* 2.1: 156 n. 4-157 n. 3).

[142] Coli 1953: 405-409. Janssen 143-165 suggests that the dictatorship of Fabius Maximus in 217 was, in fact, the first to be formally limited to six months. The idea is incapable of proof, though tempting: if indeed the limit was not yet firmly established in the fourth century, the paucity of Dictators *rei gerundae* in the third (just one before Fabius, in 249) leaves little room for such a development. Wilson 245-260 now rejects altogether the existence of a six-month limit, but offers no plausible explanation of its deep roots in the historical tradition; his claim that Fabius Maximus in 217 served well over six months, from midsummer beyond the Ides of March, 216—when the next Consuls entered office—overlooks that these Consuls were elected under an Interrex, after a Dictator *comitiorum habendorum* was compelled to abdicate (Livy 22.33.9-34.1): clearly, Fabius was no longer in office at those elections. On the obvious fiction of Livy's *lex de dictatore creando* (2.18.5) from 501 V—strangely accepted by Wittmann *StO* 699—see Mommsen *StR* 2.1: 142-143; Ogilvie 282; Magdelain 1968: 9; cf. Hartfield 4, 124; Jehne 567 n. 51; Beck 2005: 71.

4
Magister Equitum

The quarrel in 324 V between Papirius Cursor the Dictator and his Master of the Horse, Fabius Maximus Rullianus, revolved in large part—as told in the historiographical traditions we can discern through Livy—around the question to what degree, if at all, the latter was able to act independently of his superior, especially as regards their respective auspices.[1] As a magistracy, the Magister Equitum usually receives short shrift in modern studies, not least because little is known about the office. A partial remedy is offered here; again, this chapter does not aim at a comprehensive treatment, but investigates certain poorly documented features of the office, mostly from the perspective of the auspices.

4.1 The Auspices of the Magister Equitum

Fabius Rullianus maintained that his victorious battle, in the absence of the Dictator, was fought under his own command and auspices (*se cuius ductu auspicioque vicissent*, 8.31.1; *qui eius ductu auspiciisque vicissent*, 8.33.22). The Dictator insisted that, his own auspices having been found *incerta*, the Master-of-Horse was bound by the same *religio* (*illud, quae dictatori religio impedimento ad rem gerendam fuerit, num ea magister equitum solutus ac liber potuerit esse*, 8.32.5) and, therefore, had fought *turbatis religionibus ac dubiis auspiciis* (8.34.4): in other words, the Master of the Horse commanded *alienis auspiciis*, the Dictator's. In the second known case of a confrontation between the Dictator and his deputy—Fabius Maximus the Cunctator and Minucius Rufus, in 217 BC—Livy remains vague on the matter of auspices throughout; only at the very end, a clear statement issues: *sub imperium auspiciumque tuum redeo*, says the chastised Master of the Horse upon relinquishing his upgraded, now dictatorial *imperium* (22.30.4).[2] That would agree with the position taken by Papirius. Then how could Rullianus' defenders—writing in the penumbra of the Hannibalic War—with a straight face claim otherwise?

The Master-of-Horse occupied a unique position among Roman magistrates. He derived his powers not from the People through election but from being named by the Dictator; he was not answerable to the People for his actions, but to

---

[1] Chapter 1.3. [2] Chapter 3.4.3.

his superior.³ Once appointed, did his office become his own, or was it tied inseparably to the Dictator? Mommsen held that it came to an end "wahrscheinlich mit rechtlicher Nothwendigkeit" the moment the Dictator laid down. That runs against the logic of the evidence. By ancient ritual, the Dictator about to abdicate must first order his Magister Equitum also to abdicate; and we know of at least one instance when the latter stepped down only after the Dictator had resigned.⁴ If the Magister Equitum had to be ordered to resign in order to ensure he did so, and if, on the example of M. Folius in 324 V, his abdication could wait until after that of the Dictator, it must be an independent act. It follows that, without such abdication, the Master-of-Horse could remain in office even after the Dictator has stepped down: his position did not terminate automatically when the Dictator's came to an end.

A recent find offers welcome confirmation. In 2000 and 2001, excavations at Privernum brought to light fragments of *fasti consulares* for the years 45 to 43 B C that follow almost verbatim the extant text of the *Fasti Capitolini*, but contain material not preserved in the Capitoline marble. Under the year 44, we read:

C. Iulius Caesar IV dict(ator) abdic(avit) ut perpet(uo) [dict(ator) fieret]
M. Aemilius Lepid(us) II mag(ister) eq(uitum) abd(icavit) ut perpet(uo) [mag(ister) eq(uitum) fieret]
        quoad dict(ator) Caesar esset
C. Iulius Caesar desig(natus) in perpet(uum) dicta(tor)
M. Aemilius Lepidus [desig(natus) in perpet(uum) mag(ister) eq(uitum)]

Caesar's abdication of his fourth dictatorship was already known from the *FC*, and that of Lepidus is commonly supplied, along with a notation of Caesar's permanent dictatorship, [*C. Iulius C.f. C.n. Caesar in perpetuum dict(ator)*].⁵ What no one could have imagined was the appointment of Lepidus as Magister Equitum *perpetuo*. That this is not a stonecutter's error—absentmindedly repeating the words from the line above—is evident from the qualification in the line below, *quoad dictator Caesar esset*, "for as long as Caesar was Dictator."⁶ If it were understood (in keeping with Mommsen's view) that the office of Magister Equitum

---

³ See Chapter 6.6.2 with note 103.
⁴ *StR* 2.1: 175–176; Livy 9.26.20, *abdicat inde se dictatura et post eum confestim Folius magisterio equitum*; cf. 4.34.5, *iussoque magistro equitum abdicare se magistratu, ipse deinde abdicavit*; 8.15.6, *dictator magisterque equitum se magistratu abdicarunt*. Correct Wittmann *StO* 718; cf. Lange *RA* 1: 648–649. On the Dictator's *Abdikationspflicht*, see Chapter 3.4 with note 105, and below, note 79.
⁵ *FPrivern b*, lines 10–14; see Zevi 291–297 (his supplements) and *InscrItal* 13.1: 56–57, 58–59.
⁶ Cf. Zevi 297. The inscription proves Dio 53.51.8, δύο ἀντ' αὐτοῦ (sc. Λεπίδου) ἑτέρους, ἰδίᾳ γε ἑκάτερον, ἱππαρχῆσαι ἐποίησε, both right and wrong. Wrong, since Lepidus clearly was to remain Magister Equitum, *perpetuo*, upon his departure to Spain; right in that we now learn that at that point Messalla Rufus was to take office as a second Master-of-Horse in Rome: *M. Valerius Mes̄[sal(la) mag(ister) eq(uitum) desig(natus) ut, cum Lepidus] | paludatus [exisset, iniret]* (*FPrivern b*, lines 15–16; cf. *InscrItal* 13.1: 58–59, *ut, qum M.* [*Lep*]*idus paludatu*[*s exisset, iniret*]).

automatically terminated together with that of the Dictator, there would have been no need to specify that Lepidus, although *perpetuo*, could not remain in office beyond Caesar's term, whenever—and however—that came to an end.

If the Master of the Horse held his office—once conferred—as his own, to the extent that he could in principle exist without the Dictator, surely his auspices were his own once obtained. On what occasions would he auspicate? Alongside the Dictator, whenever the latter did, just as the Praetor when commanding jointly with a Consul? It seems unlikely. For Consul and Praetor, Dictator and Magister Equitum, if Iuppiter's answer came down differently to each of them, the superior's auspices, naturally, would prevail, and in practical terms the end result was the same.[7] But conceptually there was a major difference. The Praetor was an independent magistrate: he would be expected—indeed required—to auspicate, even if it was a foregone conclusion that, in case of a divergent response, the Consul's auspices took precedence; for even with the Consul present, the Praetor still performed all his actions in his own responsibility, and thus must obtain Iuppiter's permission. The Master-of-Horse held his powers from the Dictator, and was answerable to him alone; and the Dictator could order him to abdicate. It follows that, in the Dictator's presence, he was a mere assistant who had to take direct orders anytime, not couched in terms of a prohibition.[8] In consequence, a separate auspication by the Master of the Horse would be pointless: whatever action was intended on that day was the Dictator's exclusively; and Iuppiter would communicate with him alone.

At times, however, both might be separated, each engaged in different business in different locations. The Magister Equitum, holding a Senate meeting in the City while the Dictator was with the army (as did Ti. Gracchus in 216: Livy 23.24.5, 25.2–11), necessarily would do so *auspicato*; although no other instances seem to be attested in the record, Antonius in 48 and 47, and Lepidus in 46 and 45, must have auspicated routinely when managing things in Rome during Caesar's absence. Since the Dictator, being absent, would not be asking the same question for the same purpose on that day, Iuppiter's response would come to the Master of the Horse directly. Conversely, the Magister Equitum preparing to give battle, while the Dictator was in the City, necessarily must auspicate,[9] and Iuppiter's response would come to him alone. Indeed, the very fact that the Dictator should find it necessary to formally prohibit him from undertaking any military action on such occasions suggests that, without such prohibition, the Master of the Horse when on his own was fully capable of engaging in battle, which ought to mean, capable of auspicating. (It is clear that Polybios, at any rate,

---

[7] The rule is expressed *luce clarius* in Val. Max. 2.8.2: *si diversa auspicia accepissetis, cuius magis auspicio staretur? item, respondit Valerius, consulis*. See below, Subsection 4.2.1.

[8] Rullianus' gripe, *quod se magistrum equitum duxerit ac non accensum dictatoris* (Livy 8.31.4), captures his true position in a nutshell.

[9] Cf. Masi Doria 157.

understood the Magister Equitum to be fully capable of independent action in the Dictator's absence.[10])

Brennan credited the Magister Equitum with auspices, but argued that he "was never fighting *suis auspiciis*," on account of their "derivative nature."[11] Rather than describe his auspices as "derivative," one might call them "latent": he had auspices when acting in the Dictator's place, but not when assisting him, in his presence. How did he acquire them?

Again, the prohibition against fighting in the Dictator's absence provides a clue. In every known instance but one (where the sources vaguely speak of *sacra*), the Dictator had to return to Rome in order to repeat his auspices, which had become *incerta* or invalid.[12] In the Dictator's absence, the Master of the Horse certainly could auspicate. The sole reason for forbidding him to do so and engage the enemy must be the one cited by Papirius Cursor: the Magister Equitum was bound by the same *religio* as affected the Dictator. If the latter's auspices were dubious or invalid, so were his; an affirmative response, tainted by *vitium*, would carry no permission, and risk disaster.

But it is the Dictator alone who repeats the auspices: if his deputy's auspices had become invalid along with his own, the Dictator's repetition also must revalidate those of the Master-of-Horse. If the latter had no need to repeat his auspices separately, a stark conclusion emerges: he also had no need to ask for them on the day he assumed office. Like the Consul, the Dictator upon being named would ask Iuppiter for his initial auspices; and on obtaining an affirmative response,[13] would proceed with naming—again, *auspicato*—his Magister Equitum. But the latter did not then ask Iuppiter for auspices himself; for he already possessed them. When asking Iuppiter to confirm the validity of his auspices, the Dictator also asks him to confirm those of the Magister Equitum, still to be named; and in granting auspices to the Dictator at the moment he enters office, Iuppiter grants them—in the same act—to the Magister Equitum.[14]

Naming a Magister Equitum is invariably reported as the Dictator's first action, right after being named himself; in matter of fact, it will have come immediately

---

[10] Polyb. 3.87.9, οὗτος δὲ τέτακται μὲν ὑπὸ τὸν αὐτοκράτορα, γίνεται δ' οἷον εἰ διάδοχος τῆς ἀρχῆς ἐν τοῖς ἐκείνου περισπασμοῖς; similarly Plut. *Ant.* 8.4–5, possibly from Polybios.

[11] PRR 1: 46–49. See especially his statements that the Magister Equitum "never triumphed, which suggests what we would in any case expect, that he did not fight under his own auspices" (43); "never acts *suis auspiciis*" (45; note how suggestion and expectation have suddenly hardened into fact, without additional evidence); "was never fighting *suis auspiciis* and so could not triumph" (49).

[12] Note, besides the case(s) in 324 and 301 V discussed above (Chapter 1), that of Ti. Gracchus in 216 (Livy 23.19.3–5). The same prohibition was issued by the Consul to his *legati* in 252 (Val. Max. 2.7.4; cf. Frontin. *Strat.* 4.1.31; and see Konrad 2008), and can be inferred for the Consul in 215 (Livy 23.36.9–10). For an argument that in 217, too, the Dictator may have departed *ad auspicia repetenda*, see Chapter 8.2.2.

[13] On the "auspices of investiture," see Chapter 2.3.

[14] This cannot be proved, naturally, and comes with a significant caveat: below, it will be argued that in 48 Antonius took office as Magister Equitum in Rome well before Caesar, in Egypt, could have obtained his first auspices as Dictator. For discussion see below, Subsection 4.4.2.

after the Dictator took his initial auspices.[15] No separate auspication for the appointment of the Master is on record.[16] If the above reconstruction be correct, none will have been necessary: if Iuppiter confirmed the auspices of both Dictator and Magister Equitum in the same request, the Dictator should have been able to proceed and name his deputy forthwith.

The explanation developed here supports Brennan's suggestion of a "peculiar codependency of auspices" for the Dictator and his Master of the Horse. An oblative sign, sent at the precise moment the Dictator names his deputy, would signal *vitium*, and in effect render invalid the impetrative auspices that had permitted the act in progress. But if those auspices, as argued here, were identical with the Dictator's first auspication, the *vitium* extended to him: permission for the act of naming a Master-of-Horse could not be augurally separated from his "auspices of investiture." Both, therefore, must abdicate, as in the sole attested instance of this sort.[17] Not only that: even subsequently, a *vitium* in the Dictator's auspices also affected his deputy, and the same probably (we have no concrete example) held in reverse: a *vitium* incurred by the Magister Equitum while separated from the Dictator, and thus able to auspicate, would affect the Dictator as well, since his deputy could not independently repeat the auspices.

4.2 Auspices and Triumph

Let us assume there are no issues with the Dictator's auspices, but, through whatever circumstance, the Master-of-Horse is with the army by himself. Having received no orders to the contrary, he plans to engage the enemy, and asks Iuppiter for auspices; Iuppiter's response is in the affirmative, and victory ensues. Who will receive the credit, and the triumph? Four celebrated cases form an answer—of sorts.

4.2.1 Catulus and Falto

In the spring of 241 BC, the Battle off the Aegates Islands destroyed Carthage's last fleet, and ended the First Punic War. The Consul (of 242 BC) C. Lutatius Catulus

---

[15] Random examples: Livy 8.23.4; 4.23.6; 4.26.12; 4.31.5; 4.57.6; 7.12.9; 8.12.2; 25.2.3, and countless more. The apparent exception at Livy 3.27.1 is readily resolved. Cincinnatus is named Dictator *absens* by Nautius the Consul, no doubt *de nocte silentio* (cf. 9.38.14); during the (next) day, he is summoned from his farm, escorted to the City, and taken to his home, *antecedentibus lictoribus*. After an uneventful night, before dawn he goes to the Forum and names his Magister Equitum. Cincinnatus was Dictator from the moment he was *dictus* (hence the lictors), just as the Consul was Consul from midnight of the first day of the year; but he may have waited until just before dawn—the preferred moment—to confirm his auspices. Appointment of the Magister Equitum followed at once.

[16] *Pace* Mommsen *StR* 2.1: 174 ("nach besonders dafür eingeholten Auspicien").

[17] Val. Max. 1.1.5; Plut. *Marc.* 5.1–7. That famous case—Flaminius and the shrew-mouse—is discussed in Chapter 6.7. Cf. Brennan *PRR* 1: 46–49.

being ill at Lilybaeum, the Praetor Q. Valerius Falto led the Roman fleet to victory; the Senate voted a triumph—to the Consul (Val. Max. 2.8.2; Zonar. 8.17). Upon which Falto demanded a triumph, too, and Catulus objected.

Contrary to some modern claims, there is no evidence that the Senate initially denied Falto's request.[18] Nor can it be maintained that Catulus did not object to Falto's obtaining a triumph, but "simply insisted that having to share his triumph with a praetor would have leveled out unequal *potestates*" and thus would "diminish his consular *imperium auspiciumque* and slight the dignity of the supreme commander"; the Senate's award of a separate triumph to Falto in this view constituted a compromise that upheld both Catulus' point of view and Falto's claim.[19] There is not even a hint in Valerius Maximus that Falto meant to "share" the (Pro) Consul's triumph, that is, asked for both of them to parade in one and the same procession—a practice unattested prior to Titus and Vespasian in AD 71, although possible in the case of Marius and Q. Catulus in 101, and likely for Antonius' and Octavian's *ovatio* in 40 BC as well as (if it really happened) the triumphal celebration of the consuls in 207 BC.[20] There can be no doubt that Falto wanted a triumph of his own all along, and that Catulus opposed the request: *cum autem Valerius sibi quoque eum* [sc. *triumphum*] *decerni desideraret, negavit id fieri Lutatius.*

Falto then challenged Catulus to a *sponsio—ni suo ductu Punica classis esset oppressa*: was it not true that the Punic fleet had been vanquished under his command? In the end, the matter came down to two simple questions. First, if there had been a disagreement between Consul and Praetor on whether to give battle, whose orders would have carried greater weight: *utrum quod consul an quod praetor imperasset maius habiturum fuerit momentum?* The Consul's, Falto acknowledged frankly. Next, on the day of the battle, *si diversa auspicia accepissetis, cuius magis auspicio staretur*? If the two had received contradictory auspices, whose would have prevailed? The Consul's again, of course. The implications could not be more clear: the Praetor was able to issue orders on his own, though subject to being overruled by those of the Consul; and he asked, and obtained, his own auspices from Iuppiter—but he must yield if they came down differently from the Consul's.[21] Yet the *iudex*, A. Atilius Caiatinus (*cos. II* 254, *dict.* 249), never asked whether the Praetor had fought under the Consul's auspices or his own. He did not need to, for the answer was "both"; the question that really mattered was whose were superior.

---

[18] E.g., Brennan 1996: 330 n. 10; Lundgreen 194.
[19] As Vervaet 2014: 98–99, 129 (cf. also Dart–Vervaet 272), strangely persuaded himself.
[20] Joseph. *BJ* 7.121, 152; Cic. *Tusc.* 5.56; Plut. *Mar.* 27.10; 44.8; Dio 48.31.3. On the peculiar case of the Consuls' joint triumphal celebrations in 207 BC, see below, note 28.
[21] Cf. Mommsen *StR* 1: 95; Last 158–159; cf. Berthelet 149. Vervaet's reference to auspices "possibly" taken by the Praetor before the battle (2014: 97 n. 88) is needlessly hesitant.

The story has been doubted, on the grounds that it allegedly collides with the evidence of the *Acta Triumphorum*: "Valerius describes a complex (and distinctly implausible) process of legal adjudication, ending up with the decision that Catulus, not Falto, should triumph because he was in overall command."[22] That grossly misrepresents what happened, and what Valerius reports. (Indeed, the fundamental misunderstanding that the *sponsio* was to determine who should get the triumph, or whether the Praetor should get one, seems to lie at the bottom of most modern doubts about the story's authenticity, and of widespread confusion regarding its implications.)

First, the *sponsio* was an act of private litigation; it could not possibly determine who could, should, or would triumph, and Caiatinus made no ruling to that effect. Second, the question in this *sponsio* was never which of the two should triumph; Falto made no attempt to deny Catulus that distinction—he merely desired it as well. Catulus had opposed Falto's request *ne in honore triumphi minor potestas maiori aequaretur*: his argument, apparently, was that, with Consul and Praetor commanding jointly in the same *provincia*, the honor of a triumph should be restricted to the superior magistrate as the *dux* in question. Falto sought to counter this by emphasizing that in the decisive battle he, not the Consul, had held the actual command, hence served as *dux*; the *sponsio* was meant to compel Catulus to acknowledge this in open court.[23] The question before Caiatinus the *iudex* was not who should be awarded the triumph, but whether the Punic fleet had been destroyed under the Praetor's *ductus*: when the judge pronounced the words *itaque, Lutati, secundum te litem do,* he did not rule against a triumph for Valerius, nor in favor of one for Catulus, but simply rejected the former's claim that the victory had been achieved *suo ductu*. Nothing in the wording of the *sponsio* suggests that it was "carefully chosen to bypass the legal issue of *auspicia*";[24] from what followed, it is evident that the Senate's eventual decision to grant Falto a triumph did not turn on the question of who held the stronger auspices. But to Falto's chagrin, Atilius proceeded to define *suo ductu* precisely in terms of greater *imperium* and stronger auspices, and summarily ruled in Catulus' favor.[25]

---

[22] Beard 210–211, noting: "In fact, the list in the Forum attributes a triumph to both generals"; similarly already Stewart 1987: 146–147 ("the evidence of the Fasti contradicts the report of Valerius Maximus"), cf. 1998: 121, and Auliard 126 ("la présentation du moraliste est pourtant en totale contradiction avec les Actes Triomphaux").

[23] "The purpose of Falto was simply to bring his real services to full public notice": Crook 132; see ibid. for a brief explanation of the *sponsio* procedure. Cf. J. S. Richardson 1975: 51–52.

[24] As Brennan thought, *PRR* 1: 84.

[25] Inaccurate Develin 1978: 431: "It was decided that the *imperium* and *auspicium* under which the battle was fought belonged to the consul, but the *ductus* and *felicitas* could be seen as Falto's, as Valerius Maximus indicates"; thoroughly confused Dalla Rosa 2011: 256 ("after much debate the Senate decided that it was the consul that had to be credited with the victory because of his superior *imperium* and *auspicium*"). Bastien 205, besides mistaking Catulus for his brother, Q. Lutatius Cerco (*cos.* 241), maintains that Caiatinus did not address the question of *ductus* (which that scholar consistently renders as *ductio*, an unfortunate error also found in Berthelet 148–149), and focussed exclusively on the relative strength of *imperium* and auspices. That flies in the face of the evidence. Masi

Atilius' ruling, therefore, merely determined *cuius ductu* the Battle off the Aegates had been won; it had no bearing on whether Falto would be allowed a triumph.[26] That was, and always had been, for the Senate to decide; and here Falto's reasoning fell on receptive ears.[27] In the end, he triumphed two days after Catulus (*Acta Tr.* = *InscrItal* 13.1: 76–77). Nothing in Valerius Maximus, of course, contradicts the evidence of the *Acta*.

4.2.2 Salinator and Nero

In 207 both Consuls, M. Livius Salinator and C. Claudius Nero, joined their forces to defeat Hasdrubal Barqa at the Metaurus. Each requested a triumph, and each was voted one; but amongst themselves they subsequently agreed—we are told— that only one should ride in the chariot, the other follow on horseback: the battle had been fought in Livius' *provincia*, the auspices on that day were his, and his army had been brought home to Rome—an impossibility in the case of Nero's army (*quoniam et in provincia M. Livi res gesta esset et eo die quo pugnatum foret eius forte auspicium fuisset et exercitus Livianus deductus Romam venisset, Neronis deduci de provincia non potuisset*, Livy 28.9.10).[28] Did Nero not auspicate on the

---

Doria 280–284 and Dart-Vervaet 272 are among the few scholars to offer a correct account of the episode.

[26] Unlike Beard, Stewart, and Auliard (above, note 22), Itgenshorst 181–183 does not question the tale's authenticity, but misrepresents Caiatinus' ruling as setting down as indubitable the Consul's right to a sole triumph (". . . deshalb gebe es keinen Zweifel an seinem alleinigen Recht, in Rom einen Triumph zu feiern"), and—echoing Stewart 1998: 121, "the issues involved and the issues addressed are not the same"—claims that the real question of the actual military achievement was not considered at all ("obwohl die eigentliche Frage, nämlich die nach dem tatsächlich geleisteten militärischen Verdienst, überhaupt nicht erörtert worden ist"). In a similar vein, Goldbeck and Mittag 60 state that, once Falto acknowledged that the Consul held the higher *imperium* und *augurium* ([sic,] ignoring the distinction between *auspicia* and *auguria*), "war die Frage des Triumphes bereits geklärt: Nur der Träger des höheren *imperium* könne den Triumph erlangen." Lundgreen (192, 219) describes Caiatinus' role as that of an appointed mediator of the conflict ("der eingesetzte Schlichter" and "der bestellte Schlichter des Streits"; but *sponsio* constitutes an actionable judicial process in a court of law, not mediation: see Crook 135–136 who rejected Falto's request for a triumph. Bergk 72 describes the matter as a "dispute . . . about who was to be given the right to celebrate a triumph" and insists that the hierarchical distinction between Consul and Praetor "simply cannot have been so easily determined, otherwise the very discussion . . . would not have been necessary"; similar Drogula 2015: 204–205. All of them fail to understand the issue Caiatinus was asked to rule on—asked not by the Senate or some other governmental entity, but by Falto when he offered the *sponsio*, and by Catulus when he accepted it—even though Valerius could not have stated it more clearly (*cum de imperio et auspicio inter vos disceptationem susceperim*, says Caiatinus).

[27] Berthelet 149 correctly notes that the episode—with its eventual outcome of a triumph for both—confirms the precedence, within the same *provincia*, of the Consul's *imperium* and auspices over those of the Praetor, as well as the recognition that the *ductus* of military operations occurred under the independent *imperium* and auspices of the latter.

[28] There are good grounds to doubt that Nero was in fact awarded triumphal honors of any kind (be it a curule triumph or an ovation). The reasons given for the final arrangement are precisely those one would expect to be advanced by senators opposing a triumph for Nero, and ring false when ascribed to a *nobilis* who had just a day or two earlier demanded a triumph, and been granted his wish, in full and careful coordination with his colleague (as Livy makes clear, 28.9.4–7). Nor is it in the

day of the battle? Of course he did, just as Falto the Praetor had at the Aegates, and as Paullus did on days when the supreme command was Varro's.[29]

4.2.3 Furius Purpurio

In 200 BC, a major uprising prompted the Praetor L. Furius Purpurio, commanding the *provincia Gallia* with a small garrison, to request from Rome instructions and reinforcements. The Senate advised the Consul C. Aurelius Cotta, still in Rome and assigned the *provincia Italia* (Livy 31.6.2), to send his army from Etruria—where he had previously ordered it to gather—to Gaul, and either lead it in person or authorize the Praetor to take command of it and engage the enemy; the Praetor in turn was to redeploy his original force to Etruria (31.10.1–11.3). Cotta chose the second option,[30] and Furius the Praetor, commanding the Consul's legions, achieved a splendid victory over the insurgents (31.21.1–22.2). Soon after, the Consul himself arrived in Gaul, took now command of his army, and ordered the Praetor to Etruria (31.22.3, 47.4–5); the latter applied for a triumph. In the Senate, opponents objected *quod alieno exercitu rem gessisset*: he had commanded another man's army; supporters maintained that besides the actual achievement, *praeter res gestas*, only one other thing mattered: *an in magistratu suis quis auspiciis gessisset*, whether anyone (*quis*) had held command during his magistracy, under his own auspices (31.48.1–6). Their subsequent argument, however, addresses exclusively the Praetor's *res gestae* (31.48.7, 11–12) and the matter of fighting *alieno exercitu*—which, under the circumstances, was fully justified, having been expressly sanctioned by the *senatus consultum* (31.48.8–10). No further word is said, from either side, about the auspices: the Praetor had commanded *in magistratu* and *suis auspiciis*. That was self-evident.[31]

---

least plausible that the Consuls would practice a daily alternation of auspices and supreme command when engaged in a *provincia* clearly assigned to only one of them; this being the sole known instance of such a situation, it reads like an item thrown in carelessly, without consideration of the actual circumstances. For discussion, see Konrad 2017.

[29] Livy 22.42.8; cf. 22.41.3, 42.1; Mommsen *StR* 1: 95. Bleicken 1981: 268 postulated for the supreme commander of the day an exclusive right to auspicate (thus already Valeton 1890: 425); if his colleague auspicated nevertheless, the result was deemed to be oblative rather than impetrative (n. 33). That confuses the augural concepts involved. The moment a request for permission to act (*si est fas* ...) is put to Iuppiter, the process inevitably is impetrative. The result ("Ergebnis") itself is neither impetrative nor oblative, but simply Iuppiter's response to the question asked; but any time we can speak, with reference to an augural act, of a result, it must have been obtained impetratively: if Iuppiter sends a message on his own—*auspicium oblativum*—it does not constitute an answer to a question, hence not a result in any endeavor. It simply manifests his will.

[30] Cf. Pelikan Pittenger 72–73; Vervaet 2014: 108.

[31] At Livy 31.48.6, editors often emend *suis quis auspiciis* to *suisque auspiciis*, most recently Briscoe in his Teubner edition, even though the mss. reading has been sufficiently explained by Harant 158 ("intellege *an aliquis*, quaestione in universum proposita, non de L. Furio peculiariter") and McDonald (see app. crit. of his *OCT*). Furius' supporters here state a general principle. Briscoe's objection (1973: 159) that *suis quis* would make "the transition to the next sentence ... very sudden" applies

Nor do Furius' opponents allege that he had fought *in aliena provincia*: for although the Senate's decree amounted to an exchange of *provinciae* between Consul and Praetor *extra sortem*,[32] it deliberately left the effective time of that exchange a matter of the Consul's choosing—and the Consul chose to wait in Rome. Hence Gaul remained the Praetor's province at the time the battle was fought.[33] We can be certain that the Consul never auspicated for anything regarding Gaul until he arrived there, and assumed command; in fact, it is likely that he had not yet completed the ceremonies of departure (*profectio*), and thus obtained his authorization to go to war.[34] No one could argue—unlike in the case of Valerius Falto in 241—that the Consul's auspices had been superior to the Praetor's on the day of the battle, a fact that no doubt explains why no one, not even Cotta himself, ever suggested that the Consul should be awarded a triumph for this victory.

4.2.4 Helvius

In 195, the recent commander in Farther Spain, M. Helvius (*pr.* 197), was on his way back to Rome, accompanied by a picked force lent to him for his protection by the current governor, Ap. Claudius Nero (*pr.* 195). Near a town Livy calls "Iliturgi," he found himself attacked by a large force of Celtiberians; he soundly defeated them, retook the town, and slaughtered all the adults in it. On arriving at the camp of the Consul in the hither province, M. Porcius Cato, Helvius sent his force back to Ulterior—*quia tuta iam ab hostibus regio erat*—and proceeded to Rome. He was granted an ovation *ob rem feliciter gestam*; a full triumph was denied on the grounds that he had fought *alieno auspicio et in aliena provincia* (34.10.1–5).

The case of Helvius presents multiple problems, not all of them pertinent to this investigation. Ever since Schulten's masterly study it has been widely accepted

---

equally to *suisque*; for in neither case does the following sentence—the entire following paragraph, in fact, nearly a page in length—connect to the question of whether Furius was *in magistratu* and *suis auspiciis*. The only transition that exists here is the one from *res gestae*.

[32] As Brennan points out, *PRR* 1: 197–198. But there is no evidence that an arrangement had been made "for a delayed change of command" and that the Praetor "only doubtfully fought *in sua provincia*."

[33] Mommsen *StR* 1: 128 n. 3: "Das nicht vacante Commando wird niemals erworben, bevor der ablösende Beamte an Ort und Stelle eintrifft." The point is made clearly by Pelikan Pittenger 73 n. 19 ("in his own province and under his own auspices as praetor") and Vervaet 2014: 66, 110–111, but not always understood: e.g., Bastien 288 ("alors que le consul Aurélius Cotta avait reçu cette guerre comme province"); Lundgreen 194, 232 ("mit dem Heer des Konsuls C. Aurelius in dessen Provinz"); badly confused Itgenshorst 164–165, defining (correctly) Gaul as Furius' province, but describing his victory as having been won "in der *provincia* des Konsuls . . ., nämlich Italien," and misrepresenting his opponents in the Senate as arguing that the Praetor's [sic] army had been under another's auspices during the battle.

[34] See Berthelet 148 n. 5, although incorrectly describing Gaul as the Consul's province.

that there were two Iberian towns by the name of Iliturgi—one in Baetica, some 30 kilometers southwest of Castulo, and another on the east coast between Tortosa and Castellón de la Plana. In fact, the only thing (as Schulten makes clear enough) that can be said for certain is that Livy thought of the town on the east coast as bearing the name "Iliturgi": its native name was almost certainly something else.[35] And Livy wrongly imposes the name "Iliturgi" on at least one other town, Ilorci near Cartagena.[36] All of which leaves the location of Helvius' battle quite uncertain. Nor are we much better off with Cato's camp. Livy's comment that the surrounding area was safe from enemy activity by the time Helvius arrived there (34.10.3) plainly implies that Cato's great battle near Emporiae (34.11–16), at least, had already taken place.[37] It does not mean that Helvius reached Cato's camp at Emporiae: it may have been at Tarraco (34.16.6–10), or even south of the Ebro, after Cato had advanced into what Livy calls "Turdetania" (34.19.1).[38]

Not that it matters here. For Helvius had been succeeded as commander in Ulterior in 196 by Q. Fabius Buteo (*pr.* 196), who in turn had been succeeded in 195—the current year—by Ap. Claudius Nero (*pr.* 195).[39] Detained by a long illness (34.10.5), Helvius remained in Farther Spain: but it was no longer his province. For that question, it does not matter whether the "Iliturgi" of the battle was the one in Baetica, or Ilorci near Cartagena, or the town on the east coast near Castellón. The latter certainly, and Ilorci probably, lay within what was considered

---

[35] Perhaps Ilugo, to conjecture from coins reading *i-l-du-go-i-te*: Tovar 2.3: C-561. In the Roman itineraries, the town's name is *Ildum* (ibid.). See Schulten 292–293.

[36] Identified by Schulten 299–300 with modern Lorca, but more plausibly by Scullard 1970: 264 n. 70 with Lorquí: see Tipps 85–87.

[37] Attempts to deny this (e.g., Briscoe, 1981: 65–66, 70, in keeping with his untenable chronology that would place Cato's entire campaign in the year after his consulship; against which see Knapp 21–46, who accepts, however, Livy's placement of Helvius' arrival before the battle: Knapp 30) seem ill-advised. Once Helvius with his escort was in Cato's camp, the Consul could not be expected to let that force—6,000 men, supposedly—go back to Ulterior while he still faced an undefeated enemy: the fact that they were sent back shows that the area was indeed safe already. (If they had been retained until after the battle and thus augmented Cato's forces in it, we should have heard of that, given all the other detail we are presented with in Cato's campaign.)

[38] Almost certainly not the region in the Baetica commonly known by that name, but an area along the lower east coast, roughly from north of the Sucro River to New Carthage and the headwaters of the Baetis (i.e., modern Valencia, Alicante, Murcia, and Albacete provinces): see Knapp 47–54.

[39] Livy 33.26.2–3, 43.5–7. At 34.10.1, Nero is still the commander in Ulterior; but near the end of the chapter (34.10.5–6), Livy twice refers to Q. Minucius Thermus (*pr.* 196) as Helvius' successor, even though, on Livy's own evidence, Minucius had commanded in Citerior in 196 (33.26.2–3, 44.4). What concerns us is the fact that Helvius had been succeeded in command in the year after his praetorship; it does not matter by whom: cf. Stewart 1987: 301–302. For a plausible attempt to solve the puzzle, see, e.g., Martínez Gázquez 173–179, followed by Develin 1980: 365–366 and J. S. Richardson 1986: 181–182; confused Briscoe 1981: 70–71. Sumner's reconstruction (1970: 85–102, esp. 94–98; cf. 1977: 126–130), postulating an untimely death for Helvius' immediate successor, Fabius Buteo, does not really offer a solution; but his larger contention that the two *provinciae* in Spain continued to be purely military commands without fixed geographic demarcations long after 197 BC, through most of the second century and—at least in part—well into the first, has more in its favor than is generally admitted.

Hispania Citerior at that time, and outside Helvius' assigned former province; but that was immaterial to the question of Helvius' status as a commander. In 195, he held no province, and no magistracy: from the moment his successor had assumed command, anything Helvius did, including the victory he achieved, occurred *in aliena provincia*.[40] Nor did he have an army: the force he led to victory was lent to him by the current *praetor* in Ulterior. (A point Helvius plainly acknowledged when he sent them back there, rather than try to take them along to Rome, to boost his claim to triumph.) There is no evidence that his *imperium*—*pro consule*[41]—had been formally extended, for 196, by *prorogatio* beyond his year as Praetor in 197; it certainly had not been prorogued a second time for 195. It was customary for (pro)magistrates to remain in command until the arrival of their successor even when their year of office or prorogued term had run out; they evidently were considered to be *cum imperio* during such an interim, acting *pro consule* or *pro praetore* (depending on their expired appointment), but a victory achieved under that status does not seem to have normally been eligible for a triumph.[42] Yet it is not entirely certain that—prior to Sulla's *lex Cornelia de maiestate*—without formal prorogation, a commander would be considered to retain *imperium* beyond the day his successor assumed command, all the way until his return to Rome.[43]

The *Lex de provinciis praetoriis* (c.100 BC) does suggest that by the end of the second century, at least, a provincial commander retained his powers until his return to the City, even after formally laying down his command; it should be noted, though, that in the law's enumeration of such powers, anything related to

---

[40] See Versnel 178–179; Brennan *PRR* 1: 167; Vervaet 2014: 113, 116 n. 142; cf. Stewart 1998: 90–91 and, with greater clarity, 1987: 272, 298: "in the idiom of provincial assignment, 'alienus' applies to the duties or rights associated with the provincial assignment of another."

[41] Attested in the *Fasti Urbisalvienses* (*InscrItal* 13.1: 338, 552): [M. Helvius] pro co(n)s(ule) o[vans de Celtib(eris)].

[42] Mommsen *StR* 1: 640–641, adducing the case of L. Valerius Flaccus cos. 195, who defeated the Insubres and Boii in Gaul *pro consule* early in 194, clearly without *prorogatio*: the Consul of that year took over soon afterwards, and Flaccus did not triumph (Livy 34.42.2–5, 46.1–4).

[43] But see Brennan *PRR* 1: 167, cf. 145, arguing that such retention was customary even before it was "codified into law by Sulla" (318 n. 109); similarly Tarpin 284; Rafferty 37, 43. Drogula 2015: 126–129, 209–214, without offering evidence asserts this as a general rule obtaining at all times. Three of the four scholars cited in support of that view, 126 n. 264, make no such claim whatsoever; Lacey 35–37 bases a vague statement to that effect on a muddled discussion of Octavian's summoning the Senate in 32 BC, after his triumviral powers—but not, supposedly, his *imperium*—had expired. But his *imperium* could only have continued *militiae*, where, after Sulla, its persistence until crossing the *pomerium* is not in question. Convene the senate *in Urbe* (Dio's ἐπανελθών, 50.2.5, leaves no doubt of that) Octavian could only do by virtue of the *consularis potestas* (or—*vulgo*—*imperium domi*), and no one will seriously maintain that this did not expire automatically at the end of the consular term. (And, of course, Dio's φρουρὰν τῶν τε στρατιωτῶν ... περιβαλόμενος, "surrounding himself with a guard of his soldiers," 50.2.5, cannot possibly mean "no more than lictors with axes.") In reality—unless the Triumvirate did in fact not end until 31 December 32—Octavian simply acted in accordance with the principle that the powers of non-annual magistrates are not terminated until their formal abdication: see Vervaet 2010: 100–102; Coli 1953: 397–398, 404–412; and below, note 79.

military activity—*imperium* in its most fundamental sense—is notably absent.⁴⁴ In Helvius' case, his successor had already been succeeded in turn. Did he win the victory *suis auspiciis*?

The Senate ruled that he did not. Of course, as long as Helvius had a province and an army, in 197 and until his successor arrived in 196, anything he did within his province he did *suis auspiciis*; and if indeed it could be argued that he retained *imperium* until he returned to the City, then his activities during that period could be considered to occur *suis auspiciis*. But at the time of his victory, the auspices of the current commander—the Praetor Nero, if in Ulterior; Cato the Consul and Manlius the Praetor, if in Citerior—necessarily took precedence over his.

Brennan would allow such precedence as being merely "customary," on the grounds that the auspices of Nero, *pro consule*, "could not be technically superior to those of Helvius," likewise *pro consule*. As he himself points out,⁴⁵ the successor had full authority to order his predecessor out of the province, even if both had *imperium consulare*, hence equal auspices: something had to throw the balance in favor of the successor, and the allotted *provincia* is the only possible tiebreaker.⁴⁶ Indeed, of the three reasons given by Livy (28.9.10) why in 207 Claudius Nero supposedly waived a full triumph and was content with riding along, on horseback, in his colleague's procession—action in Livius' province; Livius' turn at *auspicium* on the day of battle; Livius' army disbanded, but not Nero's—the first and the third must have carried substantially more weight than the second, assuming the second is true in the first place.⁴⁷ After all, for centuries both Consuls had received triumphs for a victory won jointly, even though, on the day of the battle itself, only one of them held the supreme command, hence supreme auspices.⁴⁸ Of course, since promagistrates lacked impetrative auspices—the ability to auspicate—in the first place (as the ancient evidence makes indubitably clear, even

---

⁴⁴ Knidos Copy, col. IV, lines 33–38: . . . ἐξουσία πάντων πραγμάτων ἐ[π]ιστροφήν τε ποιεῖσθαι κολάζειν δικαιοδοτεῖν κρείνει[ν κ]ριτὰς ξενοκρίτας διδόναι ἀναδοχῶν (sive ἀναδόχων) κτημάτων ΤΕ[.]ΓΑΡΟΔΟΣΕΙΣ ἀπελευθερώσεις ὡσαύτως κατὰ τὴν δικαιοδοσίαν ἔστω καθὼς ἐν τῆι ἀρχῆι ὑπῆρχεν οὗ[τ]ός τε ὁ ἀνθύπατος ἕως τούτου ἕως ἂν εἰς πόλ[ι]ν Ῥώμην ἐπανέλθηι ἔστω (see *RStat* 1: 242, 250, 255, 266–267). Vervaet 2014: 57 n. 16 is rightly skeptical about any notion of "automatic prorogation." Rafferty 218 acknowledges that the absence of any reference to military command is problematic, but suggests "that 'to be proconsul' also entails the capacity to legitimately command troops." This ignores another problematic element in the inscription: ὁ ἀνθύπατος may be a stonecutter's error for ἀνυπεύθυνος (cf. Delphoi Copy, Block C, lines 5–6), as Crawford et. al. are inclined to think: *RStat* 1: 267 (overlooked by Rafferty, and misunderstood by Vervaet 2012: 70 n. 101).

⁴⁵ Brennan *PRR* 1: 145 (with n. 73); 167; cf. Livy 41.10.5–11.2.

⁴⁶ Mommsen *StR* 1: 93–96, 127–128; Kloft 72–73; Konrad 2004: 193–195.

⁴⁷ *Contra* Vervaet 2014: 115, unpersuasively; for doubts about an alternating supreme command at the Metaurus, see above, note 28.

⁴⁸ The statements of Versnel 167 with n. 7 that "it was unusual for two commanders to be given a triumph for one and the same victory" and that the year 254 BC "shows the only double triumph before the second century B.C." are patently incorrect: see Pelikan Pittenger's list, 81 n. 51; the most recent example would be C. Flaminius and P. Furius Philus in 223.

though modern orthodoxy says otherwise),[49] the auspices of Ap. Nero—not only *pro consule* but also Praetor—would outrank Helvius' *ipso facto*, as the latter could not even obtain a response from Iuppiter to challenge the one given to the former.

The claim to have fought under his own auspices must have rung even more hollow when Helvius could not even call the troops he led his own. (Had he been in the process of taking his own army back to Italy, after two years of uninterrupted command, the Senate's decision might have come out differently.) Five years earlier, opponents of Furius Purpurio's triumphal request had raised precisely that point—and failed; for Furius had fought *in magistratu, in sua provincia*, and he had commanded the Consul's legions at the Consul's express orders, *ex senatus consulto*, the Consul having chosen not to command them himself.

4.2.5 Suis Auspiciis

What emerges from those four cases is a picture less rigid than we might wish, perhaps, of what the Romans understood when employing the phrase *suis auspiciis*. Paradoxically—at first glance—it appears that a man could be viewed as fighting under his own auspices and under those of another at the same time, depending on one's perspective.[50] Any commander who had left the City *in magistratu* with *imperium* and auspices could legitimately claim to be operating *suis auspiciis* for as long, at least, as he held *imperium* and a *provincia*. Ambiguity arose the moment the operations of one commander—let us call him L. Titius—involved the presence, in the same theater (*provincia*), of another commander, C. Seius, whose auspices, by virtue of his magisterial rank or provincial designation, took precedence in case of conflict (however remote or hypothetical) over those of Titius. While Titius could claim to have won his victory *suis auspiciis*, and apply for a triumph, Seius could maintain that Titius had not, his own—Seius'—auspices taking precedence; and in consequence Seius could claim the triumph, and deny that Titius was entitled to one. (Such was the position taken by the Consul Catulus in 241 vis-à-vis his Praetor, Valerius Falto.)

Yet in determining the validity of a triumphal application, the mere recognition that Seius' auspices outranked, at least on the day of the battle, those of Titius did not of itself settle the issue: precisely because Titius, objectively speaking, had not fought devoid of auspices of his own. Hence other considerations might enter the decision: chiefly, the significance of Titius' *res gestae*, the particular circumstances of the victory (such as the degree of Seius' actual involvement, or lack thereof), and the respective strength of each commander's support within the

---

[49] See Giovannini 1983, esp. 35–44; Rich 1996: 101–105; North 1990a: 55; Lintott 103; Konrad 2004: 187 n. 54.
[50] Berthelet 167 n. 114.

Senate.[51] And yet, the question in whose *provincia* the victory was achieved may have carried greater weight than the rest. The Praetor and the Consul in 242/1 shared the same *provincia*, and although the latter's *imperium* and auspices were superior to those of the former—and under any but the peculiar circumstances of that battle would thus preclude all debate on whether the inferior of the two should also triumph—no one could plausibly argue that the Praetor was *in aliena provincia*. Nor could that argument be made in 200, against Furius Purpurio. Both triumphed. But the argument did apply to Nero the Consul in 207, and to Helvius (perilously close to being *privatus*) in 195. The other factors swayed the Senate to grant Nero a triumph—if the story is true. For Helvius, no such extenuating circumstances availed: without *provincia* and army, his auspices could not muster the necessary independence from those of the current commanders. As Brennan notes, even the ovation may be considered generous.[52]

The four cases may help us to better understand the position of the Magister Equitum, and how Fabius Rullianus, in the tradition that credited him with two successful battles, could claim to have won his victory *suo ductu auspicioque*. The Master of the Horse had auspices, and, when acting on his own, away from the Dictator, he could, and did, consult Iuppiter as needed. But the validity of the Master's auspices depended on the validity of the Dictator's: he could not ascertain it independently. In the ordinary course of events, when both were present with the army, there would be no reason for him to auspicate in the first place; he could not expect a triumph (or even an ovation), any more than a Praetor who had merely assisted the Consul, in a purely subordinate capacity, could expect it.

Yet nothing in principle made it impossible for him to triumph; to do so, though, would require a situation much as that of Fabius Rullianus in the "common" tradition: a significant victory in the Dictator's absence, and the validity of his auspices not in question—or their defect contested. It would not guarantee a triumph, of course, any more than the Praetor in 241 could be certain of a favorable decision. But it would permit the argument that he had fought *suis auspiciis* (the Dictator, being absent, not having auspicated for this particular action), and within the scope of the reason for which he had been named Magister Equitum.

The counterargument, just as in 241, would be that the Dictator's auspices would have taken precedence—indeed, would have been the only ones obtained—had he been present, and that his absence was irrelevant: *quae dictatori religio*

---

[51] Itgenshorst 177–178, noting the effects of *gratia*. The view espoused here is substantially in agreement with Vervaet's lengthy examination, 2014: 54–130.

[52] *PRR* 1: 167. Beard 187–218 now offers a spirited discussion of the factors governing triumphal awards, emphasizing that the extant evidence favors flexibility over rigid rules and requirements, with the outcome frequently turning on a "complex combination of demonstrable military achievement, energetic behind-the-scenes negotiation, and artful persuasion" (188). But as all cases, the one against formal requirements can be overstated. See Lundgreen's sober observations, 225–231; and cf. Dart-Vervaet 275 n. 82.

impedimento ad rem gerendam fuerit, num ea magister equitum solutus ac liber potuerit esse (Livy 8.32.4–7; cf. 8.34.4). In 324 V (and indeed in all the recorded instances of a Magister Equitum left in command of the army, except perhaps for Minucius Rufus in 217[53]), moreover, the Dictator's absence was caused by a need to repeat the auspices. That would call into question the validity of those of his deputy: he might claim that he had received an affirmative response from Iuppiter before the battle, but if the Dictator's auspices were invalid or uncertain, one could reasonably hold that those of the Master-of-Horse, obtained through having been named by the Dictator, surely were not on firmer ground. The very event—the Dictator's departure—that enabled the Magister Equitum to use his own auspices in this case also vitiated them. The defenders of Rullianus, of course, need not see it that way. If the Master's latent auspices became active only in situations where he was acting separate from the Dictator, it could be argued that their validity remained unaffected by whatever had impaired those of the latter, and that a case such as that of 241 did not, in fact, constitute a parallel. For both the Consul and the Praetor had obtained auspices pertaining to the battle on that day (hence those of the Consul would take precedence), but in Rullianus' instance the Dictator had not; and the fact that the Dictator's auspices would have taken precedence had he been present might be deemed irrelevant. How the College of Augurs would have ruled on the matter, who can say?

Leaving aside the question of valid auspices, that the Dictator in such a situation could claim a triumph for himself is evident: Rullianus burned all the spoils precisely to deny his superior that opportunity (*ne suae gloriae fructum dictator caperet nomenque ibi scriberet aut spolia in triumpho ferret*, 8.30.9).[54] As for the Magister Equitum, his claim would have to be judged by the Senate, the outcome depending on the significance of his *res gestae*, the particular circumstances of the victory, and the respective strength of his and the Dictator's support within the Senate. No Master of the Horse ever held a triumph: none ever won a battle in the absence of the Dictator.[55]

4.3 The Consul as Magister Equitum

The simultaneous holding of multiple annual "patrician" magistracies appears to have been deemed improper from earliest times, and was formally prohibited by plebiscite in 432 V. On the other hand, cumulation of an annual magistracy with one of the "regular" but non-annual offices occurred repeatedly, though not often; we know for certain of at least four men being Consul and Dictator at the same

---

[53] Above, note 12. [54] Vervaet 2014: 121.
[55] Except, of course, Minucius Rufus—whose subsequent disgrace rendered the issue moot.

time.[56] Did custom permit a Consul simultaneously to act as Magister Equitum as well? The evidence is mixed, yet generally unfavorable. (The question will acquire significance in a different context later on.)[57]

4.3.1 Cases of Cumulation

Though Livy's date for the Battle of Lake Regillus, in 499 V, would imply just such a cumulation (the Dictator Postumius Albus naming the Consul T. Aebutius Helva his Master of the Horse), he was well aware that this might be wrong; indeed, ancients and moderns alike have found the year 496 more probable—in which Aebutius did not hold the consulship.[58] In 331 V, the *Fasti* specifically note: *C. Val[e]rius L. f. L. n. Potitus, postea quam co(n)s(ulatu) abiit, mag(ister) eq(uitum)*. Livy's manuscripts (8.18.1, 13) give the Consul's praenomen as *t(itus)*, the Master's as *l(ucius)*. Now "Titus" is unattested among the Valerii, and on the basis of the *Fasti* and Diod. 17.74.1, the Consul's name in Livy is commonly corrected to "Gaius";[59] if so, Livy's Master-of-Horse that year was not identical with the Consul. But a corruption from /l/ to /t/ would appear just as easy as one from /c/ to /t/: perhaps Livy, too, thought of both as being the same man, albeit named L. Valerius. What matters is the specific note of abdication in the *Fasti*. This was almost certainly the first recorded instance of a sitting Consul being named Magister Equitum; his avoiding cumulation should have set a precedent. Oakley, thinking—with due caution—that cumulation was "probably possible," voices doubts: "It seems unlikely that a consul would have abdicated in order to be a mere *magister equitum*."[60] For what purpose would the abdication have been invented, then, if such cumulation was not perceived as problematic, at least in later times?

Confusion reigns in that *annus mirabilis*, 320 V, for which the *Fasti* record no less than three different Dictators, and L. Papirius Cursor as Consul both and Magister Equitum—not only once, but twice, under two different Dictators. Now Livy (9.15.9–10, 16.11) makes it clear that the sources he chose to follow knew of no Dictators and Masters of the Horse in that year: they ascribed the Roman capture of Luceria and subsequent triumph—in 319—to Papirius as Consul (*II* and *III*), and told of a great victory (though no triumph) at Caudium by his colleague, Q. Publilius Philo. But Livy also mentions a discrepant tradition, attributing the victories at both Caudium and Luceria—and the triumph—to the Dictator

---

[56] T. Larcius in 501 or 498; Q. Publilius Philo in 339; M. Livius Salinator in 207; C. Iulius Caesar in 48, 46, 45, and 44. (The cases of A. Postumius Albus in 396 and L. Cornelius Sulla in 80 remain uncertain.) Cf. *StR* 1: 513–515.

[57] Chapter 6.7.   [58] Livy 2.19.2–3, 21.2–4; Dion. Hal. 6.2.1–3; see Ogilvie 286.

[59] "An inevitable conjecture" (Oakley *CL* 2: 598).   [60] Oakley *CL* 2: 602; cf. 3: 168.

L. Cornelius Lentulus, with Papirius as Magister Equitum. There is no telling whether that version made Papirius step down from the consulship before becoming Master of the Horse; nor, indeed, whether it had him as Consul of that year in the first place. (What seems clear from all versions is that he was remembered as having a major part in the capture of Luceria, in whatever magistracy— and year.) That same—or possibly a third—tradition reported a L. Papirius Mugillanus,[61] not Cursor, as Consul in the following year (319 V), with Q. Aulius Cerretanus for colleague.

Of the three dictatorships the *Fasti* record in this year, 320 V, Lentulus' alone has left a trace in the literary tradition. Doubts arise, immediately, in the case of the second.

As discussed earlier,[62] the *Fasti* show C. Maenius (*cos.* 338) as Dictator in 320 V and again in 314 V, both times with M. Folius Flaccinator (*cos.* 318) for Magister Equitum; yet the literary sources know of only one dictatorship. Its date, however, was reported differently in different accounts, with a discrepancy of at least six years. The *FC*, here and no doubt elsewhere, incorporated both chronological traditions, and thus produced two dictatorships for C. Maenius.

Which leaves the *FC*'s third dictatorship in 320 V, of T. Manlius Torquatus (*cos. III* 340), with the Consul Papirius Cursor—again—as Master of the Horse. Livy knows nothing of it, in contrast to Torquatus' first two tenures as Dictator, in 353 and 349 (7.19.9–21.2; 7.26.11). It need not be fictitious in itself, but the year should be held very much in doubt. No argument, in sum, regarding cumulation can be based on the record of the *Fasti* for 320 V.

Cumulation has been inferred in 302 V from Livy, who prefers M. Aemilius Paullus as Magister Equitum over Q. Fabius Rullianus (10.3.3–8), under M. Valerius Maximus as Dictator. The problems are notorious. Paullus is commonly identified with the Consul of that year, whose praenomen, alas, is missing from Livy (10.7.1). Diodoros supplies "Marcus" (20.106.1), Cassiodorus "L." The *Fasti* are no help: the colleague of M. Livius Denter in 302 has not survived, and the dictatorship comes under 301 V, the last of the "dictator years"—with Paullus as the second of two Magistri Equitum to Valerius Corvus, Rullianus serving first. "To follow Cassiodorus would give a man otherwise unknown."[63] He would not be the only such man in the long list of Roman Consuls; and if the consulship be the only thing known about Lucius, the turn at Magister Equitum is the only certain thing known about Marcus. The names in Cassiodorus, with rare exceptions, accurately reflect those in Livy—which cannot be said of Diodoros. To follow the latter because it would allow us to identify the Consul with the Master of the Horse ("most economical," in Oakley's view) would make sense if such

---

[61] Livy 9.15.11; the tradition also crops up, unexpectedly, in the Chronographer of 354: *Murillano III et Cerritano*.
[62] Chapter 1.2.1.   [63] Oakley *CL* 4: 52.

cumulation were a common practice; which, even if permitted, it was not. Caution, rather (along with widespread trouble when it comes to names in Diodoros), should point us toward "Lucius" as the Consul's name, avoiding thus the unusual cumulation. Nor, if "Marcus" be correct, does Livy's narrative preclude the possibility that the Consul resigned before assuming office as Magister Equitum. The evidence from 302 permits no verdict but *non liquet*.

Four Consular Tribunes are reported as Masters of the Horse. First, A. Cornelius Cossus in 426 V (Livy 4.31.5, 34.5); "but our sources are not reliable on the career of Cossus."[64] Next, C. Servilius Axilla in 418 V (*FC*; Livy 4.46.11–12); but Livy notes a divergent tradition that had a Servilius Ahala. In 408, C. Servilius Ahala names a Dictator and, in turn, is named Magister Equitum (*FC*; Livy 4.57.6); the manner in which Livy refers to his re-election as Tribune for 407 (*refectus continuato honore*) very much implies cumulation. Last, T. Quinctius Capitolinus in 385 V (Livy 6.11.10, 12.10). Plutarch *Cam.* 36.4 knows him, not A. Cornelius Cossus, as Dictator: a mere slip of memory, probably, although it might suggest that, in the biographer's information, Quinctius played a more prominent part in dealing with the *Manliana seditio* than Livy allows. Again, no iron-clad evidence here, though certainly more favorable to possible cumulation than in the case of actual Consuls.

4.3.2 Lepidus as Magister Equitum

Yet we have one unequivocal statement that cumulation was contrary to *mos*. Thus Dio tells us, on the occasion of M. Aemilius Lepidus being Consul both and Magister Equitum in 46 BC. It has been suggested that what Dio found objectionable was the Consul's naming himself to that post, rather than leaving the choice to the Dictator.[65] The Greek and the context show otherwise. Having noted at the outset of the book that Lepidus served as Caesar's "colleague" in both the consulship and the dictatorship that year (43.1.1–3), Dio now closes out his account of 46 by returning to Caesar's official positions. He was Dictator and, near the end of the year, was elected Consul (in other words, again, for 45), with Lepidus as Magister Equitum convening the People for that purpose (τοῦ Λεπίδου ἐν τῇ ἱππαρχίᾳ τὸν δῆμον ἐς τοῦτο συναγαγόντος· ἱππάρχησε γὰρ καὶ τότε, αὐτὸς ἑαυτὸν ἐν τῇ ὑπατείᾳ ἐπειπὼν ἵππαρχον παρὰ τὰ πάτρια, 43.33.1): "for he was Master of the Horse at that time, too, having named, as Consul, himself Magister Equitum, contrary to ancestral custom." The emphasis here is clearly on the fact that Lepidus held the office (mentioned three times in less than three lines of text: ἐν τῇ ἱππαρχίᾳ ... ἱππάρχησε ... ἵππαρχον), not on the manner in which he acquired

---

[64] Oakley *CL* 3: 168 n. 1. He omits the strongest case favoring cumulation, Ahala in 408.
[65] Oakley *CL* 3: 168 n. 3. The notion is not new, and Mommsen knew better: *StR* 1: 514 n. 1.

it. Indeed, παρὰ τὰ πάτρια—which one would expect close to the offending item—stands next to ἵππαρχον, far from ἑαυτόν.

There exists no good reason for rejecting Dio's view that simultaneous holding of the consulship and the office of Magister Equitum was *contra morem maiorum*. But why? There clearly was no hindrance to being Consul and Dictator at the same time. An answer may be sought in the peculiar relationship between the Dictator and his deputy. The Master of the Horse, alone among magistrates, held his office at the sole discretion of another—the Dictator, who could order him to abdicate. Alone among magistrates, the Magister Equitum had to take direct orders—not merely in the form of a prohibition to act—from his superior. The Dictator could not give orders to the Consul as Consul: his superior power was grounded not in a technically higher *imperium*, but in the peculiar effect of his office that rendered the Consul powerless in his presence, reduced effectively to the status of a *privatus*. And yet the Consul was still Consul, resuming his *imperium* (and lictors) the moment he parted company with the Dictator. For the Consul simultaneously to be Dictator caused no diminution of his *dignitas*; to become the Dictator's direct subordinate while remaining Consul might well be seen as incompatible with the *maiestas* of the office.[66] It is probably no coincidence that we have no instance of a Censor being Magister Equitum. (In 210, P. Crassus assumed the latter office only after stepping down as Censor, upon the death of his colleague.)[67] What of the "Consular" Tribunes—at least one of whom, in 408, can safely be said to have held both offices simultaneously? Whatever their powers, they were not "Consuls," but *tribuni militum* acting as stand-ins for the regular chief magistracy (whatever that was called in their day): having to take orders from the Dictator would hardly diminish their prestige.

4.4 The Magister Equitum and the Augurs

Appointment of the Magister Equitum by the Consul, though, strikes one as odd, to say the least. Yet Dio tells the same procedure about Marcus Antonius in 48: Caesar entered his (second) dictatorship forthwith, even though being outside Italy (Dio thought that was improper), and chose Antonius—not yet a *vir praetorius*—as his Master of the Horse; "*and the Consul named him, too.*" The Augurs issued a protest—not against the manner of Antonius' appointment, but its duration (a whole year, like the Dictator). No hint, in Dio, at anything being wrong in a Consul naming both the Dictator and his deputy.[68]

---

[66] Cf. Wittmann *StO* 719 n. 255; Section 4.1, above, and Chapter 3.3.

[67] Livy 27.5.19, 6.18; *FC* = *InscrItal* 13.1: 46–47: *postea quam censura abiit mag. eq.* (Mommsen *StR* 1. 515 n. 1 would adduce this as an example of cumulation, "wie es scheint": certainly not.)

[68] Dio 42.21.1, καὶ ὅ τε Καῖσαρ τὴν δικτατορίαν παραχρῆμα, καίπερ ἔξω τῆς Ἰταλίας ὢν, ὑπέστη, καὶ τὸν Ἀντώνιον μηδὲ ἐστρατηγηκότα ἵππαρχον προελόμενος, καὶ εἶπε καὶ τοῦτον ὁ ὕπατος, καίτοι τῶν

4.4.1 Caesar and Antonius: the Time Frame

Could it, in fact, have happened thus, in 48 (and 46)? Cicero appears to confirm it: without Caesar's knowledge, while he was in Alexandria, Caesar's friends saw to it that Antonius was made Magister Equitum (*Phil.* 2.62, *accessit ut Caesare ignaro, cum esset ille Alexandriae, beneficio amicorum eius magister equitum constitueretur*). A fitting scenario is conceivable.

The Battle of Pharsalos was fought on August 9, 48. But Caesar himself did not send any official despatch of the event, and no honors were voted to him until after the news of Pompeius' death (September 28, 48) had reached Rome and become fully accepted when his seal-ring arrived: no earlier, probably, than late in November.[69] The Senate would have authorized the dictatorship towards the end of that month, or in the first days of December.[70] Now under the customary practice, the Consul, P. Servilius Isauricus (*cos. II* 41), would immediately perform the *dictio*; word of the event would be sent to Egypt, where the Dictator would name his Magister Equitum. Since the man chosen for that post was not in Egypt but in Rome, the Dictator would have to send word of Antonius' appointment back to the capital, and only once that missive arrived could the Master-of-Horse assume his office. By now, the calendar would read January or February, 47.

After Pharsalos, Caesar had ordered Antonius to lead several legions back to Italy (Cic. *Phil.* 2.59–61; cf. Plut. *Ant.* 8.4; Dio 42.30.1): when exactly did Caesar decide that he could spare them, and how long did it take Antonius to reach Rome? The common guess is that he arrived in October or November;[71] he is first attested there in December. On the 17th, Cicero wrote Atticus (11.7.2) from Brundisium how Antonius had sent him a copy of Caesar's letter prohibiting any Republicans from returning to Italy, for now; after Cicero explained that he had come back at Caesar's personal request, Antonius issued a general edict in accordance with Caesar's instructions, but excepting Cicero. The edict shows that he was now in office as Magister Equitum, and the exchange with Cicero occurred within a three-week window before the 17th. (It finds no mention in the previous letter, *Att.* 11.6, dated November 27.) No more than the same three-week window is available between Caesar's appointment as Dictator and Antonius' assuming

---

οἰωνιστῶν σφοδρότατα ἀντειπόντων μηδενὶ ἐξεῖναι πλείω τοῦ ἑξαμήνου χρόνον ἱππαρχῆσαι. Wittmann (*StO* 714, 717) accepts this procedure without question, for both Lepidus in 46 and Antonius in 48; likewise Vervaet 2004: 81–82 for the latter.

[69] Cic. *Att.* 11.6.5, *de Pompei exitu mihi numquam dubium fuit*; writing from Brundisium on November 27, he had apparently just learned in a letter from Atticus that the death was now confirmed beyond doubt (presumably Cicero meant to say that he had believed the earlier reports right away: Shackleton Bailey *CLA* 7: 273). Dio 42.18.1–3 describes the bad news finding slow acceptance in Rome. See Ferrary 10.

[70] Broughton (*MRR* 2: 272, 284 n. 1; cf. 3: 106–108) argued for October, once the news of Pharsalos had got to Rome; but the evidence from Cicero and Dio (see above, note 69) demands a later date.

[71] Pelling 1988: 135.

office as his Master of the Horse. Not time enough, in other words, for the requisite communications to travel from Rome to Alexandria and back.

Hence, as far as circumstances can be ascertained, it seems improbable that Antonius could have been named Magister Equitum in the normal manner, by the Dictator. What could have prompted the unusual procedure reported by Dio? If it was deemed crucial that Antonius be able to exercise his powers as Caesar's deputy immediately, as soon as the dictatorship had been agreed upon, it does seem the only way in which such a purpose could be accomplished. Against this, one must observe that there is no concrete evidence of anyone being in a hurry to see Antonius take charge in Rome. Dio has nothing to report of Antonius' activities until 47; throughout 48, it is Servilius the Consul who takes care of Italy—especially the abortive uprising of Caelius and Milo, which Dio seems to date in summer and fall.[72] Whatever the precise chronology of that spectacle, Servilius had handled the crisis firmly and successfully: Caesar had no cause to doubt his consular colleague's ability, or loyalty.

4.4.2 The Magister Equitum Named by the Consul: Constitutional Considerations

There was, however, a different—and more substantial—problem with letting Caesar name his Master of the Horse. In 210 BC, the Senate had voted that a Dictator could not be named outside Italy: *patres extra Romanum agrum—eum autem in Italia terminari—negabant dictatorem dici posse* (Livy 27.5.15).[73] Although Livy does not say so, the spatial taboo involved makes it virtually certain that an augural response lay at the bottom of the Senate decree.[74] Surely the same restriction applied to the Magister Equitum: thus Caesar, in Egypt, could not possibly name one. The identical obstacle would obtain in 46, where Dio recounts his second instance of a Consul naming the Magister Equitum: Caesar was named Dictator soon after the Battle of Thapsus, probably by the end of April, but did not return to Italy until July 25.[75]

---

[72] Dio 42.23–25; note 42.23.1, καθάπερ ἡττημένου τε αὐτοῦ (sc. τοῦ Καίσαρος) καὶ ἐφθαρμένου. Caesar himself (*BCiv* 3.20–23) recounts the incident well before Pharsalos. There need be no contradiction here. Caelius evidently started his agitation in the spring, but the affair could easily have developed over several months, and he may not have resorted to open violence—and a clear break with Caesar—until convinced that the latter was doomed in Greece. His last letter to Cicero (*Fam.* 8.17), early in 48, while expressing disgust with the Caesarians (and himself, for having joined them), and wishing for a Republican victory (politically feasible, particularly in view of changing public sentiment in Rome), remains wary about the likelihood of defeating Caesar in battle.

[73] On the ms. reading (*P = Puteaneus*, saec. V) *in Italia*, see Mommsen *StR* 2.1: 152 n. 2.

[74] Cf. Catalano 1978: 493, 499–503, 529, 534–536.

[75] [Caes.] *BAfr* 98; cf. Dio 43.14.3 (the excessive number of lictors, cumulating those of his three dictatorships, clearly had been voted by the Senate before his return, no doubt right after the news of victory arrived from Africa); and see P. Groebe "Iulius (131)" *RE* 10.1 (1918) 244; Degrassi *InscrItal*

Dio's procedure itself is not beyond constitutional comprehension. In 49, the People, by legislation (Caes. *BCiv* 2.21.5), had authorized the Praetor to name a Dictator; surely they would now empower the Consul to name a Master-of-Horse as well, if so desired. What augural law had to say about that, we simply do not know. In all likelihood, no precedent existed; the question would turn on whether there was something inherent in the Master's auspices that rendered appointment by anyone but the Dictator impossible. On the one hand, since the Consul's auspices and *imperium* sufficed to name a Dictator, they should also enable him to name the latter's deputy, especially if so directed by legislation. On the other hand, the Magister Equitum was tied to the Dictator in ways that had no parallel among other republican offices. Like the Dictator, he received his auspices and *imperium* not through election, but appointment; the formal term was *dicere* in both instances.[76] His auspices, once obtained, were his own, yet remained tied to those of the Dictator—anything that disturbed or vitiated the latter's auspices necessarily also affected his. Then again, the Master's office did not terminate automatically with that of the Dictator; the latter must order him to abdicate.

In 48, if Antonius were named by Caesar, he obviously would not be able to enter office until confirmation arrived from Egypt that the Dictator had appointed him. But what if indeed the Magister Equitum was not named by the Dictator, but the Consul? Would he have been able to assume his office right away, even before the Dictator had taken his initial auspices? In the normal way of things, as argued earlier, when Iuppiter confirmed the Dictator's auspices on the day of taking office, he also confirmed those of the Magister Equitum yet to be named.[77] The Augural College had approved the unusual circumstances of Caesar's second dictatorship, at least with regard to the length of term (Dio 42.21.2); if it was indeed the Consul who named the Magister Equitum on this occasion, it stands to reason that such a departure from traditional practice had likewise been sanctioned by the Augurs. This would have included, of necessity, special arrangements for Antonius to obtain his auspices, so as to be able to assume office right away. Having ruled that it was *fas* for the Consul to name, *dictatoris loco*, the Magister Equitum, the Augurs might well hold that it was *fas* for the Consul also to ask Iuppiter, *dictatoris loco*, for confirmation of the Master's auspices; or they could have ruled that, once the Consul had named him, the Master-of-Horse would have auspices from that moment *ac si a dictatore dictus fuerit*. (In the unlikely event that Iuppiter disapproved of Caesar's auspices when the latter asked for them in Alexandria, both would have to abdicate.) Thus the procedure described by Dio would have offered a way to enable Antonius to take over

---

13.1: 133. The recently discovered Roman treaty with Lycia (*AE* 2005 no. 1487 line 1 = *SEG* 55 no. 1452) shows that Caesar was in office as *dictator III* on July 24: see Kantor 135.

[76] Mommsen *StR* 2.1: 174 n. 8; Baroni 777 n. 13.

[77] For discussion of the Master's auspices, see above, Section 4.1.

immediately—which, seeing how he was in office by mid-December, clearly is what happened.

It passes belief, at any rate, that Caesar's friends in Rome should have chosen Antonius for Magister Equitum *Caesare ignaro*, as Cicero would have it (*Phil.* 2.62). Caesar sent no official despatch from Greece; but he sent Antony, and nothing kept him from writing, unofficially, to his friends: he "had doubtless made his wishes known."[78] Those wishes, first of all, presumably included the dictatorship: nothing compels the notion that it was voted by the Senate *sponte sua*. The dictatorship did not come under the customary limit of six months, but was to be of a whole year's duration (as the sources tell us: Plut. *Caes.* 51.1; Dio 42.20.3).[79] As with Sulla in 82, an extended term would almost certainly be sanctioned not merely by *senatus consultum* but by comitial legislation, as Dio indeed seems to indicate.[80] Now, long ago Mommsen noted that when first the *comitia* got involved in the business of installing a Dictator, allegedly in 217 and certainly in 210, their vote seems to have prescribed not only the identity of the Dictator to be named but also that of his Magister Equitum.[81] In 217, Fabius Maximus is "elected" Dictator by the People, seemingly along with his deputy (*dictatorem creavit populus Q. Fabium Maximum et magistrum equitum M. Minucium Rufum*, Livy 22.8.6). In 210, more explicitly, a plebiscite instructs the Consul to name Q. Fulvius Flaccus Dictator, who in turn, *ex eodem plebis scito*, names P. Licinius Crassus his Master-of-Horse (Livy 27.5.16–19). This may have set a precedent. In

---

[78] Pelling 1988: 134; cf. Dio 42.18.1.

[79] In line with his theory that Roman officials exercising "constituent powers" ("constituirende Gewalten") were not bound by any term limit, Mommsen had argued for an indefinite length of Caesar's first and second dictatorships, both of which he believed to be *rei publicae constituendae causa*: *CIL* I² p. 41 and (slightly less certain, "höchst wahrscheinlich") *StR* 2.2: 715–716. The first dictatorship, in 49, is now generally thought to have been *comitiorum habendorum causa*; all the others, *rei gerundae causa*: Degrassi *InscrItal* 13.1: 132–133; Broughton *MRR* 2: 284 n. 1; Wittmann *StO* 712–715. For a general critique of Mommsen's constituent-powers theory, see Bringmann 1988. But Coli 1953 (esp. 397–398, 404–412; cf. Vervaet 2010: 100–102) demonstrated that, for non-annual magistracies (such as Dictator or Censor), their nominal limit (e.g., of six or eighteen months) did not result in automatic termination: only formal abdication brought about the legal end of the office and its inherent powers.

[80] Dio 42.21.1, ταῦτ' οὖν οὕτω καὶ ἐψηφίσθη καὶ ἐκυρώθη. On Sulla, see Appian *BCiv* 1.98.459, and cf. Plut. *Sulla* 33.1–2, confirming legislation as part of the process (albeit in regard to Sulla's novel task, *legibus scribundis et rei publicae constituendae*). Pace Kantor 135 n. 2, it is unlikely that all the honors and powers given to Caesar in the fall of 48 (Dio 42.20) were voted merely by the Senate; at a minimum, the repeal of the *lex Pompeia* of 52 BC (Dio 42.20.4) should have entailed comitial legislation. As Kantor notes, the claim in Fufius Calenus' speech (Dio 46.13.1) that "both items were voted on and acceptable to us as well as the People" (ἐψηφίσθη τε ὁμοίως ἀμφότερα καὶ ἤρεσε καὶ ἡμῖν καὶ τῷ δήμῳ) refers only to the one-year terms for Dictator and Magister Equitum; but, "invented" speech or not, it is difficult to believe that Dio was not thinking of comitial legislation here. See also Wiseman 2009: 198 (notwithstanding the bizarre assertions that "Caesar's power was not usurped, but granted constitutionally by the only authority competent to do so" and that "it did not follow that Caesar was a despot, or that the rule of law had been abandoned": any modern totalitarian regime would meet that standard of lawfulness and legitimacy) and 209 (making the case that the material in Calenus' speech may have come, ultimately, from Asinius Pollio); Ferrary 12–16.

[81] *StR* 2.1: 175, "wohl aber scheint in den wenigen Fällen, wo die Comitien den Dictator bezeichnen, dies auch auf den Reiterführer erstreckt worden zu sein."

82, the Centuriate Assembly directed the Interrex, L. Valerius Flaccus (*cos.* 100), to name a Dictator; he named Sulla, and then Sulla made Flaccus his Magister Equitum.[82] In Cicero's reference to the matter (*Att.* 9.15.2), the manuscripts, with rare exceptions, read: *sed si Sulla potuit efficere ab interrege ut dictator diceretur et magister equitum, cur hic non possit?* Editors usually seclude [*et magister equitum*], perhaps unjustly.[83] Livy twice (at least) employs similar shorthand: *dictator ab consulibus ex auctoritate senatus dictus P. Cornelius Rufinus, magister equitum M. Antonius* (8.17.3); *consules . . . expressum senatus consulto est ut dictatorem dicerent . . . ; Q. Fabium Ambustum dixerunt et P. Aelium Paetum magistrum equitum* (9.7.13). The plural—Consuls—already signals that Livy here does not aim at constitutional precision; we have no cause to think that, in either instance, the Consul did in fact also name the Master-of-Horse.[84] Nor should we assume that in 82, Flaccus named not only the Dictator but himself Magister Equitum as well.[85] Yet the example of 210 may plausibly be thought to have been followed: the *lex* enacted in 82 did not merely empower the Interrex to perform the *dictio*, but specified the Dictator to be named, along with the name of the Magister Equitum to be appointed by the latter, once named.[86] A reason for this procedure may be sought in its exceptional nature: it may have been felt that comitial interference with the selection process was incompatible with the *liberum arbitrium* of the nominator. Such clearly was the objection of the Consul of 210, M. Valerius Laevinus, against this procedure when "he refused to ask the People for something that was in his power" (*cum . . . se populum rogaturum negasset quod suae potestatis esset*, Livy 27.5.17). Hence the *comitia*, once involved, had to specify both the men to be named.

In Dio's account of 48, Caesar (1) assumes office as Dictator and (2) choses Antonius as Magister Equitum; and only then (3) does the Consul name the latter (42.21.1). Taken at face value, the time lag inherent between (2) and (3) should mean that Caesar had not settled on Antonius as his deputy until he received word, in Egypt, that he had been named Dictator: an evident impossibility, as Antonius was in office by the middle of December, within three weeks at most of Caesar's appointment. Plutarch has Caesar name Antonius as Magister Equitum

---

[82] Appian *BCiv* 1.98.459–99.462; *FC* = *InscrItal* 13.1: 54–55 (Flaccus *mag. eq.* 82). On the procedure—not direct election in the *comitia* (as Broughton *MRR* 2: 66 and sundry others would have it), but *dictio* by the Interrex in consequence of special legislation—see Mommsen *StR* 2.1: 147–148, 704; Gabba 341–342; Jahn 162; Linderski *AL* 2183; Jehne 567 n. 47; Lintott 110; Vervaet 2004: 40–41; Baroni 775–777 with nn. 6, 13.

[83] See Shackleton Bailey *CLA* 4: 183.

[84] Cf. Masi Doria 138 n. 3; perhaps also Livy 22.57.9 (*inde dictator ex auctoritate patrum dictus M. Iunius et Ti. Sempronius magister equitum*).

[85] Cf. Oakley *CL* 2: 588; 3: 112. Vervaet 2004: 40–41, 79–84 insists that "Cicero explicitly records that the Valerian Law actually commissioned the *interrex* to nominate Sulla as dictator and then himself as *magister equitum.*" This both misrepresents what Cicero says (nothing about "then himself") and ignores the evidence from Livy. See Baroni 777–778 with n. 13, surely correct.

[86] Wittmann *StO* 706.

after his victory in Greece, and before sending him to Rome—but after having been named Dictator himself (*Ant.* 8.4, μετὰ δὲ τὴν νίκην δικτάτωρ ἀναγορευθείς, αὐτὸς μὲν ἐδίωκε Πομπήιον, Ἀντώνιον δ᾽ ἵππαρχον ἑλόμενος εἰς Ῥώμην ἔπεμψεν). As it stands, this cannot be; but it may reflect information that Caesar had communicated his wishes to the Senate through and for Antonius.

We may further note, in Cicero (*Phil.* 2.62), the peculiar phrasing applied to Antonius' installation: *ut . . . magister equitum constitueretur.* Not *diceretur* (as one might expect, if everything proceeded according to traditional practice). With reference to the appointment of a magistrate, *constituere* is vague, non-technical—but it perfectly suits the process described by Dio, if not his precise sequence of events. Certainly, Cicero's allegation that Antonius was made Magister Equitum *Caesare ignaro* deserves no confidence (a few paragraphs later he would claim that, at Pharsalos, Antonius had personally slain Domitius Ahenobarbus—a patently absurd notion[87]); it is expressly contradicted by Plutarch and Dio. And yet—for Cicero's jibe that Antonius had been "made" (*constitueretur*) Magister Equitum by Caesar's friends without Caesar's knowledge to have some effect, at least, four years later on his intended audience, one must allow for a greater than normal involvement of elements in Rome in the process of his appointment. Nothing more need be implied than that the law authorizing Caesar's extended dictatorship also specified the appointment, *nominatim*, of Antonius:[88] that, supposedly (and unbelievably), had been the work of Caesar's friends. After all, no one could remember an official letter from Greece announcing that Caesar demanded to be named Dictator, with Antonius for deputy.

Viewed from this angle, Cicero's comment does indeed lend support to Dio: if Antonius had in fact been pronounced Master of Horse by Servilius the Consul, in Rome, after Caesar was named Dictator, the claim, four years later, that this had been arranged by Caesar's friends might ring true in some ears. (The truly gullible might now even accept *Caesare ignaro*.)

4.4.3 No Decree for Caesar

The Augurs incurred some ridicule for their objection to Antonius' extended term, having previously approved of the Dictator's year-long appointment: how could they oppose that of the Magister Equitum?[89] Augural law was an arcane business, not easily understood among the general public (including some

---

[87] Cic. *Phil.* 2.71, *fueras in acie Pharsalica antesignanus; L. Domitium, clarissimum et nobilissimum virum, occideras.* For what actually happened, see Caes. *BCiv* 3.99.5: *L. Domitius ex castris in montem refugiens, cum vires eum lassitudine defecissent, ab equitibus est interfectus.*
[88] Vervaet 2004: 82 n. 161.
[89] Dio 42.21.2, ἀλλ᾽ ἐκεῖνοι μὲν γέλωτα ἐπὶ τούτῳ πολὺν ὠφλίσκανον, αὐτὸν μὲν τὸν δικτάτορα ἐς ἐνιαυτὸν παρὰ πάντα τὰ πάτρια λεχθῆναι γνόντες, περὶ δὲ δὴ τοῦ ἱππάρχου ἀκριβολογούμενοι.

senators), nor perhaps prompting much interest.[90] What struck the uninitiate, then or now, as nitpicking and hairsplitting may have been firmly grounded in the *disciplina*. To understand the Augurs' position, it will help to go back a year and examine their response to Caesar's demand, in 49 BC, for a decree of the *collegium* that would authorize the naming of a Dictator by a Praetor.

We must ask, first of all: Who were "the Augurs"? Of the fifteen members in the College at the beginning of 49, we know—at least—twelve.[91] Three went with the Republicans to Greece: Ap. Claudius Pulcher (*cos.* 54), Faustus Cornelius Sulla (*q.* 54), and Cn. Pompeius Magnus (*cos. III* 52). The same move may safely be assumed for P. Cornelius Lentulus Spinther (*q.* 44): he would have accompanied his father. A fifth one—unable, as always, to make up his mind promptly—followed in the summer: M. Tullius Cicero (*cos.* 63). Three others—Antonius himself, Q. Cassius Longinus (*tr. pl.* 49), and Ser. Sulpicius Galba (*pr.* 54)—were closely attached to Caesar. Two or three more, neutral or supporting Caesar's cause, remained in Italy: L. Iulius Caesar (*cos.* 64), Q. Mucius Scaevola (*tr. pl.* 54), and probably M. Valerius Messalla Rufus (*cos.* 53).[92] As did, surely, C. Claudius Marcellus (*pr.* 80), on the prudent example of his son, the Consul of 50. Whether P. Servilius Isauricus (*cos. II* 41) was a member of the *collegium* already (he is first attested in 47),[93] and whether L. Marcius Philippus (*cos. suff.* 38) was one at all,[94] remains unknown, as does the identity of the fifteenth member. Servilius certainly, and Philippus probably, stayed in Italy. Altogether, we can place seven or eight members in Italy (Antonius, Cassius, Marcellus, L. Caesar, Scaevola, Galba, Cicero, and probably Messalla) in the spring of 49.

From Cicero we learn that during March four Augurs—Galba, Scaevola, Cassius, and Antonius—were prepared to rule that a Praetor could hold consular elections, or name a Dictator. Caesar applied heavy pressure on Cicero to join them: *aberit non longe quin hoc a me decerni velit neque sit contentus Galba, Scaevola, Cassio, Antonio* (Att. 9.9.3); *volet enim, credo, senatus consultum facere, volet augurum decretum (rapiemur aut absentes vexabimur) vel ut consules rogat*

---

[90] Cf. Champion 68–71; but see now Driediger-Murphy 2019: 28–41, noting that—given the ubiquity of auspical procedures in public life—most senators must have had a working knowledge of augural principles, and suggesting that public interest in such matters may have been more common than generally thought.

[91] Broughton *MRR* 2: 254–255; Rüpke *FS* 1: 134.

[92] Messalla had been convicted in 51 under Crassus' *lex Licinia de sodaliciis* (Caelius *apud* Cic. *Fam.* 8.4.1, *absolutum Messallam, deinde eundem condemnatum*; cf. 8.2.1), but the penalty imposed is not recorded. Wiseman 1979: 134 assumed exile, R. Hanslik, "Valerius (268)" *RE* 8A.1 (1955) 168, a fine. There being not the slightest hint at the former in Caelius' curt notice, one rather is inclined towards the latter. If Messalla did go into exile, though, he would not have been able (barring an unlikely recall during 50) to return until Caesar's actual dictatorship.

[93] Rüpke *FS* 2: 1283: "... Kooptation schon in den späten 60er Jahren ... denkbar."

[94] Rüpke *FS* 2: 1138–1139 is cautiously supportive of an augurate, perhaps as early as 56 BC. If so, he may be counted in Caesar's camp politically, though with "bestehenden Pompeianischen Sympathien" (Rüpke); which does not tell us how he would have voted on the issue in question.

praetor vel dictatorem dicat; quorum neutrum ius est (9.15.2). Evidently, those four were not enough to constitute a majority of the votes necessary to produce a decree of the College: at least eight Augurs, therefore, must have been present in Rome. Messalla, although he proved an active Caesarian (at least by fall 47: Cic. *Att.* 11.22.2; [Caes.] *BAfr* 28.2), if present probably refused, as he did in a subsequent and similar case of abuse (*nos his temporibus praetore praetores creante veterum auctoritatem sumus secuti neque his comitiis in auspicio fuimus*, ap. Gell. 13.15.4).[95] How L. Caesar and Marcellus stood on the issue we are not told, but if both had agreed with Caesar, he would have had a majority of the Augurs in Italy behind him: enough to pass the desired decree, and no need to pester Cicero.[96] Even if all three of the unknown members stayed in Italy, six would constitute a majority of ten or eleven; the fact that Cicero's vote appears to have been necessary in order to produce the decree (*rapiemur aut absentes vexabimur*) suggests, however, that the total available was no more than nine—of which four (or three, if the eight we can identify were all) could not be persuaded.

It has been thought that the Augurs eventually succumbed and passed the decree;[97] but in that case, there should have been no need for legislation. (Note that Cicero, when complaining about Caesar pressuring him, only mentions a *senatus consultum* and an augural decree, but no legislation: the latter, clearly, in the end was Caesar's way around the obstacle.) Once they had ruled *fas videri a praetore dictatorem dici*, the appointment could proceed without further ado (unless the rule that only a Consul could name the Dictator was itself grounded in comitial law—a most unlikely proposition), and not only on this one occasion: the decree would permanently change the rules for naming a Dictator. In the pertinent parallel of 426 V, the antiquarian tradition saw no need for legislation; the augural decree alone extended the ability to the "Consular Tribunes": *cum ibi quoque religio obstaret ne non posset nisi ab consule dici dictator, augures consulti eam religionem exemere* (Livy 4.31.4).[98] It will not do to pretend uncertainty as to whether this decree applied only to that one occasion, and to suggest that each

---

[95] *Pace* Drummond *FRHist* 3: 386 n. 9, this incident most likely belongs during Caesar's dictatorship (thus Linderski *AL* 2192–2193). But even if one assumes a triumviral or later date, it shows that Messalla resisted Caesarian pressure in augural matters, despite his political support in general.

[96] There is no reason to think that, for a formal *responsum* or *decretum*, a majority of the members of the *collegium* (i.e., eight votes, as opposed to a majority of the Augurs present in Rome) was required. At any given time, several of them were likely to be absent from Italy, *rei publicae causa* or on private matters. Rafferty's characterization (39 n. 50) of the Augural College in 49 as "packed with Caesar's supporters and with his opponents being outside Italy" has no basis in the facts.

[97] Linderski *AL* 2183–2184; 1990: 45–46 = *RQ* 571–572, where it is presented as a fact; Giovannini 1993: 80–81; Vervaet 2004: 81–83 (with muddled reasoning that mixes the circumstances of Caesar's dictatorship in 49 with that of 48); Dalla Rosa 2011: 243 (wrongly maintaining that this is the only case in evidence "in which this procedure is attested": it is emphatically not attested in Caesar's case in 49, but very much so in 426 V, Livy 4.31.4).

[98] Linderski *AL* 2180–2181; 1990: 45 = *RQ* 571.

subsequent dictatorial nomination by a Consular Tribune may have required another such ruling. If *religio* attached to such an act, it was because of the augural characteristics relating to it: characteristics that were of necessity determined by the nature of the act, hence immutable and ever-present, not subject to changing and temporary circumstances. And if such *religio* was removed (*augures eam religionem exemere*), it was of necessity removed once and for all: not because the characteristics of the act themselves had changed, but because they were not henceforth deemed to pose an obstacle under augural law.[99]

As for the Interrex naming Sulla Dictator in 82, we are not told if that procedure was sanctioned by the Augurs. Yet Cicero's comment (*Att.* 9.15.2, *sed si Sulla potuit efficere ab interrege ut dictator diceretur, cur hic non possit?*) leaves little room for doubt. Seen in the context of Cicero's quandary, *potuit efficere* does not, on the face of it, imply an augural decree—on the contrary: the phrase strongly suggests that Sulla brought this about (by legislation empowering the Interrex to perform the *dictio*) without augural approval, just as Caesar could be expected to do, if thwarted by the Augurs.[100] And *ab interrege ut dictator diceretur*, as opposed to *dici posset*, points to a one-time event rather than a general change in the rules governing the naming of a Dictator, which an augural decree sanctioning the measure necessarily would have caused. Unlike, however, the Praetor, yet like the "Consular Tribunes" of long ago, the Interrex possessed the power to create a Consul:[101] his naming a Dictator could still be viewed, in augural terms, as keeping the process within the realm of the prerequisite capacity. Extending that ability to the Praetor, who could not even create another Praetor, let alone a Consul, would constitute a change on a different order of magnitude.

---

[99] "Livy indicates ... that the augurs simply removed the religious impediment to the appointment of 426, which is not the same as stating that the augurs ruled for once and for all that *tribuni militum* were henceforth entitled to name dictators" (Vervaet 2004: 83 n. 163). It is precisely the same. When the *pontifices* ruled (sometime in the first century AD, it seems) that the Flamen Dialis could leave the *apex* off his head when indoors (*sine apice sub dico esse licitum non est; sub tecto uti liceret, non pridem a pontificibus constitutum Masurius Sabinus scripsit*, Gell. 10.15.17), the relief thus granted applied to all holders of the priesthood, not just the one in office at that time.

[100] Vervaet 2004: 81 stands this on its head: "The essence of Cicero's argument is precisely that since Sulla already managed to bring about (*efficere ut*) a *decretum augurum* issued *ex s.c.* which officially authorized an *interrex* to nominate both a dictator and a *magister equitum*, it would be perfectly feasible for Caesar to have the same authorities authorize a praetor to organize the *comitia consularia* or to name a dictator." Cicero says nothing about Sulla's having managed to bring about a *decretum augurum*, let alone one "issued *ex s.c.*": that Sulla did so needs to be shown before it can be made the essence of Cicero's argument; Vervaet's reasoning here is perfectly circular. What still awaits demonstration mutates into fact and gross misrepresentation two pages later: "Cicero's cynical statement ... that Caesar could suit himself in 49 because the augurs had previously authorized an *interrex* to appoint a dictator" (83 n. 163; essentially followed by Rafferty 39 n. 50, "Cicero cynically expected him to obtain the augural ruling he wanted"). Hurlet 1993: 48–49 concludes, perhaps correctly, that Sulla did not even request an augural decree in 82.

[101] Cf. Wittmann *StO* 713: "Der Prätor war—im Gegensatz zum Interrex—kein Stellvertreter, sondern ein collega minor der Konsuln."

4.4.4 Lepidus' Enabling Act and the Auspices

Jerzy Linderski cautions that a comitial law "could remove legal obstacles, but not religious doubts."[102] (Not that Caesar had much concern for the latter.) That is true in principle; but it may not go very far in this case. Unless one believes that the *dictio* of a Dictator was regulated by comitial law, there were no legal obstacles under the *ius publicum* to be removed: the obstacle resided entirely in augural law. In consequence, the very fact that Caesar resorted to legislation implies that he had not succeeded in persuading the Augurs to remove the religious obstacles against his desired course of action: an augural decree *fas esse dictatorem a praetore dici* would have rendered any legislation moot and superfluous. The precedent that *tribuni militum consulari potestate* could name a Dictator was firmly established, and there can be but little doubt that this ability was grounded in their having *consularis potestas*, hence consular auspices; if we assume—for the sake of argument—that the People granted the Praetor Lepidus *consularis potestas* (which they undoubtedly could do) for one day, for the express purpose that he name Caesar Dictator, it would be difficult, even for an Augur, to deny that the precedent of the Consular Tribunes applied accordingly.[103]

In other words, it could be argued with some plausibility that such legislation would effectively remove the *religio* against the Praetor naming a Dictator, albeit only in this singular instance, not in perpetuity. We do not know, of course, if this was the form taken by the enabling act of 49 BC; the law may simply and directly have conferred on the Praetor Lepidus the power to name a Dictator, along with the necessary auspices. The People had the power to grant *imperium* to a *privatus*; and it is clear that *privati cum imperio* commanded *suis auspiciis*, just like prorogued promagistrates. Hence the grant of *imperium* must have entailed, in some form, a grant of the right to auspices: perhaps for the duration of the campaign (unlikely, unless "regular" promagistrates did in fact possess—impetrative—auspices, that is, the ability to auspicate on a daily basis); more probably, either a one-time grant of auspices to be taken, presumably, in connection with the ceremonies of *profectio*, or a legal fiction in which the *privatus* was to be treated *ac si optimo iure consul* (vel *praetor*) *fuerit*.[104] There is no reason to think that an

---

[102] *AL* 2184.

[103] Cf. Sini 1976: 420–421; Linderski *AL* 2181. The possibility of a special grant of consular power to Lepidus is envisaged by Tarpin 273. The creation in 43 BC of *IIviri comitiis consularibus habendis* (Dio 46.45.3–4) probably entailed a plebiscite authorizing the Praetor Urbanus to see to their election; if the plebiscite granted him *consularis potestas* for that purpose, it would sidestep the problem of having the Praetor create magistrates having power to create others—the Consuls—with power greater than his own: see Mommsen *StR* 2.1: 663 n. 3.

[104] Cf. Cicero's proposal to grant *imperium* to the *privatus* C. Caesar C.f. in 43 BC, *Phil.* 5.45–46: *sit pro praetore eo iure quo qui optimo . . . ob eas causas senatui placere C. Caesarem C. f. pontificem pro praetore <eo iure quo qui optimo et> senatorem esse.* (Cf. Vervaet 2014: 346 n. 140; on the text, see Shackleton Bailey 1982: 223–224.)

augural ruling was obtained in every such case, although it may well be that a decree of the *collegium* sanctioned the practice initially; and the actual acquisition of auspices would not have occurred in the vote of the *comitia centuriata* or *tributa*, but by the very act of asking for them—having been authorized by the People to do so—and receiving an affirmative response, not countermanded by an oblative sign under the *vinculum temporis*.[105]

Once the principle had been established (long before Caesar) that the People could bestow *imperium auspiciumque* on individuals outside election to a magistracy carrying those attributes, it would be difficult to argue that they could not empower a Praetor (or an Interrex, for that matter) to name a Dictator. Of course, those among the (narrow) majority in the College opposed to this procedure could still hold that any Dictator thus named was *vitio factus*; but the political circumstances would hardly encourage such a pronouncement, let alone a vote of the Senate to the effect that Caesar should abdicate. And legislation—as opposed to an augural ruling—would limit the irregular procedure to a single instance: preferable, quite possibly, to a forced and permanent change in augural law.

Caesar himself cared little about augural law: witness his election of Caninius Rebilus to the consulship of 31 December 45, without the necessary auspices, having obtained them merely for the Tribal Assembly, not the Centuriate one (*qui comitiis tributis esset auspicatus, centuriata habuit*—a flaw duly noted by the Augur Cicero, *Fam.* 7.30.1), and his ignoring the *obnuntiatio* of the Augur Antonius at Dolabella's election in 44.[106] It was not augural scruples that prompted his angling for a decree, but political expediency. In the end, when the College proved uncooperative, he did not hesitate to bypass the obstacle entirely, and resorted to legislation in the fall of 49 (Caes. *BCiv* 2.21.5; Dio 41.36.1).[107]

4.4.5 The Objection to Antonius

A year later, Cassius was in Spain (Caes. *BCiv* 2.21.3; [*BAlex*] 48.1); Cicero returned from Greece in October 48, but remained at Brundisium for a whole year, and did not arrive in Rome until October 47.[108] Neither took part in whatever augural proceedings accompanied the installation of Caesar and Antonius. We may count Marcellus, L. Caesar, Scaevola, Galba, and Messalla, and up to three unknowns (who may have returned to Italy in the meantime; absence in 49

---

[105] Magdelain 1964: 429–431 = 1990: 343–345; cf. 1968: 36–40; Linderski *AL* 2169 with n. 74; Nicholls 274 n. 36; cf. Fiori 2014b: 76–79 with n. 85. See also Chapter 2.3.

[106] Cic. *Phil.* 2.88; 3.9; 5.9. Denniston 149 showed long ago that Caesar payed no heed to Antonius' intervention and proceeded with the election.

[107] Cf. Brennan *PRR* 1: 265–266 n. 115 (". . . evidently without a hoped-for decree from the augurs").

[108] For the dates of his whereabouts, see Shackleton Bailey *CLA* 5: 270, 298; cf. Chapter 3.1.2.

does not necessarily place them in Pompeius' camp): with Antonius, who probably came back from Greece in time, no more than nine in all.[109] A majority—not necessarily all—endorsed the extended term of the Dictator, and a majority—not necessarily the same—objected to that of the Magister Equitum, himself a member (a point that should not be overlooked, although it is not easy to locate a discussion of this issue that betrays awareness of the fact). Why?

Andrew Drummond suggested that "the real target of the augural declaration was perhaps Caesar himself and his annual dictatorship," a direct attack on which would have been "perilous."[110] No more so than balking at having a Praetor name the Dictator, a year earlier; and as a means of protest, to endorse a year-long term for the Dictator but deny it to his deputy was politically inept, to say the least: the public ridicule with which their *responsum* was received could hardly have come as a surprise. Nor can we assume that there was a solidly anti-Caesarian majority among the Augurs present in 48: on the contrary, if Servilius and Philippus were Augurs at the time, Caesarians now—unlike the year before—constituted a clear majority among the nine in Rome. (And again, one of the Augurs was the man directly affected by this ruling—Antonius the Magister Equitum.) The futility of ascribing specific political motives to that body without first ascertaining its composition (hence, the political leanings of its members) cannot be stressed enough. The rational procedure is, first, to accept that the Augurs (a majority, at any rate) took their duties seriously, and discerned a problem affecting the Magister Equitum but not the Dictator; and next, to attempt to identify the problem.

It should be clear that this was not some quixotic effort to register veiled opposition to Caesar's dictatorship. The College of Augurs was not concerned with the length of a magistrate's term as such; as Brennan noted, their protest must have been prompted by a question of auspices. Now if, as regards their respective auspices, the Dictator could serve for a year (or indefinitely), but his Master of the Horse could not, it follows that the latter's auspices were separate from those of the former, even though obtained through him, and connected to his.[111] Furthermore, if it was augurally possible to name the Dictator for a period of more than six months, it is inconceivable that the same should not have been possible for his Magister Equitum. There was precedent: Sulla and Flaccus in 82. Ignoring Appian's specific statement that Sulla's dictatorship was for an indefinite term, until he should have completed his task of stabilizing and reforming the state (*BCiv* 1.98.459, οὐκ ἐς χρόνον ῥητόν, ἀλλὰ μέχρι τὴν πόλιν καὶ τὴν Ἰταλίαν καὶ τὴν ἀρχὴν ὅλην στάσεσι καὶ πολέμοις σεσαλευμένην στηρίσειεν; cf. 1.99.461, ἐς ὅσον θέλοι), Brennan held that Caesar was the first Dictator to be named for a

---

[109] Two Augurs, Appius and Pompeius, had died earlier in the year (*MRR* 2: 284; Rüpke *FS* 1: 134); since no elections were held in 48 (Dio 42.20.4, 55.4), their seats had not been filled.
[110] Drummond 1978: 571; cf. Wittmann *StO* 714; Masi Doria 148.
[111] This partly supports the argument developed above, Section 4.1. Cf. Brennan *PRR* 1: 47.

year-long term, and imagined that Sulla (and his Master of the Horse) "must have had his *auspicia* renewed each six months."¹¹² The only way a Dictator could have had his auspices renewed was through being named, by a Consul, to another term: and, patently, our evidence for Sulla contains not even the most remote suggestion of such a thing. (The *Fasti* in that case would have counted each term separately, yet the only dictatorship they list is the one that commenced in 82.) A conclusion now emerges: what Dio presents as a general prohibition (μηδενὶ ἐξεῖναι πλείω τοῦ ἑξαμήνου χρόνον ἱππαρχῆσαι, 42.21.1)¹¹³ was, in fact, an augural problem with the appointment of this particular Magister Equitum, on this particular occasion.

There is no conceivable reason why the *magister populi* (and his deputy) should have been limited to six months solely and intrinsically as a matter of augural law. The Augurs were not concerned with the duration of magistracies as such. The six-month limit acquired its augural force through the *dictio in sex menses*, which set the limit of the Dictator's valid auspices; and if no time limit was expressed in the *dictio*, there was no limit to the Dictator's term other than the one universally understood from ancient times: the expectation, overwhelming and virtually irresistible as a matter both of *fas* and *ius* already in the fourth century, that he abdicate as soon as the situation prompting his appointment had been resolved.¹¹⁴

The six-month limit must either have rested on formal legislation, or been as deeply rooted in *fas* and *ius* as the "indefinite" limit; the augural considerations revolving around it did not create the limit, but existed in consequence of it. If, at an unknown point in time before the end of the third century, a comitial law was enacted prohibiting any Dictator and his Magister Equitum from remaining in office for longer than six months, its inevitable effect in augural law would have been the limitation of their auspices to that term. No magistrate, however constituted, could have had valid auspices beyond the limits set by the People through legislation, or universally understood to have existed from the beginning of the State. If the limit was introduced by legislation, an act of the *comitia* would be necessary to create an exception, or change it altogether. But the same expectation would presumably apply to an unwritten rule that had become an accepted part of the constitution. To judge from the surviving sources (despite evidence to the contrary contained in them), by the first century BC the six-month limit had come to be seen as integral and original to the dictatorship; the Augurs very well may have

---

[112] *PRR* 1: 265 n. 107, adducing Dio 42.20.3 and Plut. *Caes.* 51.1 to show that Caesar's was the first year-long dictatorship. (Dio says no such thing here, but implies it at 42.21.2 and 46.13.1.) The first annual one, no doubt; but the point is that Sulla's appointment was neither annual nor for six months. (How long he stayed in office is another matter.)

[113] In his rendition of the Second Philippic, Dio again raised the issue, making Cicero charge that Antonius had been Magister Equitum for an entire year, which had never happened before (ὡς ἐπ' ἐνιαυτὸν ὅλον ἱππάρχησεν, ὃ μήπω πρότερον ἐγεγόνει, 45.27.5); cf. also Fufius Calenus' speech, 46.13.1. Cicero's actual speech contains not a hint of this.

[114] Chapter 3.4.

taken the position that neither *magister populi* nor *magister equitum* could have valid auspices beyond that point, unless authorized specifically by the People.

What exactly was the content of the *senatus consultum* and subsequent legislation (assuming there was legislation) that authorized Caesar's dictatorship to last a full year? Vervaet is certain that it "made explicit mention of Marcus Antonius," and directed Servilius the Consul "to appoint both his colleague and Marcus Antonius to the offices of dictator and *magister equitum* successively"; this, he insists, "Dio clearly indicates."[115] The only thing Dio actually specifies as having been voted on, by the Senate and probably the People, is the measure allowing Caesar to be named Dictator for a year, instead of six months: δικτάτωρ οὐκ ἐς ἕκμηνον ἀλλ' ἐς ἐνιαυτὸν ὅλον λεχθῆναι ἔλαβεν, 42.20.3; ταῦτ' οὖν οὕτω καὶ ἐψηφίσθη καὶ ἐκυρώθη, 42.21.1. (He does not "note," as Vervaet claims, that a law to that effect was passed by Servilius the Consul—a plausible conjecture, but nothing more; for all we know, it could have been a piece of tribunician legislation.) Caesar then assumed the dictatorship immediately, even though he was away from Italy (καὶ ὅ τε Καῖσαρ τὴν δικτατορίαν παραχρῆμα, καίπερ ἔξω τῆς Ἰταλίας ὤν, ὑπέστη, ibid.), and chose Antonius as Magister Equitum (καὶ τὸν Ἀντώνιον ... ἵππαρχον προελόμενος); and the Consul named the latter as well (καὶ εἶπε καὶ τοῦτον ὁ ὕπατος[116]). As noted earlier, this order of events clearly implies that Caesar did not communicate his choice of Antonius until he had learned of his own appointment as Dictator, in Egypt. Dio is certainly wrong about this, and may not in fact have meant to create such an impression (sloppy writing is just as likely); but he patently does not imply, let alone state, that the enabling legislation included any mention of Antonius.

Indeed, Mommsen surmised that the comitial enabling act merely specified the length of term—one year—for the Dictator, but not for his Magister Equitum: it was this failure of the law to specifically extend Antonius' term that prompted the Augurs' objection.[117] But given the character of Roman legislative language, with its obsessive repetition and striving to provide for every eventuality, it is difficult to see why in this particular situation the law should not have said *expressis verbis* that the Master of the Horse likewise should hold office for one year, if that was the intention. Nor is it plausible that the Augurs should have approved a

---

[115] Vervaet 2004: 81–82.
[116] That εἶπε here represents Latin *dixit* is clear from Dio's consistent use when reporting a dictatorial nomination: fr. 36.26, καὶ δείσαντες μὴ ὁ Ῥοῦλλος οὐκ ἐθελήσῃ αὐτὸν (sc. Παπίριον) ... εἰπεῖν ... ἐπειδὴ δὲ νὺξ ἐγένετο (νυκτὸς γὰρ πάντως ... τὸν δικτάτορα ἔδει λέγεσθαι), εἰπέ τε αὐτόν, 41.36.1, δικτάτορα τὸν Καίσαρα ... εἶπεν; 42.21.1, αὐτὸς ἑαυτὸν ἐν τῇ ὑπατείᾳ ἐπειπὼν ἵππαρχον; 54.1.3, δικτάτορά τε ἅμα δεόμενοι λεχθῆναι; and Zonar. 7.14, δικτάτωρ ἐρρήθη Οὐαλλέριος Μάρκος; 7.20, ἡ δὲ γερουσία ... δικτάτορα ... ἀνεῖπε τὸν Κυίντιον τὸν Λούκιον τὸν Κικινάτον; 7.25, δικτάτωρ ἐλέχθη Λούκιος Κάμιλλος; 8.15, δικτάτωρ μὲν ὁ Κολλατῖνος ἐλέχθη ... ἐν ᾧ δ' ὁ Κολλατῖνος δικτάτωρ ἐλέγετο; 9.2, καὶ δικτάτωρ μὲν Μάρκος Ἰούνιος, ἵππαρχος δὲ Τιβέριος Σεμπρώνιος Γράκχος ἐλέχθησαν; 10.1, ἐπεὶ δ' ἐκράτησε τῆς Ἰταλίας ὁ Σύλλας καὶ δικτάτωρ ἀνηγορεύθη. Cary's translation (in the Loeb edition) "proposed the latter's name," suggesting a legislative act, is inept.
[117] *StR* 2.1: 175 n. 5; similarly Vervaet 2004: 82.

one-year term for the Dictator but declined to do so for the Master-of-Horse. Hence if the enabling legislation said nothing about a year-long tenure for the Magister Equitum, such an omission would seem deliberate.

The Augurs had approved of the Dictator's year-long term (αὐτὸν μὲν τὸν δικτάτορα ἐς ἐνιαυτὸν παρὰ πάντα τὰ πάτρια λεχθῆναι γνόντες, Dio 42.21.2): evidently, the College had been consulted on the matter before it was put to a vote. The enabling law prescribed not only that Caesar could be Dictator for one year but also that Servilius the Consul should name both him and his Magister Equitum,[118] since the Dictator was *extra Italiam*; that much seems certain. But instead of excluding the Magister Equitum from a one-year term, the enabling act need not have directed the Consul to name a Dictator *in annum*; it may merely have authorized the extended term, without prescribing it, and done the same for the Master of the Horse. (No doubt the Augurs had approved of that as well.) If we proceed from that conjecture (and the sole item not conjectural about the measure's content is that it permitted Caesar to be Dictator for a year: δικτάτωρ οὐκ ἐς ἔκμηνον ἀλλ' ἐς ἐνιαυτὸν ὅλον λεχθῆναι ἔλαβεν, Dio 42.20.3; nothing else is actually known[119]), a more probable reconstruction offers.

From an augural point of view, what mattered was the *dictio*: for either of the two to stay in office for a year, he must be named *in annum* by the nominator, and the Augurs had ruled that it was *fas* to do so. Evidently, while Caesar had been named accordingly, Antonius had not. But *in annum* could not merely have been omitted at Antonius' *dictio*, for in that case his auspices would have been valid indefinitely, and he would have been entitled to serve until completion of his task: which, being of necessity the same as the reason for the Dictator's appointment, would mean he could remain in office just as long as Caesar. The reason for the Augurs' objection thus becomes clear: Antonius had been named not *in annum* but *in sex menses*.

An explanation is not difficult to find. For one, such a move would have provided Caesar with an opportunity to change Masters of the Horse halfway through his term, without the need to force a premature—hence embarrassing—abdication. Or, if—as is virtually certain—at the time the law was passed, Antonius was already known to be Caesar's choice, those drafting the bill (Caesar's friends, as Cicero later would have it, but not necessarily Antony's) might have thought it prudent to limit him to the traditional six months; the Dictator could always name him again for another six, if he so desired.

Caesar, between Pharsalos and Alexandria, sent word quietly to Servilius, his colleague as Consul, that he wanted Antonius to be named Magister Equitum.

---

[118] Cf. Wittmann *StO* 714; Vervaet 2004: 82 is correct in that regard.

[119] Plut. *Caes*. 51.1 notes that Caesar's second dictatorship constituted the first year-long tenure of that office (οὐδέποτε πρότερον τῆς ἀρχῆς ἐκείνης ἐνιαυσίου γενομένης), but offers no illumination as to the enabling legislation.

Servilius accordingly named Antonius, but only *in sex menses*: either because Caesar had so requested, or because Servilius himself thought it preferable to giving the man a year-long term, or—much less likely—because the enabling measure did not in fact provide for an extended tenure of the Master-of-Horse. No matter which reason obtained, the expectation would be that, six months later, either Antonius would be reappointed, or someone else would take his place.

Antonius was named Magister Equitum in late November or early December, 48.[120] His six months would thus be up around the beginning of June, 47. But at that moment no one was left who could name him (or anyone) to another term: the Dictator was still *extra Italiam*, and no Consuls had been in office since January 1. (Q. Fufius Calenus and P. Vatinius were not elected until Caesar's return to Rome, in September). Evidently with Caesar's blessing, tacit or expressed (otherwise, the Dictator could have ordered him to abdicate), Antonius simply continued in office, at which point a majority of his augural colleagues present in Rome raised their objection:[121] having been named for six months, he could not lawfully remain beyond that point. We can be confident that, contrary to the opinion of those lacking proper expertise, the Augurs did not deserve ridicule for going easy on the Dictator and his one-year term while engaging in ἀκριβολογία when it came to the Master of the Horse (42.21.2). They simply acted in accordance with the *ius augurale*.

---

[120] To judge from Cic. *Att.* 11.6 and 11.7.2, approximately between November 27 and December 17: above, Subsection 4.4.1.

[121] One may counter that Dio 42.21 notes the Augurs' intervention immediately after Antonius' appointment. But Dio's entire narrative of this period—Caesar's *dominatio*—does not follow a strict chronological order; constitutional developments in particular are grouped together, as are events in different regions (e.g., Rome, Italy, Egypt, Africa). In fact, all of 42.22–25 (the uprising of Milo and Caelius) and a good deal of 42.34–43 (Caesar in Egypt) clearly belong in the summer and fall of 48, before the appointment of Antonius; Dio would not want to interrupt his account of events in Rome during 47 (42.27–33) with a digression on augural objections to the tenure of the Magister Equitum.

5
Drowning the Chickens

The institutional studies presented in the three preceding chapters may provide a firmer foundation on which to examine a series of incidents, in the second half of the third century BC, in which Roman commanders—Consuls all—ignored prohibitive auspices, or openly mounted a challenge to the rule of auspices as such. In 324 V (or perhaps 301—who can say?), Fabius Maximus Rullianus the Magister Equitum had engaged the enemy: *incertis auspiciis*, according to the Dictator Papirius Cursor, whose own auspices were in that dubious state and affected those of his deputy. But Rullianus had not called into question the auspices themselves. Chafing at the subordination of his auspices to those of the Dictator, and asserting the independence of his own and of his *imperium*, he evidently claimed to have acted with an affirmative response from Iuppiter. (Thus, at least, is how the episode was remembered and interpreted around the turn of the third to the second century.) In the tradition as it survives in Livy, Rullianus scored a victory (or two), although in the original telling a defeat seems to have resulted from his action.[1] Not until three quarters of a century had passed—in the traditional reckoning—do we hear of attempts by Roman commanders to actually reject the auspices under which they were to go in harm's way.

The earliest three cases belong to the First Punic War. In two of them, no uncertainty or ambiguity attached to the situation, and the challenge came in the form of a flat-out refusal to let the auspices govern a military operation. The outcome, too, was unambiguous: two fleets perished—one in combat, the other in a storm. The third pursued a more subtle approach, though with more fundamental consequences had it succeeded. All three will be examined next.

5.1 The *Pulli*

In 249 BC, the Consul P. Claudius Pulcher lost most of his fleet (only 30 out of somewhere between 120 and 200 ships escaped)[2] in the Battle of Drepana. Claudius, as is well known, had the Chickens thrown into the sea when they

---

[1] Chapter 1.
[2] Polybios 1.51.11–12 seems to imply a total strength of 120, but 1.41.3, when taken with other sources' numbers, rather points to around 200; for discussion, Konrad 2015a: 197–198; cf. De Sanctis *SdR* 3.1: 170 n. 65; Walbank *HCP* 1: 114–115.

refused to eat.[3] Not only that; his colleague, L. Iunius Pullus, later in the year lost another fleet—some 120 warships and 800 transports—in a gale off Cape Pachynus. Like Claudius, he had disobeyed the auspices: his Chickens would not eat, yet he sailed anyway. From an augural perspective, in both instances the question of what happened is closely tied to the question of where it happened.

5.1.1 The Evidence

First, Claudius. When and where did he commit his outrage against the Chickens? When seeking the required auspices before the Battle of Drepana, it is generally assumed; but some scholars, pointing to a troublesome note in Servius and to the word *profectus* in the *Periochae* of Livy, thought it happened in Rome, when the Consul took his "auspices for departure" from the City.[4] Oddly enough, although several of the sources reporting the incident appear to support the *communis opinio*, none but Servius and Suetonius state a precise location. To wit:

(1) Cic. *ND* 2.7: nihil nos P. Claudi bello Punico primo temeritas movebit, qui etiam per iocum deos inridens, cum cavea liberati pulli non pascerentur, mergi eos in aquam iussit, ut biberent quoniam esse nollent? qui risus classe devicta multas ipsi lacrimas, magnam populo Romano cladem attulit. quid? collega eius Iunius eodem bello nonne tempestate classem amisit, cum auspiciis non paruisset? itaque Claudius a populo condemnatus est, Iunius necem sibi ipse conscivit.

"When the Chickens were let out of their cage and would not feed, P. Claudius, in the First Punic War, ordered them drowned in the water, so they could drink since they did not want to eat. That joke, when his fleet suffered defeat, resulted in many tears and a great catastrophe for the Roman People. And to make matters worse, Claudius' colleague, Iunius, during the same war lost his fleet in a storm because he would not obey the auspices. Claudius was condemned (in a trial) by the People, while Iunius committed suicide."

---

[3] I will not enter the tedious debate over whether this really happened; suffice it to state that I have not encountered any plausible arguments against the story's authenticity (cf. Hölkeskamp 1990: 447 = 2004: 93, with a brief survey of the pertinent literature; and see now also the well-reasoned remarks of Driediger-Murphy 2019: 183 n. 73). Invention after the fact, to explain away the horrible defeat, at any rate can be ruled out: given the number of defeats suffered by Roman commanders over the centuries, we should expect dozens, if not hundreds, of such stories to be told—and especially one for the worst of all routs, at Cannae.

[4] Reuss 1909: 415; Latte 266 n. 1; Bleicken 1955: 36 n. 1 ("diese[r] hochmütig[e], die Auszugsauspizien verachtend[e] Konsul"); 120; Hölkeskamp 1990: 437, 447 = 2004: 85, 93 ("nach eklatanter Verletzung der Auszugsauspicien"). Berthelet 228–229 imagines two separate incidents: Claudius first ignored his auspices of departure (ruled unfavorable by the Augurs) in Rome, then drowned the Chickens in Sicily just before the battle. No ancient source even hints at two such instances of violation, let alone mentions or implies an augural *responsum*.

(2) Cic. *Div.* 1.29: . . . ut P. Claudius, Appi Caeci filius, eiusque collega L. Iunius classis maxumas perdiderunt, cum vitio navigassent.

"P. Claudius, son of Appius Caecus, and his colleague L. Iunius lost huge fleets when they sailed under flawed auspices."

(3) Cic. *Div.* 2.20: si enim fatum fuit classes populi Romani bello Punico primo, alteram naufragio, alteram a Poenis depressam interire, etiamsi tripudium solistumum pulli fecissent L. Iunio et P. Claudio consulibus, classes tamen interissent.

"If it was fated for Roman fleets to perish in the First Punic War—one suffering shipwreck, the other sunk by the Carthaginians—those fleets, even if the feeding Chickens had given the most favorable 'dancing' display to the Consuls L. Iunius and P. Claudius, would still have perished."

(4) Cic. *Div.* 2.71: . . . P. Claudius L. Iunius consules, qui contra auspicia navigaverunt . . . iure igitur alter populi iudicio damnatus est, alter mortem sibi ipse conscivit.

"Of the Consuls P. Claudius and L. Iunius, who had sailed in violation of the auspices, one was rightfully condemned in a trial before the People, the other committed suicide."

(5) Livy *Per.* 19: Claudius Pulcher cos. contra auspicia profectus—iussit mergi pullos, qui cibari nolebant—infeliciter adversus Carthaginienses classe pugnavit.

"The Consul Claudius Pulcher, having set out in violation of the auspices—he ordered the Chickens to be drowned, since they refused to eat—fought badly with his fleet against the Carthaginians."

(6) Val. Max. 1.4.3 *Par.*: P. Claudius bello Punico, cum proelium navale committere vellet auspiciaque more maiorum petisset et pullarius non exire cavea pullos nuntiasset, abici eos in mare iussit dicens, "quia esse nolunt, bibant."

"P. Claudius, in the Punic War, intending to commence battle at sea and having sought auspices in the customary manner, when receiving a report from the chicken tender that the Chickens were not leaving their cage, ordered them thrown into the sea, saying 'Since they don't want to eat, let them drink.'"

(7) Val. Max. 1.4.4 *Par.*: L. Iunius P. Claudii collega neglectis auspiciis classem tempestate amisit damnationisque ignominiam voluntaria morte praevenit.

"L. Iunius, the colleague of P. Claudius, lost his fleet in a storm after disregarding the auspices; he avoided the humiliation of (trial and) conviction by dying of his own free will."

(8) Val. Max. 1.4.3 *Nep.*: P. Claudius praeceps animi primo bello Punico pullarium consuluit. quicum dixisset non vesci pullos, quod malum omen est, "bibant" inquit et in mare proici iussit. mox classem apud Aegates insulas cum multo rei pub. damno et suo exitio amisit.

"P. Claudius, being of an impetuous disposition, in the First Punic War consulted his chicken tender. When the latter told him that the Chickens were not eating—which is a bad sign—he said, 'Let them drink,' and ordered them thrown into the sea. Soon afterwards he lost his fleet at the Aegates Islands, with great damage to the State and the loss of his own life."

(9) Suet. *Tib.* 2.2: Claudius Pulcher apud Siciliam non pascentibus in auspicando pullis ac per contemptum religionis mari demersis, quasi ut biberent quando esse nollent, proelium navale iniit.

"Having drowned the Chickens in the sea, both because they would not feed and out of religious contempt (to let them drink, so to speak, since they did not want to eat), Claudius Pulcher, in Sicily, commenced a naval battle."

(10) Flor. 1.18.29: Appio [*sic*] Claudio consule non ab hostibus sed a dis superatus est [*sc.* p. R.], quorum auspicia contempserat, ibi statim classe demersa, ubi ille praecipitari pullos iusserat, quod pugnare ab iis vetaretur.[5]

"Under the Consul Appius Claudius, the Romans were defeated not by the enemy but by the gods, whose auspices he had held in contempt, and his fleet was sunk right away on the very spot where he had ordered the Chickens to be jettisoned, because he was being forbidden by them to fight."

(11) Min. Fel. *Oct.* 7.4: frequentius etiam quam volebamus deorum praesentiam contempta auspicia contestata sunt. sic Allia nomen infaustum, sic Claudii et Iunii non proelium in Poenos, sed ferale naufragium est.

"Auspices that were held in contempt have borne witness to the presence of the gods more often than we would like: thus it happened at the Allia, that unlucky name, and with Claudius and Iunius—not in battle against the Carthaginians, but in a deadly shipwreck."

(12) Min. Fel. *Oct.* 26.2: Clodius scilicet et Flaminius et Iunius ideo exercitus perdiderunt, quod pullorum solistimum tripudium exspectandum non putaverunt.

"Clodius and Flaminius and Iunius lost their armies precisely because they did not deem it necessary to wait for the feeding Chickens' most favorable 'dancing' display."

(13) Eutrop. 2.26.1: ... Claudius contra auspicia pugnavit et a Carthaginiensibus victus est.

"Claudius fought in violation of the auspices and was defeated by the Carthaginians."

---

[5] Thus Jal's Budé text. Florus commonly omits an understood subject *populus Romanus* (e.g., 1.18.5, 7, 12, 15, 27, 30, 33; see Jal, xxxix–xl); but normally in such cases, *p. R.* is the only subject. At 1.18.29, however, the subject of *contempserat, iusserat*, and *vetaretur* is clearly Claudius, not the Roman People. Two of the mss. have parts of him as the subject here: *P. Claudius consule* V(allicellianus R 33, saec. xiv–xv); *Appio Claudio consul* H (Palatinus Heidelbergensis 1568, saec. xi); though only one shows *Appius Claudius consul*: I (codicum Iordanis consensu, ca. a. p. C. n. 551).

(14) Serv. ad *Aen.* 6.198: nam Romanis moris fuit et in comitiis agendis et in bellis gerendis pullaria captare auguria. unde est in Livio quod cum quidam cupidus belli gerendi a tribuno plebis arceretur ne iret, pullos iussit adferri: qui cum missas non ederent fruges, inridens consul augurium ait "vel bibant," et eos praecipitavit in Tiberim: inde navibus victor revertens [ad Africam tendens] in mari cum omnibus quos ducebat extinctus est.

"It was the Romans' custom to obtain auspices through the Chickens both when holding assemblies and when waging war. Thus it says in Livy that, when a certain individual eager to wage war was being prevented by a Tribune of the Plebs from going, he ordered the Chicken to be brought up. When the Chickens were let out and would not eat their grains, the Consul, jeering at the auspices, said, 'Let them drink, then,' and pitched them into the Tiber. Later on, returning as victor with his ships [while heading towards Africa], he perished at sea along with all those under his command."

Of thirteen (all except #7) direct references to Claudius' violation of the auspices, seven draw an unambiguous connection to his defeat in battle (1, 3, 5, 8–10, 13); they include the two earliest sources extant (1, 3).[6] Only two of these (##9, 10), however, appear to imply clearly that the drowning of the Chickens occurred during the auspication for the battle, which is to say, on the same day; a third (6) implies the same, but without mentioning the actual battle and its outcome. One reference (11) ascribes the loss of Claudius' fleet to a storm; another by the same source (12) is too vague to determine whether the author had *naufragium* or *pugna* in mind. Two references (##2, 4) in the earliest source but one simply note that Claudius had sailed against the auspices. And then there is Servius (#14).

5.1.2 Servius, the Tribune, and the Chickens

Servius implies that the auspication took place in close proximity to the Tiber River: clearly the scholiast imagined the incident to have occurred at or near Rome. The Chickens are thrown into the Tiber, not the sea, and a Tribune of the Plebs attempts to stop the Consul from going on campaign. If so, the incident can only be understood as taking place in connection with Claudius' departure from the City: his ceremonies of *profectio*. Could Servius have been right, or was he simply confused?

---

[6] As part of his elaborate argument for dating the work of Valerius Antias to the 50s and 40s BC (about a generation later than commonly accepted), Wiseman 1979: 110–111 proposed that Cicero became aware of Claudius' treatment of the Chickens only shortly before he wrote *De natura deorum* (44 BC): in other words, soon after Antias had invented the story along with his entire evil-Claudii program. Wiseman's Antiate theory—by no means idiosyncratic, at least as regards the time of writing—is as ingenious as it is unpersuasive: see Rich *FRHist* 1: 294–296.

Conceivably, the scholiast's Tribune of the Plebs attempting to prevent the Consul's departure (above, #14) could have arisen from confusion: Polybios states that, at Lilybaeum, Claudius summoned his Military Tribunes and laid out his plan for the attack on Drepana (1.49.3-4). But Polybios insists that the Tribunes readily agreed to the design (1.49.5, προχείρως δ' αὐτῶν συγκατατιθεμένων); to postulate a mistake in Servius, one would have to assume that Livy—whom he cites here as his source—had at least one of the Military Tribunes oppose the attack. (Nor could there be any question that Livy had placed the event in Sicily.) Florus writes of a Military Tribune, ominously named Nautius, who agitated against the planned invasion of Africa in 256 among troops terrified at the thought of crossing the open sea, and had to be shown the lictor's axe by the Consul M. Regulus before mustering the courage to embark.[7] This could have happened at Rome, before the Consuls departed with their fleets for Sicily; but it might also have occurred in Sicily, during the brief refit after the Battle off Ecnomus (Polyb. 1.29.1). Confusion on the part of Servius would require, first, a false remembrance of the nature of the tribunate—*plebis* for *militum*; then, probably in consequence, transposition of the locality from Sicily to Rome (at least if stemming from Claudius' briefing at Lilybaeum); and—if the error arose out of the Nautius episode—a confusion of Atilius Regulus with Claudius Pulcher. (Of course, Florus being Florus, there is a roughly even chance that the Nautius incident really belongs to Claudius Pulcher and the Battle of Drepana, and was misattributed to Regulus and the invasion of Africa by that author, in which case Servius would have confused its location and the nature of the tribunate, but not the general circumstances.)

None of this would seem impossible. Indeed, the troubling *ad Africam tendens* found in several manuscripts might derive—if authentically Servian—from a befuddled recollection of Regulus' expedition; as the note is absent, though, from L(*ipsiensis*) and all the codices containing Servius auctus, it may be best with Thilo to seclude it.[8] Certainly Servius was confused when he credited the Consul with victory at sea (*inde navibus victor revertens*) before the waves swallowed him and all his men; and *in mari cum omnibus quos ducebat extinctus est*[9] gives no hint of a defeat in battle. One suspects a mix-up with the fleets lost in storms in 255 and 253, both times after successful operations against the enemy (Polyb. 1.36.10-37.2, 39.1-6).

---

[7] Flor. 1.18.17, *nec defuerant qui ipso Punici maris nomine ac terrore deficerent, insuper augente Nautio tribuno metum in quem, nisi paruisset, securi destricta imperator metu mortis navigandi fecit audaciam*. It would make for an evil omen indeed to permit any man named "Nautius" to remain behind, for openly expressed fear of disaster, in a naval expedition.

[8] See Thilo-Hagen *ServGr* 2: 39 *ad loc.*

[9] Some mss. have *in mari cum periit exercitu* (A = Caroliruhensis 116, later corrected to *in mari periit cum exercitu*; S = Sangallensis 861 & 862) or *in mari cum omni periit exercitu* (M = Monacensis 6394).

Nor can an even more bizarre confusion be ruled out. Frontinus (*Strat.* 2.13.9) has a story about how, after the rout off Drepana, Claudius escaped: compelled to force his way through the enemy's positions, he ordered his remaining twenty ships to be decked out as if coming from a victory, and the Carthaginians, supposing that the Romans had won the battle, in terror allowed him to pass (*P. Claudius, navali proelio superatus a Poenis, cum per hostium praesidia necesse haberet erumpere, reliquas viginti naves tamquam victrices iussit ornari; atque ita Poenis existimantibus superiores fuisse acie nostros terribilis excessit*). The ruse has been called "fantastic,"[10] and rightly so, if taken to describe a breakout through the Punic forces in the battle itself: they could hardly have failed to notice that they were winning, and the Romans turning tail. But *praesidia* seems an odd choice of word for the ships in Adherbal's line of battle. It can denote warships, of course; but normally only in the sense of an escort or guard force. In over forty references to warships, Frontinus employs the word only on three other occasions: twice it means ships guarding a harbor or shoreline, once an escort, and never ships engaged in a battle.[11]

What Frontinus was describing constitutes, in fact, not Claudius' escape from the actual battle at Drepana, but a subsequent retreat past *hostium praesidia*—naval squadrons protecting Carthaginian strongholds along the coast of Sicily—on his journey back to Rome.[12]

Servius' placing the drowning of the Chickens at Rome can be explained as the result of confusion (such as is certainly present in his apparent notion that the fleet was lost in a storm, and that the Consul perished with it); the specific mention of the Tiber river could be his own contribution, logical enough once he had come to think of Rome as the location. And yet, a case can be made for a Tribune of the Plebs seeking to block Claudius from going to war. On top of the disaster in Africa in 255 and the tremendous losses at sea in that year, and again in 253, the siege of Lilybaeum had been going poorly. As the consular year 250 was winding down (which is to say, early in 249 BC), the resourceful Carthaginian commander at Lilybaeum, Himilko, had achieved the complete destruction of the Roman siege works in a firestorm, forcing the Romans to abandon any attempt at taking the town by assault; heavy loss of life among the Roman besiegers accompanied the debacle (Polyb. 1.48.1–49.1). At the same time, famine and disease caused by rampant shortage (and perhaps spoilage) of food was ravaging the siege forces to such an extent that one of the Consuls returned home early with his army. Major political disagreements in Rome on whether and how to continue the war would not be at all surprising.[13]

---

[10] Thiel 278 n. 712.   [11] Front. *Strat.* 1.4.14; 2.7.14; 3.10.8.
[12] For a discussion of the Frontinus passage and its implications, Konrad 2015a.
[13] Diod. 24.3–4; Zonar. 8.15. Polybios omits this important detail, though perhaps Livy did not: *quod oppidum* (sc. *Lilybaeum*) ... *Romani obsidere conati, superveniente Hannibale qui Hamilcaris*

What form the Tribune's intervention would have taken is, of course, unknown; but a similar attempt two centuries later offers a serviceable model. In 55 BC, the Tribune C. Ateius Capito attempted to prevent M. Licinius Crassus (*cos. II* 55) from departing for his Parthian campaign. Ateius announced *dirae* during Crassus' *votorum nuncupatio* on the Capitol, and when these were ignored, he tried to arrest the Consul; but other Tribunes intervened. Finally, Ateius, waiting by the city gate through which Crassus was to leave, pronounced curses over him as he crossed the *pomerium*.[14] In a similar manner, the Tribune might have tried to vitiate, through a *dirarum obnuntiatio*, the ceremonies of *profectio* observed on the Capitol by the Consul on the day of his departure, and perhaps hurled curses (*exsecrationes*) at him as he was crossing the *pomerium* to leave the City.

Under no scenario, however, could the Consul have responded, as the scholiast alleges, by consulting the *auspicium pullarium*—let alone while already aboard his flagship, in the Tiber river. The Chickens conveyed Iuppiter's permission, or lack thereof, for proceeding with an intended act of state on that day; they could not override a Tribune's action. Nor could they cancel the effect of *dirae*, properly announced; and the Tribune would presumably be ready to deliver his *obnuntiatio* during any subsequent attempt to complete the ritual requirements of *profectio*.

Hence Servius, if correct about the character of the tribunate (*plebis*), is wrong in presenting the Consul's consultation of the *pulli* as his immediate reaction to the Tribune's obstruction. Indeed, it is very likely that the auspices under which a magistrate went out to war—and left the City *paludatus*—did not involve the Chickens at all. It is evident that the procedure observed whenever a commander was forced to return to Rome to repeat his auspices must have been identical to the one in which he had received them in the first place. As for the former, we

---

filius fuit victi, maiore exercitus sui parte perdita ipsi (sc. *consules*) *aegre evaserunt*, wrote Orosius (4.10.2). Cf. Konrad 2016: 186–189.

[14] Cic. *Div.* 1.29–30; 2.84; cf. Dion. Hal. 2.6.4; Vell. 2.46.3; Lucan 3.126–127; Flor. 1.46.3; Min. Fel. *Oct.* 7; additional details in Plutarch *Crass.* 16.4–8 and Dio 39.39.5–7 (probably also Appian *BCiv* 2.18.66, whose πολλὰ ἀπαίσια seem to distinguish *dirae* from the subsequent curses, ἀραί). On *dirae*, "oblative signs of especially calamitous significance," see Linderski *AL* 2203; 2200–2203, 2212–2213; on the incident in 55, also Valeton 1890: 432–436, 440–443; Simpson *passim*; Bayet *passim*; Schäublin *passim*; Konrad 2004: 181–185; Driediger-Murphy 2018. The latter (191–193) revives Mommsen's view of the curses as merely a muddled and untechnical reference to *dirae* in later sources (*StR* 1: 107 n. 2). That may be so, although Plutarch and Dio—very likely drawing on the same source here—are quite clear and specific in their distinction between *obnuntiatio* and *exsecratio*. Now, Velleius—the earliest source to mention *exsecrationes*—seems to use the word merely as a synonym for the *dira omina* employed by the Tribunes to stop Crassus (*hunc proficiscentem ... diris cum ominibus tribuni pl. frustra retinere conati; quorum exsecrationes si in ipsum tantummodo valuissent eqs.*: this does not look like an attempt to distinguish two different procedures), and Lucan ascribes to the *dirae* the effect of a vow (*Crassumque in bella secutae saeva tribuniciae voverunt proelia dirae*, "and the Tribunes' *dirae* following Crassus to the wars promised savage fighting"), without specifying curses. Similarly Cicero, in a jibe directed at the Consuls of 58 (*Sest.* 71, *exierunt malis ominibus atque exsecrationibus duo vulturii paludati*), speaks of evil omens and curses; but Piso and Gabinius were not subjected to treatment resembling anything like what Crassus was to experience in 55. Conceivably, a new set of *dirae* (different from the ones reported on the Capitol) announced by Ateius when Crassus was crossing the *pomerium* had mutated into curses by the late first century AD.

know that it entailed lying down to sleep: ... *ubi incubare posset auspicii repetendi causa* (Fest. 326.16L). Lying down on a bed inside the *tabernaculum* and then rising *silentio* between midnight and dawn constitute essential steps in obtaining *auspicia de caelo* or *ex avibus*.[15] Hence the ones to be repeated were preceded by nocturnal incubation: which does not support an auspication by means of the Chickens. (This follows whether one believes in the existence of separate "auspices of departure" or subscribes to a unitary of view of magisterial auspices, according to which the Consul derived his legitimate authority to go to war from his auspices of "investiture"—obtained *de caelo*—and the proper observance of all rituals pertaining to *profectio*.) Of course, *silentium*—in augural parlance, the absence of any *vitium*—is equally required for auspices *ex tripudiis*, and nothing prevents the Consul from obtaining the latter in the same manner as those from the sky or birds, *de nocte oriens silentio*; but the fact that auspication with the Chickens could occur anywhere, anytime, especially right before battle (the need for which would not always be apparent during the previous night) makes it virtually certain that nocturnal incubation was not among its necessary elements.[16]

5.2 The Auspices at Sea

Yet again, auspices taken in (or at) the Tiber river are entirely plausible. A little-discussed and cryptic note in Servius auctus (ad *Aen.* 1.13) informs us about the special augural status of Ostia and the Tiber with regard to war at sea:

> Ostiam vero ideo veteres consecratam esse voluerunt, sicut Tiberim, ut si quid bello navali ageretur, id auspicato fieret ex maritima et effata urbe, ut ubique coniunctum auspici, ut Tiberis, cum colonia esset.

> "The ancients wanted Ostia to be consecrated, just as the Tiber, for the reason that if any operation was conducted in a war at sea, it would be done under auspices taken from a maritime and inaugurated city; so that it would everywhere be connected, as regards *auspicium*, just as the Tiber, with the colony."

---

[15] Chapter 2.3 note 44.
[16] Livy 10.40.2, *tertia vigilia noctis ... Papirius silentio surgit et pullarium in auspicium mittit*; but Cicero's description of the procedure mentions no preparatory action beyond the establishment of *silentium* (*Div.* 2.71–72), and the circumstances of Livy 9.14.1–3 rule out auspication during the night. The detailed, though lacunose, exposition of the ceremonies before battle—from the *auspicium ex tripudio* to the soldiers' *testamentum in procinctu*—in the Veronese scholia (ad *Aen.* 10.241) have the commander auspicate while sitting in his *tabernaculum* (what one would expect in any case), *coram exercitu pullis e cavea liberatis*: the presence and participation of the entire army in this archaic version of the procedure (the *pullarii* have no part in observing the Chickens' feeding) makes it unlikely that it was carried out before dawn. Moreover, the *auspicium ex tripudio* had its origin in oblative signs (Cic. *Div.* 1.27–28; 2.73), which were not tied to a particular time of observation. Cf. Mommsen *StR* 1: 101–102; Valeton 1890: 211–215; Catalano 1960: 346 n. 38; and see Chapter 7.4.4.

Evidently, war at sea was to be waged, as on land, *auspicato*; but without the special character of Ostia and the river, this would not be possible. In other words, a Roman commander could not simply leave the City *paludatus*, go aboard his flagship, and sail in harm's way. He needed Ostia, and the Tiber.

5.2.1 Augural Waters

Water, in particular streams and rivers, poses unique problems in the augural sphere. It is unstable and unreliable.[17] Any course of running water, however small, if crossed unguardedly will disrupt—indeed, annul—impetrative auspices previously obtained; to preserve them intact, the magistrate must validate them each time he sets across a stream or river, in a procedure known as *auspicia peremnia*.[18] We do not know, in fact, if auspices could even be obtained on shipboard, wholly surrounded by water, or if they required the auspicant to be on firm land.[19] Nor do we know if and how one's auspices would be affected by entering a river without crossing it, or by emerging at its mouth into the open sea.

Wherein lay the special character of Ostia? If the scholiast's *consecrata* is used technically, it belongs to the realm of the *ius pontificium*; if untechnically, it may cover any number of augural concepts: either way, it is of no help in deciphering the town's augural significance. Like all *coloniae civium Romanorum*, Ostia ranked, augurally speaking, as an *urbs*: it had a *pomerium*, inaugurated, hence *effatum*.[20] In that regard, it did not differ from the *urbs Roma*; and both lay on the Tiber river. Unlike Rome, Ostia was an *urbs maritima*.

The Consul leaving Rome to go to war takes the auspices with him, *a domo, a publicis privatisque penatibus* (Livy 22.1.6)—in other words, *ex urbe*; this is what enables him to ask Iuppiter for auspices outside the *ager Romanus*. But for the

---

[17] Serv. ad Aen. 12.246, bene "fefellit": namque hoc augurium nec oblativum est nec inpetrativum, sed inmissum factione Iuturnae, quod carere fide indicat sedes negata: nam ubicumque firmum introducit augurium, dat ei firmissimam sedem ... in hoc autem augurio liberatum cycnum cecidisse in aquam dicit, quam instabilem esse et infirmam manifestum est.

[18] Fest. 284L, peremne dicitur auspicari, qui amnem aut aquam quae ex sacro [ex agro Mommsen, fortasse recte] oritur, auspicato transit; 296L, Petronia amnis est in Tiberim perfluens, quam magistratus auspicato transeunt, cum in campo quid agere volunt; quod genus auspici peremne vocatur; Serv. ad Aen. 9.24, ... locus autem iste dictus est secundum augurum morem, apud quos fuerat consuetudo, ut si post acceptum augurium ad aquam venissent, inclinati haurirent exinde Manibus effusis precibus vota promitterent, ut visum perseveraret augurium, quod aquae intercessu disrumpitur; cf. Cic. ND 2.9; Div. 2.77, with Pease 473–475; Mommsen StR 1: 97; Valeton 1890: 209–211; and esp. Fiori 2014a: 301–307, vindicating the text of Servius against Servius auctus and Thilo–Hagen ServGr 2: 311 (although Fiori's alternative reading, manibus <et> effusis precibus, remains attractive). As Valeton emphasizes (210), auspicia peremnia were required only to preserve auspices obtained previously, not to cross running water as such.

[19] See Catalano 1978: 535–536, on the augural distinction between terra and aqua.

[20] Varro LL 5.143, ideo coloniae nostrae omnes in litteris antiquis scribuntur urbes, quod item conditae ut Roma, et ideo coloniae et urbes conduntur, quod intra pomerium ponuntur; see Catalano 1978: 479–486.

Consul who goes to sea, it seems, it is not enough to carry the auspices with him from Rome: to wage war at sea *auspicato*, he must do so *ex maritima et effata urbe*. Rome was an *urbs effata*,[21] but not *maritima*; Ostia was both. The note in Servius auctus does not speak of auspices as such at Ostia, of course; yet the conclusion is inescapable: in order to engage in naval warfare, the commander has to take his auspices not only from Rome (as required for any war), but also from Ostia. Carrying them with him *ex urbe maritima*, the Consul may now entrust himself and his fleet to the Tiber river, without fear that the water surrounding him will disrupt his auspices: presumably the question put to Iuppiter covered this important point. The Tiber in turn leads to the open sea—and furnishes an inseparable connection with the place from which the Consul took the auspices. Be it in the waters around Sicily, off the coast of Spain, or beyond the Pillars of Hercules, the Consul will be able to wage war *auspicato*. Whether those auspices, at Ostia or at sea, could be obtained aboard ship, or had to be taken on firm land at water's edge, we cannot tell. (No source unequivocally says that Claudius pitched the Chickens over the side.)[22]

5.2.2 Making a Move, on Land and at Sea

Cicero the Augur confirms that war at sea demanded auspices not merely when battle was imminent. Twice he describes both Consuls' fault with the verb *navigare* (*Div.* 1.29, *cum vitio navigassent*; 2.71, *qui contra auspicia navigaverunt*), and not once in his four references (above, ##1–4) to those incidents does he connect the *vitium* of Claudius specifically with auspication before battle. Iunius, in any case, lost his fleet not when he engaged the enemy *contra auspicia*, but while trying to avoid a fight.[23] Hence *navigare* is significant: the act of sailing itself required Iuppiter's permission. What Cicero does not make clear is whether this permission needed to be sought only once—to take the fleet down the Tiber and into the open sea—or every time the fleet set sail from any port (or beach, or anchorage).

There is evidence that, by land, auspices must be obtained before the army could move out of a resting place—camp or city—even if no battle was expected on that day. A few days before Cannae, Hannibal attempted to lure the Romans

---

[21] We may use that common expression, although strictly speaking, only the *pomerium* was *effatum*, not the *urbs* as a whole: see Linderski *AL* 2156–2157 with n. 31.

[22] Florus, though, comes close (above, Subsection 5.1.1 #10): *ibi statim classe demersa, ubi ille praecipitari pullos iusserat*. Pease 136, commenting on Cic. *Div.* 1.29, takes this to mean "that they were thrown overboard from the fleet," and if *ibi* and *ubi* are to be understood literally, the conclusion stands. But with *ibi* and *ubi*, Florus may simply have meant Sicily and the waters around it: in which case, the Chickens could have been drowned at the shore at Lilybaeum.

[23] Polyb. 1.54.3–4; Diodor. 24.1.9; despite differences in their accounts of Iunius' movements, both are quite clear and in agreement on this point. See Section 5.3 below.

into an ambush by vacating his camp during the night, leaving behind numerous items of conspicuous material value; the Consul Varro, *penes quem imperium* that day,[24] had already ordered the army to march out of their camp and occupy that of Hannibal, filled with loot, when his colleague sent a word of caution—on top of his own hesitation, his Chickens would not eat: *Paullus, cum ei sua sponte cunctanti pulli quoque auspicio non addixissent, nuntiari iam efferenti porta signa collegae iussit* (Livy 22.42.8). Paullus, as Consul, naturally took his own auspices for his army, but in case of divergent answers from Iuppiter the auspices of his colleague as the day's supreme commander would prevail. Nothing alleges that Varro had acted inappropriately with regard to the auspices; on the contrary, he called off the sortie—albeit grudgingly—when he received the news from Paullus (22.42.9). Evidently, he too had auspicated, and obtained an affirmative response; as his auspices took precedence over those of Paullus, he could have rejected his colleague's report: yet he chose to undergo not even the slightest risk in this regard.[25] But on this day Varro had set out for plunder, not for battle.

In 209 BC, after Fabius Maximus had recaptured Tarentum, Hannibal tried a similar ruse: citizens of Metapontum went to Fabius with a—false—offer to hand their town over to him if he drew near with his forces; Hannibal meanwhile lay in ambush. Fabius fell for it, but when he prepared to march his army out of Tarentum during the night, *aves simul atque iterum non addixerunt*.[26] Like Varro, he had not expected to give battle on those days.

Unless those two examples constitute exceptions to common practice, we may conclude that auspices were required for setting out from every camp or town in which the army spent the previous night. By analogy, auspices ought to be called for whenever the fleet left the shelter of firm land. Hence the phrase *contra auspicia profectus* in the *Periocha* of Livy 19 cannot be pressed to place the drowning of the Chickens at Rome (or, rather, Ostia).

5.3 The Location of the *Vitium*: Claudius and Iunius

What makes one pause before following the majority of the sources in locating the event, at least by implication, immediately before the Battle of Drepana[27] is Cicero. In four references he never draws a clear connection between the occurrence of the *vitium* and the day of the battle; twice he terms the Consul's offense

---

[24] As follows from Livy 22.41.3, *Paullus consul, cuius eo die—nam alternis imperitabant—imperium erat*, with 22.41.6, *nocte proxima*, 22.42.1, *ubi inluxit*.
[25] Cf. Valeton 1890: 424–427; his insistence, though, that the Consul *penes quem imperium non est* lacked the right to auspicate (similarly, Bleicken 1981: 268) remains unconvincing.
[26] Livy 27.16.11–16; Plut. *Fab*. 19.7–8 (ἔμελλεν ὁρμήσειν διὰ νυκτός, a detail not in Livy).
[27] The actual auspication would have taken place before the fleet sailed from Lilybaeum, just after midnight (noted by Jal 1: 47 n. 6).

as *vitio sive contra auspicia navigare*; and on three occasions he treats Claudius and his colleague as a unit: *P. Claudius, Appi Caeci filius, eiusque collega L. Iunius* (above, #2); *L. Iunio et P. Claudio consulibus* (#3); *P. Claudius L. Iunius consules* (#4). That both had encountered the same *vitium*—the Chickens refusing to eat— is clear enough; but from Cicero it almost appears as if they encountered it together, on the same occasion. That could only have happened at their departure from Rome—again, presumably, at Ostia. Most chronologies of the First Punic War, though, have Iunius leave the City sometime after his colleague;[28] but they rely, inevitably, on a series of unprovable assumptions that cannot invalidate the evidence of Cicero, and the only source that alludes to the Consuls' leaving Rome certainly permits the conclusion that Iunius departed no later than Claudius, if not before him.[29]

On the other hand, in his most detailed—and earliest—account (#1) of Claudius' outrage against the Chickens, Cicero mentions the *vitium* of Iunius rather as an afterthought, corroborating the point just made, than as the second element in a unit, and with no hint that both incidents occurred on the same occasion; and if anywhere he implies a temporal connection between the drowning and the battle he does so here, albeit barely. Nor can we be certain that the auspices taken at Ostia involved the *pulli*; if they were conceived as a naval parallel to the ones that gave permission to the Consul to be Consul (or, if we were to accept separate "auspices of departure," to leave the City *paludatus*), one should rather think that they must be taken *de caelo* or *ex avibus*. Finally, despite a likely (and popular) groundswell of opposition against continuing the war at the beginning of consular 249, it seems doubtful that hysteria ran high enough to consume both Consuls' *pullarii* with fear so far from the prospect of battle—let alone the fact that sabotaging the departure of Iunius would in effect prevent supplies from being delivered to the starving siege forces at Lilybaeum. A random failure of the Chickens to eat cannot be ruled out, of course;[30] but that it should happen to both Consuls on the same day (or in short succession) would be *mirum* indeed. At Drepana, however, notwithstanding the apparent eagerness at least of the

---

[28] For a convenient overview, see Morgan 105–109, who favors a departure of Claudius in May or June, and of Iunius not until September. See, however, Meltzer *GdK* 2: 330–331; Reuss 1901: 119; and Walbank *HCP* 1: 116, arguing that both Consuls arrived in Sicily (hence, by implication, left Rome) at roughly the same time. For additional considerations pointing to an early departure of Iunius, see Konrad 2016: 185–186.

[29] Zonar. 8.15, τέως μέντοι Λούκιος Ἰούνιος ἡτοίμαζε ναυτικόν, Κλαύδιος δὲ Πούλχρος εἰς τὸ Λιλύβαιον ἐπειχθεὶς κτλ

[30] That the outcome of such auspications was normally effected by the *pullarii*, through starving or overfeeding the Chickens, as well as from the virtual certainty that crumbs would drop to the ground in the process of eating, is clear enough from Cicero (above, Chapter 2.2.1, note 35), although the making of a false report, as in Livy 10.40.2–4, should not be taken as a routine occurrence. But in the incidents recorded in Cic. *Fam.* 10.12.3 and Livy 41.18.8–14, it is difficult to envisage any reason why the *pullarii* should have deliberately arranged them, be it on their own initiative or under outside influence. (Cf. Driediger-Murphy 2019: 121–125, 197–198.) No technique of manipulation is fail-safe.

legionary troops (expecting lots of easy loot) embarked for the operation, uneasiness could have prevailed at the thought of going into battle with an undermanned fleet, partially untrained crews, and an unpopular commander.[31]

For Iunius Pullus, two Sicilian locations of the *vitium* can be identified. Having left Rome with a large convoy of transports to resupply the Roman siege forces at Lilybaeum, the Consul arrived at Messana, where he was joined by those ships "that had gathered there from the camp and from the rest of Sicily" (ἀφικόμενος εἰς τὴν Μεσσήνην καὶ προσλαβὼν τὰ συνηντηκότα τῶν πλοίων ἀπό τε τοῦ στρατοπέδου καὶ τῆς ἄλλης Σικελίας, Polyb. 1.52.6). The "ships from the camp" have caused much needless headache. Everywhere else in this part of Polybios' narrative (1.42–55), τὸ στρατόπεδον refers, without exception, to the Roman camp and army engaged in the siege of Lilybaeum: it cannot possibly mean something different—and entirely unknown—here.[32] The alleged difficulty arises only from a preconceived notion that if Lilybaeum is meant, the ships must have left it before Drepana, as no Roman ships could have made it from Lilybaeum to Messana after the battle, with Adherbal's (and soon, Qarthalo's) fleet blocking the way.[33] Of course, nothing (except perhaps a small Punic squadron at Herakleia) prevented them from simply sailing along the southern coast of Sicily, and past Syracuse to Messana.

From Messana, Iunius proceeded to Syracuse, with his fleet now grown to 120 warships and 800 transports. At Syracuse, he sent about half of this force ahead towards Lilybaeum, while waiting with the remainder for stragglers and additional grain from the inland. Off the south coast of Sicily, possibly in the vicinity of Phintias, the advance force was intercepted by a large Punic fleet under Qarthalo, and forced to seek shelter in a bay, where they succeeded in holding off capture by the enemy (Polyb. 1.52.5–8; 53.8–13; Diod. 24.1.7).

At this point accounts diverge. According to Polybios, when the Consul arrived with the rest of his fleet sometime later, Qarthalo prevented him from linking up with the advance force, and Iunius, not daring to fight but unable to flee, anchored along a rocky and dangerous shore, "thinking it preferable to suffer whatever must be suffered than to allow his own army, men and all, to fall into the hands of the enemy" (κρίνων αἱρετώτερον ὑπάρχειν ὅ τι δέοι παθεῖν μᾶλλον ἢ τοῖς πολεμίοις αὔτανδρον τὸ σφέτερον στρατόπεδον ὑποχείριον ποιῆσαι, 1.54.1–4). In Diodoros

---

[31] Polybios 1.50.5 insists on the troops' eagerness. He says nothing about the attitude of the naval crews—rowers and sailors—who had less prospect of plunder, and (at least the more seasoned of them) a better appreciation of the risks when fighting at sea. On their generally poor condition, see Polyb. 1.51.4, 9; on Claudius' unpopularity, Diod. 24.3; cf. Thiel 273–274.

[32] Cf. Polyb. 1.42.8; 43.1; 48.10; 49.3; especially 52.5, 7 (on either side of the passage in question!); 53.4, 7; 55.8; cf. Konrad 2015a: 199–203. W. R. Paton's translation (Loeb), "the ships from Lilybaeum," although—as often—more periphrastic than precise, meets the substance of the matter.

[33] Thus, e.g., Tarn 55 n. 38; Thiel 88 n. 84 (rejecting the words ἀπὸ τοῦ στρατοπέδου as "mak[ing] no sense"); Walbank *HCP* 1: 116; Lazenby 1996: 124 with n. 1.

(24.1.8–9), Iunius apparently was able to join his advance force; but when Qarthalo renewed his attack on the now combined fleets, the Consul, hoping to salvage the transports and their supplies, decided to retreat to Syracuse. Being overtaken by the Carthaginians, he fled towards the land, judging the fear of shipwreck to be less than the danger posed by the enemy (περικατάληπτος γενόμενος κατέφυγε πρὸς τὴν γῆν, ἐν ἐλάττονι θέμενος τὸν ἀπὸ τῆς ναυαγίας φόβον τοῦ παρὰ τῶν πολεμίων κινδύνου, 24.4). A sudden storm coming up from the open sea shattered the entire Roman fleet (Diod. 24.1.9), or both halves of it (Polyb. 1.54.5–8), on the lee shore, with tremendous losses; only two of the warships survived. (Qarthalo barely managed to round Cape Pachynus and find protection in its lee.)

No source reports the precise occasion on which Iunius disobeyed the auspices. But if auspices were necessary, as seems likely, before leaving port (whether for battle or otherwise), the *vitium* would have occurred either on his departure from Syracuse or when he chose to sail back to Syracuse from Phintias rather than risk a battle with Qarthalo's fleet. As for the Chickens, a natural loss of appetite cannot be ruled out. But If Diodoros is correct, many on the Consul's staff—including his *pullarii*—might well have considered it preferable to await the enemy in the relative safety of the anchorage at Phintias. If, on the other hand, Polybios has it right, and Iunius encountered Qarthalo somewhere before he could link up with the advance force, he would have incurred the *vitium* when auspicating before sailing from Syracuse: as he would have received the news of Drepana by then (along with the surviving ships), his *pullarii* might have found it prudent to restrain the Consul from venturing out.

Given that auspices were unquestionably required before an intended battle, and almost certainly before setting sail for any reason, we may safely assume that both Claudius and Iunius consulted the Chickens on the day of their respective disasters. The accounts of the drowning in Valerius Maximus (above, #6, cf. 8) and, to a lesser extent, Suetonius (#9) show striking verbal parallels to Cicero's (#1), but do not appear to have been culled directly from the latter: Valerius prominently features a *pullarius* and makes an explicit connection between auspication and battle; Suetonius makes the same connection and expressly locates the incident *apud Siciliam* (three elements not in Cicero). One suspects a common source that probably was also used by Livy, if not transmitted by him directly to Valerius. Since that source also contained Cicero's note of Iunius Pullus' suicide (#7; cf. 1, 4), one may conclude that it, and presumably Livy, told the story of Claudius and Iunius essentially as did Cicero, but with some added detail (the *pullarius*) and an unambiguous location, at least for Claudius, in Sicily. Of the two undeniable elements of confusion in Servius' account—fleet lost in storm, and Consul drowned with it—the first occurs already in Minucius Felix (#11); it appears to have gained currency centuries before the scholiast, and cannot have come from Livy, at least not his full text. The second is also present in Ianuarius

Nepotianus, the fifth-century excerptor of Valerius Maximus (#8).[34] The error might be due, of course, to Valerius himself; but its absence in the other excerpt—that of Iulius Paris—renders such a conclusion doubtful: Paris generally summarizes the original in a faithful and succinct manner, whereas Nepotianus is given to mistakes, and not above inserting the occasional tidbit he found elsewhere.[35] What matters is that the error did not come from Livy. Hence Servius' attribution of his version to Livy rests on shaky ground: the historian almost certainly placed the drowning immediately before the Battle of Drepana.[36] Certainty eludes us; but all in all, it appears more probable that the Consuls incurred their *vitia* involving the *pulli* on the occasion of their disasters, rather than on their departure from Rome (or Ostia).[37]

Yet Servius would not have invented out of whole cloth the Tribune's attempt to keep the Consul from leaving the City to go to war. That much he must have read somewhere, be it in Livy, be it in another author. Just as he—or probably already his source—conflated Claudius' disaster at Drepana with the catastrophic loss of fleets in storms, he mixed up the Tribune's intervention (whether or not it involved augural tools such as the annunciation of *dirae*) at the Consul's departure from Rome with the drowning of the Chickens, at dawn before the battle, in Sicily.

5.4 *Vitium* and *Perduellio*

After the disaster at Drepana, Claudius returned to Rome. The Senate now instructed him to name a Dictator. Thumbing his nose at them, Claudius named his *scriba*, who abdicated his office forthwith. Eventually, A. Atilius Caiatinus (*cos. II* 254) was installed as Dictator, and assumed command in Sicily.[38] By that time, in Rome's sole success of that year, Iunius Pullus had already seized Eryx from the Carthaginians, and perhaps been captured by them in turn (Zonar. 8.15).

The appointment of a Dictator did not, however, relieve the Consuls of personal responsibility for their violation of the auspices. Two Tribunes of the Plebs prosecuted Claudius for *perduellio*—a capital charge; on the day of the vote,

---

[34] For the date, see Briscoe's edition, 1: xxi.   [35] See Wardle 2005: 380–381.

[36] That *Per.* 19 *contra auspicia profectus* cannot be used to place the incident at Claudius' *profectio* from Rome (as Reuss 1909: 425 and Latte 266 n. 1 would have it) follows from *Per.* 22, which uses the same language for Flaminius in 217: *contra auspicia profectus signis militaribus effossis, quae tolli non poterant*—clearly thinking of auspices on the morning of the battle.

[37] Of course, if either Consul had received a negative response at Ostia and proceeded anyway, such *vitium* would render invalid and meaningless any impetrative auspices he obtained subsequently: if Claudius drowned his Chickens at Ostia, lusty feeding on the part of their replacements before Drepana would merely signify hunger, not Iuppiter's permission (cf. Konrad 2004, esp. 172–178, and Chapter 7.4.4).

[38] The appointments will be discussed in another context: Chapter 8.1.2.

vitium intervened in the form of a thunderstorm. Subsequently, the Tribunes, prevented from bringing the same charge again, persuaded the People to impose a fine of 120,000 As instead.[39]

The Bobbio scholiast attributed the ban on double jeopardy to tribunician intercession, aimed at preventing a man from being accused of treason twice by the same individuals in the same magistracy (*postea tr. pl. intercesserunt ne idem homines in eodem magistratu perduellionis bis eundem accusarent*). In fact, it arose almost certainly out of an augural rule preserved by Cicero, holding that if any event prevents the proceedings on the appointed day, be it on account of auspices or of a justifiable excuse, the entire case and trial is dropped: . . . *si qua res illum diem aut auspiciis aut excusatione sustulit, tota causa iudiciumque sublatum est* (*Dom.* 45); the augural barrier against a second prosecution is also emphasized by Valerius Maximus (*subito coorti imbris beneficio tutus fuit a damnatione: discussa enim quaestione aliam velut dis interpellantibus de integro instaurari non placuit*). The scholiast, of course, need not be altogether wrong: if this was the first time a *iudicium populi* had been interrupted by a storm, or the first time an attempt was made to resume proceedings after such an interruption, tribunician action may have been necessary to lend force to the Augurs' ruling—especially if popular rage against Claudius ran high enough to sweep aside their objections.[40] "Even the augurs must have been baffled by Jupiter's decision to save Claudius."[41]

Was Claudius tried still during his consulship? Tribunician prosecution of an incumbent magistrate was possible and did occur, but only to impose *multae*, not on capital charges—unless they involved a violation of tribunician rights, which was not the case with Claudius Pulcher.[42] In all probability, therefore, both his prosecutions took place in consular 248, after he had completed his term; less than three years later, he was dead. (In 246, Claudius' sister was fined 25,000 As for publicly expressing her wish that her brother were still alive, so that he might lose another fleet, and thus alleviate what she deemed overcrowding in the City.)[43]

His colleague, it would seem, did not outlive him, or not for long. Cicero reports that Iunius committed suicide (above, ##1, 4), and Valerius Maximus adds that he did so to escape conviction (#7); again, Livy presumably told the same essential facts as Cicero, with expanded context.

---

[39] Schol. Bob. 90.3–8St; cf. Polyb. 1.52.3; Cic. *Div.* 2.71; *ND* 2.7; Val. Max. 8.1 abs. 4.
[40] See Linderski *AL* 2176–2177 with n. 111 and Hölkeskamp 1990: 437–448 = 2004: 85–93, for a fuller discussion. Cf. also the case of the prospective *rex sacrorum* L. Cornelius Dolabella (*IIvir nav.* 180), appealing a fine imposed by the Pontifex Maximus for refusing to lay down his magistracy: as they were called up in order, the tribes voted to condemn—unless he changed his mind and obeyed. Meteorological intervention both saved Dolabella from conviction and prevented him from assuming the priesthood: *vitium de caelo, quod comitia turbaret, intervenit; religio deinde fuit pontificibus inaugurandi Dolabellae* (Livy 40.42.8–11).
[41] Thus Linderski, wryly, *AL* 2177.
[42] Mommsen *StR* 1: 705–707; 2.1: 318–322; and see esp. Bleicken 1955: 120–124; Bleckmann 201 n. 3.
[43] Gell. 10.6; cf. Livy *Per.* 19.

No charge in Iunius' prosecution is recorded, but the case of Claudius makes *perduellio* virtually certain. Not so, the date. Zonaras (8.15) notes that after capturing Eryx, Iunius himself fell into Punic hands. Unless Dio or his epitomizer made this statement in error, one may assume that Iunius was released as part of the prisoner exchange agreed upon in 247.[44] Commanders who had lost larger fleets in storms, with greater loss of life, had returned in triumph.[45] (That in itself assures that he was prosecuted not simply for the loss of his fleet, but for his violation of the auspices.) Iunius came home from captivity to a charge of treason, and found that no defense availed. He had sailed against the auspices: the fact was manifest, and nothing else mattered—not his reasons, not the circumstances. Perhaps Iuppiter would have saved him, too, as he had Claudius, on the day of the trial. Iunius chose not to wait, and took his own life.[46]

5.5 The *Sortes Praenestinae*

The events of 249 BC, when both Consuls refused to obey the auspices, may also shed new light on a mysterious incident towards the end of the First Punic War. The Consul of 241, Q. Lutatius Cerco, attempted to consult the famous oracle of Fortuna Primigenia at Praeneste before taking up his command; the Senate objected on the grounds that he should manage public affairs *auspiciis patriis, non alienigenis*, and Lutatius desisted. (Suspicion has been voiced repeatedly that "Cerco" in the manuscripts is in error for "Catulus," and indeed the latter, the famous Consul of 242, appears far more probable; for our present purpose, though, it does not matter.)[47] What exactly had been Lutatius' objective?

5.5.1 Consultation at Praeneste

The incident is reported by the two excerptors of Valerius Maximus, Iulius Paris and Ianuarius Nepotianus, under the rubric *de superstitionibus*.

> *Exc. Par.* 1.3.2: Lutatius Cerco, qui primum Punicum bellum confecit, a senatu prohibitus est sortes Fortunae Praenestinae adire: auspiciis enim patriis, non alienigenis rem publicam administrari iudicabant oportere.

---

[44] Livy *Per.* 19; Zonar. 8.16; cf. De Sanctis *SdR* 3.1: 177 n. 73; Thiel 291–292; Walbank *HCP* 1: 119.
[45] The Consuls of 255, and Sempronius Blaesus in 253.
[46] "A tragedy," Lazenby comments (1996: 141), "for he, too, like Terentius Varro in 216 . . . had not 'despaired of the Republic.'" For further notes on the prosecutions of Claudius Pulcher and Iunius Pullus, see Konrad *Hermes*, forthcoming.
[47] F. Münzer "Lutatius (4, 13)" *RE* 13.2 (1927) 2071, 2095, assuming conflation of Cerco with his brother; Briscoe 1998: 29 *ad loc.*; Shackleton Bailey *VM* 1: 44 n. 2. What follows is an abridged version of Konrad 2015b, where a full discussion of the textual problems (153–158) and of Lutatius' identity (165–169) can be found.

"Lutatius Cerco, who brought the First Punic War to an end, was prohibited by the Senate to approach the lots of Fortuna Praenestina: for they judged that the *res publica* should be managed under the ancestral auspices, not foreign ones."

Exc. Nep. 1.3.2: Lutatium Cerconem, confectorem primi Punici belli, fama extitit velle ad Praenestinam Fortunam † sortes mittere sive colligere. hoc cognito senatus inhibuit extraria responsa † consultorum disquiri. iussum legatis est aedilibusque in haec missis, ut, si consuluisset, ad supplicium Romam reduceretur. denique adeo profuit factum, ut † ex incerta ei Romana auspicia fuerint: nam ab altaribus patriis profectus Egadas opulentissimas insulas in conspectu Carthaginis populatus est.

"The story goes that Lutatius Cerco, the man who brought the First Punic War to an end, wanted † to send or collect lots at (or to?) Fortuna Praenestina. On learning of this, the Senate forbade that inquiries into foreign responses be made † of individuals consulting (?). Orders were issued to the envoys and Aediles dispatched in this regard that, should he have consulted (*sc.* the oracle), he was to be brought back to Rome for punishment. The eventual outcome of this action was highly beneficial, with the result that there were Roman auspices for him † *ex incerta*: for having set out from the ancestral altars, he plundered the Aegates islands—exceedingly wealthy—in full view of Carthage."

Despite its three vexing cruces, the text of Nepotianus, when read in tandem with Paris, offers a coherent account.[48] There can be no question of the Consul sending others to Praeneste: *sortes mittere sive colligere* simply denotes the procedure of consulting Fortuna, and *ad* here must be situational, not directional: "there was talk that Lutatius Cerco intended to cast, or rather collect, the lots at/before Fortuna Praenestina."[49] Next, with *senatus inhibuit extraria responsa consultorum disquiri* Nepotianus clearly means to say that the Senate wanted to prohibit the consultation of foreign oracles, not protect their responses by preventing investigations of such consultations. Paris' *Lutatius . . . prohibitus est sortes . . . adire* unequivocally marks the prohibition as aimed at Cerco specifically, hence not a general ban on consulting the Praenestine oracle; which also follows from Nepotianus' *ut si consuluisset . . . Romam reduceretur*. Thus *consultorum* cannot stand: perhaps *a consule Rom<ano>* (Kempf) or, preferably, *consuli Rom<ano>* (Gertz).[50] Finally, the ungrammatical *ut ex incerta ei Romana auspicia fuerint*. Both Foertsch's *exin certa* ("right away, Roman auspices were certain for him = he obtained unambiguous Roman auspices") and Halm's *ex incertis* ("instead of

---

[48] See Wardle 2005: 380–381 for a thorough discussion of the two excerptors' characteristics: Paris typically faithful to Valerius' narrative and language, if condensed; Nepotianus prone to elaborate, misunderstand, or misrepresent.
[49] Cf. Wardle 2005: 379.
[50] Cf. the apparatus criticus to Kempf's ([2]1888: 17) and Briscoe's (1998: 30) Teubner editions.

uncertain auspices he received Roman ones") furnish an acceptable meaning.⁵¹ Under either emendation, the Consul previously had either not obtained Roman auspices—which is to say, no auspices at all—or only such as were uncertain. But, throughout, the opposition evidently intended is less one of *Romana* and *incerta auspicia* than of *Romana* or *patria auspicia* and *extraria responsa* or *alienigena auspicia*. Perhaps the textual problem includes *Romana: ut ex in<certis> certa ei Roma<e> auspicia fuerint* ("with the result that, at Rome, instead of uncertain auspices he received certain ones") would yield a perfectly good sense, contrasting certain with uncertain auspices, while preserving the opposition of foreign and ancestral ones, of Rome and Praeneste.

5.5.2 An Alternative to Auspices

It is this latter element that concerns us here. Two scholars in the past thirty-odd years have tried to shed light on this strange episode, and although they arrive at divergent reconstructions of the presumed political maneuvering behind it, they both agree on a fundamental point: in proposing to consult the oracle at Praeneste, Lutatius intended not to push aside the traditional auspices or replace them altogether, but to complement them.⁵² That, however, is the question.

Both excerptors, Paris as well as Nepotianus, undeniably present the issue as a matter of alternatives: *auspicia patria* versus *extraria responsa*. Neither offers any hint that Lutatius merely aimed at consulting the lots of Fortuna in addition to the auspices, and however one restores the text, Nepotianus' account implies that, prior to the incident, the Consul had either obtained no auspices at all or only uncertain ones. If he lacked auspices altogether, Fortuna could not furnish them (for all the other advice she might offer), that being Iuppiter's prerogative; if his auspices were flawed or uncertain, the lots at Praeneste, falling outside the *ius augurale*, could be of no assistance in resolving whatever doubts existed, or remove the *vitium* that tainted them. Nor does one readily comprehend the Senate's vehement reaction, if additional guidance was the only thing at stake. Ziółkowski and Wardle both insist that Lutatius' attempt posed a serious threat to the auspices:⁵³ how so, if it was meant to be merely complementary? "The two forms of divination did not compete with one another";⁵⁴ auspices concerned

---

⁵¹ Livy 8.30.1 (cf. 8.32.7), *in Samnium incertis itum auspiciis est*, regarding L. Papirius Cursor; noted by Wardle 2005: 380, and see Chapter 1 with note 2. For the emendations, see Briscoe's apparatus, 1998: 30. Kempf (²1888: 17) and Wardle (2005: 380) accept *exin certa*, Shackleton Bailey (*VM* 1: 46) *ex incertis*; Briscoe retains *ex incerta* in his text.

⁵² Ziółkowski 1987, esp. 330–331; Wardle 1998: 147–148; 2005: 383 with n. 36.

⁵³ "Everybody ... must have been aware of the constitutional crisis which would have ensued from this appeal ... in view of the potentially disastrous consequences thereof to the augural law, the cornerstone of the state religion, and thus of the very fabric of the Republic" (Ziółkowski 1987: 332); "Cerco sought to employ sortition in a way which fundamentally struck at the heart of Roman religious practice, the auspices" (Wardle 2005: 383).

⁵⁴ Ziółkowski 1987: 330.

Iuppiter's permission to proceed with an intended action on that day, whereas oracles gave advice on how to achieve a desired result. As long as the Consul's auspices were in order, the *sortes* ought to have posed no threat; if they were not, the oracle could not help—unless the consultation was conceived to take their place.

In rejecting an intended substitution of the *sortes* for the auspices, Ziółkowksi noted the difficulty of consulting daily with the Praenestine oracle while the Consul was in Sicily. Yet that would have been the point precisely: instead of the daily auspication that *mos* demanded, a single consultation of Fortuna was to grant divine sanction to the whole campaign. If the Consul cast the lots at Praeneste, then waged his war successfully without auspices, he could create a precedent that would free future commanders from the restrictions the auspices imposed on them. It would not have put an end to auspices as such; certainly those who wished to observe the old ways would retain the ability to do so. But an alternative would have been established, and instead of being essential, auspices henceforth could be viewed as merely advisory, and optional. In light of what had happened less than a decade earlier, when one Consul displayed open contempt for the ancient practice, the other if not opposition then at least indifference to it, the probability increases considerably that this indeed was what Lutatius had in mind.

We may discern two basic scenarios of what happened. The Consul, having just left the City *paludatus*, was alerted to the fact that his auspices had become *incerta*. (If *ex incertis* could be established as the correct reading, this scenario would be nearly certain.) Instead of returning to the City to repeat them, he proposed to seek guidance from Fortuna Primigenia at Praeneste: if successful in this, he would maintain that he had no further need of auspices. Then again, Lutatius may have attempted to consult the oracle before he received any auspices: as Consul designate but still *privatus*. Instead of entering upon his consulship at Rome and obtaining his initial auspices there, followed by the usual ceremonies of *profectio*, Lutatius intended to take office in Praeneste, consulting the lots but dispensing with auspices. (A radical notion, it may seem; but within a quarter of a century a situation very similar to this was to unfold.[55])

The attempt was greeted in the Senate with a fiercely negative response. Officials were sent to Praeneste, with instructions to keep Lutatius from going through with the consultation, or bring him back to Rome should it already have occurred. Lutatius chose not to push the matter.

---

[55] Discussed in Chapter 7. A third scenario can be envisaged if one believes in the existence of "auspices of departure" (against which, see Chapter 2.4–2.6): Lutatius may have taken up his magistracy in the customary manner, with auspices in the City; but rather than observe the ritual of *profectio* and obtain the necessary auspices for war, he proposed to substitute a one-time consultation of Fortuna at Praeneste.

6
Dictator Interregni Caussa

The Consuls of 249 had sailed against the auspices and lost their fleets, to the detriment of the *res publica*. Another Consul, in 242 or 241 BC, stepped back from the brink, and brought the First Punic War to a victorious end. So far, these incidents could be seen as outliers. Yet twenty years had not passed when an objection to the rule of auspices on grounds of principle is first explicitly attested. In 223 BC, a Consul of the Roman People publicly denied the validity of a formal response by the College of Augurs, and endeavored to undermine the public belief in the practice of auspices, with reasoning and a degree of confidence that suggest he did not stand alone in such views. Given the fundamental nature of that challenge, the involvement (it will be argued) of a Dictator and his Magister Equitum in the Senate's response to it, and its unusually full documentation—in contrast to those previous instances—in the sources, the episode rewards closer examination. Incidentally, a plausible (it is hoped) explanation and understanding of what transpired in 223 will also illuminate a puzzling piece of epigraphical evidence, ostensibly relating to an event six years later. We begin with that.

6.1 An Inconvenient Document

Q. Fabius Q. f. Q. n. Maxim(us) Verrucoss(us) II dict(ator) interregni caus(sa). Thus the entry in the *Fasti consulares Capitolini*, under the year FC 536 = AUC 537, or consular 217/6 BC. It looks innocuous, and has drawn scant attention; yet beneath it lurks a mystery.

Fabius, beyond the shadow of a doubt, exercised the functions of a *dictator rei gerundae causa* in that memorable year, as abundantly documented throughout the sources. The designation *interregni causa* is attested nowhere else: most, therefore, dismiss it simply as an error, in keeping with a host of other flaws exhibited by the *Fasti*, and ask no further.[1] A few, however, have given it the scrutiny it deserves.

---

[1] E.g., Mommsen *StR* 2.1: 161 n. 1; Bandel 126 n. 1; Broughton *MRR* 1: 245 n. 2; Scullard 1951: 274; recently Golden 29 ("immaterial"). Preliminary versions of the argument made in this chapter were presented at the Annual Meeting of the American Society for Legal History (San Diego, Calif., November 8, 2002) and at the Classical Association Annual Conference (Liverpool, England, March 30, 2008).

6.1.1 Sumner's Interrex

Nearly half a century ago, G. V. Sumner launched a frontal assault on Livy's report (22.33.9–35.4) of the consular elections for 216. As the year 217 was drawing to a close, the Senate—thus Livy—by letter contacted the Consuls, Cn. Servilius Geminus and (suffect for the unfortunate C. Flaminius) M. Atilius Regulus, and requested that one of them return to Rome so as to hold elections. Both declined, citing the gravity of the military situation; they recommended that elections be conducted by an Interrex (*sine detrimento rei publicae abscedi non posse ab hoste; itaque per interregem comitia habenda esse potius quam consul alter a bello avocaretur*, 22.33.10). Instead, the Senate found it more appropriate to have a Consul name a Dictator to hold elections (*patribus rectius visum est dictatorem a consule dici comitiorum habendorum causa*, 22.33.11). One of the Consuls complied with the new instructions and named L. Veturius Philo (*cos.* 220) Dictator, who in turn chose M. Pomponius Matho (*cos.* 231) as Magister Equitum. Fourteen days later, the Dictator and his deputy abdicated without completing their task, having been found *vitio creati*; with that, *ad interregnum res rediit* (22.33.11–12). The *patres* produced as Interrex first C. Claudius Centho (*cos.* 240), then P. Scipio Asina (*cos.* 221). After a brief but intense electoral campaign, the second Interrex presided over the election of the *homo novus* C. Terentius Varro, whose supporters had directed a stream of virulent attacks against the whole procedure, accusing the Senate, the Nobles, the Consuls, and the Augurs of deliberately causing the *interregnum* in an attempt to derail their candidate's chances of winning. The other consulship remained unfilled until the next comitial day when, now under Varro's chair, the People elected as his colleague L. Aemilius Paullus (*cos. I* 219)—drafted by the *nobilitas* at the last moment, when it became clear that the original patrician candidates were ill-suited to stand up to the ebullient New Man.

Rejecting the *interregnum* reported for the opening of the year 216/5, Sumner decided that the Dictator Veturius did in fact hold the elections, and abdicated not *vitio creatus* but simply after finishing his task; but rather than eliminating Livy's two Interreges from the record altogether, Sumner proposed that they held office earlier in 217: not, however, at the beginning of that year (to elect Consuls), but in the summer—in those traumatic days following the Battle of Lake Trasumene. Panic in Rome demanded the appointment of a Dictator; but with one Consul dead and the other in Gaul, cut off from communications with Rome, there was no way to do so immediately, at least not in accordance with established practice: *consul aberat, a quo uno* (sc. *dictator*) *dici posse videbatur* (Livy 22.8.5, cf. 22.31.9). For which reason, in an unheard-of procedure the Dictator was elected by the People, along with his Magister Equitum. Hence the question, obvious and unavoidable: what magistrate presided over this electoral Assembly?

Sumner's answer was, an Interrex. He knew, of course, that the "technical conditions for an interregnum were not fully present,"[2] but appealing to an "unprecedented emergency" and a need for speedy action, he brushed aside the obvious objection that there could be no *interregnum* as long as any Consul or Praetor (at the very least) was still in office—a rule so deeply anchored in the foundation of the *res publica* that it was considered ironclad, unbreakable as late as 43 BC. In the summer of that year, both Consuls lay dead, and their replacement was urgently desired. Yet it proved impracticable, perhaps impossible, to bring about the abdication of all remaining "patrician" magistrates—Praetors, Curule Aediles, Quaestors; and thus, no *interregnum*: *dum enim unus erit patricius magistratus, auspicia ad patres redire non possunt*.[3] Sumner alleged that an *interregnum* regularly could occur with all magistrates but the Consuls still in office.[4] There is no reason to doubt Cicero's clear and unequivocal statement (it seems he very much would have preferred an *interregnum*), seeing that even lowly Quaestors possessed the *auspicia publica* (albeit *minora*).[5] At any rate, there can be no question as regards the Praetors: elected *iisdem auspiciis* as the Consuls,[6] their auspices were alive even if the Consuls were not. An *interregnum* while there still were Praetors was as impossible as one *consule vivo*. At a minimum, this presents five obstacles—four Praetors and the surviving Consul—to Sumner's hypothesis; obstacles that cannot be overcome by pleading that "at the present time Rome lacked Consuls."[7]

For yet another reason, the notion of an Interrex naming the Dictator in the middle of 217 can be ruled out. As we saw earlier,[8] in 49 BC Caesar sought to be made Dictator so as to hold consular elections, but both the Consuls were in Greece, and uncooperative. The augural college refused to sanction either of two procedures that might circumvent the obstacle: to allow a Praetor to elect Consuls or name a Dictator. Neither of which, in the considered opinion of at least one Augur (Cic. *Att.* 9.15.2), would be lawful—although if Sulla was able to have himself named Dictator by an Interrex, why should Caesar not be able to manage it? Caesar solved the problem by having legislation enacted that authorized the

---

[2] Sumner 1975: 255.
[3] Cic. *AdBrut* 1.5.4; cf. Dio 46.45.3-4, on the dilemma and its eventual solution (the People, under the Praetor Urbanus, elected *duoviri comitiis habendis* who in turn presided over the election of Consuls suffect: Chapter 4.4.4, note 103).
[4] Sumner 1975: 255 n. 19.
[5] Clear from Messalla *apud* Gell. 13.15.4: *patriciorum auspicia in duas sunt divisa potestates. maxima sunt consulum, praetorum, censorum...reliquorum magistratuum minora sunt auspicia.* Cf. *StR* 1: 92-93.
[6] Messalla *apud* Gell. 13.15.4, *censores aeque non eodem rogantur auspicio atque consules et praetores*; cf. Livy 7.1.6, *praetorem...et collegam consulibus atque iisdem auspiciis creatum*, and 3.55.11, 8.32.3.
[7] See Gruen's rebuttal, 61-74; cf. Brennan *PRR* 1: 297 n. 188. On the absence of any magistrate with auspices and *imperium* as an absolute precondition for an *interregnum*, see Mommsen *StR* 1: 651-652 with n. 5 (expressing doubts about the need for Quaestors to abdicate); Jahn 112-113; Kunkel *StO* 278; Lintott 67.
[8] Chapter 4.4.3.

Praetor M. Aemilius Lepidus to perform the *dictio* on this particular occasion: *ibi* (sc. *Massiliae*) *legem de dictatore latam seseque dictatorem dictum a M. Lepido praetore cognoscit* (Caes. *BCiv* 2.21.5). Late in 82, special legislation had enabled the Interrex to name Sulla Dictator, but that Interrex had come into existence in the normal course of an *interregnum*, the Consuls and all other magistrates having died, expired, or abdicated. If Fabius' dictatorship in 217 had offered precedent for an Interrex *consule vivo*, surely Caesar would have availed himself of it: with Sumner, he could claim that "at the present time Rome lacked Consuls." Yet he did not; and Cicero's comment makes it clear that the Augurs knew of no instance, before Sulla, for an Interrex naming a Dictator in any form whatsoever.

6.1.2 The Dictator as Interrex Substitute

Seven years after Sumner, Marianne Hartfield insisted—rightly—that *interregni caussa* can only refer to some kind of future intention and not to the procedural oddities of Fabius' appointment. As there was no actual *interregnum* in 217, she proposed that the Dictator's principal task—as identified by his designation—was not to conduct the war (that was added subsequently "with senatorial approval") but to act instead of an Interrex for the purpose of electing a Consul suffect. Although noting at first that a Dictator *rei gerundae* could "easily have solved" that problem, she then proceeded to argue that a Dictator so named, or one *comitiorum habendorum causa*, could only preside over the election of all magistrates for the coming year—unlike an Interrex, who could only see to the election "of a consul or consuls." Hence if just one Consul needed replacement, it must be handled by an Interrex or the surviving Consul. The latter being "unable to leave the field," the only options left consisted of an Interrex or a Dictator designated to act as such: "Logic in the crisis swayed the senate toward use of the dictatorship."[9]

The sole evidence of Hartfield's contention that a Dictator *rei gerundae* or *comitiorum habendorum causa* could not hold elections for a Consul suffect is the fact that none is reported to have done so prior to 217. Unfortunately, the only recorded year that shows both a Dictator and a suffect Consul is 458 V, and here the suffect—the hapless L. Minucius—was in office before the Dictator was named.[10] Even as an *argumentum e silentio* this will not do. Indeed, there are no

---

[9] Hartfield 303–307.
[10] See *MRR* 1: 39 for sources; the Consul [——-] n. Carve[tus? *an* Carvetanus?], dead in office (*in ma[g.] mortuus est*), is shown only in the *FC* and their derivative, the Chronographer of 354: *InscrItal* 13.1: 24–25, 92–93, 362–363. Likewise from the Chronographer and a fragmentary name in the *Acta Triumphorum* (*InscrItal* 13.1: 66–67), Degrassi conjectured as Consul suffect replacing M. Geganius Macerinus in 437 V one M. Valerius (Lactuca) Maximus, who would have triumphed over Veii and Fidenae instead of the Dictator Mam. Aemilius Mamercinus credited by Livy (4.17.8–20.4; cf. Eutrop. 1.19.2). Needless to say, there is no telling whether in this tradition Valerius would have been elected before or after the Dictator was named, or if it even knew of a Dictator in that year.

rational grounds to think that a Dictator could not hold elections for a Consul suffect unless specially so commissioned. As for the surviving Consul being unable to leave the field, Servilius was back in Rome long before Fabius returned from his initial encounters with Hannibal, and the election of a suffect Consul was clearly of low priority: it did not happen until much later in the year, during the debate over the Metilian proposal to give the Magister Equitum power equal to that of the Dictator.[11] Against the notion that an Interrex could have been named *consule vivo*, the same arguments apply as against Sumner.

Five years later, Giovanni Nicosia in his seminal study of the so-called "limited Dictators" briefly addressed the issue. Noting that *interregni causa* as a formal designation of the Dictator's task would make no sense ("qualifica che veramente non avrebbe senso") and that the conditions for an *interregnum* did not exist in 217, he reasoned, in a vein similar to Sumner's ("at the present time Rome lacked Consuls"), that the puzzling notation was meant to convey to readers that although there occurred no actual *interregnum*, the situation prompting the appointment of a Dictator was in fact analogous to such a state of affairs—a vacancy of all the supreme magistrates.[12] How readers of the *Fasti* in the time of Augustus, two centuries after the events in question, could be expected to extract such subtle and complex information (not available, it seems, through any literary account in circulation then) from the terse *interregni caussa*, no explanation.

6.1.3 A Very Special Interrex

More recently, Massimo Gusso, unaware of Sumner's treatise (and Gruen's rebuttal), revived the notion of an Interrex *consule vivo*, in a manner nothing short of fantastic. Gusso conjured up two distinct manifestations of the Interrex: the first and normal one ("una prima [*sc.* figura], fisiologica"), to hold elections when all regular magistrates have expired, and a second ("inconfessata," not surprisingly) "che potenzialmente porta seco tendenze patologiche," with the task of calling into existence "una magistratura straordinaria" in cases of particular emergency. The extraordinary magistrate brought about by this "second" kind of Interrex, although appearing—under the title of Dictator—familiar on the outside, was endowed with characteristics substantially different and anomalous, "quasi monarchiche," better even, "magico-carismatiche"; always named by an Interrex, even though one Consul might be alive (or both, if far enough from Rome), this special Dictator was in reality chosen by the Senate, with a semblance of popular election. Such was the appointment of M. Furius Camillus after the Gallic disaster in 390 V and, perhaps, of M. Iunius Pera after Cannae in 216; and, naturally, of

---

[11] Polyb. 3.88.8; Livy 22.11.7–9, 25.16.   [12] Nicosia 569–570.

Fabius Maximus after Lake Trasumene—extraordinary Dictators named by an extraordinary Interrex. For Fabius, Gusso divined a special treat: first produced as Interrex by the *patres*, he named himself Dictator. Hence *interregni causa*, "in occasione del suo interregno."[13]

In a parallel universe, this reconstruction might have some validity; although greater comfort would be furnished even there by a solution that stays within the generally accepted parameters of Roman institutions. It need not detain us further.[14] Yet Gusso's disquisition, like Sumner's, Hartfield's, and Nicosia's before him, has the merit of standing largely alone in asking a fundamental question: what, actually, does *interregni causa* mean, and how did the phrase attach itself to Fabius' (second) dictatorship in the *Fasti*? No other Dictator is on record *interregni causa*: it will not do with Mommsen simply to dismiss "the inconvenient document as erroneous," a mere mistake on the part of the stonecutter, or the redactor, about the nature of this dictatorship.[15] For, surely, they did not invent out of whole cloth a dictatorial designation that had no parallel anywhere else. Its very singularity calls for explanation.

6.1.4 The Missing Gerundive

Observing the analogy of *comitiorum causa*, short for *comitiorum habendorum causa*, Sumner took the mysterious phrase to mean "something like 'for the purpose of dealing with an interregnum.'"[16] This is undoubtedly correct, as far as it goes; indeed the *Fasti*, while generally scrupulous in adding the gerundive, under the year 257 BC show a Dictator [L]*atinar(um) fer(iarum) caussa*. Sumner then concluded that an *interregnum* must have existed, with an Interrex in office, "at the time when the Dictator was appointed." Now, assuming—still with Sumner— that the Interrex named the Dictator, it follows inescapably that the *interregnum* would come to an end the moment the Dictator was appointed: how, then, was the Dictator to deal with a situation that no longer existed? Surely Q. Ogulnius was not named Dictator in 257 at the time when the Latin Festival was in full swing; he was appointed to celebrate it, both Consuls being dispatched to Sicily without that customary delay.[17] The Dictator *clavi figendi causa* was not appointed because a nail was sticking from the wall of the Capitoline Temple, but to hammer a new one into it, and the Dictator *comitiorum causa* was not named to deal with elections in progress, but to see to it that elections were held. Indeed, to translate *interregni causa* "for the purpose of dealing with an *interregnum*" is to dodge the

---

[13] Gusso, esp. 318–323.   [14] Cf. Brennan *PRR* 1: 297 n. 188.
[15] Thus, rightly, Sumner 1975: 254 n. 14 and Gusso 297–298.
[16] Sumner 1975: 254 n. 14. *Comitiorum causa*, without the clarifying gerundive, is common in Livy: e.g., 7.26.11; 9.7.12; 22.34.10; 25.2.3; 27.29.6; 29.10.2; 29.11.9.
[17] Brennan *PRR* 1: 82.

issue: common Latinity as well as the universal usage in the realm of public institutions points to one meaning only (glimpsed by Gusso, and instantly dismissed[18]), straightforward if hardly of an everyday occurrence. This Dictator was named to bring about an *interregnum*: in other words, *interregni ineundi causa*.

The modalities of going about such a task will be discussed later. First, the obvious question: could this, in fact, have been Fabius' task in 217 BC? The answer, just as obvious, is "No." An *interregnum* would have required the abdication of all surviving "patrician" magistrates, followed by his own (and that of his Magister Equitum): in the middle of the year, at the height of the campaigning season, with Hannibal in Central Italy, between Rome and her only operational army (Servilius') at the moment? Certainly, if a paramount augural concern could be discovered: but nothing of the kind is mentioned in our sources, nor can it rationally be conjectured. True, Flaminius had exhibited, *suo more*, crass and deliberate neglect of auspices; yet he was dead, and nothing indicates that his behavior had vitiated his colleague's auspices, or those of all the other magistrates.[19] On the contrary, when later in the year an *interregnum* was suggested, the Senate opted for an electoral dictatorship instead: the College of Augurs, evidently, saw no need for an *auspiciorum de integro renovatio*.

The *Fasti*, therefore, are in error. Yet what is the nature of their mistake? As noted earlier, a mere slip in designation will not answer; *interregni caussa*, known of no other dictatorship, stands too alone for that. That the redactor made it up from nothing, only to place it in an impossible context, is out of the question; the puzzling designation serves no fictionalizing purpose, offers no antiquarian explanation of some archaic feature no longer understood—not, at any rate, with reference to the year 217. It follows that the designation is in itself authentic, in other words, it did occur, but not in 217 BC: we must look for a different occasion, not attested—at least not directly—in the extant record. A possible solution thus emerges. Fabius, it is well known, had been Dictator once before. The extant portions of the *Fasti*, though, do not record that first occasion, for which reason it is commonly assigned to the gap spanning the years 221 through 219. There being no serious emergency in any of these years, his first dictatorship is commonly thought to have been *comitiorum habendorum causa*, "to hold elections."[20] Yet that is a mere guess, and a designation that has actual support in the surviving evidence may claim preference. When the *Fasti* were compiled, the redactor or

---

[18] Gusso 298. Hartfield 304 with n. 10 points out correctly that *causa* with the genitive stresses "future intention"; hence "*interregni causa* cannot refer to the irregular procedure by which Fabius was named."
[19] The surviving Consul, Servilius Geminus, remained in office throughout the year (Polyb. 3.88.7; Livy 22.11.2–6; 22.25.5; 22.31.1–7; 22.32.1–3; 22.33.9–10; Plut. *Fab.* 4.3; Appian *Hannib.* 16.68; Dio fr. 57.21; Zonar. 8.26), as did the Praetors (Livy 22.9.11; 22.10.10; 22.25.6; 22.31.6; 22.33.8).
[20] Bandel 123–125; Degrassi *InscrItal* 13.1: 118–119, following De Sanctis *SdR* 3.2: 45; cf. *MRR* 2: 234–235.

the cutter switched, by accident or by design, the task of the first appointment to the year of the second.[21] It was the first of Fabius' dictatorships, not the second, that he took up *interregni causa*.

6.2 The *Fasti*

Lest an error of such magnitude be deemed improbable, a look at the *Fasti* from that perspective may prove instructive. Inscriptional evidence commands high trust in its reliability, more so than "literary" sources. All the same, the *Fasti* are not infallible; far from it. The influence and interests of the New Romulus can be detected all over the document. They are a compilation, redacted and edited to tell the Roman past from a particular point of view: and like any attempt to produce a coherent synthesis of data from the past, they are subject to—aside from deliberate manipulation—error, confusion, and the inevitable need to choose between, or attempt to resolve, conflicting pieces in the evidence. The resulting list of magistrates is arrived at by a process no different in nature than that employed by Livy, Diodoros, or Dionysios, and a priori no more credible.[22] Only the naïve will confuse the character of the evidence furnished by the *Fasti* with that of a stone preserving the actual text of, say, a *senatus consultum* or comitial law, and treat them as more reliable than a literary account of that same past merely because they are carved in stone instead of written on papyrus, or—worse—because they represent the "official," hence definitive, view. Indeed, omissions, inconsistencies, and oddities abound—some innocent, some not.

6.2.1 Death and the *Fasti*

Omitted, for example, are the deaths in office of C. Atilius Regulus (*cos.* 225), L. Aemilius Paullus (*cos. II* 216), M. Claudius Marcellus (*cos. V* 208), and—at least in the stone's original cutting—T. Quinctius Crispinus (*cos.* 208). True, in each instance the expired magistrate was not replaced by a suffect, and the *Fasti* remain silent in a number of such cases.[23] Yet by no means always. Ap. Claudius Russus (*cos.* 268) is listed dead in office, with no suffect; likewise Q. Cassius Longinus (*cos.* 164), L. Valerius Flaccus (*cos.* 152), and Cn. Octavius (*cos.* 87). We know their suffects, though not from the *Fasti*. In 272, conversely, the Censor L. Papirius Praetextatus is annotated *in mag(istratu) m(ortuus) e(st)*, but the next pair of

---

[21] A similar—albeit it far less consequential—interchange of iteration numbers has been suspected in the stone's record of 420 V: see Degrassi *InscrItal* 13.1: 96; Broughton *MRR* 1: 71 n. 1.
[22] See Broughton's salutary comments, *MRR* 1: xi–xii; cf. Wiseman 1995: 104.
[23] Degrassi *InscrItal* 13.1: 22: "Mortes quidem et abdicationes semper traduntur, ubi alter magistratus sufficitur, at, si suffectus non nominatur, mentio saepius omittitur."

Censors did not take office until three years later; moreover, Papirius' colleague, that redoubtable *exemplum* of frugal rectitude and three triumphs, M'. Curius Dentatus, is not shown to have abdicated after his fellow Censor's death—a mandatory practice since the early fourth century.[24] Are we to assume that Curius violated *mos* and tried to stay in office? An unlikely case to remain so entirely unattested. In 214, the Censor M. Atilius Regulus abdicated upon his colleague's death, and both events are duly noted; yet again, no new Censors were elected until 210. Thus twice at least, for 272 and 214, the stone records a Censor's death although no suffect was to fill his place.

The document's report on 208 BC warrants closer attention. For the first time in history, both Consuls died in office in a time of war; Livy gave due emphasis to the calamity.[25] Yet the *Fasti* have no comment. Contrast the year 176, when the same thing happened next (*InscrItal* 13.1: 48–49):

[Cn. Cor]nelius C[n.] f. L. n. Scipio Hispallus in mag(istratu) mortuus est. in eius l(ocum) f(actus) e(st) C. Valerius M. f. P. n. Laevinus

Q. Petillius C. f. Q. n. Spurinus in mag(istratu) postea quam sibi conleg(am) subrog(avit) occis(us) e(st)

Every step here is recorded. It might be said that, in 208, the Consuls' death could go unmentioned since no suffect was elected. No suffect, either, in 82 BC, though here again the stone reported the demise of both the Consuls.[26] Its silence on that fact in 208 betrays sloppiness rather than editorial policy, especially in view of the event's epochal nature. Indeed, a strange subscription to Crispinus' name, inserted between the man's filiation and cognomen, but in smaller letters and below the line, lends weight to the conclusion that death in office was omitted here by inattention, not design. The entry reads: *T. Quinctius L. f. L. n. $_{exvol}$ Crispin[us].* Surely that signifies *ex vol(nere)*;[27] noting that the letters were evidently added after the year's main entry had been cut, Degrassi suggested that the mason meant thus to indicate the death of both the Consuls: "cum uterque consul alter in proelio occisus sit, alter ex vulnere in eodem proelio accepto mortuus."[28] That lacks conviction. Marcellus died in battle, warranting the usual *in mag(istratu)* (or *in proelio*) *occis(us) e(st)*; and if *ex vol(nere)* was indeed intended to apply to him as

---

[24] *StR* 1: 215–216; 2.1: 339; cf. Livy 5.31.6–7.
[25] Livy 27.33.7, *ita quod nullo ante bello acciderat, duo consules sine memorando proelio interfecti velut orbam rem publicam reliquerant*. But, strictly speaking, it had happened before, in 463, when a pestilence claimed both Consuls while the Aequi and the Volsci raided Roman territory: 3.6.1–7.8; Dion. Hal. 9.67–68; Oros. 2.13.2. Again, the *Fasti* take no notice.
[26] Most of the right-hand column (i.e., Carbo's) of that year is missing, but the notation in the left column leaves no doubt as to what should be restored: *C. Marius C. f. C. n. in mag(istratu) occis(us) est. Cn. P[apirius Cn. f. C. n. Carbo III in mag(istratu) occ(isus) e(st)]*. See *InscrItal* 13.1: 54–55.
[27] Cf. Livy 27.33.6, *T. Quinctius consul... ex volnere moritur*.
[28] *InscrItal* 13.1: 120.

well, it should (and could: the stone has room enough) have been inserted between his name and his colleague's, viz. *M. Claudius M. f. M. n. Marcellus V*$_{ex\ vol(nere)}$ *T. Quinctius L. f. L. n. Crispinus*. The note undoubtedly pertains to Crispinus alone. *Ex vol(nere)*, though, seems harsh, even as the cutter was pressed for space; one would expect a verb, however much abbreviated, in keeping with the document's consistent practice. The note *m(ortuus) e(st)* was either omitted, or added in the right margin below the missing final letters of *Crispin[us]*, where the stone breaks off.[29]

Crispinus' death thus did find mention, after a fashion, belatedly and obliquely, when someone realized the stonecutter had missed that item. No such luck for Claudius Marcellus. A parallel is close to hand, exhibiting the same erratic efforts to correct the record. In 164 BC, a similar, though straightforward, addition marks the death in office of Q. Cassius Longinus: *in m(agistratu) m(ortuus) e(st)* was squeezed into the margin to the right of the name, "alia manu postea."[30] Yet, in the following year, the death of M'. Iuventius Thalna (*cos.* 163) remained unnoticed. Death is reported randomly in the *Fasti*—or, at the least, according to criteria that remain unfathomable.

6.2.2 More Oddities

The year 217 fares poorly in particular. The abdication *vitio facti* of the Dictator-to-Hold-Elections, Veturius Philo, and his deputy goes unmentioned. Sumner invoked this to support his argument that the abdication occurred in the normal course of business, the elections having been completed, rather than out of augural concerns; he allowed, though, that "the argument from silence here is admittedly not conclusive in itself."[31] Indeed not. The *Fasti* fail to mention quite a few other abdications: the Consuls of 392 (to renew the auspices), of 223 (*vitio creati*), of 154 (to move the beginning of the consular year up to January 1). The abdications of Consular Tribunes (444, 402, 397; the first and the last group *vitio facti*) all seem to have gone unreported.[32]

More astonishing by far, the silence of the stone regarding the two biggest issues of that year. Fabius is said to have been made Dictator in a highly irregular manner, as Livy was well aware (22.8.5–6, 31.8–11), by popular election: the stone has no comment on the unprecedented event. (Whatever the details of that mysterious procedure, it cannot explain *interregni causa*, or vice versa.) Soon Fabius' Magister Equitum, M. Minucius Rufus, disagreed with his superior about the conduct of the war, and, siding with the Master of the Horse, by plebiscite the

---

[29] Mingazzini (379, 381) and Mancini (240, 267) assume the latter.
[30] Degrassi *InscrItal* 13.1: 614.   [31] Sumner 1975: 253.
[32] The *Fasti* are extant, and silent, on the last two years; Degrassi plausibly assumes a lack of annotation also in 444 (*InscrItal* 13.1: 620).

People made his *imperium* equal to that of the Dictator. The story is well known to all the literary sources;[33] its constitutional implications, singular and remarkable, make it just the sort of notice the *Fasti* could not overlook. Yet not a word.[34] Can this be attributed to sheer ignorance? For all their imperfections, the *Fasti* constitute a marvel of antiquarian research, and ignorance is not a failing commonly imputed to their redactor. Something clearly is amiss in their treatment of Fabius' dictatorship in 217. First, *interregni caussa*, a designation that in itself appears authentic, but cannot possibly apply here; next, silence as to his irregular manner of appointment (if irregular it was); and finally, complete oblivion with regard to Minucius' special status. If ignorance is not the answer, confusion or displacement as to time and circumstance ought to be considered seriously.

Finally, the years 223 and 222. In the first, as already mentioned, the literary sources tell us that both Consuls abdicated; the *Fasti* make no note. In the second, the Consul M. Claudius Marcellus, in the great war against the Gauls, slew the Celtic chieftain in single combat, took his armor, and dedicated it as *spolia opima* to Iuppiter Feretrius on the Capitol—only the third such dedication since Romulus.[35] It seems barely credible that this feat (by a Marcellus, no less, of a family so dear to the man who commissioned the *Fasti*) should have gone unremarked in the marble; but unremarked it was. The entry for 222 forms the last line on that slab, at the bottom of the left-hand column of the third tablet; one can rule out the possibility that this information was contained at the top of the right-hand column: each column clearly began with a new year.[36] Marcellus' honor was duly noted in the *Acta Triumphorum*; but it appears that, in the *Fasti consulares*, the cutters were pressed for space.[37]

6.3 Flaminius in Gaul

In the normal way of things, a Dictator should have no connection with an *interregnum*; it commences automatically, inevitably, whenever no "patrician"

---

[33] Polyb. 3.103.3–5; Livy 22.25.10–27.9, 30.4; Plut. *Fab.* 9.3; Appian *Hannib.* 12.52; Dio fr. 57.16–17; Zonar. 8.26. Nor did the matter entirely escape the epigraphical record: see Fabius' tablet among the *Elogia Arretina* (InscrItal 13.3 no. 80): *dictator magistro equitum Minucio, quoius populus imperium cum dictatoris aequaverat,... subvenit.* Cf. Chapter 3.4.3.

[34] Degrassi *InscrItal* 13.1: 118: "Id quoque admiratione dignum ab illo qui fastos redegerit ignorari M. Minucium lege Metilia Q. Fabio Maximo dictatori collegam factum." Amazing indeed, such ignorance of a well-known fact, and quite improbable: better to assume a mix-up. As Beard 78 reminds us (in a different context), "a variety of factors, not the least of which was sheer carelessness, could lead to the exclusion of a ceremony from a particular record."

[35] For sources, *MRR* 1: 232–233.

[36] Degrassi *InscrItal* 13.1: 188; and see the top of the fourth tablet, opening with 153 (left column) and 49 (right column), respectively.

[37] *Acta Tr.* = *InscrItal* 13.1: 78–79. There is some indication that the same stonecutter worked on both the third tablet on the consular lists and the second pilaster (which contains Marcellus' triumph in 222) of the triumphal ones: see Nedergaard 120.

magistrates are in office. No circumstance that would require a Dictator to bring about an *interregnum* is conceivable, but one: if somebody were to block, obstruct, or otherwise prevent a necessary *interregnum* from taking place.

The three-year window, 221 through 219 BC, in which the first dictatorship of Fabius Maximus for want of anything better is usually placed, holds no evidence of such a situation. Yet only two years earlier, we have a full and fairly detailed report of a Consul resisting abdication to permit the inception of an *interregnum*—and it is the only such case known for certain in half a millennium of republican history.[38] As noted earlier, Fabius' designation *interregni causa* is the only one on record. Perhaps we can make the two things fit.

In 223 BC, both Consuls—Gaius Flaminius and P. Furius Philus—were sent north to fight against the Insubrian Gauls in the Po Valley. As their campaign got under way, a series of portents caused concern at home; the College of Augurs found the Consuls to be *vitio creati*.[39] The Senate resolved that they should refrain from any military action and forthwith return to Rome, and then abdicate so as to initiate an *interregnum* to renew the auspices; a letter was dispatched to Gaul with the appropriate instructions.[40] Arriving just as the Roman armies prepared for battle, the courier handed the letter to the Consuls; but they did not read it until after the battle—which the Romans won.[41]

---

[38] For the other, reported without reference to an intended *interregnum* and of dubious authenticity, see below, Subsection 6.6.1.

[39] Plut. *Marc.* 4.1–3,... οἱ δ' ἐπὶ ταῖς ὑπατικαῖς ψηφοφορίαις παραφυλάττοντες <τοὺς> οἰωνοὺς ἱερεῖς διεβεβαιοῦντο μοχθηρὰς καὶ δυσόρνιθας αὐτοῖς γεγονέναι τὰς τῶν ὑπάτων ἀναγορεύσεις; Zonar. 8.20. On the role of the Augurs acting as a college, as opposed to their individual capacity, see Linderski *AL* 2151–2190; and esp. 2162–2173, on electoral *vitium*.

[40] Plut. *Marc.* 4.4, εὐθὺς οὖν ἔπεμψεν ἡ σύγκλητος ἐπὶ στρατόπεδον γράμματα, καλοῦσα καὶ μεταπεμπομένη τοὺς ὑπάτους, ὅπως ἐπανελθόντες ᾗ τάχιστα τὴν ἀρχὴν ἀπείπωνται, καὶ μηδέν ὡς ὕπατοι φθάσωσι πρᾶξαι πρὸς τοὺς πολεμίους; Zonar. 8.20. The Augurs could advise this course of action as the proper remedy, but only the Senate could formally "order" it: Linderski *AL* 2159–2173. It bears noting how carefully Plutarch in his narrative distinguishes between the augural *responsum* declaring the Consuls *vitio facti* and the *senatus consultum* demanding that they abdicate: he was closely following a detailed and competent source. Pelikan Pittenger's treatment of the matter (39–40) is confused: the Senate did not "retaliate against the consuls for having marched off into battle despite their recall notices," and "later" force them to abdicate. The demand for abdication was part of the "recall notices," and indeed had to be; once the Consuls had been found *vitio creati*, there was no alternative.

[41] As Plutarch (*Marc.* 4.5; cf. *Fab.* 2.3, without details) tells the story, Flaminius alone received and—eventually—read the letter (if so, presumably because it was his day in the alternating supreme command). But in Zonaras 8.20, the letter is addressed jointly—as was undoubtedly the case—to both Consuls, and received and read (after the battle) by both; there is no hint of disagreement between the two until afterwards, on whether to comply with the Senate's instructions. Although Furius is mentioned at the beginning of Plutarch's narrative (*Marc.* 4.2), he disappears from the aftermath of the battle (4.5–6): the entire dispute over the Consuls' triumph features exclusively Flaminius, whom the People finally "force to abdicate together with his colleague" (ἀναγκάσας ἐξομόσασθαι τὴν ὑπατείαν μετὰ τοῦ συνάρχοντος). Here again, Zonaras makes it clear that Furius, too, suffered political ill will on account of his colleague's actions after the battle, not because of the way the letter was handled (διὰ γὰρ τὴν πρὸς τὸν Φλαμίνιον ὀργὴν ἠτίμασαν καὶ τὸν Φούριον). There can be little doubt that Plutarch chose to place all the emphasis here on Flaminius, who would soon cut a prominent—and unsympathetic—figure in the *Fabius* (2.3–3.3), and that Zonaras' account is the more accurate one.

So far, the Consuls had done nothing wrong. True, Flaminius' enemies back in Rome—of whom there were many, not least Fabius Maximus himself[42]—might grumble that he had acted irresponsibly in delaying his perusal of the letter, and going into battle without valid auspices; but as far as augural law was concerned, the rule was clear: the formal report, and only the formal report, created the augural reality. As long as the Consuls were not formally notified that the Augurs had found them *vitio creati*, they were fully within their rights in assuming that their auspices were valid; as long as they did not read the letter, they were not formally notified; and it was their decision, and theirs alone, when to read the letter.[43] It is worth noting that our sources, all uniformly hostile to Flaminius, are remarkably free of allegations that, on the day of the battle, he or his colleague had ignored any prohibitive auspices from Iuppiter.[44] We can be certain, therefore, that when Flaminius asked Iuppiter for auspices at dawn, they were affirmative. The same goes for his colleague, Furius Philus. We can be just as certain that Iuppiter, for reasons of his own, did not attempt to warn the Consuls off from giving battle by sending any negative signs, unasked: thunder "on the right," for instance, would have made the matter plain enough. But no such sign occurred; and the Consuls, as regards augural law, were in the clear.

What caused an uproar was what Flaminius did next. He flatly refused to follow the Senate's instructions, accusing his enemies of falsifying the *religio* (that is, the electoral *vitium*) discovered by the Augurs, and arguing that their very victory gave proof that his and Furius' auspices were in order, that they had been elected properly—not *vitio*. He announced that he would remain in Gaul until the campaign was finished, and in so doing teach the people back home not to let themselves be fooled by relying on birds and similar stuff and nonsense. Furius, an Augur himself,[45] at first would not cooperate with his colleague's defiant attitude, and prepared to lead his own army back to Rome; but soon he realized that this might jeopardize the safety of Flaminius' forces left behind in Gaul, and stayed while the latter completed his mop-up operations—without, however, engaging actively in them:

---

[42] Fabius had opposed Flaminius' plebiscite of 232 authorizing the *viritim* distribution of the *ager Gallicus* to Roman settlers (Cic. *Sen.* 11).

[43] Badian 1996: 200 n. 17; Linderski *AL* 2195–2198.

[44] Orosius 4.13.14, *contemptis auspiciis, quibus pugnare prohibebatur*, might mark the exception; but from the detailed accounts of Plutarch and Zonaras it is evident that the "scorned auspices" are nothing more than Flaminius' delay in opening the letter (if not a confusion with the events of 217). Lundgreen 157 n. 441 strangely misattributes Flaminius' neglect of auspices and sundry other ceremonies at the outset of his second consulship to his first in 223; the same error—apparently—in Beck 2005: 253 ("…hatte er, so die livianische Überlieferung, auf ein Einholen der Auspizien verzichtet").

[45] Bardt 18; *MRR* 1: 266; Lippold 310; Rüpke *FS* 2: 101: "…ist eine Kooptation schon deutlich vor dem Konsulat (223) nicht ausgeschlossen."

Zonar. 8.20: Μετὰ δὲ τὴν μάχην ἀναγνωσθείσης τῆς ἐπιστολῆς ὁ μὲν Φούριος ἑτοίμως ἐπείθετο, ὁ δέ γε Φλαμίνιος ἐπαιρόμενος τῇ νίκῃ τήν τε αἵρεσιν αὐτῶν ἀπεδείκνυ δι' αὐτῆς ὀρθῶς ἔχουσαν, καὶ διὰ τὸν πρὸς αὐτὸν φθόνον ἐνέκειτο καὶ τοῦ θείου τοὺς δυνατοὺς καταψεύδεσθαι. οὔτ' οὖν ἀπαναστῆναι πρὶν τὸ πᾶν καταστήσασθαι ἤθελε, καὶ διδάξειν καὶ τοὺς οἴκοι ἔφη μήτ' ὄρνισι μήτ' ἄλλῳ δή τινι τοιούτῳ προσέχοντας ἀπατᾶσθαι. καὶ ὁ μὲν κατὰ χώραν μένειν ἤθελε καὶ τὸν συνάρχοντα κατέχειν ἐπειρᾶτο, Φούριος δ' οὐκ ἐπείθετο. τῶν δὲ μετὰ τοῦ Φλαμινίου μελλόντων καταλειφθήσεσθαι φοβηθέντων μὴ μονωθέντες πάθωσί τι παρὰ τῶν ἐναντίων, καὶ δεηθέντων ἡμέρας τινὰς προσμεῖναι, ἐπείσθη, οὐ μέντοι καὶ ἔργου ἥψατο.

Zonaras' account is lucid and ungarbled, consistent with what we know of Roman auspical rules and practices related to such situations (note how Furius, although remaining in Gaul, is said to have avoided military action after reading the letter); he evidently followed Dio very closely here. Plutarch in the *Marcellus* skips the Consuls' disagreement following the battle, but in the *Fabius* notes strenuous opposition by Furius.[46] Both authors agree, in principle if not in detail, on the subsequent events.

6.4 *Consules vitio facti*

When the Consuls returned to Rome, they received a less-than-enthusiastic welcome. According to Plutarch, the people would not come to meet Flaminius outside the City gates, and came close to refusing him a triumph; after the triumph, they made him a private citizen, by forcing him and his colleague to abdicate their consulship. During the following *interregnum*, M. Claudius Marcellus was elected Consul; after entering office, he supervised the election of his colleague:

Marc. 4.6: ὡς οὖν ἐπανῆλθε μετὰ πολλῶν λαφύρων, οὐκ ἀπήντησεν ὁ δῆμος, ἀλλ' ὅτι καλούμενος οὐκ εὐθὺς ὑπήκουσεν οὐδ' ἐπείσθη τοῖς γράμμασιν, ἀλλ' ἐνύβρισε καὶ κατεφρόνησε, μικροῦ μὲν ἐδέησεν ἀποψηφίσασθαι τὸν θρίαμβον αὐτοῦ, θριαμβεύσαντα δ' ἰδιώτην ἐποίησεν, ἀναγκάσας ἐξομόσασθαι τὴν ὑπατείαν μετὰ τοῦ συνάρχοντος.

Marc. 6.1: ...ὡς δ' οὖν ἐξωμόσαντο τὴν ἀρχὴν οἱ περὶ τὸν Φλαμίνιον, διὰ τῶν καλουμένων μεσοβασιλέων ὕπατος ἀποδείκνυται Μάρκελλος, καὶ παραλαβὼν τὴν ἀρχὴν ἀποδείκνυσιν αὐτῷ συνάρχοντα Γναῖον Κορνήλιον.

---

[46] Plut. *Marc.* 4.5; *Fab.* 2.3, τῆς τε βουλῆς ἀποκαλούσης καὶ τοῦ συνάρχοντος ἐνισταμένου βίᾳ συμβαλὼν τοῖς Γαλάταις μάχῃ καὶ κρατήσας.

In Zonaras (8.20), the Consuls found themselves attacked in the Senate for not obeying promptly (Furius thus suffering "collateral damage" from the wrath mostly directed at Flaminius). The common people, which is to say, the *plebs*, however, still favored Flaminius, and—over the Senate's objections—voted a triumph to him and his colleague, after which both laid down their office:

ὀψὲ δ' οἴκαδε ἐπανελθόντες ὑπὸ μὲν τῆς γερουσίας αἰτίαν τῆς ἀπειθείας ἔσχον (διὰ γὰρ τὴν πρὸς τὸν Φλαμίνιον ὀργὴν ἠτίμασαν καὶ τὸν Φούριον), τὸ δὲ πλῆθος ἀντιφιλονεικῆσαν ὑπὲρ τοῦ Φλαμινίου ἐψηφίσαντο τὰ νικητόρια. καὶ ἀνάγοντες αὐτὰ ἐξέστησαν τῆς ἀρχῆς.

Other sources add nothing of substance, although Livy leaves no question that, at a minimum, an attempt was made to force Flaminius from office and to deny him a triumph: *memori veterum certaminum cum patribus, quae...consul prius de consulatu, qui abrogabatur, dein de triumpho habuerat* (21.63.2).

6.4.1 Augurs and Omens

Widely shared is the belief (first expressed by Flaminius himself) that party politics, raw and simple, prompted the Augurs' response *consules vitio factos videri*: an attempt to deny Flaminius the opportunity of gaining *gloria* for himself. Bleicken may serve as a vocal example, laying out a Rasputin-like portrait of Fabius Maximus, "der als erster den Wert der Ausnutzung der Auguralwissenschaft zu politischen Zwecken erkannte"—a sinister *éminence grise* who directed his eight colleagues in the Augural College like dolls having no will of their own.[47] Manipulation, even exploitation, of the augural discipline for political purposes undoubtedly occurred (we will encounter one example later on); but it cannot simply be assumed whenever it is convenient: a modicum of evidence or rational reasoning behind the assumption should not be too much to expect. In Flaminius' case, as will be seen, the claim has not a shred of evidentiary support, nor can the arguments advanced by its proponents withstand scrutiny.

When speaking of "the Augurs," it helps, again, for clarity of mind and argument, to consider who they were at the time in question.[48] (All too often, a vacuum of identity plagues scholarly encounters with the College, its members being treated

---

[47] Bleicken 1955: 30, 39; similarly Jahn 106–109, 122–123. It is depressing to see how this kind of fantasy, now fully dissociated from the evidence of the sources, can be treated as established fact today: "In 222 [*sic*] BC, in an effort to maintain his position, the noble Q. Fabius Maximus was able to induce the college of augurs to declare C. Flaminius *uitio creatus* over his election to consul" (Williams 284). For a sober treatment, accepting that there was "a real religious point to be made," see Develin 1979: 274; cf. Szemler 89–90; Eckstein 1987: 16; Champion 93–121.

[48] Cf. Chapter 4.4.

as anonymous entities acting in automaton-like unison.) In addition to Furius Philus, Fabius' fellow Augurs in 223 included such easily led men as Sp. Carvilius Ruga *cos. II* 228, M. Aemilius Lepidus *cos.* 232, M. Pomponius Matho *cos.* 231, and M. Claudius Marcellus *cos. I* 222 (and soon-to-be winner of the *spolia opima*).[49]

But if in fact they followed, meekly and thunderstruck, Fabius' lead, one would expect the electoral *vitium* to have been discovered before the Consuls left for Gaul; indeed, Bleicken confidently asserted that this was the case.[50] Citing Plutarch, Wild even claims that the evil omens were observed both at the Consuls' election and at their departure, and consequently envisages a long interval between those observations and the Senate's letter.[51] A look at the Greek will clarify the matter. Φλαμινίου δὲ καὶ Φουρίου τῶν ὑπάτων... ἐκστρατευσάντων... ὤφθη μὲν κτλ., wrote Plutarch (*Marc.* 4.2). The aorist—ἐκστρατευσάντων—leaves little room for Wild's and Bleicken's interpretation; the complete aspect in this context surely implies an action prior to that of the main verb. None of the omens listed (Plutarch's river of blood in Picenum, and three moons over Ariminum, to which Zonaras adds fire in the sky in Etruria, and a vulture settling in the Forum) could have been observed in Rome at the actual moment of election (in the Campus Martius) or departure (the ceremonies of *profectio* taking place on the Capitol and when crossing the *pomerium*). That rules out the existence, or at least its immediate recognition, of a *vinculum temporis*—the augural rule that an oblative sign pertains to a specific action only if it is observed while that action is in progress, not before or after.[52] Lacking the nexus between time and action, the portents reported were not understood to be *auspicia oblativa* but "mere" *prodigia*, of concern at first to the *pontifices* alone, not the Augurs.

It is certainly possible that the *vitium* tainting the consular elections was discovered independently of these prodigies. But given the close connection between the omens and the Augurs' ruling implied by all the sources, it will more likely have been in the course of the subsequent pontifical investigation that evidence of an actual *auspicium oblativum*, indicating a *vitium in auspicando* on the part of the presiding magistrate at the past consular elections, but not recognized or understood at the time, now came to light, and was submitted to the Augurs for a ruling.[53]

---

[49] See *MRR* 1: 230, 252, 276, 283; Szemler 70–74; Rüpke *FS* 1: 67. The remaining three members (at least two of them Plebeians) of the College are unknown, although C. Atilius Serranus *pr.* 218, first attested in 217 (Livy 22.35.2) could already have been co-opted by 223.

[50] Bleicken 1955: 30: "Der Versuch, Flaminius noch vor Beginn des Feldzuges zur Abdikation zu zwingen..."; similarly Feig Vishnia 2012: 35.

[51] Wild 123, "Plutarch... erzählt von schlechten Vorzeichen, die man beim Ausrücken der Konsuln sieht"; 126, "Vorzeichen, die man angeblich bei der Wahl und beim Ausrücken der Konsuln sah"; and 124, "Das [i.e., the Augurs' preparing their *responsum*] würde den langen Zeitraum, der anscheinend zwischen dem angeblichen *vitium* und dem Brief des Senats lag, hinreichend erklären." There is no evidence, of course, nor reason to think that it would have taken the *collegium* long to issue its report, unlike present-day investigative commissions.

[52] See Chapter 2.2.2.

[53] For a thoroughly documented example, see the celebrated case of Ti. Gracchus in 163: Chapter 8.4.3.

It passes belief that in 223 the Senate would have allowed the Consuls to depart for war after the augural college had given notice that they were *vitio creati*, or that Furius the Augur would be complicit in such an act of defiance under those circumstances. Clearly, they were already in Gaul when the portents occurred, and the Augurs did not discover the *vitium* until then.

6.4.2 Augural Sabotage (a Fantasy)

Why would Flaminius' enemies delay their augural move against him until he was in Gaul? It certainly could not aid their purpose; on the contrary. If the objective was to keep him from gaining *gloria*, it became imperative to keep him from fighting a decisive battle: in other words, he must be recalled before that battle could happen. That, however, would require the most exquisite timing. The *prodigia* setting everything in motion were observed in Ariminum, Picenum, Etruria, and Rome: they had to be staged with enough time for their report to reach the City, for someone to remember an incident at the consular election that could be a sign of *vitium*, for the Senate to submit the matter to the Augurs, deliberate on their response, and draft a letter to the Consuls, and for the courier to reach the Consuls' headquarters near the Po before the battle could be fought. To achieve all that, the man (or men) pulling the strings must have control not only of the Augural College but also of the Senate's calendar and agenda, and must be able to divine with total accuracy every delay the courier was to encounter on his way to Gaul—every washed-out bridge, impassable road, exhausted horse. And all of that would be in vain, unless he (or they) could also divine the precise day on which the Consuls were to give battle; for if the courier arrived too late (and the Romans won), nothing could deprive Flaminius of his victory and the glory that came with it. Perhaps Attus Navius could have done it; but Fabius Maximus?

These obstacles disappear if we accept that the prodigies of 223, whatever their rational explanation, were genuinely observed (in the sense that they were not staged), and caused genuine religious concern; and that the Augurs arrived at their finding *vitio consules factos videri* (however gratifying it may have been to Flaminius' enemies) within the normal parameters of their *disciplina*. Indeed, they may have chosen to exploit a political opportunity now that it offered: but that opportunity was unforeseen, just as no one could foresee whether the Senate's letter would reach the Consuls before a major battle was fought. Even so, we would have to be certain that Flaminius' enemies controlled the College, and we are not. (As a matter simply of logic and methodology, one should not have to point out that the mere fact of Fabius' augurate and known opposition to Flaminius, other than by way of circular reasoning, proves nothing.) The response affected both Consuls equally: yet one of them was a colleague of the eight Augurs deciding the case. Were five or more of them prepared to sacrifice Furius merely in order to get at Flaminius?

As one who had locked horns with Flaminius before, Fabius Maximus may at least be suspected of willingness to go so far; of course, we have no evidence that he did. As regards his colleagues, it has been suggested that Pomponius, if not an outright supporter of Flaminius, kept Fabius at a political distance.[54] Carvilius in his second consulship had refused to support his colleague, Fabius Maximus, in the latter's attacks on Flaminius, and was to clash with him again in 216; Lepidus is thought to have favored Flaminius' plebiscite *de agro Gallico dividendo*.[55] Of the rest, nothing is known:[56] a thin reed against which to lean so tall an assumption.

Even if one were to assume that such abusive manipulations of the augural discipline took place on this occasion (for which assumption, as we have seen, there is neither evidence nor reason), we should not overlook the fact that they could do but slight damage to Flaminius' career. His consulship would be cut short, certainly: but there was no humiliation, no loss of *dignitas*, for a magistrate who abdicated *vitio creatus*—the fault, after all, was not his but his predecessor's; and it did not prejudice his chance of future election.[57] On the other hand, having been found *vitio creatus* could potentially offer him unchallengeable protection against politically motivated attacks. If the Senate's letter arrived in time, and the Consuls both obeyed it (as one would expect), they would lose their bid for *gloria*: yet no one could accuse them of military failure, incompetence, or cowardice. If the letter came too late, and catastrophe had already struck, Flaminius would be untouchable: he could not be blamed, augurally speaking, for a defeat caused by divine wrath, if he had not known that he lacked valid auspices.[58] And if the letter came too late to prevent a Roman victory, nothing could detract from that. Yet if the Consuls' election, on the accumulated evidence of augural science, was truly flawed, every effort must be made to warn them. If it cost Flaminius his chance at *gloria*, so much the better; but it might with equal probability ward off disaster. (Unless, again, Fabius correctly divined the outcome of a battle still to be fought.)

The Consuls returned to Rome early in 222, with perhaps two or three months left in their term (they had taken office on 1 May 223[59]). That they faced an angry

---

[54] Bleicken 1955: 35, 39; Lippold 162, 127, 346.

[55] Cic. *Sen.* 11; Livy 23.22.4–9; cf. Scullard 1951: 54; Feig Vishnia 1996a: 32–33; 1996b: 444–447; Beck 2005: 248.

[56] Utterly baseless is Feig Vishnia's suggestion (2012: 41–42) that Marcellus engineered the *vitio facti* declaration in order to improve his chances at the consulship of 222.

[57] That *vitio factus* refers to a flaw at the magistrate's election is not understood by Drogula 2015: 70, who speaks of "any flaw in the auspices taken during a magistrate's inauguration" (another misunderstanding; magistrates were not inaugurated, unlike the *rex*, Flamines, and Augurs). M. Claudius Marcellus held three more consulships after abdicating his second, in 215; the Consuls of 162 were elected again in 156 and 155, respectively.

[58] On the virtually total protection that proper religious observation—in particular augural correctness—offered a defeated commander, see Rosenstein's fundamental study (1990), esp. 54–91.

[59] Below, Subsection 6.4.4.

reception in the Senate, as Zonaras says, cannot surprise, nor that the brunt of its wrath was directed at Flaminius, the instigator of their disobedience. One might question Plutarch's claim that the δῆμος would not meet them, but for all of Flaminius' popularity, the news of his flagrant refusal to come home immediately, despite being *vitio creatus*, had enjoyed ample time and opportunity to trouble the minds of a population that—unlike some of its leaders—seriously worried about the possibility of divine retribution. We need not assume that no one greeted the Consuls at the gate; we may be certain that there were no official delegations representing Senate and *plebs*.

6.4.3 The Triumph

All the same, now that the Consuls had returned, one could reasonably expect them to abdicate at once, and thus permit the renewal of the auspices, by way of an *interregnum*, to commence. They did not. Instead, there arose a dispute over whether they should triumph. The Senate rejected that demand, but in a plebiscite, brought about by a friendly (and unknown) Tribune, the Consuls prevailed.[60] Beck recently attempted to deny this, arguing for a *senatus consultum* authorizing the triumphs, on the grounds that Zonaras alone, but not Plutarch or Livy, contains information in that direction.[61] That will not do. While ἐδέησεν (in μικροῦ μὲν ἐδέησεν ἀποψηφίσασθαι τὸν θρίαμβον αὐτοῦ, *Marc.* 4.6) is impersonal, the logical subject is clearly ὁ δῆμος, continued with θριαμβεύσαντα δ᾽ ἰδιώτην ἐποίησεν, ἀναγκάσας ἐξομόσασθαι τὴν ὑπατείαν μετὰ τοῦ συνάρχοντος. It is true that the biographer, implausibly, makes the people the source of pressure to abdicate; but Plutarch wished to emphasize the hostile reception of Flaminius' behavior as a means to lead into his discussion of Roman religious sensibilities in the next chapter. He had no interest here in distinguishing (nor need to do so) between reactions in the Senate and the wider public. What cannot be maintained (with Beck) is that Plutarch says nothing about the *plebs* being involved in deciding the triumphs; on the contrary, the implication is clear and unambiguous, and thus supports Zonaras' explicit statement. As Zonaras distinguishes precisely between the Senate's and the *plebs*' reaction, this specific information cannot be dismissed as the compiler's own contribution: it evidently stood thus in Dio. Livy's *certamina cum patribus, quae tribunus plebis et quae postea consul prius de*

---

[60] That both Plutarch and Zonaras imply a plebiscite to authorize the triumph is generally understood: Willems *SRR* 2: 669 n. 3; Jacobs 68; Bleicken 1955: 30.

[61] Beck 2005: 254 with n. 66, suggesting that, had the Senate really refused the Consuls' triumphs, the "gängige Triumphalpraxis" in those years would suggest a triumph *in monte Albano*. Only one such event had occurred prior to 223, in 231: it hardly established a "current practice." Besides, just because Papirius Maso chose to take that route, it did not render it the sole means of overcoming senatorial opposition.

consulatu qui abrogabatur, dein de triumpho habuerat (21.63.2) does not as such imply a plebiscite granting the triumphs, naturally; but, in recalling all of Flaminius' previous clashes with the *patres* to set up and illuminate his decision, in 217, to forgo the customary rituals of assuming office, the historian implies something just as useful: none of those previous clashes had ended with Flaminius' opponents backing down. That left only the People or the *plebs* to authorize a triumph. Hence three different sources—one explicitly, two by implication—attest a plebiscite. Nothing supports the notion that the Senate gave in and awarded the Consuls a triumph.

In fact, Flaminius still could count on ample popular support, more so now that he was back in town, able to make his case directly, and aided by a significant element within the voting public: his (and no doubt Furius') troops had received a generous allocation of the war's loot (thus Zonaras, confirmed by Plut. *Marc.* 4.6), and would see no reason to oppose a triumph. As for *religio*, it did not attach to the battle and the victory—precisely because the Consuls had not read the letter, hence had not known of their flawed election and auspices, until afterwards. Flaminius would not forget to emphasize that Iuppiter, throughout the campaign, had not sent a single oblative sign (at least none that went unheeded) to him or to his colleague: all the warnings had appeared in Italy. Besides, it would be unsound to assume that many ordinary citizens were much concerned about the technicalities of augural law, or, for that matter, knew anything about it. The Consuls had won a great and decisive victory: that they could understand; and victory usually deserved a triumph.

Nor would it be wise to think that senatorial opposition to the triumph proceeded with monolithic unanimity. What goes for ordinary citizens would go for many a senator as well: we should not expect an excessive deal of familiarity with, or interest in, the *arcana* of the Augurs, except among a handful of experts—chiefly the priests themselves.[62] There appears to be no record of the Senate's ever rejecting, or overruling, the formal *responsum* of one of the priestly colleges; no doubt most members were happy to defer to those who knew.[63] Now, as regards the question of whether the Consuls were *vitio creati*, the Senate had already endorsed the Augurs' ruling; we have no grounds to think that the vote on this was narrowly split. The triumph was another matter. Some might maintain that *consules vitiosi* should not be allowed to celebrate one, but others would find it hard to argue with military victory, the touchstone of a Roman Noble's sense of achievement. Indeed, it is unlikely that opposition to the triumph could find much support in augural law: in this regard, the outcome of the battle was

---

[62] But see Chapter 4.4.3, note 90.

[63] Cf. North 1990b: 590: "Once the senate had consulted them, it seems inconceivable that their advice should not be followed."

decisive.⁶⁴ Although the Consuls were *vitio facti*, Iuppiter had granted them victory. Since their condition, by itself, posed no obstacle to that (no matter how much it might throw the issue in suspense), it ought not to pose one for a triumph. Nor should we readily assume that all of Flaminius' enemies were prepared to make Furius suffer for his colleague's sins; yet it is clear that the dispute over the triumph affected both Consuls equally. Most telling, perhaps, the fact not that a Tribune could be found to pass the enabling legislation, but that none of the other nine saw fit to veto it: a Senate acting in full concert, so one should think, would have been able to find a Tribune to champion its cause.⁶⁵ We know that the assembly's vote was close; so, it appears, was the Senate's.⁶⁶

6.4.4 Abdication and the Consular Year

Although one could hardly wish for a clearer and more precise statement than what we read in Plutarch and Zonaras, the abdication of 223/2 has met with scholarly resistance—because the *Fasti* fail to mention it.⁶⁷ Beck takes the Consuls' triumphs as evidence against their abdication, but would allow for the "scheduling" of an *interregnum* to hold the elections for 222, even though the technical requirements for it were not entirely present; he holds that no further sanctions are likely to have been imposed.⁶⁸ That simply betrays muddled thinking. If the Consuls stayed in office until the end of the year without holding elections, all the technical requirements for an *interregnum* (no "patrician" magistrates in office) would be given on New Year's Day. If an *interregnum* was "scheduled," it must have been brought about deliberately, by getting the Consuls and all other "patrician" magistrates to abdicate before the end of the year; in which case, the technical

---

⁶⁴ Develin's statement (1978: 431) that "the senate judged the element of *auspicium* to be at fault" is misleading.

⁶⁵ I owe this point to Jeffrey Tatum.

⁶⁶ Plut. *Marc.* 4.6, μικροῦ μὲν ἐδέησεν ἀποψηφίσασθαι τὸν θρίαμβον αὐτοῦ. Pace Bleicken 1955: 30 and Wild 125, we have no grounds to suspect Plutarch here of exaggerating popular displeasure with Flaminius' behavior, which was bound to divide public opinion. It is as naïve to assume that voters would back him enthusiastically and to a man as it is to assume that senators opposed him in complete unanimity. Jahn 110 n. 64 misunderstands the biographer ("nach Plutarch...triumphierten die Konsuln gegen den Willen des Volkes").

⁶⁷ Plut. *Marc.* 4.6, 6.1; Zonar. 8.20. Broughton *MRR* 1: 232–233 accepts an *interregnum* at the (regular) beginning of 222, but doubts that Flaminius and Furius actually abdicated (see, however, 2: 638, where the abdication is accepted); Linderski *AL* 2163 n. 49, joins him in doubt, invoking the "authority of the *Fasti*." Lippold 311 n. 58 wants to see the true reason for the Consuls' abdication simply in the end of their term of office, followed by an *interregnum*; but it passes credulity that either Plutarch or the Byzantine compiler would have placed such emphasis on a perfectly routine occurrence.

⁶⁸ Beck 2005: 255, "Die Triumphalfasten sprechen jedenfalls eindeutig gegen eine Abdikation"; 257, "Es ist gut möglich, daß für die Abhaltung der Wahlen für 222 tatsächlich ein Interregnum anberaumt wurde, wenngleich die technischen Voraussetzungen dafür nicht völlig erfüllt waren. Weiter wird die Maßregelung nicht gegangen sein."

conditions were, again, fully present, and the abdication cannot be doubted (besides constituting a further sanction).

Even the augural finding that the Consuls were *vitio creati* has been questioned: "In such cases," argued Vaahtera, "a Roman consul, even Flaminius, would have abdicated."[69] In an otherwise sure-footed and perceptive study, such circular reasoning surprises. Never mind how we can know what "even Flaminius" would have done; it is absurd to argue that since he did not abdicate (Vaahtera, too, prefers the silence of the *Fasti* to the explicit testimony of two sources), no one can ever have demanded that he do so. Once it is understood, as shown earlier, that the *Fasti* treat abdication in a quite erratic fashion—generally only if it resulted in *suffecti* (which obviously was not the case in 223), and even then not with consistency—their silence as to 223 loses all contrary force:[70] Flaminius' and Furius' abdication cannot be challenged on that basis.

Flaminius triumphed on March 10, Furius on the 12th.[71] Their abdication and the following *interregnum* moved the beginning of the consular year from May 1 to March 15. That, too, has been called into question; as it has bearing on the issue at hand—if the change can be shown to have occurred in a different year, the abdication becomes indeed problematic—the matter deserves brief examination.

May 1 can be established as the day of entering office from the *Acta Triumphorum* between 276/5 and 225/4, during which all Consuls triumphing *in magistratu* do so between January 18 and April 13; hence the new year cannot have started before May 1.[72] The arguments of Brind'Amour against May 1 and in favor of a permanent beginning of the consular year on March 15, from at least the fourth century down to 153 BC, are untenable, being based on the erroneous belief that C. Marius, L. Antonius, and L. Marcius Censorinus were not Consuls on the day of their triumph on January 1 of 104, 41, and 39, respectively, and that the *Acta Triumphorum* incorrectly term Cn. Scipio Asina (*cos. II* 254) *pro consule* on the day of his triumph on March 23.[73] (The document clearly identifies the year as *an. D.*, that is, *a.u.c.* [Varronian] 501, or consular 253/2 BC.)

The change from May 1 could, in theory, have occurred between 233/2, when M'. Pomponius Matho (*cos.* 233) triumphed on the Ides of March, and 225/4,

---

[69] Vaahtera 148.

[70] As Degrassi saw with greater clarity than some, "Sed in his notis parum constantiae apparet, cum eadem fere res alio anno referatur alio neglegatur. Mortes quidem et abdicationes semper traduntur, ubi alter magistratus sufficitur, at, si suffectus non nominatur, mentio saepius omittitur" (*InscrItal* 13.1: 22). The year 223 is among the examples listed there; in his year-by-year commentary, Degrassi notes: "Augures declaravisse consules vitio creatos esse auctores tradunt...id quod in fastis adnotatum non est quia consules senatui statim non paruerunt, sed consulari anno iam exeunte post triumphos actos magistratu se abdicaverunt...nec alteri consules in eorum locum suffecti sunt" (ibid. 118). See above, Section 6.2.

[71] *Acta Tr.* = *InscrItal* 13.1: 78–79.

[72] As demonstrated by Mommsen 1859: 101–102; cf. De Sanctis *SdR* 3.1: 248; Morgan 90–91; Pina Polo 14–15.

[73] Brind'Amour 175–176.

C. Papirius Maso (*cos*. 231) and L. Aemilius Papus (*cos*. 225) each triumphing on March 5; but no *interregna* are known (or likely) in the decade before 223/2. The change cannot have resulted from the puzzling situation in 220/19, for which two pairs of Consuls are on record, the first of them evidently *vitio creati*. If they never entered office (still the most probable solution), the start of the year remained unaffected; if they entered office on 1 May 220 and abdicated in the spring of 219, the new year could have started on the Ides of March, but their successors would have been counted as the Consuls of that year, not as suffects for 220. (If they were considered suffects, by definition there could be no change of year.) There was no *interregnum* (it is safe to say) in 221, 219, or 218; it stands to reason to connect the one in 223/2 with the shift from May 1 to March 15.[74] Brennan treats the shift in 223/2 as if it were an attested fact rather than inferred, and concludes: "This would explain both the literary tradition of 'deprivation of office' and the fact that nothing of this sort appears in the consular *Fasti*."[75] The implication appears to be that Flaminius and Furius were forced to abdicate because of a decision—presumably unrelated to their being found *vitio creati*—to change the beginning of the consular year; but why should that change have been deemed necessary? The change to January 1 in 153 (prompted by events in Spain) likewise went unrecorded in the *FC*, without being accompanied by a literary tradition alleging "deprivation of office."[76]

More recently, Beck argued against 223/2 on the grounds that any change in the beginning of the consular year was a "tiefgreifender Einschnitt" that affected the calendar of festivals, and that "inneraristokratische Statuskämpfe" are unlikely to have caused such a grave measure.[77] As regards the calendar, it did not care on what day Consuls took office: religious festivals (insofar as regulated by the calendar) had to be celebrated on their set day, impervious to the comings and goings of magistrates, and in any case none of them fell on the Kalends or the Ides. As for just how wrenching an event a change would have been, the rapid oscillation in the date of entering office—mostly prompted by *interregna*—during the fifth and fourth centuries[78] rather tells against Beck's claim. What of intra-aristocratic status struggles? Until it can be shown (and no one has, so far) that the *vitium* affecting the Consuls' election was deliberately manufactured, rivalries within the ruling class are not at issue here; Beck himself is rightly skeptical of claims to that effect.[79] If the Consuls were found *vitio creati*, they could not themselves produce successors untainted by the same *vitium*,[80] and the thought that a majority of

---

[74] Eckstein 1987: 16 n. 53.   [75] Brennan 1996: 334 n. 52.
[76] Livy *Per.* 47; *Fasti Praenestini* ad K. Ian. (*InscrItal* 13.2: 110); Cassiod. *Chron.* ad a.u.c. 601.
[77] Beck 2005: 410–411.   [78] See Broughton's tabulation, *MRR* 2: 637–638.
[79] Beck 2005: 255.
[80] On the fundamental principle that flawed auspices at a magistrate's election tainted all those subsequently obtained by the same magistrate, hence all actions taken by him, and any magistrates elected under his presidency, see Linderski *AL* 2163–2164, 2185; Rüpke 1990 = 2019: 46; cf. below, Section 6.5.

senators would happily watch the rest of the year go by as *consules vitiosi* continued to manage the *res publica* without Iuppiter's approval merely betrays a cavalier indifference to the fundamental role of religion in Roman political life—a role that Polybios (not a believer) recognized and emphasized (6.56.6–12).

Beck proceeds to suggest that the change to March 15 took effect in 217: Livy twice notes that date (21.63.1; 22.1.4), hence intended it as an important and evidently new piece of information for his readers.[81] The change, presumably, was prompted by Hannibal's invasion of Italy and a desire to enable the Consuls to take the field earlier in the year—the same reason, essentially, as lay behind the change to January 1 in 153 BC. But that latter change Livy did report and explain, evidently at some length, as is clear from *Periocha* 47 (*consules anno quingentesimo nonagesimo octavo ab urbe condita magistratum <Kal. Ian.> inire coeperunt; mutandi comitia causa fuit, quod Hispani rebellabant*). Nothing of that sort in Book 21 or 22. Beck argues that since *Periocha* 20 contains no mention of a change, Livy presumably did not report in that book any change that occurred by 219 BC; in consequence, if he omitted such a report in the second decade, his silence in Books 21 and 22 need not mean that no such change occurred in the years 218 or 217. This line of reasoning is hard to follow. While the *Periochae* tell us what could be found in Livy's books, they cannot tell us what he did not write about: anything the excerptor deemed insignificant would be omitted. And it took Hannibal for the Romans to realize that May 1 was a little late in the year to launch a campaign, yet Livy could not bring himself to point that out?

Livy's first mention of March 15 in 217 refers to Flaminius' edict, as Consul designate, ordering the army to assemble at Ariminum on that day (*edictum et litteras... misit ut is exercitus idibus Martiis Arimini adesset in castris*): Livy could not possibly have omitted naming the day in question, even if it had been the day of entering office for centuries. Hence no conclusions can be drawn as to whether it marked a change or not. For the second instance, Livy's *per idem tempus* (as Hannibal's setting out from his winter quarters) *Cn. Servilius consul Romae idibus Martiis magistratum iniit* simply contrasts Flaminius taking office at Ariminum that same day (21.63.13)—a decision laboriously told and criticized at great length (21.63.2–12), without the slightest hint that it went hand in hand with a change in the customary date. Worse, Livy notes Consuls taking office on the Ides of March on thirteen other occasions, ranging from 215 to 168: surely none of those instances constituted new and important information for his readers. In short, the *interregnum* of 223 remains the only plausible event to cause the shift from May 1 to March 15.[82]

---

[81] Beck 2005: 411: "Für den Leser war diese doppelte Erwähnung des neuen Datums eine wichtige und offenbar auch neue Information." For a rebuttal of Beck's thesis on different grounds, Fronda 448 n. 58.
[82] Livy 23.30.18 (215 BC); 26.1.1 (211); 26.26.5 (210); 27.7.7 (209); 31.5.2 (200); 32.1.1 (199); 33.43.1 (195); 38.35.7 (188); 39.45.1 (183); 40.35.1 (180); 41.8.4 (177); 42.22.7 (171); 44.19.1 (168). See Eckstein's sensible discussion, 1987: 16 n. 53.

The new Consuls—of 222—cannot have entered office (hence, been elected) later than March 31; otherwise, the new year would have started on April 1, or even the 13th.[83] Since they cannot have been elected until the first day of the second Interrex, the *interregnum* commenced no later than March 26, and no earlier than March 12 (if Furius stepped down immediately after completing his triumph); Flaminius and Furius, therefore, abdicated between March 12 and 26.[84] Plutarch implies that Flaminius, at least, did not go willingly.

6.5 Contesting the Auspices

It is difficult to see, indeed, how he could have gone willingly.[85] When, back in Gaul, Flaminius first chose to disobey the Senate's instructions, he did so not from wanton impudence (whatever his *inimici* might say in Rome), but with rational and coherent argument. The augural response *vitio consules factos videri* was false, contrived to derail his opportunity for *gloria*: his victory was proof that no *vitium* attached to his (and Furius') election. That line of reasoning may well have convinced the *plebs*;[86] it probably made little impression on the College of Augurs. An augural *vitium* at the election tainted all subsequent acts of the magistrate so chosen, rendering them augurally—not legally (the distinction is crucial)—flawed.[87] Elected under vitiated auspices, he possessed no valid auspices himself: in consequence, his means of communicating with Iuppiter—his impetrative auspices—were defective, and what he, unaware of his condition, took to be an affirmative response that gave permission to proceed with the intended act was, in reality, devoid of meaning.[88] Flaminius could insist for all he wanted that on the day of the battle his auspices had been affirmative; the Augurs would

---

[83] The Consuls elected under an Interrex took office *ex templo*, though it may have been customary to wait with their initial auspices until the next day, so as to enable their observation at the preferred time, between midnight and dawn (Mommsen *StR* 1: 592–593, 659; Kunkel *StO* 87–88; on the auspices, Linderski *AL* 2169 with n. 74; Vaahtera 116–122; Konrad 2004: 175 n. 12). Their term ended on the nearest Kalends or Ides (the only days used for the beginning of a regular term) a year later, without, however, exceeding a full twelve months: hence the term of Consuls entering between March 16 and 31 would cease on March 15 following.

[84] Broughton *MRR* 2: 638 suggests their successors entered office "Id. Mart."; in fact, March 18 (the first comitial day after March 12) is the earliest possible date. Koptev's attempt to deny the five-day tenure of the first Interrex (expressly attested in 52 BC: *per omnes interregni dies; fuerant autem ex more quinque*, Ascon. 38St.) in favor of a six-hour term from midnight to dawn fails to persuade.

[85] Against Jacobs's suggestion (68–69) that a compromise was worked out in which the Senate dropped its opposition to a triumph and Flaminius agreed to abdicate afterwards, thus acknowledging the augural finding that he and his colleague were *vitio creati*, see Jahn 110.

[86] As it has convinced some moderns: e.g., Wild 125: "Immerhin war nach dem großen Sieg offenkundig, daß sich die Augurn im Hinblick auf den Keltenkrieg geirrt hatten." The Augurs, of course, had not been concerned with the Gallic War at all: the question put to them was not whether the Consuls would be victorious (a matter of future prediction, hence entirely outside their *disciplina*), but whether their election had been ritually correct or not. Cf. Amat-Seguin 83 n. 7.

[87] Linderski *AL* 2163–2164, 2185; cf. Rüpke 1990 = 2019: 46.

[88] For a fuller discussion of this principle, see Konrad 2004: 172–178, and Chapter 7.4.4.

counter that, being *vitio creatus*, he had no auspices at all, and when the Chickens fed lustily that morning, it simply meant that they were hungry. What had saved him and Furius and their armies was the fact that neither was aware of that impediment, and that Iuppiter, for reasons known to him alone, had not warned them off with oblative signs. Had Flaminius engaged in battle after reading the letter from Rome, or had he received—and ignored—a prohibitive sign that Iuppiter sent on his own, he would have committed, knowingly and willfully, a flagrant violation of the auspices, and disaster would have been inevitable. Yet precisely because he and Furius had not opened the letter until after the battle, and because Iuppiter had chosen not to alert them as to their lack of valid auspices by other means, the Consuls had not acted in a culpable manner; and it is far from certain that, under these circumstances, Iuppiter would feel compelled to cause defeat, in order to get their attention. He was perfectly capable of doing so, of course; but in this instance he chose not to. Far from establishing that the Consuls' auspices were valid after all, their victory merely showed Iuppiter's forbearance: although he had not sanctioned the battle on that day, he knew the Consuls acted in accordance with the letter of the law.[89] No doubt the Augurs stood by their ruling, as did the Senate—and on this issue, unlike the matter of the triumph, Flaminius could not expect significant support. Consuls *vitio facti* must step down.

No doubt, either, that Flaminius understood all this: his and his colleague's astute move to avoid a *vitium* of their own—and, hence, personal culpability—by not reading the letter before the battle is proof enough. The claim that his victory showed the Augurs wrong about the Consuls' being *vitio creati* was logically incompatible with the rule requiring formal notification. Had he read the letter right away and then, in full and knowing violation of the auspices, engaged in battle, he would have had a valid point; indeed, the Augurs would need to resort to some creative interpretation to explain why the battle was not lost. One is

---

[89] The case of Fabius Rullianus in 324 V might have offered a precedent, although only in the—eventually—common version, according to which he was victorious. *In Samnium incertis itum auspiciis est; cuius rei vitium non in belli eventum, quod prospere gestum est, sed in rabiem atque iras imperatorum vertit*, as Livy (8.30.1-2) put it. Linderski 1993: 62 = *RQ* 617, rejecting Livy's explanation ("was the *rabies imperatorum* a sufficient disaster?"), argued that augural doctrine will have invoked the auspices' ambiguity (*incertis auspiciis*) instead: no direct prohibition, hence no direct violation. Perhaps; and if Rullianus could fight a battle, knowing that the auspices were ambiguous, and win, surely Flaminius could do so believing his auspices to be valid. But the case may be seen as more closely analogous to that of the Consul Q. Petillius Spurinus in 176 (Livy 41.18.8-14), who, having ignored a *vitium* in his own auspices, won the battle and lost his life: "the wrath of the gods descended upon the guilty general, and it could be argued that it was *eo ipso* averted from his soldiers" (Linderski *AL* 2173-2175; cf. Chapter 8.4.2). Although his own, the auspices of the Magister Equitum depended, ultimately, on those of the Dictator: and the latter had done everything, without delay, to rectify the "ambiguity." Hence divine wrath spared the army and concentrated on Rullianus, bringing him within an inch of the Dictator's *secures*. The Augurs should have had no difficulty explaining Flaminius' victory along those lines, except that in this instance the *rabies atque ira* played out between the Consul and the Senate. In reality, as we have seen, Rullianus almost certainly lost his battle, and no augural explanation would have been necessary at the time. (See Chapters 1 and 4.1.)

tempted to wonder if, in fact, that is what happened; the story of the letter not opened until afterwards would then have been created by way of justifying a victory that was augurally incomprehensible. The problem here is Furius. If he already was an Augur in 223, it borders on the unthinkable that he would go along with such a flagrant violation; if he was not, it is unthinkable that the College later on should have co-opted him. (Unless that was his reward—and price—for cooperating in the matter of Flaminius' abdication.)

But, as things stood, Flaminius could not expect his argument from victory to find acceptance with many versed in augural law, or to persuade the Senate now to overturn the Augurs' ruling and rescind its initial vote. His intended audience, surely, lay elsewhere.

For Flaminius had not merely disagreed, publicly, with the *collegium augurum*, and defied the Senate. With a splendid victory to back him up in the eyes of those who understood (and cared) little about the fine points of augural law, but whose votes in the assembly would ultimately decide his fate, he chose to challenge the role of auspices in government as such: he would "teach the people back home not to let themselves be fooled by relying on birds and similar stuff and nonsense." Zonaras' statement (8.20) deserves full credit.[90] To dismiss it simply as "hostile tradition" will not do; if we can believe that Roman politicians were ready and willing to manipulate the auspices for political purposes (which those who would dismiss the sources' portrait of Flaminius have no trouble believing), we must also believe that some at least—in particular those who felt themselves the victims of such manipulation—were ready and willing to question the practice of auspices in principle: for cynical manipulation presupposes the same personal disbelief in the reality of auspices as does outright denial. We may note that Flaminius did not, it seems, object to the routine observance of auspical ritual; no such failure on his part is alleged in 223, and in 217, although he omitted the essential auspication for entering office in Rome, he probably was willing to go through the ceremonies of "taking auspices" once he had assumed command of his army, and as long as the results did not interfere with his military judgment.[91] What he objected to was the doctrine that such ritual should be accorded greater force than a decision of the People in assembly, or of a Consul in the field.

We do not know if Flaminius continued to issue such statements after his return to Rome. It hardly matters; they would have been reported by those who had heard them in Gaul, and he was not the kind of man who would deny them.

---

[90] Briefly noted by Lippold 310. Few scholars seem to have given it proper attention; but see Wild 125: "...eine öffentliche Stellungnahme des Flaminius gegen das Auguralwesen [ist] durchaus im Bereich des Möglichen. Hier könnte sich ein Protest gegen eine Einmischung des Augurenkollegiums in die römische Politik"—never mind that the Augurs *were* politicians—"widerspiegeln. Vielleicht sah es Flaminius auch als seine Aufgabe an, den Einfluß der Auguren durch Worte und Taten zu unterminieren." Similarly Scheid 2012: 118: "Il est en effet vraisemblable que Flaminius a tenté de faire évoluer les règles rituelles dans l'intérêt de la république."

[91] Konrad 2004: 172–174, and Chapter 7.4.6; cf. Scheid 2012: 118.

Besides, he had refused to follow the Senate's instructions to come home at once and abdicate: those comments contained his justification; he could gain nothing from disavowing them now. Having prevailed against his enemies in the Senate in the plebiscite about his triumph, why would he suddenly throw away the golden opportunity to prevail against the Augurs, too? The triumph did not—could not—settle that dispute: with or without a triumph, if Flaminius stepped down as Consul now, he would be admitting, in so doing, that the Augurs had been right, and that he was *vitio creatus*. That conclusion he could not escape, whatever rationale for his abdication he might try to offer. Instead of teaching the folks back home not to be tricked by augural birds and similar superstition, he would be acknowledging—tacitly perhaps, but still acknowledging—the validity of precisely the practice he had openly dismissed as fraudulent, and defied. The public loss of face, the damage to his *dignitas*, would be severe; the gloating of his enemies, intolerable. (Had he obeyed immediately, of course, he would not have to worry about that: no shame came to those who complied with the Senate's orders, especially when *religio* was involved.) At least twice before—probably thrice—in recent memory had Consuls attempted to break the cage of auspices constraining them on the field of battle (well—at sea); but two had suffered catastrophic failure, and consequently had not found themselves in a position from which to challenge augural law, while the third stepped back from the brink.[92] Flaminius had returned in victory, and popular to boot; his savvy and determination in the warfare of politics stand not in doubt: he would not waste this opportunity to press his case. If he could stay in office through the last day of his term, without the sky come crashing down, he would have taught his fellow citizens a valuable lesson, and the business of auspices would never be the same again.

That last consideration, naturally, would concern those in the Senate most who insisted on the necessity of auspices (whether from personal belief or political expediency). To watch Flaminius triumph might be disagreeable, but it posed little danger to the State; to let an entire year go by with Consuls that were *vitio creati*, without auspices, was intolerable. And things might yet get worse. Come May the 1st, an *interregnum* would occur at last, and the auspices could be renewed from scratch: but only if Flaminius agreed not to hold elections for next year's Consuls.[93] We do not know what were his plans in that respect; but we can

---

[92] In 249 and apparently 242 or 241 BC: Chapter 5.
[93] His position in the *FC* suggests—although, again, the document is anything but consistent in that respect—that he was the *consul prior factus*, hence ordinarily the one charged with holding the *comitia*. Even if Furius were this year's electoral officer, there was little to keep Flaminius from seeing to the elections if his colleague failed to act. Barring the almost unheard-of step of a collegial veto (quite unlikely in view of Furius' deference in Gaul), the Senate could only hope for a Tribune to intercede; but none of them (as far as we know) had tried to block the plebiscite authorizing the Consuls' triumph, and none of them might be willing to challenge Flaminius on this issue. Jahn 110 invokes the rule that any Augur could prevent elections by forcing dismissal of the assembly with the words *alio die* (on which, see Linderski *AL* 2197–2198): but Flaminius had already disregarded a

easily envisage the sense of horror that would fill many a mind when pondering the possibilities. Should Flaminius insist on seeing to the election of his successors, the new Consuls taking office on May 1 would, of course, be deemed *vitio creati* like himself, since a Consul that lacked auspices could not validly create another.[94] With luck, the Consuls of the new year could be compelled to abdicate immediately, so as to make room for an *interregnum*; but what if Flaminius, with his popular appeal, were to secure election of someone who shared his views on auspices? Another year like this, and the damage might be irreversible.

6.6 Abdication, *Interregnum*, and the Need for a Dictator

Quite possibly, Flaminius would have been content with staying in office through the end of his term. Yet he could hardly be content with less; having made the auspices an issue, his *dignitas* was now at stake. More even was at stake from the viewpoint of many in the traditional ruling class. With Flaminius resisting abdication, the Senate now faced the problem of how to bring about an *interregnum* so as to allow the renovation *de integro* of the auspices.

6.6.1 The Abdication of Sergius and Verginius

An *interregnum* occurs when no "patrician" magistrate—Dictator, Consul, Praetor, Master of the Horse, Censor, Curule Aedile, Quaestor—is in office. It happens naturally when all these magistrates have completed their term, and no new Consuls have been elected; and it can be brought about deliberately, through premature abdication of all "patrician" magistrates before the election of new Consuls. (Tribunes and Aediles of the Plebs remain unaffected by this process.)

There is ample evidence, in the received tradition, for the deliberate exercise of an *interregnum*. We can count fifteen instances, recorded or inferred, ranging from 480 V to 152 BC, of Consuls (or Consular Tribunes) prematurely laying down their office.[95] Ten of these abdications are attested, one seems probable (#10 in 321 V); the remaining four, uncertain (#2 in 451 V), unclear (#12 in 220 BC),

---

decree of the entire College of Augurs. Why would he heed the *nuntiatio* of a single one? In any case, unless we accept Valeton's quite arbitrary insistence that Pompeius could not have been presiding over the *comitia* he dissolved in 55 when he heard thunder (Plut. *CatMin* 42.4; cf. *Pomp.* 52.3), hence must have intervened as Augur, there seems to be not a single recorded instance of an Augur's successfully stopping an assembly by saying *alio die*: see Valeton's list, 1891: 94–97. (Denniston 149 has shown, convincingly, that Caesar ignored Antonius' augural *nuntiatio* in 44; if Metellus Celer as Praetor and Augur in 63 BC did indeed use the phrase—Dio 37.27.3 is rather vague—it went unheeded.)

[94] Above, note 80.

[95] For sources, a detailed survey, and discussion, corresponding to the item numbers used in the text, see the Appendix.

or unlikely (#5 in 399 V, #7 in 393 V). In eight instances, the resulting *interregnum* is on record; in three more, probable (#4 in 402 V, #14 in 154 BC, and #15 in 152). The *Fasti* are extant for all but three of the attested abdications (#3 in 444 V, #9 in 341 V, and #10 in 321 V), yet mention only one (#13 in 162 BC). How many of them are authentic, no way to tell, except the final five (##11–15 in 223, 220, 162, 154, and 152 BC); but at least three of the remainder (#1 in 480 V, #6 in 397 V, and #8 in 392 V) make no particular point, constitutional, political, or otherwise, and may be considered unsuspect. Conversely, the abdication and *interregnum* of 444 V (#3) are undoubtedly fictitious. All the same, we must allow for the possibility—however remote—that no precedent of Consuls abdicating to initiate an *interregnum* was already known in 223 BC.

In the earliest example (480 V), the abdication proceeds from the Consul's own initiative; in all the others, it is prompted by a *senatus consultum*. Unpleasant though the decision might be, other than in the case of Flaminius in 223 (#11), there are no reports of resistance to the Senate's wishes—except once (#4 in 402 V). The solution found on that occasion may help illuminate the naming of a Dictator *interregni causa*.

Shaken by a defeat in the war against Veii in 402 V, the Senate voted to hold elections for new Military Tribunes immediately and have them enter office on October 1, rather than await the regular time for elections.[96] Four of the six Tribunes were willing to comply and abdicate, but L. Verginius and M′. Sergius— the ones bearing the principal responsibility for the setback at Veii—obstinately refused to step down before December 13, the end of their term.[97] Soon the Tribunes of the Plebs threatened them with jail, at which moment another of the Military Tribunes, C. Servilius Ahala, came forward both to uphold the *auctoritas* of the Senate and forestall such a worrisome display of plebeian power. He announced that, unless his two recalcitrant colleagues bowed to the Senate's vote, he would name a Dictator who would compel them to lay down their magistracy.[98] The Senate heartily approved, happy in the realization that thus had been discovered a "greater" force, a force great enough to keep even

---

[96] Livy 5.9.1, *primores patrum sive culpa sive infelicitate imperatorum tam ignominiosa clades accepta esset censuere non expectandum iustum tempus comitiorum, sed exemplo novos tribunos militum creandos esse, qui kalendis Octobribus magistratum occiperent*.

[97] Livy 5.9.2–3, *ceteri tribuni militum nihil contradicere; at enimvero Sergius Verginiusque...negare se ante idus Decembres, solemnem ineundis magistratibus diem, honore abituros esse*. December 13 had marked the beginning of the consular year since 449 V: Dion. Hal. 11.63.1 (443 V); Livy 4.37.3 (423 V); Livy 5.9.3, 11.11 (402 V); see *StR* 1: 603–604.

[98] Livy 5.9.4–6, *proinde...collegae aut facient quod censet senatus, aut si pertinacius tendent, dictatorem extemplo dicam qui eos abire magistratu cogat*. Mommsen *StR* 1: 262 n. 2 takes this as "nicht genau" understood, suggesting that the actual threat was one of suspension, i.e., the Dictator would forbid the Tribunes to exercise their office. But both here and regarding L. Minucius *cos.* 458 (*ita se Minucius abdicat consulatu*, 3.29.3), where Mommsen likewise argues for suspension, Livy is quite explicit about forced abdication, and he knew the difference: see 8.36.1, *magistro equitum Q. Fabio vetito quicquam pro magistratu agere*.

the chief magistrates in check, without having recourse to the detested power of the plebeian Tribunes.[99] Sergius and Verginius caved in, elections were held, the Military Tribunes abdicated (all of them), and their successors entered office on October 1.

Thus goes the story. It is part of the Great Veian War lore, in particular the tribulations of Sergius and Verginius, told with a heavy dose of second- and first-century political anachronism. We need not—indeed, should not—believe all of its detail; it stretches credulity that, at this early date, mere reasons of military expediency should have forced the premature abdication of all magistrates and, consequently, a change in the start of the official year. As Ogilvie notes, Livy "offers two explanations for the supersession of the military tribunes, *culpa* and *infelicitas*." Now, misbehavior, *culpa*, would be rooted in the persons of the commanders responsible for the defeat, and only those: in other words, *culpa* might lead to Sergius and Verginius being removed from office, but there is no parallel for such personal failure prompting the abdication of an entire college. Ill luck, however, was another matter: the gods might—indeed, very likely did—have a hand in this, and who could say for certain that the taint was limited to the two Tribunes directly involved in the defeat? That all six were forced to abdicate ought to make it evident that *infelicitas* was indeed the reason—or, more precisely, the manifestation of a fundamental flaw: surely, the Tribunes had been *vitio creati*. If so, a *renovatio auspiciorum* would be necessary; from which it follows that the Military Tribunes cannot have presided over the election of their successors: instead, they abdicated, and an *interregnum* ensued. When sixty years later, in 341, the Senate out of military considerations instructed the Consuls to abdicate early, *religio incessit ab eis quorum imminutum imperium esset comitia haberi*: hence, an *interregnum* (Livy 8.3.4).[100]

If such an "augural" version of the story did in fact exist (whether known to Livy, one cannot say), it evidently was not reflected in the source that Livy followed here. That source was not concerned with the tale's augural implications: it either failed to understand them, if indeed it imagined *tribuni vitiosi* creating their own successors, or deliberately crafted a version that omitted all reference to auspices and related matters, and presented the conflict in purely "political" terms. Of course, the source could have done so *ex nihilo*, without an "augural" version to begin with; in which case we should not hesitate to deem the Tribunes' abdication in 402 fictional. (Not that the "augural" version, were it extant, would prove otherwise.)

---

[99] Livy 5.9.7, *gauderentque patres sine tribuniciae potestatis terriculis inventam esse aliam vim maiorem ad coercendos magistratus.*
[100] Ogilvie 645; Jahn 61; cf. Appendix ## 4 and 9.

6.6.2 Abdication Forced by a Dictator?

The abdication's historicity, however, is of little consequence to this investigation: if the story was invented, its purpose renders it just as illuminating. Without reference—deliberately so, it appears—to augural law, Livy's source here aimed at making a specific constitutional point that matters to us: a Dictator had the power to force a Consular Tribune—hence, by implication, a Consul—from office.

Mommsen did not think so. The very notion was incompatible with his vision of Roman popular sovereignty: as the People alone could bestow a magistracy, so the People alone could take it away—and even that remained a mere concession to constitutional theory, until the last century of the Republic. A magistrate with *imperium*—"das unbedingte Befehlsrecht," in Mommsen's inimitable definition—possessed sweeping powers over lower magistrates, including the right of forbidding them to carry out any of their duties and functions.[101] Yet while *maior potestas* enabled the Consul to rescind or prohibit a lower magistrate's acts, it did not, *sensu strictu*, allow him to directly order the lower magistrate to perform a specific action. All magistrates derived their powers from the People, and were responsible to them alone, not to magistrates of higher rank; Praetors, Aediles, even Quaestors (to some extent) carried out the functions of their office independently and as they saw fit, not under instructions from above. The higher magistrate did not (and could not) assume responsibility for the action of a lower one, even when performed at his behest: it was the lower magistrate who remained accountable for carrying it out, as part of his powers and duties of office. Conversely, the lower magistrate could not be held responsible for omitting an action forbidden him by *maior potestas*, any more than anyone could be held responsible for failing to carry out an action vetoed by his colleague: accountability in such cases rested with the magistrate issuing the prohibition. We need not imagine that in everyday affairs at home Praetors and Aediles would stand on ceremony and refuse to comply when told by the Consul to do this or that; nor should we imagine that the Consul would have much occasion to tell them so. Yet even abroad, *militiae*, the Praetor usually commanded his own army in his own right and—quite unlike, for instance, a *legatus*—was not subject to direct orders. In case of disagreement about what to do in a particular situation, the Consul's *maior potestas* naturally prevailed, and the Praetor must defer to the Consul's *maius imperium* when engaged in joint military operations;[102] but any attempt to

---

[101] *StR* 1: 224–227, 258–263, 627–630.
[102] The point is neatly set out in Val. Max. 2.8.2, relating the dispute between Q. Lutatius Catulus (*cos.* 242) and Q. Valerius Falto (*pr.* 242): *si dimicandum necne esset contrariis inter vos sententiis dissedissetis, utrum quod consul an quod praetor imperasset maius habiturum fuerit momentum*. Valerius acknowledged that the Consul's orders would take precedence. See Chapter 4.2.1.

make the lower magistrate do something against his will had to be couched in terms of forbidding him to do the thing he wanted to.[103]

Thus the Consul could forbid the Praetor (and lower magistrates) to act; he could not order him to abdicate. Did the same apply to the Dictator?

Aside from the question of popular sovereignty, Mommsen's answer was also consistent with his view of the Dictator as a *collega maior* of the Consuls: just as the Consul could not order the Praetor—his *collega minor*—to abdicate, so the Dictator could not force a Consul from office. That view, however, now seems mistaken. If indeed the Dictator's *imperium* was considered *valentius* in the sense that no other magistrate could exist, as magistrate, in his presence, it could presumably be argued that the Dictator had the power to order a Consul to formally abdicate his office: the Consul would not be in a position to refuse the order, suspended and without constitutional standing while face to face with the former.[104]

That an argument in favor of the Dictator's ability to remove a Consul from office was put forward at some point follows with some certainty from the story Livy tells of the Consular Tribunes under the year 402 (presupposing the Dictator's ability to force abdication), and an even more famous one. In 458 V, Cincinnatus the Dictator, having rescued the army of the Consul L. Minucius at the Algidus and preparing to return to Rome (and his plow), orders the hapless Consul to resign, and remain with the army as a mere Legate: *"Et tu, L. Minuci, donec consularem animum incipias habere, legatus his legionibus praeeris." ita se Minucius abdicat consulatu iussusque ad exercitum manet.*[105]

It is difficult to see how those two tales should have come into existence if no one ever raised the question, and answered it accordingly. Dismissal by invoking "antiquarian speculation"—that convenient tool enabling us to set aside what evidence we have, and substitute our own imagination—would be hazardous: when Roman annalists during the second and first centuries crafted the history of the City, the dictatorship had already receded from the living constitution, and they had little incentive to create a precedent in the distant past for dealing with a situation that had never occurred and, even theoretically, could no longer seriously be expected to occur. We ought to assume, therefore, that the tales reflect an actual concern, prompted by an actual situation, and that they were formed at a time when that situation could still be expected to recur—at a time when a Consul might still feel strong enough to resist a *senatus consultum* ordering him to abdicate, and when appointing a Dictator could still be perceived as a feasible way

---

[103] Mommsen *StR* 1: 258 n. 2, noting "...es ist dasselbe, ob dem Consul befohlen wird in Rom zu bleiben oder verboten zum Heere abzugehen." Mommsen buried this important principle in a footnote; for a full elaboration, see Kunkel *StO* 186–187; cf. Last 158–159; Drogula 2015: 66–67 (without reference to Mommsen); also Chapters 3.3.5 and 4.1.

[104] Cf. Chapter 3.2 and 3.3.5.

[105] Livy 3.29.2–3; cf. 8.33.14, *dictatorem Quinctium Cincinnatum in L. Minucium consulem...non ultra saevisse quam ut legatum eum ad exercitum pro consule relinqueret*; Dion. Hal. 10.25.2, τὸν Μηνύκιον ἀποθέσθαι τὴν ἀρχὴν ἀναγκάσας.

of dealing with incompetent or recalcitrant officials, or outright sedition. Not probably in 458 and 402; but also not after the first half of the second century. The Consuls of 162 abdicated without further ado, and no resistance is known in connection with the abdications in 154 and 152, or with that of a Praetor (who had every reason to hang on to the immunity and protection his magistracy extended to him) in 63 BC; in 133, 121, and 100, the Senate apparently gave no serious thought to having a Dictator confront the political upheavals of those years. Livy's narrative being extant from 218 to 167, the situation should best be sought in the seventy-four-year gap between 292 and 218, and surely more towards the end than the beginning of that period: for the early annalists, such a crisis within comparatively recent memory would make the creation of a distant precedent seem more worth their while than an event that had held its place in constitutional tradition already for several generations. Certainly L. Minucius' demotion to *legatus* cannot have occurred until two or three centuries after his consulship, when *legati* had become standard fixtures in Roman armies. We need not assume that this "actual situation" in the (late) third century did precisely parallel either of the tales in Livy: a Dictator need not in the end have been appointed (in the "precedent" of 402, the mere threat was enough to secure the desired effect), or he may have compelled the Consul's abdication by means other than a direct order.

In connection with Flaminius' second consulship, in 217, Livy (21.63.2) cryptically recalls his struggle with the Senate *prius de consulatu qui abrogabatur, dein de triumpho*. He had told the story, evidently, in Book 20, and unfortunately saw no need to repeat it here: all we can tell from it is that an attempt was made to force Flaminius from his consulship—which is clear enough, already, from Plutarch and Zonaras. What form it took, that is the question. Conceivably, a Tribune could have tried, and failed, to pass legislation that would remove the Consul—or both of them?—from office.[106] Now Livy's *prius... dein* places the fight over the consulship before that over the triumph; yet the imperfect *abrogabatur* carries no implication that the first was settled before the second broke out. The imperfect is best taken as conative, covering the entire attempt to remove Flaminius from office, from the initial finding that he was *vitio creatus* and the corresponding demand that he resign—which indeed falls well before the struggle over the triumph—to the dispute's eventual resolution. The conative use, though, need not imply failure:[107] Livy uses the same phrase on the *lex Oppia, quae abrogabatur* in 195 (34.1.7). Nor need *abrogare*, in Livy, imply a legislative procedure. In recalling the forced abdication of the Consular Tribunes of 402, he has two of them comment, *quippe et collegis abrogatum imperium*—but, of course, there was no vote of the *comitia*, no *abrogatio imperii* in the technical sense.

---

[106] Wild 124 imagines a Praetor attempting the same thing. Not likely; the Consul could simply forbid it, *vi maioris imperii*.
[107] See K–S 1: 120–121.

6.7 The First Dictatorship of Fabius Maximus

Short of comitial *abrogatio*, no power on earth could legally force a Roman Consul from office before his term; except, probably, a Dictator. We have discussed the constitutional situation in this respect above, in particular the episodes Livy told under the years 458 (3.29.2–3) and 402 (5.9.1–8), which strongly suggest that at some point—not necessarily in the fifth century—the question did come up, and was answered in the affirmative by at least one school of thought. The crisis unfolding in 223 BC would have offered an obvious opportunity to entertain such considerations: a Dictator, under this view, could force Flaminius to abdicate. Not everyone would necessarily have agreed, or thought such a course of action advisable.

But, without question, the Dictator could suspend the Consuls, one or both, from office, for the remainder of the year; and thus prevent the travesty of having new Consuls elected by a predecessor who was *vitio creatus* and lacked auspices. Hence a Dictator, appointed now, would ensure at least that an *interregnum* could commence on the Kalends of May, so that the auspices could be renewed, untainted. A Dictator named for this purpose would be termed, naturally, *interregni* (sc. *ineundi*) *causa*, "for reason of an *interregnum* (to be entered)."

It is here, in the spring of 222, that we should seek the first dictatorship of Fabius Maximus. It is the only credibly recorded instance in five hundred years of republican history of a situation that could have called for the appointment of a Dictator to bring about an *interregnum*. Somehow in between preparing the draft of the *Fasti* (on stacks and stacks of waxen tablets) and executing them in marble, the designation *interregni causa* slipped from the year of Fabius' first dictatorship to that of his second—and to make confusion worse, the first dictatorship was omitted altogether under its proper year, even though the second remained duly identified as such.[108]

6.7.1 Removing Flaminius: a Moderate Solution

The procedure would require the cooperation of Flaminius' colleague, since only a Consul could name the Dictator.[109] (We need not canvass the possibility that the Senate tried to persuade Flaminius to do it.) Although Furius had stayed with Flaminius in Gaul after the letter was read, he made it clear that he was doing so under duress, entreated by his colleague's own troops, and he pointedly abstained

---

[108] As noted above, in Subsection 6.2.2, the cutters of the *Fasti* seem to have been running short of space for the years 223 and 222.
[109] Against the notion that a Praetor, too, could name a Dictator, see (conclusively) Brennan *PRR* 1: 121; cf. Konrad 2003: 344–346.

from all military activity. Still, he had not, it seems, escaped opprobrium altogether (Zonar. 8.20), and surely had not opposed the plebiscite authorizing his triumph. But through all of this he had been careful not to endorse Flaminius' aggressive disdain of the auspices; indeed, he would have been well advised to close ranks with the other members of the *collegium* on the question of *abdicatio*. With the triumph behind him, he was free now to assume the role of champion of augural law and senatorial *auctoritas*. Of course, he could not abdicate until Flaminius did so as well: the *res publica* would be ill served by handing the wild man sole control of it.

We may conclude, then, that soon after his triumph on March 12, 222, Furius named Fabius *dictator interregni causa*. By March 26 at the latest, both Consuls had laid down their office, and the *interregnum* took its course.[110] Did the Dictator command Flaminius outright to abdicate, or forbid him henceforth to act as Consul?

An unstated yet fundamental principle of the Roman constitution held that nothing should be taken to its theoretical limit. This was true of political opportunity, personal enmities, and—in particular—the official powers of a magistrate. The *res publica* was based on restraint, both mutual and self-imposed, on the part of those who managed it; consensus (*concordia*), however slow and arduous to forge, was preferred at all times over blunt coercion. Mommsen had seen this, and Badian has forcefully reminded us of it:[111] we forget it at our peril.

Barring the remote possibility that the incident reported under 402 is indeed authentic, Rome had never faced a situation such as this. "As long as an act of a certain kind had not been attempted, *mos maiorum* gave no guidance on what to do about it, except by inferences that could be disputed."[112] That certainly was true of the argument that a Dictator had the power to remove a Consul from office; not everyone might agree. (No one knew yet, probably, that Cincinnatus had done so with L. Minucius long, long ago.)[113] Nor can we be entirely certain that the fifth- and fourth-century precedents of Consuls abdicating *vitio creati* were already known: without them, the demand now being made on Flaminius and Furius would multiply in magnitude. Yet even if the principle were universally admitted, its practical application would constitute just the sort of pushing official powers to their logical limit ("die letzte Consequenz," as Mommsen put it) that was discouraged and, if at all possible, avoided. Flaminius had enemies in plenty, and he was a New Man, subject to all the disdain the Nobles could muster; yet he had achieved a consulship, and his son would be a *nobilis*: like it or not, he had arrived. The public humiliation of being peremptorily dismissed, by the

---

[110] It is generally agreed that the appointment of a Dictator could not be blocked by tribunician or collegial veto: Mommsen *StR* 2.1: 148. On the date, see above, Subsection 6.4.4.
[111] *StR* 2.1: 725–726; Badian 1972: 710, 714–716, 722; 1990: 473–474; cf. Brennan *PRR* 1: 111.
[112] Badian 1983: 162; cf. 1972: 706–712. On the incident in 402, see above, Subsection 6.6.1.
[113] Cf. J. H. Richardson 2012: 62.

Dictator, from a magistracy the Roman People had bestowed on him was something few of them could watch with equanimity. Nor was it free of grave political risk: what if Flaminius, invoking the lack of precedent and clear constitutional guidance, were to challenge the Dictator's power, and refuse the order to step down? The Dictator then must resort to physical force—not against a private citizen such as the uppity Sp. Maelius, but against a Consul of the Roman People: what precedent was there for that? And if Flaminius, backed against the wall with no way out, chose to resist with force? The plebiscite about the triumph, however close the vote, demonstrated that he still enjoyed solid popular support, and to attack his *dignitas* might cause a public backlash:[114] if force came into play, there was no telling where it would end—and how.

Perhaps Fabius found a different way. A well-known story tells how a *sorex*, a shrew-mouse, squeaked just as a Dictator named his Magister Equitum, and thus caused both to abdicate.[115] Now the appointment of a Master of the Horse, like that of the Dictator himself, had to be made *auspicato*, in accordance with proper augural procedure; but as argued earlier, it is doubtful that this entailed a separate auspication: the Dictator's initial request for auspices comprised the permission to name a Magister Equitum, and affirmation of the latter's auspices before he named him.[116] Hence the rodent's intervention must have occurred not when the Dictator asked Iuppiter to confirm the validity of his auspices, but precisely at the moment he announced his choice of Magister Equitum; a *vitium* at the initial auspices would have prevented him from naming one in the first place.[117] Differently put, the *sorex* constitutes an oblative *auspicium*, not an impetrative one.

The oblative sign rendered null and void the impetrative auspices previously obtained for the action at hand, and thus could be seen as conveying Iuppiter's disapproval of the choice. Yet absent a separate auspication for permission to name a Magister Equitum, the impetrative auspices annulled of necessity were those of the Dictator himself: hence both must abdicate.[118] One has difficulty imagining, though, that Iuppiter, having granted the Dictator auspices in the first place, would then allow him to make a bad choice for Master of the Horse; if that happened, it must be because of a flaw in the Dictator's own appointment. The augural explanation of the sign (assuming the College was called upon to interpret it[119]), no doubt, was that he was *vitio factus*, and his deputy as well.

---

[114] Note Badian's comments, 1990: 474, on Cato's praetorian candidacy in 55.
[115] Val. Max. 1.1.5; Plut. *Marc.* 5.1–7.   [116] Chapter 4.1.
[117] As, in fact, we read in Plutarch: δικτάτορος ἵππαρχον ἀποδείξαντος (*Marc.* 5.6); cf. Amat-Seguin 86 n. 14. On the augural theory of the *vinculum temporis* (the nexus of oblative sign observed and action in progress), see Chapter 2.2.2.
[118] Chapter 4.1; Konrad 2004: 177; cf. the similar case of Marcellus' in 215 BC, Chapter 8.3.
[119] Pliny *NH* 8.223 notes: *nam soricum occentu dirimi auspicia annales refertos habemus.* The case under discussion, however, is the only such instance in the surviving record. Unless Pliny was exaggerating wildly, we should seriously consider the possibility that the *occentus soricis* constituted an established, i.e., "standard," omen signalling *vitium* in connection with the appointment of a Dictator

The incident is reported without date or context. What makes it interesting—not to say, intriguing—is the name of the Magister Equitum: Gaius Flaminius.

6.7.2 The Name of the Dictator

Even more intriguing, though problematic, the name of the Dictator. According to Valerius Maximus (1.1.5), it was Fabius Maximus; but Plutarch (*Marc.* 5.6) has Μινίκιος, which is to say, Minucius. Which should we believe?

The biographer's notice is part of a long digression on the paramount importance of proper religious observance (μαντειῶν δὲ καὶ πατρίων ὑπεροψία) in Roman public life (*Marc.* 4.7). It commences immediately after the Consuls' abdication (4.6), and continues all through chapter 5; Plutarch does not return to the actual story until 6.1 (*interregnum* and Marcellus' election). All of the intervening material serves to illustrate the point made in 4.7. First (5.1–4) comes the famous case of Tiberius Gracchus in 163 and 162, told at length (and with considerable confusion on the augural issue involved): as it concerned the abdication of both Consuls *vitio creati*, and without any complaint on their part, it held obvious relevance to the situation in 223/2.[120] (That observation alone should suffice to dispel the notion that Plutarch misunderstood what happened in 223, and erred in thinking that the Consuls abdicated.) Next (5.5) come two *flamines*—Cornelius Cethegus, having improperly handled the victim's entrails, and Quintus Sulpicius, whose *apex* fell off his head during a sacrifice—that were forced to abdicate because of the ritual errors committed in the exercise of their duties. Plutarch notes that these incidents, unlike that of Gracchus, occurred at the same time as the trouble with Flaminius in 223/2 (ἀλλὰ ταῦτα μὲν ὕστερον ἐπράχθη· περὶ δὲ τοὺς αὐτοὺς ἐκείνους χρόνους καὶ δύο ἱερεῖς ἐπιφανέστατοι τὰς ἱερωσύνας ἀφῃρέθησαν...). Then (5.6), the *sorex*: Μινικίου δὲ δικτάτορος ἵππαρχον ἀποδείξαντος Γάϊον Φλαμίνιον, ἐπεὶ τρισμὸς ἠκούσθη μυὸς ὃν σόρικα καλοῦσιν, ἀποψηφισάμενοι τούτους, αὖθις ἑτέρους κατέστησαν. The biographer concludes (5.7) with the remark that such Roman precision even in the smallest matters did not lead to superstition (δεισιδαιμονία), since it reflected the unaltered, and unalterable, ancestral custom.

This runs exactly parallel to what we find in Valerius Maximus: first, the case of Ti. Gracchus (1.1.3); then three *flamines*—P. Cloelius Siculus, M. Cornelius Cethegus, and C. Claudius—forced to resign their priesthoods *propter exta*

(not necessarily of other magistrates), and that it was this same sign that prompted the abdication of the five or six other Dictators found *vitio facti* (in 368 [?], 337, 333, 327, 321, and 217). If so, the augural college need not have to be consulted after the sign was first observed: knowing its meaning, the Dictator who encountered it would be expected to step down forthwith.

[120] Chapter 8.4.3.

parum curiose admota deorum immortalium aris (1.1.4); finally, *Q. Sulpicio inter sacrificandum e capite apex prolapsus idem sacerdotium abstulit* (1.1.5). Then, in the same paragraph, *occentusque soricis auditus Fabio Maximo dictaturam, C. Flaminio magisterium equitum deponendi causam praebuit* ("the squeak of a shrew-mouse that was heard provided the reason for Fabius Maximus to resign his dictatorship, and for C. Flaminius to resign his mastership of the horse"). If it were not for Plutarch's extra detail, especially in the Gracchus segment, one would not hesitate to conclude that he lifted the chapter directly from the Roman compiler of *memorabilia*, whose work he knew—in fact, he cites it later in this same *Life* (*Marc.* 30.5).[121] Clearly, though, the biographer culled all his examples from the same source, as did Valerius Maximus; and all six incidents reported by Valerius were already grouped together in that common source: Plutarch did not, just by coincidence, pick from a larger pool the very same examples, in the same order, as did Valerius.[122]

To what he took from the common source, Plutarch added detail regarding the *vitium* of Gracchus that he found elsewhere. Nothing here will come as a surprise to those familiar with Plutarch's method of work. His account is crafted from multiple sources, and highly selective in the use of the material he had available. Which brings us back to the question, oft debated: What was the name of the Dictator appointing Flaminius as Magister Equitum—Fabius (Valerius Maximus) or Minucius (Plutarch)?

One thing is certain from their use of the common source: Plutarch and Valerius refer to one and the same incident, and Flaminius did not fall victim to the same *vitium* twice in a row. As for which name, Minucius (M. Minucius Rufus, cos. 221; *mag. eq.* 217) has had its defenders, chiefly on the grounds that Μαξίμου is unlikely to be corrupted into Μινικίου; that for Fabius to name an old enemy such as Flaminius as his deputy was inconceivable; and that Minucius is on record as having set up an altar to Hercules while Dictator: *Hercolei sacrom M. Minuci. C. f. dictator vovit* (*CIL* 1².2.607 = *ILS* 11).[123] Against the latter point (and, by implication, in favor of Fabius), Badian supplied the decisive argument

---

[121] Plut. *Brut.* 53.5; Val. Max. 4.6.5. Beck 2005: 258 rashly names Valerius as Plutarch's direct source.

[122] Of the priests, he omitted Cloelius and Claudius. Were they too far in time from 223 BC? Claudius (the only one whose abdication we can date with certainty: Livy 26.23.8, *C. Claudius flamen Dialis quod exta perperam dederat flamonio abiit*) resigned in 211; one doubts that the biographer—not a stickler for chronological precision—would have had qualms including him among those περὶ δὲ τοὺς αὐτοὺς ἐκείνους χρόνους. More likely he found it tedious to list all three who had trouble with the *exta* (he generally knew how to keep a narrative flowing, even in digressions such as this), and chose the name he remembered first, or best. Without sufficient caution, Palmer (85 n. 36; 87; followed by Rüpke *FS* 3: 1571) takes Plutarch's phrase as evidence of a precise date, 223 BC, for the abdications of Cethegus and Sulpicius.

[123] Thus chiefly Dorey 92–96; cf. Bleicken 1955: 30 n. 4; Jahn 112–115; Wild 134; Dalla Rosa 2003: 204; Vervaet 2007: 228–232 (reviving Dorey's reasoning). Fabius and Flaminius had clashed over the latter's plebiscite (passed during his tribunate in 232) authorizing the *viritim* distribution of the *ager Gallicus* to Roman settlers (Cic. *Sen.* 11).

long ago.[124] The *vitium* occurred at the precise moment (δικτάτορος ἵππαρχον ἀποδείξαντος, Plut. *Marc.* 5.6) when the Dictator in question had just named his Magister Equitum, on the day he himself had entered office; the abdication cannot have been much delayed, and it strains the imagination to detect what sort of vow to Hercules (!) a *dictator comitiorum habendorum causa* (as the supporters of "Minucius" would have it) could have made, and seen fulfilled—for if his prayer were not granted, he would not have erected the altar—in so short a time. No special pleading that the *vitium* must have been manufactured by Fabius Maximus and his fellow Augurs (that tired red herring, naturally, cannot be missing from the "evidence" adduced), and that therefore "it would have been some little time" before the abdication could have been effected—enough to allow Minucius to make his vow—can help the case.[125] Nor will it do to argue that Minucius made his vow when campaigning against the Istri as Consul in 221, and only fulfilled it as Dictator in 220 or 219; *dictator vovit* is unambiguous.[126] The wording might, however, suggest that he offered his vow while Dictator, but did not fulfill it until after he stepped down: *vovit* stands out among republican dedicatory inscriptions, which usually combine the commander's title with *cepit* or *dedit*.[127] That he should have made a vow to Hercules, of all gods, as Dictator *comitiorum habendorum causa* to commence his tenure calls for a better explanation than the mere assertion that it could have happened, let alone speculation—entirely without support in the evidence of the sources—about political and augural machinations that could accommodate a dictatorship for Minucius between 221 and 219.[128]

---

[124] Badian 1961: 497; cf. Bandel 123 n. 7; Lippold 144; Càssola 1968: 261–267; Meyer 1972: 976; Develin 1979: 271–273.

[125] Thus Dorey 94–95; cf. Vervaet 2007: 230.

[126] Dorey 95 adduced Marcellus' inscription, on the base of a statue looted from Sicily, as a parallel (*M. Claudius M. f. consol Hinnad cepit*, *CIL* 1².2.608 = *ILS* 12): presumably Marcellus acquired the statue at the Romans' sack of Henna in 213, when he was *pro consule*, but set up the inscription in 210 as Consul (*IV*). If this was a dedication *ex voto* (as Dorey assumed), Marcellus would have made the vow before he took up the command in Sicily, as Consul (*III*), in 214. But it forces the Latin beyond plausible limits to interpret the text as meaning "Marcellus took this from Henna (i.e., in 213), and set it up as Consul (in 210)," thus cutting *cepit* off *consol*, and requiring a second verb (*dedit* vel sim.) to be supplied. L. Flamininus had no trouble making the distinction: *[L. Quinctius L. f. Le]ucado cepit* (as his brother's Legate in 197), *[eidem conso]l dedit* (in 192, *CIL* 1².2.613 = 14.2935 = *ILS* 14); and neither had L. Mummius: *quod in bello voverat* (as Consul in 146)…*imperator dedicat* (after his triumph in 145, *CIL* 6.331 = *ILS* 20). Fulvius Nobilior, who captured Ambrakia as Consul in 189, said so unequivocally (*M. Folvios M. f. Ser. n. Nobilior cos. Ambracia cepit*, *CIL* 1².2.615 = 6.1507 = *ILS* 16), even though he could not have dedicated the image until after his triumph in 187. De Sanctis (*SdR* 3.2: 330–331) notwithstanding, there are no cogent grounds to date the sack of Henna to 213 instead of 214; Livy refers to Marcellus as *consul* four times in that context (24.37.9, 11; 24.38.9; 24.39.2).

[127] See, e.g., *ILS* 3, 12–14, 16–17, 21b, 36.

[128] Note the bewildering proliferation of scenarios entertained by Vervaet 2007: 230–232, who ventures to maintain that it is "not inconceivable that Minucius, in the face of his opponents' machinations to force him and Flaminius out of their offices, defiantly fulfilled his vow to Hercules as dictator, as to record it for posterity and ostentatiously parade his military and political bravado" (230 n. 40). Military bravado for a Dictator named to hold elections? All that is pure fantasy.

The altar surely belongs to 217 BC, when Minucius, his *imperium* having been made equal to that of the Dictator, "proceeded to interpret" his elevation "as having equated the titles together with the powers."[129] A vow to Hercules at that point would make eminently good sense.[130] Corruption of Μαξίμου to Μινικίου is improbable, it is true; but as Càssola points out, the transformation of "M. Minucius" to "Fabius Maximus" (the latter name is spelled out in full in Valerius Maximus) is no less improbable.[131] There is no reason, though, to think that anything is wrong with Plutarch's text. Relying heavily on memory, the biographer frequently puts down the wrong name when noting incidental detail such as here.[132] He makes no mention, in the *Fabius*, of the Cunctator's first dictatorship, nor of anything that fell into the fifteen years between his first consulate in 233 (2.1) and his finest hour in 217 (2.2); but he gives ample attention to Minucius (4.1; 5–13)— whose *praenomen*, it appears, he misremembered at the first occasion.[133] Those who would prefer a name in Plutarch over one in a Latin author walk treacherous ground. The Dictator's name was, in the common source as in Valerius, Fabius Maximus.

6.7.3 The *Sorex*

That leaves the politically odd combination of Fabius and Flaminius. Why would Fabius Maximus choose a man he had opposed before to be now his deputy? The hypothesis developed here provides an answer: if we are right about the occasion of Fabius' first dictatorship, Flaminius was the obvious choice—indeed, the only

---

[129] Badian 1961: 497; cf. Chapter 3.4.3.
[130] Beck 2005: 289 n. 103 offers the attractive suggestion that the choice of Hercules—ancestor of the *gens Fabia*, Plut. *Fab*. 1.2—was made in return for Fabius' rescue of Minucius at Gereonium.
[131] Càssola 1968: 262.
[132] See *Cam*. 36.4, where Plutarch knows T. Quinctius Capitolinus as Dictator in 385 V, when according to Livy—surely more trustworthy in such things—the Dictator was A. Cornelius Cossus, with Quinctius Capitolinus as his Magister Equitum (6.11.10, 12.10); or *TiGrac* 20.6, where the biographer names Scipio Nasica instead of C. Laelius, quite by mistake: Cic. *Amic*. 37; cf. Val. Max. 4.7.1; Badian 1972: 708 n. 120.
[133] Ziegler, like most editors, prints Μᾶρκον Μινούκιον (*Fab* 4.1), but the mss. have λεύκιον: an unfortunate slip, caused perhaps by the intrusion, into the biographer's mind, of the man's hapless ancestor, the Consul of 458. At 12.3, Plutarch got it right; but he never noticed, and corrected, his earlier error. Beck 2005: 257–258, after making a good case against "Minucius," suggests that the biographer deliberately substituted the latter for Fabius, on the grounds that this resulted in an ideologically more suitable pair, since Fabius—*homo religiosus* par excellence—did not well fit into his "Beispielliste für mangelnde religiöse Observanz." Perhaps; but knowing Plutarch, a simple error appears far more likely. In any case, Plutarch's point with his list of examples is not the failure to observe proper ritual (no fault of the Dictator's is implied), but the contrary: the Roman determination to follow correct religious procedure in even the smallest things (*Marc*. 5.7, τὴν ἐν οὕτω μικροῖς ἀκρίβειαν φυλάττοντες; cf. 4.7).

one. It cleared the way for overcoming Flaminius' resistance and letting the *interregnum* take its course.[134]

Whatever stand contemporaries might take on the suggestion that a Dictator could force a Consul to resign, there could be no doubt as regards the Magister Equitum. Not only did the Dictator have the power to order him to abdicate, he was—by *mos*, at least—required to give that order before he himself stepped down.[135] The all-important difference lay in that no shame, no humiliation, attached to such an abdication: it was the normal manner in which those two offices terminated. If Fabius named Flaminius his Magister Equitum, then commanded him to abdicate while preparing to do the same himself, Flaminius' *dignitas* would remain untarnished. The same was true of the Consul who resigned his office in order to become Magister Equitum. Nor would Flaminius be acknowledging that he was *vitio creatus*: he would step down not because it was demanded thus of him, not because he was forced to, but because he answered the call of the *res publica*. It was an offer he could not refuse.

Resign as Consul, though, he must, before assuming office as Magister Equitum: the deal would of necessity require that. Although the matter has been doubted, we have it on good authority that combining both those offices was contrary to custom, unlike a man being Consul and Dictator all at once, and not a single unequivocal case of cumulation prior to 46 BC is attested in the record.[136]

Thus in 223 BC, in making Flaminius his deputy, Fabius Maximus solved the problem of how to force him to resign his consulship; and once Flaminius was his deputy, Fabius could order him outright to resign that post, and thereby clear the way for an *interregnum*. Yet in so doing, Fabius also took care to let Flaminius save face. There was no loss of *dignitas* in abdicating one's consulship so as to become Magister Equitum (at least one precedent, from 331, could be adduced, and possibly more); nor was there any humiliation in resigning as Magister Equitum, if so ordered by the Dictator immediately before he himself stepped down. It mattered not one whit that the true reason for these proceedings was clear for everyone to see; in a society so closely regulated by proper form and ritual, it was the formal, stated reason that counted, not whatever was the practical intent behind it. Had Fabius attempted to use his dictatorial powers to force the

---

[134] Plutarch notes that after the Romans had removed "Minucius" and Flaminius from office, they appointed others (ἀποψηφισάμενοι τούτους, αὖθις ἑτέρους κατέστησαν, *Marc.* 5.6). Neither "Minucius" nor the notion of removal from office (rather than abdication) encourages much trust in the biographer's accurate representation of the event; Valerius Maximus (1.1.5) says nothing beyond abdication. If, as seems probable, Plutarch found the episode in a collection of *exempla*, without accompanying historical context, he would naturally assume that another Dictator would be needed to perform whatever task "Minucius" had originally been chosen for; the statement should not be taken as reflecting a concrete piece of information the biographer had in front of him.

[135] Mommsen *StR* 2.1: 175–176, making an artificial and unpersuasive distinction between the "abdicirende Dictator," who has power to dismiss his Master-of-Horse, and the Dictator in mid-term, who has not. Cf. Chapter 4.1, note 4.

[136] Dio 43.33.1; see Chapter 4.3.

Consul from office directly, without the detour of making him his Magister Equitum, it may be doubted that Flaminius would have dared to resist; but it would have caused a major blow to the *dignitas* of a man who was now a fellow member of the ruling class, and the Nobles still knew better than to push things to the limit. The moment Fabius was named Dictator, Flaminius was bound to know that he had lost this power struggle with the Senate and the Augurs; but his political prestige, his *dignitas*, remained unharmed, and he conceded nothing with regard to the very issue that had led to this constitutional crisis: he could continue to deny that he was *vitio creatus*, and maintain that his auspices, as Consul, had been intact no matter what the Augurs said. Or so he thought.

The *sorex* squeaked, and gave the Augurs the last word. Their verdict was the same on Flaminius the Magister Equitum as it had been on Flaminius the Consul: *vitio creatus*, appointed under an augural flaw, and thus required to step down immediately. But this time he could not possibly resist: the Dictator would order him to abdicate, and that was that. Not that Flaminius would have expected to remain Magister Equitum for longer than a day or so; the whole purpose of his appointment was, after all, to make him give up his consulship without loss of face, and thus allow his colleague and all the other magistrates to abdicate. Once this had been achieved, there was no point for the Dictator and his deputy to hang on; on the contrary, both would abdicate as speedily as possible, to let the *interregnum* take its course. But had Flaminius foreseen the shrew-mouse?

To those familiar with augural law, the *sorex* comes as no surprise; in fact, it was inevitable. The Dictator naming his Magister Equitum had first to be named, with auspices from Iuppiter, by one of the Consuls: and both the Consuls had earlier been found *vitio creati*. Which meant that they lacked valid auspices: which meant in turn that any Dictator named by Furius the Consul was *vitio creatus*, just like the Consul naming him; and so, of course, was the Magister Equitum named by the Dictator. Hence both of them must abdicate immediately, to put things right again between the Roman State and Iuppiter. And so they did. With that, the Augurs had established once and for all the point Flaminius had denied so vigorously: that his and his colleague's election to the consulship was augurally flawed, and that their auspices were null and void. Iuppiter, of course, was in on it: note how he waited with the oblative sign until the Magister Equitum was announced. It would not do to force Fabius from office before he had a chance to name Flaminius. Those with a soft heart for small rodents may rest confident that this particular *sorex* was cared for lovingly in his augural employ all the remaining days of his life.

7
The Road to Perdition

For all his belligerent rejection of the augural science, Gaius Flaminius in 223 BC had not at any point failed to observe the auspices. Although—like his colleague— *vitio creatus*, he had achieved a great victory over the dread Gauls. His open declaration—the first so recorded by a Consul of the Roman People—that auspices were stuff and nonsense represented as remarkable an attack on the constitutional foundations of the Republic as did his refusal to accept the Augurs' verdict and the Senate's directive to abdicate his consulship. Yet no harm had come, in the end, to the *res publica*, thanks to the ingenious solution (devised by we know not whom, and put into effect by Fabius Maximus) of naming a Dictator to bring about an *interregnum*, with Flaminius as Magister Equitum.

Five years after the *sorex* squeaked, Flaminius was again presented with an opportunity to establish his—and, if successful, future Consuls'—independence from auspices and other augural interference in military operations. He seized it without hesitation. This time, he would go beyond rejecting the science: he decided to dispense with auspices altogether, like Lutatius in 242, but without offering a substitute. As had happened in 249, when the Consuls proceeded *contra auspicia*, calamity ensued.

7.1 Hannibal's Pass

The consular elections for 217 BC, held in the wake of the devastating defeat suffered at the River Trebia, had returned Flaminius (*iterum*), together with Cn. Servilius Geminus. In the first days of March, Flaminius, still Consul-elect, in fear that his political rivals would attempt to detain him in the City through sundry manipulations of religious and procedural demands (*auspiciis ementiendis Latinarumque feriarum mora et consularibus aliis impedimentis*), quietly left Rome and travelled to Ariminum, pretending to make a private journey (*simulato itinere privatus clam in provinciam abiit*, Livy 21.63.5). His true objective was to enter office at Ariminum on the Ides of March. In consequence, it could be argued, he lacked valid auspices, having received none in Rome on the day of taking office: for such auspices could not be obtained *in externo solo*.[1] Nor had

---

[1] Livy 22.1.7, *nec privatum auspicia sequi nec sine auspiciis profectum in externo ea solo nova atque integra concipere posse*. The lack of valid auspices, of course, did not affect the status of Flaminius'

he departed, *paludatus*, in the ritually prescribed manner from the City to go to war.

Thus says Livy. He is often disbelieved: in the early days of spring, Polybios tells us, the Consul led his army through Etruria to Arretium, and encamped there (ἐνισταμένης δὲ τῆς ἐαρινῆς ὥρας, Γάιος μὲν Φλαμίνιος ἀναλαβὼν τὰς αὑτοῦ δυνάμεις προῆγε διὰ Τυρρηνίας καὶ κατεστρατοπέδευσε πρὸ τῆς τῶν Ἀρρητίνων πόλεως, 3.77.1). Saying nothing about Flaminius' taking office at Ariminum, the statement is frequently cited as proof that he took his army to Arretium directly from Rome, and that Livy's story about the Consul entering office at Ariminum and failing to acquire his auspices must be false.[2] That conclusion does not hold up to scrutiny of Polybios' own account. To show this, we must start with an examination of Hannibal's movements in the spring of 217.

7.1.1 Hannibal's Options

According to Polybios, Hannibal contemplated several routes of advance into Italy: some were long and, from the enemy's point of view, constituted an obvious choice; one leading through marshy land into Etruria was difficult but direct, and suitable for taking Flaminius unawares (τὰς μὲν ἄλλας ἐμβολὰς τὰς εἰς τὴν πολεμίαν μακρὰς εὕρισκε καὶ προδήλους τοῖς ὑπεναντίοις, τὴν δὲ διὰ τῶν ἑλῶν εἰς Τυρρηνίαν φέρουσαν, δυσχερῆ μὲν, σύντομον δὲ καὶ παράδοξον φανησομένη τοῖς περὶ τὸν Φλαμίνιον, 3.78.6). He chose the second option, and having against all expectation crossed the marshes, he found that Flaminius was encamped at Arretium (διαπεράσας δὲ παραδόξως τοὺς ἑλώδεις τόπους καὶ καταλαβὼν ἐν Τυρρηνίᾳ τὸν Φλαμίνιον στρατοπεδεύοντα πρὸ τῆς τῶν Ἀρρητίνων πόλεως, 3.80.1). We are not told specifically where Hannibal emerged from the swamps, but since he set out, after resting his troops, from the vicinity of Faesulae (ὡς γὰρ θᾶττον ποιησάμενος ἀναζυγὴν ἀπὸ τῶν κατὰ τὴν Φαισόλαν τόπων, 3.82.1), a reasonable assumption holds that this is where he reached dry ground.[3] (See Map 1.)

Thus Hannibal with his choice of route meant to surprise Flaminius: but how? To cross the Appennines from Cisalpine Gaul into Etruria, he had available some

---

consulship under public law: the rule *magistratus vitio creatus nihilo setius magistratus* (Varro *LL* 6.30; cf. Linderski, *AL* 2163–2164) applied accordingly; although a Consul *vitiosus* (not, to be sure, *vitio creatus*), he was Consul nonetheless, with all the legal powers of the office. For a fuller discussion of the status of Flaminius' auspices, see Konrad 2004: 170–178, where the existence of "auspices for war" was still accepted unquestioningly; and Chapter 2.4–2.6.

[2] Seeck 162–166; Jung 1902: 186; Pareti 1912a: 257–258; De Sanctis *SdR* 3.2: 109; Schmitt 87–89, 105–106; Seibert 1993b: 147 n. 55; Meißner 101–104. Walbank *HCP* 1: 410–411 labels Livy's account "suspect," but acknowledges that the reassignment of the previous Consuls' armies could explain Flaminius' presence at Ariminum. Develin 1979: 276 is undecided; Lazenby 1978: 61–62 accepts Livy's version.

[3] Kromayer *AS* 3.1: 117; Walbank *HCP* 1: 413; Lazenby 1978: 61; Seibert 1993a: 219. For an ingenious if unconvincing argument against this view, see Fuchs 1904: 125–127, 130–135.

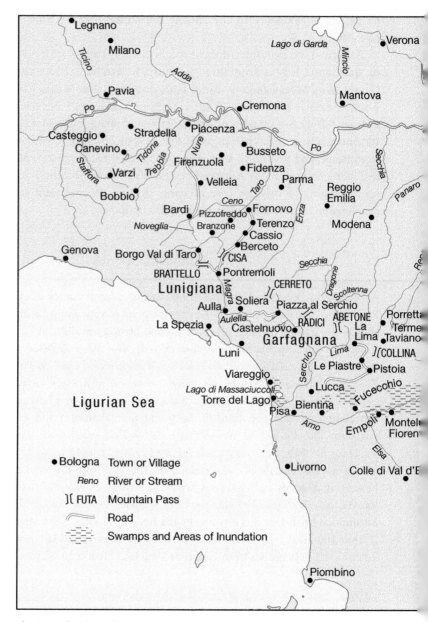

Map 1. North-Central Italy and Appennine Passes. (Place names in modern Italian; for ancient equivalents, see General Index.)

THE ROAD TO PERDITION 215

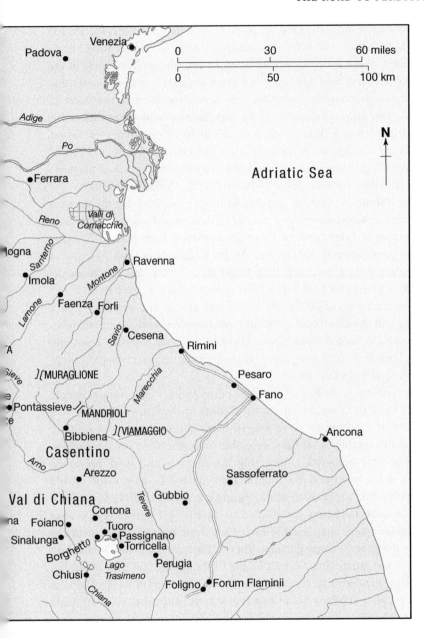

twenty passes that reduce to essentially three options: those to the west, ending on or near the Ligurian coast, between Luna and Luca, which would bring him to the lower course of the Arno; those that emerged onto the middle course of the river near Pistoriae and Faesulae; and the eastern ones, leading to the Casentino region along the headwaters of the Arno, a mere 20 kilometers northeast of Arretium. The prevailing opinion now holds that Hannibal took the middle route, most likely from Bologna (then Felsina) up the Reno valley to Porretta Terme, then over Taviano and Spedaletto to the Passo della Collina, and down to Pistoia.[4] There followed the grueling march through the inundated area north of the Arno towards dry land near Faesulae, about 70 kilometers northwest of Arretium.

Explaining Hannibal's intended surprise, Kromayer reasoned that the Romans would be guarding any route leading directly to their consular armies—the later Via Aemilia towards Ariminum, the Passo dei Mandrioli from Forlì to Bibbiena on the upper Arno towards Arezzo, and the Passo della Futa from Bologna to Fiesole and on to Arezzo; and each army could move, by the Pass of Viamaggio, from Rimini to Arretium (c.105 kilometers) or vice versa in a week or less, thus effecting a concentration of all forces with relative ease in one location.[5] Hence Polybios' long and obvious routes—the ones the Romans would expect Hannibal to take—must have been the western passes, leading to the Ligurian coast and lower Arno; Hannibal's surprising move was to pick the one that brought him to the middle Arno at Pistoriae instead.

This view runs into difficulties. Both the Collina and the Futa route originate at Bologna, a mere 10 kilometers apart: the Collina up the Reno valley, the Futa up the Savena. If the Romans were able to block access to the Futa route at Bologna, one should think that they were able to do the same for the Collina. They may not have bothered, considering the marshes and their presumed impassability at the other end; but Hannibal's army and its movements would have been within easy range of observation, and it is hard to believe that a force of over 50,000 men could have approached so close yet escaped all notice: after all, if the Romans were guarding the Futa, they must have reckoned with the possibility of the enemy's coming near it. They might have been surprised to find that Hannibal was attempting to cross by the Collina route, but they could not have failed to realize what he was doing and send word ahead to Flaminius at Arezzo. The surprise Polybios has in mind must have resulted in some strategic advantage for Hannibal, or at least held out the hope of such; Kromayer's preferred route does neither.

---

[4] Kromayer AS 3.1: 133–134; De Sanctis SdR 3.2: 37, 106; Walbank HCP 1: 413; Lazenby 1978: 60–61; Seibert 1993b: 147–148. For a lucid assembly and discussion of possible (and impossible) routes, see Kromayer AS 3.1: 104–135.
[5] Kromayer AS 3.1: 137–138 with n. 2.

7.1.2 The Floods of the Arno

There is more. During springtime, the entire coast from the Serchio to the Arno rivers, from Viareggio to Pisa, in Hannibal's day would have presented a continuous area of flooded swamps and marshes extending some 60 kilometers inland: wholly impassable for an army as late as the early twentieth century. The only way from the western Appennine passes into Etruria would have been via Luca to Pistoriae, hugging the foothills of the mountains, and then through the inundation area of the middle Arno to Faesulae.[6] In other words, Kromayer's "obvious" route in the end would have brought Hannibal to the same point, 70 kilometers from Arretium, as the "surprising" one. And if Hannibal did in fact go by the Collina Pass, he first must have advanced in Gaul as far east as Bologna: would the Romans, at that point, still expect him to turn back and take a route—the "obvious" one—leading to the Ligurian coast? Perhaps; but only if they were convinced that the route by the Collina Pass itself—not on account of the marshes at the other end—was not feasible: something we have no grounds to assume. The marshes of the middle Arno posed an obstacle that Hannibal would have to overcome regardless, whether he emerged from the Appennines near Luca or near Pistoriae—unless he waited for a drier time of year. From Faesulae, finally, the way into central Italy led south, towards Arezzo. From the Roman point of view, the western passes to the lower Arno, at this time of year, were no more obvious or probable than the central ones as far east as the Collina: no matter which of them he took, Hannibal would have to make his way across the marshes. Success in the latter attempt, depending on where exactly it deposited Hannibal's army in relation to that of Flaminius, may have constituted Polybios' "surprise": the choice of lower versus middle Arno assuredly did not.

In consequence, the longer and—to the Romans—obvious routes can only have been either those that led into Etruria by one of the passes east of Bologna,[7] all of which would bring Hannibal through the Sieve valley to Faesulae (or farther east to Pontassieve) without touching any marshes or inundated area; or those that did not lead into Etruria at all—across Emilia-Romagna to Ariminum, and from there to Umbria (and Rome) or Picenum (and the South). The more direct and difficult one would take him to Etruria instead, and in a way the enemy did not expect: which is precisely how Polybios put the contrast (τὰς μὲν ἄλλας ἐμβολὰς τὰς εἰς τὴν πολεμίαν . . . τὴν δὲ διὰ τῶν ἑλῶν εἰς Τυρρηνίαν φέρουσαν,

---

[6] Kromayer AS 3.1: 112–119, pointing out (115) that the road from Lucca to Pistoia (basically today's Via Lucchese) would have posed no difficulties of terrain or flooding; De Sanctis SdR 3.2: 106; Walbank HCP 1: 413; Capecchi et al. 142–143, 150–159.

[7] Besides the Futa from Bologna, these would be the routes up the Santerno valley from Imola, the Lamone valley from Faenza, and the Montone valley from Forlì; also from Forlì or Cesena, the Mandrioli Pass led directly to the headwaters of the Arno northeast of Arezzo.

3.78.6), and how Strabo understood it.[8] This route was unexpected insofar as the Romans thought the marshes impassable at this time of year, and doubtless kept the eastern passes—the ones avoiding the marshes—under close observation. It follows, in turn, that Hannibal launched his march from a position to the west of Bologna, well beyond the range of sustained Roman observation (otherwise, there could have been no surprise); as noted already, if he did not take the Futa route, it is virtually certain that he did not take the one over the Collina Pass either.

Hence we may conclude that Hannibal chose one of the westerly routes that brought him to the middle Arno at Pistoriae. Up to five may have offered. Which one he used will depend on where he spent the winter, and on how far he had advanced eastward from his winter quarters before crossing the Appennines.[9]

The easternmost route would have been from Mutina up the Panaro and Scoltenna valleys across the Passo del Abetone and down the Lima; from La Lima, Pistoia could be reached over San Marcello, Pontepetri, and Le Piastre. It is doubtful, however, whether there existed a viable road across the Abetone prior to its development in the eighteenth century. Also from Modena, there may have been a route up the Secchia and Dragone valleys over the Foce delle Radici, from Pievepelago to Castelnuovo di Garfagnana, and along the Serchio river to Lucca; but the viability of the Radici Pass in antiquity appears even more questionable than the Abetone route.[10]

From Reggio Emilia, following the Secchia valley one could reach the Passo del Cerreto and descend the mountains via Sassalbo to Soliera Apuana, then along the Aulella and Magra rivers to the Tyrrhenian Sea at Luna; but rather than march down the coast and confront the vast marshes of Lake Massaciuccoli, Hannibal could have availed himself of a route leading east from Soliera Apuana (more or less similar to today's Strada Regionale 445) to Piazza al Serchio and through the Garfagnana to Lucca.[11] The Cerreto route itself does not seem to have entailed—unlike the Abetone and the Passo delle Radici—major difficulties, but is not known to have been used in antiquity.

Still farther west, from Parma up the Taro to Fornovo, then via Terenzo, Cassio, and Berceto (roughly along today's Strada Statale 62), the Passo della Cisa led to

---

[8] Strabo 5.2.9 C226-227. Too much should not be made of this, though; the historian-geographer has Hannibal gain control of his route only after defeating Flaminius, and imagines the marshes to be those of the Po Valley (5.1.11 C217).

[9] The exact location of his winter quarters remains unknown: Polyb. 3.77.3; Livy 21.59.1; Appian *Hannib.* 7.30. All three suggest a location west of Placentia: cf. Lazenby 1978: 60; Seibert 1993b: 137–140. Pareti 1912a: 255 and Kromayer *AS* 3.1: 138 had argued for a place between Modena and Bologna; against this, see the compelling reasoning of Banti (115–120), who makes a strong case for Clastidium (Casteggio). From Luca, Hannibal would march along the foothills to Pistoriae, then through the inundated area of the middle Arno to Faesulae. If the Romans maintained a force guarding Luca through the winter and the spring, as is often thought (below, note 76), this route could be eliminated; but the inability, due to the marshlands and spring flooding, of moving anywhere from Luca but to Faesulae would render such a force superfluous. See Banti's detailed discussion (98–114) of available routes in this sector of the Appennines.

[10] Kromayer *AS* 3.1: 121 n. 2.   [11] For a detailed description, see Banti 108.

Pontremoli and down the Lunigiana along the Magra to Luni; as with the Passo del Cerreto, Hannibal could turn east at Aulla and march up the Aulella to Piazza al Serchio, the Garfagnana, and Lucca. It would surprise if that great medieval route across the Cisa had been unknown in antiquity; Fornovo (Forum Novum *sive* Municipium Foronovanorum) and the names Terentium, Cassium, and Bercetum suggest as much.[12] Yet noting a complete absence of Roman remains along the Cisa road between Fornovo and Pontremoli, Banti proposed an archaeologically better supported route parallel to the left bank of the Taro, from Fornovo past Pizzofreddo, Branzone, and the church of San Cristoforo in Val Vona to Borgo Val di Taro (Borgotaro for short), then over the Passo del Brattello to Pontremoli.

That same pass, the Brattello, finally, is part of the only securely attested route across the northern Appennines from Placentia to Luca in Roman times. It led up the Nure river (as well as on roads from Firenzuola and Fidenza) to Velleia, then via Bardi along the Noveglia to San Cristoforo-Borgotaro; from there over the Brattello Pass to Pontremoli and Lucca.[13] The route was accessible, moreover, from points farther west as far as Pavia—and Clastidium: either up the Stàffora valley via Varzi and Bobbio to Bardi, or via Stradella and Canevino to Bobbio and Bardi, or through the northern foothills across the Tidone, Trebbia, and Nure past Velleia to Bardi.[14]

A further conclusion follows: Flaminius must have expected Hannibal to arrive in Etruria, should he be headed there, by one of the eastern passes, from the Futa to the Mandrioli,[15] those farther west being deemed unsuitable in springtime on account of the marshes they inevitably led to. All the eastern routes would bring Hannibal to the vicinity of Faesulae, except the Mandrioli Pass; but as long as the latter could not be ruled out, Arretium marked the northernmost point at which to position an army with intent to intercept the invader. Hence Hannibal's arrival at Faesulae could not have come as a surprise as such. All roads led to Arezzo, where Flaminius was waiting. Or was he?

7.1.3 Where was Flaminius?

Polybios certainly implies that Flaminius was waiting at Arretium. As we have seen, he reports the Consul marching his army through Etruria to Arretium early

---

[12] Schütte 22, arguing for use of the Cisa road in antiquity; Banti 104–107 ("il passo della Cisa fu probabilmente conosciuto, ma non deve esser stato molto frequentato").

[13] See Banti's painstaking reconstruction, 101–105.

[14] Jung 1899: 523–530; the latter route was taken in 1268 by the army of the last Staufer, Konradin, Duke of Schwaben (Jung 546–547; Schütte 132–133; Banti 102, 105).

[15] Kromayer *AS* 3.1: 112 n. 1 in fact suggests the latter, in contradiction to his more developed view at 137–139. Fuchs 1904: 122–125 valiantly argued that Hannibal did take the Mandrioli Pass, but Kromayer's rebuttal, 107–122, seems decisive.

in the spring, and pitch camp there (3.77.1). Yet Hannibal next moves to take Flaminius by surprise (3.78.6), and, having made his way unexpectedly through the marshes, finds the Consul in camp at Arretium: διαπεράσας δὲ παραδόξως τοὺς ἑλώδεις τόπους καὶ καταλαβὼν ἐν Τυρρηνίᾳ τὸν Φλαμίνιον στρατοπεδεύοντα πρὸ τῆς τῶν Ἀρρητίνων πόλεως (3.80.1). Now this is strange: if Flaminius was waiting for Hannibal at Arretium, whatever route the latter chose could not have caused much of a surprise, as shown above; and if Hannibal knew in advance, before setting out from Gaul, that Flaminius was waiting at Arretium, he could hardly have expected to take the enemy unawares by choosing a route that would bring him to just the area where Flaminius had anticipated his arrival. Nor is it clear why Hannibal still needed to find out, on arriving at Faesulae, about the Consul's position—and character. That καταλαβών must be allowed its full force—Hannibal learned of Flaminius' presence at Arretium now, not before his departure from Gaul[16]—is confirmed by the need to make extensive inquiries (βουλόμενος τήν τε δύναμιν ἀναλαβεῖν καὶ πολυπραγμονῆσαι τὰ περὶ τοὺς ὑπεναντίους καὶ τοὺς προκειμένους τῶν τόπων, 3.80.2) while resting his forces: inquiries about the enemy in general and the Consul's background and habits in particular (πυνθανόμενος ... τὸν δὲ Φλαμίνιον ὀχλοκόπον μὲν καὶ δημαγωγὸν εἶναι τέλειον, πρὸς ἀληθινῶν δὲ καὶ πολεμικῶν πραγμάτων χειρισμὸν οὐκ εὐφυῆ, πρὸς δὲ τούτοις καταπεπιστευκέναι τοῖς σφετέροις πράγμασι, 3.80.3), and, even more significantly, about the character of the country that lay ahead—one of wealth and abundance, as it turned out (τὴν μὲν χώραν ... πολλῆς γέμειν ὠφελείας). Only now, in light of this intelligence, does Hannibal develop his strategy for confronting the enemy (3.80.4–5).[17] Yet he had faced no difficulty, it seems, in obtaining accurate information, before setting out from Gaul, on the nature of the marshes he would have to cross: why would he not attempt to gather the necessary facts about Etruria and Flaminius at the same time? The impression here is one of a move made in some haste, not planned long in advance—and clearly not in full knowledge of Flaminius' position at Arretium.

Perhaps Livy can furnish some clarity. After taking office in Ariminum, Flaminius begins to move his army on mountain paths across the Appennines toward Etruria (*in Etruriam per Appennini tramites exercitus duci est coeptus*, 21.63.15); we are not told its exact destination. Next Hannibal, under pressure from his Gaulish allies to take the war into Italy proper, and exposed to constant Gaulish attempts on his life, leaves his winter quarters as early as possible

---

[16] A point well made by Fuchs 1904: 125; cf. 1897: 50–54, with extensive examination of καταλαμβάνω in Polybios.

[17] Although Polybios makes this clear enough, it is not always understood; Amat-Seguin 97 is a notable exception. Pareti 1912b: 269–270 argued that Polybios meant to say that Hannibal realized—with relief—that Flaminius was *still* at Arretium, rather than having moved up to Faesulae to cut down the Punic forces as they emerged from the marshes. If that was Polybios' point, he hid it well; a simple ἔτι in front of στρατοπεδεύοντα would hardly have encumbered the narrative with an attack of loquacity.

(22.1.1–4).[18] Having set out, he chooses the shorter route through the swamps over the longer and more convenient one, since he hears by way of rumor that the Consul had already arrived at Arretium: *Hannibal profectus ex hibernis, quia iam Flaminium consulem Arretium pervenisse fama erat, cum aliud longius, ceterum commodius ostenderetur iter, propiorem viam per paludes petit* (22.2.1–2). The march through the swamps is narrated in much the same terms, and details, as in Polybios (22.2.3–11; cf. Polyb. 3.79). On emerging from the marshes, his scouts confirm that the Roman army is encamped under the walls of Arretium (*ubi primum in sicco potuit, castra locat, certumque per praemissos exploratores habuit exercitum Romanum circa Arreti moenia esse*, 22.3.1). He then proceeds to make inquiries about his opponent's character and manner of arriving at decisions, and about the nature of the surrounding country (*consulis deinde consilia atque animum et situm regionum itineraque et copias ad commeatus expediendos et cetera quae cognosse in rem erat summa omnia cum cura inquirendo exsequebatur*, 22.3.2).

All in all, this is rather close to Polybios—too close, indeed, to come from a different tradition. But unlike Polybios, Livy specifies that Hannibal had heard rumors—hence nothing certain yet—that Flaminius was already (*iam*) at Arretium, and establishes a clear causal connection between this information and the choice of route: *quia* speaks for itself. The rumor, as opposed to confirmed intelligence, of Flaminius' presence at Arretium ties in smoothly with the need to reconnoiter upon arrival in Etruria to determine the enemy's dispositions: it evidently constitutes an element inherent in the tradition common to both authors, and must not be dismissed as an extraneous addition on the part of Livy, or some other of his sources.[19] Nor have we grounds for assigning a different origin to the causal connection between the rumor and Hannibal's choice of route. It, too, was part of the tradition Polybios followed here. Behind Livy's *quia* (the Patavian eschewed spelling out the notion of a surprise) lurks Polybios' παράδοξον τοῖς περὶ τὸν Φλαμίνιον.

Unfortunately, Livy would not specify the nature of the causal connection, as he understood it. One possibility offers right away. Having reason to believe that Flaminius might already be at Arezzo, Hannibal chose a route that would take him to a part of Etruria where the enemy could not easily interfere with his further advance into Italy—a route that did not lead to Faesulae, but to a point well south of Arretium. The strategic advantage gained would be self-evident.

---

[18] The famous story of Hannibal's wigs and other disguises (*mutando nunc vestem nunc tegumenta capitis errore etiam sese ab insidiis munierat*, 22.1.3) is told by Polybios more like an isolated matter, before mention of the Gauls' growing dissatisfaction at the prospect of the war against the Romans being waged in their country (3.78.1–5; cf. also Zonar. 8.24). One must admit that Livy here provides, or preserves, a more coherent arrangement.

[19] The same applies to Livy's note that the flooding of the Arno exceeded its normal state that year (22.3.1): *pace* Pareti 1912b: 264, that piece of information clearly lies at the bottom of Polybios' description of the terrain (3.79.1), the river and precise location being of no interest to him, and does not reflect a conjecture of Livy or his source.

By default, such a scenario would require one of the western passes, leading to the lower Arno at Luca. Instead of taking the dry route hugging the foothills from Luca to Pistoriae, thence through the inundation area of the Arno to Faesulae, Hannibal would have to march in a southeasterly direction across the vast marshland between the Serchio and Arno rivers toward Empoli, and up the Elsa valley to Siena. Continuing east-southeast in the direction of Cortona, he would reach the plains of the Chiana near Sinalunga or Foiano, about 35 kilometers south of Arezzo, roughly on the same latitude as the north shore of Lake Trasumene.

7.1.4 Where was Faesulae?

Some such itinerary has found champions, if few recently.[20] It certainly would furnish Hannibal with the strategic advantage implied in Polybios' "surprise"; yet, attractive though it is, it cannot be reconciled with the evidence.

From Polybios it is evident that Hannibal, having crossed the marshes, continued his advance from somewhere in the vicinity of Faesulae. Whatever one makes of the notorious *crux* in Livy (*laeva relicto hoste †Faesulas petens† medio Etruriae agro praedatum profectus*, 22.3.6),[21] it is equally evident, if not more so, that Faesulae figured prominently in the latter's understanding of the situation. Now, Faesulae (modern Fiesole) lies about 100 kilometers north of Foiano: if Hannibal went by the route under discussion, it cannot be the place where he emerged from the swamps. In consequence, Faltin postulated the existence of a second town of that name, located somewhere in the triangle formed by Siena, Cortona, and Clusium;[22] a less drastic assumption would be that in the tradition common—clearly enough—to both Livy and Polybios in this part of their narratives, Faesulae was mistakenly believed to have stood in central rather than northern Etruria.

---

[20] Faltin offers the most cogently argued case. Diana 109–111 suggested this itinerary in reverse direction; supposedly Hannibal was moving westward through the lower Serchio–Arno marshlands, trying to link up with a Carthaginian fleet at Pisa. How this could have taken Flaminius by surprise at Arezzo remains a mystery.

[21] If Faesulae is the known town of that name, neither the manuscripts' *petens* nor Conway's emendation *praeteriens* make any sense (Walbank *HCP* 1: 414). If Faesulae is thought of as a town (existing or in error) in central Etruria, *petens* could work, if one envisions Hannibal as proceeding from a point farther west, e.g., Siena. But Livy's close agreement with Polybios in this chapter renders it inconceivable that he should have consciously written something to the opposite effect of the latter's ποιησάμενος ἀναζυγὴν ἀπὸ τῶν κατὰ τὴν Φαισόλαν τόπων, "making his departure from the area around Faesulae" (3.82.1); and it seems improbable—though not impossible—that either author misunderstood a common source in a simple matter of "departing from" or "heading towards." Livy should have written essentially the same as Polybios, and an emendation along the lines proposed by Eisen (*Faesulis cedens*) and Jordan (secl. *Faesulas petens*) may be in order; but we cannot rule out an error in his understanding of what he had in front of him. Best, therefore, to obelize.

[22] Faltin 82.

The notion is not as far-fetched as it may seem. On making his inquiries about the country he now was in, Hannibal found that it constituted one of the most fertile parts of Italy: the plains of Etruria, between Faesulae and Arretium, abounding in grain and livestock and everything else (*regio erat in primis Italiae fertilis, Etrusci campi, qui Faesulas inter Arretiumque iacent, frumenti ac pecoris et omnium copia rerum opulenti*, Livy 22.3.3). He found out, by inquiry, essentially the same in Polybios: the country lying ahead of him abounded in resources of all kinds (πυνθανόμενος δὲ τὴν μὲν χώραν τὴν πρόσθεν πολλῆς γέμειν ὠφελείας, 3.80.3). One has some difficulty, indeed, imagining the Arno valley from Fiesole to Arezzo as the Etruscan plains, let alone as the focal area of Tuscan agricultural wealth;[23] yet Livy repeats that image a few sentences later, when he has Hannibal plunder the center of Etruria, in some directional connection to Faesulae (the *crux* at 22.3.6).

In fact, the details of his march, as Polybios reports them, do preclude a route that would have brought Hannibal directly to the triangle Siena–Clusium–Cortona, without passing by Fiesole and Arezzo first. The marshes through which he led his army did not form deep quagmires, but possessed a firm and solid ground covered with shallow water (πᾶς τις . . . ὑφορώμενος βάραθρα καὶ τοὺς λιμνώδεις τῶν τόπων· Ἀννίβας δ' ἐπιμελῶς ἐξητακὼς τεναγώδεις καὶ στερεοὺς ὑπάρχοντας τοὺς κατὰ τὴν δίοδον τόπους κτλ., 3.78.8–79.1): as has been pointed out more than once, this can only mean that he did not pass through continuous natural swamps or marshlands, but through an area subject to temporal or seasonal inundation.[24] Recent hydrological and geomorphological studies have confirmed earlier views that the great swamps—still extant in the eighteenth century—of Bientina and Fucecchio, which Hannibal could not have avoided crossing on a march from Luca to the Val d'Elsa and Siena, would have been utterly impassable; the Padule di Fucecchio in particular in his day formed an actual lake.[25]

Even allowing that somehow Hannibal managed to skirt the deeper waters by staying on the slightly higher ground just east of Fucecchio, he must still—in order to get to Siena—cross the Arno between Fucecchio and Montelupo Fiorentino, where deep flooding appears to have been inevitable. To reach from there a "Faesulae" near Foiano della Chiana would first mean a march of some 130 kilometers up the Val d'Elsa, through dry country: there is no way Polybios could have presented this "Faesulae" as the location where Hannibal emerged from the "swamps," and rested his army. This leaves only the plain between Pistoia and Firenze–Fiesole, littered with individual ponds and swampy patches, and prone to flooding, but not forming a permanent marsh: a route to be avoided at any cost—unless cost was no object.

---

[23] Faltin 82; Kromayer *AS* 3.1: 135 n. 1; but see 132 n. 3.
[24] Fuchs 1904: 123, 127–129; Kromayer *AS* 3.1: 114, 124–127.
[25] Capecchi et al. 142–143 with n. 36, "un vero e proprio lago," cf. 150–159, and Kromayer *AS* 3.1: 112–113.

Nor do Hannibal's movements after emerging from the "swamps" agree with a starting position south of Arretium. On learning of Flaminius' presence at Arretium, he made inquiries about the enemy and about the country that lay ahead (βουλόμενος . . . πολυπραγμονῆσαι τὰ περὶ τοὺς ὑπεναντίους καὶ τοὺς προκειμένους τῶν τόπων, 3.80.2–3): "ahead" evidently in the direction of the enemy at Arretium. He decided to pass beyond the Roman army and move into the region in front of it (παραλλάξαντος αὐτοῦ τὴν ἐκείνων στρατοπεδείαν καὶ καθέντος εἰς τοὺς ἔμπροσθεν τόπους, 3.80.4), in the hope of provoking Flaminius into following him wherever he led (εἰς πάντα τόπον ἑπόμενος) rather than watch the country being ravaged. This accords precisely with an advance from Fiesole southward past Arezzo into the Val di Chiana, and on toward Cortona, Clusium, or Lake Trasumene; it cannot be squared with a move in an easterly direction from Siena or Foiano across the Chiana valley toward Cortona or the lake. Polybios repeats this scenario in his narrative: Hannibal, after setting out from the vicinity of Faesulae (ὡς γὰρ θᾶττον ποιησάμενος ἀναζυγὴν ἀπὸ τῶν κατὰ τὴν Φαισόλαν τόπων), marched a small distance beyond the Roman position at Arretium (καὶ μικρὸν ὑπεράρας τὴν τῶν Ῥωμαίων στρατοπεδείαν), and then launched his attack on the country lying in front (ἐνέβαλεν εἰς τὴν προκειμένην χώραν, 3.82.1): it was not the region between Faesulae and Arretium that was being plundered, but only that on the far side (in Hannibal's direction of march) of Arezzo—in other words, the region between him and Flaminius, the latter now being to his rear. Again, this makes no sense if Hannibal was moving towards Lake Trasumene eastward from a hypothetical "Faesulae" in the triangle between Siena, Cortona, and Clusium; but it completely agrees with a march from Fiesole south past Arretium towards the Val di Chiana.[26] It is clear enough that in Livy's mind, too, the ravaging of the countryside only commenced after Hannibal had bypassed the enemy on his left, which is to say, after Hannibal had advanced beyond Arretium: a virtual absurdity if he was heading east from Foiano, some 35 kilometers slightly west of south from Arezzo. While Livy's source describing Hannibal's position after he emerged from the marshes (22.3.1–5) appears to have imagined, more clearly in fact than visible in Polybios, a Faesulae nearer Foiano, the actual directions given for Hannibal's subsequent advance require, just as in Polybios, that it commenced near Fiesole, the only Faesulae attested.

7.2 Hannibal's Surprise

Thus evaporates the notion that Hannibal took his army through the marches to a point well south of Arretium, and in this way sought to surprise Flaminius (to put it in Polybios'—not Livy's—terms). Which brings us to a second possibility as to how Livy may have understood the situation.

---

[26] Kromayer *AS* 3.1: 110–111.

7.2.1 The Race to Arezzo

Hannibal took the shorter, faster route, through the marshes of the Arno, not because he intended to outwit the Consul at Arretium with his choice of route per se, but because he hoped yet to get there before Flaminius. If he could reach Arretium while the Consul's army was still in transit from Ariminum *per Appennini tramites*, he would find no Roman forces between him and Etruria, or Rome, or the Adriatic coast. Again, the strategic advantage gained would be self-evident. The move, of course, contained an element of uncertainty: rumor, after all, had it that the Consul had arrived already. But rumor was just that, not a confirmed fact; quick action might yet yield the hoped-for result. As we have seen, Polybios' narrative suggests a decision taken in some haste, and without thorough information (other than the particulars of the road) about the character of the country and the opponent Hannibal would be facing there. Moreover, it was the rumor that triggered this decision. In other words, when Hannibal made his initial plans, in early spring 217, for the upcoming campaign, he had not yet decided on a trek across the marshes: a strike into Etruria, quite possibly; but perhaps by a more convenient route. Nor did he expect a Roman army at Arretium—at least not so soon.

Zonaras (8.25) offers an account of the year's opening maneuvers that is apt to compound the puzzle: widely divergent from Polybios and Livy all in all, yet close to the second scenario posed above. At the onset of spring, Hannibal, learning that both the Consuls were marching against him, turned towards deceiving them (Ἀννίβας δ᾽ ἄρτι τοῦ ἔαρος ἐπιστάντος ὡς ἔγνω τὸν Φλαμίνιον μετὰ τοῦ Σερουιλίου Γεμίνου χειρὶ πολλῇ ἐπ᾽ αὐτὸν ἰόντα, πρὸς ἐξαπάτην αὐτῶν ἐτράπη). He put on a show of staying in place and giving the impression that he would join battle (πλαττόμενος ἐνδιατρίψειν ἐκεῖ καὶ μάχην συνάψειν), and the Romans, assuming that he would retain his position, relaxed their watch over the roads (ἐπεὶ νομίσαντες αὐτὸν οἱ Ῥωμαῖοι κατὰ χώραν μένειν ἀμελῶς τῶν ὁδῶν ἔσχον). Leaving his cavalry behind in his camp, he set out during the night, marched quietly through the mountain passes, and hurried towards Arretium (ἐπὶ τοῦ στρατοπέδου τοὺς ἱππέας κατέλιπεν, αὐτὸς δ᾽ ὑπὸ νύκτα ἄρας τά τε στενόπορα μεθ᾽ ἡσυχίας διῆλθε καὶ πρὸς Ἀρίτιον ἠπείγετο); the cavalry eventually followed, after Hannibal had progressed a considerable distance (οἱ ἱππεῖς δέ, ἐπεὶ πολὺ προῆλθεν, ἀπῄεσαν αὐτῷ ἐφεπόμενοι). On realizing that they had been outwitted, the Consuls divided their forces: Servilius remained where he was, in order to retaliate against defectors and prevent them from giving aid to the enemy (οἱ δὲ ὕπατοι γνόντες ἠπατημένοι, Γέμινος μὲν αὐτοῦ ὑπέμεινε τούς δ᾽ ἀφεστηκότας κακώσων καὶ κωλύσων ἐπικουρῆσαι Καρχηδονίοις); Flaminius alone went in pursuit, so that the victory—as he imagined—would be his work alone (Φλαμίνιος δὲ μόνος ἐδίωκεν, ἵν᾽ αὐτοῦ μόνου τὸ ἔργον τῆς νίκης, ὡς ᾤετο, γένηται). He reached Arretium before Hannibal (καὶ τὸ Ἀρίτιον προκατέλαβεν). The latter had taken a more direct route, but run into difficult terrain, and lost many men, animals, and one of his eyes (ὁ γὰρ Ἀννίβας συντομωτέραν τραπόμενος δυσόδοις ἐνέτυχε, καὶ ἀνθρώπους συχνοὺς καὶ πολλὰ ὑποζύγια καὶ τὸν ἕτερον τῶν ὀφθαλμῶν ἀπέβαλεν); thus he arrived late at Arretium, and found Flaminius already there (ὀψὲ δ᾽ οὖν πρὸς τὸ Ἀρίτιον ἐλθών, καὶ εὑρὼν ἐκεῖ τὸν Φλαμίνιον).

Hence Dio, it appears, spelled out what Livy seems to imply, and what apparently lies behind Polybios' surprise: Hannibal made a move to reach Arretium before Flaminius. The context, though, is presented in exact opposition: in Polybios and Livy, Hannibal acts to forestall, if still possible, a move Flaminius is rumored to have made already; in Dio/Zonaras, Flaminius reacts to an unexpected move of Hannibal. And Dio seems to have been explicit about another point that Livy made: Flaminius, like his colleague, launched his campaign in Cisalpine Gaul, which is to say, at Ariminum. This, at least—some with relief will say—Polybios disproves.

Perhaps not. Hannibal waited for several days at Faesulae before moving toward Arretium, a distance of about 70 kilometers, or three days' march, at most four; and Flaminius made no move until Hannibal had advanced past his position (Polyb. 3.80.1–82.7).[27] From Arretium, the invader would need two days, more likely three, to reach Lake Trasumene (38 kilometers to the northwest shore, at Borghetto, but 56 kilometers to the northeast corner, at Torricella/Montecolognola, the most probable site of the battle).[28] The Consul arrived at the lake very late in the day (ὀψὲ τῆς ὥρας, Polyb. 3.83.7; *solis occasu*, Livy 22.4.4), evidently after a forced march that covered the whole distance in a single day.[29]

We have already seen how the historian's actual narrative strongly implies, at a minimum, that Hannibal had no certain information as to whether Flaminius was already at Arretium when he commenced his march across the Appennines, and that he had reason to believe that a surprise could be effected. Given that little more than about two weeks can have elapsed between Hannibal's arrival at Faesulae and the battle at Lake Trasumene on June 22, uncertainty regarding Flaminius' whereabouts is not, of course, impossible, military intelligence being

---

[27] For Hannibal's normal rate of march, see Proctor's sensible discussion, 26–34. In good terrain, without enemy interaction, his army can be expected to have covered *c.*20 kilometers per day, rest days included. In difficult terrain or when encountering hostilities along the march, the rate of speed would drop rapidly, to about 15–18 kilometers per day, or less.

[28] Hannibal reached the lake with plenty of time left in the day to examine the topography of the surroundings, and plan his ambush: Polyb. 3.82.11–83.5. This implies arrival by early afternoon at the latest, and an average progress from Arretium of *c.*19 kilometers per day over two days, if the battle took place on the northwest shore. If the battle was fought along the northeast shore of the lake, between Passignano and Torricella, a journey of three days from Arretium is virtually certain, averaging just under 19 kilometers. On the location of the battle, with ample surveys of the controversy, see Kromayer *AS* 3.1: 163–197 (still decisive); more recently, Walbank *HCP* 1: 415–418; Lazenby 1978: 62–63; Seibert 1993a: 220–222, all in favor of Passignano–Torricella; *contra*, Sadée 54–63; De Sanctis *SdR* 3.2: 110–116; Susini 1956–60 and 1961–4; Schmitt 115–121, 334–335, variously locating the battle in the area between Mt. Gualandro, Sanguineto, and Tuoro.

[29] Thus Kromayer *AS* 3.1: 162; cf. Appian *Hannib.* 9.38, οὐ διαναπαύων τὴν στρατιάν: perhaps from a good source, despite Appian's general inability to understand the strategic moves involved.

sketchy even in good conditions.[30] But it is difficult to understand if Flaminius took his army to Arretium directly from Rome: unless the Consul was moving at a glacial pace, there should have been no doubt about his presence in northern Etruria (a presence Polybios had earlier stated as fact when describing the Roman dispositions for the upcoming campaign, 3.77.1) now, three months after his entrance into office, especially as Hannibal had no difficulty obtaining current information about the condition of the roads leading to the area. Nor is it clear how Hannibal could hope to take Flaminius by surprise, if the latter was still approaching Arretium from the south: all Flaminius had to do was to avoid battle, and wait for Servilius to march his army across the mountains, by the Marecchia valley and the Viamaggio Pass, and the Romans would have Hannibal between their armies. By implication, at the time Hannibal was considering his move, or until shortly before that, both consular armies must have been located north or east of the Appennines, and not in Etruria.

More significant than this, though, the account of Livy. As we have seen, his narrative of Hannibal's movements from setting out towards Etruria to his arrival at Lake Trasumene (22.2.1–4.1) is virtually identical to that of Polybios. The only points of overlap with Zonaras exist in Flaminius' initial presence in Gaul, and the apparent notion that Hannibal's longer and more difficult route constituted an alternative merely to a shorter and easier one leading to the same destination, Etruria, as opposed to Polybios' clear implication that the longer route extended to an altogether different target—Ariminum and points in Italy south of there. But in Zonaras, both Consuls spend considerable time in Gaul, conducting a joint operation in the belief, deliberately stoked by Hannibal, that the enemy had no intention of leaving the Po Valley; then Hannibal and Flaminius engage in a race toward Arretium, each using a different path, with Hannibal making the first move and the Consul hurrying to catch up. In Livy, Flaminius' move to Arretium (21.63.15) occurs soon after he takes command at Ariminum, and without any hint at a previous campaign in Gaul; Servilius is not even mentioned in this context—if anything, one gets the impression that he was still in Rome (22.2.1). There is no race against time and Hannibal to reach Arretium; on the contrary, Flaminius makes the decision to transfer his army completely free of influence by any action on the enemy's part, and even though Hannibal knows of his presence at Arezzo only by way of rumor (22.2.1), it is quite evident that Livy knew, and meant his readers to know, that Flaminius was already there when Hannibal launched his march across the Appennines. It should be obvious that Livy's version of Flaminius' move from Ariminum to Arretium cannot have come from the tradition preserved in Dio and Zonaras. It should be obvious, likewise, that in its essentials Livy's version corresponds to that of Polybios. Hannibal confirms

---

[30] For the date of the battle (June 22 rather than 21), see Konrad *RhM*, forthcoming.

Flaminius' presence at Arretium only after he arrives at Faesulae (3.80.1); since he had hoped to surprise the man, however (3.78.6), he must have had reason to deem such presence probable (in other words, Livy's rumors); and Polybios knew, and meant his readers to know, that the Consul was in fact already there: he earlier had told us so, at 3.77.1. It follows that the story of Flaminius' taking his army from Ariminum to Arretium did not originate with the tradition followed by Dio/Zonaras, but was part of the tradition common to Livy and Polybios.[31]

Polybios concerned himself with matters of grand strategy, and intricacies of battle tactics; he refused to burden his narrative with detail he judged irrelevant to his purpose, and took no interest in the political squabbles going on in Rome— let alone the religious dimensions attaching to them—unless they had an impact on the conduct of the war. (In other words, he tended to ignore the very things that exercise modern historians the most.) That Flaminius took office on March 15 at Ariminum instead of Rome, and his reasons why, were of no consequence for the historian's presentation (and his audience's grasp) of the war with Hannibal; nor was the reshuffling of Roman armies in late winter or early spring from Placentia to Rimini and on to Arretium. What mattered, strategically, was that, when the campaign of the year 217 opened, one Roman army was located at Ariminum, and the other, at Arretium: that is the situation he wants the reader to understand at 3.77. The peculiar circumstances under which Flaminius travelled to Etruria had no effect on the war (except, of course, in the eyes of those who believed in the necessity of auspices—Polybios assuredly not among them); they could, indeed should, be omitted, given the priorities of his narrative.[32] There is no mystery here: if anything calls for explanation, it is the obsessive and obtuse insistence of so many scholars, for so many years, that the silence of Polybios in such a matter proves that what we read in Livy must be false.

7.2.2 The Campaign in Gaul

Again, there is more. Throughout the winter, Hannibal had to deal with discontent among his Gaulish allies, who resented the prolonged waging of the war in their land, and were eager to invade that of their enemies: it was for that reason, Polybios makes clear, that he decided to move on Italy as soon as possible and indulge the desires of his troops (θεωρῶν δὲ τοὺς Κελτοὺς δυσχεραίνοντας ἐπὶ τῷ

---

[31] Given that nothing else in Livy's entire narrative of Hannibal's march agrees with Zonaras, his apparent understanding of the longer and the shorter route as both being limited to ways into Etruria—not to Arretium, in any case—should not be attributed to the tradition behind the latter. More likely, Livy did not fully grasp the difference between the two routes, and in any case the longer route always entailed the option of crossing into Etruria by one of the eastern passes, rather than going all the way to Ariminum and the coast.

[32] Cf. Amat-Seguin 80, 101–102.

τὸν πόλεμον ἐν τῇ παρ' αὐτῶν χώρᾳ λαμβάνειν τὴν τριβήν, σπεύδοντας δὲ καὶ μετεώρους ὄντας εἰς τὴν πολεμίαν . . . ἔκρινε τὴν ταχίστην ἀναζευγνύειν καὶ συνεκπληροῦν τὰς τῶν δυνάμεων ὁρμάς, 3.78.5). Now, surely the Gauls would not expect him to invade Italy in midwinter: but if they had reason to assume that he planned to do so come spring, their mounting anger—enough to cause Hannibal serious fear of assassination, 3.78.2—becomes inexplicable.[33] Evidently, all through the winter he said and did nothing to dispel their concerns about a resumption of warfare in Cisalpine Gaul in the spring. If from his behavior the Gauls derived the impression that he intended to renew the campaign in the Po Valley, so, presumably, would the Romans. Had he indeed planned to fight there initially, or was this from the start an attempt to deceive the Romans into concentrating their forces north of the Appennines while he struck suddenly across the mountains into Etruria?

A campaign in Gaul would leave the Romans with the longer lines of communication, and Hannibal in friendly territory: it could have been an inviting prospect, until the depth of his allies' resentment became clear. Once he decided on invading Italy proper, he may well have continued to pretend otherwise; despite the risks it carried, the deception, if successful, could bring a huge strategic payoff. Viewed in this light, the "surprise" was not merely a matter of getting to Arretium before Flaminius: it was the key move in a scheme designed to make the Romans believe that Hannibal planned to fight the spring campaign—initially at least—in Gaul, most likely intending to push east toward the Adriatic, along the route of the later Via Aemilia. The true attack was to come by way of Etruria, wide open and undefended.

Nor need the Romans be adverse to a renewed campaign in Gaul.[34] They had plenty of experience and success in fighting there, Flaminius in particular (whatever childish interpretation his detractors might be putting on his battle against the Insubres[35]), and a campaign in Gaul possessed the undeniable advantage of keeping the war away from Italy. It had been the Roman strategy in the previous year: they might as well try it again, especially if Hannibal seemed to comply. It is clear that no measures were taken to prepare the defenses of the City until after the Battle at Lake Trasumene.[36] Such complacency is more easily understood if neither the Consuls nor the Senate seriously expected Hannibal to be operating freely on their side of the Appennines, let alone attempt a march on Rome, during the first few months of consular 217.

It appears, then, that Dio/Zonaras, Livy, and Polybios all followed a tradition in which both Consuls opened the campaign of 217 in Cisalpine Gaul, with their

---

[33] Miltner 16–17. [34] Amat-Seguin 96 with n. 36.
[35] Polyb. 2.33.7, cf. Kromayer AS 3.1: 368 n. 1; Walbank HCP 1: 208–209.
[36] Livy 22.8.7; Appian Hannib. 11.48; Zonaras 8.25, explicitly; cf. Polyb. 3.75.4–8 (no mention of defensive measures for the City).

armies based on Ariminum. Yet at some point both Hannibal and Flaminius crossed the Appennines in an attempt to establish a position at Arretium. Who made the first move, that is the question.

Zonaras' account exhibits obvious problems. The stratagem ascribed to Hannibal is reasonable in itself; but it is virtually identical to one employed by the Gauls in Etruria during their great raid of 225 (Polyb. 2.25.2–7): one may wonder if the Romans would have so easily been duped by it so soon again. There is a clear affinity to Polybios: he, too, notes how Hannibal's cavalry came last in the trek across the mountains—but with a different purpose. Instead of tricking the enemy into believing that Hannibal was still in camp, it carried out the more mundane task of bringing up the rear, making sure especially that the Gauls did not indulge in their tendency to straggle (3.79.4). Zonaras further implies that Hannibal and the Roman armies were in close proximity, which would mean that the latter had advanced as far west at least as Bologna (leading to the easternmost pass, the Collina, that the Carthaginian could have taken into the marches of the Arno). Most perplexing, though, is the statement that, when the Consuls realized the ruse, they decided to divide their forces—Servilius staying in Gaul, Flaminius going after Hannibal to gain all the glory for himself. There is implicit criticism of Flaminius' move here, as if Servilius saw no strategic need for his colleague to leave the theater, any more than he did see such a need for himself.

Clearly this cannot be right. The ruse employed by Hannibal could only serve to delay the Romans' realizing where he was headed; it could not cloak his objective—Arretium—altogether. Once his cavalry had left camp, and the Romans found it empty, the tracks made by his army—50,000 men and counting—could not possibly be missed, nor could the pass he took into Etruria remain a mystery for long. Within two days or three, at most, the Roman commanders would have understood that Hannibal was crossing the Appennines to invade Etruria, and by what route. Indeed, nothing in Zonaras hints that they had any doubt as to Hannibal's objective: quite the contrary. With no forces between him and the rest of Italy, it is utterly inconceivable that they would have disagreed about what should be done, let alone divided their forces, with one of them staying behind in Gaul—to discomfort defectors, of all things. Both would have marched toward Arretium by the fastest route available.

Divide their forces, though, they did; the question is when and where. In Polybios and Livy, Hannibal lacks certainty about Flaminius' movements: he might already be at Arretium, or not. The Consul, obviously, was not acting in response to Hannibal's sudden and dramatic disappearance from his camp; yet the latter's uncertainty indicates that Flaminius cannot have been at Arretium for very long before the Carthaginian arrived at Faesulae. Servilius' campaign in Gaul may help. As just noted, it cannot have commenced (as Zonaras would have it) after the Romans realized that Hannibal was on his way across the Appennines, or even close to undertaking such a move. It follows that when Flaminius moved his army to Arezzo, his colleague either had already launched the campaign (unlikely to have ranged far from Ariminum, in any case), or felt that he had time to embark on it before he might be called on to intervene south of the Appennines, should Hannibal make a move in that direction. Zonaras' story about Hannibal outwitting the Consuls cannot be accurate as told.

It might, however, reflect—by accident or spun from a source familiar with Hannibal's initial intentions, such as Sosylos or Silenos—in general terms how Hannibal at first had planned his invasion of Italy proper. The consular armies had wintered in Placentia and Cremona, at no great distance, apparently, from Hannibal's own quarters; just before spring, they were withdrawn to Ariminum.[37] The move would not go unnoticed in his headquarters. Yet clearly Hannibal had no speedy and reliable intelligence about Roman operations beyond that point; he may not have learned of the Consuls' arrival at Ariminum (first Flaminius, then Servilius) for some time. Livy certainly creates the impression (21.63.15 and 22.2.1) that Flaminius departed Ariminum for Etruria soon after he assumed command, while his colleague was still in Rome, conducting levies. It appears improbable, though, that Flaminius should have left Ariminum exposed: he did not know yet, after all, whether Hannibal would make for Etruria or the Adriatic coast. Conditions on the ground being what they were, the Consul need not worry (not until summer, and drier times) about any route into Etruria west of the Futa Pass. As long as Hannibal did not approach the area of Bologna or beyond, Etruria was safe; and from Ariminum, Flaminius could transfer his forces to Arretium (c.105 kilometers) in a week or less (if pressed for time) by the Pass of Viamaggio. From Bologna to Arezzo by the Futa route would be more than half as far again. As long as he kept a close watch over the routes leading to the eastern passes between Bologna and Ariminum (c.110 kilometers), Flaminius ought to be able to anticipate a hostile turn towards Etruria. Such surveillance would not be feasible from a position at Arretium, the mountains impeding prompt communication: the news that Hannibal was coming across the Appennines, or approaching Ariminum, might not by much precede his arrival. (That same obstacle, of course, attaches to the popular scenario that has Flaminius go to Arretium directly from Rome, while Servilius remained in the City— Ariminum unprotected, and the only commander in the field left without reliable means of knowing what was happening in Gaul.)

Once Servilius had brought his new levies to Ariminum, Flaminius would be free to move his army to Arretium. The task of keeping Hannibal under observation would fall to Servilius, naturally. If the Carthaginian took one of the passes east of Bologna towards Etruria (all except the Mandrioli leading to Faesulae), Servilius should have sufficient notice to take his army to Arretium by the

---

[37] Livy 21.56.9, 63.1; Appian *Hannib.* 7.30; see below, Subsection 7.5.1.

Viamaggio Pass, and link up with Flaminius before Hannibal could put distance enough between himself and the Roman armies to make an attack on Rome feasible. If Hannibal kept pushing east instead, Servilius should be able to hold him off at Ariminum until Flaminius arrived there. Indeed, Servilius' entire campaign in Gaul may have been tied to the attempt to keep an eye on Hannibal's movements.

At what point Hannibal realized the nature of those Roman dispositions we cannot tell. But he would have had reason to believe that for some time in the spring, a month at least past March 15, no Roman army would be covering Arretium, and that at some point both Consuls would be at Ariminum, if only perhaps briefly. If he marched east past Bologna and, say, Faenza, the Romans very likely would conclude that he was going to force the issue at Ariminum, and hold both armies there. Then, at the last opportunity, near Forlì he could suddenly turn south across the Appennines, either by the Passo del Muraglione to Fiesole/Pontassieve, or by the Mandrioli Pass directly to Arezzo. If he could hide his change of direction for a day or two, by a stratagem such as in Zonaras, he would gain enough of a head start to make it to Arretium before the Romans could get there from Ariminum, the distance from Forlì via the Mandrioli Pass being only marginally farther. When rumors reached him that Flaminius had taken his army to Arretium, indicating that such a move was at least held in contemplation, the scheme unraveled; he now must go against Ariminum, or risk a march through the swamps—the only chance left to take his adversaries by surprise.

It will not do. If Hannibal was aiming at one of the eastern passes with the elaborate feint envisaged here, it surely was because he knew that any route farther west would be impassable at the Etruscan end. That means that he had made his inquiries about what routes availed before he formed this hypothetical initial plan, and before he was compelled to abandon it when Flaminius was reported to be moving to Arretium. Which means in turn that he already knew, almost certainly, that the stretch from Pistoriae to Faesulae, while under water, could be traversed in principle, if at enormous pain and cost. If so, why not take this chance immediately, without the long detour across Emilia-Romagna, and gain access to Etruria unopposed for certain, while all the Roman forces were still at Ariminum? The deception necessary at Forlì (or thereabouts) might fail: in weighing its risk against that of a march through the swamps, the latter easily might seem preferable.

Nor was he likely to gain much of a strategic advantage by that deception, if it worked. Both Roman armies would be in Etruria within two days or three after his own arrival: too short a time for him to march on Rome. Just like the Gauls in 225 had abandoned that idea when confronted first by the Praetor's army, then the Consul's (having come in haste down from Ariminum),[38] Hannibal would

---

[38] Polyb. 2.25.1–26.7.

lack the time to reduce the City by siege before relief arrived; nor could he hope to seize it by surprise. He might be able to ravage Etruria and Umbria, and cross the Appennines toward the Adriatic, while keeping the consular armies at arm's length; but the slightest unforeseen obstacle or misstep might bring them within range, and force a battle—not necessarily in a location and under circumstances of Hannibal's choosing, nor in his favor.

It follows that Zonaras' (hence, presumably, Dio's) version of Hannibal's "surprise" reflects neither the actual events nor any previous but unrealized plans on Hannibal's part. The version of Polybios and Livy is surely correct: Flaminius took up his position at Arretium before Hannibal made his move, and Hannibal's decision was based on, or at least influenced by, the rumor that Flaminius had already got there. But when he reached Etruria, Hannibal found a Roman army waiting for him at Arretium, just as rumor had alleged. Clearly, such news, however unwelcome, was not wholly unexpected; and nothing indicates that Hannibal considered his grueling march, his attempt to take Flaminius unawares, a failure. Which leads to a third possibility as to the strategic advantage he had sought to gain.

7.2.3 Flaminius at Arretium

During the early part of spring, Hannibal had the choice of essentially two routes into Roman Italy: the longer, easier, and obvious one through Emilia-Romagna, and the shorter, difficult, and unsuspected one into Etruria through the inundations and marshes of the middle Arno. Ariminum was guarded by a consular army, eventually—briefly—by both; he could cross into Etruria by one of the eastern Appennine passes, but the Romans would keep the area east of Bologna under close observation, and be able to follow him speedily enough to prevent free-ranging operations once in Italy, let alone an attack on Rome. (Advancing against him from Ariminum, they might even force a battle while he was still in Gaul.) The way through the marshes, if launched from a point well to the west of the Roman range of observation, offered the chance of entering Etruria without advance warning: word of his arrival, rather than of his departure, would first have to travel to Ariminum before countermeasures could be taken. Risky though the route might be, it would furnish Hannibal, once in Italy, the freedom of operation that he sought.

Ideally, then, he would attempt to make his way along the shorter but difficult route before the Romans redeployed one of their armies to Etruria. (That they would do so as soon as they had assembled sufficient forces to cover both Ariminum and Arretium he may have expected.) The weather, though, could render this impossible: spring might be blossoming in the plains of the Po while winter still ruled the heights of the Appennines. The five passes that would serve his purpose, from the Brattello to the Abetone, are among the tallest of the

Appennines, covered in snow often well into May.[39] To invade Etruria without alerting the enemy, he would have to wait.

On hearing reports that Flaminius was already at Arretium, Hannibal realized that the moment for this might have passed. Yet Flaminius' move to Arretium, once confirmed upon Hannibal's arrival at Faesulae, also offered an opportunity, albeit fraught with uncertainty and risk. As long as both Consuls were at Ariminum, Hannibal had to assume that they together would move against him, be it in Gaul if he chose to advance across Emilia-Romagna, or in Etruria once they learned of his arrival there. With word of Flaminius' redeployment, Hannibal now must choose whether to try to get past the latter in Etruria, or past Servilius at Ariminum; but either way, he might be able to confront his opponent before the Roman armies could unite. If he marched down the later Via Aemilia towards the Adriatic coast, his objective would become evident very soon, and word of his advance might reach Flaminius, directly or via his colleague, from patrols watching the eastern passes along the north slope of the Appennines, in time to redeploy his army, by the Viamaggio Pass, to Ariminum before Hannibal was able to overpower Servilius. The route across the marshes, unexpected and unobserved, might allow him to prevent the Roman commanders from correctly predicting his move and joining forces in time to confront him together. If Hannibal made for Etruria from a point much farther west, outside the area of Roman reconnaissance coverage (which will have extended as far as Bologna, or even Modena[40]), he stood a good chance of arriving there before the enemy realized his intention; Flaminius might not find out about it until a day or two after Hannibal had reached Faesulae, and Servilius not until his colleague notified him.

All of this renders the two westernmost routes most probable: either from Parma—far enough from Mutina and Bologna to elude Roman observation—via the Cisa or the Brattello, or directly from the vicinity of Ticinum and Clastidium (following Banti) across the Pass of Brattello. Both led to Luca, hence along the foothills to Pistoriae. Again, the route he chose was shorter and more difficult, not in comparison with an alternative leading to the same destination (as Livy might imply, and Zonaras certainly does[41]), but with an alternative leading to the other Roman army.

---

[39] See Kromayer *AS* 3.1: 120–121. The Brattello Pass lies at 953 meters above sea level, La Cisa at 1041, the Cerreto at 1261, the Foce delle Radici at 1528, and the Abetone at 1388 meters. (Admittedly, the latter two seem the least probable.)

[40] Mutina had been fortified and in Roman hands in 218: Polyb. 3.40.8–14; Livy 21.25.2–26.2; but the failed attempt to relieve it when under attack by the Gauls renders it doubtful that its garrison was retained through the winter. Cf. Banti 117, stressing Hannibal's absolute need to keep his movements unobserved in order to achieve the desired surprise.

[41] Starting from winter quarters in the region of Pavia and Placentia, both routes were in fact shorter than a march down Emilia-Romagna to Bologna and across the Collina Pass, as Banti 114–119 notes.

It was not, then, Hannibal's appearance in the vicinity of Faesulae that surprised Flaminius; the Consul would have expected him to appear precisely there, from all but one (the Mandrioli) of the eastern passes across the Appennines. The surprise lay in the lack of any advance warning, not only to Flaminius but, more importantly, to his colleague at Ariminum: the Roman strategy had counted on both Consuls being alerted to any attempt at crossing by one of the eastern passes, and on Servilius' being able to link up with Flaminius in the time it would take Hannibal to reach Arretium. Instead, Flaminius now must send word to Ariminum, and wait for his colleague's response and eventual arrival—or face Hannibal alone.

That, surely, must be what Hannibal had hoped to achieve with his surprise, when he learned that Flaminius might already be at Arretium. Once the Consul's presence was confirmed, there no longer existed an opportunity of slipping into Etruria while both consular armies were on the wrong side of the Appennines. But if Hannibal could inflict a defeat on Flaminius before Servilius arrived from Gaul, he would enjoy considerable freedom of operation throughout central Italy—long enough to march his army across Umbria to the Adriatic, and on to the South, to implement his Italian strategy.[42] (Depending on the exact circumstances, eliminating Flaminius' force might even allow him an attack on Rome.) But if he failed in this, his situation could deteriorate quickly; sooner rather than later, it would become necessary to fight both Roman armies together. At the Trebia, he had won such an encounter; the new commanders might prove more dangerous, and circumstances, less advantageous. Hence his immediate inquiries: not merely into the nature of the country or the size and composition of the forces opposing him, but into the character of the man who held command. For to achieve his purpose, and gain the strategic advantage sought at such cost and trouble, Hannibal must find a way to make Flaminius abandon his position at Arretium, and engage in battle before his colleague could arrive. A prudent commander would not easily be thus compelled.

7.3 Going after Hannibal

One might think that Flaminius, bursting with self-confidence and hungry for glory, would have loved nothing better than to comply with Hannibal's designs; but once reported fact is stripped of commentary (Polybios' or Livy's, both evidently following the same general tradition), it becomes clear, abundantly, that such action was far from the Consul's mind. He made no move against Hannibal in the days the latter rested his army near Faesulae, nor to oppose him on his march south. After crossing the latitude of Arretium (we do not know how closely

---

[42] As Kromayer pointed out, *AS* 3.1: 138–139.

he approached the town), Hannibal upped the pressure by laying waste to the countryside, aiming to draw out Flaminius, and thus delay the link-up with Servilius, who about this time would have received his colleague's first report. From Arretium to Lake Trasumene and his ambush position (an opportunity that offered unexpectedly[43]), Hannibal would need at least two days, most likely three; yet Flaminius covered the distance in a single day's forced march, reaching the lake late in the evening. Evidently, he did not set out as soon as the reports of Punic depredations started coming in, but held still for another day at least, probably two.[44]

From Polybios it follows that Flaminius had notified Servilius of the enemy's presence in Etruria as soon as he found out, while Hannibal was still encamped at Faesulae (Σερουίλιος . . . ἀκούσας εἰσβεβληκότα τὸν Ἀννίβαν εἰς Τυρρηνίαν ἀντιστρατοπεδεύειν τῷ Φλαμινίῳ, 3.86.1–3).[45] The Consul's subsequent holding in position at Arretium implies of necessity a decision (reached graciously or grudgingly, it does not matter) to wait for his colleague's arrival, or at least, response: it would be natural, indeed crucial, for Servilius to let Flaminius know when to expect him—and where. For Servilius was not coming, from Ariminum by the Pass of Viamaggio, to Arretium: he chose to take the Via Flaminia instead. The choice profoundly altered the strategic situation.

As long as Flaminius could expect his colleague to come straight to Arezzo (as initial plans presumably had called for), he obviously must wait; their armies then together would follow Hannibal to whatever point he would have reached. Even if the Roman armies were a week or so behind, the Carthaginian could not risk an attempt on Rome, and would eventually be forced to face them both. But now Servilius was coming by Flaminius' great road: to suggest that the best course of action remained to sit still at Arretium and wait for Servilius to turn off the highway at Forum Flaminii, swing westward by Perusia and the Lake, and north again towards Arezzo for the link-up, with Hannibal all the while loose in central Italy, unfettered, unhampered, and perhaps unobserved—such would be plain idiocy. Coming down the Via Flaminia, Servilius' advance would intersect with Hannibal's somewhere between Forum Flaminii and Rome, depending on the latter's movements and direction: the logical, indeed self-evident, course for

---

[43] From Polybios 3.82.11, it is clear that Hannibal did not head for the lake with ambush on his mind; it simply was the most direct route towards Perusia and farther east. Only while marching past the lake's northern shore did he realize the suitability of its terrain for such an attempt. Initially, he no doubt had hoped to bring Flaminius to battle somewhere between Perusia and the Via Flaminia.

[44] Pol. 3.83.7, ὀψὲ τῆς ὥρας; Livy 22.4.4, solis occasu; cf. above, notes 23 and 24. When read with care, Polybios himself suggests such a delay: first, reports come that Hannibal had now advanced south of Arretium (3.82.1), to which Flaminius reacts with anger at being slighted—but evidently without taking further action (3.82.2); later on (μετὰ δὲ ταῦτα), when Hannibal ravages the countryside, his anger mounts: only now does he judge the situation intolerable (ἐσχετλίαζε δεινὸν ἡγούμενος τὸ γινόμενον, 3.82.3). The council of war follows (3.82.4–6): clearly not all on the same day.

[45] De Sanctis SdR 3.2: 38; Seibert 1993b: 151 n. 72.

Flaminius to take was to move in a southeasterly direction from Arezzo toward the great road, and join his colleague as close to Hannibal's position as was feasible. With any luck, they might be able to pin the enemy between their armies, and force him to fight on two fronts at once, as they had done to the Gauls at Telamon in 225. Regardless of the outcome of such a pincer attempt (if that indeed was the idea), it would be pointless for Flaminius to stay at Arretium once he learned of Servilius' decision; on the contrary, it was now crucial that he remain in contact with Hannibal—without, of course, allowing himself to be drawn into a fight.[46]

What prompted the Consul's decision to go after Hannibal, then, was not so much the devastation inflicted by the enemy, but word from Servilius that he would take the Via Flaminia. Whether this choice of route was Servilius' alone, or had been discussed by both of them as a contingency before, or was suggested to Servilius by Flaminius along with his report of Hannibal's arrival in Etruria, we cannot say. What we can say with confidence is that the debate in Flaminius' general staff at Arretium did not unfold quite as portrayed in Polybios (3.82.4–6) and Livy (22.3.7–10, clearly from the same tradition). If the Consul's officers advised him to hold at Arretium before they learned of Servilius' response, it cannot have amounted to a difference of opinion, since Flaminius was doing so anyway; if they persisted in staying put after hearing from Servilius, such advice was neither cautious nor prudent, but that of imbeciles. (This would not, naturally, keep Flaminius' haters in Rome from praising it as sage and salutary, after the catastrophe.) In all likelihood, none of the officers ever argued thus, although those who survived Lake Trasumene no doubt found it beneficial to pretend they did.

Yet it is possible that Flaminius, once notified of Servilius' plans, decided that to merely shadow Hannibal was not enough, and that the devastation visited upon the countryside called for immediate and full-fledged confrontation: in other words, he now—but only now—chose not to wait for the eventual link-up with his colleague at some point farther east, but to challenge Hannibal alone. If so, the disagreement in the council of war would not have been over whether to remain at Arretium (as both Polybios and Livy very much aver: αὐτῶν δὲ κατόπιν τῶν πολεμίων ἐν Τυρρηνίᾳ στρατοπεδευόντων, 3.82.6; *immo Arreti ante moenia sedeamus*, 22.3.10), but whether to merely follow Hannibal, or follow him and force a fight. On the morning of June 22, Flaminius certainly expected to make contact with the enemy later in the day (εὐθέως ἐπὶ τὴν ἑωθινὴν ἦγε ... βουλόμενος ἐξάπτασθαι τῶν πολεμίων, Polyb. 3.83.7); whether he meant to fight a battle once he caught up, we probably will never know.[47] But the evident misrepresentation of the debate among his general staff already in the earliest Roman tradition, when an accurate report should have posed no obstacle, suggests that there was

---

[46] Kromayer *AS* 3.1: 140–141; De Sanctis *SdR* 3.2: 38–39.
[47] Cf. Sadée 52–55. De Sanctis *SdR* 3.2: 38 believes that Flaminius had no intention to fight before being able to join forces with his colleague; see also Scullard's sober assessment, 1951: 45.

never any serious disagreement: either the Consul's officers agreed that they should take on Hannibal alone, or Flaminius made it clear (to everyone's relief) that for now he would merely shadow the enemy, but decline battle. On balance, the latter seems more probable.

There may have been, however, a difference of opinion on a tactical issue: just how closely should they follow Hannibal? Clearly the Consul intended to shadow the enemy aggressively, with the entire army, at a distance of no more than a few hours' march, and not merely because of his personal temperament. Close quarters would make it more difficult for Hannibal's troops to linger while ravaging the country, and Flaminius had every reason to believe that Hannibal was unaware of Servilius' pending approach down the Via Flaminia: he would want to make sure to push the Carthaginian towards his colleague's army, and deny him the opportunity of slipping away at the last moment. At the same time, he would want to slow down Hannibal as much as possible, to give Servilius time enough to appear on the scene before Hannibal was able to cross the Via Flaminia, and the Appennines again, towards the Adriatic. (By now, Flaminius will have had no doubts about the enemy's objective: it was not Rome, at any rate.)[48] Many of his officers may have judged such an approach too close for comfort, as it could afford the enemy an opportunity to suddenly turn and attack, should he come upon a suitable location, especially in view of his vast superiority in cavalry;[49] and they could make a reasonable case that the countryside could be more effectively protected by detaching cavalry and light infantry (Livy 22.3.9), while keeping the bulk of the army a day or two from Hannibal, to avoid any unpleasant surprises. (That argument alone disproves that Flaminius' officers wanted to stay put at Arretium: the mobile forces would soon have reached the limits of their effective range as Hannibal moved south or east.)

7.4 *Ostenta Flaminiana*

Yet did not Flaminius ignore the Chickens, and the standards stuck to the ground, and sundry other signs of evil presage? No doubt he did; but none of them need prove that he intended to do battle on that day.

7.4.1 The Signs

Four negative signs are reported to have been sent to him before the catastrophe.[50] On the day he took office at Ariminum, he offered sacrifice; instead of going

---

[48] Cf. Kromayer *AS* 3.1: 140–141.   [49] Polyb. 3.82.4; cf. De Sanctis *SdR* 3.2: 39.
[50] See Konrad 2004: 170–181 for a more extensive discussion of the *Flaminiana ostenta* (where that phrase, from Cic. *Div.* 2.67, is mistakenly attributed to Valeton) and their augural implications.

willingly, a calf, already stricken, broke free and splattered the bystanders with blood (*paucos post dies magistratum iniit, immolantique ei vitulus iam ictus e manibus sacrificantium sese cum proripuisset, multos circumstantes cruore respersit*, Livy 21.63.13). Next, as the Consul led his army out of camp at Arretium, his horse bucked and threw him headlong to the ground, right in front of the image of Iuppiter Stator.[51] Then it was reported to him that the *pulli* would not eat; and, finally, that one of the standards appeared fixed in the ground and could not be raised.

The last three pose an intriguing question. On which day did they occur—that of setting out from Arretium, or that of the battle? Cicero alone, in an account generally agreed to derive from Coelius Antipater,[52] records the Consul's fall off his horse, the Chickens, and the standard, in that order (*Div.* 1.77–78):

> Quid? bello Punico secundo nonne C. Flaminius consul iterum neglexit signa rerum futurarum magna cum clade rei publicae? qui exercitu lustrato cum Arretium versus castra movisset et contra Hannibalem legiones duceret et ipse et equus eius ante signum Iovis Statoris sine causa repente concidit nec eam rem habuit religioni obiecto signo, ut peritis videbatur, ne committeret proelium. idem cum tripudio auspicaretur pullarius diem proelii committendi differebat. tum Flaminius ex eo quaesivit si ne postea quidem pulli pascerentur quid faciendum censeret. cum ille quiescendum respondisset, Flaminius: 'praeclara vero auspicia, si esurientibus pullis res geri poterit, saturis nihil geretur!' itaque signa convelli et se sequi iussit. quo tempore cum signifer primi hastati signum non posset movere loco nec quicquam proficeretur plures cum accederent, Flaminius re nuntiata suo more neglexit. itaque tribus iis horis concisus exercitus atque ipse interfectus est. (78) Magnum illud etiam, quod addidit Coelius, eo tempore ipso cum hoc calamitosum proelium fieret tantos terrae motus in Liguria, Gallia, compluribus insulis totaque in Italia factos esse ut multa oppida conruerint, multis locis labes factae sint terraeque desederint, fluminaque in contrarias partes fluxerint atque in amnes mare influxerit.

"What? In the Second Punic War, did not C. Flaminius, Consul for the second time, ignore the signs of things to come, with great disaster for the Republic? When, with the army purified, he had moved his camp to Arretium and was leading his legions against Hannibal, both he and his horse suddenly fell down,

---

[51] Cic. *Div.* 1.77; Livy 22.3.11; Val. Max. 1.6.6; Plut. *Fab.* 3.1. "The ominous significance of falling before the statue of the god who stays the rout is obvious" (Pease 226).

[52] Coelius HRR F 20/FRHist 15 F 14b; cf. Cic. *ND* 2.8 (HRR F 19/FRHist 15 F 14a), *C. Flaminium Coelius religione neglecta cecidisse apud Trasumennum scribit cum magno rei publicae vulnere.* Livy 22.3.11–13 and Valerius Maximus 1.6.6. omit the *pulli*. Ovid *Fasti* 6.763–768 and Silius Italicus 5.54–62, 66 omit the Consul's fall, but allude to the Chickens and the standards (Ovid in reverse order); in between, Silius inserts the bloody sacrifice gone wrong (5.63–65). Plutarch *Fab.* 3.1 only mentions Flaminius getting thrown off his horse, Florus 1.22.14 and Servius auctus *ad Aen.* 11.19 only standards refusing to budge.

without cause, in front of the image of Iuppiter Stator, he did not deem this event a religious impediment—notwithstanding the sign put in his way, in the view of the experts—against engaging in battle. Likewise, when he was auspicating by means of the *tripudium*, his *pullarius* told him to postpone the day of commencing battle. Then Flaminius asked him what he thought should be done if even later on the Chickens would not eat. When the *pullarius* said that no move was to be made, Flaminius retorted: 'Splendid auspices indeed, if war may be waged when chickens are hungry, but nothing will happen when they're well-fed!' And so he ordered the standards to be raised and to follow his lead. At that point, when the standard-bearer of the first *Hastati* maniple was unable to move his standard from its place, and no headway was made when several others came to help, Flaminius on receiving the report ignored it in his customary manner. And so in those three hours, his army was cut to pieces, and he himself was killed. (78) Of great significance also is that which Coelius added, namely, that at the very time when this disastrous battle was happening, there took place such enormous earthquakes in Liguria, Gaul, quite a number of islands, and all over Italy: in consequence, many towns were toppled down; in many locations, landslides occurred and sinkholes opened up; rivers flowed in their opposite direction, and the sea surged back into the rivers."

7.4.2 The Fall off the Horse

First, the horse. Livy places this indubitably at Arretium: as he has Flaminius put it, "Hannibal ... *ad Romana moenia perveniat, nec ante nos hinc moverimus quam, sicut olim Camillum ab Veiis, C. Flaminium ab Arretio patres acciverint." haec simul increpans cum ocius signa convelli iuberet et ipse in equum insiluisset, equus repente corruit consulemque lapsum super caput effudit* (22.3.10–11). Plutarch, on the other hand, creates the impression that the fall occurred at Rome: Fabius Maximus cautions against an aggressive strategy—a warning obviously issued in Rome—for dealing with Hannibal (*Fab.* 2.4), but Flaminius is not persuaded; declaring himself unwilling to let the war reach Rome and fight in the City, like once upon a time Camillus, for its survival, he orders his Tribunes to lead out the army, and is thrown off his horse (οὐ μὴν ἔπεισε τὸν Φλαμίνιον, ἀλλὰ φήσας οὐκ ἀνέξεσθαι προσιόντα τῇ Ῥώμῃ τὸν πόλεμον οὐδ' ὥσπερ ὁ παλαιὸς Κάμιλλος ἐν τῇ πόλει διαμαχεῖσθαι περὶ αὐτῆς, τὸν μὲν στρατὸν ἐξάγειν ἐκέλευσε τοὺς χιλιάρχους, αὐτὸς δ' ἐπὶ τὸν ἵππον ἁλάμενος, ἐξ οὐδενὸς αἰτίου προδήλου παραλόγως ἐντρόμου τοῦ ἵππου γενομένου καὶ πτυρέντος, ἐξέπεσε καὶ κατενεχθεὶς ἐπὶ κεφαλήν, Fab. 3.1). It changes nothing in the Consul's determination; the next thing he does is arrange his army in battle order at Lake Trasumene (ὅμως οὐδὲν ἔτρεψε τῆς γνώμης, ἀλλ' ὡς ὥρμησεν ἐξ ἀρχῆς ἀπαντῆσαι τῷ Ἀννίβᾳ, περὶ τὴν καλουμένην Θρασυνίαν λίμνην τῆς Τυρρηνίας παρετάξατο).

Now, Schmitt argued that Rome was in fact the place where Flaminius took his tumble, and that this version—contained in a source common to Coelius/Cicero and Plutarch, but accurately reported solely by the biographer—represents the earliest tradition of the event.[53] Doubting that an image of Iuppiter Stator could be found in a Roman army camp, he insists that the Consul's fall must have occurred in front of the god's temple in Rome, near the Porta Mugonia. That will not do. The temple just north of the Palatine, possibly on the site of the Neronian Atrium Vestae, but at any event between the hill and the Basilica of Maxentius, was located deep inside the *pomerium*: an utterly improbable point of departure for a Consul setting out to war *paludatus*—a pageant that, in turn, surely did not involve (except in the movies) mounting a horse; and the event would have been impossible for the army (in the Campus Martius) to witness.[54] (Nor does *ante signum Iovis* suggest a fall in front of a temple: the cult image would hardly have been visible from there.) And lastly, Cicero alone specifies that the fall happened in front of that statue; and he clearly places it at Arretium: *qui exercitu lustrato cum Arretium versus castra movisset et contra Hannibalem legiones duceret... et ante signum Iovis Statoris... repente concidit* leaves no doubt that Flaminius had already deployed his army to Arretium (*movisset*) and was now leading (*duceret*) it against Hannibal when he fell (*concidit*).[55]

It is obvious that Plutarch here, as so often, compresses and connects material disparate in time and substance.[56] The sole item in his narrative that can be tied to Rome in terms of location is Fabius' warning: an anachronistic anticipation of his eventual strategy, hence clearly fictitious. As for the rest, the parallel with Livy's and Cicero's accounts is unmistakable; any notion that Plutarch was working from a source that actually placed the fall at Rome, untenable.

7.4.3 The Chickens and the Standard

This first incident is specifically placed at Arretium, if unambiguously so alone by Cicero and Livy. The Chickens and the standard, in principle, could have signalled trouble either there or on the following day. But the Consul's altercation with his *pullarius* leaves no doubt that Cicero (hence, presumably, Coelius) envisaged the Chickens to have been uncooperative immediately before the battle,

---

[53] Schmitt 104–106.
[54] See Wiseman 2017 on the topography. The second temple of Iuppiter Stator, in the Circus Flaminius next to that of Iuno Regina (now both enclosed within the Porticus Octaviae), would be suitably located; but we know that its cult image was created by Polykles and Dionysios Sons of Timarchides (Pliny *NH* 36.35), hence not before the mid-second century: L. Richardson 1992: 225; cf. C. Robert "Dionysios (161)" *RE* 5.1 (1907) 1000–1001; G. Lippold "Polykles (10)" *RE* 21.2 (1952) 1725; G. Lippold "Timarchides (4)" *RE* 6A.1 (1936) 1233–1234.
[55] As Schmitt 105 acknowledges.
[56] On this aspect of his method, see Pelling 1980: 127–130.

which is to say, on the day after the departure from Arretium—the day of the battle. The omen of the immovable standard, in turn, immediately follows (*itaque signa convelli . . . iussit*) the one of the Chickens, as one would expect in any case. (The commander would not give the order to raise the standards and march out against the enemy until he had auspicated *ex tripudio*.)

But did the auspication happen at all? Livy does not mention it: a notable omission, given his usual interest in such matters. His narrative shows signs that he recast his material here to quite an extent. Encountering opposition from his general staff, Flaminius angrily rushes out of the meeting and gives the signal both for getting under way, and for battle: *iratus se ex consilio proripuit signumque simul itineris pugnaeque cum <proposuisset, "Quin> immo Arreti ante moenia sedeamus" inquit* (22.3.9–10). Taken literally, a signal for battle on this occasion appears highly implausible: he had a long day's march ahead of him before he could even hope to close with Hannibal, and surely he did not aim on commencing battle as the sun was setting. Next, he orders the standards to be raised, and jumps on his horse, which promptly throws him on his head (22.3.11). While the bystanders are struggling to absorb the shock of such an evil omen, report comes that a standard will not budge: *territis omnibus, qui circa erant, velut foedo omine incipiendae rei insuper nuntiatur signum omni vi moliente signifero convelli nequire*. The Consul orders it dug out (22.3.12–13). All this, of course, is taking place at Arretium—the day before the battle.

That time frame, however, renders the sequence of events improbable. We may envisage, certainly, the Consul mounting his charger after issuing the order to raise the standards; but one has difficulty believing that if both omens occurred on the same day, Iuppiter would first knock him off his horse, and only then alert him to the recalcitrant standard. That the latter constituted an (oblative) augural sign is well attested; in consequence, the *vinculum temporis* would make it desirable to keep the omen and its report closely tied to the Consul's order, and cause his horse to throw him only after he had disobeyed the first warning.[57] Hence Livy here rearranged what happened, no doubt in the interest of dramatic effect, creating a shift from the ludicrous toward the ominous.[58]

His omission of the Chickens similarly can be explained on literary grounds. Between the vivid portrait of Flaminius jumping up onto his mount, only to find himself prostrate on the ground a moment later, and the command—contemptuous of auspices, and foreboding disaster—to dig up the standard, the *pulli* might

---

[57] Serv. ad Aen. 11.19: *vellere signa adnuerint superi: ne in mora sitis, cum captatis auguriis ad bellum exire coepimus. "vellere" autem proprie dixit, quia Romani signa figebantur in castris, et cum ad bellum eundum fuisset, captatis auguriis avellebantur e terra . . . sed inter auguria etiam hoc habebatur, si avellentem facile sequerentur, adeo ut cum filio in Orodis bello sit Crassus occisus, qui iturus ad proelium avellere signa vix potuit*. Servius auctus: *quod etiam Flaminio contigit, qui cum imperasset signa tolli eaque non possent moveri, effoso solo in quo erant fixa, vi magna extrahi praecepit, et infeliciter apud Trasimenum pugnavit*. Cf. Konrad 2004; on the *vinculum temporis*, Chapter 2.2.2.

[58] Cf. Hall 34–36; Levene 1993: 41–42; 2010: 134–135.

be deemed distractive: one omen too many, perhaps, for Livy's purpose. The shift in location, too—from Lake Trasumene, on the morning of the battle, as in Coelius, to Arretium on the day before—may be attributed to a desire to create a scene of dramatic unity and concentration, focussing Flaminius' recklessness into a single moment.

One wonders, though. There is reason to believe that the standard refusing to budge posed more than a general warning of impending doom: it was an oblative sign that conveyed a specific alert to the effect that the commander's auspices were invalid, or *incerta*.[59] As such, it need not occur in connection with the *auspicium pullarium*; Iuppiter could send it on any occasion on which the Consul's action in progress raised the question of whether he had valid auspices—as he was taking office in the wrong place, Ariminum; as he led his army out against the enemy at Arretium; on the morning of the eventual encounter; and on any number of other opportunities in between. And when Cicero—this time, Marcus in his own voice, the Augur albeit unbeliever, not his credulous brother—returns to the warnings issued to Flaminius, the Chickens, just as in Livy, are notably absent: *atque etiam a te Flaminiana ostenta collecta sunt: quod ipse et equus eius repente conciderit; non sane mirabile hoc quidem! quod evelli primi hastati signum non potuerit; timide fortasse signifer evellebat quod fidenter infixerat* (*Div*. 2.67). Now this is odd: what to us, at first glance, would appear to mark the most egregious example of the Consul's dismissing a prohibitive sign is passed over—by an Augur, no less—in silence.

7.4.4 Auspices Valid and Invalid

The Consul must enter office in Rome, because only there could he obtain his initial auspices, on which depended all his subsequent ones, including any obtained on campaign, having set out from the City *paludatus*, in observance of all prescribed ritual for going to war; if he failed to do so, he lacked—valid—auspices: which is to say, he had no auspices at all.[60] "Valid" (or as the Romans would put it, *habere auspicia*), to be clear, refers to impetrative auspices alone: an oblative sign always carried its full force, and did not depend on whether its recipient

---

[59] Konrad 2004.

[60] Livy 22.1.5–7, *quod enim illi iustum imperium, quod auspicium esse? magistratus id a domo, publicis privatisque penatibus, Latinis feriis actis, sacrificio in monte perfecto, votis rite in Capitolio nuncupatis secum ferre; nec privatum auspicia sequi, nec sine auspiciis profectum in externo ea solo nova atque integra concipere posse*. The view expounded here need not have been unanimously espoused by all the Augurs; but it agrees with our entire body of knowledge about the *ius augurale*, and not a shred of evidence permits us to suggest that it was located on the fringes of augural theory. In most instances, of course, the lack of valid auspices would be due not to a willful failure to obtain them, but to the Consuls' being *vitio creati*, i.e., to a flaw—not immediately discovered—in the auspices that governed their election. For a fuller discussion, Konrad 2004: 172–178; and see Chapter 2.3–2.6.

"had auspices" or not. Without auspices, the Consul lacked the ability to ask Iuppiter's permission for any intended act of state (and, consequently, permission—under augural law—to attend to such an act); if he auspicated anyway, from indifference to the rules or because he was unaware of his defective state, an affirmative sign, whether by way of birds on the left or a *fulmen sinistrum*, would hold no meaning, since he had no power to elicit such a response from Iuppiter.

In consequence, a negative response given (whether *ex avibus* or *de caelo*) to the Consul lacking auspices would likewise hold no meaning, and ignoring it should, strictly speaking, not constitute a violation of the auspices. But in most circumstances, the fact that the magistrate lacked valid auspices would not be known yet at that time, and ignoring the response—valid or not, Iuppiter had not granted permission—would manifest an attitude of contempt.

The same, presumably, applied to the *pulli*. The *auspicium ex tripudio* originally was an oblative sign that could be conveyed by any bird; in historical times it had been repurposed as a quasi-impetrative sign exclusively employing the Chickens.[61] Cicero repeatedly terms it an *auspicium coactum*, noting that given the circumstances under which it was obtained—hungry birds kept in a cage and fed in a manner that inevitably caused crumbs of food to drop to the ground—it could not fail to produce an affirmative result. It is not entirely clear whether such "forced" auspices by way of the *pulli* involved, as did all genuinely impetrative ones, a specific question being put to Iuppiter; both Cicero's rendering of the procedure (*Div.* 2.71–72) and the description in the Scholia Veronensia (ad *Aen.* 10.241), which may preserve a more archaic form of it, are silent on that point.[62] If no question was asked, the *vinculum temporis* (here referring not to the battle itself—which was not yet in progress—but to the act of preparing to give battle, or to perform a sacrifice or some other act) would have to provide meaning, as with all oblative signs. But the clear purpose of the Chickens was to obtain Iuppiter's approval of an action intended to be performed later during the same day, which would seem to render a question essential. (We cannot exclude, of course, the possibility that the Chickens represent an archaic stage of divination that does not yet reflect the fully developed augural distinction between oblative and impetrative auspices, and the respective rules governing them.) In any case, the Chickens were only consulted on the magistrate's order. Hence we may assume that Iuppiter, while agreeing (not always, though most of the time) to cooperate in this extortion of an affirmative—oblative—sign, did so only on condition that the magistrate ordering the procedure was in possession of valid impetrative auspices. Lacking those, a pair of Chickens feeding, no matter how voraciously, simply meant that they were hungry, not that Iuppiter gave permission.

---

[61] Cic. *Div.* 1.27–28; 2.73; and see Pease 131–133, 468–469.
[62] See Chapter 5.1.2 with note 16.

Hence the standard stuck to the ground belongs to a narrative complex that emphasized Flaminius' lack of impetrative auspices, and its consequences under the augural theory on display in Livy; the other elements that naturally connect with it are the Consul's tumble off his horse when leading his army out of camp at Arretium, and the bloody mess at the sacrifice when he took office in Ariminum. Both are *prodigia*, obviously; but their context—on both occasions, the Consul was engaged in an act of state that required valid auspices, which he did not possess—allows us to see them as oblative *auspicia* as well: the *vinculum temporis* reveals them to be Iuppiter's attempt to alert to that disability.[63] (Not that Flaminius was unaware of it; he simply was indifferent.) On the other hand, whether Flaminius heeded the Chickens did not matter, fundamentally, in this line of reasoning: had they eaten lustily, it still would not have signified Iuppiter's approval to engage in battle on that day. Such a narrative, focussing more on the Consul's original sin of not obtaining his first auspices in Rome than on his neglect of proper procedure right before the battle (irrelevant augurally—though not politically and polemically—on account of the underlying flaw), might well omit the *pulli*.

7.4.5 Coelius, Cicero, and Livy—an Augural Perspective

Since no other extant source mentions the combination of Flaminius' tumble, the Chickens, and the standard, it has been suggested that Coelius alone reported all three *omina*.[64] Perhaps so; more to the point, did any author before him report the Chickens, with or without the other warnings? *Magnum illud etiam, quod addidit Coelius*: at the height of the battle, an earthquake of tremendous magnitude struck the Mediterranean from Gaul to Italy, yet the combatants at Lake Trasumene, absorbed in their struggle, never noticed it (Cic. *Div.* 1.78). The perfect *addidit* leaves no doubt that Coelius did not merely continue his story with this piece of information, but that it could not be found in other—earlier—accounts: he was the first to discover it.[65] Conversely, it follows that the warning signs were present already in other accounts, and had become part of the tradition before Coelius; not necessarily, though, all together or at the same time.

That "Quintus" culled from Coelius all that he could find about Flaminius is a safe conclusion; the earthquake, after all, though a *prodigium*, could hardly count

---

[63] On both the difference and overlap of *prodigia* and *auspicia oblativa*, see Linderski 1993: 58–59 = RQ 613–614; cf. Chapter 2.2.2.
[64] Beck–Walter *FRH* 2: 54.
[65] Cicero's consistent practice is to use the present when simply stating that certain information could be found in a given author: e.g., *Div.* 1.33, *quod scriptum apud te est*; 1.48, *Hannibalem Coelius scribit eqs.*; 1.49, *hoc item in Sileni, quem Coelius sequitur, Graeca historia est*; 1.56, *et se audisse scribit Coelius et dixisse <eum> multis*. Hence Coelius' addition is not merely one to his own story, but to the pre-existing body of knowledge. Cf. Herrmann 113; Beck–Walter *FRH* 2: 54.

as an oblative sign in the augural sense, let alone as a *signum rerum futurarum*.⁶⁶ Which prompts an intriguing observation: Coelius did not report the first such warning issued to the Consul, on the day he entered office at Ariminum, when the stricken calf escaped from the altar and spattered blood all over the sacrificial party. In the sequence of oblative signs, this is not only the first but the one most closely and clearly connected with the underlying problem—the Consul's lack of valid auspices, which must and could be obtained only in Rome on that occasion.⁶⁷

As Cicero presents it, Coelius' collection of *Flaminiana ostenta* appears, from an augural point of view, quite unsystematic. Now, Linderski has shown how "Quintus" is concerned here (all through *Div*. 1.72–79) with examples of divination based on *coniectura*, from signs that require interpretation as to their meaning. The *pulli* have no place in such a context; as with all impetrative auspices, there could be no doubt as to the meaning: if the birds refused to eat, it signified a negative response to the request for permission sought. No *coniectura* was involved.⁶⁸ Sure enough, in his eventual refutation, "Marcus" ignores the Chickens (*Div*. 2.67).

In fact, the Chickens need not have entered the tradition until Coelius discovered them; he clearly wanted to stress Flaminius' religious misconduct in the immediate context of the battle as much as possible, without striving for an augurally consistent picture. The identification of the earthquake as Coelius' own contribution may seem to render this unlikely, on the assumption that all three of the warnings listed by "Quintus" were already present in the pre-existing tradition. That assumption, while reasonable, is not quite as certain as it might seem. At *ND* 2.8, Cicero had noted earlier: *C. Flaminium Coelius religione neglecta cecidisse apud Trasumennum scribit cum magna rei publicae vulnere*—almost verbatim how his brother opens the list of *Flaminiana ostenta*. The earthquake cannot be deemed a case of *religio neglecta*; since Flaminius' tumble off his horse and the recalcitrant standard evidently belong to an earlier tradition, the reference to Coelius ought to suggest that he offered something of relevance beside it: presumably, the Chickens. If so, Cicero accepted Coelius' contribution at face value in the *ND*; when he came to write *De divinatione*, he realized the augural inconsistency (and perhaps the shaky evidence for the *pulli*) in Coelius' laundry list of signs neglected by Flaminius: he decided to let "Quintus" repeat it intact in 1.77–78,

---

⁶⁶ As Wardle points out, 2006: 296.

⁶⁷ The unmovable standard, to be sure, was even more clearly connected, if the view that it signalled a problem with the commander's auspices is correct; but the sign occurs only in a military context, and would have been unsuitable for the occasion of the Consul's entering office.

⁶⁸ Linderski, *AL* 2231–2232 with n. 337: in wanting to group together "all examples showing Flaminius' lack of religiosity," Cicero "forgot . . . that by doing so he undermined the augural logic of his presentation." More precisely, perhaps, the logic of his brother's presentation, taken wholesale (though clearly not verbatim) from Coelius. Even if the Chickens were still technically considered an oblative sign (above, Subsection 7.4.4), there was no need for interpretation: failure to eat would indubitably indicate Iuppiter's disapproval of the action at hand.

then silently corrected it at 2.67, ignoring the Chickens and the earthquake, and limiting his comments to the two items that were augurally significant.

Nor does the Coelian assemblage betray an interest in the issue that so exercised Livy: the Consul's willful failure to obtain his auspices in Rome, and take them with him from there to war. Coelius surely knew that Flaminius opened his campaign in Gaul: hence, presumably, that he took office at Ariminum. Did he fail to recognize the augural significance of that event? Perhaps. More likely, he simply preferred a different emphasis for his history: a cumulation of acts demonstrating Flaminius' *neglegentia auspiciorum* in the immediate context of battle and catastrophe, rather than the slow—if far more ominous—buildup that we see in Livy. (Coelius' approach, precisely because of its lack of augural systematic, would also be more accessible to a readership little versed in the arcane theories of the *auguralis disciplina*.)

In contrast, Livy's narrative presents an augurally coherent and consistent theme, surely not by accident. It omits the Chickens not because the tradition it follows did not know about them (it well may have, at least since Coelius), but because that tradition saw them as irrelevant for the purpose of establishing Flaminius' *neglegentia auspiciorum*. The Consul chose to skip the rituals of investiture and *profectio* in Rome: therein lay his fundamental contempt for *caerimoniae* and auspices, and the source of the calamity. Once he had done so, nothing could mend the fatal flaw short of his return to Rome, to carry out those procedures; it did not matter whether he observed the *auspicium pullarium*, and heeded its report. What mattered was that he persisted in his contempt when he refused to heed the signs—the oblative ones—that did have relevance. Such a view, naturally, cannot be separated from the circumstances under which he assumed office. A priori, it would appear far more likely that the augural interpretation here at work was applied to an actual event, rather than that the event was created to suit a complex augural theory. As we have sought to demonstrate, the circumstances in question—taking office at Ariminum, not Rome—were present already in the historiographical tradition on which Polybios based his narrative. It stands to reason that Livy's interpretation of Flaminius' fault stood in that same tradition. Given that, from a strategic perspective, the Consul's movements under that tradition make eminent good sense (better indeed than the alternative—from Rome directly to Arretium—espoused by many scholars), the grounds for rejecting it become exceedingly thin, nay arbitrary, there being no positive evidence to do so in the first place.

7.4.6 Flaminius at the Lake

When and where did Flaminius encounter the sign of the recalcitrant standard? Livy's arrangement remains doubtful: both augurally and psychologically, the morning of the battle seems more plausible. At Arretium, Iuppiter had sent his second warning (after the sacrifice gone awry at Ariminum) by causing the Consul's horse to stumble; it went unheeded. The third and final warning would come just before the calamity. As we have seen, there probably was no basic disagreement among Flaminius' staff with the decision to go after Hannibal, and we should not expect any attempts to delay or block that move at this point.[69] The next morning may have posed a different picture: despite impenetrable fog rendering their surroundings (and the enemy's position—evidently near, but how near exactly, and where?) precarious and the army virtually blind, the Consul insisted that they press on immediately at dawn, without bothering to reconnoiter:[70] whether the objective was to engage Hannibal or merely to pursue him, some, if not most, of the officers may have found the situation too dangerous to move. Persuasion having no effect, perhaps the standard unwilling to budge would do the trick. Nor would its bearer necessarily need prompting: a superstitious soldiery had had a day and a night to mull over the evil omen of seeing their *imperator* flung off his horse in front of Iuppiter Stator, and the fog brought little in the way of reassurance.

Hence the omen of the standard stuck to the ground was reported, in all likelihood, on the morning of the battle, and entered the tradition in that context. Whether Livy himself repositioned the event to Arretium, or found it told thus in an earlier source, we cannot say; the dramatic effect achieved by the new arrangement, though, would seem to point toward the Patavian.

What about the *pulli*? If Flaminius did consult them, they probably were disinclined to eat that morning. Yet having chosen to ignore the auspices on a much more fundamental level from the day he entered his second consulship, it is conceivable that he also chose to dispense with the *auspicia ex tripudio* altogether; in which case, their absence in the tradition preserved in Livy may simply reflect the earliest version of the story. On the other hand, Flaminius may have seen no harm in going along with what he considered a meaningless ritual: as we have seen, a case can be made that auspication was required whenever the army set out from camp, whether battle was planned for that day or not.[71] If so, his troops would expect the ceremony: why undermine their confidence by suppressing it needlessly?[72] The Chickens had not caused him trouble before (in his first consulship, they were not an issue); no reason to think that they would now, unless the *pullarii* lost confidence in his leadership. Yet so it happened, at the fog-clad dawn of

---

[69] Above, Section 7.3.

[70] Livy's *inexplorato* (22.4.4.) is clearly borne out by Polybios' account (3.83.7–84.2) in general, and probably paralleled in οὐ καιρόν, οὐ τόπον προορώμενος (3.82.7); cf. Kromayer *AS* 3.1: 140 n. 3. Meißner 102 states that Flaminius' advance into the narrow passage along the lake would indeed have been foolish, had he not intended to use the pass to slow down Hannibal's advance: to occupy the narrows and attack Hannibal "unter Ausnutzung des Geländes." It remains a mystery how Flaminius could have hoped to ambush Hannibal—ahead of him—in the narrows: the known laws of physics militate against his being able to levitate above and in front of the enemy "by exploiting the terrain."

[71] Chapter 5.2.2.

[72] Similarly Scheid 2012: 118; 2015: 253; cf. Rosenstein 1990: 83; Wardle 2006: 293 ("Flaminius was prepared to observe religious rites ... but not the kind that could be used against him by the elite").

June 22; and the Consul, naturally, would not step back. Quite the contrary—if the day passed without calamity, in defeat of Hannibal or simply by staying hard on his heels, Flaminius would again have taught the people, in the army and back home, not to put faith in birds and similar stuff and nonsense. His victory over the auspices would be complete.

Was Flaminius looking for a fight? Of the four signs he would not heed, the first two—the sacrifice at Ariminum and the horse at Arretium—have no connection to an impending battle, hence cannot prove anything as to the man's intent. The standard that would not budge belongs, probably, to the morning of the battle; but in itself the sign merely alerts to a problem with the Consul's auspices, or—if that interpretation be rejected—to impending doom: it implies no intent one way or the other. (That it occurred on the day of the catastrophe is irrelevant: Iuppiter knew what was coming, Flaminius did not.) Which leaves the *pulli*. If their consultation was customary only before an expected battle (and not every time the army set out from camp), and if consultation did occur on the shores of Lake Trasumene that day, it would indicate that Flaminius meant to fight. All of which is entirely possible, and not at all certain. After the catastrophe, any negative response received and ignored immediately prior to it would readily lend itself to reinterpretation as to the Consul's intention, all the more in a hostile political—and historiographical—atmosphere ripe with accusations that he had recklessly sought battle without waiting for his colleague, lest he must share the glory: an accusation that could not stand without establishing the intent to fight. What Flaminius had in mind that day remains as irrecoverable as his body.

7.5 *Inauspicato Consul*

We may now reconstruct the strategic decisions arrived at in Rome with regard to the upcoming campaign of 217, and Flaminius' movements in particular. As will be seen, his presence, as reported by Livy, at Ariminum served a specific, and crucial, strategic objective. The choice, however, to dispense with his initial auspices in Rome on his first day in office, along with the ceremonies of *profectio*, served a larger purpose. Victory under such circumstances would establish, incontestably, that Roman commanders had no need of auspices.

7.5.1 Redeployments for 217

Hannibal had spent the winter in Cisalpine Gaul, somewhere west of Placentia.[73] The remnants of the consular armies of 218 were wintering in Placentia

---

[73] Above, note 9.

(Sempronius) and Cremona (Scipio).[74] For the new year, the Romans faced a choice between essentially two options: resume the war offensively in Gaul, and try to defeat Hannibal there; or adopt a defensive posture aimed at either prohibiting a Punic breakthrough into Italy proper, or—perhaps more realistically—confronting the invader with all available forces at the earliest opportunity after such a breakthrough had occurred.

Polybios notes how, during the winter, the Romans built up supply depots at Ariminum and in Etruria, with the aim of making those locations their bases for the upcoming operations.[75] This does not in itself preclude a planned offensive in Gaul, but in view of Flaminius' arrival at Arretium, whether from Ariminum or from Rome, at a point in time not long before Hannibal crossed—and could be expected to cross—the Appennines (such a timeline follows inevitably from both Polybios and Livy), it strongly suggests that the defensive strategy was the one eventually adopted. Instead of resuming the campaign in Gaul, it was decided to confront Hannibal either in Etruria or on the Adriatic coast, depending on which way he chose to advance into Italy—along the north slope of the Appennines past Bologna towards the Adriatic, or directly across the mountains into Etruria.

As for Etruria, all through the spring conditions on the ground would render the area between the lower Serchio and Arno rivers, from the Tyrrhenian coast to Florence, impassable for any army: there was no need to post a force at Luca. If Hannibal came by one of the western passes to the lower Arno region, he would have no choice but to move along the foothills to Pistoriae, and on to Faesulae. The obvious places at which to station an army to await the enemy, therefore, were Ariminum on the Adriatic coast, and Arretium in northern Etruria.[76] From either location to the other, an army could cross the Umbrian mountains quickly and with relative ease, by the Pass of Viamaggio and the Marecchia valley, thus effecting a concentration of both consular armies against Hannibal once his target became evident.

Of those two locations, however, Ariminum was the more pivotal—and the more vulnerable. The colony served as the principal base of operations for all

---

[74] Livy 21.56.9, 59.1–2, 63.1; Appian *Hannib.* 7.30; see De Sanctis *SdR* 3.2: 34; Walbank *HCP* 1: 410–411; Lazenby 1978: 61; Seibert 1993b: 137.

[75] Polyb. 3.75.6, παρῆγον δὲ καὶ τὰς ἀγορὰς τὰς μὲν εἰς Ἀρίμινον, τὰς δ' εἰς Τυρρηνίαν, ὡς ἐπὶ τούτοις ποιησόμενοι τοῖς τόποις τὴν ἔξοδον; cf. Miltner 15, 20.

[76] Seibert 1993b: 141 nn. 28–29 (following earlier authors), in an attempt to explain Livy 21.59.10 (*Hannibal in Ligures, Sempronius Lucam concessit*), assumes an unattested *prorogatio imperii* for Sempronius for 217, with orders (and an army, likewise unattested) to guard eastern Etruria towards Liguria, at Luca. Such would have been a waste of men and effort. When facing the same uncertainty again in 207, the Romans guarded Etruria with Varro's two legions—at Arretium (Livy 27.36.13, cf. 27.22.13, 24.1–7, 35.2); nothing indicates a separate force around Luca. There are no grounds to assume one in 217. The existence of Luca as a town, prior to the foundation of the Latin Colony in 180, is not certain: E. Honigmann "Luca" *RE* 13.2 (1927) 1535–1537; Schmitt 85 (who believes, nevertheless, not only that Sempronius and his army spent the winter in Luca but that Servilius assumed command of that army there—not at Ariminum—in 217: ibid. 86–87, 164–165). Kahrstedt *GdK* 3: 169 rightly dismissed the entire Liguria–Luca episode.

Roman activity in Gaul;[77] to withdraw the forces wintering in Placentia and Cremona directly to Etruria, across the central Appennines, would leave Ariminum exposed to an attack by Hannibal, if he moved rapidly enough; and not just Ariminum: he would see his way free into Italy, through Umbria or Picenum, without a Roman army within striking distance to engage him. Nor would it do to split up the forces at the Po, sending some to Etruria, others to Ariminum: the losses at the Trebia had been severe, reaching nearly half the combined strength of the consular armies;[78] if the remainder were divided, Ariminum would be protected by what essentially amounted to no more than one legion and *ala sociorum*. From the standpoint of logistics, in any case, it would be easier, and probably faster, to move the entire Po Valley force to Ariminum: at the time of year in question, late winter or early spring, even the lower passes across the central Appennines, such as the Futa or Collina (both at over 900 meters), might not be open, whereas from Ariminum, reinforced by the new levies, the army destined for Etruria could cross over to Arretium without difficulty, a month or so later.[79] As long as the central passes were unusable due to the season, Etruria in any case was safe: not so Ariminum. It follows that the strategy adopted for the spring of 217 made necessary the redeployment of both armies from the Po to Ariminum first.[80]

Time, however, would be of the essence. If both Consuls remained in Rome for a month or two after taking office, overseeing the recruitment of additional forces and celebrating the Latin Festival,[81] Hannibal might arrive at Ariminum (and

---

[77] See Amat-Seguin, esp. 93–96, on the strategic significance of Ariminum. When Sempronius' army was redeployed from Sicily to Placentia in 218, it went via Ariminum, not by the more direct route through Etruria; and while Hannibal's presence in western Cisalpine may explain why an even shorter route, along the Tyrrhenian coast and through Liguria, was not chosen, nothing indicates (*pace* Amat-Seguin 89–90) that the passes from Pistoriae (the Collina) or Faesulae (the Futa) to Bologna were no longer safe for a Roman army to take: no Carthaginian activity east of Placentia is attested, or conjecturable, before the Battle at the Trebia (Polyb. 3.61.9–10, 64.1–68.8, 68.13–69.14; cf. Livy 21.51.6-7).

[78] See Brunt 419 n. 4, for an estimate (from Polyb. 3.72.11, 74.6-8) of between 15,000 and 20,000 lost.

[79] De Sanctis *SdR* 3.2: 35 thought that, at the beginning of spring, Sempronius moved his army from Placentia first to Luca, then on to Arretium in preparation of the upcoming campaign. But the flooded Arno swamps between Pistoriae and Faesulae would have posed the same obstacle to a Roman army as they did to Hannibal; the move makes no sense when a far more practical alternative was available.

[80] Miltner 17 n. 1 made this point clearly enough, but few have considered its implications for the credibility of Livy's account. (On the fashionable out-of-hand dismissal of the latter, note also Miltner's pithy comment, 14 n. 3: ". . . so kann man sich nur darüber wundern, daß Livius überhaupt noch gelesen werden darf.")

[81] Between April 14 and May 15 in 217: *Fasti Fer. Lat.* = *InscrItal* 13.1: 148–149. Pace Seibert 1993b: 147 n. 55 (more cautious Schmitt 302 with n. 80: "Mindestens einer der Konsuln muß vor seinem Abmarsch aus Rom daran teilgenommen haben"), the putative presence of both Consuls' names (neither is extant) on the stone does not prove that Flaminius attended the festival. The absence of one Consul is known in 176: the Latinae were held on August 11, but Petillius Spurinus had left for his province on August 5 (Livy 41.16.5, 17.6). Throughout the document, the Consuls' names serve merely to date the event, not to attest their participation, as is clear from the notes on the years 27

points farther south) or in Etruria before any Roman army could challenge him. According to Livy (21.63.1), Flaminius wrote to Sempronius, still Consul, asking that the force wintering in the Po Valley be in camp at Ariminum on March 15. This makes eminent good sense from a purely military perspective: the move would ensure that Flaminius could lead an army toward Etruria without delay, should Hannibal already be on the march.

7.5.2 Strategy

The overall strategy for 217 had no doubt been worked out in the Senate during the last weeks of the old year, once the new Consuls had been elected.[82] In the assignment of *provinciae*, by sortition or *comparatio*,[83] Flaminius had drawn Arretium/Etruria, while Servilius received Ariminum/Gallia. There ought to be no serious doubt that the Consuls' armies in 217 consisted of those commanded by their predecessors, heavily reinforced with new levies (attested by Polybios 3.75.5); the notion especially would be absurd that Flaminius intended to face the enemy with nothing but raw recruits when a veteran force (even one that had experienced defeat) was available.[84] Yet how the two armies of 217 were distributed among the new Consuls remains unclear. From Livy (21.63.1 and 63.15) it is fairly certain that Flaminius took charge of the remnants of Sempronius' army. Appian *(Hannib.* 8.33) states that Servilius went to the Po and there received from Scipio the command over the latter's forces. But Appian clearly thought of Scipio as commanding the entire force, both consular armies, that was wintering at Placentia and Cremona (*Hannib.* 7.29–30); by implication—not necessarily apparent to that author—Flaminius would have commanded an all-recruit army. Conversely, Livy (21.63.15) gives Flaminius all four legions of the previous year; by implication, Servilius' army would have consisted of new levies only.

Although Livy notes specifically only that the army wintering at Placentia— that of Sempronius—was withdrawn to Ariminum (21.63.1), it is out of the question that Scipio's army remained at Cremona; hence both ended up at Ariminum. Flaminius would naturally have assumed command of both on his arrival, being the sole Consul present. He would not have taken the entire force to Arretium, and left Ariminum unprotected, unless he had evidence that Hannibal was

---

through 23 BC (*InscrItal* 13.1: 150–151): both Consuls are given under each year, followed by [*Imp. Caesar vale*]*tudin(e) inpeditus fuit* (27); [*Imp. Caesar in*] *Hispania fuit* (26, 25); [*Imp.*] *Caesar valetud(ine)* [*inpedit(us) fuit*] (24); and—at last!—[*Imp. Cae*]*sar in monte fuit* (23); see Degrassi, *InscrItal* 13.1: 143–144, 156–157; and, long ago, Mommsen 1871: 380; cf. Marco Simón 124. For what it is worth, Livy clearly implies that Flaminius was not present: *ratus auspiciis ementiendis Latinarumque feriarum mora et consularibus aliis impedimentis retenturos se in urbe*, 21.63.5.

[82] Soon after the Trebia, hence perhaps in January: Livy 21.57.3–4; cf. Walbank *HCP* 1: 401–403.
[83] Mommsen *StR* 1: 52–57; cf. 2.1: 208.
[84] Walbank *HCP* 1: 410–411; Brunt 419 n. 1; Amat-Seguin 95 n. 33; Seibert 1993b: 142 n. 31.

moving towards Etruria; but if such was the case, he had no other choice—and Ariminum would be safe until Servilius got there. In all probability, however, Flaminius remained at Ariminum until his colleague arrived with the new levies; in which case Servilius likely enough took over the remains of Scipio's army, and Flaminius that of Sempronius, each now boosted to full strength or more. As Livy appears to have been under the impression that Flaminius moved to Etruria shortly after his arrival at Ariminum (an impression firmly at odds with the evidence, from his own account and that of Polybios, of the events to follow), it would fit that he mistook Flaminius' initial if temporary assumption of command over the entire Po Valley force for the final arrangement. In the end, it appears that Hannibal as well as Flaminius did not start out until late April or early May.[85]

We may with confidence now dismiss the notion that Flaminius' movements at the start of 217, as reported in Livy, reflect nothing but an elaborate scheme concocted by annalists bent on blackening the man's reputation, and who in doing so came up, miraculously, with a chain of events that corresponds, step by step, to hard and rational strategic objectives—objectives that were in dispute, it seems, neither with the Senate nor with Flaminius' colleague, Servilius Geminus. Certainly nothing in Livy's account ties the latter to the vociferous attacks launched against Flaminius in the Senate on the Ides of March (Livy 22.1.4–7). Servilius observed all the proper rituals before making, with new levies, his own journey to Ariminum (*dum consul placandis Romae dis habendoque dilectu dat operam*, 22.2.1); it does not follow that he believed in their unalterable necessity. Once in the field, he and Flaminius cooperated as closely as the circumstances would allow.[86]

7.5.3 The Fog of Contempt

Flaminius' attempt to push aside the auspices in 217 did not go entirely unchallenged. As his intention became known, a storm of protest rose in the Senate. Two envoys were dispatched to make him return to Rome and observe all customary procedures before taking up his command. The same, essentially, had transpired in 242 or 241, when Lutatius (Catulus or Cerco) had embarked on a similar venture. Lutatius yielded to the Senate, took his auspices, and went to Sicily; and on to triumph. But in 217, the Senate's envoys proved unable to dissuade Flaminius.[87] On March 15, he entered his consulship without auspices, at Ariminum.

---

[85] On the chronology, see Walbank *HCP* 1: 412–413.   [86] Above, Section 7.3.
[87] Livy 21.63.11, *revocandum universi retrahendumque censuerunt et cogendum omnibus prius praesentem in deos hominesque fungi officiis quam ad exercitum et in provinciam iret.* Lazenby 1978: 59 makes a strong case for believing that, contrary to the portrait drawn by Polybios and Livy, Flaminius enjoyed considerable backing within the Senate. If so, the Consul's friends lacked the votes to

Yet had Flaminius departed for Ariminum from Rome on March 17, *auspicato in Capitolio votis nuncupatis, paludatus cum lictoribus* (and staying put on the day after the Ides), he would have achieved all his strategic aims (a week's delay in assuming command, perhaps less, travelling on his high road, would have made no difference), and no one could have objected and hoped to be taken seriously. Whether he truly feared that his enemies would attempt through augural machinations to unduly detain him in the City, or deprive him of command altogether, we cannot know.[88] But if bitterness on both sides lingered, as it surely did, from the unpleasant business of five years ago, prudence alone might suggest that he minimize any such possibility. And not just prudence: having once challenged the Nobles and the Augurs on the auspices in principle, the strategic necessities at the dawn of his second consulship presented an opportunity that would not soon come again. In contrast to Lutatius in 242 (or 241), Flaminius did not bother to substitute another divinatory rite: as before, in 223, he preferred to invoke success in battle as proof that he was right, and his augural opponents wrong. As noted earlier, Flaminius may have been perfectly willing to go along with the practice of auspices where it suited him and caused no complications. The same, indeed, may have been Lutatius' aim in 242: to observe the auspices when convenient, and ignore them when not.[89] But to ignore them safely at any time it would be essential to establish an acceptable alternative, or demonstrate their lack of efficacy. Flaminius chose the latter approach.

To take office at Ariminum not only would preserve his command from all interference aided by religion, and frustrate any *inimici* harboring such designs: it would—even better—enable him to strike a blow directly at the auspices, revealing their utter futility. This time, victory would demonstrate nothing less than the fact that auspices were unnecessary.[90] Henceforth, no commander leading an army of the Roman People in harm's way could be compelled to make decisions based on the appetite of birds, or sundry other practices of that nature: good judgment, aided by experience and ability, alone should govern a military campaign.

For those who hoped to free themselves and future commanders from the cage of auspices, the Battle at Lake Trasumene would prove catastrophic in more ways than one. And so Gaius Flaminius, *inauspicato* and *inexplorato*, led his army into the fog along the lake, and perished with fifteen thousand of his men. The reader may judge which fault was more reprehensible.

---

altogether block the attempt to recall him; but they were strong enough to dilute the measure, and prevent a follow-up.

[88] Cf. Develin 1979: 276.   [89] Above, Subsection 7.4.6; and see Chapter 5.5.2 on Lutatius.

[90] Cf. Magdelain 1968: 41 (with nn. 3 and 4): "Flaminius avait voulu, dans sa hâte de quitter Rome, s'affranchir des prescriptions de droit sacré. Il considérait son élection et sa loi curiate suffisantes pour justifier l'exercise du pouvoir militaire. Il se faisait une conception purement laïque de l'*imperium*."

8
The Auspices Prevail

The aftermath of the catastrophe at Lake Trasumene in 217 BC bears examination under several perspectives. First, the decision to appoint a Dictator. When viewed together with the same move following the defeats at Drepana in 249 BC and Cannae in 216, a common denominator emerges: the presence of *vitium*, actual or suspected, caused by commanders going into battle *contra auspicia*, and resulting in the need to obtain the *pax deorum*.[1] Next, the likelihood (incapable of proof, unfortunately) that a question of auspices lay at the bottom of the falling out between Fabius Maximus the Dictator and his Master-of-Horse, Minucius Rufus. Of greatest consequence, though, was the reaction of M. Claudius Marcellus to being found *consul vitio factus* by the Augurs in 215: abdication without complaint, thus setting a demonstrative example in support of the auspices. In effect, the events of those two years shut the door to any further public questioning of the rule of auspices. The second century would see one major case of negligence in 176, whose outcome essentially confirmed the augural *disciplina*; and the uncontentious abdication of both Consuls, ruled *vitio creati*, in 162 may be seen as the final word on an issue first touched upon by Fabius Rullianus in the late fourth century, and raised to dramatic prominence by a number of commanders during the third. A brief look at a few ambiguous cases in the late second and first century rounds out the study.

8.1 Disaster and Dictator

In June 217, Hannibal annihilated the army of Gaius Flaminius at Lake Trasumene; no trace of the Consul was found afterwards. In Rome the news caused consternation—indeed, a state of near panic, soon amplified by word of the destruction of a large force of cavalry under C. Centenius in Umbria. Polybios notes a reaction marked by prolonged debate and—initially—indecision: the

---

[1] The traditional view of the *pax deorum* as a (regular) state of relations between the Romans and the divine power has recently been called into question, with strong arguments, by Santangelo 2011: 162–172 and Satterfield *passim*. The evidence suggests that *pax deorum* was not understood as a state that could be maintained and ruptured, but as "the outcome of a process, or indeed a process itself . . . rooted in a background of conflict and struggle" (Santangelo 163). The peace with the gods had to be sought and gained again and again, whenever a perceived threat to the safety of the State could be identified; securing it constituted a single event, and did not establish an ongoing condition.

double impact of Lake Trasumene and Centenius' defeat left not only the People perplexed, but even the Senate; and thus they agreed to forgo the annual management of affairs and the election of magistrates, and to appoint a commander with unlimited powers, as called for by the situation.[2] Livy concurs: presided over by the Praetors in the City, the Senate met in daily session; eventually, it was decided to address the crisis by resorting to an almost-defunct instrument: the appointment of a Dictator *rei gerundae causa*, for probably only the second time in some eighty years.[3]

8.1.1 Emergency

What prompted the decision to name a Dictator in 217, and why was it reached only after some debate? The military emergency resulting from the catastrophe at Lake Trasumene offers a ready reason, commonly espoused by scholars.

But the emergency, while real, can be exaggerated: the Praetors were capable of seeing to the immediate defense of the City and its environs (and did so), and by the time the decision was finally made—not before the last days of June—it was probably becoming evident that Hannibal had turned east towards the Adriatic, and was not moving on Rome.[4] Once Fabius Maximus had taken office, certainly neither he nor the Senate exhibited signs of military urgency.

The Dictator as his first order of business addressed religious matters and persuaded the Senate to order a consultation of the Sibylline Books (*quo die magistratum iniit vocato senatu ab dis orsus . . . pervicit ut, quod non ferme decernitur nisi cum taetra nuntiata sunt, decemviri libros Sibyllinos adire iuberentur*, Livy 22.9.7–8: *pervicit* strongly suggests that this move, too, encountered resistance). The Decemvirs reported that the war's initial vow to Mars had been *non rite factum* and must be repeated *de integro et amplius*; for Iuppiter, *ludi magni* must be held, and to Venus Erycina and Mens, temples built; a *supplicatio* and a *lectisternium* must be organized, and a *ver sacrum* vowed (Livy 22.9.9–10). Since the Dictator was going to be—but was not yet, evidently—occupied with military matters (*quoniam Fabium belli cura occupatura esset*), the Senate instructed the

---

[2] Polyb. 3.86.6–7: . . . οὐ μόνον τὸ πλῆθος, ἀλλὰ καὶ τὴν σύγκλητον αὐτὴν συνέβη διατραπῆναι. διὸ καὶ παρέντες τὴν κατ' ἐνιαυτὸν ἀγωγὴν τῶν πραγμάτων καὶ τὴν αἵρεσιν τῶν ἀρχόντων . . . νομίζοντες αὐτοκράτορος δεῖσθαι στρατηγοῦ τὰ πράγματα καὶ τοὺς περιεστῶτας καιρούς.

[3] Livy 22.8.5, *itaque ad remedium iam diu neque desideratum nec adhibitum, dictatorem dicendum, civitas confugit*. The most recent Dictator *rei gerundae causa* had been A. Atilius Caiatinus, in 249, and before him (it seems) M. Valerius Maximus in 301 V. (The three undatable dictatorships between 292 and 285, cf. *MRR* 2: 187, are unlikely to have been *rei gerundae causa*.) For the Praetors (M. Aemilius, *praetor urbanus*, and M. Pomponius, *praetor peregrinus*), Livy 22.7.14, 9.11; cf. Broughton *MRR* 1: 244; Brennan *PRR* 2: 727.

[4] On this, see Lesiński 138–140, 152.

Praetor Urbanus, M. Aemilius, to see to the speedy execution of all these measures, *ex collegii pontificum sententia* (22.9.11).

Not so fast, though: before anything could be carried out, the People had to vote on the *ver sacrum*; thus the Pontiffs ruled, after the Senate had passed its decrees.[5] A Praetor, presumably—though not necessarily—Aemilius, called an assembly, and the People approved the Sacred Spring.[6] Even if the decision to name a Dictator was reached on June 28 or 29, the popular vote in which Fabius was allegedly elected (Livy 22.8.5–6; 22.31.8–10) could not have happened before June 29; but if Quinctilis had already come, the first comitial day would be the 10th.[7] That also constitutes the earliest opportunity for the People's vote on the *ver sacrum*.

Next, great games were vowed to Iuppiter; then, the *supplicatio* was announced. Not only the City population took part in this, but also many of the country folk (22.10.7–8): some days would pass before it actually took place. A three-day *lectisternium* followed (22.10.9). *Tum*—only then—*aedes votae*: that of Mens by a Praetor, T. Otacilius, but the one for Venus of Eryx by the Dictator himself, as prescribed in the Books (*quia ita ex fatalibus libris editum erat ut is voveret cuius maximum imperium in civitate esset*, 22.10.10). By now we are well into July, three weeks or more after the Battle at Lake Trasumene. With religious matters thus taken care of, now—only now—the Dictator briefed the Senate concerning the war and affairs of state: *ita rebus divinis peractis, tum de bello reque publica dictator rettulit* (22.11.1).

If resorting to a Dictator in an emergency had been a common practice, no explanation would be needed why it happened here: but for the past eight decades no such practice had been observed. The only Dictator *rei gerundae causa* between 301 V and 217 was A. Atilius Caiatinus in 249. The massive and terrible Gaulish raid on Italy in 225, penetrating deep into Etruria while one Consul was away in Sardinia (and then killed in the battle with the Gauls), had not triggered a dictatorship; nor had any of the military crises during the Third Samnite War or the Gaulish and Etruscan wars of the late 280s—not to mention Pyrrhos. This constitutes a remarkable departure from the ubiquity of the office in the surviving tradition about the fourth century. Whatever the historical reality of the dictatorship in that period, it is evident that, in the third century, Dictators *rei gerundae causa* were appointed only with great reluctance: it stands to reason that the

---

[5] Livy 22.10.1, *his senatus consultis perfectis, L. Cornelius Lentulus pontifex maximus consulente collegium praetore omnium primum populum consulendum de vere sacro censet: iniussu populi voveri non posse*.

[6] Livy 22.10.2–6. The actual vow of the *ver sacrum* was pronounced by the Praetor A. Cornelius Mammula (Livy 33.44.2); he may also have convened the *comitia*.

[7] The earliest dates plausible, assuming the Battle at Lake Trasumene was fought on June 22 (Chapter 7.2.1, note 25). Lesiński 154 proposed the 26th. I hope to examine in a separate study the tradition of a popular vote in the appointment of Dictators.

decision to do so was prompted by specific and unusual circumstances that went beyond a military challenge.

Viewed in this light, what happened in 249 BC may be more significant than commonly realized. Having lost most of his fleet in the Battle of Drepana, the Consul P. Claudius Pulcher on his return to Rome was instructed by the Senate to appoint a Dictator. Did the defeat at Drepana indeed constitute a military emergency of such magnitude as to call for a Dictator, for the first time in half a century? There was no fear, as far as can be told, of the enemy now invading Italy, and Atilius proceeded to take command of the land forces in Sicily—the first Dictator to hold command outside Italy, and the only one down to Caesar.[8] In magnitude, Claudius' losses of ships and men fell well short of those suffered in the storms of 255 and 253.[9] Nor had the need been felt for a Dictator when Rome's invasion of Africa had ended in catastrophe six years earlier—two legions and their *alae* lost, the Consul captured. Those who would invoke practical concerns—the need for a second commander in Sicily, once Claudius had returned to Rome—will have to explain why such a need had not been felt in 260, when Cn. Scipio the Consul was taken alive by the enemy early in the year, and why it could not be met in 249 by sending out the Praetor, with one Consul back safely in the City.

What sets Claudius' defeat at Drepana apart from others is a feature it shares with that of Flaminius at Lake Trasumene. A charge of *vitium* hangs over both.[10]

8.1.2 *Vitium*

After the disaster at Drepana, Claudius returned to Rome. The Senate now instructed him to name a Dictator. We have no means of determining when exactly the Consul got to Rome, and where his colleague was at that moment. The two could have met in Messana, or passed each other in transit from and to Sicily; but Polybios' specific note (the perfect συνηντηκότα, 1.52.6) that the ships from Lilybaeum were already at Messana when Iunius arrived there opens up the serious possibility that he was still in Rome when news arrived of Drepana. If this could be shown for certain, it would demonstrate that the decision to name a

---

[8] Contrary to what Dio puts in Catulus' mouth in 67 BC, during the debate over the *lex Gabinia* (36.34.2–3), there probably existed no rule, augural or legal or otherwise, limiting a Dictator's military operations to Italy; the point was that he could not be *named* outside Italy (Livy 27.5.15), the *dictio* requiring a piece of *ager Romanus*. Cf. Konrad 2008 and Chapter 4.4.2 with note 73.

[9] Polyb. 1.37, 39.6.

[10] As it does for the disaster at the Allia river, prompting—eventually—the appointment of Camillus as Dictator: Livy 5.38.1, *nec auspicato nec litato instruunt aciem*; Min. Fel. *Oct.* 7.4, *frequentius etiam quam volebamus deorum praesentiam contempta auspicia contestata sunt; sic Allia nomen infaustum . . . est*. That our surviving tradition refused to elaborate on this point is remarkable; but its matter-of-fact appearance in Minucius Felix indicates that in other strands, now lost, the Battle at the Allia was well documented as having been fought *contra auspicia*. For similar observations concerning *vitium*, defeat, and the appointment of Dictators, see Rosenstein 1990: 34–37, 56–67, 77–87.

Dictator was not taken immediately, in response to military defeat alone: for in that case the Senate presumably would have instructed Iunius to make the appointment, and not waited for Claudius to return. Alas, we do not know; all we can tell is that by the time the Senate ordered Claudius to name a Dictator, his colleague certainly had left the City. Even so, we have evidence that the process proved contentious.

As is well known, when directed to appoint a Dictator, Claudius named his *scriba*, M. Claudius Glicia, who, under pressure from the public outrage sparked by this defiant mockery of the ancient office, abdicated the same day without ever naming a Magister Equitum.[11] Perhaps the Consul's move should not be attributed solely to inbred arrogance, nor to resentment at being superseded in his command. Claudius or not, after a defeat such as he had suffered, he could not realistically expect to be sent back to Sicily right away in charge of fleet or army; and having a Dictator take over for him was less humiliating than being replaced by the Praetor—an option the Senate would have been free to exercise. In other words, the objective of removing Claudius from command could have been achieved by less dramatic means than naming a Dictator—unless the Consul refused outright to yield to the Senate's wishes, and made it clear that he intended to return to Sicily at the earliest opportunity. That certainly is possible.[12] But there are grounds to think that other considerations were at work—both as regards the reason for naming a Dictator, and for Claudius' reaction to the attempt.

Roman commanders had survived defeat before without lasting damage to their standing in the *res publica*. Indeed, the degree of forbearance shown in Roman politics to failure in high command is nothing but remarkable. Such forbearance had its limits; but the limits were not set by (as one might think) the magnitude of the military failure, the severity of the defeat, but by a failure of an altogether different kind: the failure to abide by certain rules. Personal cowardice was held inexcusable in a commander; so was failure to observe the requirements of *religio*—first and foremost, the auspices. Had the Chickens given Claudius a *solistimum tripudium* at Drepana, he might still have lost the battle (as noted by Cicero, *Div*. 2.20): but he would have been untouchable politically, or in the courts. Instead, he had gone into battle *contra auspicia* and, in so doing, stripped himself of what would have furnished him with an impenetrable armor in the

---

[11] FC = *InscrItal* 13.1: 42–43; Livy *Per.* 19, *Claudius Pulcher cos. contra auspicia profectus ... infeliciter adversus Carthaginienses classe pugnavit, et revocatus a senatu iussusque dictatorem dicere Claudium Gliciam dixit, sortis ultimae hominem, qui coactus abdicare se magistratu postea ludos praetextatus spectavit*; Suet. *Tib*. 2.2. It would be disappointing if no one had conjured up "die politische Instrumentalisierung der Auguralwissenschaft" (Bleckmann 191) as the mechanism to force Glicia from office. In that case, one should expect *vitio factus abdicavit* in the FC (e.g., the Consuls of 162 BC), instead of *coact(us) abd(icavit)*, a phrase that clearly implies abdication forced under political pressure.

[12] Bleckmann 189–190 deems it likely.

hour of defeat.[13] The protection offered by having scrupulously observed the auspices, should anything go wrong in battle, surely played a significant role in the Roman elite's tenacious holding on to this archaic practice, cumbersome and inconvenient though it might be when on campaign. Those inclined to dismiss reports of unfavorable auspices as convenient excuses invented after the fact "to explain away the defeat" (if so, why only on a handful of occasions in a long litany of defeats?) may want to ponder that.

Yet Claudius had gone beyond failing to observe the ritual: he cast the Chickens into the sea, and thus not only mocked the gods but challenged the entire practice of auspices itself. Had he emerged victorious from Drepana, the Augurs would have been hard-pressed to explain how this could happen: and precisely because the violation was so spectacular, it could not have been swept under the rug, in hopes that it would soon be forgotten (as might be possible with a case of merely ignoring a negative response). Nor would the lesson be lost on future commanders. If Claudius could win a battle *contra auspicia*, so could they, and they were free to base their decision when and where to fight solely on their military judgment, with no interference from scared *pullarii* or the animals' random loss of appetite. (Not all would draw such a conclusion; many no doubt did believe in auspices, or at least in the political and psychological benefit of maintaining them. But it would become difficult henceforth to constrain those who had their doubts.)

It is here that we should seek at least one reason for naming a *dictator rei gerundae causa* in 249, the first in half a century.[14] From a purely military point of view, a Dictator brought no improvement to the situation in Sicily: unity of command was not an issue, as the Consuls had not had disagreements with each other—indeed, had never served in the same theater together—and Iunius, now the only Consul in the field, would automatically be superior to the Praetor, were the latter sent. Having recourse to that ancient office, perhaps liberally used until two generations ago but half-forgotten now, best made sense if there was hope or expectation that its occupant somehow could provide succor simply by being what he was—*dictator*, "the one who speaks," and the *magister populi* of the *libri augurales*. After the Consul's affront to Iuppiter, a higher authority—*is cuius maximum imperium in civitate esset*—was needed to put things right with the divine power, especially if the Consul refused to acknowledge his fault, and hence the need for remedy. That this Dictator should be named *rei gerundae causa*, not for some other reason, follows logically from the crisis's origin in the sphere of war; only the *magister populi* in the ancient meaning of the word would do. Scrupulously observing the auspices, and presiding over a host of expiatory ceremonies before

---

[13] On this, see Rosenstein's fundamental study (1990), esp. 46–49, 54–91, 114–152, 157–164.
[14] Lippold 154 n. 320 saw this correctly ("auch 249/48 hatte eine religiöse Verfehlung des geschlagenen Konsuls zum Entschluß, eine Diktatur zu errichten, beigetragen").

he took the field, he would be able to restore the situation, and with his *imperium valentius* neutralize the Consul who, through *vitium* deliberately incurred, had brought such calamity on the Roman People.[15]

Thus naming a Dictator did not merely replace the Consul as commander in Sicily: it could be seen as a public statement that the battle had been lost through *religio*—a statement that the fault was his, and not (as was theoretically possible) due to some sacrilege or ritual error committed by a third party. Claudius' reaction leaves little doubt that he took it to mean precisely that; and he responded with the same contempt that he had shown the Chickens. He had challenged the auspices at Drepana: he continued to challenge the underlying principles here in Rome.

A. Atilius Caiatinus (*cos. II* 254) was named Dictator next;[16] we do not know how soon, nor what prompted Claudius now to abide by the Senate's wishes. Possibly the pressure brought on Glicia, the hapless *scriba*, warned the Consul that his fellow Nobles, even though some of them might privately share his dismissive view of auspices, would form a united front in public against him on this issue; perhaps a Tribune (if not all ten) threatened *abrogatio imperii* by plebiscite. Even so, a late (unfortunately) source offers a hint that he may not have succumbed at once.

Zonaras, after noting the decision to name a Dictator, tells us that, "while Caiatinus was being named Dictator, during that time Iunius captured Eryx, and Qarthalo . . . took Iunius prisoner" (ἐν ᾧ δ' ὁ Κολλατῖνος δικτάτωρ ἐλέγετο, ἐν τούτῳ τὸν Ἔρυκα παρεστήσατο ὁ Ἰούνιος, καὶ ὁ Καρθάλων . . . ἐζώγρησε τὸν Ἰούνιον, 8.15). The imperfect here (ἐν ᾧ . . . ἐλέγετο) instead of a simple aorist is odd: it could reflect a more protracted than normal process of appointing a Dictator. At a minimum, it must cover two attempts: one abortive (Glicia), not specifically mentioned; one successful (Caiatinus).

We cannot say for certain whether the attempt to install a Dictator was launched immediately on learning what Claudius had done to the Chickens, or only after news arrived of Iunius' catastrophe at sea, likewise attributable to *vitium*. Zonaras mentions the decision right after noting how the frequent disasters at sea caused the Romans much distress (8.15, πολλάκις δὲ τοῦ ναυτικοῦ κινδυνεύοντος ἐβαρύνοντο οἱ Ῥωμαῖοι τῇ συνεχεῖ τῶν νεῶν φθορᾷ). What cannot be argued from Zonaras is that only Iunius' capture by the enemy prompted the naming of a Dictator, "because the consuls of 249 had now both been

---

[15] It is widely held today that the first *ludi saeculares* were staged in 249 BC; see Wissowa 309–311; M. P. Nilsson "Saeculares ludi" *RE* 1A.2 (1920) 1700–1705; Cichorius 1, 47; Latte 246–247; Bleckmann 193. No doubt the disasters in Sicily contributed to a general sense of doom, but the immediate event that prompted consultation of the Sibylline Books (which prescribed the games) was a lightning strike on the City wall (Censor. 17.8), not the defeat at Drepana. On the near-magical properties associated with the dictatorship, see Chapter 3.3.

[16] *FC* = *InscrItal* 13.1: 42–43; Livy *Per.* 19; Zonar. 8.15; cf. Dio 36.34.2.

eliminated."[17] We may take the epitomizer's ἐν ᾧ δ'... ἐλέγετο to signify that Caiatinus' appointment did not come until the seizure of Eryx and the capture of Iunius had occurred. Yet we must give full weight to the imperfect and all that it implies: the process of appointing a Dictator unfolded over the period in which these two events took place—in other words, it could have concluded afterwards, but not commenced. And we must give full weight to the rest of his narrative: the fact that he reports the decision to name a Dictator, and the actual appointment, immediately after the naval disasters.[18]

It appears improbable that the Senate would be inclined to overlook the first instance of violating the auspices but not the second, and the motion to name a Dictator was probably made as soon as the details of Claudius' action became known. Such details—specifically, that the Consul had fought *contra auspicia*—need not have been contained in his initial report, and may have become available only as he, and some of his crews, arrived in Rome. The Senate, though, was not always thinking with one mind; some influential members might have sympathized, initially, with Claudius and his attempt to free himself from the constraints of auspices, and succeeded in stalling the decision until word came that the other Consul, too, had lost his fleet *cum vitio navigasset*—at which point, resistance would have become politically impossible.

By the time the Dictator took command in Sicily, Iunius Pullus had already seized Eryx from the Carthaginians; and Caiatinus, in Dio's words, "accomplished nothing."[19] Not in the military sphere, it is true; but if our interpretation of the evidence is correct, the Dictator's foremost task was to set things right with the divine power: only thus and then could the course of the war be restored in Rome's favor. In that regard, Atilius Caiatinus certainly fulfilled his duty.

8.1.3 After Cannae

Our reconstruction of the considerations that prompted the naming of a Dictator in 249 BC is of necessity conjectural. Yet the connection of catastrophe, in battle and in storm, with the commanders' failure to obey the auspices sets the events of 249 aside from all the other disasters suffered, on land and sea, between the Samnite Wars and Lake Trasumene in 217: it is difficult to believe in mere coincidence.

---

[17] Thus Thiel 291 n. 741; *contra* De Sanctis *SdR* 3.1: 177 n. 74.

[18] While noting, correctly, that Zonaras "actually places this before Iunius' capture," Lazenby 1996: 141 maintains that the latter event "might explain the nomination of a dictator." Assuredly it does not. What Zonaras says here is "both unusual and specific," and must be considered carefully and fully, not accepted or ignored piecemeal. (The quote is from Morgan 92 n. 15, in a different context.)

[19] Dio 36.34.3, μηδὲν πράξαντος; cf. Zonaras 8.15, οὐδὲν δὲ μνήμης ἔπραξαν ἄξιον, of the Dictator and his Magister Equitum.

This is not to say that every Dictator *rei gerundae causa* was appointed in response to an action *contra auspicia*. Certainly later tradition did not see such a connection at work among the numerous dictatorships of the fifth and fourth centuries (the historical reality of which is probably irretrievable). But in the third century, the evidence strongly suggests that recourse was had to this particular manifestation of the office in connection with catastrophe: a situation being deemed catastrophic not merely because of the magnitude of losses suffered, but because its circumstances gave reason to believe that the divine power was visiting punishment on the Roman People for acts, of commission or omission, that resulted in *religio*. Twice, in 249 and 217, augural *vitium* was deemed to have accompanied the defeat; indeed, Fabius Maximus—now Dictator—publicly blamed the disaster at Lake Trasumene not on Flaminius' shortcomings as a commander, but on his indifference to ritual and the auspices: *plus neglegentia caerimoniarum auspiciorumque*[20] *quam temeritate atque inscitia peccatum a C. Flaminio consule esse* (Livy 22.9.7). There are signs that on the third (and last) occasion of a Dictator *rei gerundae causa*, the same fault was initially suspected, too.

After the Battle of Cannae, on reading Varro's dispatch sent from Canusium, the Senate instructed him to come to Rome *primo quoque tempore quantum per commodum rei publicae fieri posset* (Livy 22.57.1). Word of the terrible defeat had already reached the City a day or two before, but without detail (22.54.7–55.8). Earlier in the year, acts of sacrilege—the *stuprum* of two Vestal Virgins—had been uncovered and dealt with *more maiorum*: now these *prodigia*, with their warning of impending doom, acquired heightened significance. The Decemvirs were ordered to approach the Books, and reported the need for human sacrifice, duly carried out, to avert further disaster; Q. Fabius Pictor travelled to Delphi to seek advice from the highest authority (22.57.2–6).[21] It would be surprising—indeed, inconceivable—if no questions were raised in those days as to whether the Consuls, one or both, might have engaged in battle *contra auspicia*. The memory of Flaminius and Lake Trasumene was still raw; Varro and Flaminius shared the same friends and enemies: the latter would not overlook this opportunity to bring the Consul down, should he prove vulnerable. As witnesses became available, they (and eventually Varro and his *pullarii*, once back in Rome) would be closely questioned on the subject.

Varro, however, proved untouchable. Better still, we are told expressly (Min. Fel. *Oct.* 26.3) that Aemilius Paullus, too, received favorable auspices before the battle: *pullos edaces habuit et Paullus apud Cannas*—a conclusion which, in any

---

[20] Dorey in his Teubner text and Briscoe in his new *OCT* (2016) rightly adopt Sigonius' *auspiciorum<que quam>* for the manuscripts' *auspiciorum*; Walters' (*OCT* 1929) seclusion of that word misses the point.
[21] Eckstein 1982: 73–75.

case, Cicero renders inescapable: Flaminius disobeyed the auspices, and thus perished with his army; but in the following year, Paullus did obey, and perished in the Battle of Cannae with his army all the same (*Div.* 2.71, *Flaminius non paruit auspiciis, itaque periit cum exercitu; at anno post Paulus paruit: num minus cecidit in Cannensi pugna cum exercitu?*). In light of which, the incident a few days before Cannae gains in significance: Varro, *penes quem* (as at Cannae) *imperium*, had ordered the army out of camp, clearly under affirmative auspices (no violation is alleged); but when his colleague sent word that his Chickens would not eat, Varro called off the undertaking (Livy 22.42.1–10; cf. 22.41.2). One may wonder if this was seen as noteworthy at the time. But now it could be adduced as proof that Varro the Consul, however rash in his decisions as a field commander, did not permit *temeritas* to encroach on the religious side of warfare; on the contrary, he scrupulously observed the auspices, and exercised extra caution when, as supreme commander on that day, he could have properly ignored his colleague's divergent auspices, his own taking precedence.[22] Following the catastrophe, Varro and his friends could not fail to cite this event, and make the most of it to dispel questions about a possible *vitium* at Cannae. There can be no doubt that on the day of Cannae, his Chickens had fed lustily: he could not have survived the aftermath politically otherwise.[23]

It would take some time to sort it all out, of course. In the meantime, the Praetor M. Claudius Marcellus (*cos. I* 222) was ordered to Canusium, to assume command of what was left, under the Consul, of the *exercitus Cannensis*. When Marcellus arrived, Varro as directed by the Senate named a Dictator, M. Iunius Pera (*cos.* 230): clearly *in castris*, at Canusium.[24] His instructions to do so must have come either in the letter summoning him back to Rome or separately with Marcellus:[25] either way, the decision was probably made before all the evidence was in on whether the auspices had been obeyed.

Again, this is not to say that had there never been a question of auspices at Cannae—in fact, we can only conjecture, not say for certain, that there was—no Dictator would have been appointed in 216. The *incestum* of the Vestals, and the response of the *libri fatales*, offered proof positive that divine anger had led to the calamity, which made it imperative to secure the *pax deorum*; and taking place in the sphere of war, prudence would dictate that the State have resort to a man endowed with *imperium valentius*. The details are lost, but Iunius Pera, like Fabius Maximus before him, did not take the field until he had completed the *res divinae* (Livy 23.14.2; cf. 22.11.1, on Fabius Maximus: *ita rebus divinis peractis*). What the

---

[22] Cf. Mommsen *StR* 1: 95 with n. 3; Vervaet 2014: 46–47.   [23] Rosenstein 1990: 84–85.

[24] Livy 22.57.8–9: *Marcellus . . . Canusium magnis itineribus contendit. inde dictator ex auctoritate patrum dictus M. Iunius eqs.* Varro did not arrive in Rome for some time afterwards, when he was summoned back (the Dictator by now having taken the field, 23.14.2–4) to name a second Dictator, *qui senatum legeret* (23.22.10–11).

[25] Cf. Lippold 166 n. 373.

evidence does point toward is that, in the third century, the naming of a Dictator *rei gerundae causa* could be seen not merely as a practical response to a military emergency, driven by practical considerations of military expediency and necessity. Naturally, it contained that element as well: a Dictator could bring practical benefits, chiefly that of replacing a commander killed or captured, or manifestly incompetent—such as T. Otacilius Crassus (*pr. II* 214), at least in the Cunctator's judgment: *si consul esses, dictatorem dicendum exemplo maiorum nostrorum censeremus, nec tu indignari posses aliquem in civitate Romana meliorem bello haberi quam te* ("If you were Consul, we would think it necessary to name a Dictator in the manner of our ancestors, and you would not be able to take umbrage at someone else in the Roman state being deemed better at war than you," Livy 24.8.17). But if that were a principal objective, one should expect Dictators to be named left and right throughout the Punic Wars; and if Fabius in fact had used those words (they surely are Livy's, or an earlier annalist's), the only *exemplum maiorum* he could realistically have had in mind would have been the one of 249 BC.

For reasons that are beyond the purview of this study, in the third century the office of Dictator *rei gerundae causa* receded drastically from the frequency—not to say, ubiquity—with which it had been employed, according to the surviving tradition, in the late fifth and throughout the fourth. The three attested occasions on which this manifestation of the dictatorship was employed—"revived" might be a better way of putting it—after 301 V, in 249, 217, and 216, can all be tied to severe losses in which *vitium* caused by willful disregard of auspices was either present or suspected, and a need to secure the *pax deorum* manifest. To have recourse to a Dictator, with his *imperium valentius*, in such circumstances would be a prudent move towards obtaining the peace with the gods. Yet insofar as it could be seen as an affirmation of the auspices and their overriding importance in the conduct of the *res publica*, the move was bound to draw opposition from those within the ruling class who, like the unfortunate commanders themselves, were skeptical of the practice of auspices, and who wished for greater flexibility in making public decisions, especially when at war. Hence both the push to name a Dictator in 249 and 217, and the resistance to it implied by the surviving evidence.

The appointment of a Dictator in a time of crisis should be understood, first and foremost, as an attempt to regain divine goodwill by placing the State under the command of a man untainted—since not currently in charge—by whatever *religio* constricted it. (This would also explain the evident reluctance, other than for a few instances mostly in the high and far-off times, to name an incumbent magistrate to the office.)[26] The tales of Cincinnatus and Camillus furnish the

---

[26] In 207, the Consul M. Livius Salinator was named Dictator *comitiorum habendorum causa*, evidently *ex s.c.* (*per dictatorem comitia haberi placuisset*, Livy 28.10.1): a puzzling case, since both Consuls were present in Rome at election time. W–M *ad loc.* suggest (unidentified) religious concerns, no doubt correctly (*contra*, unpersuasively, Bandel 140). That was after the Battle at the Metaurus; no possible concern could be raised about Livius being free of all religious blemish.

archetypal model: no man could have been farther removed from the *res publica*—in seclusion away from Rome the one, in exile the other. (In that sense, the two final occupants of the office, outlaws and rebels both, fittingly close the circle.)

8.2 Contra Auspicia

On five occasions in a span of little more than thirty years, between 249 and 217 BC, four Consuls commanding armed forces of the Roman People chose not to obey the requirements imposed by the traditional observance of *auspicia*. They either knowingly and willfully ignored the auspices (in 249, twice, and 217), or refused to accept a ruling by the *collegium augurum* that they were *vitio creati* (in 223), or attempted to replace their auspices with a more convenient form of divination (in 242 or 241). It is difficult to say whether these were mere individual outliers, or representatives of a more broadly based minority view within the ruling class. A few observations, though, can be ventured that point in the latter direction.

8.2.1 The Challengers

One of the challengers, C. Flaminius, stated openly that he aimed at breaking the hold the ancient practice had over the *res publica*, both in general terms and in particular as a tool for a commander's political enemies to interfere with his conduct of a military campaign.[27] Whether Claudius Pulcher pronounced his intentions in similar manner we do not know; that he shared Flaminius' view of auspices is evident, and his actions once back in Rome make it a fair conclusion that he was not content with a one-time act of contempt, but under attack now hoped to challenge the practice itself. Only Iunius Pullus can be presumed to have ignored the auspices to avoid a potentially devastating military setback rather than out of contempt; but that he chose to disobey them at all shows that he believed neither in their reality nor in the absolute necessity of maintaining them *rei publicae causa*. Lutatius' outlook—be he Catulus or Cerco—cannot have differed much, and, like Flaminius after him, he sought to challenge the practice of auspices on a fundamental level; unlike Flaminius, he stepped back from the brink when confronted by the Senate. Coming so close on the trials of Claudius and Pullus, it would surprise if Lutatius could not count on a measure of—at least tacit—support.

---

[27] Zonar. 8.20, καὶ διδάξειν καὶ τοὺς οἴκοι ἔφη μήτ' ὄρνισι μήτ' ἄλλῳ δή τινι τοιούτῳ προσέχοντας ἀπατᾶσθαι (in 223 BC); Livy 21.63.5, *ob haec ratus auspiciis ementiendis ... retenturos se in urbe* (in 217).

In this light, the claim carries little conviction that the tradition of Flaminius the contemptor of auspices, hostile as it certainly is, emerged as a concerted effort to make him a scapegoat designed to exonerate the political class of its collective failure against Hannibal.[28] It would be absurd to blame the Nobles for Flaminius' defeat at Lake Trasumene, and nothing short of delirious imagination could support the notion that, as a class, they ever were touched by the slightest sense of having failed in their conduct of the war. Terentius Varro had suffered, at Cannae, a far more devastating catastrophe, and was blamed for it with far less justification—as far as their respective military dispositions are concerned—than Flaminius was for his. Yet Varro retained the respect—grudging perhaps, but respect nonetheless—of his contemporaries, continuing in several commands down to 207, and other assignments beyond. The difference lies not in their political allegiances (largely the same), nor in the degree of hostility directed at them by the established political class (also largely the same), but in a stark fact: Varro had played by the rules of *religio*, and obeyed the auspices; Flaminius (like Claudius Pulcher) had not.[29] His demonstrative rejection of augury was not invented after his catastrophe to create a scapegoat; it simply opened the door wide to his posthumous vilification.

Both in 249 and 217, we find indications that the decision to name a Dictator was not made immediately and unanimously, but only after some hesitation and resistance. Opponents will have had a variety of reasons, discomfort with the sweeping powers of that office being not the least of them; but insofar as the appointment of a Dictator *rei gerundae causa* appears to have been driven in large part by considerations of *religio*, and within that realm, on those two occasions, by charges that a Consul had fought *contra auspicia*, one should assume that a number of senators, and not merely those without influence, agreed with Claudius and Flaminius in their fundamental sentiments regarding the matter.

The tale of Papirius Cursor the Dictator and his Magister Equitum, Fabius Rullianus, offers further indication that the proper role of auspices in the conduct of the *res publica*, at least insofar as warfare was concerned, was a subject of debate in the late third century. As we have seen, the story, as told by Livy, received its essential shape in the penumbra of the Hannibalic War. The "Papirian" version, that is to say, Pictor's, to the extent that we can identify it, focussed on the point that the Dictator's auspices had been found *incerta*; that he must return to the City to repeat them; that the same *religio* necessarily must extend to the auspices of his Magister Equitum; and hence that Fabius Rullianus, in fighting a battle against his superior's orders, did commit not only an act of disobedience but an offense against the auspices as well. The versions favorable to Rullianus are so closely tied, in their presentation of the facts and in their line of argument, to the

---

[28] Meißner 104. [29] Cf. Rosenstein 1990: 35, 85, 90–91.

268 THE CHALLENGE TO THE AUSPICES

dispute between the Cunctator and his Master of the Horse, Minucius Rufus, that they could not well have arisen much after the war. (Which does not exclude subsequent elaboration on either side of the issue.) The pro-Rullianus view takes a three-pronged but internally consistent approach: apart from a brief assertion that the Magister Equitum held his auspices independently of the Dictator's (and thus, by implication, was not subject to the *religio* that attached to the latter), the question of auspices is studiously ignored; the main thrust of the argument is directed at the fact that Rullianus was victorious, that victory gave proof of divine favor, and thus justified disobedience, even towards the Dictator (and, again, by implication towards the auspices); and in a concluding threat, the power of the people and their Tribunes is invoked against that of the Dictator.[30] To those who saw in auspices a bedrock element of republican government, such reasoning would have posed a serious challenge.

8.2.2 The Cunctator and his Deputy

One wonders, indeed, if auspices played a part in the quarrel between Fabius and Minucius. After making so much of Flaminius' neglect of the auspices and letting Fabius open his first Senate meeting with the judgment that this neglect, more than military error, had brought about the disaster (21.63.5–9; 22.1.5–7, 3.11–13, 9.7), Livy's narrative of the dictatorship falls strangely silent on that account: the word occurs only once more, at the end, when Minucius acknowledges the error of his ways (*sub imperium auspiciumque tuum redeo*, 22.30.4). Minucius' fortunes rose when the Dictator was compelled to return to Rome and leave his Magister Equitum in command. What had occasioned that return?

Inde sacrorum causa Romam revocatus, says Livy (22.18.8). Which agrees with Polybios, who has Fabius forced to return to Rome for certain religious rites (καταναγκασθεὶς δὲ μετ' ὀλίγας ἡμέρας ἐπί τινας ἀπελθεῖν θυσίας εἰς τὴν Ῥώμην, 3.94.9), although Plutarch offers a detail: it was the priests who summoned Fabius to Rome for those ceremonies (μετὰ δὲ ταῦτα τῶν ἱερέων καλούντων αὐτὸν εἰς Ῥώμην ἐπί τινας θυσίας, *Fab.* 8.1). On reflection, this appears odd: we hear of commanders being recalled from the field on numerous other occasions (to hold elections, most often)—but never, it seems, *sacrorum causa*.[31] Even stranger, the summons being issued by "the priests," as Plutarch avers: which priests? If *sacra* were at stake, the Pontiffs, presumably; again, we have no parallel for such a

---

[30] See Chapter 1.3.
[31] The instances of subordinate officers returning to Rome in order to sacrifice (Livy 43.11.1, a Military Tribune; 43.23.6, a *legatus*) offer no parallel: the *sacra* in question there could only be private ones, as in the case of P. Licinius Crassus and M. Cornelius Scipio Maluginensis, who as Praetors in 176 refused to go to their provinces in Spain, claiming that solemn sacrifices prevented them (41.15.9–10, cf. 42.32.2). See Palmer 94–95.

summons. And Livy took care to note how all the religious measures voted at the start of the dictatorship had in fact been implemented before Fabius even discussed the military situation in the Senate, let alone took the field (22.9.9–11.1). Private *sacra* requiring his attention are ruled out by Livy's *revocatus*, not to mention Plutarch's priests.[32]

If Polybios were all we had on this question, one would not hesitate to conclude that θυσίαι here simply stands for religious ritual in general, and that the Dictator was forced to return to Rome in order to repeat the auspices.[33] (Nothing in Polybios about his being recalled; nor would the historian, distinctly uninterested in such matters, have found it worth his while to spell things out.) Let us, for argument's sake, briefly pursue that trail. Repetition of the auspices would be necessary because they had been discovered, somehow, to be or have become *incerta* or invalid. On the prevailing (we might say, "Papirian") theory, *religio* attaching to the Dictator equally affected his Magister Equitum: if the former's auspices had to be repeated, those of the latter could hold no validity until such repetition had taken effect. Any battle in the meantime would be fought *vitio*. Minucius fought a battle—and won. It would pose an interesting quandary: either the auspices of the Master-of-Horse were fully independent of the Dictator's, after all, and no *vitium* had occurred, or Iuppiter had granted victory to a commander who had engaged the enemy, at will and in full knowledge of the fact, *contra auspicia*. (Unless, of course, Fabius had already repeated his when the battle occurred.) Those inclined to question the practice of auspices would seize on the second interpretation as the obvious one; Minucius had finally succeeded where Claudius Pulcher and Flaminius had come to grief. To those who, from personal belief or political consideration, deemed auspices indispensable, that view would be unacceptable; the alternative, unpalatable.

But Minucius did not remain victorious; his fall from grace proceeded as rapidly as his rise to eminence. When the strategy he advocated suffered total meltdown at Cannae, few will have wanted to continue an open challenge of the auspices: not because they had come to believe in their efficacy, but because questioning the auspices now had become politically inadvisable, perhaps impossible, and certainly unprofitable. If Minucius' victory at Gereonium was achieved *contra auspicia* (or, at a minimum, *incertis auspiciis*), the moment to exploit it had already passed; the failed commander, now dead at Cannae, no longer served to make the case. Fabius Rullianus, though, might prove a useful substitute, if treated with caution: the issue of the auspices to be just touched on, not made the core of the argument.

---

[32] Smith 1996: 201 is unsure "whether it was for *sacra* of his own *gens*, or because his presence as dictator was necessary for state cults." But for gentilician *sacra*, any Fabius ought to have sufficed, like Dorsuo during the Gaulish occupation (Livy 5.46.2–3); there should have been no need to call the Dictator away from "managing the Thing."

[33] As Oakley suggests, *CL* 4: 583. Champion 109 with n. 144 assumes as much.

The "Papirian" school, too, might be content to sidestep the questions of *auspicia* in the story of Minucius, and focus instead on the dramatic potential of the conflict: the Dictator reviled, threatened with *abrogatio*, and humiliated; the Master of the Horse elevated, unaware of his own limitations, and brought low again by too much self-confidence. For Rullianus, this approach would offer scant relief as his story evolved: disobedience remained disobedience, and until informed of the contrary, he must assume that his auspices, like the Dictator's, were *incerta*. (Besides, there were still those who remembered the oldest version of that tale, the one in which Rullianus lost his battle.) But once his victory had prevailed even in the "Papirian" (in other words, Fabius Pictor's) version, a fudge became inevitable: contrary to expectations, his *vitium*, instead of causing the ruin of his army, recoiled on the *res publica* by way of his quarrel with Papirius: *cuius rei vitium non in belli eventum, quod prospere gestum est, sed in rabiem atque iras imperatorum vertit* (Livy 8.30.1). A "lame explanation," perhaps, from the Augurs' point of view, who may have preferred to argue that the Dictator's auspices were *incerta*, but not manifestly invalid: hence the Magister Equitum could have won a battle without causing distress to the theory.[34] It would have worked equally well for Minucius.

If Fabius went to Rome to repeat his auspices, what we read in Livy would serve both sides' interests in covering up that element. That he did cannot, however, be established.

8.3 Upholding the Auspices

Another opportunity to challenge the auspices arose not long after Cannae. Yet this time, the man whom they had put at a disadvantage chose not to avail himself of it.

8.3.1 The Second Consulship of Marcellus

On the Ides of March, 215, Ti. Sempronius Gracchus (*mag. eq.* 216) entered office as Consul, without a colleague: the Consul designate L. Postumius Albinus (*cos. II* 229) had been killed in Gaul a few weeks earlier.[35] Gracchus was slow in scheduling *comitia* to choose a suffect, which prompted an outcry in the Senate, where M. Claudius Marcellus (*cos. I* 222)—temporarily absent from the City to oversee a major reshuffling of armies in the South—was a clear favorite to occupy the vacant spot; the Consul assured the senators that he was waiting to call elections

---

[34] Linderski 1993: 62 = *RQ* 617.
[35] Livy 23.30.18; cf. 23.24.6–25.9; Polyb. 3.118.6; Zonar. 9.3; Oros. 4.16.11.

solely in order to enable Marcellus to be back in Rome as a candidate, *ut vos consulem quem tempus rei publicae postularet, quem maxime voltis, haberetis* (Livy 23.31.7–8). When elections were held at last, Marcellus won *ingenti consensu*, as expected (we do not know of any competitors). As he entered office, thunder was heard; on being summoned, the College of Augurs found Marcellus *vitio creatus*, and the *patres*—not the Senate as a whole, clearly, and more importantly, not the Augurs—spread the word that the gods disapproved of two Plebeians as Consuls; Marcellus abdicated, and the People elected Fabius Maximus in his stead.[36]

The incident has been seen as yet another egregious example of the Cunctator's total control, and use to his political benefit, of the Augural College.[37] Not a shred of evidence supports such claims, whereas ample evidence exists to the contrary. Marcellus enjoyed the backing of much of the Senate, and of the Consul presiding at his election. If Fabius was so eager to secure the consulship of 215 for himself, because, after Cannae, he thought it imperative to maintain the strategy he had adopted while Dictator,[38] why did he not engineer a *vitium* to overturn the original elections, and disqualify Postumius Albinus, a man not known for operating with an excess of caution? (Or was Fabius able to predict that the Gauls would take care of that?) If the Cunctator was so keen on keeping Marcellus from the consulship, why would he later in the same year, in a show of public humiliation that has scant rivals in Roman annals, block the election of his own niece's husband, T. Otacilius Crassus, in a move clearly calculated to get Marcellus elected instead (Livy 23.7.10–9.3)?[39] And why do we have no evidence of serious rivalry or disagreement between Fabius and Marcellus in the years to come?

---

[36] Livy 23.31.13, *cui ineunti consulatum cum tonuisset, vocati augures vitio creatum videri pronuntiaverunt; volgoque patres ita fama ferebant, quod tum primum duo plebeii consules facti essent, id deis cordi non esse.*

[37] E.g., Münzer "Fabius (116)" *RE* 6.2 (1909) 1823; Münzer 74; Scullard 1951: 57–60; Lippold 169–171, 348; more cautiously, Levene 1993: 51. Seibert 1993b: 227 treats fantasy as established fact: "Gegen die Wahl ... brachte Q. Fabius Maximus religiöse Bedenken vor." Vervaet 2012: 90 imagines, without evidence and against Livy's unequivocal implication that Marcellus was elected without significant—if any—competition (*ingenti consensu*, 23.31.13; cf. 23.31.8, *ut vos consulem ... quem maxime voltis haberetis*), that "at least one ranking patrician senator had run against Marcellus": none other, we are to suppose, than Fabius Maximus, "who also happened to be the chief augur of the day." Chief Augur? The notion that there was an *augur maximus* is not new, but nonetheless untenable: see Linderski *AL* 2154 n. 26.

[38] Thus Lippold 383 *ad* n. 394; similarly Lazenby 1978: 94, 100; *contra*, persuasively, Beck 2005: 309–310; Lundgreen 149 n. 421.

[39] It should not be necessary to point out that, as a Patrician, Fabius could not take Otacilius' place once he had effectively rejected him as a viable candidate. His rejection of the leading Patrician contender, M. Aemilius Regillus, the Flamen Martialis (thus Livy 29.11.14, 38.6, surely correct, not Quirinalis as at 23.8.10; see Broughton *MRR* 1: 305; Rüpke *FS* 2: 741), was based on good precedent: in 241, the Flamen Martialis, A. Postumius Albinus, although Consul, had been prohibited from leaving the City to go to war (Livy 37.51.1–2; *Per.* 19; Val. Max. 1.1.2; Tac. *Ann.* 3.71.3). Back then, the situation had not required two Consuls capable of military command. That any Roman Noble should avail himself of *mos* to further his own career is only to be expected, and ought not to be taken for a remarkable example of scheming. Cf. Lippold's fairly level-headed assessment (341–351) of how Fabius used religious considerations in the political arena; for the undoubtedly correct interpretation

The siege of Casilinum in 214 (Livy 24.19) is sometimes cited as evidence of "fundamental differences" between the two.[40] In that episode, Fabius called on Marcellus for assistance, suggesting several courses of how he could offer it; Marcellus chose the one that Fabius clearly preferred (24.19.3–5). After unsuccessful attempts to take the town, the Consuls disagreed on how to proceed next; Fabius yielded to Marcellus, and both made preparations for a full-fledged assault (24.19.6–8). When some of the townsfolk opened a gate in an effort to reach Fabius' camp and implore him to allow them safe passage to Capua, Marcellus seized the opportunity to throw his troops into the town and capture it, with huge loss of life among its inhabitants; the survivors were partly sent to Rome (if they had served in Hannibal's army), partly distributed among neighboring communities for imprisonment (24.19.9–11). The episode shows a difference in temperament and approach to military problems, true enough. It also shows, on both Fabius' and Marcellus' part, a ready willingness to cooperate—something not to be taken for granted among Roman commanders. And while Fabius did indeed issue a safe conduct to Capua to the few who had made it to his camp, nothing indicates that he quarreled with Marcellus over the disposition of the remaining survivors.[41]

Marcellus was an Augur himself (indeed, *augur optumus*, Cic. *Div*. 2.77), *vir triumphalis*, dedicator of the *spolia opima*, and riding high in favor with both the People and the Senate: not a man lightly trifled with, or easily crossed. We have no indications that, within the College, his voice went unheard and his views counted for little. Seven of the nine—or perhaps eight: a vacancy is possible—Augurs in 215 are known.[42] Besides Fabius Maximus, the patrician members were P. Furius Philus (*cos*. 223) and Cn. Cornelius Lentulus (*cos*. 201). The successor of M. Aemilius Lepidus (*cos*. 232, died 216) has escaped all record, but presumably was also a Patrician; he may, however, not yet have been chosen at the time Marcellus' case came up.[43] The Plebeians in the College were, in addition to Marcellus, Sp. Carvilius Ruga (*cos. II* 228), M. Pomponius Matho (*cos*. 231), and C. Atilius Serranus (*pr*. 218); the fifth plebeian member remains unidentified.[44]

---

of the entire Marcellus episode, see Linderski *AL* 2168–2173; cf. Müller-Seidel 241–249; Beck 2005: 293–295, 309–310; Lundgreen 149–150.

[40] Lippold 383 *ad* n. 394.

[41] See North's (1967: 427–429) and Levene's (2010: 200–202) perceptive discussions.

[42] For convenient tabulation, see Rüpke *FS* 1: 69–70.

[43] Conceivably Lentulus, whose co-optation date is not recorded, could have succeeded Lepidus; again, not necessarily in time to judge Marcellus' case. Either way, one (presumably) patrician member of the College is unknown.

[44] Rüpke *FS* 1: 68–71, cf. 2: 1186, accepting (like, e.g., Szemler 73 n.1) the manifestly botched account of Livy 27.6.15–16 (*C. Servilius pontifex factus in locum T. Otacilii Crassi, Ti. Sempronius Ti. filius Longus augur factus in locum T. Otacilii Crassi; decemvir item sacris faciundis in locum Ti. Sempronii C. filii Longi Ti. Sempronius Ti. filius Longus suffectus*), lists T. Otacilius Crassus (*pr. II* 214; *pontifex*) in this slot, and explains the resulting double priesthood—both Pontiff and Augur—with the "Stellung der Familie und der engen Verbindung mit den dominierenden Fabiern und Marcelli" (*FS* 2: 1186). That family had produced a grand total of two Consuls (the last in 246): hardly a position of

At least two of these can be suspected of not being in the Cunctator's camp politically. Lentulus' father, L. Cornelius Lentulus (*cos.* 237), Pontifex Maximus, had disagreed with Fabius in 218 on how to respond to Hannibal's sack of Saguntum: Lentulus had advocated an immediate declaration of war, and lost (Zonar. 8.22). Pomponius has been deemed closer to "the Cornelii" and "the Aemilii" than to Fabius, and even been located in the political circle of C. Flaminius.[45] Family connections did exist between the Atilii Reguli and the Fabii,[46] which tells us nothing, however, about Atilius Serranus' attitude. A majority of the Augurs agreed that Marcellus was *vitio creatus*; to assert that they did so—four of them, at a minimum, *viri consulares*—in blind obedience to Fabius' bidding, without independent judgment of the augural issue and political situation before them, would be preposterous.

We have no record of what the Augurs identified as the actual cause of the *vitium* that had occurred at Marcellus' election. But it is evident from Livy, who distinguishes clearly between *augures vitio creatum videri pronuntiaverunt* and *volgoque patres ita fama ferebant*, that their *responsum* contained nothing about the issue of having two Plebeians for Consuls: that interpretation was grafted on the augural ruling—perhaps even spread before the verdict had been rendered—by the *patres* (here clearly not just "senators," but specifically the Patricians in the Senate). This does not prove, naturally, that the Augurs were not motivated in their decision by a concern about two plebeian Consuls; but ever since the *lex Ogulnia*, a majority of the College must be Plebeians—five out of nine;[47] and at this moment there may have been five out of eight. One should not automatically

---

prominence from which to propel this military and political underachiever into the exclusive club of men combining those two priesthoods—only one such individual, Fabius Maximus, being securely attested during the entire period of the Republic. (And Fabius became a Pontiff only in 216: Rüpke would have Otacilius hold both priesthoods since at least 218.) As regards his connection with the Fabii (he had married the Cunctator's niece) and Marcelli, the open and public contempt with which Fabius derailed his bid for the consulship of 214 seeks its equal; and four years later the voters unceremoniously dropped Otacilius from consideration for the consulship of 210 when the patrician front runner, T. Manlius Torquatus (*cos. II* 224), withdrew his name. Both times, Marcellus was elected in Otacilius' place (as Rüpke acknowledges, *FS* 2: 1186): if such humiliating setbacks constitute evidence of the man's influence, one wonders why no one else ever succeeded in becoming both Augur and Pontifex. Badian demonstrated long ago (1968a: 32) that the notice of Otacilius' replacement as Augur cannot be correct, especially in view of Livy's identifying the man simply as *pontifex* when reporting his death at 26.23.7–8; in that same context, Livy did not miss the co-optation of M. Servilius Geminus as Augur for the deceased Sp. Carvilius. It does not follow, certainly, that Otacilius' name should be replaced with Atilius Serranus' (thus Bardt's solution, 19–20), although Badian's suggestion that no Augur died at all in 211 carries no conviction: what purpose would the supposed "pure invention by an annalist" have served? Massive confusion appears more likely; as Badian notes, Livy consistently ignores the fifth plebeian slot in the College. Perhaps it intruded here.

[45] Bleicken 1955: 35, 39, concluding that his abdication as Magister Equitum (with the Dictator *comitiorum habendorum* L. Veturius Philo) in 217 was therefore "mit aller Wahrscheinlichkeit ein Werk des Q. Fabius"; similarly if with more caution Lippold 162, cf. 127, 346. The ready eagerness with which, on this view, Roman Augurs—*viri consulares* and *triumphales*, no less—cooperated in their own emasculation whenever their colleague Fabius brandished his *lituus* is astonishing.

[46] Lippold 116, 127, 136 n. 241, 158 n. 338.

[47] Livy 10.9.1–2; see Bardt 22; Ross Taylor 386; Szemler 29 n. 1; Rüpke *FS* 3: 21, 1421, 1621.

assume that a majority could readily be assembled in support of a view that found two plebeian Consuls unacceptable.

We must not overlook that, for the Augurs to get involved, the thunder had to be reported by someone—and, of course, the fact could have been manifest, a clap of thunder (the meteorological phenomenon is known to occur in Italy), heard by numerous witnesses, having actually sounded.[48] Either way, once thunder "had been heard," the matter could not simply be ignored, especially if the report was made not by some L. Titius but by influential senators such as, for example, T. Manlius Torquatus (*cos. II* 224; *cens.* 231) or M. Cornelius Cethegus (*cens.* 209; *cos.* 204): Patricians both, and on record—albeit not before 210—as Marcellus' *inimici* (Livy 26.26.5–8, 32.1–5). The Consul Gracchus had no choice but to summon the Augurs, with or without first consulting the Senate.[49] Given the apparent singularity of the event (no other instance of an oblative sign vitiating a magistrate's auspices for entering office is on record), the Augurs could have found it difficult to come up with a harmless explanation, with patrician senators losing no time exploiting the occasion by publicly announcing their view of what was wrong.

8.3.2 The Nature of the *Vitium*

But could Marcellus not have solved his quandary by simply repeating his auspices the next day? Adducing this incident as particularly characteristic of Fabius' augural activity ("ganz besonders bezeichnend für die Augurentätigkeit des Fabius"), Bleicken complained that Marcellus was not allowed to repeat his auspices, "gegen jedes Herkommen, denn für gewöhnlich stand der Wiederholung der Antrittsauspizien nichts im Wege."[50] Since we have no attested case of a negative answer to a magistrate's impetrative auspices on entering office, we do not know what was "gewöhnlich" with regard to repeating them. But that is beside the point. To think that Marcellus, in this particular situation, could have repeated his auspices is to misunderstand the augural nature of the event. To signal a negative response when asked for auspices, Iuppiter will either withhold the desired affirmative sign (the Chickens will not eat), or send an adversative sign of the same kind as requested. Marcellus, like every Consul, would have asked for a *fulmen sinistrum*, the flash of lightning "on the left," to confirm that he had valid auspices; a negative answer would have taken the form of no lightning to be observed at all, or a flash in the west. But thunder, although a sign *de caelo*, was

---

[48] Cf. Beck 2005: 310; Lundgreen 149–150.
[49] Lippold's discussion, 170–171 with n. 393, of whether the Augurs might have been summoned by the Senate or the Consuls, or acted on their own initiative, is moot: *vocati augures*, says Livy.
[50] Bleicken 1955: 39 n. 1.

not the same as lightning: Marcellus had not asked for a *tonitrus sinister*. When Marcellus asked for the customary *fulmen sinistrum*, he very likely observed the desired flash; it was the *tonitrus* (on the right) heard simultaneously or in close order that caused trouble: an oblative sign, and clearly negative. And oblative signs, when negative in character, do not simply deny permission for the day, but alert to the presence of *vitium*.[51] The question then was not if Marcellus could, or should, repeat his auspices: if *vitium* attached to his auspices at the moment he first asked Iuppiter to confirm them, it attached to his entire consulship, and no repetition could mend the flaw.[52]

Münzer called the incident and Marcellus' subsequent election for 214 "ein abgemachtes Spiel": troubled by the prospect of two plebeian Consuls, Fabius Maximus arranged the *vitium* that forced Marcellus to abdicate, then made sure—by way of compensation—that Marcellus was elected Consul for the following year.[53] That patrician opposition to having two Plebeians as Consuls, not opposition to Marcellus being one of them, was at the bottom of the episode is certainly possible;[54] less obvious—and plausible—is the assumption that the motivation for such opposition must have been driven by mere patrician–plebeian status rivalry. As Beck points out, the plebeian Marcellus lacked the "sakrale Autorität" of a Patrician, and, in the wake of the catastrophic course of the war with Hannibal, concerns that now was not the time to experiment with an all-plebeian consulship were probably genuine: and if a clap of thunder had in fact sounded, it would have been impossible, under the prevailing circumstances, to ignore it.[55]

If we strip Münzer's reconstruction of the claim, which has no basis in the evidence, that Fabius Maximus and the Augural College were the driving force behind it, we may be getting close to what happened. Unknown individuals (perhaps patrician opponents of a two-Plebeians consulship) reported thunder immediately after Marcellus had completed his initial auspices. Unable to quickly find a means of explaining away the obvious—one could not wish for a stronger and more explicit *vinculum temporis* than this—the Augurs had no choice but to follow precedent (and some earlier verdicts of this kind likely enough had been based on weaker evidence), and declare their colleague *vitio creatus*. Marcellus stepped down, and Fabius took his place as Consul—with an understanding that he would do everything in his power to see to Marcellus' election for the

---

[51] Chapter 2.2.2.
[52] Linderski *AL* 2169–2171; Konrad 2004: 176–177; Van Haeperen 2012: 78; cf. Chapter 2.3.
[53] Münzer 1920: 74; similarly Scullard 1951: 57–58.
[54] Linderski *AL* 2171–2172; Lundgreen 149–150. Càssola 1968: 316–318 sees the *vitium* as the work of unidentified enemies of Marcellus within the *collegium*, but pointedly excludes Fabius as one of them.
[55] Beck 2005: 310; see also Champion's sensible discussion, 109–111.

following year. It forms the only rational explanation for Fabius' unparalleled intervention against the front runners, Aemilius and Otacilius, on that occasion.

8.3.3 *Augur Optumus*

Marcellus abdicated forthwith, and without complaint—which has led to strange flights of fancy. One scholar took Marcellus' habit of always travelling in a litter with the curtains drawn *si quando rem agere vellet, ne impediretur auspiciis* (Cic. *Div.* 2.77) as a learning experience from his abortive second consulship ("Marcellus aber scheint aus dem Vorgang gelernt zu haben, daß man sich den Zeichen der Götter notfalls entziehen mußte, wenn man ein Vorhaben durchführen wollte").[56] How anyone could have learned this particular lesson from this particular incident remains a mystery; without taking his initial auspices as Consul, Marcellus could not enter office; the thunder was an oblative sign observed, surely, by a third party, and reported, probably, not to him but to his colleague. At which point, the matter was out of his hands (except insofar as that, in the College, he had a say in its interpretation): no enclosed litter could have saved his consulship that day.

Another scholar ventured yet a step further: Marcellus travelled in the closed litter both to protest his rejection and to demonstrate his faith, in quiet opposition. "Es war ihm möglich, trotz der schmachvollen Erniedrigung weiterhin sein Gesicht zu wahren: Die Götter hatten ihn zum Rücktritt gebracht, nicht aber sein persönliches Fehlverhalten."[57] How else? No one found *vitio creatus* was ever implicated in the *vitium*: the fault was, of necessity, that of the magistrate presiding at the election, not the nominee's. There was no "humiliating degradation," no face to be kept, since no face was lost; the consulship counted—*consul iterum*.

There is, of course, nothing in Cicero's account to indicate that Marcellus adopted his peculiar practice only in reaction to the episode of 215. The *imperator* and *augur optumus*[58] simply availed himself of a fundamental rule of augury: for an oblative sign to have augural effect, it must be observed and accepted (or rejected); a sign not perceived—nor reported by a third party—held no force. This is well known, and attested, with inimitable clarity, as early as Cato Censorius: *domi cum auspicamus honorem me deum immortalium velim habuisse. servi, ancillae, si quis eorum sub centone crepuit, quod ego non sensi, nullum mihi vitium facit. si cui ibidem servo aut ancillae dormienti evenit, quod comitia prohibere solet, ne id quidem mihi vitium facit* (apud Fest. 268L).[59] Cicero continues with an

---

[56] Bergemann 94.   [57] Rosenberger 217.
[58] Since *c*.226: Plut. *Marc.* 2.3; Rüpke *FS* 2: 884.
[59] Cf. Pliny *NH* 28.17, *in augurum certe disciplina constat neque diras neque ulla auspicia pertinere ad eos qui quamque rem ingredientes observare se ea negaverint*; Serv. ad *Aen.* 12.260, *nam in oblativis auguriis in potestate videntis est, utrum id ad se pertinere velit, an refutet et abominetur*; Augustin.

example from the Augurs' own practice: *huic simile est quod nos augures praecipimus, ne iuges auspicium obveniat, ut iumenta iubeant diiungere.*

Consul now for the third time, Fabius Maximus in 215 took command of the army in Campania, near Teanum (Livy 23.32.1). Having advanced to Cales, he was forced to postpone the crossing of the Volturnus river: first it became necessary to repeat his auspices, then he had to see to the procuration of a host of prodigies, with considerable difficulty (23.36.9–10, *nec Fabius, qui ad Cales castra habebat, Volturnum flumen traducere audebat exercitum, occupatus primo auspiciis repetendis, dein prodigiis quae alia super alia nuntiabantur; expiantique ea haud facile litari haruspices respondebant*). Where did he repeat the auspices—*in castris* at Cales, or back in Rome? In the camp, if the auspices in question were merely unfavorable ones (obtained day by day) that prevented his moving the army; but *repetere auspicia* in Livy normally refers to the commander's returning to Rome to repeat his "auspices of investiture," which had become *incerta* or invalid. The *prodigia* should eliminate all doubt: they surely had to be dealt with in Rome.[60] The Consul's return to the City, at the cost of delaying his campaign, set a clear example so soon after Marcellus' abdication without complaint. To conduct war with any hope of victory, the auspices must come first.

His fifth and final consulship, in 209, furnished the old Augur with another demonstration of the importance and efficacy of auspices. As he prepared to march his army from Tarentum to Metapontum, unaware of the trap Hannibal had set for him there, the birds repeatedly refused to signal Iuppiter's permission (*Fabio auspicanti priusquam egrederetur ab Tarento aves simul atque iterum non addixerunt*, Livy 27.16.15). Fabius stayed put. When the men from Metapontum returned to inquire about his delay, the threat of enhanced interrogation made them reveal Hannibal's plot.[61] Abiding by the auspices, the Cunctator had saved his army from grave risk, and perhaps annihilation. The example required no elaboration.

Doctr. Christ. 2.2.4, *illa signa, quibus perniciosa daemonum societas comparatur, pro cuiusque observationibus valent; quod manifestissime ostendit ritus augurum, qui et antequam observent et posteaquam observata signa tenuerint id agunt ne videant volatus aut audiant voces avium; quia nulla ista signa sunt, nisi consensus observantis accedat.* See Valeton 1889: 428–429; 1890: 433–434; Linderski *AL* 2195–2196, 2200–2201, 2203 n. 198; and cf. 1993: 60–61. Driediger-Murphy 2019: 51–125 rejects, perhaps rightly, the view that a clearly observed sign could simply be nullified by its observer through a declaration of not having seen it; but she agrees that, for a sign to have effect, it must be perceived by, or reported to, its intended recipient.

[60] Chapter 2.6; on Livy's usage, Linderski 1993: 69 n. 31 = *RQ* 624. Cf. Livy 23.39.5, *et circa Capuam transgresso Volturnum Fabio post expiata tandem prodigia ambo consules rem gerebant*; Driediger-Murphy 2019: 178 n. 63; Koortbojian 54.

[61] Livy 27.16.11–16; Plut. *Fab.* 19.7–8; cf. Chapter 5.2.2. His *haruspex* also had warned him to beware of treachery and ambush (*hostia quoque caesa consulenti deos haruspex cavendum a fraude hostili et ab insidiis praedixit*), but precautions could have been taken while on the march: what prevented a move were the auspices.

8.4 The Triumph of the Augurs

We have no indications that Marcellus' *vitium* in 215 was used by anyone to question the auspices and their oversight by the College of Augurs.[62] Yet little more than a year earlier, another case of magistrates found *vitio creati* apparently had triggered such a protest. On that occasion, it involved a Dictator—and may have dragged Marcellus' name into the debate.

8.4.1 The *Vitium* of the First Marcellus

Under the year 327 V, Livy reports the appointment of a Dictator *comitiorum causa*: M. Claudius Marcellus (*cos.* 331), named by the Consul L. Cornelius Lentulus *in castris* in Samnium (8.23.13). The appointment, however, prompted questions; the Augurs were summoned, and ruled that Marcellus was *vitio creatus* (8.23.14, *consulti augures vitiosum videri dictatorem pronuntiaverunt*). Some Tribunes of the Plebs took issue with this: how could the Augurs, sitting in Rome, know that a *vitium* had occurred in the Consul's camp, when the latter, rising from his bed at nighttime, had to name the Dictator in ritual silence, and when neither the Consul had given public or private communication to anyone concerning the matter, nor any living soul had come forward to state that he had seen or heard anything that would disrupt the auspices? It must be obvious to everyone that the true *vitium*, in the Augurs' eyes, was the Plebeian as Dictator.[63] Such protests notwithstanding, Marcellus abdicated, and an *interregnum* ensued; the fourteenth Interrex eventually completed the elections (8.23.17).

The historicity of the first Marcellus' dictatorship has its doubters and defenders;[64] what concerns us is the reasoning attributed here to the Tribunes. The Augurs' apparent desire to avoid a plebeian Dictator carries an obvious

---

[62] Plutarch says that the "priests" judged the thunder to be a negative sign, but were hesitant to oppose Marcellus' election openly, for fear of the People; hence he stepped down on his own accord (ἐπιβροντήσαντος δὲ τοῦ θεοῦ καὶ τῶν ἱερέων οὐκ αἴσιον τιθεμένων τὸ σημεῖον, ἐμφανῶς δὲ κωλύειν ὀκνούντων καὶ δεδιότων τὸν δῆμον, αὐτὸς ἐξωμόσατο τὴν ἀρχήν, *Marc*. 12.2). Of course, the Augurs had been formally summoned (*vocati*), and had rendered an official *responsum* to the Consul and—or—the Senate (Livy 23.31.13); it does not get any more open than that. Plutarch's version might conceivably derive from a source ascribing sinister machinations to the Augurs; but his emphasis on Marcellus' voluntary abdication, without any public calls for it (a manifestly untrue element), make it far more likely that all we have here is the biographer's attempt to focus on the hero's qualities.

[63] Livy 8.23.15–16: *nam neque facile fuisse id vitium nosci, cum consul oriens de nocte silentio diceret dictatorem, neque ab consule cuiquam publice privatimve de ea re scriptum esse nec quemquam mortalium exstare qui se vidisse aut audisse quid dicat quod auspicium dirimeret, neque augures divinare Romae sedentes potuisse quid in castris consuli vitii obvenisset; cui non apparere, quod plebeius dictator sit, id vitium auguribus visum?* See Linderski, *AL* 2172, on the concentration of augural technical language in this passage.

[64] Skeptical: Münzer "Claudius (218)" *RE* 3.2 (1899) 2737–2738; Bandel 88; Linderski *AL* 2172. In favor: Jahn 87–89.

resemblance to the case of 215. But the main point of the complaints against their ruling in 327—that no one had reported any sign indicative of *vitium*, and that, absent such a report, the Augurs in Rome could not possibly know what had gone wrong in the Consul's camp—do not fit the latter situation:[65] in 215, we do have a report, and everything took place in Rome, in full view of the public. One could argue over the significance of thunder, or whether it indeed had occurred; but no one could possibly advance the arguments ascribed to the Tribunes of 327 against the Augurs' ruling of 215.

Those arguments, however, could have been eminently suited to circumstances that had developed late in 217. Unwilling to return to Rome in order to hold elections, the Consuls, Cn. Servilius Geminus and M. Atilius Regulus (suffect), proposed an *interregnum*; the Senate instead voted for a dictatorship *comitiorum habendorum causa*, and L. Veturius Philo (*cos.* 220) was named—we do not know by which Consul—with M. Pomponius Matho (*cos.* 231; *augur*) for Magister Equitum. Fourteen days into their term, they abdicated *vitio creati*; an *interregnum* commenced, out of which emerged as Consuls C. Terentius Varro and L. Aemilius Paullus (*cos. I* 219).[66]

The *interregnum*, apparently, proved politically contentious: in certain quarters, it was perceived as an attempt, in a compact of all the Nobles (*id foedus inter omnes nobiles ictum*, Livy 22.34.7), to prevent the election of the *novus homo* Varro, through the greater control Patricians allegedly exercised over the election process under an Interrex.[67] The speech Livy puts in the mouth of one of Varro's supporters, the Tribune Q. Baebius Herennius, twice directly accuses the Augurs of deliberately manufacturing, in the Nobles' interest, the *vitium* to bring about the Dictator's abdication: *criminando non senatum modo sed etiam augures, quod dictatorem prohibuissent comitia perficere* ("attacking not only the Senate but also the Augurs, because they had prevented the Dictator from completing the elections," 22.34.3); *id postea, quia invitis iis dictator esset dictus comitiorum causa, expugnatum esse ut vitiosus dictator per augures fieret* ("finally, because a Dictator to hold elections had been named against their will, it had been forcibly brought about that the Dictator was rendered ritually flawed by the Augurs," 22.34.10).[68] Baebius here gives no reasons why anyone should think that the Augurs had

---

[65] Jahn 88 notes the discrepancy. [66] Livy 22.33.9–34.1, 35.1–4.
[67] For a fundamentally plausible, if in parts problematic, theory of how this would have worked, see Staveley 1954–55 *passim*. Jahn's contrary attempt (26, 50–52) to show that the Interrex held fewer means of influencing elections than the Consul fails to convince, although he may be correct in contending that the Interrex created only a single Consul, who then took office and oversaw the election of a colleague. The matter needs further study, but not here.
[68] From its position right after *id consules ambo ad exercitum morando quaesisse*, one normally would take *invitis iis* as referring to the Consuls (thus W–M *ad loc.*). The latter had recommended an *interregnum* so as not to have to come to Rome for the elections. But a Dictator could be named *in castris*; the Consuls should have no objections to that solution on grounds of military expediency. Although harsh, the sense rather favors *iis* to go with *omnes nobiles* at 22.34.7, as *habere igitur interregnum eos* at 22.34.11 certainly must. Levene 2010: 44 n. 109 appears to understand it in that sense,

made things up. He would have found the necessary ammunition in the unnamed Tribunes' attacks on the Augurs in 327 V. For the Dictator Veturius, in 217, was certainly named *in castris*,[69] like Marcellus in 327, and every one of the arguments made on the latter occasion fits the situation in 217 like a glove. Perhaps a Marcellus was Dictator in 327 and abdicated *vitio creatus*; the pontifical records just might contain a note to that effect. (One cannot help notice, though, the Dictator's abdication after fourteen days in 217, and the fourteen Interreges in 327.)

That the tribunician attacks on the Augurs ascribed to the earlier occasion present an authentic memory of the past we may with serenity discount. Yet such attacks, and the arguments put forward, were real enough: they reflect a struggle over the position of the auspices and those who oversaw them, the *collegium augurum*, in the workings of republican government—a struggle that played out over the second half of the third century. The Augurs won.

In his first challenge to the auspices, Flaminius was outmaneuvered (as argued above)[70] by the appointment of a Dictator that forced him to step down as Consul *vitio creatus*. His second attempt ended at Lake Trasumene, enabling the champions of augury to turn the tables on their opponents and interpret the catastrophe as confirming their view; Fabius Maximus lost no time making the point in the Senate—*plus neglegentia caerimoniarum auspicior<umque quam> temeritate atque inscitia peccatum a C. Flaminio consule esse* (Livy 22.9.7). The inability of Minucius Rufus to assert his independence—from the Dictator and, we may suspect, the auspices—with success, and the catastrophe at Cannae in the following year further undermined what had undoubtedly been a minority view to begin with. The firm and pointed refusal of no less an augural and military authority than Marcellus to challenge the finding that he was *vitio creatus* in 215 settled the issue.

8.4.2 *Vitium* and Its Consequences

And yet—despite the victory of augural practice and theory, every so often, in the century or so that followed, a commander would choose to go to war in the face of prohibitive, or at least questionable, auspices. The most egregious case occurred in 176.

The Consul Q. Petillius Spurinus, campaigning in Liguria, committed an error during auspication yet ignored it. Then, preparing to assault a fortified position

---

noting how Livy, in explicitly stating the Senate's preference for a Dictator over an *interregnum* (22.33.11), contradicts Baebius' accusation.

[69] Livy does not specifically say so, but as both Consuls had refused to come home to hold elections, it stands to reason that neither would be willing to return for the naming of a Dictator.

[70] Chapter 6.

named Letum, he announced to his troops that, on this day, he would take Letum (*se eo die Letum capturum esse*); Iuppiter could not tell whether the Consul had meant Letum or *letum* and, assuming the latter, let him be felled by an enemy missile, while sparing the army and granting the Romans a splendid victory. During the subsequent augural investigation in Rome, the Consul's *pullarius* unequivocally stated that there had been a flaw in the auspices, of which the Consul was fully aware (*vitium in auspicio fuisse, nec id consulem ignorasse*).[71] Evidently, Petillius went into battle without valid auspices knowingly and deliberately; but with his ill-omened choice of words, he enabled Iuppiter to make his sin recoil on him alone, and avert detriment from the *res publica*. Forty-one years after Flaminius' catastrophe at Lake Trasumene, Petillius' indifference to auspices strikes one as remarkable: the skepticism so well attested for intellectuals of the Late Republic apparently was not a recent development, but can be seen two centuries earlier.

The incident, moreover, threw into question the conduct of the upcoming elections. Earlier in the year, Petillius' original colleague, Cn. Cornelius Scipio Hispallus, had died of a stroke during his return from the Latin Festival, which, for other reasons, the Pontiffs had ruled faulty and to be repeated; the death under such circumstances was seen as adding to *religio* (Livy 41.16.1–3). C. Valerius Laevinus was chosen as Consul suffect. But now, a fragment of Livy tells us, those versed in religion and public law argued that, with both the original Consuls dead, the suffect was not qualified to hold elections: *periti religionum iurisque publici, quando duo ordinarii consules eius anni, alter morbo, alter ferro perisset, suffectum consulem negabant recte comitia habere posse.*[72]

The identity of the *periti religionum iuris publici* is debated. Weissenborn–Müller and Linderski took them to be the Augurs; Jahn, noting that the death of both Consuls surely constituted a *prodigium*, argued for the Pontiffs as the priesthood responsible for its procuration, and suggested that they were asked by the Senate whether the suffect should hold the elections, or whether a *renovatio auspiciorum* through an *interregnum* was advisable. But auspices are the exclusive responsibility of the Augurs; there appears to be no known case of the Pontiffs ever commenting on the conduct of elections. The *prodigium*, in any case, could also function as an oblative *auspicium*; since it led to questioning the Consul's ability to hold elections, and nothing but defective auspices is ever attested or conceivable as a religious hindrance to his doing so, we may be confident that the

---

[71] Livy 41.18.7–15; cf. Val. Max. 1.5.9. The gaps in the sole manuscript make it impossible to be certain whether the *vitium* attested by the *pullarius* is the one caused by Petillius during the Consuls' sortition for their theaters of operation (41.18.7–8), or a separate one at the auspication before his final battle; at any rate, the Augurs ruled the sortition faulty (*id vitio factum postea augures responderunt*, 41.18.8), which could only have happened later in Rome. See Linderski *AL* 2173-2175; Briscoe 2012: 97–99.

[72] Livy 41.18.16 = Priscian *Inst.* 17.29, 150 = *GramLat* 3: 126, 182.

portent here indeed was deemed an oblative sign—a determination that was for the Augurs to make, not the Pontiffs. In which case, it surely meant that *vitium*, almost certainly contracted at their election, attached to the original Consuls: and since Valerius the Consul suffect had been elected under Petillius' auspices, he, too, was *vitio creatus*—hence unsuitable to elect new Consuls.[73]

Briscoe has pointed out that if with *periti religionum iurisque publici* Livy had meant the Augurs, "one would expect [him] simply to have said so, not used, or added, the phrase."[74] The same, however, goes for the Pontiffs (Briscoe offers no suggestion as to who should be understood behind the expression), and *periti religionum* rules out a concern solely grounded in the *ius publicum*, such as a general prohibition (unattested) against suffects holding elections that might have been waived, for instance in 215 BC, during the Hannibalic War. Now Priscian quoted the passage to illustrate the use of a nominative where strict grammar demands a genitive (*duo ordinarii consules* for *duorum ordinariorum consulum*); he was not concerned with the question of elections. We do not know what had come in Livy immediately before the fragment; but we can be fairly confident that in his narrative he did not introduce the subject abruptly with *periti religionum eqs*. It is possible, even probable, that leading up to the fragment, he told of the question arising in the Senate, where opinions differed, perhaps vehemently. The Senate submitted the matter to the appropriate experts—the *augures*, without doubt, and so termed by Livy at that point; and they, the *periti religionum iurisque publici*, responded as in the fragment. An augural explanation of the issue may have followed.[75]

We cannot say for certain how the eventual decision fell regarding the elections; but it would be an extraordinary departure from *mos* for the Senate to reject the advice given by the experts. Thus the *interregnum* postulated by Jahn almost certainly did follow. Given that the year was well advanced by now (Petillius had departed for his province on August 5, Laevinus sometime later: Livy 41.17.6, 18.6), rather than have the Consul abdicate and, after the renewal of auspices through the *interregnum*, install a new pair of suffects (none are on record), Laevinus was apparently allowed to serve out his term, and the *interregnum* commenced on March 15, 175.[76]

---

[73] W-M *ad loc.*; Linderski AL 2184–2185 (cf. Giovannini 1998: 106). Jahn 150–151, after arguing for the Pontiffs, would allow for a consultation of the Augurs on a possible error committed at the election of the original Consuls of 176 (Linderski's view), and in the end splits the difference: Livy's phrase "legt . . . nahe, daß zwei religiöse Körperschaften mit der Frage befaßt wurden."

[74] Briscoe 2012: 99.   [75] For a similar explanation, see North 1967: 396–398.

[76] Jahn 150–152. A Dictator to hold the elections can be ruled out: if Laevinus was *vitio creatus*, he could no more name a Dictator, *rite*, than hold elections. Linderski AL 2185 is cautious, noting that the *Fasti* do not record an *interregnum* in 176/5; but while the *Fasti* note (sometimes) abdications, they never record *interregna* as such. An abdication likely would have prompted (barring an extended *interregnum*) a change in the start of the consular year. Conversely (barring the remote possibility that the objection was not grounded in a formal *responsum* of the College of Augurs), had Laevinus indeed proceeded with the election contrary to the advice given, the new Consuls would undoubtedly have

That much we can surmise, yet not be certain of. The loss of Livy's full account deprives us of the information we would really want. Were there attacks, as back in 217, on the Augurs for their ruling?[77] Did Valerius Laevinus cooperate willingly, or—initially at least—resist? We cannot say. Three events, though, surrounding this episode within a decade and a half, suggest that open resistance to the auspices and related ceremonies was now a thing of the past.

8.4.3 The Final Test

A year before Petillius' unfortunate experience, in 177 BC, the Consul C. Claudius Pulcher sought to take command of the army in his assigned province without having performed the customary rituals of *profectio* before his departure from the City: the *votorum nuncupatio* on the Capitol, the procession to the *pomerium*, and the solemn change, by his lictors and himself, from civilian into military garb—the donning of the *paludamentum*. The outgoing commanders (the Consuls of the previous year) flatly refused to hand over the army to him. Forced to return to Rome, he completed the prescribed ceremonies, and proceeded again to his province; only now did his predecessors relinquish their command to him.[78]

Forty years earlier, Gaius Flaminius had gone to his province under circumstances even less legitimate: without having entered office in Rome, hence without auspices (those of Claudius' were never in question); without lictors; and without any of the rituals attached to solemn *profectio*. Protests had arisen in the Senate, but not strong enough to trigger effective measures to prevent him from taking up command, and neither his predecessor nor the army at Ariminum had shown any hesitation in accepting him. Now such an attempt was met with universal resistance, even ridicule.

In 168, the Consul C. Licinius Crassus failed to auspicate before entering the *templum* from where he announced the day on which his army was to assemble.[79] It appears to have been a simple mistake, not deliberate omission. The matter was submitted to the Augurs, who ruled that the day had been set *vitio*. In consequence, his legions (already levied) did not join him in Gaul, but remained at Rome; only the allied troops—not being Roman citizens, they were not affected by the *vitium*—accompanied him on what proved to be an undistinguished

---

been found *vitio creati* in turn, and been forced to abdicate; yet the *Fasti* show only a normal pair in 175.
[77] Above, Subsection 8.4.1.   [78] Livy 41.10.4–11.2; cf. Chapter 2.6.3.
[79] The announcement had to be made from an inaugurated place (*templum*), such as the Rostra (e.g., Livy 34.56.3–4, *Minucius consul . . . in rostra escendit et edixit ut legiones . . . post diem decimum Arretii adessent*) or the podium of the Temple of Castor; similarly, sortitions had to be carried out in a *templum*: Linderski *AL* 2173–2175; Briscoe 2012: 640.

campaign, and a disappointing consulship.[80] Not a word of protest from Crassus is reported.

The most serious test presented itself six years later. Ti. Sempronius Gracchus, having completed a second consulship in 163 BC, found himself *pro consule* in Sardinia in 162. While reading in his scientific manuals, the *summus augur* discovered the explanation to a puzzling event that had occurred when he was presiding, *auspicato* (naturally), over the election of this year's Consuls. The *primus rogator* (the vote-taking clerk of the *centuria praerogativa*), just as he reported the century's vote in favor of the eventual winners, P. Cornelius Scipio Nasica Corculum and C. Marcius Figulus, suddenly died. Gracchus nonetheless continued with the election; but afterwards, sensing concern among the public that the death might constitute a *prodigium*, hence threat of *religio*, he submitted the matter to the Senate. The *haruspices* (foreign divinatory experts, employed on a case-by-case basis, but unrelated to Roman augury, and not Roman priests)[81] were summoned from Etruria; they concluded that Gracchus was not a *iustus comitiorum rogator*—a lawful holder of the election. The Consul (and Augur) was unimpressed, and dismissed them. Note that the Augural College remained uninvolved: the *prodigium* was not—yet—understood or even suspected to be an *auspicium* alerting to a pre-existing *vitium*. Now in Sardinia, reading in the technical books, Gracchus suddenly realized what had been the problem.

Earlier on election day he had forgotten to carry out a necessary auspication, and never noticed the omission. The *prodigium* of the *primus rogator* dying while the consular election was under way, Gracchus now understood, had functioned as an oblative sign—under the *vinculum temporis*—meant to alert the Consul that his auspices for holding the election had become invalid.[82] He promptly sent a letter to the College, reporting his mistake and concluding that the Consuls elected on that day were *vitio creati*. The Augurs concurred, and referred the matter to the Senate; the Senate instructed the Consuls to abdicate to let an *interregnum* take its course, and thus renew the auspices. The Consuls, both of whom had already taken up their provinces, returned from Corsica and Gaul to Rome and resigned their office. No source even hints at any resistance on their part.[83] No Dictator was called upon to effect their abdication, nor would one be needed in

---

[80] Livy 45.12.10, *cum legionibus ad conveniendum <diem> dixit, non auspicato templum int<travit>. vitio diem dictam esse augures, cum ad eos relatum est, decreverunt*; 45.12.12, *legiones Romanae, quod vitio dies exercitui ad conveniendum dicta erat, Romae manserant*. North 1967: 402–411 offers a perceptive discussion of Claudius' and Crassus' cases.

[81] On the *haruspices* and—since the Late Republic—the *ordo haruspicum LX* (drawing pay, hence not *sacerdotes publici p. R.*), Wissowa 543–549; North 1990a: 53–69; 1990b: 583–584.

[82] On the relation of *prodigia* to oblative auspices, see Chapter 2.2.2. On the episode's augural aspects, see Linderski *AL* 2160–2161, 2166; Fiori 2014a: 310; cf. Chapter 2.4.2, note 62.

[83] Cic. *ND* 2.10–11; *Div.* 1.33; 2.74; *QFr.* 2.2.1; Val. Max. 1.1.3; Plut. *Marc.* 5.1–4; Gran. Lic. 28.25–26 Criniti; Auct. *De vir. ill.* 44.2. The abdication *vitio facti* is noted in *FC* = *InscrItal* 13.1: 50–51.

154 and 152.[84] And Gracchus himself, it appears, deposed his province and returned to Rome: before the end of the year—too soon for a regular succession in command—we find him there, about to be chosen as a *legatus* to go East.[85]

The incident, unsurprisingly, has prompted desperate searches for a political motivation, or at least evidence of conflict. Already Münzer, intimating doubts ("wie es heißt") about the religious scruples involved, wanted to see here the origin of the enmity between Gracchus' and Nasica's sons, never mind the complete lack of evidence for such enmity prior to Tiberius' tribunate in 133.[86] Noting that Corsica was usually joined to Sardinia as a province, Astin surmised that Scipio Nasica was to be Gracchus' successor in Sardinia/Corsica, and that ("incidentally") with his abdication, Gracchus "secured an extension of his command."[87] Although rare, separate commands on the two islands are not unheard of: at least four previous instances are known.[88] More to the point, if—as we must assume—Sardinia was Gracchus' consular province, such a split had been in effect during his consulship: his colleague, M'. Iuventius Thalna, died in Corsica after conducting a successful campaign (Val. Max. 9.12.3); which makes it far more probable that Scipio was to succeed Iuventius in Corsica alone, not Gracchus in both.[89]

Rüpke noted—unattested—"politische Spannungen" and voiced suspicion that Gracchus invented a correctable error in order to avoid further attacks on him. Lundgreen treats Gracchus' concern less as a belated realization of an error than a change in deciding how to deal with the matter ("bevor er sich dann später anders entschied"), and suggests a political motivation—perhaps turf conflicts between Gracchus and Scipio. He offers no further evidence or reasoning, but notes, in fairness, that the Consuls' abdication was not accompanied by controversy.[90] How that could be so if political motives were at work (if we can surmise those, they should have been glaringly obvious to contemporaries), not a word. Yet the lack of

---

[84] On the probable abdications and *interregna* of those two years, see Appendix ##14 and 15.

[85] Polyb. 31.15.9-11; MRR 1: 443 n.1; cf. Walbank *HCP* 3: 463, 478, on the chronology.

[86] Münzer 1920: 104 ("Die Anfänge dieser Feindschaft gingen auf die Väter zurück, denn der ältere Ti. Gracchus hatte . . . Nasica Corculum zum Consulat verholfen, dann aber nachträglich—wie es heißt, aus religiösen Bedenken—die Wahl rückgängig gemacht"); similarly Astin 1967: 36. Wardle 1998: 23, entertaining "self-seeking political motives," claims "evidence of personal animosity" between Gracchus and Nasica, without offering any.

[87] Astin 1964: 435. He did not consider that, if Nasica indeed was meant to be Gracchus' successor in Sardinia/Corsica, one of the Consuls suffect would presumably have been sent there soon after the *interregnum*: a drastic maneuver to secure a couple of months' extension, at the most. Jahn 154-155 imagined, among other fantastic speculation, that Gracchus feared being pushed out of his province (Sardinia) by Nasica from Corsica.

[88] In 234 BC (Consul in Corsica, Praetor in Sardinia); 231 (one Consul in each); 174 (Praetor Corsica, Propraetor Sardinia); 173 (ditto): MRR 1: 224, 226, 404, 408.

[89] Sardinia is attested for Gracchus in 163/2 by Cic. *QFr* 2.2.1; given his colleague's recent military activity on Corsica, Gracchus surely would have gone there directly, had it been part of his *provincia*. (The complete lack of evidence that it ever was must be stated clearly.) For a similar argument as here against Astin's and cognate speculations, see also North 1967: 417-419; Driediger-Murphy 2019: 175-176.

[90] Rüpke 1990: 33 = 2019: 35 with n. 36 = 35; Lundgreen 150-151 with n. 425.

controversy has significance from another perspective. Even if contemporaries, including the two Consuls, suspected political machinations behind the Augurs' ruling, they did not see fit to challenge it: a notable contrast to Flaminius in 223.

Most recently, Görne, eschewing a purely political explanation, saw Gracchus as "dienstältester Augur" in a "Kompetenzstreitigkeit mit dem Kollegium der *haruspices*" after ignoring an oblative sign at the elections.[91] Now the *haruspices* (not a College, but Etruscan contractors who held no place in the religious institutions of the Roman state), no matter how highly prized their expertise, had no public competence as such, in contrast to the *augures publici populi Romani*; there could be no *Kompetenzstreitigkeiten*, properly speaking, between the latter and the former. The Augurs dealt with augural law, hence auspices; the *haruspices* were consulted on *prodigia*—never on questions of the auspices. A *prodigium* could, of course (as in this case), also constitute an oblative *auspicium*: but it was for the Augurs, not the *haruspices*, to determine that; and in the immediate wake of the election in 163, none of them apparently saw any reason to think so. (Hence Gracchus cannot be said to have ignored an oblative sign.) As Görne notes, however, in declaring that the election lacked a *iustus rogator*, a lawful holder, the *haruspices* apparently alleged a *vitium in auspicio* that would require the resignation of the Consuls designate; certainly the Consul and Augur took their answer to be trespassing onto augural territory (*itane vero, ego non iustus, qui et consul rogavi et augur et auspicato? an vos Tusci ac barbari auspiciorum populi Romani ius tenetis et interpretes esse comitiorum potestis?* Cic. *ND* 2.11). Yet whatever they said did not offer specifics that would have triggered Gracchus' recollection on the spot, or permit anyone else to identify the alleged *vitium*; and without that, the *prodigium* was not understood to be an oblative *auspicium*. It was as Consul— not as Augur—that Gracchus presided over the Senate meeting with the *haruspices*, and as Consul that he dismissed them and their explanation of the *prodigium*: the Augurs (other than in their capacity as senators) were not involved—yet. When they eventually did address the matter, at Gracchus' insistence, they agreed with the *haruspices*.

Such efforts to imagine an ulterior motivation for Gracchus' actions utterly fail to convince. If he wanted to keep Scipio from becoming Consul, the *prodigium* and the *haruspices*' explanation offered him a god-sent opportunity; he did not take it. If he experienced a change of heart and now wanted to sabotage Nasica's command in Corsica, why wait with his revelation until both Consuls (animosity between Gracchus and Figulus has yet to be alleged) had already reached their

---

[91] Görne 52 n. 62; 220 with note 63. An Augur since 204, Gracchus would be the senior member if M. Servilius Pulex Geminus (*cos.* 202; Augur since 211) was dead by now; but Servilius was alive and well just five years earlier (Livy 45.37–39); *MRR* 1: 276, 309; Rüpke *FS* 2: 1270, 1284. In any case, there is no evidence that seniority amounted to a dominant influence in the College of Augurs: cf. note 37, above. For a close examination of the incident under the aspect of Gracchus' attitude toward the *disciplina Etrusca*, see Santangelo 2013: 751–752.

provinces—a month or two, at least, into their term? The *vitium* could be revealed the day they took office, or even before, and they would have to resign. And would it have been worth the considerable embarrassment of admitting, publicly, that he had been wrong, and the *haruspices* right?[92]

8.5 Last Notes

For the remainder of the Republic, the issue of auspices in war crops up on just three occasions. But the instances noted below did not entail frontal and dramatic challenges of the principle, such as had enlivened the period of the Punic Wars; in fact, none of them indicate the persistence of principled opposition to the ancient practice—as opposed to individual indifference and carelessness—among the political class, let alone a desire to emancipate commanders from the constraints the auspices might pose.

In 137, C. Hostilius Mancinus proceeded to Spain and ruin despite encountering a horrible example of *dirae*: as he was auspicating to sacrifice at Lavinium, the Chickens flew out of their cage, and disappeared.[93] (This, surely, could not have been staged.) But the question Mancinus had put to Iuppiter undoubtedly was whether it was *fas* to offer sacrifice that day, not whether he had permission to go to Spain. He ignored the warning signalled by the sign he witnessed, and failed to take precautions; but he had not acted in direct contravention to a response from Iuppiter. Unlike Claudius Pulcher and Flaminius (and perhaps Petillius Spurinus), he made no effort to advertise his neglect as a matter of disdain for auspices.

In 105, allegations that both commanders had gone into battle *contra auspicia* may have followed the double defeat at Arausio, and may have played a role in their eventual condemnation; the evidence is tenuous in the extreme. There are grounds to think that an oblative sign—a standard would not let itself be pulled, and was dug out—was observed in the army of Cn. Servilius Caepio (*cos.* 106, now *pro consule*), and that Cn. Mallius the Consul had received a negative

---

[92] *Peccatum suum, quod celari posset, confiteri maluit quam haerere in re publica religionem; consules summum imperium statim deponere quam id tenere punctum temporis contra religionem.* No facts are known, or can plausibly be conjectured, to call Cicero's understanding of the matter (*ND* 2.11) into question. Cf. Scheid 1985: 29, 35; Potter 154 ("It . . . appears that the issue here did not have anything to do with politics on the human plane but rather involved the perception that the state was in danger from the gods if something was not done to correct the situation"); Champion 72; and see Driediger-Murphy 2019: 178, noting with North (1967: 418) the embarrassment the affair must have caused Gracchus.

[93] Val. Max. 1.6.7, *cum Lavinii sacrificium facere vellet, pulli cavea emissi in proximam silvam fugerunt*; Obseq. 24 [83], *cum Lavinii auspicarentur, pulli e cavea in silvam Laurentinam evolarunt neque inventi sunt*; Livy *Per.* 55, *C. Hostilio Mancino cos. sacrificante pulli ex cavea evolaverunt*. On *dirae*, see Chapter 5.1.2, note 14. The same omen would signal the impending doom of the Emperor Galba: Suet. *Galba* 18.3.

response in his impetrative auspices.⁹⁴ It is not certain, however, whether Caepio ever received a formal report of the recalcitrant standard, or, for that matter, of the Consul's prohibitive auspices (if such there were); it is certain, on the other hand, that Mallius had not wanted to join battle on that day, but only did so when it became evident that Caepio's army was being slaughtered. In other words, we cannot demonstrate that Caepio was culpable, and if Mallius indeed did act against his auspices, it was not out of contempt: he faced a choice similar to that of Iunius Pullus in 249.

Finally, another commander dared set out from Rome under auspices called into question, with predictably deplorable consequences. Even then, there is some reason to think that for all his open contempt of matters divinatory, Marcus Crassus, when confronted with the *dirae* announced to him by Ateius Capito at the crucial moment of his *votorum nuncupatio* on the Capitol late in 55, had received and followed poor advice from none other than the Augur Cn. Pompeius Magnus. (Which could not, of course, absolve him from ignoring a host of oblative signs—most telling, the standards refusing to budge—encountered once in Syria.)⁹⁵

The increased use, in the Late Republic, of augural mechanisms to impede and prevent the meeting of popular assemblies for legislation or election is not a subject of this book. The remarkable thing in that regard, however, is the near-universal acceptance of the augural rules that made such obstruction possible.⁹⁶ And even in the death throes of the Republic, at the height of the crisis brewing around Mutina, a crucial Senate meeting on April 7, 43 BC, was adjourned when the *pullarii* reported that the Praetor presiding, M. Caecilius Cornutus, had taken the auspices for the meeting without the requisite diligence; the College of Augurs concurred (*oblata religio Cornuto est pullariorum admonitu non satis diligenter eum auspiciis operam dedisse; idque a nostro collegio comprobatum est*, Cic. *Fam.* 10.12.3). As Driediger-Murphy points out in her perceptive discussion of the political surroundings, the postponement can be seen as favoring Antonius and his supporters; but his enemies, still in the majority, accepted it without complaint,

---

⁹⁴ On the battle, Livy *Per.* 67; Vell. 2.12.2; Tac. *Germ.* 37.4; Flor. 1.34.8; Gran. Lic. 33.1–17 Criniti; Dio fr. 91.1–4; Oros. 5.16.1–7; on the fate of Caepio and Mallius, Cic. *De orat.* 2.124–125, 164, 167, 197–203; *Brut.* 135; *Balb.* 28; [*Rhet. ad Herenn.*] 1.24; Livy *Per.* 67; Val. Max. 4.7.3; Gran. Lic. 33.24 Criniti; on the standard, *Schol. Bern.* ad *Georg.* 4.108. For discussion, Konrad 2004: 188–201.

⁹⁵ Cic. *Div.* 1.29–30; 2.84; Vell. 2.46.3; Val. Max. 1.6.11; Plut. *Crass.* 16.4–8 (noting Pompey's presence); 18.5; 19.4–8; 23.1–2; *synkr.* 5(38).3; Flor. 1.46.3–4; Dio 39.39.5–7; 40.12.2–13.4, 18.1–5; 19.1–3; Obseq. 54 [124]; Serv. *ad Aen.* 7.606; 11.19; Eutrop. 6.18.1. For discussion, Konrad 2004: 181–187; cf. Chapter 5.1.2.

⁹⁶ Cf. Chapter 2.2.1, notes 37 and 38. Despite occasional accusations of laws being passed in violation of the auspices, rather few are on record as having been ruled a *lex vitio lata* by the College of Augurs: the legislation of the Tribune Sex. Titius in 99 BC appears to be the sole unequivocally attested example (Cic. *Leg.* 2.31). On the same grounds, the Senate annulled the laws of M. Livius Drusus (*tr. pl.* 91) as advised by the Consul and Augur L. Marcius Philippus, but evidently without a decree of the College (Cic. *Leg.* 2.31): see North 1967: 442–459; Linderski *AL* 2165 n. 54; on the uncertain case of Saturninus in 100, Linderski 1984: 458 = *RQ* 540.

and Cicero, however unhappy with the delay, allows not the slightest hint that the *vitium* might have been manufactured for political gain.[97]

By the early second century, attempts to challenge the auspices by way of practical politics had ceased. Individual instances of neglect still occurred sporadically, but no principled opposition to their role in governing the *res publica* manifested itself henceforth: the ruling class—as well as those who aspired to it—had achieved consensus on the auspices' abiding necessity, and maintained them categorically for as long as the *res publica* remained theirs. The efficacy of auspices continued to be questioned, though, and their truthfulness rejected; but no longer in the realm of politics and government. Opposition now unfolded on a different plane. Skeptics and disbelievers, though senators all, and sometimes Augurs, voiced and developed their views in private discussion and philosophical treatises.[98] And from those practitioners of governance, the debate about the merits and significance of auspices was taken up by those who shaped the memory of the Roman past.

By Livy's time, as we have noticed repeatedly in the course of this study, there existed a branch of the historical tradition that paid slight or no attention to the complex of auspices in its narratives; indeed, one strand of that tradition may have systematically excluded all reference to the practice, in deliberate contrast to the legitimacy (in some instances, perhaps, sole legitimacy) bestowed on magistrates by a popular vote, or by military success. This tradition was not necessarily rationalist: some of it apparently acknowledged, even emphasized, the importance of other areas of religion (the *sacra*, chiefly), perhaps even other forms of divination, in the conduct of the *res publica*. (Coelius Antipater clearly put great stake in *religio* and divination, including auspices ignored, yet his treatment of Flaminius suggests a fundamental lack of understanding of augural theory, and perhaps lack of interest in it.)[99] How far back this tradition goes, no way of telling; but nothing precludes an early origin in the second century. The pro-Rullianus and pro-Minucius versions of those epic quarrels, with their consistent aim to diminish the Dictator and the validity of auspices, are too closely tied to issues of the Hannibalic War to have arisen long after its conclusion.

Livy, though, based most of his history on traditions that acknowledged fully the augural underpinnings of the *res publica*. But even as he wrote, the auspices and all that went with them were being placed under new management, so to

---

[97] Driediger-Murphy 2019: 198–200; cf. Linderski *AL* 2213–2214. Champion 36 n. 51, citing the incident as a "singular exception" to the Senate's "ultimate authority in religious matters," apparently misunderstood the process involved: it was not the Augurs that adjourned the meeting; they merely confirmed that the *pullarii* had correctly diagnosed a *vitium in auspicio*. The decision to adjourn (like a decree requiring Consuls *vitio facti* to abdicate, or annulling a *lex vitio lata*) was made by the Senate; there was nothing exceptional here. (Driediger-Murphy 2019: n. 126 is surely correct to suggest that such delays were common.)

[98] For a concise presentation, focussing on Cicero's attitude toward divination, see Linderski 1982.

[99] Chapter 7.4.5.

speak, unable any longer to affect the conduct of affairs of state, and to trigger disagreement and debate. With the exception of Galba's disastrous auspication on January 1, AD 69, not a single prohibitive response to impetrative auspices is reported throughout the imperial period, at least at the level of Emperor or Consul. The perfect record of approval from Iuppiter would be astounding, were it not for the inescapable conclusion that it reflected his endorsement of the new dispensation. Caesar the Dictator had pushed aside any augural obstacle in his way, but never felt the need to attack, or omit, the practice as such (or mention it in his commentaries): in case of conflict, he simply treated it as irrelevant. His heir, as in so many other things, found the ideal solution. He saw to it that all observed the auspices scrupulously, and that Iuppiter did not withhold permission, evermore. "Man war nicht in allen Dingen vorwärts gekommen, aber gewiss in der Frömmigkeit."[100]

---

[100] Mommsen *StR* 2.1: 20.

APPENDIX
Consular Abdication and *Interregnum*

The following survey comprises all instances of Consuls or Consular Tribunes abdicating before the end of their term that are **attested** (number and date shown in **bold type**) or can *plausibly be inferred* (number and date in ***bold italics***), along with uncertain or improbable cases (number and date in regular type). In most though not all occurrences, the ensuing *interregnum* is likewise on record.[1]

(1)   **480 V**. One Consul having been killed in action, his colleague declined a triumph and abdicated two months before the regular end of his term; an *interregnum* followed.[2]

(2)   451 V. The sources cannot agree on whether the Consuls abdicated after taking office (Cic. *Rep.* 2.61 and the *FC* = *InscrItal* 13.1: 26–27), or desisted from taking office altogether (Dion. Hal. 10.54.3–56.2; Livy 3.33.4). If abdication was involved, an *interregnum* may have followed; but Dionysios seems to imply that the Decemvirs were elected under the outgoing Consuls of 452 V, and the "abdication" tradition may have envisaged their election by the Consuls of 451.

(3)   **444 V**. The Military Tribunes with Consular Power—the first holders of that puzzling office—abdicated after three months in accordance with an augural decree, having been found *vitio creati*; an *interregnum* followed.[3]

Unfortunately, the new Consuls elected during the *interregnum* are clearly marked as *suffecti* (Livy 4.7.11; cf. Dion. Hal. 11.62.3), merely filling the remainder of the year when in fact they should have held office for a full twelve-month term.[4] Dionysios notes that most of his sources only know of either the Tribunes in that year or the alleged suffect Consuls, although a few have both (πλὴν οὐκ ἐν ἁπάσαις ταῖς Ῥωμαϊκαῖς χρονογραφίαις ἀμφότεραι φέρονται, ἀλλ' ἐν αἷς μὲν οἱ χιλίαρχοι μόνον, ἐν αἷς δ' οἱ ὕπατοι, ἐν οὐ πολλαῖς δ' ἀμφότεροι). Livy states that the names of these suffects appear in neither the early annals nor the *fasti* (*neque in annalibus priscis neque in libris magistratuum inveniuntur*): it was Licinius Macer who unearthed them from both the *libri lintei* and the Roman treaty with Ardea concluded in that year (4.7.10–12; cf. 4.7.4–7). Since the Tribunes' abdication, however, apparently did not cause a change in the consular year (which, on Mommsen's reconstruction, began on December 13 continuously from 449 to 402[5]), it must be considered fictional as told.

---

[1] For a complete list of known *interregna*, see Willems *SRR* 2: 10–12; Jahn *passim*.
[2] Dion. Hal. 9.13.4–14.1 (abdication and *interregnum*); cf. Livy 2.47.7–12. The *interregnum* was overlooked by Jahn 57.
[3] Dion. Hal. 11.62.1–3 (Tribunes resign after 73 days); Livy 4.7.1–12.
[4] Mommsen 1859: 92–94; cf. 82 n. 112. Prior to 162 BC, there is simply no credible evidence of two suffects completing the original Consuls' term, although the practice could have commenced in 220, if the first pair of Consuls reported under that year did in fact enter office (below, #12). Instead, an *interregnum* due to early termination, whether prompted by death or abdication, seems invariably to have resulted in a new, full consular term, i.e., a change in the beginning of the official year. Cf. Jahn 30–32, 75.
[5] *StR* 1: 603–604. The date is attested for 443 V, Dion. Hal. 11.63.1; 423 V, Livy 4.37.3; and 402 V, Livy 5.9.3, 11.11.

The electoral *vitium* adduced may furnish a clue: *quod C. Curiatius qui comitiis eorum praefuerat parum recte tabernaculum cepisset* (Livy 4.7.3). This evidently falls in the same category of mistake as happened to that *summus augur*, Ti. Sempronius Gracchus, when holding the consular *comitia* in 163: *qui . . . tabernaculum vitio cepisset*.[6] When the *vitium* was discovered several months into the next year, 162, the Consuls elected under it promptly abdicated; yet the subsequent *interregnum* did not lead to a change in the beginning of the official year: instead, it produced a pair of *suffecti* to complete the current term.[7] Unless the story from 444 be true as told, the solution adopted in 162 is the first of its kind unambiguously attested, and may serve as a *terminus post quem* for the first occurrence of the Tribunes' abdication in the record, or at any rate, of such a detailed reason for their abdication.

As Frier showed long ago, there are no grounds for doubting the basic authenticity of Macer's information: the pair of Consuls (L. Papirius Mugillanus and L. Sempronius Atratinus) he found in the Linen Books constitute the actual successors of the Military Tribunes of 444—successors who, for reasons irrecoverable, had fallen out of the "established" *fasti* and were unknown to the earlier annalists. Macer understood that this pair of Consuls had to come between the Tribunes of 444 and the Consuls of 443, but did not realize (or did not want to propose such an invasive alteration to the "established" chronology) that, to correct the record, an entire year (which we may call "444-A"), with Papirius and Sempronius as its regular Consuls, would have to be inserted between 444 V and 443 V. Instead, he made the Tribunes abdicate, to be succeeded, after an *interregnum*, by Papirius and Sempronius as suffects for the remainder of the year 444. Dionysios and Livy both accepted Macer's reconstruction.[8]

(4) 402 V. Political and military considerations led to a *senatus consultum* instructing the Military Tribunes to leave office two-and-a-half months early, allegedly after first securing the election of their successors and without recourse to an *interregnum*. In consequence, the new Tribunes entered office on October 1 instead of December 13. There are grounds, however, to postulate an *interregnum*, if the premature termination of office in this year reflects historical reality at all.[9]

(5) 399 V. Broughton assumed another early abdication of Military Tribunes, based on Plutarch (*Cam.* 2.9).[10]

As is clear from λαχὼν Φαλερίοις καὶ Καπηνάταις πολεμεῖν (*Cam.* 2.10), Plutarch here conflates Camillus' campaigns against Falerii (in 401, Livy 5.12.5) and Capena (in 398, Livy 5.14.5-7), but the context of his narrative evidently follows Livy's (or a common source's) account of 402 and 401, not 399 and 398: συνεστάλησαν ἐς τὰ τείχη surely corresponds to a *M. Furio in Faliscis et Cn. Cornelio in Capenate agro hostes nulli extra moenia inventi*

---

[6] Cic. *Div.* 1.33, 36; cf. *ND* 2.11, *vitio sibi tabernaculum captum fuisse*; Val. Max. 1.1.3, *vitio tabernaculum captum comitiis consularibus*; for elucidation of the phrase, see Linderski *AL* 2164, and for the incident, Chapter 8.4.3.

[7] Below, # 13.

[8] Frier 1975, esp. 83–90. On Macer and the *libri lintei*, see Ogilvie 7–12, 542–545; Frier 1979: 153–159; Walt 75–85; Oakley *FRHist* 1: 322–326; on the problem in 444 V, Walt 246–254; Beck–Walter *FRH* 2: 330–332; Oakley *FRHist* 3: 431–436. Jahn 58–59 rejects (following, inter alia, Mommsen 1859: 93–98) the abdication of the Military Tribunes and considers the suffect Consuls spurious; but he accepts an *interregnum* at the end of the year 444, on the grounds (no evidence: Zonaras 7.19 says nothing of that sort) that Consular Tribunes initially lacked the auspices necessary to conduct elections. Frier's solution is clearly preferable.

[9] Livy 5.9.1–8; see Ogilvie 645; Jahn 61; and Chapter 6.6.1.   [10] *MRR* 2: 638.

(Livy 5.12.5, in 401), and the reason given for the magistrates' premature termination (τοὺς ἄρχοντας ἐν αἰτίᾳ γενέσθαι καὶ μαλακῶς πολιορκεῖν δοκοῦντας) is exactly the same as Livy's in 402 (*sive culpa sive infelicitate imperatorum tam ignominiosa clades accepta*, 5.9.1). The mistaken numeration of Camillus' military tribunate of 401 as his second (cf. *MRR* 1: 82 n. 1, 84 n. 1) is likewise common to both authors.[11] Thus there remains no evidence for an early abdication in 399. (Dion. Hal. 12.10, adduced by Broughton under 398 V for additional support, says nothing about Tribunes entering or leaving office.)

(6)   397 V. The Military Tribunes were deemed *vitio creati* and ordered to abdicate; an *interregnum* followed (Livy 5.17.1–4).

(7)   393 V. Abdication followed by an *interregnum* has been suggested, since the *Fasti* list a pair of suffect Consuls along with those originally elected. Degrassi (*InscrItal* 13.1: 30–31) restored [*vitio facti abdicaru*]*nt*, but Mommsen's [*non inieru*]*nt* (*CIL* 1².1: 19) is much preferable.

(8)   392 V. Pestilence struck the City, and the Senate instructed the Consuls to abdicate, so as to enable a renovation of the auspices through an *interregnum* (Livy 5.31.5–8).

(9)   341 V. With the (First) Samnite War under way and the Latin War threatening, the Consuls of that year were prompted to abdicate early, so as to enable their successors to devote a greater part of their term to the campaign; religious scruples, however, prevailed to the effect that Consuls whose *imperium* had been curtailed in such fashion ought not to hold elections, and an *interregnum* ensued.[12]

(10)   321 V. After the disaster at the Caudine Forks the Consuls refrained from all public activity, except to appoint a Dictator *comitiorum causa*, who soon abdicated, *vitio creatus*; another Dictator followed, but likewise failed to carry out elections, for reasons unknown. Eventually, an *interregnum* came to pass: perhaps at the normal end of the consular year, though Livy's *quia taedebat populum omnium magistratuum eius anni* rather suggests that the Consuls left office early.[13]

(11)   223 BC. The Consuls were found *vitio creati* and compelled to abdicate immediately after their triumphs. An *interregnum* followed, and the start of the consular year shifted from (probably) May 1 to March 15.[14]

(12)   220 BC. The Chronographer of 354 has *Levino et Scevola*, meaning M. Valerius Laevinus and an unidentified Mucius Scaevola, perhaps Q. *pr.* 215. The other sources show C. Lutatius Catulus and L. Veturius Philo; both campaigned in Gaul (Zonar. 8.20). Since Valerius Laevinus is attested with a second consulate in 210 (*FC* = *InscrItal* 13.1: 46–47; Livy 29.11.3; 30.23.5), the Chronographer's notice must be correct, and both Consuls must have been *vitio facti*. But it remains unknown whether they abdicated early into their term, or never entered office.[15] If the former, an *interregnum* must have followed; if their

---

[11] *MRR* 1: 82 n. 1, 84 n. 1.

[12] Livy 8.3.4–5, *religio incessit ab eis quorum imminutum imperium esset comitia haberi*.

[13] Livy 9.7.12–14, supported by Zonaras 7.26 (τοὺς δ' ὑπάτους μὲν παραχρῆμα ἔπαυσαν, ἑτέρους δ' ἀνθελόμενοι). Jahn 92 needlessly rejects the latter's account as an "anachronism"; but no Greek source (even less, a Byzantine compiler) can rationally be expected to understand, let alone care about, the distinction between Consuls deposed and Consuls ordered to resign.

[14] Plut. *Marc.* 4.3–6; 6.1; Zonar. 8.20. Livy 21.63.2, ... *de consulatu qui abrogabatur* ..., alludes to the same situation. For the beginnings of the official year, see Mommsen 1859: 101–103; Broughton *MRR* 2: 638–639; and Chapter 6.4.4.

[15] *MRR* 1: 235; cf. Degrassi *InscrItal* 13.1: 119.

successors took office on or after April 1, they were the first *suffecti* proper, completing the original Consuls' term without a change in the beginning of the consular year.

(13) 162 BC. The Consuls abdicated, having been deemed *vitio creati*; in a major departure (unless this happened already in 220) from previous practice, however, the ensuing *interregnum* apparently produced two suffects to complete the term, rather than regular Consuls starting a new official year.[16]

(14) 154 BC. The Consuls left office two-and-a-half months early so as to enable their successors to take command in Spain sooner; in consequence, the beginning of the official year shifted from March 15 to January 1.[17]

An *interregnum* is not attested but probable enough: if the precedent of the year 341 (see #9 above) was already known, it could hardly be ignored in 154; if not, it is difficult to see why it should have been invented without an actual case to serve as a model (and, presumably, in need of a justifying precedent). Unless, of course, the Consuls of 153 had already been elected when the decision was made to accelerate their entrance into office; but elections completed some three months before year's end, though possible, command scant likelihood in the second century.

(15) 152 BC. A *prodigium* is said to have prompted the abdication of all magistrates; an *interregnum* must have followed, but it yielded no suffects to complete the term, nor another shift in the start of the consular year.

The notice has not always attracted credence: Broughton ignored it. However, Jahn's explanation may well point in the right direction: although all the magistrates in Rome resigned, a delay in communication with the Consul M. Claudius Marcellus, on campaign in Spain, was inevitable; and notice of his abdication (assuming he learned of the necessity before it became moot, that is, still in 152) did not reach Rome until close to the end of the year—too close to make electing suffects worth the while, or move up the start of the next official year.[18]

---

[16] Cic. *ND* 2.10–11; *Div.* 1.33, 2.74; *QFr.* 2.2.1; Plut. *Marc.* 5.1–4; Val. Max. 1.1.3; Gran. Lic. 28.25–26 Criniti; Auct. *De vir. ill.* 44.2. The suffects are not mentioned in the literary sources, but attested in *FC* (*InscrItal* 13.1: 50–51) and the *Fasti Antiates*. See above, note 4 and #12; cf. Chapter 8.4.3.

[17] Livy *Per.* 47; *Fasti Praenestini* ad K. Ian. (*InscrItal* 13.2: 110); Cassiod. *Chron.* ad AUC 601. The Capitoline *Fasti* take no notice of it.

[18] Obseq. 18 [77], *cumque aruspices respondissent magistratuum et sacerdotum interitum fore, omnes magistratus se protinus abdicaverunt.* Cf. Broughton *MRR* 1: 45; Jahn 155–158.

Bibliography

Alföldi, A. (1965) *Early Rome and the Latins*. Ann Arbor.
Amat-Seguin, B. (1986) "Ariminum et Flaminius." *RSA* 16: 79–109.
Astin, A. E. (1964) "Leges Aelia et Fufia." *Latomus* 23: 421–445.
Astin, A. E. (1967) *Scipio Aemilianus*. Oxford.
Auliard, C. (2001) *Victoires et triomphes à Rome: Droits et réalités sous la République*. Paris.
Badian, E. (1961) "Review of T. R. S. Broughton, *Supplement to The Magistrates of the Roman Republic*" (New York, 1960). *Gnomon* 33: 492–498.
Badian, E. (1968) "Sulla's Augurate." *Arethusa* 1: 26–46.
Badian, E. (1972) "Tiberius Gracchus and the Beginning of the Roman Revolution." *ANRW* I.1: 668–731.
Badian, E. (1983) "The Silence of Norbanus: A Note on Provincial Quaestors under the Republic." *AJP* 104: 156–171.
Badian, E. (1990) "Magistratur und Gesellschaft." In *Staat und Staatlichkeit in der frühen Römischen Republik*, ed. W. Eder, 458–475. Stuttgart.
Badian, E. (1996) "*Tribuni Plebis* and *Res Publica*." In *Imperium Sine Fine: T. R. S. Broughton and the Roman Republic*, ed. J. Linderski, 187–213. Stuttgart.
Bailey, D. R. Shackleton. (1965–70) *Cicero's Letters to Atticus*. 7 vols. Cambridge.
Bailey, D. R. Shackleton. (1977) *Cicero: Epistulae ad Familiares*. 2 vols. Cambridge.
Bailey, D. R. Shackleton. (1982) "Notes on Cicero's *Philippics*." *Philologus* 126: 217–226.
Bailey, D. R. Shackleton. (2000) *Valerius Maximus: Memorable Doings and Sayings*. 2 vols. Cambridge, Mass., and London.
Bandel, F. (1910) *Die Römischen Diktaturen*. Breslau.
Banti, L. (1932) "Via Placentia–Lucam: Contributo allo studio della guerra annibalica." *A&R* 13: 98–132.
Bardt, C. (1871) "Die Priester der vier grossen Collegien aus römisch-republikanischer Zeit." *K. Wilhelms-Gymnasium in Berlin: Jahresbericht*, 1–41.
Baroni, A. (2007) "La titolatura della dittatura di Silla." *Athenaeum* 95: 775–792.
Bastien, J.-L. (2007) *Le triomphe romain et son utilisation politique à Rome aux trois derniers siècles de la république*. Rome.
Bayet, J. (1960) "Les malédictions du tribun C. Ateius Capito." In *Hommages à George Dumezil*, 31–45. Paris.
Beard, M. (2007) *The Roman Triumph*. Cambridge, Mass., and London.
Beck, H. (2003) " 'Den Ruhm nicht teilen wollen': Fabius Pictor und die Anfänge des römischen Nobilitätsdiskurses." In *Formen römischer Geschichtsschreibung von den Anfängen bis Livius: Gattungen—Autoren—Kontexte*, ed. U. Eigler, U. Gotter, N. Luraghi, and U. Walter, 72–92. Darmstadt.
Beck, H. (2005) *Karriere und Hierarchie: Die römische Aristokratie und die Anfänge des cursus honorum in der mittleren Republik*. Berlin.
Beck, H., and U. Walter. (2004–5) *Die Frühen Römischen Historiker*. 2 vols. (1: 2nd ed.). Darmstadt.

Bellomo, M. (2019) *Il comando militare a Roma nell'età delle guerre puniche (264–201 a. C.)*. Stuttgart.
Bergemann, C. (1992) *Politik und Religion im spätrepublikanischen Rom*. Stuttgart.
Bergk, A. (2011) "The Development of the Praetorship in the Third Century BC." In *Consuls and Res Publica: Holding High Office in the Roman Republic*, ed. H. Beck, A. Duplá, M. Jehne, and F. Pina Polo, 61–74. Cambridge.
Berthelet, Y. (2015) *Gouverner avec les dieux: Autorité, auspices et pouvoir, sous la République romaine et sous Auguste*. Paris.
Birt, Th. (1927) "Was heisst βασιλεύς? Was heisst *dictator*?" *RhM* 76: 198–204.
Bleckmann, B. (2002) *Die römische Nobilität im Ersten Punischen Krieg: Untersuchungen zur aristokratischen Konkurrenz in der Republik*. Berlin.
Bleicken, J. (1955) *Das Volkstribunat der klassischen Republik: Studien zu seiner Entwicklung zwischen 287 und 133 v. Chr*. 2nd ed. 1968. Munich.
Bleicken, J. (1981) *Zum Begriff der römischen Amtsgewalt: auspicium—potestas—imperium*. (Nachrichten der Akademie der Wissenschaften in Göttingen, I: philologisch-historische Klasse, 1981, no. 9, 257–300.) Göttingen.
Blösel, W. (2003) "Die *memoria* der *gentes* als Rückgrat der kollektiven Erinnerung im republikanischen Rom." In *Formen römischer Geschichtsschreibung von den Anfängen bis Livius: Gattungen—Autoren—Kontexte*, ed. U. Eigler, U. Gotter, N. Luraghi, and U. Walter, 53–72. Darmstadt.
Botsford, G. W. (1909) *The Roman Assemblies from Their Origin to the End of the Republic*. New York.
Brennan, T. C. (1996) "Triumphus in Monte Albano." In *Transitions to Empire: Essays in Greco-Roman History, 360–146 B.C., in Honor of E. Badian*, ed. R. W. Wallace and E. M. Harris, 315–337. Norman and London.
Brennan, T. C. (2000) *The Praetorship in the Roman Republic*. 2 vols. Oxford and New York.
Brind'Amour, P. (1983) *Le calendrier romain: Recherches chronologiques*. Ottawa.
Bringmann, K. (1988) "Das Zweite Triumvirat: Bemerkungen zu Mommsen's Lehre von der außerordentlichen konstituierenden Gewalt." In *Alte Geschichte und Wissenschaftsgeschichte: Festschrift für Karl Christ zum 65. Geburtstag*, ed. P. Kneissl and V. Losemann, 22–38. Darmstadt.
Briscoe, J. (1973) *A Commentary on Livy Books XXXI–XXXIII*. Oxford.
Briscoe, J. (1981) *A Commentary on Livy Books XXXIV–XXXVII*. Oxford.
Briscoe, J., ed. (1998) *Valeri Maximi Facta et dicta memorabilia*. 2 vols. Leipzig.
Briscoe, J. (2008) *A Commentary on Livy Books 38–40*. Oxford.
Briscoe, J. (2012) *A Commentary on Livy Books 41–45*. Oxford.
Broughton, T. R. S. (1951–2) *The Magistrates of the Roman Republic*. Vols. 1–2. New York. Vol. 3, *Supplement*. (1986) Atlanta.
Brunt, P. A. (1971) *Italian Manpower, 225 B.C.–A.D. 14*. Oxford.
Buecheler, F. (1880) "Altes Latein." *RhM* 35: 627–630.
Bunse, R. (1998) *Das römische Oberamt in der frühen Republik und das Problem der "Konsulartribunen."* Trier.
Capecchi, F., P. L. Dall'Aglio, and G. Marchetti. (1988) "L'attraversamento dell'Appennino da parte di Annibale: Valutazioni storico-topografiche e geomorfologiche." In *L'età annibalica e la Puglia*. Atti del II convegno di studi sulla Puglia romana, 24–26 marzo 1988, 133–159. Mesagne.
Càssola, F. (1968) *I gruppi politici romani nel III secolo a.C.* Rome.
Càssola, F. (1999) "Problemi della tradizione orale." *Index* 28: 1–34.
Catalano, P. (1960) *Contributi allo studio del diritto augurale, I.* Turin.

Catalano, P. (1978) "Aspetti spaziali del sistema giuridico-religioso romano: Mundus, templum, urbs, ager, Latium, Italia." *ANRW* II.16.1: 440–553.
Champion, C. B. (2017) *The Peace of the Gods: Elite Religious Practices in the Middle Roman Republic*. Princeton.
Chaplin, J. D. (2000) *Livy's Exemplary History*. Oxford.
Cichorius, C. (1922) *Römische Studien: Historisches Epigraphisches Literargeschichtliches aus vier Jahrhunderten Roms*. Leipzig and Berlin.
Cohen, D. (1957) "The Origin of Roman Dictatorship." *Mnemosyne* 10: 300–318.
Coli, U. (1951) " 'Regnum.'" *SDHI* 17: 1–168.
Coli, U. (1953) "Sui limiti di durata delle magistrature romane." In *Studi in onore di Vincenzo Arangio-Ruiz nel XLV anno del suo insegnamento*, 4: 395–418. Naples.
Cornell, T. J. (1995) *The Beginnings of Rome: Italy and Rome from the Bronze Age to the Punic Wars (c. 1000–264 BC)*. London and New York.
Cornell, T. J., E. H. Bispham, J. W. Rich, C. J. Smith, et al. (2013) *The Fragments of the Roman Historians*. 3 vols. Oxford.
Crawford, J. W. (1994) *M. Tullius Cicero: The Fragmentary Speeches*. Atlanta.
Crook, J. (1976) "*Sponsione Provocare*: Its Place in Roman Litigation." *JRS* 66: 132–138.
Dalla Rosa, A. (2003) "*Ductu auspicioque*: Per una riflessione sui fondamenti religiosi del potere magistratuale fino all'epoca augustea." *SCO* 49: 185–255.
Dalla Rosa, A. (2011) "Dominating the Auspices." In *Priests and State in the Roman World*, ed. J. H. Richardson and F. Santangelo, 243–269. Stuttgart.
Dart, C. J., and F. J. Vervaet. (2011) "The Significance of the Naval Triumph in Roman History (260–29 BCE)." *ZPE* 176: 267–280.
Daube, D. (1969) *Roman Law: Linguistic, Social and Philosophical Aspects*. Edinburgh.
de Libero, L. (1992) *Obstruktion: Politische Praktiken im Senat und in der Volksversammlung der ausgehenden römischen Republik (70–49 v. Chr.)*. Stuttgart.
Denniston, J. D. (1926) *M. Tulli Ciceronis in M. Antonium orationes Philippicae prima et secunda*. Oxford.
De Sanctis, G. (1907–23) *Storia dei Romani*. 4 vols. Turin.
Develin, R. (1978) "Tradition and the Development of Triumphal Regulations in Rome." *Klio* 60: 419–438.
Develin, R. (1979) "The Political Position of C. Flaminius." *RhM* 122: 268–277.
Develin, R. (1980) "The Roman Command Structure and Spain 218–190 B.C." *Klio* 62: 355–367.
Diana, B. (1987) "Annibale e il passaggio degli Appennini." *Aevum* 61: 108–112.
Dorey, T. A. (1955) "The Dictatorship of Minucius." *JRS* 45: 92–96.
Driediger-Murphy, L. G. (2018) "Falsifying the Auspices in Republican Politics." In *Institutions and Ideology in Republican Rome*, ed. H. van der Blom, C. Gray, and C. Steel, 183–202. Cambridge.
Driediger-Murphy, L. G. (2019) *Roman Republican Augury: Freedom and Control*. Oxford.
Drogula, F. K. (2007) "*Imperium, Potestas*, and the *Pomerium* in the Roman Republic." *Historia* 56: 419–452.
Drogula, F. K. (2015) *Commanders and Command in the Roman Republic and Early Empire*. Chapel Hill.
Drummond, A. (1978) "The Dictator Years." *Historia* 27: 550–572.
Eckstein, A. M. (1982) "Human Sacrifice and Fear of Military Disaster in Republican Rome." *AJAH* 7: 69–95.
Eckstein, A. M. (1987) *Senate and General: Individual Decision Making and Roman Foreign Relations, 264–194 B.C.* Berkeley, Los Angeles, and London.

Faltin, G. (1885) "Der Einbruch Hannibals in Etrurien." *Hermes* 20: 71–90.
Feig Vishnia, R. (1996a) *State, Society, and Popular Leaders in Mid-Republican Rome, 241–167 B.C.* London and New York.
Feig Vishnia, R. (1996b) "The Carvilii Maximi of the Republic." *Athenaeum* 84: 433–456.
Feig Vishnia, R. (2007) "The Delayed Career of the 'Delayer': The Early Years of Q. Fabius Maximus Verrucosus, the 'Cunctator'." *SCI* 26: 19–38.
Feig Vishnia, R. (2012) "A Case of 'Bad Press'? Gaius Flaminius in Ancient Historiography." *ZPE* 181: 27–45.
Feldherr, A. (1998) *Spectacle and Society in Livy's History.* Berkeley, Los Angeles, and London.
Ferrary, J.-L. (2010) "À propos des pouvoirs et des honneurs décernés à César entre 48 et 44." In *Cesare: Precursore o visionario? Atti del convegno internazionale Cividale del Friuli, 17–19 settembre 2009*, ed. G. Urso, 9–30. Pisa.
Fiori, R. (2014a) "Gli auspici e i confini." *Fundamina* 20: 301–311.
Fiori, R. (2014b) "La convocazione dei comizi centuriati: Diritto costituzionale e diritto augurale." *ZRG* 131: 60–176.
Flower, H. I. (1995) "*Fabulae Praetextae* in Context: When Were Plays on Contemporary Subjects Performed in Republican Rome?" *CQ* 45: 170–190.
Flower, H. I. (1996) *Ancestor Masks and Aristocratic Power in Roman Culture.* Oxford.
Forsythe, G. (1994) *The Historian L. Calpurnius Piso Frugi and the Roman Annalistic Tradition.* Lanham.
Forsythe, G. (1999) *Livy and Early Rome: A Study in Historical Method and Judgment.* Stuttgart.
Forsythe, G. (2005) *A Critical History of Early Rome: From Prehistory to the First Punic War.* Berkeley, Los Angeles, and London.
Frier, B. W. (1975) "Licinius Macer and the *Consules Suffecti* of 444 B.C." *TAPA* 105: 79–97.
Frier, B. W. (1979) *Libri Annales Pontificum Maximorum: The Origins of the Annalistic Tradition.* 2nd ed. 1999. Ann Arbor.
Frolov, R. M. (2019) "*Lictoresque habent in urbe et Capitolio privati*: Promagistrates in Rome in 49 B.C." *Phoenix* 73: 114–133.
Fronda, M. P. (2011) "Polybius 3.40, the Foundation of Placentia, and the Roman Calendar (218–217 BC)." *Historia* 60: 425–457.
Fuchs, J. (1897) *Hannibals Alpenübergang: Ein Studien- und Reiseergebnis.* Vienna.
Fuchs, J. (1904) "Hannibal in Mittelitalien." *WS* 26: 118–150.
Gabba, E. (1958) *Appiani Bellorum civilium liber primus: Introduzione, testo critico e commento con traduzione e indici.* Florence.
Gaertner, J. F. (2008) "Livy's Camillus and the Political Discourse of the Late Republic." *JRS* 98: 27–52.
Gelzer, M. (1968) *Caesar: Politician and Statesman.* Trans. P. Needham. Cambridge, Mass.
Giovannini, A. (1983) *Consulare Imperium.* Basel.
Giovannini, A. (1984) "Les origines des magistratures romaines." *MH* 41: 15–30.
Giovannini, A. (1993) "Il passagio dalle istituzioni monarchiche alle istituzioni repubblicane." In *Bilancio critico su Roma arcaica fra monarchia e repubblica*, 75–96. Rome.
Giovannini, A. (1998) "Les livres auguraux." In *La mémoire perdue: Recherches sur l'administration romaine.* École française de Rome, 103–122. Rome.
Gladigow, B. (1972) "Die sakralen Funktionen der Liktoren: Zum Problem von institutioneller Macht und sakraler Repräsentation." *ANRW* I.2: 295–313.
Goldbeck, F., and F. P. Mittag. (2008) "Der geregelte Triumph: Der republikanische Triumph bei Valerius Maximus und Aulus Gellius." In *Triplici invectus triumpho:*

Der römische Triumph in augusteischer Zeit, ed. H. Krasser, D. Pausch, and I. Petrovic, 55–74. Stuttgart.
Golden, G. K. (2013) *Crisis Management During the Roman Republic: The Role of Political Institutions in Emergencies*. Cambridge.
Görne, F. (2020) *Die Obstruktionen in der Römischen Republik*. Stuttgart.
Grandazzi, A. (1986) "La localisation d'Albe." *MEFRA* 98: 47–90.
Grandazzi, A. (2008) *Alba Longa, histoire d'une légende: Recherches sur l'archéologie, la religion, les traditions de l'ancien Latium*. 2 vols. Rome.
Gruen, E. S. (1978) "The Consular Elections for 216 B.C. and the Veracity of Livy." *CSCA* 11: 61–74.
Gusso, M. (1990) "Appunti sulla notazione dei Fasti Capitolini *interregni caus(sa)* per la (pro-)dittatura di Q. Fabio Massimo nel 217 a.C." *Historia* 39: 291–333.
Hall, L. G. H. (1990) "Flaminius at Arretium: A Joke in Livy." *LCM* 15.3: 34–36.
Harant, A. (1880) *Emendationes et adnotationes ad Titum Livium*. Paris.
Hartfield, M. E. (1982) "The Roman Dictatorship: Its Character and Its Evolution." Diss., University of California. Berkeley.
Herrmann, W. (1979) *Die Historien des Coelius Antipater: Fragmente und Kommentar*. Meisenheim am Glan.
Hesselbarth, H. (1889) *Historisch-kritische Untersuchungen zur dritten Dekade des Livius*. Halle.
Heuß, A. (1944) "Zur Entwicklung des Imperiums der römischen Oberbeamten." *ZRG* 64: 57–133.
Heuß, A. (1982 [1983]) *Gedanken und Vermutungen zur frühen römischen Regierungsgewalt*. (Nachrichten der Akademie der Wissenschaften in Göttingen, I: philologisch-historische Klasse, 1982, no. 10, 377–454.) Göttingen.
Hölkeskamp, K.-J. (1987) *Die Entstehung der Nobilität: Studien zur sozialen und politischen Geschichte der römischen Republik im 4. Jhdt. v. Chr*. Stuttgart.
Hölkeskamp, K.-J. (1990) "Senat und Volkstribunat im frühen 3. Jh. v. Chr." In *Staat und Staatlichkeit in der frühen römischen Republik. Akten eines Symposiums, 12.–15. Juli 1988, Freie Universität Berlin*, ed. W. Eder, 437–457. Stuttgart.
Hölkeskamp, K.-J. (2004) *Senatus Populusque Romanus: Die politische Kultur der Republik—Dimensionen und Deutungen*. Stuttgart.
Hölkeskamp, K.-J. (2011) "The Roman Republic as Theatre of Power: The Consuls as Leading Actors." In *Consuls and Res Publica: Holding High Office in the Roman Republic*, ed. H. Beck, A. Duplá, M. Jehne, and F. Pina Polo, 161–181. Cambridge.
Holloway, R. R. (2012) "A Little Noticed Synchronism in Livy and the Working Methods of the Annalists." *Klio* 94: 122–129.
Humm, M. (2012) "The Curiate Law and the Religious Nature of the Power of Roman Magistrates." In *Law and Religion in the Roman Republic*, ed. O. Tellegen-Couperus, 57–84. Leiden and Boston.
Hurlet, F. (1993) *La dictature de Sylla: Monarchie ou magistrature républicaine? Essai d'histoire constitutionelle*. Brussels and Rome.
Hurlet, F. (2010) "Recherches sur la *profectio* de la dictature de Sylla à la *lex Pompeia* (82–52): Le cas des gouverneurs de rang prétorien." In *Administrer les provinces de la République romaine. Actes du colloque de l'université de Nancy II, 4–5 juin 2009*, ed. N. Barrandon and F. Kirbihler, 45–75. Rennes.
Instinsky, H. U. (1937) "Die Weihung des Heiligtums der Latiner im Hain von Aricia." *Klio* 30: 118–122.
Irmscher, J. (1976) "Die Diktatur—Versuch einer Begriffsgeschichte." *Klio* 58: 273–287.

Itgenshorst, T. (2005) *Tota illa pompa: Der Triumph in der römischen Republik*. Göttingen.
Jacobs, K. (1937) *Gaius Flaminius*. Leiden.
Jahn, J. (1970) *Interregnum und Wahldiktatur*. Kallmünz.
Jal, P., ed. (1967) *Florus: Oevres*. 2 vols. Paris.
Janssen, L. F. (1960) *Abdicatio: Nieuwe Onderzoekingen over de Dictatuur*. Utrecht.
Jehne, M. (1989) "Die Diktatur optima lege." *ZRG* 106: 557–572.
Jordan, H. (1882) *Quaestiones Umbricae*. Königsberg.
Jung, J. (1899) "Bobbio, Veleia, Bardi." *MIÖG* 20: 521–566.
Jung, J. (1902) "Hannibal bei den Ligurern." *WS* 24: 152–193.
Kahrstedt, U. *See* Meltzer, O., and U. Kahrstedt. (1879–1913).
Kantor, G. (2014) "Roman Treaty with Lycia (*SEG* LV 1452) and the date of Caesar's Third Dictatorship." *ZPE* 190: 135–136.
Keaveney, A. (1982) "Sulla Augur." *AJAH* 7: 150–171.
Kempf, C., ed. (1888) *Valerii Maximi Factorum et dictorum memorabilium libri novem*. 2nd ed. Leipzig.
Kloft, H. (1977) *Prorogation und außerordentliche Imperien 326–81 v. Chr.: Untersuchungen zur Verfassung der römischen Republik*. Meisenheim am Glan.
Klotz, A. (1935) "Über die Quelle Plutarchs in der Lebensbeschreibung des Q. Fabius Maximus." *RhM* 84: 125–153.
Klotz, A. (1940/41) *Livius und seine Vorgänger*. Leipzig.
Knapp, R. C. (1980) "Cato in Spain, 195/194 B.C.: Chronology and Geography." In *Studies in Latin Literature and Roman History II*, ed. C. Deroux, 21–54. Brussels.
Konrad, C. F. (2003) "Review of T. C. Brennan, *The Praetorship in the Roman Republic* (2 vols., Oxford and New York, 2000)." *CJ* 98: 341–347.
Konrad, C. F. (2004) "*Vellere signa*." In *Augusto augurio: Rerum humanarum et divinarum commentationes in honorem Jerzy Linderski*, ed. C. F. Konrad, 169–203. Stuttgart.
Konrad, C. F. (2008) "*Ager Romanus* at Messana?" *CQ* 58: 349–353.
Konrad, C. F. (2015a) "After Drepana." *CQ* 65: 192–203.
Konrad, C. F. (2015b) "Lutatius and the *Sortes Praenestinae*." *Hermes* 143: 153–171.
Konrad, C. F. (2016) "Polybios and the Consulship of Iunius Pullus." *Hermes* 144: 178–193.
Konrad, C. F. (2017) "Nero's Triumph." In *Entre los mundos: Homenaje a Pedro Barceló/ Zwischen den Welten: Festschrift für Pedro Barceló*, ed. J. J. Ferrer-Maestro, C. Kunst, D. Hernández de la Fuente, and E. Faber, 195–208. Besançon.
Konrad, C. F. (Forthcoming) "Das Datum der Schlacht am Trasumenischen See." *RhM*.
Konrad, C. F. (Forthcoming) "Pullus, Pullius, and Pulcher." *Hermes*.
Koortbojian, M. (2020) *Crossing the Pomerium: The Boundaries of Political, Religious, and Military Institutions from Caesar to Constantine*. Princeton.
Koptev, A. (2016) "The Five-Day Interregnum in the Roman Republic." *CQ* 66: 205–221.
Kragelund, P. (2016) *Roman Historical Drama: The Octavia in Antiquity and Beyond*. Oxford.
Kromayer, J., and G. Veith. (1903–31) *Antike Schlachtfelder: Bausteine zu einer antiken Kriegsgeschichte*. 4 vols. Berlin.
Kunkel, W., and R. Wittmann. (1995) *Staatsordnung und Staatspraxis der Römischen Republik*. Part 2, *Die Magistratur*. Munich.
Lacey, W. K. (1996) *Augustus and the Principate: The Evolution of the System*. Leeds.
Lange, L. (1863–71) *Römische Alterthümer*. 3 vols. Berlin.
Last, H. (1947) "*Imperium Maius*: A Note." *JRS* 37: 157–164.
Latte, K. (1960) *Römische Religionsgeschichte*. Munich.
Lazenby, J. F. (1978) *Hannibal's War: A Military History of the Second Punic War*. Warminster. (Repr. 1998 with new preface. Norman, Okla.)

Lazenby, J. F. (1996) *The First Punic War: A Military History*. Stanford.
Lesiński, J. (2002) "Quintus Fabius Maximus Verrucosus: A Dictator in 217 BC?" In *ΕΥΕΡΓΕΣΙΑΣ ΧΑΡΙΝ: Studies Presented to Benedetto Bravo and Ewa Wipszycka by Their Disciples*, ed. T. Derda, J. Urbanik, and M. Wecowski, 131–158. Warsaw.
Levene, D. S. (1993) *Religion in Livy*. Leiden.
Levene, D. S. (2010) *Livy on the Hannibalic War*. Oxford.
Liebeschuetz, J. H. W. G. (1979) *Continuity and Change in Roman Religion*. Oxford.
Linderski, J. (1982) "Cicero and Roman Divination." *PP* 37: 12–38.
Linderski, J. (1984) "A Witticism of Appuleius Saturninus." *RFIC* 111: 452–459.
Linderski, J. (1985) "The *Libri Reconditi*." *HSCP* 89: 207–234.
Linderski, J. (1986a) "The Augural Law." *ANRW* II.16.3: 2146–2312.
Linderski, J. (1986b) "Watching the Birds: Cicero the Augur and the Augural *templa*." *CP* 81: 330–340.
Linderski, J. (1990) "The Auspices and the Struggle of the Orders." In *Staat und Staatlichkeit in der frühen römischen Republik*, ed. W. Eder, 34–48. Stuttgart.
Linderski, J. (1993) "Roman Religion in Livy." In *Livius: Aspekte seines Werkes*, ed. W. Schuller, 53–70. Konstanz.
Linderski, J. (1995) *Roman Questions: Selected Papers*. Stuttgart.
Linderski, J. (2006) "Founding the City." In *Ten Years of the Agnes Kirsopp Lake Michels Lectures at Bryn Mawr College*, ed. S. B. Faris and L. E. Lundeen, 88–107. Bryn Mawr.
Linderski, J. (2007) *Roman Questions II: Selected Papers*. Stuttgart.
Lintott, A. W. (1999) *The Constitution of the Roman Republic*. Oxford.
Lipovsky, J. P. (1981) *A Historiographical Study of Livy: Books VI–X*. Salem.
Lippold, A. (1963) *Consules: Untersuchungen zur Geschichte des römischen Konsulates von 264 bis 201 v. Chr*. Bonn.
Luce, T. J., jr. (1961) "Appian's Magisterial Terminology." *CP* 56: 21–28.
Lundgreen, C. (2011) *Regelkonflikte in der römischen Republik: Geltung und Gewichtung von Normen in politischen Entscheidungsprozessen*. Stuttgart.
Luzzatto, G. I. (1956) "Appunti sulle dittature 'imminuto iure': Spunti critici e ricostruttivi." In *Studi in onore di Pietro de Francisci*, 3: 403–459. Milan.
Magdelain, A. (1964) "Auspicia ad patres redeunt." In *Hommages à Jean Bayet*, ed. M. Renard and R. Schilling, 427–473. Brussels.
Magdelain, A. (1968) *Recherches sur l' imperium: La loi curiate et les auspices d'investiture*. Paris.
Magdelain, A. (1990) *Jus imperium auctoritas: Études de droit romain*. Paris and Rome.
Mancini, G. (1925) "Un nuovo frammento dei fasti consolari capitolini." *BCAR* 53: 238–270.
Manuwald, G. (2001) *Fabulae praetextae: Spuren einer literarischen Gattung der Römer*. Munich.
Manuwald, G. (2011) *Roman Republican Theatre: A History*. Cambridge.
Marco Simón, F. (2011) "The *Feriae Latinae* as Religious Legitimation of the Consuls' *imperium*." In *Consuls and Res Publica: Holding High Office in the Roman Republic*, ed. H. Beck, A. Duplá, M. Jehne, and F. Pina Polo, 116–132. Cambridge.
Marshall, A. J. (1984) "Symbols and Showmanship in Roman Public Life: The Fasces." *Phoenix* 38: 120–141.
Martínez Gázquez, J. (1974) "La sucesión de los magistrados romanos en Hispania en el año 196 a. de C." *Pyrenae* 10: 173–179.
Masi Doria, C. (2000) *Spretum imperium: Prassi costituzionale e momenti di crisi nei rapporti tra magistrati nella media e tarda repubblica*. Naples.

Mazzarino, S. (1967) " 'Dicator' e 'dictator.'" *Helikon* 7: 426–427.
Meißner, B. (2000) "Gaius Flaminius—oder: wie ein Außenseiter zum Sündenbock wurde." In *Von Romulus zu Augustus: Große Gestalten der römischen Republik*, ed. K.-J. Hölkeskamp and E. Stein-Hölkeskamp, 92–105. Munich.
Meister, J. B. (2013) "Adventus und Profectio: Aristokratisches Prestige, Bindungswesen und Raumkonzepte im republikanischen und frühkaiserzeitlichen Rom." *MH* 70: 33–56.
Meltzer, O., and U. Kahrstedt. (1879–1913) *Geschichte der Karthager*. 3 vols. Berlin.
Meyer, E. (1961) *Römischer Staat und Staatsgedanke*. 2nd ed. Zurich.
Meyer, E. (1972) "Die römische Annalistik im Lichte der Urkunden." *ANRW* I.2: 970–986.
Mignone, L. M. (2016) "Rome's Pomerium and the Aventine Hill: From Auguraculum to Imperium sine fine." *Historia* 65: 427–449.
Miltner, F. (1943) "Zwischen Trebia und Trasimen (218/17 v. Chr.)." *Hermes* 78: 1–21.
Mingazzini, P. (1925) "Un frammento inedito dei Fasti Capitolini." *NSA* 376–382.
Momigliano, A. (1930) "Ricerche sulle magistrature romane, I: Il 'dictator clavi figendi causa.'" *BCAR* 58: 29–42.
Mommsen, Th. (1859) *Die römische Chronologie bis auf Caesar*. 2nd ed. Berlin.
Mommsen, Th. (1871) "Die neuen Fragmente der Jahrtafel des latinischen Festes." *Hermes* 5: 379–385.
Mommsen, Th. (1881–6) *Römische Geschichte*. 5 vols. 7th (5: 3rd) ed. Berlin.
Mommsen, Th. (1887–8) *Römisches Staatsrecht*. 3 vols. (1–2: 3rd ed.). Leipzig.
Mommsen, Th. (1899) *Römisches Strafrecht*. Leipzig.
Morgan, M. G. (1977) "Calendars and Chronology in the First Punic War." *Chiron* 7: 89–117.
Müller-Seidel, I. (1953) "Q. Fabius Maximus Cunctator und die Konsulwahlen der Jahre 215 und 214 v. Chr." *RhM* 96: 241–281.
Münzer, F. (1920) *Römische Adelsparteien und Adelsfamilien*. Stuttgart.
Nedergaard, E. (2001) "Facts and Fiction about the Fasti Capitolini." *ARID* 27: 107–127.
Nicholls, J. J. (1967) "The Content of the *lex curiata*." *AJP* 88: 257–278.
Nicosia, G. (1987) "Sulle pretese figure di '*dictatores imminuto iure*'." In *Studi in onore di C. Sanfilippo*, 7: 529–592. Milan.
North, J. A. (1967) "The Inter-Relation of State Religion and Politics in Roman Public Life from the End of the Second Punic War to the Time of Sulla." D.Phil. diss., University of Oxford. Oxford.
North, J. A. (1990a) "Diviners and Divination at Rome." In *Pagan Priests: Religion and Power in the Ancient World*, ed. M. Beard and J. A. North, 51–71. Ithaca.
North, J. A. (1990b) "Religion in Republican Rome." In *The Cambridge Ancient History*. Vol. 7.2: *The Rise of Rome to 220 BC*, 573–624. 2nd ed. Cambridge.
Northwood, S. J. (2000) "Livy and the Early Annalists." In *Studies in Latin Literature and Roman History X*, ed. C. Deroux, 45–55. Brussels.
Oakley, S. P. (1997–2005) *A Commentary on Livy, Books VI–X*. 4 vols. Oxford.
Ogilvie, R. M. (1965) *A Commentary on Livy, Books 1–5*. Oxford.
Palmer, R. E. A. (1996) "The Deconstruction of Mommsen on Festus 462/464 L., or the Hazards of Restoration." In *Imperium Sine Fine: T. Robert S. Broughton and the Roman Republic*, ed. J. Linderski, 75–101. Stuttgart.
Pareti, L. (1912a) "Una reduplicazione in Livio e le mosse romane nell'inverno 218–217: Contributi per la storia della guerra annibalica, 3." *RFIC* 40: 246–258.
Pareti, L. (1912b) "Sul passaggio di Annibale per l'Appennino: Contributi per la storia della guerra annibalica, 4." *RFIC* 40: 258–271.

Paschall, D. (1936) "The Origin and Semantic Development of Latin Vitium." *TAPA* 67: 219–231.
Pease, A. S. (1920–3) *M. Tulli Ciceronis de Divinatione libri duo*. Urbana. Repr. Darmstadt, 1963.
Pelikan Pittenger, M. R. (2008) *Contested Triumphs: Politics, Pageantry, and Performance in Livy's Republican Rome*. Berkeley, Los Angeles, and London.
Pelling, C. B. R. (1980) "Plutarch's Adaptation of His Source-Material." *JHS* 100: 127–140.
Pelling, C. B. R. (1988) *Plutarch: Life of Antony*. Cambridge.
Peter, H. (1865) *Die Quellen Plutarchs in den Biographieen der Römer*. Halle.
Petrucci, A. (1996) *Il trionfo nella storia costituzionale romana dagli inizi della repubblica ad Augusto*. Milan.
Philipp, G. B. (1959) "Politische Wortstudien." *Gymnasium* 66: 97–127.
Pina Polo, F. (2011) *The Consul at Rome: The Civil Functions of the Consuls in the Roman Republic*. Cambridge.
Potter, D. S. (2010) "Roman Religion: Ideas and Actions." In *Life, Death, and Entertainment in the Roman Empire*, ed. D. S. Potter and D. J. Mattingly, 137–191. 2nd ed. Ann Arbor.
Proctor, D. (1971) *Hannibal's March in History*. Oxford.
Rafferty, D. (2019) *Provincial Allocations in Rome, 123–52 BCE*. Stuttgart.
Ramsay, W. M. (1898) "Varia." *CR* 12: 335–343.
Rauh, S. H. (2015) "The Tradition of Suicide in Rome's Foreign Wars." *TAPA* 145: 383–410.
Reuss, F. (1901) "Zur Geschichte des ersten punischen Krieges." *Philologus* 60: 102–148.
Reuss, F. (1909) "Der erste punische Krieg." *Philologus* 68: 410–427.
Rich, J. W. (1996) "Augustus and the spolia opima." *Chiron* 26: 85–127.
Rich, J. W. (2005) "Valerius Antias and the Construction of the Roman Past." *BICS* 48: 137–161.
Richardson, J. H. (2012) *The Fabii and the Gauls: Studies in Historical Thought and Historiography in Republican Rome*. Stuttgart.
Richardson, J. S. (1975) "The Triumph, the Praetors and the Senate in the Early Second Century B.C." *JRS* 65: 50–63.
Richardson, J. S. (1986) *Hispaniae: Spain and the Development of Roman Imperialism, 218–82 BC*. Cambridge.
Richardson, J. S. (1991) "*Imperium Romanum*: Empire and the Language of Power." *JRS* 81: 1–9.
Richardson, L., jr. (1992) *A New Topographical Dictionary of Ancient Rome*. Baltimore and London.
Ridley, R. T. (1979) "The Origin of the Roman Dictatorship: An Overlooked Opinion." *RhM* 122: 303–309.
Ridley, R. T. (1989 [1991]) "The Historical Observations of Jacob Perizonius." *MAL* 32: 181–295.
Ridley, R. T. (2013) "The Historian's Silences: What Livy Did Not Know—Or Chose Not to Tell." *JAH* 1: 27–52.
Ridley, R. T. (2014) "Livy the Critical Historian." *Athenaeum* 102: 444–474.
Rix, H. (1992) "Wonach haben die Römer ihre Beamten benannt?" In *Verstehen, Übernehmen, Deuten*, ed. P. Neukam, 83–105. Munich.
Rosenberger, V. (1998) *Gezähmte Götter: Das Prodigienwesen der römischen Republik*. Stuttgart.
Rosenstein, N. S. (1990) *Imperatores Victi: Military Defeat and Aristocratic Competition in the Middle and Late Republic*. Berkeley, Los Angeles, and Oxford.

Rosenstein, N. S. (1995) "Sorting Out the Lot in Republican Rome." *AJP* 116: 43–75.
Rudolph, H. (1935) *Stadt und Staat im römischen Italien*. Leipzig.
Rüpke, J. (1990) *Domi militiae: Die religiöse Konstruktion des Krieges in Rom*. Stuttgart.
Rüpke, J. (2005) *Fasti sacerdotum: Die Mitglieder der Priesterschaften und das sakrale Funktionspersonal römischer, griechischer, orientalischer und jüdisch-christlicher Kulte in der Stadt Rom von 300 v. Chr. bis 499 n. Chr*. 3 vols. Stuttgart.
Rüpke, J. (2019) *Peace and War in Rome: A Religious Construction of Warfare*. Stuttgart. (English trans., D. M. B. Richardson, of Rüpke 1990.)
Sadée, E. (1909) "Der Frühjahrsfeldzug des Jahres 217 und die Schlacht am trasimenischen See." *Klio* 9: 48–69.
Sánchez, P. (2014) "Le fragment de L. Cincius (Festus p. 276 L) et le commandement des armées du Latium." *CCG* 25: 7–48.
Santangelo, F. (2011) "*Pax Deorum* and Pontiffs." In *Priests and State in the Roman World*, ed. J. H. Richardson and F. Santangelo, 161–186. Stuttgart.
Santangelo, F. (2013) "Priestly *auctoritas* in the Roman Republic." *CQ* 63: 743–763.
Satterfield, S. (2015) "Prodigies, the *Pax Deum*, and the *Ira Deum*." *CJ* 110: 431–445.
Schäublin, C. (1986) "Ementita Auspicia." *WS* 20: 165–181.
Scheid, J. (1985) *Religion et piété à Rome*. Paris.
Scheid, J. (2012) "Le rite des auspices à Rome: Quelle evolution? Réflexions sur la transformation de la divination publique des Romains entre le IIIe et le Ier siècle avant notre ère." In *La raison des signes: Présages, rites, destin dans les sociétés de la Méditerranée ancienne*, ed. S. Georgoudi, R. Koch-Piettre, and F. Schmidt, 109–128. Leiden and Boston.
Scheid, J. (2015) "Auspices et autres pratiques divinatoires des magistrats romains à l'époque medio-républicaine." *CCG* 26: 251–260.
Schmitt, T. (1991) *Hannibals Siegeszug: Historiographische und historische Studien vor allem zu Polybios und Livius*. Munich.
Schulten, A. (1928) "Iliturgi." *Hermes* 63: 288–301.
Schütte, L. (1901) *Der Apenninenpass des Monte Bardone und die deutschen Kaiser*. Berlin.
Schwegler, A. (1853–8) *Römische Geschichte*. 3 vols. Tübingen.
Scullard, H. H. (1951) *Roman Politics, 220–150 B.C*. Oxford. 2nd ed. 1973.
Scullard, H. H. (1970) *Scipio Africanus: Soldier and Politician*. Ithaca.
Seeck, O. (1874) "Der Bericht des Livius über den Winter 218/17 v. Chr." *Hermes* 8: 152–166.
Seibert, J. (1993a) *Forschungen zu Hannibal*. Darmstadt.
Seibert, J. (1993b) *Hannibal*. Darmstadt.
Simpson, A. D. (1938) "The Departure of Crassus for Parthia." *TAPA* 69: 532–541.
Sini, F. (1976) "A proposito del carattere religioso del 'dictator': Note metodologiche sui documenti sacerdotali." *SDHI* 42: 401–424.
Skutsch, O. (1985) *The Annals of Quintus Ennius*. Oxford.
Smith, C. J. (1996) *Early Rome and Latium: Economy and Society ca. 1000 to 500 BC*. Oxford.
Smith, C. J. (2011) "The Magistrates of the Early Roman Republic." In *Consuls and Res Publica: Holding High Office in the Roman Republic*, ed. H. Beck, A. Duplá, M. Jehne, and F. Pina Polo, 19–40. Cambridge.
Soltau, W. (1870) *De fontibus Plutarchi in secundo bello Punico enarrando*. Bonn.
Soltau, W. (1914) "Der Ursprung der Diktatur." *Hermes* 49: 352–368.
Stasse, B. (2005) "La loi curiate des magistrates." *RIDA* 52: 375–400.
Staveley, E. S. (1953) "The Significance of the Consular Tribunate." *JRS* 43: 30–36.

Staveley, E. S. (1954-5) "The Conduct of Elections during an *Interregnum*." *Historia* 3: 193-211.
Staveley, E. S. (1956) "The Constitution of the Roman Republic 1940-1954." *Historia* 5: 74-122.
Staveley, E. S. (1963) "The *Fasces* and *Imperium Maius*." *Historia* 12: 458-484.
Stewart, R. (1987) "Sors et Provincia: Praetors and Quaestors in Republican Rome." Diss., Duke University. Ann Arbor.
Stewart, R. (1998) *Public Office in Early Rome: Ritual Procedure and Political Practice*. Ann Arbor.
Stolle, F. (1912) *Das Lager und Heer der Römer*. Straßburg.
Sumner, G. V. (1970) "Proconsuls and *Provinciae* in Spain, 218/7-196/5 B.C." *Arethusa* 3: 85-102.
Sumner, G. V. (1973) *The Orators in Cicero's Brutus: Prosopography and Chronology*. Toronto.
Sumner, G. V. (1975) "Elections at Rome in 217 B.C." *Phoenix* 29: 250-259.
Sumner, G. V. (1977) "Notes on *Provinciae* in Spain (197-133 B.C.)" *CP* 72: 126-130.
Suolahti, J. (1976) "M. Claudius Glicia, qui scriba fuerat, dictator." *Arctos* 10: 97-103.
Susini, G. (1956-60) "Ricerche sulla battaglia del Trasimeno." *Annuario dell'Accademia Etrusca di Cortona* 11 (NS 4): 1-93.
Susini, G. (1961-4) "L'archeologia della guerra annibalica." *Annuario dell'Accademia Etrusca di Cortona* 12 (NS 5): 111-139.
Syme, R. (2016 [1958]) "How Many *Fasces*?" In Syme, R., *Approaching the Roman Revolution: Papers on Republican History*, ed. F. Santangelo, 255-271. Oxford.
Szemler, G. J. (1972) *The Priests of the Roman Republic: A Study of Interactions Between Priesthoods and Magistracies*. Brussels.
Tarn, W. W. (1907) "The Fleets of the First Punic War." *JHS* 27: 48-60.
Tarpin, M. (2015) "*Imperium*, promagistrats et triomphe au Ier siècle av. J.-C.: Quelques affaires..." *CCG* 26: 261-288.
Tatum, W. J. (2012) *A Caesar Reader: Selections from Bellum Gallicum and Bellum Civile, and from Caesar's Letters, Speeches, and Poetry*. Mundelein.
Taylor, L. Ross. (1942) "Caesar's Colleagues in the Pontifical College." *AJP* 63: 385-412.
Thiel, J. H. (1954) *A History of Roman Sea-Power before the Second Punic War*. Amsterdam.
Tietz, W. (2020) "*Praetor maximus*—eine vage Formulierung aus den Anfangsjahren der römischen Republik." *Historia* 69: 185-207.
Timpe, D. (1972) "Fabius Pictor und die Anfänge der römischen Historiographie." *ANRW* I.2: 928-969.
Tipps, G. K. (1991) "The *Rogum Scipionis* and Gnaeus Scipio's Last Stand." *CW* 85: 81-90.
Tovar, A. (1974-89) *Iberische Landeskunde. Teil 2: Die Völker und die Städte des antiken Hispanien*. 3 vols. Baden-Baden.
Vaahtera, J. (2001) *Roman Augural Lore in Greek Historiography: A Study of the Theory and Terminology*. Stuttgart.
Valditara, G. (1988) "Perché il dictator non poteva montare a cavallo." *SDHI* 54: 226-238.
Valditara, G. (1989) *Studi sul magister populi: Dagli ausiliari militari del rex ai primi magistrati repubblicani*. Milan.
Valeton, I. M. J. (1889) "De modis auspicandi Romanorum, I-II." *Mnemosyne* 17: 275-325, 418-425.
Valeton, I. M. J. (1890) "De modis auspicandi Romanorum, II-III." *Mnemosyne* 18: 208-263, 406-456.
Valeton, I. M. J. (1891) "De iure obnuntiandi comitiis et conciliis." *Mnemosyne* 19: 75-113, 229-270.

Van Haeperen, F. (2007) "Les rites d'accession au pouvoir des consuls romains: Une part intégrante de leur entrée en charge." In *Le pouvoir et ses rites d'accession et de confirmation. Actes de la table ronde organisée par le Centre de Recherches en Histoire du Droit et des Institutions, le 9 décembre 2005*, ed. J.-M. Cauchies and F. Van Haeperen, 31–45. Brussels.

Van Haeperen, F. (2012) "Auspices d'investiture, loi curiate et légitimité des magistrats romains." *CCG* 23: 71–112.

Van Haeperen, F. (2017) "Les comices curiates, une assemblée garante de la norme?" In *La norme sous la République et le Haut-Empire romains: Élaboration, diffusion et contournements*, ed. T. Itgenshorst and P. Le Doze, 389–397. Bordeaux.

Versnel, H. S. (1970) *Triumphus: An Inquiry into the Origin, Development and Meaning of the Roman Triumph*. Leiden.

Vervaet, F. J. (2004) "The *lex Valeria* and Sulla's Empowerment as Dictator." *CCG* 15: 37–84.

Vervaet, F. J. (2007) "The Scope and Historic Significance of the 'lex Metilia de aequando M. Minuci magistri equitum et Q. Fabi dictatoris iure' (217 B.C.E.)." *SDHI* 73: 197–232.

Vervaet, F. J. (2010) "The Secret History: The Official Position of Imperator Caesar Divi filius From 31 to 27 BCE." *AncSoc* 40: 79–152.

Vervaet, F. J. (2012) "The Praetorian Proconsuls of the Roman Republic (211–52 BCE): A Constitutional Survey." *Chiron* 42: 47–96.

Vervaet, F. J. (2014) *The High Command in the Roman Republic: The Principle of the summum imperium auspiciumque from 509 to 19 BCE*. Stuttgart.

Vervaet, F. J. (2018) "The Date, Modalities and Legacy of Sulla's Abdication of his Dictatorship: A Study in Sullan Statecraft." *Studia Historica: Historia Antigua* 36: 31–82.

Voci, P. (1953) "Per la definizione dell' *imperium*." In *Studi in memoria di Emilio Albertario*, ed. V. Arangio-Ruiz and G. Lavaggi, 2: 65–102. Milan.

Walbank, F.W. (1957–79) *A Historical Commentary on Polybius*. 3 vols. Oxford.

Walt, S. (1997) *Der Historiker C. Licinius Macer: Einleitung, Fragmente, Kommentar*. Stuttgart and Leipzig.

Wardle, D. (1998) *Valerius Maximus: Memorable Deeds and Sayings, Book I*. Oxford.

Wardle, D. (2005) "Valerius Maximus and the End of the First Punic War." *Latomus* 64: 377–384.

Wardle, D. (2006) *Cicero on Divination: De Divinatione, Book I*. Oxford.

Wild, H. (1994) *Untersuchungen zur Innenpolitik des Gaius Flaminius*. Munich.

Willems, P. (1878–85) *Le sénat de la république romaine: Sa composition et ses attributions*. 3 vols. Louvain and Paris.

Williams, P. (2004) "The Roman Tribunate in the 'Era of Quiescence' 287–133 BC." *Latomus* 63: 281–294.

Wilson, M. B. (2021) *Dictator: The Evolution of the Roman Dictatorship*. Ann Arbor.

Wiseman, T. P. (1979) *Clio's Cosmetics: Three Studies in Greco-Roman Literature*. Leicester.

Wiseman, T. P. (1994) *Historiography and Imagination*. Exeter.

Wiseman, T. P. (1995) *Remus: A Roman Myth*. Cambridge.

Wiseman, T. P. (1998) *Roman Drama and Roman History*. Exeter.

Wiseman, T. P. (2009) *Remembering the Roman People: Essays on Late-Republican Politics and Literature*. Oxford.

Wiseman, T. P. (2017) "Iuppiter Stator in Palatio: A New Solution to an Old Puzzle." *MDAI(R)* 123: 13–45.

Wissowa, G. (1912) *Religion und Kultus der Römer*. 2nd ed. Munich.

Wittmann, R. *See* Kunkel, W., and R. Wittmann. (1995).

Yaron, R. (1974) "Semitic Elements in Early Rome." In *Daube Noster: Essays in Legal History for David Daube*, ed. A. Watson, 434–457. Edinburgh and London.
Zevi, F. (2016) "I Fasti di *Privernum*, 1. Il Documento. Le liste consolari. I *magistri equitum* di Cesare." *ZPE* 197: 287–305.
Ziółkowski, A. (1987) "Q. Lutatius Cerco cos. 241 and the 'sortes Fortunae Primigeniae'." *CCC* 8: 319–332.
Ziółkowski, A. (2011) "The Capitol and the 'Auspices of Departure'." In *Studia Lesco Mrozewicz ab amicis et discipulis dedicata*, ed. S. Ruciński, K. Balbuza, and K. Królczyk, 465–471. Poznań.

General Index

Note: All ancient dates are BC, unless indicated otherwise. Roman names are alphabetized in the customary manner: family name/*nomen* followed by surname/*cognomen* (if any; sometimes multiple), given name/*praenomen* (in standard abbreviation); identical names are arranged in chronological order. Roman Emperors and most ancient authors are listed under their conventional English names (e.g., Augustus, Livy, Plutarch); most persons of the Regal Period are listed under their first names (e.g., Tullus Hostilius).

For the benefit of digital users, indexed terms that span two pages (e.g., 52–53) may, on occasion, appear on only one of those pages.

abdication:
    of consul(s) 60, 128, 178–9, 189–93, 197–8, 201–2, 284–6, 291–4 *passim*; *see also* Claudius Marcellus, M. (*cos. V* 208): consulship (second), abdication of; Flaminius, C.: consulship (first), abdication of; Furius Philus, P.: consulship, abdication of
    of consular tribunes 178, 197–9, 202, 291–4 *passim*
    of dictator, *see* dictator
    of *flamines* 206–7
    of magister equitum, *see* magister equitum
    of magistrates 61–2, 76, 123n.43, 135n.79, 171, 175, 189–90, 294
    of praetor 72n.15, 201–2
abrogation 108, 202–3, 261, 270
Acta Triumphorum 118–19, 172n.10, 179, 190
Adherbal (Carthaginian commander 249) 154, 161
adiutor 35–6, 116–19, 126
Adriatic Sea 225, 229, 231–5, 238, 250, 256
Aebutius Helva, T. (*cos.* 499, *mag. eq.* 499 or 496) 6n.10, 128
Aebutius Parrus, T. (*pr.* 178) 35–6
aediles 166, 200–1
    curule 12–13, 171, 197
    plebeian 12n.25, 197
Aegates islands, battle of 36, 116–17, 119–20
Aelius Tubero, L. (or Q.) (historian):
    on aediles of 299 12–13
Aemilius Lepidus, M. (*cos.* 232, *augur*) 183–4, 186, 272–3
Aemilius Lepidus, M. (*cos. II* 42, *IIIvir r.p.c., pont. max.*) 114–15
    consul and magister equitum 130–1
    names Caesar dictator 104, 133, 141–2, 171–2
    magister equitum *perpetuo* 113–14

Aemilius Mamercinus, L. (*cos. II* 329, *dict.* 316) 110–11
Aemilius Mamercinus, Mam. (*tr. mil. c. p.* 438, *dict. III* 426) 172n.10
Aemilius Papus, L. (*cos.* 225) 190–1
Aemilius Paullus, L. (*cos. II* 216) 119–20, 170
    auspicates before moving army 158–9, 263–4
    death in office 176–7
Aemilius Paullus, M. (*cos.* 302, *mag. eq.* 301) 4–5, 9–10, 129–30
Aemilius Regillus, M. (*pr.* 217) 256–7, 256n.3, 271n.39, 275–6
Africa 28–9, 133n.75, 147n.121, 153
    Roman invasion of 153–4, 258
ager 58–9
    effatus 58–9, 61
    Romanus 41–2, 54–9, 61, 258n.8
Alba Longa 89–90, 90n.70, 92
Albanus mons 53, 90n.70
Alexandria 132–5, 146–7
Algidus 19–20, 201
Allia river, battle of the 62, 258n.10
annalists/annalistic 15–16, 30, 66–7, 84n.50, 87n.60, 110–11, 291
    elaboration/invention/reconstruction 6, 21, 21n.38, 201–2
    see also reconstruction
Annius Milo, T. (*pr.* 55) 133, 147n.121
antiquarian(s) 48, 111, 139–40
    explanation 175–6
    research 178–9
    speculation 29, 94, 201–2
Antonius, L. (*cos.* 41) 190
Antonius, M. (*cos. II* 34, *IIIvir r.p.c., augur*) 52n.65, 69, 80, 288–9
    augur 138–9, 142–3, 196n.93

Antonius, M. (*cont.*)
  magister equitum and Caesar's deputy 114–15, 115n.14, 132–3
  magister equitum with extended appointment 131, 142–3, 146–7
  named magister equitum by consul 131, 133–5, 145
  ovatio in 40 117
Appennine passes 232, 235, 250–1
  Abetone, Passo del 218, 233–4
  Brattello, Passo del 218–19, 233–4
  Cerreto, Passo del 218–19
  Cisa, Passo della 218–19, 234
  Collina, Passo della 213–18, 230, 234n.41, 250–1
  Futa, Passo della 216–19, 231, 250–1
  Mandrioli, Passo dei 216, 217n.7, 219, 231–2, 235
  Muraglione, Passo del 232
  Radici, Passo (or Foce) delle 218
  Viamaggio, Passo di 216, 226–7, 231–2, 234, 236, 250
  see also Hannibal Barqa: Appennine passes, choice of
Appennines 213, 218–19, 225, 250
  see also Flaminius, C. (*cos. II* 217): movements in 217
  see also Hannibal Barqa: Arretium, surprises Flaminius at
Appian of Alexandria 110–11
  on magistrates under dictator, termination of 79, 82, 84
  on Sulla's dictatorship 143–4
Appuleius, L. (*pr.* by 59) 73
Appuleius Saturninus, L. (*tr. pl. II* 100) 288n.96
Arausio, battle of 287–8
Arezzo, see Arretium
Aricia 89n.69, 90
Ariminum (Rimini) 184–5, 216–18, 228, 249–53
  pivotal to Roman strategy 250–2
  see also Flaminius, C.: Ariminum
Arkhidamos (Aitolian ambassador) 51n.63
Arno river 213–16, 218n.9, 223
  flooding of 216–19, 222–3, 232, 250, 251n.79
  see also Hannibal Barqa: Arno, crosses marshes of
Arretium (Arezzo) 250, 252–3
  see also Flaminius, C.: Arretium; movements in 217; Hannibal, pursuit of
  see also Hannibal Barqa: Arretium, surprises Flaminius at
Arx 49n.59, 56n.75
Asinius Pollio, C. (*cos.* 40) 135n.80

assemblies, see *comitia*; *contio*
Ateius Capito, C. (*tr. pl.* 55) 155, 288
Atilius Caiatinus, A. (*cos. II* 254, *dict.* 249) 163, 255–8, 261–2
  iudex in Catulus–Falto *sponsio* 117–19
Atilius Regulus, C. (*cos.* 225):
  death in office 176–7
Atilius Regulus, M. (*cos. II* 256) 153
Atilius Regulus, M. (*cos. II* 217, *cens.* 214) 78–9, 82n.48, 107–8, 170, 176–7, 279
Atilius Serranus, C. (*pr.* 218, *augur*) 184n.49, 272–3
Attus Navius (*augur*) 185
augur(s) 35n.18, 40–2, 50, 61–2, 188–9, 243n.60, 254, 289
  augural books 89–90, 92–4, 260–1, 284
  augural law, see *ius augurale*
  augural science, *see* augurs, college of
  augurium 40n.31, 50n.61, 58n.81
  comitia, dismissed by 196n.93
  inaugurated 61–2, 186n.57
  inauguration, performed by 40n.31
  interpretes Iovis 39–40
  not responsible for *prodigia* 43–4, 184
augurs, college of 35n.18, 126–7, 175, 183, 193–4, 270
  and Antonius as magister equitum, extended term of 131, 137–8, 142–3, 145–7
  and Caesar as dictator, extended term of 134–5, 142–3, 145–6
  and consular tribunes naming dictator 139–40
  and *haruspices* 286
  and interrex naming dictator 140
  and magistrates ruled *vitio creati*, see *vitio creatus/-ti* or *factus/-ti*
  and magistrates, terms of 144–5
  and Marcellus, *vitium* of 273–4
  and praetor naming dictator 104, 138–40, 142–3, 171–2
  and Ti. Gracchus, *vitium* of 284–6
  augural rulings, falsification of, for political purposes 170, 181, 183–7, 195, 212–13, 254, 275–6, 278–80, 278n.62, 285–6, 288–9
  augural science (*disciplina*) 185–6
  augural science, manipulation of, for political purposes 183, 185–7, 207–8, 212–13, 259n.11
  auspices, exclusive responsibility for 39–42, 281–2, 286
  auspices, critics of, power struggle with 280
  decrees and responses of 41–2, 133, 138–43, 149n.4, 164, 169, 180, 184n.51, 188–9, 283–4, 288–9, 291
  members in 223 183–6, 203–4

members in 215 272–3
members in 49 138–9
members in 48 142–3
no *augur maximus* 271n.37
periti religionum iurisque publici 281–2
auguraculum 49n.59, 56n.75
Augustus (Imp. Caesar Divi f. Aug., *cos. XIII* 2) 123n.43, 141n.104, 173, 176
  and auspices 289–90
  and lictors 75–6
  and Marcellus 179
  at Latin Festival 251n.81
  ovatio in 40 117
Aulla 218–19
Aulella river 218–19
Aulius Cerretanus, Q. (*cos. II* 319) 128–9
Aulius Cerretanus, Q. (*mag. eq.* 315) 6n.10, 14–15
Aurelius Cotta, C. (*cos. II* 248) 24–5, 115n.12
Aurelius Cotta, C. (*cos.* 200) 120–1
Aurelius Pecuniola, P. (*leg.* 252) 25
auspication 38n.25, 40–2, 44–5, 49, 58–60, 76, 100–1, 114–16, 119–21, 124–6, 141–2, 152, 168, 205, 280–1, 287, 289–90
  at *pomerium* 50n.62
  before battle 149, 152, 155–6, 158, 160–3, 181, 241–4, 281n.71
  before moving of army/sailing of fleet 158–9, 159n.27, 162–3, 248–9, 277
  initial 45–7, 47n.51, 59, 65, 195; *see also* auspices: of investiture
  omitted 40–2, 283–5
  see also Flaminius, C.: auspices
  see also *pulli*
auspices:
  acquired through initial auspication 46–7, 54–6, 141–2
  alternatives to 167–8, 212, 254
  and *agri* 58–9
  and historical tradition 2–3, 16–17, 19, 126, 139–40, 199, 240–3, 245–9, 258n.10, 263, 267, 289–90
  and naval warfare 157–8
  and *res publica* 32, 39–43, 169, 191–2, 265, 280–1, 289–90
  and water 156–9
  auspicato 40–1, 47, 50n.61, 52–4, 56n.75, 98, 114–15, 157–8, 205, 254, 284
  contra auspicia 158–60, 163n.36, 169, 212, 255, 258n.10, 259–60, 262–3, 267, 269, 287–8; *see also* auspices: (dis)respect for
  distinct from *prodigia* 44n.39; see also *prodigium/-gia*
  impetrative 43, 59–60, 120n.29, 163n.37, 193–4, 205, 243–4, 246
  impetrative, negative response to/cancellation of 44–5, 205, 244, 274–5, 284–5, 289–90
  inauspicato 54n.70, 254
  incertis auspiciis 1n.2, 17, 24, 60, 62–3, 112, 115, 148, 166–8, 194n.89, 243, 269–70, 277
  manipulation of 42–3
  oblative 45–8, 54n.70, 59–60, 62–3, 83, 120n.29, 184, 188–9, 193–4, 205, 211, 242–6, 274–5, 281–2, 284–8
  obtained by magistrate 40–1, 43
  of censor 43, 97–8, 101
  of consul 35–6, 43, 54–6, 97–8, 114, 117, 120–1, 124–7, 141, 157–8, 212–13
  of consular tribune 292n.8
  of departure/war 30, 48–52, 55–6, 61n.88, 63n.96, 64–5, 149, 155–6
  of departure/war, evidence for 50–2
  of dictator 2–3, 16, 43, 85, 97–8, 100–2, 112–16, 126–7, 143–5, 269
  of investiture 45–8, 53–6, 59–60, 62–3, 115, 155–6, 168, 212–13, 243–5, 247, 274–5
  of magister equitum 1, 16, 19, 112–16, 126–7, 134–5, 143–5, 269
  of patricians 97–8
  of praetor 35–6, 43, 97–8, 114, 117, 120–1, 124–7
  of promagistrates 124–5, 141–2
  of quaestor 35–6, 171
  praetor elected under same as consuls 16, 171
  precedence of 263–4
  procedures and orientation 40–1, 44n.41
  protection against defeat in battle 259–60
  renovation of 62n.94; see also *interregnum*
  repetition of 1, 3, 9, 24–5, 26n.48, 56–65, 115n.12, 126–7, 155–6, 274–5, 277
  report, significance of 181, 193–4, 274–9, 287–9
  requiring interpretation 246
  (dis)respect for 16–17, 142, 148–9, 152, 165, 175, 244, 265, 280–1; *see also* auspices: *contra auspicia*; auspices: rule of, questioned
  rule of, accepted 288–9
  rule of, questioned 168, 193–5, 254, 260–2, 265–9, 280, 287, 289
  suis/alienis auspiciis 16, 112, 115, 120–1, 123–7, 141–2
  tied to City of Rome 57–8
  uncertain, *see* auspices: *incertis auspiciis*
  valid for current day only 40–1, 43–5
  validity of magistrate's 17, 40–1, 46–7, 59–63, 126–7, 144, 193–4, 205, 243–5, 284–5
  water, interrupted by 157

auspices (*cont.*)
see also augur(s); augurs, college of;
    auspication; *auspicium/-cia*; *dirae*;
    inauguration; *incubatio*; lightning;
    obnuntiatio; *pulli*; *silentium*; standards;
    tabernaculum; thunder; *vinculum temporis*;
    vitio creatus/-ti or *factus/-ti*; *vitium*
  see also Fabius Maximus Verrucosus,
    Q.: auspices
  see also Flaminius, C.: auspices; *vitio creatus*
auspicium/-cia 32, 40–1, 58n.81, 124–5
  ave sinistra 45n.44, 85–6, 100–1, 243–4
  coactum 244
  de caelo 40–1, 44–5, 58, 61, 155–6, 160–1,
    243–4, 274–5
  distinct from *augurium/-ia* 40n.31
  domi and *militiae* 32, 43, 61–2, 64–5
  ex acuminibus 58–9, 65n.102
  ex avibus 40–1, 44–5, 155–6, 159–61,
    244, 277
  maxima 43, 85, 97–8, 101
  minora 97–8
  peremnia 58–9, 157
  pertermine 58–9
  pullarium, see *auspicium ex tripudio*
  urbanum 58n.80, 64n.99
  see also auspices; lightning; *pulli*; *silentium*;
    tabernaculum; thunder; *vitium*
auspicium/-cia ex tripudio/-iis 40–2, 58–60,
    155–6, 243, 248–9
  not used for investiture or departure 45n.45,
    155–6, 160–1
  originates in oblative signs 156n.16, 244
  see also *pullarius/-rii*; *pulli*
axes, see lictors

Baebius, Egerius, see Laevius
Baebius Herennius, Q. (*tr. pl.* 216) 279–80
Baetica 121–3
Bardi 219
Berceto 218–19
Bibbiena 216
Bientina, Lago di 223
birds, see *auspicium ave sinistra*; *auspicium
    ex avibus*
Bobbiensia Scholia:
  on Claudius Pulcher, trial of 164
Bobbio 219
Bologna (Etruscan Felsina) 213–18, 218n.9,
    230–2, 234, 250, 251n.77
Borghetto 226
Borgotaro (or Borgo Val di Taro) 218–19
Branzone 218–19
Brennus 84

brothel 74
Brundisium 69–70, 75–6, 142–3

Caecilius Cornutus, M. (*pr.* 43):
  vitium in auspicio 288–9
Caecilius Metellus Celer, Q. (*cos.* 60,
    augur) 196n.93
Caecilius Metellus Nepos, Q. (*cos.*
    57) 72nn.14,16
Caelius Rufus, M. (*pr.* 48) 69, 133, 147n.121
Caesena, see Cesena
calendar, see chronology
Cales 277
Calpurnius Bibulus, M. (*cos.* 59) 49n.58
Calpurnius Piso, L. (*cos.* 133; historian):
  on aediles of 299 12–13
Calpurnius Piso Caesoninus, L. (*cos.* 58) 50n.62,
    155n.14
Campania 10, 277
Campus Martius 50n.62, 184
Caninius Rebilus, C. (*cos.* 45) 142
Cannae, battle of 66–7, 105, 149n.3, 158–9, 255,
    263, 269, 280
  auspices at 263–4
Canusium 263–4
Capitol 45–6, 46n.46, 48–54, 53n.67, 56n.75,
    58–61, 63–4, 155, 179, 184, 288
  Capitoline temple 174–5
Capua 10–11, 272
Carve[tus?] (*cos.* 458) 172n.10
Cartagena (New Carthage) 121–3
Carthage/Carthaginian(s) 11n.20, 116–17,
    163, 165
  prisoner exchange 165
  see also Punic War(s)
Carvilius Maximus, Sp. (*cos. II* 272) 12–13
Carvilius Ruga, Sp. (*cos. II* 228, *augur*) 183–4,
    186, 272–3
Casentino 213–16
Casilinum 272
Cassio 218–19
Cassiodorus Senator (historian) 129–30
Cassius, Q. (*tr. mil.* 252) 25
Cassius Longinus, C. (*cos. des.* 41) 67, 98
Cassius Longinus, Q. (*cos.* 164):
  death in office 176–8
Cassius Longinus, Q. (*tr. pl.* 49, *augur*) 138–9, 142–3
Casteggio, see Clastidium
Castellón de la Plana 121–3
Castelnuovo di Garfagnana 218
Castulo 121–2
Caudine Forks 11, 62, 293
Caudium, battle of 128–9
censor(s) 33n.10, 43, 97–8, 131, 135n.79, 176–7

GENERAL INDEX 313

Centenius, C. (*praef. eq.* 217) 255–6
Cesena (Caesena) 217n.7
Chiana river, *see* Val di Chiana
chickens, augural, see *auspicium ex tripudiis*; *pulli*
Chiusi, *see* Clusium
Chronicon Paschale 9
Chronographer of 354 9, 172n.10, 293–4
chronographers, late 9–10
chronology:
  calendar and festivals 191–2
  fourth-century confusion and dislocation 9–13, 129–30
  Ides 190–2, 193n.83, 212–13, 253–4, 270–1
  Kalends 191–2, 193n.83, 203
  of Antonius' appointment as magister equitum 132–3, 147n.121
  of magistrates in 444 V 291–2
  of measures taken after Lake Trasumene 257
  of naming dictator in 249 258–9, 261–2
  of Cato's campaign 122n.37
  of First Punic War 159–60
  of Roman campaign in 217 252–3
  see also consular year, start of; dates
Cilicia 68–71, 70n.5
Cincius, L. (antiquarian) 48–50
Cincius Alimentus, L. (*pr.* 210; historian) 48n.57
Civil War, Second 35n.18, 68–71, 104
Clastidium (Casteggio) 218n.9, 219, 234
Claudius, C. (*flamen Dialis* 211) 206–7
Claudius Caesar Aug. Germanicus, Ti. (*cos. V* AD 51) 86
Claudius Centho, C. (*cos.* 240, *interrex* 216, *dict.* 213) 170
Claudius Glicia, M. (*scriba*; *dict.* 249) 104, 163, 259, 261
Claudius Marcellus, C. (*pr.* 80, *augur*) 138, 142–3
Claudius Marcellus, C. (*cos.* 50) 138
Claudius Marcellus, M. (*cos.* 331, *dict.* 327): dictator *vitio creatus* 278–80
Claudius Marcellus, M. (*cos. V* 208, *augur*) 65n.102, 182, 186n.57, 206, 264
  augur 183–4, 186n.56, 272–3, 276–7, 280
  auspices of investiture 274–6
  auspices, oblative, avoidance of 276
  consul *vitio creatus* 255, 270–3, 275–6
  consulship (second), abdication of 255, 270–1, 274–6
  cooperation with Fabius Maximus 272
  death in office 176–8
  dedication at Henna 208n.126
  enemies of 274
  spolia opima 179, 183–4, 272–3
  see also *vitium*: of Marcellus

Claudius Marcellus, M. (*cos. III* 152) 294
Claudius Nero, Ap. (*pr.* 195) 35–6, 121–5
Claudius Nero, C. (*cos.* 207) 117, 119–20, 124–6
  triumph or ovation doubtful 119n.28
Claudius Pulcher, Ap. (*cos.* 185) 71–3, 75n.26, 76
Claudius Pulcher, Ap. (*cos.* 54, *augur*) 67, 70–1, 138
Claudius Pulcher, C. (*cos.* 177, *augur*):
  attempts army command without *profectio* 63–4, 283
Claudius Pulcher, P. (*cos.* 249):
  after Drepana 154, 258–9
  attack on Drepana 153
  auspices, practice of, attacked by 260–1, 266–7, 269, 287
  dictator, named by 163, 257–9, 261
  perduellio, tried for 163–4
  profectio 152
  pulli, drowned by 148–9, 152, 157–60, 162–3
  unpopularity 161n.31
  see also *vitium*: of Claudius Pulcher
Claudius Pulcher, P. (*cos.* 184) 71
Claudius Russus, Ap. (*cos.* 268):
  death in office 176–7
Cloelius Siculus, P. (*flamen*) 206–7
Cloelius Siculus, Q. (*cos.* 498) 83–4
Clusium (Chiusi) 222–4
Coelius Antipater, L. (historian) 106n.118
  augural inconsistency of account 245–7, 289
  on earthquake at Lake Trasumene 245–7
  on Flaminius' neglect of auspices 239–43, 245
Coelius Dionysius, M. (*lictor*) 76n.29
coercitio 33, 37, 61
comitia 39, 46
  elect dictator and magister equitum 170
  grant *imperium* and right to auspices 141–2
  legislation 63, 70–1, 139–40, 176
  legislation affecting terms of dictator and magister equitum 101–2, 135–6, 144–6
  legislation authorizing praetor to name dictator 134, 139–42, 171–2
  legislation authorizing interrex to name dictator 136n.82, 140, 171–2
  legislation authorizing *ver sacrum* 257
  legislation awarding triumph 182–3, 187–8, 204–5
  obstruction of, see *obnuntiatio*
  prescribe name of dictator and magister equitum 103–4, 135–6
comitia centuriata 33, 50n.62, 135–6, 141–2
  formula for convening of 93n.81
  must meet *extra pomerium* 58

comitia curiata 57, 62
comitia tributa 141–2
consul(s) *passim*
　abdication of, *see* abdication
　alternate *fasces* 74–6
　alternate military command 119–20, 124–5, 158–9, 263–4
　as dictator 127–8, 131
　as magister equitum 130–1
　both dead in office 177–8, 281
　constitutional position vis-à-vis dictator, *see* dictator
　constitutional position vis-à-vis praetor, *see* praetor
　departure for war, *see profectio*
　fail to enter office 291, 293
　hold elections 71–2
　iudices, originally called 92–4
　killed in battle 170–1, 175, 177, 239–40, 254, 257–8, 270–1, 280–1, 291
　March 15, take office on 52–3
　prior factus 196n.93
　suffect 82, 108, 170, 171n.3, 172–3, 176–8, 190–1, 270–1, 279, 281–2, 285n.87, 291–4
　see also auspices: of consul; consular year, start of; consulship; *imperium*: of consul; *vitio creatus/-ti* or *factus/-ti*
consular year, start of 189–93, 294
　April 1 193, 293
　April 13 193
　December 13 198–9, 291–2
　January 1 190, 192, 293
　July 1 109–10
　March 15 190, 192–3, 293–4
　May 1 190, 196–7, 203, 293
　October 1 198–9, 292
　see also chronology
consulship 31n.5
　origins of 93n.81
contio 1, 8, 22, 100
Corfinium 67–8, 70–1, 77–8
Cornelius Balbus, L. (*cos.* 40) 69–70
Cornelius Cethegus, M. (*flamen*) 206–7
Cornelius Cethegus, M. (*cos.* 204) 274
Cornelius Cossus, A. (*tr. mil. c. p.* 426, *mag. eq.* 426) 6n.10, 130
Cornelius Cossus, A. (*dict.* 385) 209n.132
Cornelius Dolabella, L. (*IIvir nav.* 180) 164n.40
Cornelius Dolabella, P. (*cos.* 44) 142
Cornelius Lentulus, Cn. (*cos.* 201, *augur*) 272–3
Cornelius Lentulus, L. (*cos.* 327, *dict.* 320) 128–9, 278
Cornelius Lentulus Caudinus, L. (*cos.* 237) 272–3

Cornelius Lentulus Sura, P. (*cos.* 71, *pr. II* 63) 72n.15, 201–2
Cornelius Mammula, A. (*pr.* 217) 257n.6
Cornelius Scipio, P. (*cos.* 218) 249–50, 252–3
Cornelius Scipio Asina, Cn. (*cos. II* 254) 190, 258
Cornelius Scipio Asina, P. (*cos.* 221, *interrex* 216) 170
Cornelius Scipio Hispallus, Cn. (*cos.* 176): death in office 177, 281
Cornelius Scipio Maluginensis, M. (*pr.* 176) 268n.31
Cornelius Scipio Nasica Corculum, P. (*cos. II* 155) 284
　consulship, abdication of 284–6
　Corsica, consul in 284–7
　Ti. Gracchus, enmity with, alleged 285–6
Cornelius Scipio Nasica Serapio, P. (*cos.* 138) 209n.132, 285
Cornelius Spinther, P. (*q.* 44, *augur*) 138
Cornelius Sulla, Faustus (*q.* 54, *augur*) 138
Cornelius Sulla Felix, L. (*cos. II* 80, *dict.* 81, *augur*) 29, 70–1, 87n.60, 101, 122–3, 128n.56
　Camillus, model for 110
　dictator 135–6, 140, 143–4, 171–2, 265–6
Corsica 284–7
Cortona 222–4
Cremona 249–53
cumulation:
　of annual magistracies prohibited 127–8
　of censorship and *magisterium equitum* 131
　of consular tribunate and *magisterium equitum* 130–1
　of consulship and dictatorship 127–8, 131, 210
　of consulship and *magisterium equitum* 130–1, 210
Cunctator, *see* Fabius Maximus Verrucosus
Curius Dentatus, M'. (*cos. III* 274) 176–7

dates:
　Varronian 1n.1, 190
　see also chronology; consular year; dictator years; triumph(s): third-century dates of
decemviri legibus scribundis 74n.22, 83–4, 93n.81, 291
decemviri sacris faciundis 45n.45, 256–7, 263
　and *prodigia* 39–40, 43–4
defeat in battle, *see* failure in command
dictator 1–29 *passim*, 66–111 *passim*, 169–211 *passim*
　abdication 10, 78–9, 100–2, 111–14, 135n.79, 170, 175, 178, 205n.119, 278–80, 293
　abdication of consul, forced by 19–20, 83, 200–5, 210–11, 284–5

also called *dicator* 90–2
and *interregnum* 179–80
appointed after calamity caused by *vitium* 257–8, 260–6
appoints magister equitum 115–16, 132–3, 143, 205
approached by consul without lictors 66–7, 82, 95–8
assumes office 116n.15, 131
authority over/suspension of other magistrates 16–17, 30, 33–4, 78–9, 81–2, 84, 95–6, 98–9, 201, 203
constitutional position vis-à-vis consul 30, 33–4, 66–7, 85–7, 95–6, 98–9, 131
dictio of, see *dictio*
elected by the people 170, 178–9
emergency, named in 256–8
horse, permission to ride on 66–7, 82, 87n.57
imminuto iure 101–2
imperium (military) *in urbe* 37, 61
Italy, not to be named outside of 133, 258n.8
Latin towns, in 89–90, 92
Latin League, of 90–2
lictors, twenty-four 66–7, 82, 85–6
named by consul 79, 83–4, 97–105, 108, 170, 203–4
named by consular tribune 139–41
named by interrex 135–6, 140, 171–2
named by praetor 35n.18, 104, 134
optima lege 101n.110
origin of office 92–4
origin of title 79, 87–9
religious-magical dimension 86–7, 95–6, 98–9
resistance to appointment of 267
speaks with effect 88–9, 91–4, 260–1
term limited by *dictio* 100–4, 144, 146
term limited to six months 100, 109–11, 144–5
without magister equitum 100, 102–5, 108–9, 259
see also *auspices*: of dictator; *imperium*: of dictator; *vitio creatus/-ti* or *factus/-ti*
dictator *interregni caus(s)a* 174–6, 178–80, 198, 204, 212
and *Fasti Capitolini* 169
dismissed by scholars 169n.1, 174
explained by Gusso 173–4
explained by Hartfield 172–3
explained by Nicosia 173
explained by Sumner 170–2
interregni ineundi causa 174–5, 203
unattested except in *Fasti* of 217 169, 174–6, 179–80
dictator, reason (*causa*) for appointment of:
clavi figendi 92–4, 101–2, 111, 174–5

comitiorum habendorum 14n.28, 111n.142, 135n.79, 170, 172–6, 207–8, 265n.26, 278–9, 282n.76, 293
feriarum constituendarum 92–4
feriarum Latinarum 102n.111, 174–5
legibus scribundis et rei p. constituendae 101, 135n.79
ludorum faciendorum 92–4
rei gerundae 10–11, 33–4, 94n.85, 100–3, 111, 135n.79, 169, 172–3, 255–8, 260–1, 263–5, 267
perpetuo 113–14
quaestionibus exercendis 10–11
seditionis sedandae 111n.141
senatus legendi 100–3, 105
special purpose 100–3, 111
dictator years 4n.8, 9–12, 111; see also chronology
dictio 47, 79, 92–4, 132, 141, 144, 258n.8
establishes dictator's powers 100–3
includes authorization to name magister equitum 102–4, 134–5, 205
of Minucius Rufus 108
dignitas 77n.36, 131, 186, 195–6, 204–5, 210–11
Dio, L. (?) Cassius (*cos. II* AD 229; historian) 19–20, 25, 75–6, 107–8
language of dictatorial appointments 145n.116
on Antonius as magister equitum 131, 134–7, 143–5
on Caesar's dictatorships 104, 130–1, 135n.80, 145
on Crassus' departure for Parthia 155n.14
on Iunius Pullus 165
on Lepidus as magister equitum 130–1, 133–4
see also Zonaras
Diodoros of Sicily (historian):
and reconstruction of the past 176
on Camillus and the Gauls 110
on C. Maenius as dictator 10–11
on magistrates of 301 V 129–30
Dionysios of Halikarnassos (historian):
and reconstruction of the past 176
on auspices 45n.45
on lictors and fasces 74–6
on magistrates of 444 V 291
on magistrates under dictator 79, 82–4
on title of dictator 87–8
dirae 155, 163, 287–8
Domitius Ahenobarbus, L. (*cos.* 54) 137
Corfinium, abandons *fasces* at 67–8, 70–1, 78
Domitius Calvinus Maximus, Cn. (*cos.* 283) 12–13
Dragone river 218
drama:
as historical source 21–3, 28
fabula praetexta 22

Drepana, battle of 148-9, 153-4, 159-63, 255, 258-9, 261n.15
ductus/suo ductu/dux 36, 117-19, 126
duumviri comitiis consularibus habendis 141n.103

Ebro river 121-2
Egypt 115n.14, 132-7, 145, 147n.121
Elsa river, *see* Val d'Elsa
Emilia-Romagna 217-18, 232, 234n.41
Empoli 222
Emporiae, battle of 121-2
Eryx 163, 165, 261-2
Etruria 6, 120-1, 184-5, 250-3, 284
  plains of 223
  see also Flaminius, C.: Arretium, with army at; movements in 217
  see also Hannibal Barqa: Appennine passes, choice of; Arretium, surprises Flaminius at; Italy, routes available into
Etruscan(s) 6, 32n.8, 39-40, 257-8, 286
exauguratio 61-2
exsecratio 155

Fabia *gens* 18-19, 21
Fabius Ambustus, C. (*mag. eq.* 315) 6n.10
Fabius Ambustus, M. (*cos. III* 354, *dict.* 351) 15-20, 23-4
Fabius Ambustus, M. (*mag. eq.* 322) 6n.10
Fabius Buteo, M. (*cos.* 245, *dict.* 216) 100-7
Fabius Buteo, Q. (*pr.*196) 122-3
Fabius Dorsuo, K. 269n.32
Fabius Maximus Gurges, Q. (*cos. II* 276) 4-5, 12-13, 28
Fabius Maximus Rullianus, Q. (*cos. V* 295, *mag. eq.* 324, *dict.* 315):
  abdication or suspension 5, 8-10, 15, 23-5
  auspices, claims independence of 1, 16, 112, 126-7, 148
  curule aedile, not in 299 12-13
  dictator, disobedience toward 1-2, 9-10, 16-17, 19-21, 25, 148, 270
  dictatorship, year-long 110-11
  letter to senate 21-2
  magister equitum, not in 301 V 4-6, 9-11, 13, 129-30
  Papirius Cursor, dispute with 1-29 *passim*, 267-8
  tradition of defeat or no battle fought 1-4, 6, 9-10, 13-15, 148, 194n.89, 270
  tradition of victory 1-3, 5-8, 13-14, 17, 19-26, 28, 126, 148, 194n.89, 270
  see also drama: as historical source; Fabius Pictor; Livy; Papirius Cursor, L. (*cos. V* 313, *dict.* 324)

Fabius Maximus Verrucosus, Q. (*cos. V* 209, *dict. II* 217, *augur*) 28n.50, 115n.12, 173-4, 264-5
  augural college, alleged control of/augural science, alleged manipulation of 183-5, 207-8, 271-6
  augur and pontiff 272n.44
  auspices, before moving army 159, 277
  auspices, repeated/upheld by 26n.48, 59n.84, 115n.12, 269-70, 277, 280
  consul, removed from command by 66-7, 78-9, 82, 95-6, 96n.93
  dictator, addresses religious concerns as 256-7, 263, 268-9
  dictator, elected by the people 135-6, 170, 178-9
  dictator *interregni causa* (in 223/2) 169, 173-6, 203
  dictator *rei gerundae causa* (in 217) 169
  dictatorship, first of 175-6, 203-11
  Flaminius, cautioned by 240-1
  Flaminius' *dignitas*, preserved by 210-11
  Flaminius, named magister equitum by 206-12
  Flaminius, opponent of 181, 186, 207n.123
  magister equitum, conflict with 26-9, 105-9, 255, 267-8
  Marcellus, cooperation with 272
  Marcellus, replaced as consul by 270-1, 275-6
  Papirius Cursor-Rullianus quarrel, parallels to 27-8
  prodigia, procurated by 277
  recalled to Rome *sacrorum causa* 26, 115n.12, 268-9
  Venus Erycina, temple of, vowed by 257
Fabius Pictor, Q. (*pr.* by 218?; historian):
  and events of 324 V 8, 13-14, 18-19, 21-6, 28
  and Livy, *see* Livy: and Fabius Pictor
  and Rullianus' letter 21-2
  common source for Fabius Maximus–Minucius Rufus dispute 26n.48, 106n.120
  critical of Fabius Rullianus 2-3, 8, 19
  Delphi, mission to 263
  on constitutional position of dictator and magister equitum 2-3, 16-17, 19, 29, 270
  Plutarch's *Fabius*, source for 106n.118, 106n.120
fabula praetexta, *see* drama
Faenza (Faventia) 217n.7, 232
Faesulae (Fiesole) 213-19, 218n.9, 222, 227-8, 232, 234-5, 250, 251nn.77,78
  location of 222-4
  failure in command, reactions to 259-60

fasces, see lictors
Fasti Capitolini 104, 113, 143–4
   and abdication of magistrates 178–9, 189–90, 282n.76
   and changes in start of consular year 190
   and C. Maenius 10–11, 129
   and death of magistrates 176–8
   and Fabius Rullianus 4–7, 9–10
   and *interregna* 282n.76
   and reconstruction of the past 176
   on consul and magister equitum in 331 V 128
   on *dictator interregni caus(s)a* 169, 173–6, 203
   on Fabius Maximus as dictator by popular election 195
   on *imperium* of magister equitum made equal to dictator's 178–9
   on magistrates in 420 V 176n.21
   on magistrates in 320 V 128–9
   on magistrates in 301 V 4–5, 9, 129–30
   on *spolia opima* 179
Fasti Hydatiani 9–10
Fasti Privernates 113–14
Faucia *curia* 62–3
Faventia, *see* Faenza
Festus, Sex. Pompeius (grammarian) 48n.57, 49, 52–3
Fidentia, *see* Fidenza
Fidenza (Fidentia) 219
Fiesole, *see* Faesulae
Firenze, *see* Florence
Firenzuola (Florentiola) 219
flamen(s) 39–40, 40n.31, 97–8, 186n.57, 206–7
   and chariot 87n.57
   and *commoetaculum* 76n.29
   Dialis 87n.57, 140n.99, 207n.122
   Martialis 271n.39
   Quirinalis 271n.39
Flaminia Via 236–8, 236n.43
Flaminius, C. (*cos. II* 217) 59n.84, 163n.36, 169–211 *passim*, 212–54 *passim*, 272–3, 289
   Ariminum, consulship (second) entered at 52–3, 55–6, 192, 212–13, 220–1, 228, 238–9, 247, 249, 253, 283
   Ariminum, orders army to assemble at 192, 251–2
   Ariminum, sacrifice at 238–9, 245–6, 249
   Arretium, fall of horse at 238–42, 245–9
   Arretium, staff debate at 237–8, 242
   Arretium, warning signs at 238–43
   Arretium, with army at 213, 216, 219–22, 224, 235–8, 250
   auspices, contempt for/neglect of 175, 181, 212, 241–9, 267

   auspices, lacks valid 53–5, 186, 193–4, 196–7, 202–3, 211–13, 243–7, 253, 283
   auspices, observed by 181, 194–5, 212, 241–2, 254
   auspices, practice of, attacked by 169, 181, 195–6, 212, 249, 253–4, 266, 269, 287
   elections for 222 196–7
   enemies of 181, 183, 185–6, 188–9, 204–5, 212–13, 254, 263, 267
   campaign in Gaul in 223 180–1, 184–5, 229, 247
   consulship (first), abdication of 182, 187–93, 206, 210–11
   Hannibal, pursuit of 236–8, 242
   magister equitum, forced to abdicate 206–7, 210–11
   magister equitum, named by Fabius 206
   magister equitum, named by Minucius 206
   movements in 217 220–1, 225–35
   reconnoiter, failure to 247–8, 254
   senate, letter of 180–2, 184–6, 188, 193–5, 203–4
   senate's envoys, not heeded by 253
   senate's order to abdicate, defied by 169, 180–1, 193–4, 197, 204–5, 212
   sorex, squeak of 116n.17, 206–7, 211–12
   Trasumene Lake, with army at/defeat at 240, 247–8, 254–6, 258, 267, 280–1
   triumph, by popular vote 182–3, 187–90, 195–6, 202, 204–5
   vitio creatus, augural ruling of being, rejected by 169, 181, 193–6, 210–12, 280
   vitio creatus consul 180, 183n.47, 186–91
   see also pulli: refuse to eat
Flaminius Circus 241n.54
fleet(s):
   Carthaginian 161–2
   Iunius Pullus, of 161–2
   lost in storms 30, 148–9, 153, 161–3, 165, 258
flogging 19, 25
Florence (Florentia, now Firenze) 223, 250
Florentiola, *see* Firenzuola
Florus, L. Annaeus (or P. Annius; historian) 153, 158n.22
Foiano della Chiana 222–4
Folius Flaccinator, M. (*cos.* 318, *mag. eq.* 314) 10–11, 129
Forlì (Forum Livii) 216, 217n.7, 232
Fornovo 218–19
Fortuna Primigenia 165, 167–8
Forum Cornelii, *see* Imola
Forum Flaminii 236–7
Forum Livii, *see* Forlì
Frontinus, Sex. Iulius (*cos. III* AD 100; historian) 25, 154

Fucecchio, Padule di 223
Fufius Calenus, Q. (*cos.* 47) 135n.80, 144n.113, 147
Fulvius Flaccus, Q. (*cos. IV* 209, *dict.* 210) 135–6
Fulvius Nobilior, M. (*cos.* 189) 208n.126
Furius Camillus, M. (*tr. mil. c. p. VI* 381, *dict. V* 367) 19–20, 57, 80, 84, 173–4, 240, 258n.10, 265–6, 292–3
  dictator for over six months 109–10
Furius Medullinus, L. (*tr. mil. c. p. II* 370) 19–20
Furius Philus, P. (*cos.* 223, *augur*):
  abdication of Flaminius, cooperates in 194–5, 203–4
  augur 183–6, 194–5, 272–3
  auspices, observed by 181–2, 194–5
  consulship, abdication of 182, 188–91, 193, 203–4
  Gaul, with Flaminius in 180–1, 203–4
  names Fabius Maximus dictator 204
  senate, letter of, *see* Flaminius, C.
  triumph, by popular vote 130–1, 182–3, 190, 204
  vitio creatus consul 180, 186–91, 211
Furius Purpurio, L. (*pr.* 200, *cos.* 196) 120–1, 125–6

Gabinius, A. (*cos.* 58) 155n.14
Galba (Ser. Galba Imp. Caesar Aug., *cos. II* AD 69) 287n.93, 289–90
Gallia 104, 120–1, 170, 180–2, 184–5, 219–20, 245, 249–50, 252, 293
  Cisalpina 213–16, 228–9, 251n.77
  Roman campaign in 229–30, 250
  Transalpina 67
Garfagnana 218–19
Gaul, *see* Gallia
Gauls 228–9, 271
  Insubrian 180, 229
  Rome, captured by 62, 84–5, 109–10
  war against 179, 230, 232–3, 257–8
Geganius Macerinus, M. (*cos. III* 437) 172n.10
Gereonium, battle of 26, 269
gerundive:
  dative of 10–11
  genitive of, with *causa* 10–11, 174–5
Greece 133n.72, 135–6, 138, 142–3, 171–2

Habinnas (*VIvir augustalis*) 74n.19
Hannibal Barqa (Carthaginian commander 221–201) 26, 28–9, 158–9, 172–3, 175, 192, 255, 267, 272, 277
  Appennine passes, choice of 213–19, 233–4, 250
  Arno, crosses marshes of 213–17, 222–5, 230, 232

Arretium, surprises Flaminius at 213–35
Faesulae, at 213, 222–4
Gaul, in 220–1, 228–30
Italy, routes available into 213–19, 221–4, 233–4
march, rate of 226n.27
Rome, march on 229, 232–3, 235, 256
Trasumene Lake, move toward 224, 226–8, 235–6
haruspex/haruspices 39–40, 43–4, 277n.61
  and Ti. Gracchus (*cos. II* 163) 284, 286–7
  auspices, not concerned with 286
Hasdrubal Barqa (Carthaginian commander 218–207) 119–20
Henna 208n.126
Helvius, M. (*pr.* 197) 121–6
Himilko (Carthaginian commander 250–241) 154
Hispala Faecenia 74n.19
Hispania 142–3, 268n.31, 287, 293–4
  Citerior 35–6, 121–3
  Ulterior 35–6, 121–3
Histria 63
Horatius (*leg.* 43) 73n.17
Hostilius Mancinus, C. (*cos.* 137):
  ignores *dirae* 287

Iliturgi 121–3
Ilorci 121–3
Imola (Forum Cornelii) 217n.7
imperator 51n.63, 64, 68–70, 276–7
  iustus 64
  Latinus 91n.76
imperium:
  defined by Bleicken 32
  defined by Drogula 32–7
  defined by Heuß 31–2
  defined by Mommsen 30–1, 33
  genera imperii 34n.15
  in sphere *domi* 30–4, 37
  in sphere *militiae* 30–4, 37–8, 61, 64, 122–4, 200–1
  in urbe, not applicable except of dictator 33, 37, 61
  iustum 54–5
  maius and *minus* 34–5, 85, 94–6, 98–9, 200–1
  military valid only outside *pomerium* 77–8, 77n.39, 123n.43
  of consul (*consulare*) 34–6, 38–9, 54–5, 77n.38, 85–6, 94–5, 117, 124–6, 293
  of dictator 16, 26, 28, 34n.15, 85–6, 94–100
  of *magister equitum* 26, 102–3, 105–8, 112
  of praetor (*praetorium*) 34–7, 94–5, 117, 125–6

of *privati* 77n.39, 141n.104
of promagistrate 38n.24, 68, 70–1, 77–8, 122–5
valentius 86, 94–100, 201, 260–1, 264–5
inauguration 40n.31, 50n.61, 61–2, 164n.40, 186n.57
incubatio 45–6, 155–6
intercessio, see veto
interregnum 62n.94, 174–5, 179–80, 190–1, 291–4 *passim*
   auspices, renovation of, through 175, 178, 180, 187–8, 196–7, 199, 203, 281–2, 284–5, 293
   deliberate exercise of 197–8
   impossible with patrician magistrates in office 171–3, 175, 189–90, 197, 211
   in 327 236–7, 279–80
   in 223/2 189–90, 192–3, 196–7, 204, 206, 209–12
   in 217/6 170, 175, 279–80
   in 176/5 281–2
   in 162 284–5
   patrician control of elections during 279–80
interrex 33n.10, 97–8, 111n.142, 193n.83, 278
   dictator, named by 135–6, 140, 171–2, 174–5
   elections in 217/6 170–1, 279
Iulius Caesar, C. (*cos. V* 44, *dict. perpetuo*) 128n.56, 258, 265–6
   and Cicero in civil war 68–70
   at Alexandria 132–5
   augural law, ignored by 142, 196n.93, 289–90
   despot, (not) a 135n.80
   dictatorships authorized/modified by comitial legislation 104, 134–6, 141–2, 145–6
   dictator in 49, named by praetor 104, 134, 141–2
   dictator in 48/7 131–3, 135–6, 142–3, 145
   dictator in 46 130–1, 133
   dictator *perpetuo* 113–14
   dictator, wants praetor to name 35n.18, 137–40, 171–2
   dictator with extended term 135–7
   dictator without magister equitum 104
   lictors, excessive number of 133n.75
   lictors, restores alternation of 74–5, 77n.37
   praefecti, governs city through 81n.46
   praetor, suspended as 72–3, 75n.26, 76
Iulius Caesar, L. (*cos.* 64, *augur*) 138–9, 142–3
Iunius Brutus, M. (*cos.* 178) 63
Iunius Bubulcus, C. (*cos. III* 311, *mag. eq.* 309) 6n.10, 62
Iunius Pera, M. (*cos.* 230, *dict.* 216) 100, 105–7, 173–4, 264
   dictator, addresses religious concerns as 264–5
   horse, permission to ride on 66–7

Iunius Pullus, L. (*cos.* 249):
   auspices, ignored by 148–9, 158–60, 162–3, 266, 287–8
   Carthaginians, prisoner of 163, 165, 261–2
   Sicily, operations in 161–3, 258–9, 261–2
   perduellio, prosecuted for 148
   see also *vitium*
Iuppiter *passim*
   and sortition 54n.70
   auspices, grants/withholds permission through 39–50, 53–6, 59–62, 65, 88–9, 96, 100–1, 103–4, 134–5, 155, 158, 167–8, 211, 243–4
   response 114–15, 120n.29, 124–5
   response affirmative 40–2, 44–7, 47nn.51, 53, 115–16, 126–7, 141–2, 148, 243–4
   response negative 40–2, 44–5, 47, 47n.51, 59–60, 62, 244, 274–5
   saves Claudius Pulcher 164–5
   warning signs, sent by 181, 188, 193–4, 238–9, 242–3, 245, 247–8
Iuppiter Feretrius 179
Iuppiter Stator 238–9
   temple of 241
ius:
   agendi 33, 77–8
   augurale 1, 39–42, 46–7, 54n.70, 100–2, 104, 134, 137–8, 141–2, 144–5, 167–8, 181, 188–9, 193–5, 203–4, 211, 243n.60, 286
   civile 31n.5, 38n.24
   pontificium 157
   publicum 1, 46, 47n.51, 101–2, 141, 212n.1, 281–2
Iuventius Thalna, M'. (*cos.* 163):
   death in office 178, 285

king(s) 32n.8, 40n.31, 50n.61, 85, 91–2, 94n.84, 186n.57
   military command of questionable 87n.57, 92n.80, 93n.82
Konradin (Duke of Schwaben) 219n.14

Laelius, C. (*cos.* 140, *augur*) 209n.132
Laevius, Egerius (*dict. Latinus*) 90–1
La Lima 218
Lamone river 217n.7
Larcius, T. (*cos. II* 498, *dict.* 501 or 498) 83, 128n.56
Latinae feriae 51, 53–4, 89n.69, 102n.111, 109–10, 174–5, 251–2
   and consuls of 217 251n.81
   repeated in 176 281
Latin Festival, see *Latinae feriae*
Latin<i?>us (*leg.* 43) 73n.17

Latin League 50
  dictator of 90–1
  praetor(s) of 46n.48, 48–9, 91n.76
Lautulae, battle of 6n.10, 14–15
Lavinium 287
law, see *ius*
lectisternium 256–7
legate(s) 3–4, 6–7, 19–20, 22–3, 99n.104, 115n.12, 200–2, 208n.126, 268n.31, 284–5
  granted lictors 73
legislation, see *comitia*
legitimacy 135n.80
  of magisterial power 1, 46–7, 54–5, 64, 124n.44, 125
  of Caesar's dictatorship 35n.18, 111n.140
Le Piastre 218
Letum 280–1
lex:
  centuriata (for censors) 97–8
  Cornelia de maiestate 70n.8, 122–3
  curiata 31–3, 37–9, 54nn.71–72, 62, 64
  de dictatore creando 111n.142
  de provinciis praetoriis 123–4
  Gabinia 258n.8
  Licinia de sodaliciis 138n.92
  Metilia 28, 107–8, 172–3
  Ogulnia 273–4
  Oppia 181
  Pompeia de provinciis ordinandis 135n.80
  vitio lata 288n.96
Licinius Crassus, C. (*cos.* 168):
  fails to auspicate 283–4
Licinius Crassus, M. (*cos. II* 55) 138n.92
  dirae, ignored by 288
  Parthia, departure for 155
Licinius Crassus, P. (*cos.* 171) 268n.31
Licinius Crassus Dives, P. (*cens.* 210, *mag. eq.* 210, *cos.* 205) 131, 135–6
Licinius Macer, C. (*pr.* 68?; historian) 14n.28
  and *libri lintei* 291–2
  on aediles of 299 12–13
  on magistrates of 444 V 291–2
  on dictatorship, origin of 89–90
lictor(s) 19, 22, 53, 63–4, 66–7, 116n.15, 283
  axes 37, 50n.62, 61, 64, 74–5, 123n.43
  fasces 37, 61, 64, 74–6
  fasces, alternation of 74–6, 94–6
  fasces laureati 68–71
  fasces, municipal without 69n.4, 75–6
  needed by magistrate to exercise powers 64, 71–4, 76–8, 94–6
  needed by promagistrate to retain *imperium* 67–71, 77–8
  not with praetor in *lupanar* 74
  of legates and quaestors 73

pomerium, dismissed at 69–70
pomerium, without axes inside 50n.62, 74–5
proximus 74
see also dictator: approached by consul without lictors; Cicero: and *fasces*/lictors
lightning 40–1, 44–6, 62–3, 243–4, 274–5;
  see also *auspicium de caelo*; thunder
Liguria 71, 213–17, 250n.76, 251n.77, 280–1
Lilybaeum 116–17, 158n.22, 258–9
  siege of 153–4, 160–1
Lima river 218
Livius Denter, M. (*cos.* 302) 9, 129–30
Livius Drusus (*mag. eq.* 324?) 9–10, 23–4
Livius Drusus, M. (*tr. pl.* 91) 288n.96
Livius Salinator, M. (*cos. II* 207, *dict.* 207) 117, 119–20, 124–5, 265n.26
Livy (T. Livius, historian):
  and augural language 62–4
  and augury in *res publica* 289–90
  and elections in 217 170
  and Fabius Pictor 2–3, 8, 14–17, 20–1, 25, 29
  and Fabius Maximus–Minucius Rufus dispute 26n.48, 106–8, 112, 268–9
  and Fabius Rullianus as magister equitum in 301 V 4–5, 8
  and Fabius Rullianus–Papirius Cursor dispute 1–29 *passim*, 30, 267–8
  and Fabius Rullianus–Papirius Cursor dispute, epilogue on 23–4
  and Fabius Rullianus–Papirius Cursor dispute, sources for 1–17, 19–24, 28–9
  and fourth-century chronology 10–12
  and reconstruction of the past 176
  on aediles of 299 12–13
  on consul and magister equitum in 331 V 128
  on consul, dictator, and magister equitum in 301 V 3–6, 129–30
  on consular tribunes in 402 V, abdication of 199
  on consul(s) naming dictator 135–6
  on consuls taking office on Ides of March 192
  on dictator and other magistrates 66–7, 81–2, 84–5, 94
  on dictator riding on horse 66–7
  on dictator's term of office 27, 100, 109–11
  on *fasces*, alternation of 74–5
  on Flaminius at Arretium 237
  on Flaminius' departure in 217 53–7, 212–13
  on Flaminius' dispute with Senate 202
  on Flaminius' movements in 217 220–1, 224–5, 227–8, 234, 251n.80, 252–3
  on Flaminius' neglect of auspical warnings 240–3, 247–9

on Hannibal at Faesulae 222–4
on Hannibal's surprise of Flaminius,
   see Flaminius, C.: movements in 217;
   Hannibal Barqa: Arretium, surprises
   Flaminius at
on magister equitum, nomination of 103–4
on magistrates of 444 V 291
on magistrates of 320 V 128–9
on Marcellus' abdication 273–4
on *pulli*, drowning of 162–3
Luca (Lucca) 213–19, 218n.9, 222, 234, 250
Lucca, *see* Luca
Lucan (M. Annaeus Lucanus, *q. c.* AD 62, *augur*;
   poet) 155n.14
Luceria, capture of 128–9
ludi:
   magni 256–7
   plebei 28
   Romani 28, 94n.85
   saeculares 261n.15
   scaenici 22n.40
Luna (Luni) 213–16, 218–19
Luni, *see* Luna
Lunigiana 218–19
lustrum 33n.10
Lutatius Catulus, C. (*cos.* 242) 125–6, 165, 253–4
   triumph, dispute with praetor over 36,
      116–19, 200n.102
Lutatius Catulus, C. (*cos.* 220) 293
Lutatius Catulus, Q. (*cos.* 102) 117
Lutatius Catulus, Q. (*cos.* 78) 258n.8
Lutatius Cerco, Q. (*cos.* 241) 118n.25, 253
   and *sortes Praenestinae* 165–7
   auspices, attempts alternative to 167–8, 212,
      254, 266
   auspices questionable 166–7
Lycia, Roman treaty with 133n.75

Macedonia 50n.62, 73
Maenius, C. (*cos.* 338, *dict.* 314) 10–11, 129
Maelius, Sp. 204–5
magister equitum 1–29 *passim*, 112–47 *passim*, 169
   abdication 112–13, 116, 134–5, 146, 170, 175,
      178; *see also* Fabius Maximus Rullianus, Q.:
      abdication or suspension
   abdication ordered by dictator 112–14, 131,
      134, 147, 210–11
   acting as dictator 105–9
   action, capable of independent 82, 114–15, 126
   army, command of 1, 3–4, 8, 15, 25–6, 112,
      114–16, 126–7
   auspicates in absence of dictator 114–15,
      126, 148
   auspices of, acquired through *dictio* by
      dictator 115–16, 134, 205
   auspices of, codependent with dictator's 116,
      126, 134, 143, 148, 194n.89, 269
   constitutional position vis-à-vis dictator 16–17,
      19, 25, 29–30, 66, 112–16, 126–7, 131, 148
   consulship, cumulation with contrary to
      mos 130–1, 210
   election, by popular vote 170
   elections, held by 130–1
   imperium of, made equal to dictator's 26,
      71–2, 105–8, 178–9, 209
   Italy, not to be named outside of 133
   named by consul instead of by dictator 130–1,
      133–7, 145–7
   perpetuo 113–14
   senate, convened by 114–15
   triumph, right to 115n.11, 126–7
   see also auspices: of magister equitum;
      auspices: *suis*/*alienis auspiciis*
   see also dictator: appoints magister equitum;
      dictator: without magister equitum
magister populi 45n.44, 85, 87n.57, 89–90, 97–8,
   144–5, 260–1
   originally distinct from dictator 92–4
magistrate(s):
   entering office 45–6, 55–6
   function independently of superior
      magistrates 96, 112–14, 200–1
   have auspices 42–3, 59
   non-annual, cumulation of with others 127–8
   non-annual, termination of 123n.43, 135n.79
   not inaugurated 40n.31
   patrician 17, 78–9, 97–8, 127–8, 171, 175,
      179–80, 189–90, 197
   see also abdication: of magistrates;
      vitio creatus/-ti or *factus/-ti*
Magra river 218–19
Mallius Maximus, Cn. (*cos.* 106) 287–8
Mamilius, L. (*dict.* of Tusculum) 89n.69
Mamilius, Octavius (*dux Latinus*) 91n.76
Manlius, P. (*pr.* 195) 35–6, 124
Manlius Capitolinus, P. (*tr. mil. c. p. II* 367,
   dict. 368) 111n.141
Manlius Imperiosus, L. (*dict.* 363) 101–3, 111
Manlius Torquatus, T. 20
Manlius Torquatus, T. (*cos. III* 340, *dict.* 320?) 129
Manlius Torquatus, T. (*cos. II* 224) 272n.44, 274
Manlius Vulso, A. (*cos.* 178) 63
manumission 74, 77n.37, 88
Marcius Censorinus, L. (*cos.* 39) 190
Marcius Figulus, C. (*cos. II* 156) 286–7
   abdicates consulship 284–5
Marcius Philippus, L. (*cos.* 91, *augur*) 288n.96
Marcius Philippus, L. (*cos.* 38; *augur*?) 138, 143
Marecchia river 226–7, 250
Marius, C. (*cos. VII* 86, *augur*) 72n.15, 117, 190

Marius, C. (*cos.* 82):
  death in office 177n.26
Mars, Field of, *see* Campus Martius
Marsi 3, 6
Massaciuccoli, Lago di 218
Massilia 104
master-of-horse/master of the horse,
  see magister equitum
Mater Matuta 109–10
Mens, temple of 256–7
Messalla (augural writer), *see* Valerius
  Messalla Rufus
Messana 24–5, 161, 258–9
Metapontum 159, 277
Metaurus, battle of the 119–20, 265n.26
Metilius, M. (*tr. pl.* 217) 26–8, 80
  and *rogatio Metilia* 108
Minucius Augurinus, L. (*cos.* 458) 19–20, 83,
  172–3, 198n.98, 201–2, 204–5
Minucius Rufus, M. (*cos.* 221, *mag. eq.* 217) 82,
  126–7, 127n.55, 135–6, 280
  auspices, victory without (?) 269–70
  dictator, conflict with 26–9, 255, 267–8
  dictator, considered to be 105–9, 207–9
  Fabius Rullianus–Papirius Cursor dispute,
    parallels to 27–8
  imperium made equal to dictator's 26, 102–3,
    105, 107–8, 178–9, 209
  Hercules, altar dedicated to 207–9
  names Flaminius magister equitum (?) 206–8
  reputation 28–9, 109
Minucius Thermus, Q. (*pr.* 106, *cos.* 193) 122n.39
Mucius Scaevola, Q. (*cos.* 220) 293
Mucius Scaevola, Q. (*tr. pl.* 54, *augur*) 138–9,
  142–3
Modena, *see* Mutina
Montecolognola 226
Montelupo Fiorentino 223
Montone river 217n.7
mos (maiorum) 21, 48, 63, 74–6, 77nn.37, 39,
  100n.106, 103, 130–1, 168, 176–7, 204–5,
  210, 263, 282
Mugonia Porta 241
Mummius, L. (*cos.* 146) 208n.126
Mutina (Modena) 218, 218n.9, 234, 288–9

Nautius (*tr. mil.* 256) 153
Nautius Rutilus, C. (*cos. II* 458) 83, 116n.15
new man (*homo novus*) 170, 204–5, 279–80
noble(s)/*nobilitas* 10, 170, 188–9, 204–5, 254,
  271n.39, 279–80, 289
  and Second Punic War 267
Noveglia river 219
Numitor Procae f. 89–90
Nure river 219

obnuntiatio 43n.38, 76, 142, 155, 288–9
Octavian, *see* Augustus
Octavius, Cn. (*cos.* 87):
  death in office 176–7
Ogulnius Gallus, Q. (*cos.* 269, *dict.* 257) 174–5
omen(s), *see prodigium*
opinion, public 1, 147, 189n.66, 204–5, 259, 284
Oppius, C. (*eques R.*) 69–70
Ostia 96n.93, 159–60
  augural significance of 156–8, 160–3
Otacilius Crassus, T. (*pr. II* 214) 257, 264–5,
  271, 275–6
  not an augur 272n.44
ovation(s) 117, 119n.28, 121, 125–6

Pachynus, Cape 148–9, 161–2
paludamentum/paludatus (-dati) 49–55, 61,
  63–4, 155–7, 160–1, 168, 212–13, 241,
  243–4, 254, 283
Papirius Carbo, Cn. (*cos. III* 82):
  death in office 177n.26
Papirius Crassus, L. (*cos. II* 330) 5, 8, 10n.15
Papirius Cursor, L. (*cos. V* 313, *dict.* 324,
  309) 27, 167n.51
  auspices and *imperium*, claims supremacy of
    dictator's 16, 30, 112, 115, 148
  auspices, repeated by 1, 60n.85, 62–3
  clemency/*comitas* 8, 17–18, 23
  elogium 9
  Fabius Rullianus, dispute with 1–29 *passim*,
    267–8, 270
  Fabius Rullianus, punishment of 1, 17–18, 23
  offices held in 320–319 V 128–9
  saevitia/severitas 4, 7–8
  triumph 7–8, 23
Papirius Cursor, L. (*cos. II* 272) 12–13, 59n.84
Papirius Maso, C. (*cos.* 231) 187n.61, 190–1
Papirius Mugillanus, L. (*cos.* 444) 292
Papirius Mugillanus, L. (*cos.* 319?) 128–9
Papirius Praetextatus, L. (*cens.* 272):
  death in office 176–7
Parma 218–19, 234
Passignano sul Trasimeno 226n.28
patrician(s) 12n.25, 31–2, 170; *see also*
  magistrate(s): patrician
Pavia (Ticinum) 219, 234
pax deorum 43–4, 255, 264–5
perduellio 163–5
Perugia, *see* Perusia
Perusia (Perugia) 236–7, 236n.43
Petillius Spurinus, Q. (*cos.* 176) 194n.89, 281–2
  death in office 177, 280–1
  Latin Festival, absent from 251n.81
  vitium in auspicio, ignored by 280–1, 287
Pharsalos, battle of 132–3, 137, 146–7

GENERAL INDEX 323

Phintias 161–2
Piacenza, *see* Placentia
Piazza al Serchio 218–19
Picenum 184–5, 217–18, 250–1
Pictor (historian), *see* Fabius
Pievepelago 218
Pisa 217
Piso (historian), *see* Calpurnius
Pistoia, *see* Pistoriae
Pistoriae (Pistoia) 213–18, 222–3, 232, 234, 250, 251nn.77,79
Pizzofreddo 218–19
Placentia (Piacenza) 218n.9, 219, 234n.41, 249–53
Plancius, Cn. (*q*. 58, *aed. cur.* 54) 73, 76, 77n.37
plays, *see* drama
plebiscite 26, 105, 127–8, 135–6, 178–9, 185–6, 204–5, 207n.123
Plutarch of Khaironeia (biographer):
  and Fabius Maximus–Minucius Rufus dispute 105–9, 268–9
  and Valerius Maximus 206–7
  memory, reliance on 209
  on abdication of Flaminius and Furius 180nn.40–41, 182, 186–7, 206
  on alternation of *fasces* 74–5
  on Antonius as magister equitum 136–7
  on Crassus' departure for Parthia 155n.14
  on dictator and other magistrates 66–7, 79–82, 96
  on dictator riding on horse 66–7, 82
  on dictator's term of office 110–11, 110n.134
  on Flaminius as magister equitum 206–9, 210n.134
  on Flaminius' fall off horse 240–1
  on *prodigia* in 223 184
  on title of dictator 87–8
  on triumphs of Flaminius and Furius 187–8
  sources for *Fabius* 106nn.118, 120
  sources for *Marcellus* 206–7
Po river/valley 217n.7, 227–8, 250–3
  battle at 180, 185–6
Polybios of Megalopolis (historian):
  and Fabius Maximus–Minucius Rufus dispute 26n.48, 105–9, 268–9
  and Gauls' sack of Rome 110
  archaeologia 84
  on Flaminius at Arretium 237
  on Flaminius' movements in 217 213, 227–8, 230, 233, 247, 252–3
  on dictator's term of office 110–11
  on Hannibal's crossing of Arno marshes 219–20
  on Hannibal's routes into Italy 213, 217–18

  on Hannibal's surprise of Flaminius 217, 219–20, 224–5
  on magister equitum 114–15
  on suspension of magistrates under dictator 78–9, 81–4
pomerium 241
  divides spheres *domi* and *militiae* 30–1, 50–1, 57–8, 61, 65, 155, 184
  effatum 58n.80, 158n.21
  imperium retained until crossing of 70–1, 123n.43
  imperium (military) valid only outside 77–8, 77n.39
  inaugurated 157, 158n.21
  lictors dismissed at 69–70
  lictors without axes inside 50n.62, 74–5
Pompeius Magnus, Cn. (*cos. III* 52, *augur*) 69, 132, 138, 142–3, 196n.93, 288
Pompeius Trimalchio Maecenatianus, C. (*VIvir augustalis*) 74n.19
Pomponius, M. (*pr.* 217) 256n.3
Pomponius Atticus, T. (*eques R.*) 67–8
Pomponius Matho, M'. (*cos.* 233) 190–1
Pomponius Matho, M. (*cos.* 231, *mag. eq.* 217, *augur*) 170, 183–4, 186, 272–3, 279
Pontassieve 217–18, 232
Pontepetri 218
pontiff(s):
  elections, not concerend with 281–2
  pontifex maximus 164n.40, 272–3
  pontifical college 39–40, 140n.99, 256–7, 268–9, 282
  pontifices Albani 90n.70
  prodigia, managed by 43–4, 184, 281–2
  records of 279–80
Pontremoli 218–19
Porcius Cato, M. (*cos.* 195, *cens.* 184; historian) 35–6, 90–1, 121–2, 124
Porretta Terme 213–16
portent(s), see *prodigium*
Postumius Albinus, A. (*cos.* 242) 271n.39
Postumius Albinus, L. (*cos. II* 229) 270–1
Postumius Albus, A. (*cos.* 496, *dict.* 499 or 496) 128n.56
potestas:
  and *imperium* 37–9
  censoria 98n.99, 100
  consularis 33–4, 37–8, 39n.27, 71–2, 77–8, 85n.53, 98n.99, 99n.104, 141
  dictatoria 38
  maior and *minor* 33–4, 37, 72n.16, 200–1
  praetoria 33–5, 37–8, 72–3
  regia 16, 30, 85, 98n.99
Praeneste 165–8
Praenestinae sortes 167–8

praetor(s):
  army/fleet, command of 37, 116–17, 120–1, 200–1, 232–3, 258–9
  assisting consul, see *adiutor*
  auspices, elected under same as consuls 16, 171
  city, defense of 256
  collega minor of consul 85, 201
  constitutional position vis-à-vis consul 30, 33–5, 85, 96–8, 114, 117–18, 125–6, 200–1
  dictator, named by 35n.18, 104, 134, 140–2
  elections, held by 35n.18
  maximus 93n.81
  origin of title 93n.83
  senate, convened by 255–6
  see also auspices: of praetor; *imperium*: of praetor
praetorship 31n.5
privatus/-ti 53, 56–7, 67, 71–4, 76, 95–6, 125–6, 168
  auspices, lack of 54–5, 59, 141–2
  cum imperio 77n.39, 141–2
proconsul (*pro consule*) 33–6, 38n.24, 49, 122–3, 124n.44
  not subordinate to consul 77–8
prodigium/-gia 39–40, 43–4, 62–3, 86, 245–6, 277, 284–5, 294
  auspices, distinct from/overlap with 43–4, 44n.39, 62–3, 245, 281–2, 284–6
  Cannae, surrounding 263
  observed in 223 180, 184–5
profectio 49–51, 56, 60–1, 141–2, 155–6
  evidence for 51–2
  of consul(s) 53–5, 63–4, 120–1, 152, 155, 159–60, 163n.36, 168, 184, 212–13, 241, 243–4, 247, 283
  of dictator 61
promagistrate(s) 49, 68, 77–8
  auspices, lack of 124–5, 141–2
  imperium, retained by, until return to City 122–4
propraetor (*pro praetore*) 33–4, 49, 122–3
proquaestor (*pro quaestore*) 63
prorogatio 122–3, 250n.76
provincia 73, 282, 284–5
  imperium, exercise of, affected by 33–6, 63
  naval 96n.93
  sortition of 35–6
  triumph, award of, affected by 34–6, 118–21, 119n.27, 125–6
provocatio 22, 31–2, 37, 61
  dictator (not) subject to 16–17, 19, 86–7
Publilius Philo, Q. (*cos. IV* 315, *dict.* 339) 128–9, 128n.56

pullarius/-rii 1, 22, 45n.45, 59n.84, 60n.85, 156n.16, 160–3, 241–2, 260, 263, 280–1, 288–9
pulli 40–1, 45n.45, 59–60, 244–7
  drowning at Drepana 148–9, 162–3
  drowning at Rome/Ostia 149n.4, 152, 154–9, 162–3
  drowning, evidence for 148–56
  escape 287
  feeding eagerly 44–5, 163n.37, 193–4, 245, 259–60, 263–4
  rarely fed 42, 160n.30, 244
  refuse to eat 148–9, 158–62, 238–9, 241–2, 245, 248–9, 263–4, 274–5
Punic War(s):
  First 12–13, 116–17, 148–9, 161–2, 165, 169
  Second (Hannibalic) 26, 28–9, 66–7, 96n.93, 275, 282, 289
  see also Carthage/Carthaginian(s)
Pyrrhos of Epeiros (king 297–272) 257–8

Qarthalo (Carthaginian commander 249) 161–2, 261
quaestor(s) 35–6, 63, 200–1
  not entitled to lictors 73
  pro praetore 73
Quinctius Capitolinus, T. (*tr. mil. c. p. III* 384, *mag. eq.* 385) 6n.10, 130, 209n.132
Quinctius Cincinnatus, L. (*cos.* 460, *dict.* 458) 83, 116n.15, 265–6
  abdication of consul, compelled by 19–20, 83, 201, 204–5
Quinctius Crispinus, T. (*cos.* 208):
  death in office 176–8
Quinctius Flamininus, L. (*cos.* 192, *augur*) 208n.126
Quinctius Flamininus, T. (*cos.* 198) 35–6, 51n.63
Quinctius Poenus, T. (*cos. II* 351, *dict.* 361) 14n.28

reconstruction:
  annalistic and Livy's 21n.38
  scholarly/speculative 34n.13, 37–8, 50, 94n.84
  see also annalists/annalistic
Reggio Emilia (Regium Lepidum) 218
Regillus Lake, battle of 128
Regium Lepidum, *see* Reggio Emilia
religio 16, 51n.63, 72n.15, 112, 115, 126–7, 139–42, 181, 188–9, 193–4, 259–61, 263, 265–7, 281, 289
Reno river 213–16
res publica 72–5, 98–9, 203–4, 210, 265–6, 270, 289
  and auspices, *see* auspices: and *res publica*

and *prodigia* 43–4
based on restraint 204
rex/reges, see king(s)
Rimini, *see* Ariminum
rogator primus 284–5
Romulus Martis f. 46, 87n.57
Rusellae, battle of 6

sacra 26, 39–40, 57, 115, 268–9, 289
  privata 268nn.31,32
sacrifice, human 263
Saena, *see* Siena
Samnites/Samnium 1, 6, 19–20, 278
  Samnite Wars 11, 21, 257–8, 293
San Cristoforo in Val Vona 218–19
San Marcello 218
Santerno river 217n.7
Sardinia 35–6, 257–8, 284–5
Sassalbo 218
Saticula, battle of 14–15
Savena river 216
Scribonius Curio, C. (*tr. pl.* 50) 69, 81–2
Secchia river 218
self-advertisement, aristocratic 2–3
Sempronius Atratinus, L. (*cos.* 444) 292
Sempronius Atratinus, A. (*mag. eq.* 380) 6n.10
Sempronius Blaesus, C. (*cos. II* 244) 165n.46
Sempronius Gracchus, Ti. (*cos. II* 213, *mag. eq.* 216) 74n.18, 114–15, 115n.12
  augurs, summoned by 274
  elections in 215, held by 270–1
Sempronius Gracchus, Ti. (*cos. II* 163, *augur*):
  elections, *vitium* at 50n.62, 206–7, 284–7, 292
  haruspices, dispute with 284, 286–7
  political motives, alleged 285–7
  Sardinia, *pro consule* 284–5
Sempronius Gracchus, Ti. (*tr. pl.* 133, *augur*) 285
Sempronius Longus, Ti. (*cos.* 218) 249–53, 250n.76, 251nn.77,79
Sempronius Sophus, P. (*tr. pl.* 310, *cos.* 304) 10–11
Sempronius Tuditanus, M. (*cos.* 185, *pontifex*) 71
senate 5, 21, 39–42, 45–6, 55, 70n.5, 71–3, 210–11, 270–1, 288–9
  consular tribunes, ordered to abdicate by 198–9, 292
  consuls, ordered to abdicate by 180, 201–2, 284–5, 293–4
  consuls, recalled by, to hold elections 170
  convened by Octavian 123n.43
  dictator, appointment of ordered by 163, 255–6, 258–9, 262, 264
  responsa of priestly colleges, accepted by 188–9

senatus consultum 101–2, 133, 135–6, 145, 176
sortes Praenestinae, consultation of prohibited by 165–8
triumph(s), awarded/denied by 116–17, 119–21, 183, 187–8
senator(s) 39–40
granted lictors 73
Serchio river 217–18, 222, 250
Sergius Fidenas, M'. (*tr. mil. c. p. II* 402) 198–9
Servilius Ahala, C. (*tr. mil. c. p.* 408, *III* 402, *mag. eq.* 408) 130
  threatens to name dictator 198–9
Servilius Axilla, C. (*tr. mil. c. p.* 418, *mag. eq.* 418) 130
Servilius Caepio, Cn. (*cos.* 106) 287–8
Servilius Geminus, Cn. (*cos.* 217) 54, 78–9, 107, 170, 172–3, 175, 212–13, 250n.76, 279
  command, removed from by dictator 66–7, 82, 95–6, 96n.93, 98
  Gaul, campaign in 225–8, 230–2
  Hannibal, campaign against 226–7, 234–8, 252–3
Servilius Glaucia, C. (*pr.* 100) 72n.15
Servilius Isauricus, P. (*cos. II* 41, *augur*) 133, 138, 143
  names Antonius magister equitum 131, 137, 145–7
  names Caesar dictator 132, 137, 145
Servilius Pulex Geminus, M. (*cos.* 202, *augur*) 272n.44, 286n.91
Servius (grammarian):
  on drowning of *pulli* 152–6, 162–3
Servius auctus *sive* Danielis 153
  on augural character of Ostia and Tiber 156–8
Sestius, P. (*pr.* by 50) 70n.5
shrew-mouse, see *sorex*
Sibylline Books 39–40, 256–7, 261n.15, 263–5
Sicily 11n.20, 148–168 *passim*, 149n.4, 174–5, 208n.126, 251n.77, 253, 258–61
Siena (Saena) 222–4
Sieve river 217–18
silence, augural/ritual, see *silentium*
silentium 155–6, 278
Silenos of Kale Akte 231
Sinalunga 222
Soliera Apuana 218
sorex 116n.17, 205–7, 205n.119, 211–12
sortition 54n.70, 283n.79
  of provinces 35–6, 252
Sosylos of Lakedaimon 231
Spain, *see* Hispania
Spedaletto 213–16

Spoletium 90–1
sponsio/spondere 36, 93n.83, 117–19
spring, sacred, see *ver sacrum*
Stàffora river 219
standards, refuse to be moved 238–9, 241–3, 245–9, 246n.67, 287–8
Strabo (historian–geographer) 217–18
Stradella 219
strategy, Roman, in 217 249–53
    armies and *provinciae* 252–3
    consuls, cooperation of 253
    redeployments 249–52
Suetonius Tranquillus, C. (*eques R.*; biographer):
    and the Livii Drusi 9–10
    on drowning of *pulli* 162–3
Sulpicius, Q. (*flamen*) 206
Sulpicius Galba, Ser. (*pr.* 54, *augur*) 138–9, 142–3
Sulpicius Longus, Q. (*tr. mil. c. p.* 390) 84
supplicatio 256–7
Syracuse 161–2
Syria 288

tabernaculum 155–6, 292
taboo 66–7, 87n.57, 133
Tarentum 159, 277
Taro river 218–19
Tarquinius, Sex. 91n.76
Tarraco 121–2
Taviano 213–16
Telamon, battle of 236–7
templum 54n.70, 283–4
Terentius Varro, C. (*cos.* 216) 28–9, 119–20, 165n.46, 250n.76, 267
    auspices at Cannae, questioned about 263
    auspices, observed by 158–9, 263–4, 267
    dictators, named by 98, 102–3, 105, 264
    election of 170, 279–80
    enemies of 263, 267
    see also Cannae, battle of
Terentius Varro, M. (*pr.* by 67; polymath) 33n.10, 48n.57, 50n.62
    on magistrate *vitio creatus* 88, 89n.66, 94
    on title of dictator 79, 87–8
Terenzo 218–19
terminology 31n.4, 33, 34n.15, 38–9, 79
    augural 44n.41
Tevere river, see Tiber
Thessalonica 73, 77n.37
thunder 40–1, 44–5, 59–60, 181, 196n.93, 270–1, 274–6, 278–9; see also *auspicium de caelo*; lightning
Tiber river:
    augural significance of 156–8
    pulli, drowning of 152, 154–5

Ticinum, see Pavia
Tidone river 219
Titius, Sex. (*tr. pl.* 99) 288n.96
Titus (Imp. Titus Caesar Vespasianus Aug., *cos.* VIII AD 80) 117
toga praetexta 45–6, 50–1, 55–6, 66–7, 72, 95–6
Torricella 226
Tortosa 121–2
Trasimeno, Lago di, see Trasumene Lake
Trasumene Lake 222, 224, 226–8, 235–7
    battle of 170, 226–7, 229, 237, 242–3, 245, 254–8, 263
Trebia (Trebbia) river 219
    battle of the 212–13, 235, 250–1
Trebbia, see Trebia
tribune(s), military 94n.84, 240, 268n.31
    as magister equitum 130–1
    in First Punic War 153
    with consular power 19–20, 39n.27, 130–1, 139–41, 198–9, 201
    tribuni celerum 92n.80
tribune(s) of the Plebs 70n.5, 72n.16, 187–9, 198–9, 261
    augurs, accused by 278–80
    Claudius Pulcher, *profectio* opposed by 152–6, 163
    Claudius Pulcher, prosecuted by 163–4
    dictator, retain powers under 78–82, 84–5, 95–6, 98–9
    not affected by *interregnum* 197
    sacrosancity of 98
    support Fabius Rullianus against dictator 1, 5, 17–19, 22, 28–9
    technically not magistrates 78–82
triumph(s) 2, 6–8, 20, 23, 30–1, 34–5, 83, 94n.85, 109–10, 111n.141, 165, 172n.10, 176–7, 179, 253, 291, 293
    by Romulus on foot 87n.57
    Cicero's hope of 68–71
    disputes over 36, 125–7, 187–9, 200n.102
    in monte Albano 187n.61
    of Catulus and Falto 36, 116–19
    of Flaminius and Furius Philus 180n.41, 182–3, 187–91, 193–7, 202–5
    of Furius Purpurio 120–1
    of Helvius 121–5
    of Salinator and Nero 119–20
    third-century dates of 190–1
triumvirs/triumvirate 123n.43
Tubero (historian), see Aelius
Tullius Cicero, M. (*cos.* 63, *augur*) 35n.18, 288–9
    and Antonius 132–3, 137, 146
    and Caesar 69–70
    and *fasces*/lictors 68–71, 78

augur 138, 142–3, 171–2, 243
divination, attitude toward 289n.98
on Crassus' departure for Parthia 155n.14
on drowning of *pulli* 159–63
on Flaminius' neglect of auspices 239–47
on *vitium* at trials 164
imperium and triumph 68–71
Tullius Cicero, Q. (*pr.* 62) 243, 245–7
Tullus Hostilius 91
Tuoro sul Trasimeno 226n.28
Turdetania 121–2
Tusculum 89n.69, 90
Twelve Tables 93n.81
Tyrrhenian Sea 218, 250, 251n.77

Umbria 217–18, 232–3, 235, 250–1, 255–6
urbs/ad urbem/in urbe 54–5, 58–9, 61, 123n.43
(not) *effata* 58n.80, 157–8
maritima 157–8

Val d'Elsa 222–3
Val di Chiana 222, 224
Valerius Antias (historian) 106nn.118–120, 152n.6
Valerius Corvus, M. (*cos. VI* 299, *dict. II* 301) 4n.8, 129–30
Valerius Falto, Q. (*pr.* 242, *cos.* 239) 119–21, 125–6
  triumph, dispute with consul over 36, 116–19, 200n.102
Valerius Flaccus, L. (*cos.* 195) 123n.42
Valerius Flaccus, L. (*cos.* 152):
  death in office 176–7
Valerius Flaccus, L. (*cos.* 100, *interrex* 82, *mag. eq.* 81) 135–6, 143–4
Valerius Lactuca Maximus, M. (*cos.* 437?) 172n.10
Valerius Laevinus, C. (*cos.* 176) 177, 281–3
Valerius Laevinus, M. (*cos. II* 210) 135–6, 293
Valerius Maximus (author of *exempla*):
  on consultation of *sortes Praenestinae* 165–7
  on Cotta punishing officers 25
  on drowning of *pulli* 162–3
  on Fabius Rullianus 5–7, 19–20
  on Flaminius as magister equitum 206–7, 209
  on Lutatius Catulus–Valerius Falto dispute 117–19, 118n.25
  on trial of Claudius Pulcher 164
Valerius Maximus, M'. (*dict.* 494) 111n.141
Valerius Maximus (Corvinus), M. (*cos. II* 289, *dict.* 301) 4, 9, 13, 15, 129–30, 255
Valerius Messalla Rufus, M. (*cos.* 53, *augur*) 35n.18, 43, 113n.6, 138–9, 142–3
  on auspices of magistrates 85, 97–8, 101

Valerius Poplicola, M. (*cos. II* 353, *mag. eq.* 358) 6n.10
Valerius Poplicola, P. (*cos. IV* 504) 74–5
Valerius Potitus, C. (*cos.* 331, *mag. eq.* 331) 128
Varro (polymath), *see* Terentius
Varzi 219
Vatinius, P. (*cos.* 47, *augur*) 147
Veii 57–8, 109–10, 198–9
Velleia 219
Velleius Paterculus (*pr. des.* AD 15; historian):
  on Crassus' departure for Parthia 155n.14
Venuleius (*leg.* 43) 73n.17
Venus Erycina, temple of 256–7
ver sacrum 256–7
Verginius Tricostus, L. (*tr. mil. c. p. II* 389) 198–9
Veronensia Scholia 156n.16, 244
Verres, C. (*pr.* 74) 56n.75, 61n.88
Verrius Flaccus, M. (grammarian) 48n.57, 49
Vespasian (Imp. Caes. Vespasianus Aug., *cos. IX* AD 79) 117
Vestal Virgins 39–40, 87n.57
  stuprum of 263–5
  virgines Albanae 90n.70
veto 76, 86–7, 98, 188–9, 196n.93, 200–1, 204n.110
Veturius Philo, L. (*cos.* 220, *dict.* 217) 170, 178, 273n.45, 279–80, 293
Viareggio 217
vinculum temporis 43–5, 47, 47n.54, 59–60, 62–3, 141–2, 184, 205n.117, 242, 244–5, 275–6, 284–5
Vipsanius Agrippa, M. (*cos. tertium* 27) 75–6
vitio creatus/-ti or *factus/-ti*
  consul(s) 17, 46n.49, 47n.54, 50n.62, 180–1, 183–6, 188–91, 193–4, 196–7, 206, 210–12, 243n.60, 255, 270–1, 275–6, 281–2, 284–5, 293–4
  consular tribunes 199, 291–3
  dictator 142, 170, 178, 205, 207–8, 211, 278–80, 293
  magister equitum 211
  magistrates 47nn.51,54, 61–2, 77n.37, 88, 212n.1
  fault of magistrate presiding at election 186, 276
  see also vitium
vitium 13–14, 40–1, 43–5, 47, 54–5, 59–60, 62–3, 97–8, 116, 155–6, 260–1, 270, 274–5
  at auspices for battle 255, 258, 263, 265, 269
  at elections 88–9, 180n.39, 181, 184–5, 191–4, 206, 271, 281–2
  at naming of dictator and/or magister equitum 205n.119, 207–8, 211, 278
  of Claudius Pulcher 158–60, 162–3
  of consuls in 176 281–2

vitium (*cont.*)
 of Crassus (*cos.* 168) 283–4
 of Iunius Pullus 158–63
 of Marcellus 273–6
 of Ti. Gracchus 50n.62, 206–7, 284–7, 292
 prevents repeated prosecution 163–4
 taints magistrate's subsequent actions 40–1, 56, 59–60, 100–1, 115, 163n.37, 167–8, 191n.80, 193–4
 see also *vitio creatus/-ti* or *factus/-ti*
Volturnus river 277
votorum nuncupatio 45–6, 48–55, 59–61, 63–4, 155, 254, 283, 288
vow(s) 2–3, 17, 45–6, 207–9, 256–7;
 see also *votorum nuncupatio*

winter quarters in 218/7:
 of Hannibal 218, 231, 249–50
 Roman 231, 249–50

Zonaras (historian):
 on abdication of Flaminius and Furius 180n.41, 183, 186–7
 on appointment of dictator in 249 261–2
 on Flaminius' defiance of augurs and senate 181–2
 on Flaminius' movements in 217 225–8, 230, 233–4
 on Iunius Pullus 165, 261–2
 on *prodigia* in 223 184
 on triumphs of Flaminius and Furius 187–8

Index Locorum

Note: Further discussion of ancient authors can be traced through the General Index. Authors and works are alphabetized by their commonly used names.

For the benefit of digital users, indexed terms that span two pages (e.g., 52–53) may, on occasion, appear on only one of those pages.

ACTA TRIUMPHORUM (*Acta Tr.*)
  InscrItal 13.1: 66–67 111n.141
  InscrItal 13.1: 70–71 94n.85
  InscrItal 13.1: 76–77 119
  InscrItal 13.1: 78–79 179n.37, 190n.71
APPIAN
  BCiv (*Bella civilia*)
    1.98.459–99.462 136n.82
    1.98.459 135n.80, 143–4
    1.99.461 143–4
    2.5.16 72n.15
    2.11.37 75n.27
    2.18.66 155n.14
  Hannib. (*Hannibalica*)
    7.29–30 252
    7.30 218n.9, 231n.37, 252n.74
    8.33 252
    9.38 226n.29
    11.48 229n.36
    12.50 79
    12.51–52 26n.47
    12.52 107n.123, 179n.33
    13.55 107n.123
    16.68 175n.19
ASCONIUS (ed. Stangl)
  Mil. (*In Milonianam*)
    36.23St. 90n.70
AUGUSTINUS
  Doctr. Christ. (*De doctrina Christiana*)
    2.2.4 276n.59
CAESAR
  [*BAfr*] (*Commentarius belli Africi*)
    28.2 138–9
    98 133n.75
  [*BAlex*] (*Commentarius belli Alexandrini*)
    48.1 142–3
  BCiv (*Commentarii belli civilis*)
    1.6.6 52
    1.6.7 77n.39

    1.23.4 68
    2.21.3 142–3
    2.21.5 104, 134, 142, 171–2
    2.32.9 67
    3.2.1 104
    3.20–23 133n.72
    3.99.5 137n.87
CASSIODORUS
  Chron. (*Chronica*)
    ad a.u.c. 601 191n.76, 294n.17
CATO the Elder
  Orig. (*Origines*)
    HRR F 58/FRHist 5 F 36 90
CENSORINUS
  De die natali
    17.8 261n.15
CHRONICON PASCHALE 49
CHRONOGRAPHER of 354 9, 172n.10
CICERO
  AdBrut (*Epistulae ad Brutum*)
    1.5.4 171n.3
  Amic. (*De amicitia*)
    37 209n.132
  Att. (*Epistulae ad Atticum*)
    5.20.3 68–9
    8.14.3 67
    8.15.1 67
    8.15.3 67
    7.10 68–9
    7.12.14 68–9
    7.21.2 67n.2
    8.1.3 68–9
    8.3.5 68–9
    8.3.6 68–9
    9.1.3 68–9, 78
    9.1.4 67n.2
    9.2a 69
    9.3.3 35n.18

CICERO (cont.)
  9.7.2–5 69
  9.7.5 71n.10
  9.9.1 69
  9.9.3 99n.103, 138–9
  9.10.3 69
  9.11A.3 69
  9.12.4 69
  9.15.1 69
  9.15.2 135–6, 138–40, 171–2
  9.18 69
  9.19.3 69
  10.1.2 69
  10.1a 69
  10.4.10 69
  10.10.1 69
  11.6 132–3, 147n.120
  11.6.2 69–71, 71n.10, 76n.31
  11.6.5 132n.69
  11.7.1 68–70
  11.7.2 132–3, 147n.120
  11.22.2 138–9
Balb. (*Pro Balbo*)
  28 288n.94
Brut. (*Brutus*)
  135 288n.94
Cat. (*In Catilinam*)
  3.14 72n.15
  3.15 72n.15
  4.5 72n.15
De orat. (*De oratore*)
  2.124–125 288n.94
  2.164 288n.94
  2.167 288n.94
  2.197–203 288n.94
Div. (*De divinatione*)
  1.3 39n.28, 64
  1.27–28 156n.16, 244n.61
  1.27 42n.35
  1.29–30 155n.14, 288n.95
  1.29 150, 158–60, 158n.22
  1.33 245n.65, 284n.83, 292n.6, 294n.16
  1.36 292n.6
  1.48 245n.65
  1.49 245n.65
  1.56 245n.65
  1.72–79 246
  1.77–78 246–7
  1.77 42n.35, 59n.84, 239n.51
  1.78 245
  2.20 150, 158–60, 259–60
  2.67 238n.50, 243, 246–7
  2.71–72 156n.16, 244
  2.71 150, 158–60, 162–4, 164n.39, 263–4
  2.72 42n.35
  2.73 42n.35, 156n.16, 244n.61
  2.74 45n.45, 284n.83, 294n.16
  2.77–78 239
  2.77 65n.102, 157n.18, 272–3, 276
  2.83 42n.35
  2.84 155n.14, 288n.95
Dom. (*De domo sua*)
  41 40n.30
  42 40n.30
  45 164
Fam. (*Epistulae ad familiares*)
  1.9.25 70n.8
  2.16.2 69–71
  2.17.6 49n.58
  7.30.1 142
  8.4.1 138n.92
  8.10.2 52n.66
  10.12.3 160n.30, 288–9
  12.21 73n.17
  12.30.7 73n.17
  13.61 52n.66
  14.7 69
  14.11.3 68–9
  15.3.2 49n.58
  15.17.3 52n.66
  15.19.2 52n.66
  18.17 133n.72
Har. resp. (*De haruspicum responso*)
  18 40n.30
Leg. (*De legibus*)
  2.20 39–40
  2.21 58n.81
  2.31 288n.96
  3.8 93n.81
  3.9 45n.44, 85–6
Leg. agr. (*De lege agraria*)
  2.26 97–8
  2.93 69n.4, 76n.31
Lig. (*Pro Ligario*)
  7 69–70
ND (*De natura deorum*)
  1.122 40n.30
  2.7 149, 158, 160–4, 164n.39
  2.8 239n.52, 246–7
  2.9 157n.18
  2.10–11 284n.83, 294n.16
  2.11 286, 292n.6
  3.5 40n.29
Off. (*De officiis*)
  3.112 101–2
Phil. (*Orationes Philippicae*)
  2.59–61 132–3
  2.62 132, 135–7
  2.71 137n.87
  2.88 142n.106

3.9 142n.106
5.9 142n.106
5.24 52
5.45–46 141n.104
11.30 98
Pis. (In Pisonem)
 31 52n.66
 55 50n.62, 52n.66
Planc. (Pro Plancio)
 98–99 73
QFr (Epistulae ad Quintum fratrem)
 2.2.1 284n.83, 285n.89, 294n.16
Rep. (De re publica)
 1.63 79n.45, 84, 86n.54, 87–90, 89n.68
 2.55 74n.23
 2.56 85n.53
 2.61 291
[Rhet. ad Herenn.] (Rhetorica ad Herennium)
 1.24 288n.94
Scaur. (Pro Scauro)
 29–30 86n.56
Sen. (De senectute)
 11 181n.42, 186n.55
Sest. (Pro Sestio)
 71 52n.66, 155n.14
Tusc. (Tusculanae disputationes)
 5.56 117n.20
Verr. (In Verrem)
 2.1.67 73n.17
 2.1.72 73n.17
 2.1.104 56n.75
 2.1.149 61n.88
 2.5.34 52, 61n.88
COELIUS ANTIPATER
 HRR F 19/FRHist 15 F 14a 239n.52
 HRR F 20/FRHist 15 F 14b 239n.52
CORNELIUS NEPOS
 Hann.(Vita Hannibalis)
 5.3 107n.123
CORPUS INSCRIPTIONUM LATINARUM (CIL)
 1^2.2.607 207–8
 1^2.2.608 208n.126
 1^2.2.613 208n.126
 1^2.2.615 208n.126
 6.331 208n.126
 6.1507 208n.126
 6.1898 76n.29
 6.2161 90n.70
 6.2168 90n.70
 6.2170 90n.70
 6.2171 90n.70
 6.2172 90n.70
 9.782 91n.73
 9.1595 90n.70

11.4766 90n.72
14.2264 90n.70
14.2410 90n.70
14.2935 208n.126
14.2947 90n.70
Auctor DE VIRIS ILLUSTRIBUS
 43.3 107n.123
 44.2 284n.83, 294n.16
 72.6 95n.90
DIGESTAE Iustiniani
 1.2.2.18 (Pomponius) 99n.102
 40.2.7 (Gaius) 74nn.18,21
 40.2.8 (Ulpian) 74n.21, 77n.37
Cassius DIO
 Romaica
 fr. 36.2 19–20
 fr. 36.26 145n.116
 fr. 57.16–17 179n.33
 fr. 57.16 107n.123
 fr. 57.17 107n.123
 fr. 57.19 107n.123
 fr. 57.21 175n.19
 fr. 91.1–4 288n.94
 fr. 102.12 53n.69
 36.34.2–3 258n.8
 36.34.2 261n.16
 36.34.3 262n.19
 36.41.2 95n.90
 37.27.3 196n.93
 37.34.2 72n.15
 39.39.5–7 155n.14, 288n.95
 40.12.1–13.4 288n.95
 40.18.1–5 288n.95
 40.19.1–3 288n.95
 41.36.1 142, 145n.116
 41.36.2 104
 42.18.1–3 132n.69
 42.20 135n.80
 42.20.3 135–6, 144n.112, 145–6
 42.20.4 135n.80, 143n.109
 42.21 147n.121
 42.21.1 131n.68, 135n.80, 136–7, 143–5, 145n.116
 42.21.2 134–5, 137n.89, 144n.112, 146–7
 42.22–25 147n.121
 42.23–25 133n.72
 42.23.1 133n.72
 42.23.3 95n.90
 42.27–33 147n.121
 42.30.1 132–3
 42.34–43 147n.121
 42.55.4 143n.109
 43.1.1–3 130–1
 43.14.3 133n.75

Cassius DIO (*cont.*)
    43.33.1 130–1, 210n.136
    45.27.5 144n.113
    46.13.1 135n.80, 144nn.112,113
    46.45.3–4 171n.3
    46.45.3 141n.103
    48.31.3 117n.20
    50.2.5 123n.43
    53.1.1 75–6
    53.1.3 145n.116
    53.51.8 113n.6
DIODOROS of Sicily
  Bibliotheca Historica
    14.117 110
    17.74.1 128
    19.73.1 10
    19.76.3–5 10, 87n.59
    20.106.1 129–30
    24.1.7 161
    24.1.8–9 161–2
    24.1.9 158n.23, 161–2
    24.3–4 154n.13
    24.3 161n.31
    24.4 161–2
DIONYSIOS of Halikarnassos
  Antiquitates Romanae
    2.5.1–2 45n.44
    2.5.1 46
    2.5.2 45n.45, 46n.46
    2.6.1–2 45n.44
    2.6.1 46
    2.6.2 45n.45, 46n.46
    2.6.4 155n.14
    2.34.2 87n.57
    3.6.1–7.8 177n.25
    3.34.3 91n.76
    3.35.5–6 47n.51
    4.62.4 45n.45
    5.1 74–5
    5.19.3 75n.25
    5.37.1 88n.61
    5.61.3 91n.76
    5.70.1–2 83
    5.70.4 83
    5.72.3 83
    5.74.4 90n.70
    5.75.2 87n.60
    5.77.1 83
    5.77.2 83
    6.2.1–3 128n.58
    6.4.1 91n.76
    6.39.2 87n.60
    9.13.4–14.1 291n.2
    9.67–68 177n.25

    10.25.2 83, 201n.105
    10.25.4 83
    10.54.3–56.2 291
    11.20.3 83
    11.62.1–3 291n.3
    11.62.3 291
    11.63.1 198n.97, 291n.5
    12.10 292–3
ELOGIA ARRETINA
  InscrItal 13.3: 61 no. 80 179n.33
ELOGIA FORI ROMANI
  InscrItal 13.3: 39 no. 62 9
EUTROPIUS
  Breviarium ab Urbe condita
    1.19.2 172n.10
    2.26.1 151
    6.18.1 288n.95
FASTI CAPITOLINI (FC)
  InscrItal 13.1: 24–25 172n.10
  InscrItal 13.1: 26–27 291
  InscrItal 13.1: 30–31 293
  InscrItal 13.1: 32–33 111n.141
  InscrItal 13.1: 36–37 10–11
  InscrItal 13.1: 38–39 5, 9–10
  InscrItal 13.1: 42–43 104n.115,
    259n.11, 261n.16
  InscrItal 13.1: 44–45 169
  InscrItal 13.1: 46–47 131n.67, 293
  InscrItal 13.1: 48–49 177
  InscrItal 13.1: 50–51 284n.83, 294n.16
  InscrItal 13.1: 54–55 136n.82, 177n.26
  InscrItal 13.1: 56–57 113n.5
  InscrItal 13.1: 58–59 61n.90, 113nn.5,6
  InscrItal 13.1: 66–67 172n.10
FASTI FERIARUM LATINARUM
  InscrItal 13.1: 146–147 109n.131
  InscrItal 13.1: 148–149 251n.81
  InscrItal 13.1: 150–151 251n.81
FASTI HYDATIANI 9–10
FASTI PRAENESTINI
  InscrItal 13.2: 110 191n.76, 294n.17
FASTI PRIVERNATES (ed. Zevi)
  b.10–14 113, 113n.5
  b.15–16 61n.90, 113n.6
FASTI URBISALVIENSES
  InscrItal 13.1: 338 123n.41
  InscrItal 13.1: 552 123n.41
FESTUS (ed. Lindsay)
  De verborum significatu
    17.14–15L 49n.59
    56.29L 76n.29
    71L 87n.57

128.15-16L 90
176.7-9 L 52
232.23-28L 58n.79
268L 276-7
27615-277.2L 46n.48, 48, 53n.67, 91n.76
284L 157n.18
285L 42n.35
296L 157n.18
326.16L 45n.44, 155-6
470.35L 45n.44
474.7-15L 45n.44

FLORUS
  Epitomae de Tito Livio
    1.18.5, 7, 12, 15, 27, 29, 30, 33 151n.5
    1.18.17 153n.7
    1.18.29 151, 158n.22
    1.22.14 239n.52
    1.34.8 288n.94
    1.46.3-4 288n.95
    1.46.3 155n.14

FRONTINUS
  Strat. (Strategemata)
    1.4.14 154n.11
    2.7.14 154n.11
    2.13.9 154
    3.10.8 154n.11
    4.1.31 25n.45, 56n.77, 115n.12

GAIUS
  Inst. (Institutiones)
    1.20 74nn.18, 21
    see also *DIGESTAE*

Aulus GELLIUS
  Noctes Atticae
    2.2.1-10 74n.19
    3.2.10 45n.44
    10.6 164n.43
    10.15.3 87n.57
    10.15.17 140n.99
    13.12.6 (Varro) 33n.12, 73
    13.14.1 58n.81
    13.15.4: (Messalla) 33n.12, 35n.18, 38n.25,
      43, 85n.51, 97-8, 99n.103, 101, 138-9,
      171nn.5, 6
    13.15.4 (Tuditanus) 33n.12
    15.17.5 (Laelius Felix) 33n.10

GRANIUS LICINIANUS (ed. Criniti)
  28.25-26 Criniti 284n.83, 294n.16
  33.1-17 Criniti 288n.94
  33.24 Criniti 288n.94

INSCRIPTIONES LATINAE SELECTAE (ILS)
  3 208n.127
  11 108, 207-8
  12-14 208n.127

12 208n.126
14 208n.126
16-17 208n.127
16 208n.126
20 208n.126
21b 208n.127
36 208n.127
212 86
887 90n.70
1345 90n.70
2749 90n.70
4911 90n.72, 91n.73
4912 91n.73
4955 90n.70
4956 90n.70
5010 90n.70
5011 90n.70
6190 90n.70

JOSEPHUS
  BJ (Bellum Iudaicum)
    7.121 117n.20
    7.152 117n.20

LAELIUS FELIX, *see* GELLIUS
LEX de PROVINCIIS PRAETORIIS
  RStat 1: 242, 250, 255, 266-267 124n.44

LICINIUS MACER
  HRR F 10/*FRHist* 27 F 15 90n.70

LIVY
  Ab Urbe condita
    1.15.6 65n.100
    1.36.6 39n.28, 64
    2.1.7-8 85n.53
    2.1.8 74n.23
    2.8.9 65n.100
    2.18.3-4 90n.71
    2.18.5 111n.141
    2.18.6 99n.102
    2.18.9 87n.59
    2.19.2-3 128n.58
    2.19.10 91n.76
    2.20.7-9 6n.10
    2.20.7 91n.76
    2.21.2-4 128n.58
    2.30.4 87n.58
    2.31.3 111n.141
    2.47.7-12 291n.2
    2.49.3 52n.66
    3.17.11 55n.73
    3.18.2 89n.69
    3.18.7 89n.69
    3.27.1 116n.15
    3.29.2-3 19-20, 203
    3.29.3 198n.98, 201n.105

LIVY (cont.)
   3.33.4 291
   3.33.8 74n.22
   3.55.11-12 93n.81
   3.55.11 171n.6
   4.2.8 85n.53
   4.3.9 85n.53
   4.7.1-12 291n.3
   4.7.3 291
   4.7.4-7 291
   4.7.10-12 291
   4.7.11 291
   4.17.8-20.4 172n.10
   4.23.6 116n.15
   4.26.12 116n.15
   4.29.8 11n.20
   4.31.4 139-40, 139n.97
   4.31.5 116n.15, 130
   4.33.7 6n.10
   4.34.5 113n.4, 130
   4.37.3 198n.97, 291n.5
   4.46.11-12 130
   4.57.6 116n.15, 130
   5.9 203
   5.9.1 198n.96, 292-3
   5.9.2-3 198n.97
   5.9.3 198n.97, 291n.5
   5.9.4-6 198n.98
   5.9.7 199n.99
   5.10.1 65n.100
   5.11.11 198n.97, 291n.5
   5.12.5 292-3
   5.14.5-7 292-3
   5.17.1-4 293
   5.17.3 62n.94
   5.9.1-8 292n.9
   5.19.1 109n.131
   5.23.7 109n.131
   5.31.5-8 293
   5.31.6-7 177n.24
   5.32.1 109-10
   5.38.1 258n.10
   5.46.2-3 269n.32
   5.48 110n.133
   5.49.2 81-2, 84
   5.49.9 109-10
   5.52.2-3 57
   5.52.5 57
   5.52.15-16 57
   5.54.7 57
   6.1.4 109-10
   6.1.5 110n.132
   6.11.10 130
   6.12.10 6n.10, 130
   6.23.3-25.6 19-20

   6.28.4 87n.59
   6.29.1-2 6n.10
   6.38.3 99n.102
   6.41.4 39n.28, 64
   7.1.6 171n.6
   7.3.8 99n.102
   7.3.9 101-2
   7.9.3-5 14n.28
   7.12.9 116n.15
   7.15.6-7 6n.10
   7.19.9-21.2 129
   7.20.1 87n.59
   7.26.11 129, 174n.16
   8.3.4-5 293n.12
   8.3.9 91n.76
   8.4.3 199
   8.12.2 116n.15
   8.15.6 113n.4
   8.17.3 135-6
   8.17.12 65n.100
   8.18.1 128
   8.18.13 128
   8.18.4-5 12n.23
   8.22.6 55n.74
   8.23.4 116n.15
   8.23.13 278
   8.23.14 278
   8.23.15-16 278n.63
   8.23.15 45n.44
   8.23.17 278
   8.29.6-14 10n.15, 92-4
   8.30.1-2 56n.77, 60n.85, 194n.89
   8.30.1 13-14, 167n.51, 270
   8.30.4 2, 17
   8.30.6 5-6
   8.30.7 1-3
   8.30.8-9 2
   8.30.9 17, 21-2, 127
   8.30.10 21, 27
   8.30.11 16, 20, 30
   8.31 7
   8.31.1 16, 112
   8.31.2-3 27
   8.31.3-4 27
   8.31.4 16, 114n.8
   8.32.2-11 19
   8.32.3 16, 85, 99n.102, 171n.6
   8.32.4-7 16, 126-7
   8.32.4 55n.74, 60n.85, 62n.94
   8.32.5 112
   8.32.8-10 18-19
   8.32.14-15 18-19
   8.32.15 18-19
   8.32.16 18-19
   8.32.18 18-19

INDEX LOCORUM   335

8.33.8   16–17, 19, 27
8.33.12   16–17
8.33.14–15   16–17
8.33.14   19–20, 201n.105
8.33.15   19–20
8.33.17   16–17, 19–20, 27
8.33.18–19   20
8.33.21   15–17
8.33.22   16, 112
8.34.2–3   16
8.34.2   20n.37
8.34.4–11   17–18
8.34.4   16, 112, 126–7
8.34.5–6   16
8.34.6   16–17
8.34.9   20n.37
8.35.1–9   17–18
8.35.2   18–19
8.35.5   16
8.35.7–9   23
8.35.10–12   23
8.35.10–11   3–4, 7
8.36   6
8.36.1   5, 8, 10n.15, 23, 198n.98
8.36.2–7   8
8.36.2–4   23
8.36.5–7   23
8.36.8–10   23
8.38.1–39.15   94n.85
8.38.14–39.5   6n.10
8.40   94n.85
8.43.2   87n.58
9.7.12–14   293n.13
9.7.12   174n.16
9.7.13   135–6
9.14.1–3   156n.16
9.15.9–10   128–9
9.16.11   128–9, 129n.61
9.21.1   110–11
9.22   14–15
9.22.1   110–11
9.22.2   55n.74
9.22.4–10   6n.10
9.23.4   14–15
9.23.5   14–15
9.23.6   6n.10
9.23.7–17   14–15
9.23.15   6n.10
9.24.1   110–11
9.26.7   10, 87n.59
9.26.14   10
9.26.20   113n.4
9.34.14   10–11
9.38.14   45n.44, 92–4, 116n.15
9.38.15–39.1   62

9.38.15   97–8
9.40.8–10   6n.10
10.3   15
10.3.3–8   129–30
10.3.3–4   4
10.3.5–6   3
10.3.6   7, 23, 56n.77, 62n.94
10.3.7–4.4   6
10.3.7–8   4
10.3.7   14–15
10.3.8   5
10.4.3–4   5
10.4.6–5.11   5
10.4.7   6
10.5.1–13   6
10.5.7–8   5
10.7.1   129–30
10.8.9   65
10.9.1–2   273n.47
10.9.10–13   12–13
10.9.10–11   12–13
10.11.9   12–13
10.31.9   12n.23
10.40   59n.84
10.40.2–4   160n.30
10.40.2   156n.16
21.1.6–7   54
21.25.2–26.2   234n.40
21.51.6–7   251n.77
21.56.9   231n.37, 252n.84
21.57.3–4   252n.82
21.59.1–2   252n.84
21.59.1   218n.9
21.59.10   250n.76
21.63.1   192, 231n.37, 251–3, 252n.84
21.63.2–12   192
21.63.2   183, 187–8, 202, 293n.14
21.63.5–9   268
21.63.5   53n.68, 212–13, 251n.81, 266n.27
21.63.8–9   51–3
21.63.9   49, 53n.68, 64n.97
21.63.10   55–6
21.63.11   253n.87
21.63.13   192, 238–9
21.63.15   220–1, 227–8, 231, 252
22.1.1–4   220–1
22.1.3   221n.18
22.1.4–7   253
22.1.4   192
22.1.5–7   243n.60, 268
22.1.6–7   51–3, 59
22.1.6   157–8
22.1.7   55n.72, 212n.1
22.2.1–4.1   227–8
22.2.1–2   220–1

336 INDEX LOCORUM

LIVY (cont.)
    22.2.1 227–8, 231, 253
    22.2.3–11 220–1
    22.3.1–5 224
    22.3.1 220–1, 221n.19
    22.3.2 220–1
    22.3.3 223
    22.3.6 222–3
    22.3.7–10 237
    22.3.9–10 242
    22.3.9 238
    22.3.10–11 240
    22.3.10 237–8
    22.3.11–13 239n.52, 268
    22.3.11 239n.51, 242
    22.3.12–13 242
    22.4.4 226, 236n.44, 248n.70
    22.7.14 256n.3
    22.8.5–6 178–9, 257
    22.8.5 170, 256n.3
    22.8.6 135–6
    22.8.7 229n.36
    22.9 96n.91
    22.9.7–8 213
    22.9.7 268, 280
    22.9.9–11.1 268–9
    22.9.9–10 213
    22.9.11 175n.19, 213, 256n.3
    22.10.1 257n.5
    22.10.2–6 257n.6
    22.10.7–8 257
    22.10.9 257
    22.10.10 99n.102, 175n.19, 257
    22.11.1 257, 264–5
    22.11.2–6 175n.19
    22.11.5 66n.1
    22.11.6 96n.93
    22.11.7–9 173n.11
    22.11.7 96n.93
    22.12.11–12 26n.47
    22.14.4–15 26n.47
    22.15.1 28n.51
    22.15.5 26n.47
    22.18.8 268–9
    22.18.9–10 26n.48
    22.18.9 28n.51
    22.24 26n.48
    22.25–26 26n.49
    22.25.2 27
    22.25.5 175n.19
    22.25.6 27, 175n.19
    22.25.8–9 27
    22.25.10–27.9 179n.33
    22.25.10 27, 106, 108
    22.25.11 108
    22.25.13 26n.48
    22.25.16 108, 173n.11
    22.26.7 107n.123
    22.27.3–4 107n.121
    22.27.3 107, 107n.121
    22.27.11 107n.121
    22.30.1 107n.121
    22.30.2 107n.121
    22.30.3 107n.121
    22.30.4 107, 108n.124, 112, 179n.33, 268
    22.30.5 107n.121
    22.31.1–7 175n.19
    22.31.6 175n.19
    22.31.7 108n.126
    22.31.8–11 109n.128, 178–9
    22.31.8–10 257
    22.31.9 170
    22.32.1 107, 108n.126
    22.33.8 175n.19
    22.33.9–34.5 170
    22.33.9–34.1 111n.141, 279n.66
    22.33.9–10 175n.19
    22.33.10 170
    22.33.11–12 170
    22.33.11 170, 279n.68
    22.34.3 279–80
    22.34.7 279–80, 279n.68
    22.34.10 174n.16, 279–80
    22.34.11 279n.68
    22.35.1–4 279n.66
    22.35.2 184n.49
    22.41.2 263–4
    22.41.3 159n.24
    22.41.6 159n.24
    22.42.1–10 263–4
    22.42.1 159n.24
    22.42.8 158–9
    22.42.9 158–9
    22.49.7–9 76n.33
    22.54.7–58.8 263
    22.57.1 263
    22.57.2–6 263
    22.57.8–9 264n.24
    22.57.9 136n.84
    23.7.10–9.3 271
    23.8.10 271n.39
    23.14.2–4 264n.24
    23.14.2 66n.1, 87n.57, 264–5
    23.19.3–5 115n.12
    23.19.3 56n.77, 62n.94
    23.19.5 19n.36
    23.22.4–9 186n.55
    23.22.10–11 98, 264n.24
    23.22.10 102–3
    23.22.11–23.2 100n.106, 108

INDEX LOCORUM 337

23.22.11 101
23.23.2 106
23.24.5 114–15
23.24.6–25.9 270n.35
23.30.18 192n.82, 270n.35
23.31.7–8 270–1
23.31.8 271n.37
23.31.13 271nn.36,37, 278n.62
23.32.1 277
23.36.9–10 56n.77, 115n.12, 277
23.36.10 62n.94
23.39.5 277n.60
24.8.17 264–5
24.9.1–2 50n.62
24.19 272
24.19.3–4 272
24.19.6–8 272
24.19.9–11 272
24.37.9 208n.126
24.37.11 208n.126
24.38.9 208n.126
24.39.2 208n.126
25.2–11 114–15
25.2.3 116n.15, 174n.16
25.17.1 74n.18
25.18.10 55n.73
26.1.1 192n.82
26.12.9 55n.74
26.23.7–8 272n.44
26.23.8 207n.122
26.26.5–8 274
26.26.5 192n.82
26.32.1–5 274
27.5.10 135–6
27.5.15 133, 258n.8
25.5.16–19 135–6
27.5.19 131n.67
27.6.15–16 272n.44
27.6.18 131n.67
27.7.7 192n.82
27.16.11–16 159n.26, 277n.61
27.16.15 59n.84, 277
27.22.13 250n.76
27.24.1–7 250n.76
27.33.6 177n.27
27.33.7 177n.25
27.35.2 250n.76
27.36.13 250n.76
28.9.4–7 119n.28
28.9.10 119–20, 124–5
28.10.1 265n.26
28.10.6 65n.100
29.10.2 174n.16
29.11.3 293
29.11.9 174n.16

29.11.14 271n.39
29.38.6 271n.39
30.23.5 293
30.24.3 99n.102
31.5.2 192n.82
31.6.2 120–1
31.10.1–11.3 120–1
31.14.1 51, 64n.97
31.21.1–22.2 120–1
31.22.3 120–1
31.47.4–5 120–1
31.48.1–6 120–1
31.48.6 120n.31
31.48.7 120–1
31.48.8–10 120–1
31.48.11–12 120–1
32.1.1 192n.82
33.26.2–3 122n.39
33.43.1 192n.82
33.43.5 35–6
33.43.6 35–6
33.43.8 35–6
33.44.2 257n.6
33.44.3 63
33.44.4 122n.39
34.1.7 202
34.10.1–5 121
34.10.1 122n.39
34.10.3 121–2
34.10.5 122–3
34.10.5–6 122n.39
34.11–16 121–2
34.16.6–10 121–2
34.19.1 121–2
34.42.2–5 123n.42
34.46.1–4 123n.42
34.56.3–4 283n.79
35.48.13 51n.63
36.3.14 52n.66
36.10.1 55n.74
37.4.3 52n.66
37.51.1–2 271n.39
38.35.7 192n.82
38.48.16 51
39.12.2 74n.19
39.12.3–13.14 74n.19
39.32.5–9 71
39.32.10–11 71
39.32.11 71–2
39.32.15 65n.100
39.45.1 192n.82
40.26.6 52n.66
40.33.4 55n.74
40.35.1 192n.82
40.42.8–11 164n.40

LIVY (cont.)
   41.8.4 192n.82
   41.5.8 52n.66
   41.10.4–11.2 283n.78
   41.10.4–5 63
   41.10.5–11.2 124n.45
   41.10.5 52, 64n.97
   41.10.6–7 63
   41.10.7 51, 64n.97
   41.10.11–13 63
   41.10.11 52
   41.10.13 51, 64n.97
   41.11.2 63
   41.15.4–7 35–6
   41.15.9–10 268n.31
   41.16.1-3 281
   41.16.5 251n.81
   41.17.6 52n.66, 251n.81, 282
   41.18.6 282
   41.18.7–15 281n.71
   41.18.7–8 281n.71
   41.18.8–14 160n.30, 194n.89
   41.18.8 281n.71
   41.18.16 281n.72
   41.27.3 52
   42.22.7 192n.82
   42.27.8 52n.66
   42.32.2 268n.31
   42.49.1 52
   42.49.6 52n.64
   43.5–7 122n.39
   43.11.1 268n.31
   43.23.6 268n.31
   44.19.1 192n.82
   45.12.10 284n.80
   45.12.12 284n.80
   45.17.7 55n.74
   45.24.12 55n.73
   45.37–39 286n.91
   45.39.11 52, 64n.97
   45.39.18 65n.100
   Per. (Periochae)
     19 104n.115, 150, 159, 163n.36, 164n.43, 165n.44, 259n.11, 261n.16, 271n.39
     20 192
     22 163n.36
     47 191n.76, 192, 294n.17
     55 287n.93
     67 288n.94
LUCAN
   De bello civili
     3.126–127 155n.14

MACROBIUS
   Sat. (Saturnalia)
     1.3.7 45n.44
MARIUS VICTORINUS
   Ars gramm. (Ars grammatica)
     4.42 (GramLat 6: 4.21–22) 58n.82
MESSALLA, see GELLIUS
MINUCIUS FELIX
   Oct. (Octavia)
     7 155n.14
     7.4 151, 162–3, 258n.10
     26.2 151
     26.3 263–4
Iulius OBSEQUENS
   Prodigiorum liber
     18 [77] 294n.18
     24 [83] 287n.93
     54 [124] 288n.95
OROSIUS
   Historiae adversum paganos
     2.13.2 177n.25
     4.10.2 154n.13
     4.13.14 181n.44
     4.16.11 270n.35
     5.16.1–7 288n.94
OVID
   Fasti
     2.682 58n.79
     6.763–768 239n.52
   Pont. (Ex Ponto)
     4.4.30 53n.69
PETRONIUS
   Satyr. (Satyrica)
     65.3–4 74nn.18,19
PLINY the Elder
   NH (Naturalis historia)
     8.223 205n.119
     28.17 276n.59
     28.146 87n.57
PLUTARCH
   Ant. (Antony)
     8.4 132–3, 136–7
     8.4–5 80, 115n.10
     8.5 79
   Brut. (Brutus)
     53.5 206–7
   Caes. (Caesar)
     51.1 135–6, 144n.112, 146n.119

INDEX LOCORUM 339

Cam. (Camillus)
  2.9 292
  2.10 292–3
  5.1 80
  18.6 80
  29.3 80, 84n.50
  30.1 110n.133
  31.3 110n.134
  36.4 130, 209n.132
CatMin (Cato minor)
  42.4 196n.93
Cic. (Cicero)
  19.3 72n.15
Crass. (Crassus)
  16.4–8 155n.14, 288n.95
  18.5 288n.95
  19.4–8 288n.95
  23.1–2 288n.95
  synkr. 5(38).3 288n.95
Fab. (Fabius)
  2.1 209
  2.2 209
  2.3–3.3 180n.41
  2.3 180n.41, 182n.46
  2.4 240
  3.1 239nn.51,52, 240
  3.6–7 80
  4.1 209, 209n.133
  4.1–3 82
  4.1–2 66n.1, 87n.57
  4.3 66n.1, 82, 96, 175n.19
  4.4–5.1 96n.91
  5–13 209
  5.5–6 26n.47
  8.1 26n.48, 268–9
  9.1–3 26n.49
  9.2 80
  9.3 179n.33
  9.3–4 106
  9.4 66–7
  9.5 106–7
  10.1 106–7
  12.3 209n.133
  13 106
  13.4 106
  14.1 82
  17–18 106–7
  19.7–8 159n.26, 277n.61
Flam. (Flamininus)
  synkr. 2(23).6 51n.63
Mar. (Marius)
  27.10 117n.20
  44.8 117n.20

Marc. (Marcellus)
  2.3 276n.58
  4.1–3 180n.39
  4.2 180n.41, 184
  4.3–6 293n.14
  4.4 180n.40
  4.5–6 180n.41
  4.5 180n.41, 182n.46
  4.6 182, 187–8, 189nn.66,67, 206
  4.7 206, 209n.133
  5 206
  5.1–7 116n.17, 205n.115
  5.1–4 206, 284n.83, 294n.16
  5.5 206
  5.6 205n.117, 206–8, 210n.134
  5.7 206, 209n.133
  6.1 182, 189n.67, 206, 293n.14
  12.2 278n.62
  24.10 79
  24.11 79
  24.12–13 79
  24.12 88n.61
  25.1 79
  25.2 79
  30.5 206–7
Pomp. (Pompeius)
  52.3 196n.93
Popl. (Poplicola)
  12.5 74n.23
QR (Quaestiones Romanae)
  40 (*Mor.* 274C) 87n.57
  81 (*Mor.* 283B–D) 79–80
Rom. (Romulus)
  16.7–8 87n.57
  27.1 90n.70
Sulla
  33.1–2 135n.80
TiGrac (Tiberius Gracchus)
  20.6 209n.132

POLYBIOS
  Historiae
    1.29.1 153
    1.36.10–37.2 153
    1.37 258n.9
    1.39.1–6 153
    1.39.6 258n.9
    1.42–55 161
    1.42.8 161n.32
    1.43.1 161n.32
    1.48.1–49.1 154
    1.48.10 161n.32
    1.49.3–4 153

POLYBIOS (cont.)
  1.49.3 161n.32
  1.49.5 153
  1.50.5 161n.31
  1.51.4 161n.31
  1.51.9 161n.31
  1.51.11–12 148n.2
  1.52.3 164n.39
  1.52.5–8 161
  1.52.5 161n.32
  1.52.6 161, 258–9
  1.52.7 161n.32
  1.53.4 161n.32
  1.53.7 161n.32
  1.53.8–13 161
  1.54.1–4 161–2
  1.54.3–4 158n.23
  1.54.5–8 161–2
  1.55.8 161n.32
  2.18.2–3 110
  2.22.4–5 110
  2.22.5 110n.133
  2.25.1–26.7 232n.38
  2.25.1–7 230
  2.33.7 229n.35
  3.40.8–14 234n.40
  3.61.9–10 251n.77
  3.64.1–68.8 251n.77
  3.68.13–69.14 251n.77
  3.72.11 251n.78
  3.74.6–8 251n.78
  3.75.4–8 229n.36
  3.75.5 252
  3.75.6 250n.75
  3.77 228
  3.77.1 213, 219–20, 227–8
  3.77.3 218n.9
  3.78.1–5 221n.18
  3.78.2 228–9
  3.78.5 228–9
  3.78.6 213, 217–20, 227–8
  3.78.8–79.1 223
  3.79 220–1
  3.79.1 221n.19
  3.79.4 230
  8.80.1–82.7 226
  3.80.1 213, 219–20, 227–8
  3.80.2–3 224
  3.80.2 219–20
  3.80.3 219–20, 223
  3.80.4–5 219–20
  3.80.4 224
  3.82.1 213, 222n.21, 224, 236n.44
  3.82.2 236n.44
  3.82.3 236n.44
  3.82.4–6 236n.44, 237
  3.82.4 238n.49
  3.82.6 237–8
  3.82.7 248n.70
  3.82.11–83.5 226n.28
  3.82.11 236n.43
  3.83.7–84.2 248n.70
  3.83.7 226, 236n.44, 237–8
  3.86.1–3 236
  3.86.6–7 256n.2
  3.87.7–9 110–11
  3.88.7 175n.19
  3.87.8 78
  3.87.9 81–2, 115n.10
  3.88.8 78–9, 82, 96n.93, 173n.11
  3.90.6 26n.47
  3.92.4 26n.47
  3.94.9 26n.48, 268–9
  3.102 26n.48
  3.103 26n.49
  3.103.3–5 179n.33
  3.103.3–4 108
  3.103.4 105
  3.105.10 107n.122
  3.106.2–9 82n.48
  3.106.2 78–9, 106, 108n.126
  3.106.6–7 82n.48
  3.118.6 270n.35
  6.11a 84n.49
  6.12.2 81n.47
  6.56.6–12 191–2
  31.15.9–11 285n.85

POMPONIUS, see *DIGESTAE*

PRISCIAN
  Inst. (*Institutiones grammaticae*)
    4.21 (*GramLat* 2: 129.11–15) 90–1
    8.78 (*GramLat* 2: 432.25) 87–8
    17.29 (*GramLat* 3: 126) 281n.72
    17.150 (*GramLat* 3: 182) 281n.72

SALLUST
  Cat. (*Catilinae coniuratio*)
    47.3 72n.15

SCHOLIA AMBROSIANA
  ad Cic. *Scaur.* (ad *Ciceronis Scaurianam*)
    274St. 86n.56

SCHOLIA BERNENSIA
  ad *Georg.* (ad *Vergilii Georgica*)
    4.108 288n.94

SCHOLIA BOBIENSIA
  Ciceronis duodecim orationum scholia
    90.3–8St. 164n.39

SCHOLIA VERONENSIA
  ad *Aen.* (ad *Vergilii Aeneidem*)
    10.241 156n.16, 244
SENECA the Elder
  Contr. (*Controversiae*)
    9.2.17 74
SENECA the Younger
  Ep. (*Ad Lucilium epistulae morales*)
    108.31 89n.68
SERVIUS Grammaticus
  ad *Aen.* (*In Vergilii Aeneidem commentarii*)
    1.448 87n.57
    3.20 58–9
    4.200 45n.44
    6.197 58n.81
    6.198 152–3
    7.606 288n.95
    9.24 157n.18
    11.19 242n.57, 288n.95
    12.246 157n.17
    12.260 276n.59
SERVIUS AUCTUS (*sive* DANIELIS)
  ad *Aen.*
    1.13 156
    8.552 87n.57
    11.19 239n.52, 242n.57
SILIUS ITALICUS
  Punica
    5.54–62 239n.52
    5.63–65 239n.52
    5.66 239n.52
STRABO
  Geographica
    5.1.11 C217 218n.8
    5.2.9 C226–227 218n.8
    5.3.2 C230 58n.79
SUETONIUS
  DIul (*Divus Iulius*)
    16.1 72
    16.2 72
    20.1 75n.26
  Galba
    18.3 287n.93
  Tib. (*Tiberius*)
    2.2 104n.115, 151, 162–3, 259n.11
    3.1 9
TACITUS
  Ann. (*Ab excessu Divi Augusti*)
    3.71.3 271n.39
  Germ. (*De origine et situ Germanorum*)
    37.4 288n.94

TUDITANUS, *see* GELLIUS
TWELVE TABLES
  RStat 2: 557 93n.81
  RStat 2: 719 93n.81
ULPIAN, see *DIGESTAE*
VALERIUS MAXIMUS
  Facta et dicta memorabilia
    1.1.2 271n.39
    1.1.3 206–7, 284n.83, 292n.6, 294n.16
    1.1.4 206–7
    1.1.5 116n.17, 205n.115, 206–7, 210n.134
    1.3.2 *Nep.* 166
    1.3.2 *Par.* 165
    1.4.3 *Nep.* 150, 162–3
    1.4.3 *Par.* 150, 162–3
    1.4.4 *Par.* 150, 162–4
    1.5.9 281n.71
    1.6.6 239nn.51, 52
    1.6.7 287n.93
    1.6.11 288n.95
    2.2.4 74
    2.6.4 25
    2.7.4 56n.77, 115n.12
    2.8.2 36, 114n.7, 116–17, 200n.102
    3.2.9 5–6, 14, 19–20, 56n.77
    3.8.2 107n.123
    4.6.5 206–7
    4.7.1 209n.132
    4.7.3 288n.94
    5.4.3 102n.112
    8.1 abs. 4 164n.39
    9.12.3 285
VARRO
  LL (*De lingua Latina*)
    5.33 58n.79, 58n.82
    5.80 93n.83
    5.82 79n.45, 87–8
    5.143 64n.99, 157n.20
    6.30 46n.49, 47n.51, 77n.37, 88, 212n.1
    6.53 58n.81
    6.61 87–8
    6.86 45n.44
    6.88 33n.10, 93n.81
    6.93 33n.10
    6.95 33n.10
    7.37 50n.62, 52n.66
  see also GELLIUS
VELLEIUS Paterculus
  Historiae
    2.12.2 288n.94
    2.46.3 155n.14, 288n.95

ZONARAS
Epitoma historiarum
   7.11 45n.45
   7.13 87n.57
   7.14 145n.116
   7.20 145n.116
   7.19 292n.8
   7.25 145n.116
   7.26 94n.85, 293n.13
   8.14 25
   8.15 145n.116, 154n.13, 160n.29, 163, 165, 261–2, 261n.16, 262n.19
   8.16 165n.44
   8.17 116–17
   8.20 180nn.39–41, 182–3, 188, 189n.67, 195, 203–4, 266n.27, 293, 293n.14
   8.22 272–3
   8.24 221n.18
   8.25 225–6, 229n.36
   8.26 26n.47, 107–8, 107n.123, 108n.124, 175n.19, 179n.33
   9.2 145n.116
   9.3 270n.35
   10.1 145n.116